OTHER A TO Z GUIDE
THE SCARECROW PRESS, INC.

1. *The A to Z of Buddhism* by Charles S. Prebish, 2001.
2. *The A to Z of Catholicism* by William J. Collinge, 2001.
3. *The A to Z of Hinduism* by Bruce M. Sullivan, 2001.
4. *The A to Z of Islam* by Ludwig W. Adamec, 2002.
5. *The A to Z of Slavery & Abolition* by Martin A. Klein, 2002.
6. *Terrorism: Assassins to Zealots* by Sean Kendall Anderson and Stephen Sloan, 2003.
7. *The A to Z of the Korean War* by Paul M. Edwards, 2005.
8. *The A to Z of the Cold War* by Joseph Smith and Simon Davis, 2005.
9. *The A to Z of the Vietnam War* by Edwin E. Moise, 2005.
10. *The A to Z of Science Fiction Literature* by Brian Stableford, 2005.
11. *The A to Z of the Holocaust* by Jack R. Fischel, 2005.
12. *The A to Z of Washington, D.C.* by Robert Benedetto, Jane Donovan, and Kathleen DuVall, 2005.
13. *The A to Z of Taoism* by Julian F. Pas, 2006.
14. *The A to Z of the Renaissance* by Charles G. Nauert, 2006.
15. *The A to Z of Shinto* by Stuart D. B. Picken, 2006.
16. *The A to Z of Byzantium* by John H. Rosser, 2006.
17. *The A to Z of the Civil War* by Terry L. Jones, 2006.
18. *The A to Z of the Friends (Quakers)* by Margery Post Abbott, Mary Ellen Chijioke, Pink Dandelion, and John William Oliver Jr., 2006
19. *The A to Z of Feminism* by Janet K. Boles and Diane Long Hoeveler, 2006.
20. *The A to Z of New Religious Movements* by George D. Chryssides, 2006.
21. *The A to Z of Multinational Peacekeeping* by Terry M. Mays, 2006.
22. *The A to Z of Lutheranism* by Günther Gassmann with Duane H. Larson and Mark W. Oldenburg, 2007.
23. *The A to Z of the French Revolution* by Paul R. Hanson, 2007.
24. *The A to Z of the Persian Gulf War 1990–1991* by Clayton R. Newell, 2007.
25. *The A to Z of Revolutionary America* by Terry M. Mays, 2007.

76. *The A to Z of World War II: The War Against Japan* by Anne Sharp Wells, 2009.
77. *The A to Z of Witchcraft* by Michael D. Bailey, 2009.
78. *The A to Z of British Intelligence* by Nigel West, 2009.
79. *The A to Z of United States Intelligence* by Michael A. Turner, 2009.
80. *The A to Z of the League of Nations* by Anique H. M. van Ginneken, 2009.
81. *The A to Z of Israeli Intelligence* by Ephraim Kahana, 2009.
82. *The A to Z of the European Union* by Joaquín Roy and Aimee Kanner, 2009.
83. *The A to Z of the Chinese Cultural Revolution* by Guo Jian, Yongyi Song, and Yuan Zhou, 2009.
84. *The A to Z of African American Cinema* by S. Torriano Berry and Venise T. Berry, 2009.
85. *The A to Z of Japanese Business* by Stuart D. B. Picken, 2009.
86. *The A to Z of the Reagan–Bush Era* by Richard S. Conley, 2009.
87. *The A to Z of Human Rights and Humanitarian Organizations* by Robert F. Gorman and Edward S. Mihalkanin, 2009.
88. *The A to Z of French Cinema* by Dayna Oscherwitz and MaryEllen Higgins, 2009.
89. *The A to Z of the Puritans* by Charles Pastoor and Galen K. Johnson, 2009.
90. *The A to Z of Nuclear, Biological, and Chemical Warfare* by Benjamin C. Garrett and John Hart, 2009.
91. *The A to Z of the Green Movement* by Miranda Schreurs and Elim Papadakis, 2009.
92. *The A to Z of the Kennedy–Johnson Era* by Richard Dean Burns and Joseph M. Siracusa, 2009.
93. *The A to Z of Renaissance Art* by Lilian H. Zirpolo, 2009.
94. *The A to Z of the Broadway Musical* by William A. Everett and Paul R. Laird, 2009.
95. *The A to Z of the Northern Ireland Conflict* by Gordon Gillespie, 2009.
96. *The A to Z of the Fashion Industry* by Francesca Sterlacci and Joanne Arbuckle, 2009.
97. *The A to Z of American Theater: Modernism* by James Fisher and Felicia Hardison Londré, 2009.
98. *The A to Z of Civil Wars in Africa* by Guy Arnold, 2009.

The A to Z of
African American Cinema

S. Torriano Berry
Venise T. Berry

The A to Z Guide Series, No. 84

THE SCARECROW PRESS, INC.
Lanham • Toronto • Plymouth, UK
2009

Published by Scarecrow Press, Inc.
A wholly owned subsidiary of
The Rowman & Littlefield Publishing Group, Inc.
4501 Forbes Boulevard, Suite 200, Lanham, Maryland 20706
http://www.scarecrowpress.com

Estover Road, Plymouth PL6 7PY, United Kingdom

British Library Cataloguing in Publication Information Available

Library of Congress Cataloging-in-Publication Data

The hardback version of this book was cataloged by the Library of Congress as follows:

Berry, Torriano.
  Historical dictionary of African American cinema / S. Torriano Berry, Venise T. Berry.
      p. cm. — (Historical dictionaries of literature and the arts ; no. 12)
  Includes bibliographical references.
  1. African Americans in motion pictures. 2. African Americans in the motion picture industry–Biography–Dictionaries. I. Berry, Venise T. II. Title.
PN1995.9.N4B433 2007
791.43089'96073–dc22   2006019070

ISBN 978-0-8108-6871-7 (pbk. : alk. paper)
ISBN 978-0-8108-7034-5 (ebook)

Printed in the United States of America

We are thankful to our God and our guardian angel, Toni, for our many blessings. We are thankful to our parents and family members for their ongoing love and support. We are thankful to our friends and colleagues who have encouraged and fostered this effort. We are thankful to Jon Woronoff, Nicole McCullough, Scarecrow Press, and the Rowman & Littlefield Publishing Group, Inc., for providing the opportunity to document this extraordinary enterprise. We are thankful to the talented African American actors, actresses, directors, producers, writers, and other film industry personnel who have enriched our lives and our culture through their creative endeavors.

Contents

Editor's Foreword

African American cinema is in a very different category from the various "national cinemas" included in this subseries. Unlike the French, Russians, or Germans, the African Americans first had to reclaim their own cinematic image before they could turn it into a thing of representation and beauty. Launched just over a century ago, most of the early films actually had white actors with burnt cork-covered faces portraying black roles, and the stories were humiliating, to say the least. It took decades before there were enough black actors, producers, directors, scriptwriters, and film companies to address the stereotypes and attempt to turn the situation around. Eventually, since there was money to be made, Hollywood joined in. Nowadays, African American cinema is considered quite normal. It can deal not only with the discrimination and hardships of the past, but virtually any subject can be presented on the screen from love and marriage to hatred and revenge, in every genre, whether comedy or tragedy, farce or science fiction. True, it has gained its own movies and stars, but these have increasingly become part of the mainstream, and its contribution to cinema both as an industry and an art has become indispensable.

The fact that this has been a long, hard climb from a particularly low level is shown clearly in the chronology, without which this volume might be hard to understand. The various stages in the progression are characterized in the introduction. But the dictionary section will be of greatest interest to readers, with hundreds of entries on notable actors and actresses, singers, dancers, and comedians, as well a growing circle of directors, producers, cinematographers, and scriptwriters. Some general topics, such as race movies, film genres, and stereotypes, are also included. Other entries briefly summarize the better-known films, old and new, good and bad, Academy Award winners and cult classics.

Details on casts and filmographies only enhance the value of these entries. The bibliography points readers toward other sources of information on a cinema that deserves to be better known.

A brother and sister team wrote this latest volume in the subseries on cinema. Both of them have a very strong interest and impressive standing in the field. S. Torriano Berry has written two novels and also produced several independent film and television productions, including two episodic series that showcase black films. He is currently an associate professor at Howard University's Department of Radio, Television, and Film in Washington, D.C. Venise T. Berry has written three best-selling novels and co-edited a nonfiction work. She is presently an associate professor of Journalism and Mass Communications at the University of Iowa in Iowa City. Together, S. Torriano Berry and Venise T. Berry collaborated on *The 50 Most Influential Black Films,* a very useful reference work, which helped pave the way for this latest contribution, *Historical Dictionary of African American Cinema,* which finally fills many gaps.

Jon Woronoff
Series Editor

Acronyms and Abbreviations

ABC	American Broadcasting Company
AFI	American Film Institute
BACS	Black American Cinema Society
BET	Black Entertainment Television
BFC/A	Black Film Center/Archive
BFF	Black Filmmakers Foundation
BFHF	Black Filmmakers Hall of Fame
BHERC	Black Hollywood Education and Resource Center
BCC	Black Cinema Cafe
CBS	Columbia Broadcasting System
DVD	Digital Video Disc
FOX	20th Century Fox
HBO	Home Box Office
MGM	Metro Goldwyn Mayer
NAACP	National Association for the Advancement of Colored People
NBC	National Broadcasting Company
NBPC	National Black Programming Consortium
NFL	National Football League
SAG	Screen Actors Guild
TV	Television
UCLA	University of California, Los Angeles
UPN	United Paramount Network
USC	University of Southern California
VCR	Video Cassette Recorder

Chronology

1824   Peter Mark Roget receives credit for discovering a phenomenon known as persistence of vision. Scientists and inventors develop flipbooks, twirling coins, and spinning disks to help prove his theory.

1839   New photographic processes are developed in France and England. Louis Daguerre's *Daguerreotype* becomes the rave in Paris, while Henry Fox Talbot's *Collotype* raises eyebrows in London.

1872   Photographer Eadweard Muybridge and John D. Isaacs invent a process for taking motion pictures.

1887   George Eastman receives a patent on Celluloid film.

1889   Thomas Edison sets up the "Black Maria," the world's first movie studio that utilizes his Kinetoscope technology.

1895   Louis Lumiere invents the Cinematographe. He holds the first public film exhibition in France.

1902   George Melies advances the artistic merits of film in *Off to Bloomingdale Asylum,* and uses special effects and trick photography to awe and entertain.

1903-1905   Played mostly by white actors in blackface, films like *Uncle Tom's Cabin, The Wooing and Wedding of a*

Coon, and *A Nigger in a Woodpile*, denigrate the African American image on film to the lowest common denominator.

1908   Edwin S. Porter explores the power of the cut in *The Great Train Robbery*.

1909   Sigmund Lubin produces his highly successful *Sambo* series of all-black comedies. He follows it with *The Rastus Films*.

1910   The Jack Johnson vs. Jim Jeffries fight film is banned from exhibition after the black fighter wins.

1912   William Foster produces *The Railroad Porter*, a Keystone Cops-style comedy, becoming the first African American to control his own-filmed image.

1914   Sam Lucas becomes the first black actor to be cast in a lead role for a major film production for the third re-make of *Uncle Tom's Cabin*.

1915   D. W. Griffith's film epic *The Birth of a Nation* is released. Based on the novel *The Clansman*, about the birth of the Ku Klux Klan, the film advances the creative and technical art of filmmaking while increasing recruitment for the Klan and undermining race relations around the world.

1916   The Lincoln Motion Picture Company is established in Los Angeles by character actors Noble Johnson and Clarence Brooks. They take on as partners Dr. James T. Smith, a local druggist, and Universal Studios camera operator Harry Gant.

1918   Film pioneer Oscar Micheaux produces *The Homesteader* based on his self-published novel. Emmett Scott releases *The Birth of a Race* as a direct response to D. W. Griffith's racist film *Birth of a Nation*. Black and white children play together in Hal Roach's *The Our Gang Series*, with Farina.

1920-1927   Race movies or sepia flicks are produced and shown at black-owned movie houses, as well as at Midnight

Rambles held for coloreds in white theaters, and at makeshift screening facilities set up across the South due to segregation and Jim Crow laws. Production companies making these movies included Reol Picture Company, Ebony Films, and Norman Film Manufacturing Company. Many of these are white-owned but produce only black product.

1922 In Kansas City, Missouri, Tressie Souder directs *A Woman's Error*, considered to be the first feature-length film directed by an African American woman.

1923 Sound comes to Tinseltown. Inventor Lee de Forest develops the technology to record sound on film.

1927 Talking pictures are introduced to the masses when Al Jolson stars as *The Jazz Singer*. His musical number of "Mammy," performed in blackface, is considered to be a stereotypical insult to African Americans. Expensive sound film technology eventually puts many independent film companies out of business.

1928 The Academy Awards for Motion Picture Excellence is established to honor the best in Hollywood film productions. Blues singer Bessie Smith stars in the musical short *St. Louis Blues*.

1929 *Hearts In Dixie*, the first all-black talkie, is released by Fox Studios. The film stars Clarence Muse and introduces Stepin Fetchit in his first major role. The U.S. stock market crashes on 29 October, leading to an economic depression.

1930 James and Eloyce Gist distribute *Hellbound Train*, a religion-based film and successfully "four-wall" their film to churches, schools, and rent it to civic organizations for fundraiser screenings. Oscar Micheaux partners with Leo Brecher and Frank Shiffman, two white Harlem Theater owners, to make sound films.

1932 Technicolor Corporation develops the three-color film process.

1933   Paul Robeson appears on the screen as *The Emperor Jones*, a role that catapults him to international stardom.

1938   Herbert Jeffrey (a.k.a. Herb Jeffries) becomes known as "The Bronze Buckaroo," a singing cowboy in a series of black Western films beginning with *Harlem on the Prairie*. Ralph Cooper, the emcee who created Amateur Night at the Apollo, organizes Million Dollar Productions to produce and star in a series of black gangster films beginning with *Dark Manhattan*.

1939   Hattie McDaniel wins the best supporting actress Oscar for her role as Mammy in *Gone with the Wind*. She is the first African American to win an Academy Award.

1940   Ted Toddy organizes Toddy Pictures to produce light comedies and musical adventure films such as *Mantan Messes Up*, with funny man Mantan Moreland, *House-Rent Party*, with former vaudeville star Pigmeat Markham, and *Here Comes Louis Jordan*, with music man Louis Jordan.

1941-1946   Spencer Williams Jr. writes, produces, directs, and stars in a series of nine films for Sack Amusement Co. These include *The Blood of Jesus*, *The Girl in Room 30*, and *Juke Joint*.

1943   The studios release big-budget musicals like MGM's *Cabin in the Sky* and Fox's *Stormy Weather*. Both films star the now-legendary Lena Horne and are highly successful. World War II brings this active age of African American screen images to an end.

1947   The McCarthy Era hits Hollywood hard. Blacklisting begins and African Americans considered to have communist ties are hit even harder.

1948   *No Time for Romance* is the first all-black cast musical shot on color film.

1949-1952   Problem pictures emerge as Hollywood begins to address the mounting racial tension in America with films like *Home of the Brave*, 1949; *Pinky*, 1949; *No Way Out*, 1950; and *Intruder in the Dust*, 1952.

1949-1954   Sports heroes move to the Silver Screen. Champion pugilist Joe Louis plays himself in *The Fight Never Ends*, 1949. Jackie Robinson, Brooklyn Dodgers' second baseman and modern-day color barrier breaker, plays himself in *The Jackie Robinson Story*, 1950. Actor Coley Wallace portrays boxing champion Joe Lewis in *The Joe Lewis Story*, 1954.

1950s   Television takes on Tinseltown. Theater audiences dwindle as people stay home to watch moving images in their living rooms on small electronic tubes. The box office and theater attendance continues to decline over the next two decades. Eastman Kodak introduces its Integral Tripac film that produces an improved color image and motion pictures begin to move away from black and white.

1954   *Carmen Jones* is released by Fox. Shot in Technicolor, its star Dorothy Dandridge becomes the first African American actress nominated for a Best Actress Oscar for her title role. The film wins a Golden Globe Award for best picture, musical/comedy.

1961-1967   Sidney Poitier becomes a major box office star. He portrays strong and dignified black men in mainstream films like *Paris Blues*, 1961; *The Long Ships*, 1964; *The Bedford Incident*, 1965; *Duel at Diablo*, 1966; and *To Sir with Love*, 1967. Independent filmmakers produce powerful and controversial films such as *Nothing But a Man*, 1964, with Ivan Dixon; *One Potato, Two Potato*, 1964, with Bernie Hamilton; *Black Like Me*, 1964, with Roscoe Lee Brown and Al Freeman Jr.; and *The Dutchman*, 1967, with Al Freeman Jr.

1960   *Orfeu Negro* (Black Orpheus), a film from Brazil, wins the Academy Award for Best Foreign Language Film. Woody Strode portrays powerful black roles as a Buffalo Soldier in *Sergeant Rutledge*, a Nubian warrior in *Spartacus*, and a valiant seaman in *The Last Voyage*.

1962   Duke Ellington becomes the first African American nominated for a non-acting Oscar for his music score to the film *Paris Blues.*

1963   Sidney Poitier becomes the first African American to win the Best Actor Oscar for his role in *Lilies of the Field.*

1968   The Film Rating System is instituted by the Motion Picture Association of America to warn viewers of potentially violent, profane, or sexually offensive motion pictures.

1969   Still photographer Gordon Parks becomes the first African American to direct a feature-length motion picture for a Hollywood studio. Parks writes, produces, directs, and composes the original music score for *The Learning Tree*, based on his autobiographical novel.

1970   Hugh A. Robertson becomes the first African American film-technician nominated for an Academy Award for his editing work of the film *Midnight Cowboy.*

1970-1976   The blaxploitation era is kindled by films like *...tick...tick...tick*, 1970, starring Jim Brown, and the hit comedy *Cotton Comes to Harlem*, 1970, starring the detective duo of Raymond St. Jacques and Geoffrey Cambridge. This hard-edged evolution of African American cinema explodes onto the screen with maverick filmmaker Melvin Van Peebles's hip and independent release of *Sweet Sweetback's Baadasssss Song*, 1971. Hollywood follows suit with *Shaft*, 1971, starring Richard Roundtree; *Superfly*, 1972, starring Ron O'Neil; *Coffy*, 1973, with Pam Grier; and a plethora of other black theme films. In the wake of stiff competition from television, this onslaught of low-budget, high-grossing black movies saved many financially struggling Hollywood studios from bankruptcy. Lonnie Elder III and Suzanne De Passe become the first African American screenwriters nominated for Oscars. Elder wrote *Sounder*, 1973; De

Passe co-wrote *Lady Sings the Blues*, 1973. Inspired by National President Lillian Benbow, Delta Sigma Theta Sorority finances and produces *Countdown at Kusini*, 1976, a film of music, romance, and political intrigue. A bold model for alternative film financing.

1980s   Despite the huge profits generated by the blaxploitation boom, Hollywood studios pare down their output of African American films to just a trickle, while stand-up comics gain a huge on-screen presence. Richard Pryor stars in *Bustin' Loose*, 1981, and *Some Kind of Hero*, 1982. Eddie Murphy goes from television to the big screen in *48 Hours*, 1982, and *Beverly Hills Cop*, 1984. Whoopi Goldberg stars in *Jumpin' Jack Flash*, 1986, and *Burglar*, 1987. Sidney Poitier becomes the first black director to gross over $100 million at the box office with his film *Stir Crazy*, starring Richard Pryor and Gene Wilder.

1985   *The Color Purple* brings Alice Walker's Pulitzer Prize-winning novel to the screen. It gives a new image to African American women and introduces talk show host Oprah Winfrey to the big screen. The film is nominated for 11 Oscars but receives none.

1986-1987   Independent filmmaker Spike Lee's *She's Gotta Have It*, 1986, ushers in a new crop of African American images and image-makers. Robert Townsend's *Hollywood Shuffle*, 1987, and Keenon Ivory Wayans' *I'm Gonna Get You Sucka*, 1987, help to confirm the trend.

1989-1990   Sound mixer Russell Williams becomes the first African American to win two technical Oscars for his work on *Glory*, 1989, and *Dances with Wolves*, 1990.

1990s   In Hollywood, a new wave of African American directors get the green light to helm their cinematic visions of the world. These are all male directors that include brothers Warrington and Reginald Hudlin, Ernest Dickerson, Mario Van Peebles, John Singleton, Matty Rich, and twin brothers Allen and Albert Hughes. African American-owned film and video distribution companies, such as Urban Entertainment in

Los Angeles, Urban World, and Life Films in New York are formed, thus entering an area of the industry previously denied to African Americans. Rap music artists expand beyond the concert stage to become a major influence on the silver screen. Talented entertainers, such as Ice Cube, Ice T, Queen Latifah, Will Smith, DMX, and L. L. Cool J, become major movie stars as well as rap music icons.

1990-1992   *House Party*, Warrington and Reginald Hudlin's low-budget teen comedy film grosses over $26 million at the box office. Their tribute to comedian Robin Harris, *Bebe's Kids*, 1992, is the first feature-length cartoon produced by African Americans.

1991   Julie Dash becomes the first African American female director to receive national distribution for a feature length film for *Daughters of the Dust*.

1991-1993   John Singleton's urban drama *Boyz N the Hood*, 1991, shifts the cinematic focus to inner city street life. Mario Van Peebles's *New Jack City*, 1991; Ernest Dickerson's *Juice*, 1992; Steve Anderson's *South Central*, 1992; and The Hughes Brother's *Menace II Society*, 1993, confirm the trend.

1994   Ethiopian-born filmmaker Haile Gerima "four-walls" his independently produced *Sankofa*, to over a million-dollar box-office gross.

1995   *Waiting to Exhale*, Terry McMillan's best-selling novel becomes a highly anticipated film and helps to transform the African American female image.

1998   Black Entertainment Television buys the Arabesque line of African American romance novels from Kensington Publishing and begins adapting these stories to film.

1999   Malcolm Lee's *The Best Man* helps to bring the long overlooked genre of black romance to the silver screen as he takes the African American male image away from guns, drugs, and violence, and out of the 'hood. Similar films like *The Wood*, 1999; *The*

Brothers, 2001; *Two Can Play That Game*, 2001; *Brown Sugar*, 2002; and *Deliver Us from Eva*, 2003, confirmed the trend. The popular novel-based film *How Stella Got Her Groove Back*, 1999, wins three top Image Awards.

2000   Keenen Ivory Wayans's *Scary Movie* becomes the highest-grossing film written and directed by an African American. The sequel, *Scary Movie II*, 2001, also directed by Keenen, becomes another blockbuster hit.

2002   Halle Berry becomes the first African American actress to win a best actress Oscar for her role in *Monster's Ball*. Denzel Washington receives his second Oscar for his role as a rogue cop in *Training Day*. And Sidney Poitier receives a Lifetime Achievement Award from the Academy of Motion Picture Arts and Sciences. The comedy film *Barbershop* receives serious criticism from critics and civic leaders for disrespecting civil rights leaders Martin Luther King Jr., Jesse Jackson, and Rosa Parks. These protests bring national attention to the film, boosting the box office gross, but also causing a massive out-of-context exposure to these questionable statements on television news networks worldwide.

2003   Three films directed by African Americans gross over $100 million at the box office: John Singleton's *2 Fast, 2 Furious*, Clarke Johnson's *S. W. A. T.*, and F. Gary Gray's *The Italian Job*.

2004   Headquartered in Los Angeles, Simmons Lathan Media Group (SLMG) is established to produce, acquire, and distribute original urban/hip-hop themed media content including original motion picture productions. Founded by media entrepreneur Will Griffin, in partnership with hip-hop mogul Russell Simmons and television producer/director Stan Lathan, SLMG's vision is to redefine the way urban media content is developed and distributed to an ethnically diverse urban consumer audience.

2005   Five African Americans receive Oscar nominations in top categories by the Academy of Motion Pictures

Arts and Sciences. Best Actor: Don Cheadle, *Hotel Rwanda*, and Jamie Foxx, *Ray*. Best Supporting Actor: Morgan Freeman, *Million Dollar Baby*, and Jamie Foxx, *Collateral*. Best Supporting Actress: Sophie Okonedo, *Hotel Rwanda*. Jamie Foxx won and he is the first black actor to be nominated twice in the same year.

Introduction

Throughout human history, the art of visual communication and interpretation has played a significant role in fostering understanding both within and across cultures. From the earliest primitive cave drawings, to today's modern computer generated art and graphics, the old saying, "a picture paints a thousand words," still rings true. But, how about ten pictures, one thousand pictures, or several million still photographs moving rapidly across the bright flicker of a film projector's magical lamp? This multitude of fast flowing forms will not only paint words, but they will speak volumes.

Photographs and still pictures can evoke thought, cause an emotional response, or provoke a profound reaction while the moving image, when presented as a narrative sequence of events, can motivate and inspire us to action. The stories seem to unfold continuously on the screen, in real time, and it is often difficult to separate these constructed images from social realities. We take in this information, digest it, and draw conclusions from what we see. And, far too often, we accept these conclusions as truth without question. We buy into their validity, and, having no other source information to draw upon, we accept these filmed representations as fact.

The daunting subject of race and ethnicity permeated life in America at the turn of the 20th century and due to the effect of a certain few films, specific television images, and an often-biased news media, it still plagues us today. The United States Constitution plainly declares that "all men are created equal." However, in an attempt to justify the existence of slavery in America, society set out to define its darker hue population as "something less than." The awesome power of this new moving image was employed to perpetuate such racist beliefs, and created degrading stereotypes that would endure for years.

Thomas Edison was at the dawn of motion pictures when he stated that "whoever controls the motion picture industry controls the most powerful medium of influence over the people." And, he was right. Many social constructs and early anthropological theories, such as Darwinism, held that blacks were racially inferior to whites and therefore, deserve to be enslaved. As if to support this theory, the early-filmed images of Negroes portrayed them as such, practically incapable of being or doing anything else.

Even without sound the awesome power of the filmed image was realized virtually from its inception and its enormous potential for promotion, distortion, and vilifying propaganda has not gone to waste. The indoctrination potential of the moving image was quite effective and in the over one hundred years that have followed, there has been a constant struggle between Hollywood and the African American community over how their lives, images, and culture are portrayed on the silver screen.

THE DARK AGE OF AFRICAN AMERICAN CINEMA

There is no doubt that the images we are exposed to on film can influence our beliefs, motivate our actions, and manipulate the politics of society. Despite decades of collective protest and criticism over Hollywood's packaging and selling of black culture, blacks still have virtually no influence within the Hollywood film industry, or in the mainstream media institutions of America. So the purposeful selection of images and news stories allowed to grace both the big and the small screen are seldom very flattering, which has a powerful impact on the individual perceptions of how African Americans see themselves within society, and how others perceive them as well. This can all be too clearly seen from the first filmed images of African Americans, visions which should never have been allowed to fade up from black. These portrayals were degrading to say the least, and nothing more than purposeful attempts to belittle the Negro race before the eyes of an ever-growing world audience. Films like *The Watermelon Eating Contest, A Nigger in the Woodpile,* and *The Wooing and Wedding of a Coon* relegated the African American image to the lowest common denominator.

Many early cinematic depictions of blacks were merely unrehearsed coonery performed just to entertain the white masses, or simply minstrel shows from the vaudeville stage featuring happy darkies, dancing around as buffoons and jigaboos. White actors with burnt cork-covered faces portrayed the majority of these early characterizations, as they had done for many years in vaudeville skits, depicting these most degrading interpretations of black life. Later, black actors were paid to darken their faces even more and play similar roles, usually, with unemployment as their only alternative. However, when considering the volatile racial climate of the times, even if early Hollywood had wanted to make films that presented a more progressive or tolerant attitude when it came to the race question, theaters showing such films probably would have been burned to the ground.

Through the turn of the century, a dark exodus of Southern blacks was abandoning old Dixie to seek jobs and a better way of life in the industrialized northern cities, but the opportunities they sought were not always easy to find. By 1904, there was a new administration in the White House. President Teddy Roosevelt met with Booker T. Washington to address the concerns of the country's colored populations, and several Negroes were appointed to government positions. However, the dismal plight of the average black job seeker remained virtually the same. The white industrialists in the north often refused to hire blacks, and there was strong resentment from the white workers as well. Black applicants were sometimes beaten and lynched for trying to find employment, which led to the realization that Negroes were regarded as lower-class citizens in America, regardless of where they lived.

Then, on 4 July 1910, film cameras rolled at an outdoor boxing ring in Reno, Nevada. The odds were 10:6 in favor of former heavyweight champion Jim Jeffries, who was brought back from retirement to be the Great White Hope against challenging pugilist Jack Johnson. When the underdog Negro fighter won, at least 10 people died and hundreds more were injured due to riots and angry white retaliation. For the first time ever, there was an indisputable black heavyweight champion of the world and, as a historical record, the defeat had been captured on film for the whole world to see. But the print was instantly banned from public screenings around the globe, and the United States Congress even passed a special law making it a federal offense to transport films of prize fights across a state line. The most powerful image of a black man ever recorded was quickly made to disappear, while the more degrading images of African Americans continued, and even increased.

The first African American actor hired for a lead role in a major film production was Sam Lucas. He was cast as the title character in the third remake of *Uncle Tom's Cabin*, 1914. Based on the pre-Civil War novel on the cruelty of slavery and the racist old South, Harriet Beecher Stowe's book was a passionate indictment of what it was like to actually be a slave, and tried to portray its enslaved characters as human beings. However, the film version shifted the focus and used its propaganda power to negate all of that and the story became a sappy melodrama with Uncle Tom transformed into a shining example of black subservience, and Lucas' role became a despised character archetype in the black community. Even today, the term Uncle Tom is synonymous with any African American who seems too eager to please or to service the "white man," and for any black person considered to have too many white friends.

In an attempt to reflect and reinforce social attitudes that were safe and acceptable for the times, many other racist stereotypes would join the Uncle Tom on the silvery screen, such as Mammies, Mulattoes, Bucks, Sambos, and the popular good-for-nothin', lazy, lovable Coon. Stepin Fetchit, whose real name was Lincoln Perry, is credited with perfecting the coon role on the screen, and he became one of the highest-paid actors in Hollywood while doing it. Off-screen, however, he became known as "The High-Stepin Fetchit" because of his glamorous lifestyle of fancy cars, pretty women, and living the nightlife.

As despicable and degrading as the tom and coon stereotypes are considered to be, these strong and identifiable character archetypes are hard to shake loose. Many more questionable coon-like portrayals would appear in films to come, and even today, several stand-up comedians who have turned to acting are often criticized for portraying modern-day Uncle Toms and sophisticated coon roles. And, just like Stepin Fetchit before them, they are often among the highest-paid actors in Hollywood.

To be fair, Tinseltown is not the only culprit when it comes to presenting negative portrayals of African Americans on the screen. Black images on film are often called into question even when there is a black producer or director involved, and they can often get away with portraying far worse images as well. To be sure, in the early days most films perpetuated black myths and stereotypes with white characters in superior social positions and maintaining ultimate control. This eventually became a Hollywood staple and, if a change was to be made, it appeared that African American filmmakers would have to make it themselves.

THE GOLDEN AGE OF AFRICAN AMERICAN CINEMA

Several African American filmmakers emerged out of a need to address and counteract the blatant negativity of D. W. Griffith's epic but racist film *The Birth of a Nation*, in 1915. Although it was a revolutionary motion picture in style and cinematic technique, it played a major role in influencing, shaping, and distorting America's volatile race relations, and the world still suffers from its impact today.

However, three years before, William Foster of Foster Photoplay Company in Chicago independently raised the money to produce *The Railroad Porter*, 1912, a one-reel, Keystone Cops-style comedy, and became the first African American to control his own image on film. Foster was a hardworking jack of all trades with multiple careers as a talent agent, vaudeville performer, and sportswriter and circulation manager for the *Chicago Defender* newspaper. He even served a short stint as a Hollywood publicist, and was best known for promoting the famous vaudeville comedy team of Bert Williams and George Walker. Foster realized the tremendous commercial potential of this new-filmed entertainment medium and set out to capitalize on it. After *The Railroad Porter*, he continued to make a series of short films that featured local negro talent from Chicago's Robert Mott's Peking Theater Stock Company. His other films are *The Fall Guy*, 1913, another comedy; *The Butler,* 1913, a detective story; and *The Grafter and the Maid*, 1913, a melodrama.

Then, the one-two punch of *The Birth of a Nation*'s racist distortions in 1915, followed by the movie version of Edward Sheldon's despicable stage play entitled *The Nigger,* released just one month later, catapulted Emmett Scott, Noble Johnson, Clarence Brooks, Oscar Micheaux, and others into action.

In Los Angeles, two character actors, Noble Johnson and Clarence Brooks, established The Lincoln Motion Picture Company with the expressed purpose of portraying positive images and uplifting the race. As partners, they took on Dr. James T. Smith, a local druggist, and Harry Grant, a white Universal Studios camera operator. Their counter measure film was titled, *Realization of a Negro's Ambition*, 1916, about a college-educated black man (played by Noble) who leaves the family farm to seek his fortune in the world, only to return one day to find his fortune right there at home.

In the wake of the success of their first picture, George P. Johnson, a mailman from Omaha, Nebraska, and Noble's brother, joined the company. They made three additional films with dramatic story lines that stressed hard work, self-pride, and an individual's ability to reach his goals through persistence, decency, and integrity. *The Trooper of Company K*, released in 1918, was based on the Spanish-American War and the historic all-black 10th Cavalry's valiant fight against the Carramzita's soldiers at Carrizal, Mexico. A year later, in 1919, they released their first feature-length film, *A Man's Duty*, which dramatized a black man's right to participate freely in American life. In 1920, Noble returned to a steady paycheck as an actor with Universal Studios while George took over the company's business affairs. Their final film was *By Right of Birth*, 1921, and starred company co-founder Clarence A. Brooks. It was a middle-class success story about the pressures of racism, and a light-skinned black person who passes for white in hopes of experiencing the American dream. Despite his many promotional schemes devised to sell tickets and woo moviegoers into the theaters,

George Johnson could not fill the seats because of the limited income levels in black communities. Strapped for cash to make additional movies and keep the company going, he sought bank loans, but the banks saw no profit in the making of black films. The Lincoln Motion Picture Company was forced to close its doors in 1922.

Emmitt Scott was a personal secretary to scholar and civil rights leader Booker T. Washington. As a direct response to the negative portrayals of the Negro race as seen in Griffith's film, Scott spent years trying to produce a film entitled *Lincoln's Dream*, but securing the budget quickly became a daunting task. There was also talk of teaming up with the National Association for the Advancement of Colored People (NAACP) to turn Washington's autobiographical book *Up from Slavery* into a movie, but Washington died before the contracts could be signed. After much effort and many other broken alliances, a movie was finally released entitled *The Birth of a Race*, 1918, but not until financial difficulties forced Scott to take on white investors. When these new financiers came in, Scott no longer had any creative control. Most of the footage already shot was left on the cutting room floor, and not only was the name of the film changed, but the project took on a more universal theme and ceased to represent the hopes and aspirations of the Negro race. After straying from its original vision, purpose and intent, the budget grew to over $1 million and soon after its premiere at the Blackstone Theater in Chicago, the film was quickly declared an artistic and financial flop.

The most prolific black independent filmmaker of them all during the early years was Oscar Micheaux. From 1918 through 1948, Micheaux produced, directed, and often personally distributed over 30 feature length films. Ironically, The Lincoln Motion Picture Company contacted Micheaux to buy the movie rights to his self-published novel, *The Homesteader*, but passed when the brash young author insisted on directing the film himself. Undaunted by their rejection, he decided to make his book into a film anyway. As a filmmaker, Micheaux devised a very unique, one-man system of making and distributing his movies. He raised money by selling copies of his book and shares of stock in his publishing company. Once his film was complete, he hired a car and driver and "four-walled," or personally took the film print around the theater circuit to be screened. Micheaux had his next script, head shots of the leading actors and provocative production stills with him, and he would talk the theater owners into investing a portion of the night's proceeds in his next project. Once the screening tour was complete and the budget had been raised, he would start all over again. To keep down his production costs, Micheaux would use existing locations to shoot his scenes and would often only allow one take per shot. This often led to a rough quality in the performances and production value of his films, but he knew his work had limited draw at the box office regardless of the film's overall quality.

In an attempt to capitalize on Hollywood's tremendous influence, Micheaux built his ad campaigns around his stable of stars which included Bee Freeman as the Colored Mary Pickford, Evelyn Preer as the Negro Harlow, Slick Chester as the Colored Cagney, and Lorenzo Tucker as the Black Valentino. During these early days of black cinema, Anita Bush, Evelyn Preer, and Alice B. Russell, graced the screen in a variety of roles in these all-black cast independent films, while in Hollywood, black actresses were often relegated to mammy and housekeeper roles. Years later, Hattie McDaniel, the first African American to receive an Oscar for her role as "Mammy" in *Gone with the Wind,* 1939, is quoted as saying, "I'd rather make $750 dollars a week playing a maid than $7.50 a week being one."

Dozens of companies in the early to mid-1920s produced what were called race movies or sepia flicks. These all-black cast productions were shown at the hundreds of black-owned movie theaters and makeshift-screening facilities that existed in the South because of segregation and at Midnight Rambles held by segregated movie theaters when screenings for colored patrons started at midnight. They included Reol Films of New York, The Colored Players of Philadelphia, Norman Film Manufacturing Company of Jacksonville, Florida, Sack Amusement of Dallas, Texas, Ebony Pictures of Chicago, and many others. Most of these companies were white-owned, but the films they made were produced strictly to make money off a colored audience that was starved for images of themselves. The most notable was perhaps Richard C. Norman of the Norman Film Manufacturing Company, who produced the silent films *The Crimson Skull,* 1921, with Anita Bush; *The Flying Ace,* 1926, with Lawrence Criner; and *Black Gold,* 1928, with Kathryn Boyd.

With the advent of sound picture technology in 1927, most independent film companies were forced out of business because they could not afford the expensive sound equipment required to keep up. The first sound film, or "talkie" as it was called, made for a theatrical release was *The Jazz Singer,* 1927. In it, Al Jolson performs his famous song "Mammy" while in blackface, thus carrying this degrading stereotype from the vaudeville stage into the new era of sound film technology. Realizing the added entertainment value of sound, the big studio productions of Fox's *Hearts in Dixie,* and MGM's *Hallelujah,* both released in 1929, soon introduced the talkie to the black community.

Hearts in Dixie was billed as "the first all black, all-talking and singing musical." The film was a post-Civil War story about an illiterate tenant farmer who wants better for his family's future. Unfortunately, the film is seen today as a stereotypical representation of poor Southern blacks who seem quite happy and resigned to sing and dance their way through a life of hard field work and oppression. It starred Clarence Muse, Mildred Washington, and introduced Lincoln Perry (a.k.a. Stepin Fetchit) in his first major role. In fact, this is the film that made Stepin Fetchit a star, and the original script was expanded to exploit his on-screen image of a lazy, lovable coon.

Hallelujah is a story of redemption and salvation. After an unfortunate personal tragedy involving a huge gambling loss, a Southern cotton picker becomes a traveling preacher, only to be lured off the righteous path by a beautiful vixen. The film starred Daniel L. Haynes and introduced 16-year-old Nina Mae McKinney to the screen as the talkies, first, black love goddess, and tragic mulatto character.

As sound pictures became more mainstream and the hardships of the Great Depression raged on, race movies and the companies that made them all but ceased to exist. This brought an unfortunate end to the bold and assertive pioneer black filmmakers of the silent era. Meanwhile, Oscar Micheaux, being the wise entrepreneur he was, partnered with Leo Brecher and Frank Shiffman, two white businessmen who operated five of Harlem's seven movie theaters. This way, he made sound films and got them seen, but he no longer owned the company and had much less control. His first production with this new alliance was *The Exile*, 1932, and he continued to produce a wide variety of timely and controversial films until 1948.

Entertainment became a highly prized relief from the doldrums of everyday life during the hardship and squalor of the Great Depression. People could escape into a better world up on the screen and live vicariously through the two-dimensional, lifelike characters that were living a much better life than they were. When it came to an outlet for African American content, Hollywood released several specialty films that addressed specific themes within the black community, and a few based around the single black star of that time, Paul Robeson.

Robeson began his cinematic career in Oscar Micheaux's *Body and Soul*, 1924. In this silent film, he plays an escaped convict posing as a man of God. He drinks, gambles, and takes advantage of a young girl in his congregation one night after they are trapped in a storm. He is a real life wolf in minister's clothing, but in true dramatic form, his past and his shady dealings eventually catch up with him. After performing on stage in Europe, Robeson was brought to Hollywood to star as *The Emperor Jones*, 1933. As the title character of Brutus Jones, he is an ambitious Pullman Porter who steals his pal's girl, and then accidentally kills the jilted lover in a bar fight. He is sentenced to hard labor in a rock quarry, but escapes after killing a brutal prison guard who was harassing him. To avoid angry white protests, the shots of the actual killing of the guard were cut from the film. He takes a job as a stoker on a steamship headed for Haiti, but jumps ship early and uses tricks and superstition to take political control of a remote Caribbean island. Once in power he becomes callous and greedy, and constantly pushes his luck, until the people rise up and turn against him. Robeson played other powerful roles in films like *Saunders of the River*, 1935, with Nina Mae McKinney; *Showboat*, 1936, with Hattie McDaniel; and in the mainstream film *Tales of Manhattan*, 1942, with Ethel Waters. Robeson was often required to sing in his films, but refused to take any role he felt was stereotypical or demeaning. He eventually became disillusioned, however, over how his performances would sometimes be undermined in the editing process. His career was cut short when he was labeled a communist during the McCarthy Era for being an outspoken critic of America's unfair racial policies and practices toward the Negro, while often praising his unbiased acceptance and personal experiences in the Soviet Union.

Hollywood's specialty films of the post-Depression period covered a wide variety of topics and film genres. These included the thriller *Drums of Voodoo*, 1934, which featured a voodoo princess out to save her small town from being taken over by the local villain; the religion-based *Green Pastures*, 1935, which was a series of vignettes based on characters and events from the Old Testament of the Bible; and, the action-packed Western *Harlem on the Prairie*, 1938.

Having "Harlem" in the film's title was a quick way to let distributors know it was an all black cast film. It starred Herbert Jeffrey, who became known as "the Bronze Buckaroo." He plays Jeff Kincaid, a singing cowboy who helps the daughter of an old-time medicine show performer recover a stash of hidden gold. Jeffrey was a well-known vocalist with the Earl Hines Big Band at the time and he croons the film's title song with his backup singers, The Four Tones. Jeffrey would later change his name to Herb Jeffries and continue his singing and recording career. Crime dramas were added to the mix when former Apollo Theater emcee Ralph Cooper formed a partnership with producer Harry Popkin to create Million Dollar Productions. Through this collaboration Cooper, as an on-screen mobster, ruled the numbers racket in *Dark Manhattan*, 1937, fleeced the syndicate in *Bargain With Bullets*, 1939, and gets pinned for a jewelry store robbery he did not commit in *Double Deal*, 1939.

Also very popular around this time was a series of black musical shorts featuring the talents of Louis Armstrong in *A Rhapsody in Black and Blue*, 1932, and Cab Calloway in *Hi-De-Ho*, 1935, and *Blow My Top Blues*, 1936. Unlike music videos of today, which have gained their own venues of distribution and exhibition, these short productions were spliced at the beginning of white cast films often shown at black theaters. It was this string of musical shorts that set the stage for Hollywood's next push in African American based films that consisted of spectacular, big-budget, all-black cast musicals.

THE SILVER AGE OF AFRICAN AMERICAN CINEMA

On 7 December 1941, America was dragged into World War II when Japanese fighter planes attacked the U.S. naval base at Pearl Harbor, Hawaii. Meanwhile in Hollywood, the on-screen shooting stopped in gangster films like *Gang War*, 1940, and the music started with two grand-scale musicals produced by MGM and 20th Century Fox.

Fox's *Stormy Weather*, 1943, has been hailed as the most important black musical of its time, if not of all time. It was Lena Horne's first major starring role since going from a Cotton Club chorus line to being discovered in the independent film *The Duke is Tops*, 1938. *Stormy Weather* is told mostly in flashback as Bill, a retired hoofer, tells a group of neighborhood children about his days on the stage and the woman he loved but lost to show business. When some of his friends decide to throw a tribute in his honor, the whole gang returns, including his lost love, Selena. The film also stars Bill "Bojangles" Robinson, Cab Calloway, Fats Waller, Emmit "Babe" Wallace, The Katherine Dunham Dancers, and the legendary dancing of the Nicholas Brothers. All of these acts are at their performing peaks and their artistry on the screen is unparalleled.

MGM's *Cabin in the Sky*, 1943, was adapted to the screen from the highly successful stage play and took most of the theatrical cast with it. The film has been described as a religious musical fantasy and tells the story of Little Joe Jackson, a good hearted, back-sliding sinner with an "appointment with repentance." His wife, Petunia, is a godly woman with powerful prayers for her husband's salvation. When a hot-tempered gambler named Domino Johnson nearly takes Little Joe's life, a battle for his soul begins between Lucifer Jr., and The General, an emissary for The Lord.

By the mid-1940s, the fighting in Europe and Asia had taken its toll on vital resources and all-black cast films became casualties of war. Independent producers, such as Spencer Williams and Teddy Toddy, turned out an occasional release, while white producers, such as Jed Buell and Alfred Sack, continued to keep black actors working as well. But the dark film producers had to do battle with an even darker presence while pursuing their craft. The almost insurmountable wall of prejudice and racial hatred still permeated the mindset of many white Americans, and it often appeared that those in Hollywood thought no differently. Access to skilled and qualified Negro technicians was difficult because technical trade unions were closed to Negroes, and their chances of receiving bank loans to cover production costs and equipment purchases was virtually nonexistent.

But, like the pioneering efforts of William Foster, Noble and George Johnson, Emmett Scott, and Oscar Micheaux before them, these sepia storytellers forged ahead against the odds to assert control over their own-filmed images. Spencer Williams struck a production deal with Sack Amusement Company of Dallas, Texas, to write, direct, and star in a string of nine films over a seven-year period. These included *Son of Ingagi*, 1940; *Blood of Jesus*, 1941; *Go Down Death*, 1941; *The Girl in Room 20*, 1945; *Dirty Gertie from Harlem U.S.A.*, 1946; and *Juke Joint*, 1947. Williams was an all-around filmmaker who had worked in the industry for years, including playing the heavy in three of the Herbert Jeffrey Westerns. He observed while on the set, asked questions, and learned to work easily on both sides of the camera. However, he is perhaps best remembered for portraying Andy Brown, in the highly controversial television series *Amos 'n' Andy*, which aired from 1951 to 1953 on CBS.

Teddy Toddy set out to produce a series of musicals and romantic comedy adventures through his company Toddy Pictures. His first film, *The Duke is Tops*, 1940, starred recently discovered Lena Horne, who ironically portrayed a musical celebrity, and then became one. The Toddy Pictures comedies starred former vaudeville comedians like Pigmeat Markham in *House-Rent Party*, 1946; Eddie Green in *Eddie's Laugh Jamboree*, 1947; and funnyman Mantan Moreland in *Mantan Messes Up*, 1946; and *Come On Cowboy*, 1948. Moreland became better known as Charlie Chan's bug-eyed, taxi-driving sidekick, in the long-running detective series of films. Toddy's string of light musical adventures included *Beware*, 1946; *Reet, Petite and Gone*, 1947; and *Here Comes Mr. Jordan*, 1948, all starring scat-singing music-man Louis Jordan.

Outside of the box office, there was an ever-expanding chasm growing between the races due to America's policy of bigotry and Jim Crow Laws. African Americans had proudly fought during World War II expecting to find progress, appreciation, and social change upon their return to America. It never happened. However, in an attempt to become socially conscious, Hollywood set out to explore and define the boundaries of this harsh and divisive social ill.

The problem pictures began with producer Stanley Kramer's wartorn *Home of the Brave,* 1949, in which a black soldier returns home paralyzed from a reconnaissance mission on a Japanese-held island with no sign of any physical trauma. We learn that his problem is not only psychological, but it is also more universal than one might think because the film was adapted from a stage play in which the soldier was not black, but Jewish. *Pinky*, 1949, explores the world of a light-skinned girl who leaves home in search of a better life, and forsakes her loving black grandmother to pass for white. *Lost Boundaries*, 1949, is another passing film based on a true story, in which a prominent doctor and his family live happily in an all-white neighborhood, until it is discovered they are not "white." Staying true to the Hollywood form, these films cast white actors in the passing roles, but they at least attempted to shine what was meant to be a healing light on America's ailing problems of race prejudice, bigotry, and miscegenation. They also exposed the perception that there is something intrinsically wrong if you are born with the slightest bit of black blood in your veins.

THE TV AGE AND AFRICAN AMERICAN CINEMA

When television was first introduced in the early 1950s, many in Hollywood believed that it was just a fad. They said that nobody would be crazy enough to sit at home and stare into a tiny square box for hours a day, but they did not realize how "crazy" the American public actually was. People did stay home to watch the little box and Hollywood almost went bankrupt. It tried to entice audiences back into the theater with tricks and gimmicks like Wide Screen Cinemascope, 3-D movies, and even Smell-a-Vision, trying to make the theater-going experience spectacular and far beyond anything that television could ever provide. Unfortunately, nothing seemed to work.

At the same time, Negroes were again being denied representation, but now on both the big and the small screen. The black population of the United States had reached about 15 million, but this growth was not being reflected on the silver screen, and Negroes were not treated as full equals. Black soldiers were now being shipped off to fight and die for freedom in the Korean War, while racism still ran rampant in the self-proclaimed "land of the free."

This era brought biography films on black sports heroes like *The Jackie Robinson Story,* 1950. Jackie Robinson actually plays himself in this biopic about the ball player's life and career struggles. He is credited with breaking the color line in modern major league baseball, and the film depicts not only his dreams, but the courage, determination, and restraint it took to withstand the initial hatred and resentment from his teammates, the fans, and white society at large. Robinson had to endure it all while turning the proverbial "other cheek," until he helped the Brooklyn Dodgers win the pennant. After that, just like in the black community, Jackie Robinson was everybody's hero. Although boxing champion Joe Lewis had played himself in two films, *Spirit of Youth,* 1938, and *The Fight Never Ends,* 1949, appearing with Clarence Muse and Ruby Dee, respectively, the real "The Brown Bomber" was portrayed by actor Coley Wallace in *The Joe Lewis Story*, 1954.

As black roles continued into the 1950s, Hollywood harvested a new crop of stars and on-screen black images. Dorothy Dandridge and Harry Belafonte starred in *Bright Road*, 1953, a film about schoolteachers and stressing the importance of an education. The romantic duo sizzled on the screen and they were teamed up again in *Carmen Jones*, 1954, for which Ms. Dandridge became the first of her race to receive the top Oscar nomination for Best Actress. An adaptation of the Bizet opera of *Carmen*, Dandridge plays a detained parachute factory worker who entices Belafonte, the military GI ordered to lock her up for fighting, to go AWOL with her. The manipulative vixen soon tires of him and when a champion prizefighter takes her fancy, the rejected GI takes her life.

Another bronze bombshell to hit the big screen toward the end of the 1950s was Eartha Kitt, who starred in *Anna Lucasta*, 1958, and *St. Louis Blues*, 1958. In *Anna Lucasta*, Kitt plays a prostitute torn between pleasing her family and her life on the streets. The American Negro Theater adapted the story from a play about a Polish family and turned it into a Broadway hit. In the film version, Kitt plays opposite three leading men of that time, Sammy Davis Jr., Rex Ingram, and Frederick O'Neil. In *St. Louis Blues*, Kitt plays voluptuous GoGo Germaine, a tempting nightclub singer who helps to put W. C. Handy's music on the map. Known as the father of jazz music, Handy, played by Nat King Cole, is persecuted at an early age by his strict minister father. He encounters rejection, rebellion, and even blindness in pursuit of the music he loves. Many years later, GoGo performs an entire show of his songs at Carnegie Hall, as Handy and his style of music are honored as an original American art form.

In 1957, due to mounting pressures from the civil rights movement, President Dwight D. Eisenhower signed the Voting Rights Act into law, but there was still much resistance and open hostility to blacks exercising their right to vote. However, the tide was about to turn as the African American communities refused to accept lower-class treatment and widespread racial discrimination any longer. The emphasis was being shifted from that of nonviolent resistance to the bold and assertive tactics being stressed by the oncoming Black Power movement.

As if a prelude to the approaching change in the political trend, actors Sidney Poitier and Woody Strode stood tall and strong in on-screen performances throughout the 1960s. Poitier starred in many socially conscious films like *A Raisin in the Sun*, 1961; *In the Heat of the Night*, 1967; and *Guess Who's Coming to Dinner*, 1967. Strode portrayed a series of unique and powerful characters, such as a falsely accused Buffalo Soldier in *Sergeant Rutledge*, 1960; a Nubian warrior in *Spartacus*,

1960; and a deadly gunfighter in *Once Upon a Time in the West*, 1968. Strode mostly appeared in mainstream films, however, and was often the only dark face on the screen.

Despite these previous two examples, such strong and dignified roles for black actors were in short supply. But as always, the independents were working to help fill the void. Several art house films made it to the big screen that attempted to comment on the mental anguish that just being black in America often brought to bear with its strict codes of separatism and racial inequities. These included Shirley Clark's *The Cool World*, 1963, introducing Clarence Williams III; Robert Young's *Nothing But a Man*, 1964, with Ivan Dixon and Abby Lincoln; Larry Peerce's *One Potato Two Potato*, 1964, with Bernie Hamilton; and Anthony Harvey's *Dutchman*, 1967 starring Al Freeman Jr.

In 1969, *The Learning Tree*, a film based on still photographer Gordon Park's autobiography, was released. This powerful portrait of a young black kid coming of age in a racist Midwestern town brought a quiet and dignified humanity to the screen. Newt Winger is a curious and fun-loving pre-teenager growing up in Cherokee Flats, Kansas, in the 1920s under the crippling effects of Jim Crow laws. As he comes of age, he loses his innocence and learns about racial hatred, the unfairness of life, and the inevitability of death. Parks made history by becoming the first African American to direct a major motion picture for a Hollywood studio. He also wrote the script, produced the film, and composed the original music score. Ground had been broken, progress had been made, and there was a strong wind blowing through the inner cities that would hit Hollywood with hurricane force.

THE BRONZE AGE OF AFRICAN AMERICAN CINEMA

In the 1960s, "Say it loud, I'm black and I'm proud" became the battle cry for African Americans to accept our dark skin and turn a perceived negative aspect of our very being that could not be changed into a positive. A new race pride had been spawned, a social awareness had been raised, and a generation of filmed images was about to hit the screen to help solidify this fresh black consciousness.

Salted by former NFL football star Jim Brown's role as a tough Southern sheriff in ...*tick*...*tick*...*tick*, 1970, and peppered by the hip-talking cop duo of Raymond St. Jacques and Godfrey Cambridge in *Cotton Comes to Harlem*, 1970, the scene was being set for something exciting and new. Something that would give birth to a whole new film genre and light up once-darkened movie screens like never before.

Melvin Van Peebles's independent film *Sweet Sweetback's Baadasssss Song*, 1971, with its rebellious anti-hero lead, literally kicked what became known as The Blaxploitation Era into high gear. It lasted from 1971 to 1976, and consisted of five years of angry soul brothers and sisters kicking "The Man's" butt all over the big screen. These films hit the screen strong with hard-hitting titles like *Shaft, Superfly, Slaughter, Sheba Baby, Trouble Man, Hit-Man, Coffy, Cleopatra Jones, Hammer, Hell Up in Harlem, Black Belt Jones, Blackula,* and *Thomasine & Bushrod,* just to name a few. Ivan Dixon's drama based on Sam Greenlee's ex-CIA novel, *The Spook Who Sat by the Door,* 1973, gave black characters on the screen a power and identity like never before. These characters were taking control, fighting against the white establishment for influence and respect, and famished filmgoers who, for years, had been denied and disenfranchised, lived vicariously through these empowering cinematic experiences.

These movies made instant stars out of Richard Roundtree, Ron O'Neil, Max Julien, Robert Hooks, Bernie Casey, Pam Grier, Tamara Dobson, Fred Williamson, Jim Kelly, Gloria Hendry, William Marshall, and Vonetta McGee. It also introduced comedian Richard Pryor to the big screen in a small role in the popular pimp drama, *The Mack,* 1973. Controversy soon erupted over how negative many of these images actually were. Rudy Ray Moore's now ghetto classic *Dolemite,* 1975, was independently produced but did nothing to improve upon the black image on film. To some, the glorification of pimps, hookers, and drug dealers was no better than the olden-day stereotypes of mammies, coons, bucks, brutes, and uncle toms.

While Hollywood was serving us "Rock'em–Sock'em Negroes," the independents were producing a variety of alternative films. Bill Gunn's *Ganja and Hess,* 1973, Haile Gerima's *Bush Mamma,* 1976, Larry Clark's *Passing Through,* 1977, along with Charles Burnett's *Killer of Sheep,* 1977, which is now a part of the American Film Institute's Film Registry, all dealt with a different perspective of African American life and showed a more human side of the black experience.

However, by 1976, black films were again on their way out. Just as it seemed they were gaining a foothold, getting some clout, and possibly building a little power in the industry, it was all gone again. What happened? Despite all the discussion and criticism as to the overall merits of these films, black people were tired of seeing themselves portrayed as pimps, pushers, and prostitutes. And, although these images may have saved some Hollywood studios from filing bankruptcy, they refused to change these images and simply concluded that black films were no longer profitable.

THE DAWN OF THE CROSSOVER COMEDIANS

In the late 1970s, Richard Pryor became the single black star of the time and could be seen in films like *Car Wash,* 1976; *Which Way is Up?* 1977; and *Greased Lightning,* 1977, all directed by Michael Schultz. Hollywood even turned the hit Broadway play *The Wiz,* 1978, into a film and cast Pryor in the title role. Once again, black actors were singing and dancing in a big-budget, all-black cast musical, but as usual, a black director could not be trusted to direct.

As black images trickled into the 1980s, most of the black presence came from comedians turned actors like Richard Pryor, Eddie Murphy, Whoopi Goldberg, and Bill Cosby. They worked constantly in films such as *The Toy,* 1982; *Beverly Hills Cop,* 1984; *Jumpin' Jack Flash,* 1986; and *Leonard Part 6,* 1987. However, these were predominantly white-cast films with the comedian's lead role intended to help cross the movie over to the black audience and boost the box office appeal. This successful formula opened the door for a host of future funny men and women to make people laugh on the big screen, such as Bernie Mac, Steve Harvey, Mo'Nique, Chris Tucker, and Chris Rock.

This period brought forth a series of new images for African American women as well. Talk show host Oprah Winfrey first graced the silver screen in *The Color Purple,* 1985, a film based on Alice Walker's Pulitzer Prize–winning novel. This highly anticipated film actually flipped the script and relegated the male characters to subordinate and supporting roles. Winfrey would go on to become a media powerhouse, as well as the first African American woman billionaire with film production as a major part of her empire.

THE NEW BLACK FILM RENAISSANCE

The influence of Spike Lee's independently produced, *She's Gotta Have It,* 1986, began a new era black film productivity. His tale of an African American woman who could not get satisfaction from the three men in her life did satisfy the ravenous taste buds of a famished black audience. Then came Robert Townsend's *Hollywood Shuffle* and Keenon Ivory Wayans's *I'm Gonna Get You Sucka.* Then, Hollywood turned the 1970s boom 180 degrees around when Mario Van Peebles's *New Jack City,* 1991, ushered in an era where instead of kicking The Man's butt all over the screen, black people were kicking each other's butts all over the screen. And, far too often, these films were blasting black butts completely off the screen as well. John Singleton's *Boyz N the Hood,* 1991; Ernest Dickerson's *Juice,* 1992; Steve Anderson's *South Central,* 1992; and the Hughes Brother's *Menace II Society,*

1993, all lead to a series of films depicting drugs, guns, and blatant inner-city violence starring "black on black" crime.

Several African American women also entered the fold during this new wave. Julie Dash with *Daughters of the Dust*, 1991, Darnell Martin with *I Like It Like That*, 1994, and Kasi Lemmons with *Eve's Bayou*, 1997, have all helmed the director's chair and shown their version of African American life from a softer and more feminine side.

Hollywood caught a serious case of rappermania in the last decade of the 20th century as rap and hip-hop artists such as Ice Cube, Ice T, Queen Latifah, Tupac, DMX, L.L. Cool J, Eve, and Bow Wow became serious movie stars, and were bringing their already-established music following to the box office. Often, these artists also contributed to the film's soundtrack album, which, at times, would outsell the movie. Although entertainer extraordinaire Prince tried but failed to meld his music persona into films like *Under the Cherry Moon*, 1986, and *Graffiti Bridge*, 1990, the audience readily accepted films like *Friday*, *Trespass*, *Like Mike*, *All about the Benjamins*, *Brown Sugar*, and *Barbershop*. One major difference was that these already-established musical talents actually acted in these films and only rapped on the movie soundtracks. Even multi-talented rapper Will Smith followed his successful TV sitcom *The Fresh Prince of Bel Air* to the big screen in mega-hits like *Independence Day*, *Men in Black I & II*, *Enemy of the State*, *Bad Boys I & II*, and *Ali*. He also carried the sci-fi thriller *I-Robot*, to a huge box-office success, becoming one of the hardest-working and highest-paid actors in the industry.

AFRICAN AMERICA CINEMA: INTO A NEW MILLENNIUM

Thanks to broader access and advancing media technologies heading into the 21st century, the black film stream has been relatively steady. With the advent of VCRs, DVDs, video stores, satellite TV, and cable channels such as BET and TV-One, access to images that represent African Americans have been plentiful. Nearly 100 years of black films and television movies can be purchased, rented, or borrowed to watch any time. Consumers can also order programs off the Internet or download movie trailers and streaming video directly into our home computers. This expands not only our program access but also our product need. There have been times when we may have been put on a diet from a lot of new black films, but there has been no 10-year famine as in the decades before. *Waiting to Exhale*, 1995, the long-awaited film based on Terry McMillan's best-selling novel, might have been the catalyst for a new black film feast, but it was not. It also was not an independent film, and historically, it has taken an independent project to create a major shift in the way that Hollywood does business with blacks.

The film version of Tyler Perry's popular and highly successful stage production of *Diary of a Mad Black Woman*, hit the big screen in 2005. If the box office gross matches its theatrical receipts, this independent film has the potential to motivate Hollywood into another wave of African American-based productions. Films like *Ray*, 2004; *Hotel Rwanda*, 2004; and the long-awaited movie based on the Zora Neal Hurston novel *Their Eyes Were Watching God*, 2005, may also have an affect on the type and numbers of films Hollywood will produce in the future.

However, despite all of the progress African Americans have made in Hollywood, the National Association for Colored People still complains that, as of 2005, there is still no person of color at any of the major studios who can green light a film project. African American directors are being assigned to big-budget mainstream film productions, but the images on the screen continue to be controlled and filtered through a bevy of decision-makers who do not posses the cultural experience or sensibilities of the target audience these films are meant to represent.

On the independent side, however, the latest digital video production formats that are now available, affordable, and more acceptable by mainstream industry standards will play a major role in the future of African American cinema. In the years to come, more independently produced stories will be shot on digital video and possibly transferred to film for distribution, or simply exhibited over television, cable, and Internet outlets. These stories will be told more and more by everyday people who have something to say, and by those who have never seen their voice and image adequately represented on screen. As new technologies bring the power of the moving image to the masses, African Americans will shoot with hand-held digital cameras, edit on home computers, and share their stories with a global audience via the Internet and the World Wide Web. These independently produced visions will add to the diverse cache of African American images being displayed on an ever-expanding silver screen. This wide range of stories, topics, views, and genres will finally give the world a glimpse of African American life that has long been ignored, and has yet to be seen.

Cinema is the youngest of all of the creative arts and these new and innovative means of visual storytelling will continue to entertain, motivate, inspire, educate, and encourage not only African Americans to record and share their most intimate visions of life, but all the people of the world for many years to come.

The Dictionary

A

AALIYAH (1979-2001). Singer, actress. She was born Aaliyah Dana Haughton in Brooklyn, New York, and she was destined to be a star. Aaliyah was first noticed when she appeared on the TV series *Star Search*, and recorded her first album, *Age Ain't Nothing but a Number*, with the help of singer R. Kelly. Her second album, *One in a Million*, was a huge success and more opportunities soon followed. Producer Joel Silver cast her in *Romeo Must Die*, 2000, his action-packed martial arts film starring Jet Li, after seeing her perform at the Grammys. Her next film role was as the title character in *Queen of the Damned*, 2002, a vampire film based on the book by Anne Rice. In 2001, her self-titled third album was released, *Aaliyah*. She died months later in a plane crash while returning from a music video shoot in the Bahamas.

Filmography: *Romeo Must Die*, 2000; *Queen of the Damned*, 2002.

AARON LOVES ANGELA. 1975. (R) 99 min. Urban Romance. *Romeo and Juliet* meet *West Side Story*. It is the story of an undying love between a Puerto Rican girl and an African American boy, set amidst the harsh, often-divisive realities of the inner city. Cast: **Kevin Hooks**, **Irene Cara**, **Moses Gunn**, **Robert Hooks**, Jose Feliciano. Director: **Gordon Parks**. Music: Jose Feliciano.

ABBY. 1974. (R) 89 min. Horror. Abby is a sweet, mild-mannered marriage counselor who is married to a minister. When her father-in-law goes on an archeological dig in Africa, he unleashes an ancient

Nigerian sex demon that possesses her soul. Cast: **Carol Speed, William Marshall, Terry Carter, Juanita Moore,** Austin Stocker, Elliott Moffitt, Nathan Cook, Nancy Lee Owens, Claude Fulkerson, William P. Bradford. Director: William Girdler.

ABDUL-JABBAR, KAREEM (1947-). Basketball player, athlete, actor. The long-time star 7'2" center for the Los Angeles Lakers was born Lew Al Cindor, but changed his name to Kareem Abdul-Jabbar when he converted to the Muslim faith. Having achieved celebrity status, he occasionally guest starred in films, including the basketball flick *The Fish That Saved Pittsburgh*, 1979, with star forward Julius Irving; *Game of Death*, 1979, with martial arts master Bruce Lee; and in the sports spoof *BASEketball*, 1998.

Filmography: *The Fish That Saved Pittsburgh*, 1979; *Game of Death*, 1979; *Airplane*, 1980; *Fletch*, 1985; *Purple People Eater*, 1988; *Stephen King's The Stand*, 1994; *D2: The Mighty Ducks*, 1994; *Slam-Dunk Ernest*, 1995; *Rebound: The Legend of Earl "The Goat" Manigault*, 1996; *BASEketball*, 1998.

ABOVE THE RIM. 1994. (R) 97 min. Urban Drama. A high school basketball star is torn between accepting a college scholarship offer and making money hustling in street games. Cast: **Duane Martin, Tupac Shakur, Leon, Marlon Wayans,** Tonya Pinkins, **Bernie Mac.** Director: Jeff Pollack. Writers: Jeff Pollack, Barry Michael Cooper. Music: Marcus Miller.

ACADEMY AWARDS. A gala awards ceremony held each year in Hollywood, California, by the **Academy of Motion Picture Arts and Sciences.** Awards of merit are presented to film artists and technicians to recognize exceptional work within the industry. Up to five nominees in each specialty area are selected by members of 13 art and craft branches. Actors choose actors, directors choose directors, cinematographers choose cinematographers, etc. The nominees are voted on in a secret ballot by the entire 5,000 Academy membership. The ceremony is telecast around the world and reaches over one billion viewers. The coveted award is represented by a 13-1/2-inch-high gold-plated statuette and known as an **Oscar.** African American Oscar winners include **Hattie McDaniel,** Best Supporting Actress, *Gone with the Wind*, 1939; **Sidney Poitier,** Best Actor, *Lilies of the Field*, 1963; **Louis Gossett Jr.,** Best Supporting Actor, *An Officer and a Gentleman*, 1982; **Denzel Washington,** Best Supporting Actor, *Glory*, 1989; **Whoopi Goldberg,** Best Supporting Actress, *Ghost*, 1990; **Cuba Gooding Jr.,** Best Supporting Actor, *Jerry Maguire*, 1996; **Halle Berry,** Best Actress, *Monster's Ball*, 2001; **Denzel Washington**, Best Actor, ***Training Day***, 2001.

ACADEMY OF MOTION PICTURE ARTS AND SCIENCES. Established in 1927 as a nonprofit organization to "improve the artistic quality of the film medium, provide a common forum for the various branches and crafts of the industry, foster cooperation in technical research and cultural progress, and pursue a variety of other stated objectives." Membership is by invitation only. It is mostly known for its annual **Academy Awards** presentation.

ACADEMY OF TELEVISION ARTS AND SCIENCES. The Academy of Television Arts and Sciences Foundation utilizes the resources and membership of the Television Academy to develop and sponsor educational and archival programs addressing a variety of issues, including career guidance, student achievement, personal skill development, diversity, and the documentation of television's evolution. The Foundation is a nonprofit organization with a primary focus to use the history and artistry of television to preserve our past for posterity and to guide those who will be our future. The organization is a co-sponsor of the **Emmy Awards**.

ACROSS 110TH STREET. 1972. (R) 102 min. Drama. Filmed on location in Harlem, this hard-core, violent, and gritty cop thriller follows three black thieves as the cops and the Mafia chase them after robbing a mob-controlled bank. Cast: Anthony Quinn, **Yaphet Kotto**, Tony Franciosa, Paul Benjamin, Ed Bernard, **Antonio Fargas, Richard Ward**. Director: Barry Shear. Writer: Luther Davis.

AJAYE, FRANKLIN (1949-). Actor, comedian. This popular standup comic was a popular talk-show guest throughout the 1970s and 1980s, and was the host *of National Lampoon's Hot Flashes*, a syndicated variety series. In 1975, he was a regular on the summer-replacement comedy series *Keep on Trucking*. His feature film roles include *Car Wash*, 1977, and *The 'burbs*, 1990.

Filmography: *Car Wash*, 1976; *Convoy*, 1978; *The Jazz Singer*, 1980; *Get Crazy*, 1983; *Fraternity Vacation*, 1985; *The Wrong Guys*, 1988; *The 'burbs*, 1990; *American Yakuza*, 1994.

ALEXANDER, ERIKA (1969-). Actress. She was born in Winslow, Arizona, and attended school at the Philadelphia High School for Girls. She also studied acting at the Freedom Theater. Her big break came when she landed the role of Pamela Tucker on *The Cosby Show*. She would later be cast as a regular in the **television**

series *Going to Extremes*, and portrayed the role of Maxine Shaw in the sitcom *Living Single*. Her notable film roles include *The Long Walk Home*, 1990; *Full Frontal*, 2002; and the TV movie *Mama Flora's Family*, 1998.

Filmography: *My Little Girl*, 1986; *The Long Walk Home*, 1990; *He Said, She Said*, 1991; *Fathers & Sons*, 1992; *30 Years to Life*, 2001; *Love Liza*, 2002; *Full Frontal*, 2002; *Tricks*, 2003.

ALEXANDER, KHANDI (1957-). Actress, dancer. A native of New York City, she was educated at Queensborough Community College. She has appeared on Broadway and was once dance choreographer for **Whitney Houston**. On **television**, she has had roles in such shows as *News Radio* and *ER*. Alexander is currently co-starring as coroner Alexx Woods on *CSI: Miami*.

Filmography: *What's Love Got to Do with It?* 1993; *CB4: The Movie*, 1993; *Sugar Hill*, 1994; *Greedy*, 1994; *Robin Cook's Terminal*, 1996; *There's Something About Mary*, 1998; *Thick as Thieves*, 1999; *Dark Blue*, 2003.

ALEXANDER, WILLIAM (1916-1991). Producer. He was born in Denver, Colorado, and educated at Colorado State University and the University of Chicago. During World War II, Alexander became the official state filmmaker for Ethiopia under Emperor Haile Selassie, and also did film work for Liberia under President William S. B. Tubman. He was an organizer of the Associated Producers of Negro Motion Pictures in New York City in 1945, shot two military documentaries in 1946, and became producer-director of *All-American Newsreel*. His early films include *Flicker Up*, 1946, with Billy Eckstine and Marylou Harris; *Love in Syncopation*, 1946, with **Ruby Dee** and June Eckstine; and the musical short *Jivin' in Be-Bop*, 1946, featuring Dizzy Gillespie. Alexander's first feature film was *The Fight Never Ends*, 1948, starring ex-boxing champion Joe Lewis. His other features include *Souls of Sin*, 1949, and *The Klansman*, 1974, for Paramount Pictures starring **O. J. Simpson** in his film acting debut. Alexander was a 1995 inductee into the **Black Filmmakers Hall of Fame**.

ALI. 2001. (R) 158 min. Biopic. This film chronicles a decade in the life of former world heavyweight boxing champion **Muhammad Ali**, from 1964 to 1974. Cast: **Will Smith, Jamie Foxx**, John Voight, **Mario Van Peebles**, Ron Silver, **Jeffrey Wright, Mykelti Williams, Jada Pinkett Smith, Michael Michele, Joe Morton**, Paul Rodriquez, **Nona Gaye**, Bruce McGill, Barry Henley, **Giancarlo Esposito**, Laurence Mason, **LeVar Burton, Albert Hall,**

David Cubitt, Ted Levine, David Elliott, Michael Bentt, James N. Toney, Charles Shuford, Malick Bowens, Shari Watson, **Victoria Dillard**, Kim Robillard, Gaillard Sartain, Rufus Dorsey, Robert Sale, Damien Wills, Michael Dorn. Director: Michael Mann. Writers: Michael Mann, Stephen J. Rivele, Christopher Wilkinson, Eric Roth. Cinematographer: Emmanuel Lubezki. Music: Lisa Gerrard, Pieter Bourke.

ALICE, MARY (1941-). Actress. The Mississippi-born Alice began her career with the Negro Ensemble Company and played many roles off-Broadway. Later, she won a Tony Award for her performance in the August Wilson play *Fences*, and played Broadway in *Having Our Say: The Delaney Sisters' First 100 Years*, with veteran actress **Gloria Foster**. Her television credits include guest spots on *Sanford and Son, Good Times, The Cosby Show*, and *A Different World*. Her television movies include *The Women of Brewster Place* and the HBO miniseries *Laurel Avenue*. Alice won an **Emmy** for her performance in an episode of *I'll Fly Away*. She has played many powerful mother roles in films like *Sparkle*, 1976; *To Sleep With Anger*, 1990; and *Down in the Delta*, 1998. She recently took over the role as The Oracle in the final installment of the Matrix Trilogy, replacing her friend and former co-star, the late Gloria Foster.

Filmography: *Sparkle*, 1976; *He Who Walks Alone*, 1978; *Killing Floor*, 1985; *Charlotte Forten's Mission: Experiment in Freedom*, 1985; *The Women of Brewster Place*, 1989; *To Sleep with Anger*, 1990; *Laurel Avenue*, 1993; *Down in the Delta*, 1998; *Catfish in Black Bean Sauce*, 2000; *Sunshine State*, 2002; *The Matrix Revolutions*, 2003.

ALI, MUHAMMAD (1942-). Born Cassius Marcellus Clay in Louisville, Kentucky, Ali became the dominant heavyweight boxing champion throughout the 1960s and 1970s. He won the boxing gold medal in the 1960 Summer Olympic Games in Rome, Italy, and with his loud mouth and flamboyant style, he quickly became a celebrity in the world of sports. He labeled himself as the greatest fighter of all time and actually lived up to that claim by capturing the world heavyweight title on three separate occasions. Controversy surrounded him in the 1960s as he spoke out against and refused to fight in the Vietnam War, advocated black pride, and converted to the Muslim faith. He starred in his Hollywood biopic *The Greatest*, 1977, and would occasionally guest star on film and television. He retired from boxing in 1981, but remained an international public figure. Rapper turned actor **Will Smith** portrayed the famous pugilist in the recent biopic *Ali*, 2001.

Filmography: *Requiem for a Heavyweight*, 1962; *The Greatest*, 1977; *Freedom Road*, 1979; *Body & Soul*, 1981; *Doin' Time*, 1985.

ALL ABOUT THE BENJAMINS. 2002. (R) 98 min. Comedy. A bounty hunter and the con man he is chasing join forces to recover a winning lottery ticket and, in the process, they become involved in a mobster's diamond heist. Cast: **Ice Cube, Mike Epps,** Tommy Flanagan, Eva Mendes, Carmen Chaplin, **Roger Guenveur Smith,** Anthony Michael Hall, Valarie Rae Miller, **Bow Wow.** Director: Kevin Bray. Writers: Ice Cube, Ronald Lang. Cinematographer: Glen McPherson. Music: John Murphy.

ALLEN, DEBBIE (1950-). Dancer, actress, producer, director, choreographer. She was born in Houston, Texas, and educated at Howard University in Washington, D. C. Allen began her dancing career in Broadway musicals before moving on to **television** and films. Her performance in the 1979 stage production of *West Side Story* earned her a Drama Desk Award, plus a Tony Award nomination. She received a second Tony nomination for her performance in the 1986-87 production on *Sweet Charity*. Allen's success on stage led to television guest appearances in popular **sitcoms,** such as *Good Times* and *The Love Boat*, as well as the TV miniseries *Roots: The Next Generation.* Other TV appearances include the 1977 NBC series *3 girls 3*, the 1980s hit series *Fame*, and the 1985 sitcom *In the House.* Allen became the first African American woman hired as a director by a major network for a prime time show when she directed several episodes of *Fame.* She later co-wrote, produced, directed, choreographed, and starred in her own 1989 variety show *The Debbie Allen Special*, for ABC, for which she received two **Emmy** nominations for direction and choreography. Allen took over the reins as a producer/director of the *Cosby Show* spin-off *A Different World*, and turned it into a long-running series by addressing important social and political issues within the comedic plot lines. In television, she has also directed the made-for-TV movies *Pollyanna*, and *Stompin' at the Savoy*, as well as the pilot episode of the hit sitcom *Fresh Prince of Bel-Air*. Allen choreographed the dance numbers for the 1982 **Academy Awards.** In film, she acted in and choreographed the cheerleading routines for the basketball flick *The Fish That Saved Pittsburgh*, 1979, and appeared in **Richard Pryor**'s autobiographical film *Jo Jo Dancer, Your Life is Calling*, 1986. Her film directing debut was *Out-of-*

Sync, 1995. For her many achievements in the fields of television and film, Allen received her star on the Hollywood Walk of Fame in October 1991.

Filmography: *Roots: The Next Generation*, 1979; *The Fish That Saved Pittsburgh*, 1979; *Fame*, 1980; *Ragtime*, 1981; *Jo Jo Dancer, Your Life is Calling*, 1986; *The Old Settler*, 2001.

ALWAYS OUTNUMBERED, ALWAYS OUTGUNNED. 1998. (R) 110 min. Drama. This is a cable movie based on a book by **Walter Mosley**. A recently released ex-convict must now make his way through the tough streets of Los Angeles, where getting a job as a convicted felon is hard, but getting into more trouble is easy. Cast: **Laurence Fishburne, Bill Cobbs**, Natalie Cole, Daniel Williams, Laurie Metcalf, **Bill Nunn, Cicely Tyson, Isaiah Washington**. Director: Michael Apted. Writer: Walter Mosley. Cinematographer: John Bailey. Music: Michael Franti.

AMERICA'S DREAM. 1995. (PG-13) 87 min. Drama. Three short stories exploring a glimpse of the African American experience between 1938 and 1958. *Long Black Song* is from a short story by Richard Wright. A hardworking Alabama farmer goes to town for supplies. In his absence, a white traveling salesman pays a visit to his farm, meets the farmer's wife, and takes advantage of their mutual attraction, but their sinful union has a deadly aftermath. *The Boy Who Painted Jesus Black* deals with a young student who causes a great deal of controversy when he paints a black portrait of Jesus in 1948 Georgia. *The Reunion* is a short story by writer/poet **Maya Angelou** about a jazz pianist in Chicago who encounters the daughter of a white family her parents once served. Cast: **Danny Glover**, Tina Lifford, Tate Donavan, Dan Kamin, **Wesley Snipes, Jasmine Guy, Vanessa Bell Calloway**, Norman B. Golden II, Timothy Carhart, Yolanda King, Rae'ven Kelly, Lorraine Toussaint, Susanna Thompson, **Carl Lumbly**. Directors: **Bill Duke, Kevin Rodney Sullivan, Paris Barclay**. Writers: Ron Stacker Thompson, Ashley Tyler. Cinematographer: Karl Hermann. Music: Patrice Rushen.

AM I GUILTY? 1940. 70 min. Drama. A man becomes a criminal to help the poor. Cast: **Ralph Cooper**, Sybil Lewis, Sam McDaniel, **Lawrence Criner**, Marcella Moreland, Arthur Ray, Reginald Fenderson, **Monte Hawley, Clarence Brooks**, Jess Lee Brooks, Ida Coffin, **Cleo Desmond**, Alfred Grant, Mathew Jones. Lillian Randolph, Mae Turner, Napoleon Simpson, Edward Thompson.

Guernsey Morrow. Director: Sam Newfield. Writers: Sherman L. Lowe, George Wallace Sayre.

AMISTAD. 1997. (R) 152 min. Drama. This is a film version of the 1839 rebellion on the Portuguese slave ship *La Amistad*. Cinque, a Mende tribesman, leads the other African captives in a rebellion and they take over the ship until it is intercepted in U.S. waters. Cinque and the others are thrown back in chains as they await a trial that will once again determine their freedom and their fate. Championed by property attorney Robert Baldwin, their defense is argued and won before the Supreme Court by former president John Quincy Adams. Cast: Paul Guifoyle, **Djimon Hounsou**, Anthony Hopkins, Matthew McConaughey, **Morgan Freeman**, Nigel Hawthorne, David Paymer, Pete Postlethwaite, Stellan Skarsgard, Anna Paquin, Austin Pendleton, Tomas Milian. Director: Steven Spielberg. Writer: David Franzoni. Cinematographer: Janusz Kaminski. Music: John Williams.

AMOS, JOHN (1941-). Actor. Born in Newark, New Jersey, Amos played professional football before becoming a stand-up comedian and comedy writer for TV shows in the 1960s. His most notable role was as a strong, hard-working father figure in the TV sitcom *Good Times*. He was also cast as the adult Kunta Kinte in the highly acclaimed TV miniseries *Roots*, 1977. Film roles included *Let's Do It Again*, 1975; *Coming to America*, 1988; and *Die Hard 2: Die Harder*, 1990. He appeared on numerous television series, including *The West Wing*.

Filmography: ***Sweet Sweetback's Baadasssss Song***, 1971; *The World's Greatest Athlete*, 1973; *Let's Do it Again*, 1975; *Future Cop*, 1976; *Roots*, 1977; *Willa*, 1979; *Touched by Love*, 1980; *The Beastmaster*, 1982; *Dance of the Dwarfs*, 1983; *American Flyers*, 1985; *Coming to America*, 1988; *Lock Up*, 1989; *Two Evil Eyes*, 1990; *Die Hard 2: Die Harder*, 1990; *Ricochet*, 1991; *Mac*, 1993; *Mardi Gras for the Devil*, 1993; *Hologram Man*, 1995; *For Better or Worse*, 1995; ***The Players Club***, 1998; ***Disappearing Acts***, 2000.

AMOS 'n' ANDY. As a throwback to the old vaudeville minstrel shows *Amos 'n' Andy* was begun in the 1920s as a radio program with the characters performed by whites. A movie version was produced by RKO Pictures in 1929 called *Check and Double Check*, which also starred white actors performing in **blackface**. The concept became a historic and controversial 1950s **television** series that was quickly boycotted by the NAACP and eventually taken off the air after two seasons for projecting visual representations of what were considered to be racist and stereotypical black characters. It was the first all-black cast television series ever, and despite its early cancellation, (1951-1953), CBS continued to make money on reruns until 1966. The entire collection is now available on home video and DVD. Broadway actor Alvin Childress portrayed Amos Jones, while notable actor, producer, writer, and director **Spencer Williams Jr.** played Andrew Hogg Brown. Cast: Alvin Childress, Spencer Williams Jr., Harry Tim Moore, Johnny Lee, Ernestine Wade, Amanda Randolph, and Lillian Randolph.

ANDERSON, EDDIE "ROCHESTER" (1905-1977). Actor, comedian. The son of a minstrel performer father and circus tight wire-walking mother, Eddie Anderson was born to be an entertainer. As the character Rochester on the *Jack Benny Show,* he was among the first black regulars to work on a network radio program. Anderson had performed for years in small clubs until a guest appearance on Benny's radio show on *Easter Sunday,* 1937, made him a star. He followed the Benny show onto television, and starred in many Hollywood movies.

Filmography: *False Faces,* 1932; *Green Pastures,* 1936; *You Can't Take it With You,* 1938; *Thanks for the Memory,* 1938; *Jezebel,* 1938; *You Can't Cheat an Honest Man,* 1939; *Honolulu,* 1939; *Gone with the Wind,* 1939; *Topper Returns,* 1941; *Birth of the Blues,* 1941; *Tales of Manhattan,* 1942; *Star Spangled Rhythm,* 1942; *Cabin in the Sky,* 1943; *Broadway Rhythm,* 1944; *Brewster's Millions,* 1945; *The Show-Off,* 1946; *It's a Mad, Mad, Mad, Mad World,* 1963.

ANDERSON, MADELINE. Producer, director, editor. As a child growing up in Lancaster, Pennsylvania, Anderson was inspired by how images seemed to come to life as she flipped through her flicker books. Despite being told that black men, let alone a little black girl, can't be filmmakers, she was determined to prove them wrong, and she did. After attending a Pennsylvania teacher's college, she enrolled at New York University. While in New York, she took a babysitting job in exchange for room and board with renowned **documentary** filmmaker Richard Leacock, and gained experience by working with his production company. Anderson's self-financed first film, *Integration Report 1,* 1961, documented America's earliest sit-ins, and established her as a serious filmmaker. She worked as assistant director and assistant editor with Shirley Clark on her feature film *The Cool World,* 1963, and then went to work for WNET-TV in New York. While there, she made broadcast history with *Black Journal*, working alongside noted documentary filmmakers **Stan Lathan**, **St. Clair Bourne**, and **William Greaves**. From 1971 to 1975, she was supervising film editor and in-house film producer/director for *Sesame Street* and *The Electric Company*. In 1975, Anderson founded her own production company, Onyx Productions, and became the first African American woman to executive produce a television series with *Infinity Factory*, a math show targeted at inner-city youth.

Filmography: *Integration Report 1*, 1961; *I Am Somebody*, 1970.

ANDLAUER PRODUCTIONS. Early race movie production company. It produced the film *As the World Rolls On*, 1921, which stars ex-heavyweight boxing champion Jack Johnson.

ANGELOU, MAYA (1928-). Author, poet, director. She is best known for her writing, but her book *I Know Why the Caged Bird Sings*, 1979, about growing up in the rural South during the 1930s, was a made-for-TV movie in 1979. It starred **Diahann Carroll**, **Ruby Dee**, and **Esther Roll**. Angelou made her directing debut with *Down in the Delta*, 1998, which starred **Angela Bassett** and **Wesley Snipes**.

ANTWONE FISHER. 2002. (PG-13) 113 min. Drama. This film is based on the screenwriter's true experience of growing up in abusive foster homes and the lasting psychological damage these bad experiences had. Now grown, he is in the U.S. Navy with a bad attitude, a long history of fighting, and an overall negative view of authority figures until a Navy psychiatrist helps him to confront his past, find his real family, and slay his past demons. This was **Denzel Washington**'s directorial debut. Cast: **Derek Luke**, Denzel Washington, Joy Bryant, **Salli Richardson**, Earl Billings, Kevin Connolly, Viola Davis, Rainoldo Gooding, Novella Nelson, Vernee Watson-Johnson, **Jenifer Lewis**, Kente Scott, Yolanda Ross, Stephen Snedden. Director: Denzel Washington. Writer: Antwone Fisher. Cinematographer: Philippe Rousselot. Music: Mychael Danna. Awards: Independent Spirit Awards 2003: Best Actor (Luke).

APOLLO THEATER. This is the most famous theater in Harlem, New York, to showcase black talent. Located at 253 West 125th Street, just down the street from the world-famous Cotton Club, it began as a burlesque house in 1914. Well known for making or breaking acts, its audiences have a distinct reputation for being hard to please. While working as an emcee at the theater in the 1930s, **Ralph Cooper** began *Amateur Night at the Apollo*, a competition to highlight up-and-coming acts. A modern version titled *Showtime at the Apollo* is still being taped and syndicated to television stations around the world.

ARE WE THERE YET? 2005. (PG) 95 min. Comedy. A road-trip movie where two kids set out to sabotage the burgeoning relationship between their mother and their unwitting chauffeur, who offers to drive them from Portland, Oregon, to Vancouver, British Columbia, where their mom is waiting. The kids test his nerves and trash his car in the process, but all is forgiven in the end. Cast: **Ice Cube, Nia Long**, Aleisha Allen, Philip Daniel Bolden. Director: Brian Levant. Writers: Steven Gary Banks, Claudia Grazioso, J. David Stem, David N. Weiss.

ARMSTRONG, DANIEL LOUIS (1900-1971). Jazz musician, trumpeter. Armstrong was raised in a poor section of New Orleans by his grandmother. He learned to play the cornet at the age of 12, after being sent to the Colored Waif's Home after a New Year's Eve prank. By the age of 17, he was being mentored by Joe "King" Oliver, who played cornet with Kid Ory's Jazz Band, and later, filled Oliver's position when he left the band. Armstrong received the nickname "Satchelmouth," which was eventually shortened to just "Satchmo." He became famous for not only his superb style of playing, but also for his gruff voice and scat style of singing, or spitting out a series of syllables instead of words. His songs include "Ain't Misbehavin'," "Hello Dolly," and "What a Wonderful World." Armstrong would later move to New York and become one of the greatest jazz musicians in the world. He and his band toured Europe several times and appeared in several films, including *A Rhapsody in Black and Blue*, 1932. Armstrong would also take on a cameo role as one of Lucifer, Jr.'s henchmen in **Cabin in the Sky**, 1943, and would appear on many **television** shows.

Filmography: *Cabin in the Sky*, 1943; *New Orleans*, 1947; *Here Comes the Groom*, 1951; *The Glenn Miller Story*, 1954; *High Society*, 1956; *The Five Pennies*, 1959; *Paris Blues*, 1961; *A Man Called Adam*, 1966; *Hello, Dolly!*, 1969.

ARNOLD, TICHINA (1971-). Actress, singer. She was born in Queens, New York, and made her film break as a background singer in the musical remake of *Little Shop of Horrors*, 1986, with *Tisha Campbell*. She would work with Campbell again in the role of Pamela "Pam" James in the popular **television** sitcom *Martin*,

1992. Arnold was Zena Brown, 1987-89, in the daytime drama *Ryan's Hope*, and also appeared as Sharla Valentine, 1989-1990, in the daytime series *All My Children*. Her additional film work includes roles in *Fakin' Da Funk*, 1997; *Dancing in September*, 2000; and *Civil Brand*, 2002.

Filmography: *Little Shop of Horrors*, 1986; *Starlight: A Musical Movie*, 1988; *How I Got into College*, 1989; *Scenes From a Mall*, 1991; *Fakin' Da Funk*, 1997; *A Luv Tale*, 1999; *Dancing in September*, 2000; *Big Momma's House*, 2000; *Civil Brand*, 2002; *Yo Alien*, 2002; *On the One*, 2004; *Getting Played*, 2005.

ASHES AND EMBERS. 1982. (NR) 120 min. Drama. A black Vietnam veteran returns home to Los Angeles but has a hard time of fitting back into society. His isolation and alienation eventually sets him on a collision course with the law. Cast: John Anderson, Evelyn Blackwell. Writer/Director: **Haile Gerima**.

ASUNDER. 1999. (R) 102 min. Drama. This independently made thriller explores love, loss, and betrayal. After a family tragedy, a man takes his best friend in, totally unaware of a prior affair between the friend and his own wife. Cast: **Blair Underwood, Debbie Morgan, Michael Beach**, Marva Hicks. Director: **Tim Reid**. Writer: Eric Lee Bowers. Cinematographer: **Johnny Simmons**. Music: Lionel Cole.

ATKINS, ESSENCE (1972-). Actress. She began her career in **television**, guest starring on shows, such as *Moesha, Family Matters*, and *The Parent Hood*. She had a recurring role on *Sabrina, The Teenage Witch*, and she was a regular on *The Smart Guy, Malibu Shores*, and *Under One Roof*. She starred in the UPN series *Half and Half*. Her film roles include *How High*, 2001, and *Deliver Us from Eva*, 2003.

Filmography: *Love Song*, 2000; *Nikita Blues*, 2000; *XCU: Extreme Close Up*, 2001; *How High*, 2001; *Looking Through Lillian*, 2001; *Deliver Us from Eva*, 2003.

ATLANTA CHILD MURDERS, THE. 1985. (TV) 245 min. Miniseries. This is a film based on the true story of a series of child murders that occurred in the black communities of Atlanta, Georgia, in the 1970s. A black photographer is arrested and charged for these crimes, but is he truly guilty, or just a scapegoat? Cast: **James Earl Jones**, Jason Robards, **Morgan Freeman**, Rip Torn, Calvin Levels, **Lynn Moody, Ruby Dee, Gloria Foster**, Paul Benjamin, Martin Sheen, Andrew Robinson, Christopher Allport, Guy Boyd, Gary Graham, Bill Paxton. Director: John Erman. Writer: Abby Mann.

AUTOBIOGRAPHY OF MISS JANE PITTMAN, THE. 1974. (TV-PG) 110 min. Drama. This is a made-for-TV movie based on the novel by Ernest J. Gaines. A 110-year-old former slave retells her life's story, which spans the history of America from the Civil War to the Civil Rights movement. It received nine **Emmy Awards**. Cast: **Cicely Tyson**, Odetta, Joseph Tremice, Richard Dysart, Michael Murphy, Katherine Helmond. Director: John Korty. Writer: Tracy Keenan Wynn. Cinematographer: James A. Crabe.

AVENGING DISCO GODFATHER, THE. 1976. (R) 99 min. Blaxploitation. This is a parody of *The Godfather* movie and martial arts films. The "Disco Godfather" is a retired cop turned celebrity disc jockey at the Blueberry Hill disco. When his favorite nephew takes a bad trip on a new drug called "angel dust" or PCP, the deejay becomes a butt-kicking kung-fu master and sets out to bring down the drug kingpin and close his PCP-producing warehouse. This film includes plenty of fighting, rapping, rollerskating, and disco-dancing action. Cast: **Rudy Ray Moore, Carol Speed**, Jimmy Lynch, Jeny Jones, Lady Reeds, James H. Hawthorne, Frank Finn, Julius J. Carey III. Director: J. Robert Wagoner. Writers: J. Robert Wagoner, Cliff Roquemore. Cinematographer: Arledge Armenaki. Music: Ernie Fields Jr.

AVERY, MARGARET. Actress. She was born in Mangum, Oklahoma, and worked throughout the 1970s' **blaxploitation** era, landing roles in *Melinda*, 1972; *Louis Armstrong–Chicago Style*, 1976; and *Which Way is Up?*, 1977. Her acting career hit a slow period in the early 1980s, but revived when she was cast as Shug Avery in *The Color Purple*, 1985, the film version of Alice Walker's Pulitzer Prize-winning novel in which Avery received an **Oscar** nomination for Best Supporting Actress. Her **television** guest appearances include *The Rookies, Kojak, Baby, I'm Back, Murder She Wrote, Miami Vice, Amen*, and *Walker, Texas Ranger*.

Filmography: *Melinda*, 1972; *Cool Breeze*, 1972; *Terror House*, 1972; *Hell Up in Harlem*, 1973; *Lewis Armstrong: Chicago Style*, 1976; *Which Way is Up?* 1977; *The Fish That Saved Pittsburgh*, 1979; *The Color Purple*, 1985; *For Us the Living*, 1988; *Riverbend*, 1989; *Return of Superfly*, 1990; *Heat Wave*, 1990; *The Jacksons: An American Dream*, 1992; *Mardi Gras for the Devil*, 1993; *Night Trap*, 1993; *Lightning in a Bottle*, 1993; *Cyborg 3: The Recycler*, 1994; *White Man's Burden*, 1995; *The*

Set Up, 1995; *Love Kills*, 1998; *Second to Die*, 2001; *Waitin' to Live*, 2002.

B

BAADASSSSS! 2003. (R) 108 min. Docudrama. **Mario Van Peebles** pays homage to his filmmaker father, **Melvin Van Peebles**, and his maverick, controversial film *Sweet Sweetback's Baadasssss Song*, 1971. It portrays an honest and revealing portrait of independent filmmaking as he struggles to raise money while sidestepping the unions under the guise of making a porno film and his dogged determination to pursue his vision. Despite countless production problems, including crew arrests, death threats, and being hassled by creditors, Van Peebles masters the art of guerilla filmmaking to create a landmark film credited with creating a new genre of black film. Cast: Mario Van Peebles, Joy Bryant, T. K. Carter, Terry Crews, **Ossie Davis**, **David Alan Grier**, **Nia Long**, Paul Rodriguez, Saul Rubinek, Vincent Schiavelli, Khleo Thomas, Rainn Wilson, Karimah Westbrook, Len Lesser, Sally Struthers. Director: Mario Van Peebles. Writers: Melvin Van Peebles, Mario Van Peebles.

BABATUNDE, OBBA. Actor. He was born in Jamaica, Queens, New York, to become a noted actor of stage, **television**, and film. He received a Tony Award nomination for his portrayal of C. C. White in the original Broadway production of *Dreamgirls*, and portrayed the legendary jazz artist Jelly Roll Morton in the world premier of *Jelly's Last Jam*. On television, he has portrayed **Berry Gordy** in the telepic *The Temptations*, 1998, and he showed off his dancing talents as **Harold Nicholas** in the HBO original movie ***Introducing Dorothy Dandridge***, 1999. Notable film roles include *Life*, 1999; *John Q*, 2002; and *The Black Man's Guide to Understanding Black Women*, 2005.

Filmography: *The Silence of the Lambs*, 1991; *Undercover Blues*, 1993; *Philadelphia*, 1993; *That Thing You Do*, 1996; *Soul of the Game*, 1996; *Multiplicity*, 1996; *Miss Evers' Boys*, 1997; *The Temptations*, 1998; *Life*, 1999; *Introducing Dorothy Dandridge*, 1999; *The Visit*, 2000; *How High*, 2001; *John Q*, 2002; *The Manchurian Candidate*, 2004; *After the Sunset*, 2004; *The Celestine Prophecy*, 2005; *The Black Man's Guide to Understanding Black Women*, 2005.

BABY BOY. 2001. (R) 129 min. Drama. A grown, unemployed, 20-year-old man who still lives with his mom has a hard time growing into emotional maturity. He has two children by different women that he barely supports, he is unfaithful to his current girlfriend, and he would rather sell hot clothes out of the trunk of her car than get a job. Things get rough when his mother's ex-con boyfriend moves in, his girl's ex-boyfriend gets out of the joint, and then decides to camp out at her apartment. Through it all, he must come to terms with who he is, what he wants, and accept the responsibilities of being a man. Cast: **Tyrese Gibson**, Omar Gooding, Taraji P. Henson, **A. J. Johnson, Snoop Dogg**, Tamara La Seon Bass, **Ving Rhames**, Angell Cromwell. Writer/Director: **John Singleton**. Cinematographer: **Charles Mills**. Music: David Arnold.

BACK ROAD DINER, 2003. (NR) 89 min. Drama. This is the chilling story of four lifelong friends from the mean streets of the New York City ghetto on a cross-country trip recalling the hilarious and wild adventures of their younger days. When they are approached by a group of redneck bigots, racial tension erupts into violence and sets off a chain reaction, and lets them know that the back roads of America can be more dangerous than the mean streets of Harlem. Cast: Andre M. Carrington, Winston I. Dunlop II, Job Langione, Steve Schroke, Bruce Bearman, Phil Mills, Edward Olmedo. Writer/Director: Winston I. Dunlop II. Cinematographer: Joe Matina. Music: Bill Brown.

BAD BOYS. 1995. (R) 118 min. Action/Drama. Two Miami narcotics officers try to recover $100 million worth of heroin missing from the evidence room before internal affairs takes action on their precinct. One is a single playboy with a trust fund, the other a family man working hard to do his job, pay his bills, and maintain his marriage. They are later teamed with a female eyewitness to the pursued drug dealer's murderous ways, as she becomes targeted for death herself. It spawned the sequel ***Bad Boys 2***, 2003. Cast: **Martin Lawrence, Will Smith**, Tcheky Karyo, Tea Leoni, **Theresa Randle**, Marg Heigenberger, Joe Pantoliano, John Salley. Director: Michael Bay. Writers: Michael Barrie, Jim Mulholland. Cinematographer: Howard Atherton. Music: Mark Mancina. Awards: Blockbuster Awards 1996: Best Male Newcomer (Smith).

BAD BOYS II. 2003. (R) 147 min. Action/Drama. The Miami-based drug-fighting duo takes on a web of dangerous ecstasy dealers. More action tinged with a bit of romance when one of the cops falls for the other one's little sister. Cast: **Will Smith, Martin Law-**

rence, **Gabrielle Union**, Joe Pantoliano, **Thereasa Randle**, Jordi Molla, Peter Stormare. Director: Michael Bay. Writers: Ron Shelton, Jerry Stahl, John Lee Hancock. Cinematographer: Amir M. Mokri.

BAILEY, PEARL (1918-1990). Singer, actress. Pearl Bailey's unconcerned style and informal rapport with an audience made her an endearing and respected entertainer. After singing in small clubs in Scranton, Pennsylvania, and Washington, D. C., her career took off when she became the vocalist for the Cootie Williams Band, which led to a stint with Count Basie. In the early 1940s, Bailey played the Village Vanguard and the Blue Angel Club in New York, before touring with the U. S. O. during World War II. She received the Donaldson Award, in 1946, as that year's most promising new performer for her stage debut in *St. Louis Woman*. She was called to Hollywood in 1954 to appear as Frankie in the movie *Carmen Jones*, 1954, with **Dorothy Dandridge**. That same year, she starred in the Broadway musical *House of Flowers*. Miss Bailey has made countless television appearances and headlined at the country's leading nightspots. Her hit recordings include "Two to Tango," "Tired," "Row, Row, Row," and the title song to the movie *Variety Girl*, 1947. She retired after a 1975 all-black revival run of *Hello, Dolly*. She was appointed U. S. representative to the United Nations.

Filmography: *Carmen Jones*, 1954; *Norman, Is That You?* 1976; *The Fox and the Hound*, 1981; *The Member of the Wedding*, 1983; *Peter Gunn*, 1989.

BAKER, JOSEPHINE (1906-1975). Singer, dancer, actress. Josephine Baker became a legend for her bold and risqué stage performances in 1920s Paris. After running away from home at age 13 to join a traveling road show, she ended up in Philadelphia. There, she was hired as a dresser for Noble Sissle's musical comedy review *Shuffle Along*. She learned all of the songs and dances, and later, she stole the show one night when a performer dropped out and she filled in. In 1923, at age 17, she was in "Chocolate Dandies," Sissle's all-black Broadway show, and performed material written especially for her. Soon after, she was introduced to Paris in the 1925 production of *La Revue Négre*. Miss Baker's most sensational role may have been as the "Dark Star" of the *Folies-Bergére*, in which she appeared topless in a skirt of bananas. This dance made her the toast of Paris, and she reveled in her success by catering to her cadre of fans, and flamboyantly walking her pet leopard down the Champs Elysées. After a successful around-the-world tour, Miss Baker branched out as a singer and comedienne at the Casino de Paris. She later starred in the French films *La Creole*, with Jean Gabin, and also *Zou Zou*, 1934, and *Princess Tam Tam*, 1935. She was quite active during World War II as a Red Cross volunteer and as an Italian Embassy attaché. At the end of the war, she was decorated with the Legion of Honor by the French government. By the early 1950s, Baker retired and used her fortune and notoriety to adopt and care for an interracial mix of orphaned children. After only three years, the lack of income, her lavish lifestyle, and her "rainbow family" had depleted her savings. She was forced to return to her career and starred in *Paris, Mes Amours*, a musical based on her own amazing life.

Filmography: *Zou Zou*, 1934; *Princess Tam Tam*, 1935; *The French Way*, 1949.

BAMBOOZLED. 2000. (R) 135 min. Drama. A frustrated African American writer creates a modern-day minstrel show for the TV network that he works for and expects to be fired. The show is a big hit and the network's ratings rise. Militant groups angered over the stereotypical depictions mount their own protests over the despicable buck dancing, shuck-and-jive routines, and actors performing in blackface. This was one of the first movies to be shot on digital video and blown up to 35mm film for distribution. Cast: **Damon Wayans, Jada Pinkett Smith, Savion Glover, Tommy Davidson**, Michael Rapaport, **Thomas Jefferson Byrd, Paul Mooney**. Writer/Director: Spike Lee. Cinematographer: Ellen Kuras. Music: **Terence Blanchard**.

BANKS, TYRA (1973-). Model, actress. This Los Angeles-born beauty signed with the Elite Modeling Agency after graduating from high school and moved to Paris, where she modeled for Chanel and Ralph Lauren. She became the first African American woman to sign for a cosmetic company, and to appear on the cover of *Sports Illustrated*'s swimsuit issue, the cover of *GQ* magazine and the Victoria's Secret catalog. Her feature film debut came with a role in **John Singleton**'s *Higher Learning*, 1995. She followed with roles in *Coyote Ugly*, 2000; *Halloween: Resurrection*, 2002; and co-starred in the telefilm *Life-Size*, 2000. Her **television** guest appearances include *New York Undercover*, *The Hughleys*, and *Soul Food*. She is creator, writer, and producer of the UPN reality series *America's Next Top Model*.

Filmography: *Higher Learning*, 1994; *A Woman Like That*, 1997; *Love Stinks*, 1999; ***Love and Basketball***, 2000; *Life-Size*,

2000; *Coyote Ugly*, 2000; *Halloween: Resurrection*, 2002; *Larceny*, 2004.

B*A*P*S. 1997. (PG-13) 91 min. Comedy. A talent audition in Los Angeles lures two ambitious waitresses from Georgia. While waiting in line, they are offered a chance to make even more money by posing as a wealthy man's granddaughter by his black mistress, who was the love of his life. They lose their country roots and are taught to appreciate the finer things in life, but as relationships grow and develop, the thought of pulling off the scam becomes more and more unbearable. Cast: **Halle Berry**, Natalie Desselle, Martin Landau, Ian Richardson, **Troy Beyer**, Luigi Amodeo, Johnathan Fried, Anthony Johnson. Director: **Robert Townsend**. Writer: Troy Beyer. Cinematographer: Bill Dill. Music: **Stanley Clarke**.

BARBERSHOP. 2002. (PG-13) 102 min. Comedy. This is an ensemble comedy about the daily grind of a barbershop located on Chicago's South Side. Calvin inherited the business from his father but now sees it as a waste of time. He rents out the cutting stalls to an eclectic group of barbers who tell jokes, relate stories, and often clash with one another throughout the course of the day. Wanting out, Clyde sells the shop to a ruthless loan shark, but reconsiders when he learns the new owner plans to close the shop down. The film received serious criticism for denigrating remarks toward several civil rights leaders. Cast: **Ice Cube, Anthony Anderson, Cedric the Entertainer, Sean Patrick Thomas**, Eve Jihan Jeffers, Troy Garity, **Michael Ealy**, Leonard Earl Howze, **Keith David**, Jazsmin Lewis, Lahmard J. Tate, Tom Wright, Jason Winston George, DeRay Davis, Sonya Eddy. Director: Tim Story. Writers: Mark Brown, Don D. Scott, Marshall Todd.

BARBERSHOP 2: BACK IN BUSINESS. 2004. (PG-13). 106 min. Comedy. This sequel to *Barbershop*, 2002, finds Calvin, the barbershop owner having to step up his business plan after a corporate franchised hair salon opens up across the street and starts taking his clients. Cast: **Ice Cube, Cedric the Entertainer, Sean Patrick Thomas**, Eve, **Queen Latifah**. Director: **Kevin Rodney Sullivan**. Writers: Don D. Scott, Kevin Rodney Sullivan, Norman Vance Jr.

BARCLAY, PARIS (1956-). Director, producer, writer, actor. This native of Illinois has done it all. He directed **television** series, such as *Law & Order, Silk Stalkings, The West Wing, The Shield, and Cold Case*. He has co-executive produced *City of Angels, The Big*

Time, The Street Lawyer, and was also a writer on the first season of *City of Angels.* His acting credits include guest-starring roles in the series *Sliders, NYPD Blue,* and he appeared in and directed the telepic *The Cherokee Kid,* 1996. Barclay made his film directorial debut with ***Don't Be a Menace to South Central While Drinking Your Juice in the Hood,*** 1996.

Filmography: *Don't Be a Menace to South Central While Drinking Your Juice in the Hood,* 1996; *America's Dream,* 1996; *The Cherokee Kid,* 1996; *The Chang Family Saves the World,* 2002; *The Big Time,* 2002; *The Street Lawyer,* 2003.

BARNETTE, NEEMA (1949-). Director, producer. She was born in New York City and began her career directing television series, such as *The Cosby Show, What's Happening Now,* and *The Redd Foxx Show.* Her dramatic made-for-TV movies include ***My Name is Zora,*** 1989; *Better Off Dead,* 1993; ***Run for the Dream: The Gail Devers Story,*** 1996; and the miniseries *Miracle Boys,* 2005. Barnette produced and directed the female prison-based ***Civil Brand,*** 2002.

Filmography: *Sky Captain,* 1985; *My Name is Zora,* 1989; *Different Worlds: A Story of Interracial Love,* 1992; *Better Off Dead,* 1993; *Scattered Dreams,* 1993; *Sin & Redemption,* 1994; *Spirit Lost,* 1996; *Run for the Dream: The Gail Devers Story,* 1996; *Close to Danger,* 1997; *Civil Brand,* 2002.

BASSETT, ANGELA (1958-). Actress. She was born in St. Petersburg, Florida, and as a teenager was inspired to act after seeing a play starring **James Earl Jones.** After graduating from high school with a high GPA, Bassett received her master's degree in drama from Yale University. Moving to New York, she worked in television commercials and on the CBS daytime drama *The Guiding Light.* She made her Broadway debut in August Wilson's musical play *Ma Rainey's Black Bottom.* Turning to film, she appeared as Tre's concerned mother in **John Singleton's** *Boyz N the Hood,* 1991, and John Sayles' *City of Hope,* 1991. **Spike Lee** cast Bassett as Betty Shabazz in his 1992 biography film on *Malcolm X,* and serious recognition followed her portrayal of pop star Tina Turner in ***What's Love Got to Do with It,*** 1993, for which she received a **Golden Globe** and two NAACP **Image Awards.** Further acclaim followed her performance in the ensemble cast of ***Waiting to Exhale,*** 1995, and ***How Stella Got Her Groove Back,*** 1998, both made from best-selling novels by Terry McMillan.

Filmography: *F/X,* 1986; *Critters 4,* 1991; *City of Hope,* 1991; *Boyz N the Hood,* 1991; *Passion Fish,* 1992; *Malcolm X,* 1992;

The Jacksons: An American Dream, 1992; *Innocent Blood*, 1992; *What's Love Got to Do with It?*, 1993; *Waiting to Exhale*, 1995; *Vampire in Brooklyn*, 1995; *Strange Days*, 1995; *Contact*, 1997; *How Stella Got Her Groove Back*, 1998; *Supernova*, 1999; *Music of the Heart*, 1999; *Boesman & Lena*, 2000; *Ruby's Bucket of Blood*, 2001; *Sunshine State*, 2002, *The Rosa Parks Story*, 2002.

BEACH, MICHAEL (1963-). Actor. This native of Roxbury, Massachusetts, is a graduate of the Julliard School, whose work has spanned the artistic worlds of theater, television, and film. His early film work includes *One False Move*, 1991; *Lean on Me*, 1989; and *In a Shallow Grave*, 1988. He received rave reviews for his appearances in the hit films *Soul Food*, 1997, and *Waiting to Exhale*, 1995. On the small screen, Beach had a recurring role on the **Emmy Award**-winning drama *ER*, and starred as Monte "Doc" Parker in the Warner Brothers fire rescue series *Third Watch*. He has also performed off-Broadway and in Los Angeles regional theater.

Filmography: *Lean on Me*, 1989; *Cadence*, 1989; *Internal Affairs*, 1990; *One False Move*, 1991; *Bad Company*, 1994; *Waiting to Exhale*, 1995; *Soul Food*, 1997; *Ruby Bridges*, 1998; *Made Men*, 1999; *Asunder*, 1999; *Crazy as Hell*, 2002.

BEAH: A BLACK WOMAN SPEAKS. 2003. (NR) 90 min. Documentary. This film celebrates the life of legendary actress, poet, and political activist **Beah Richards**, perhaps best remembered for her Oscar-nominated role in *Guess Who's Coming to Dinner*, 1967. Throughout her career, Richards worked to overcome racial stereotypes on stage and on screen. Interviews are woven together with archival material on Richards' work as an actress and activist. It is the directorial debut of actress **Lisa Gay Hamilton**, who was inspired to make the film after meeting and working with Richards during the filming of *Beloved*, 1998.

BEALS, JENNIFER (1963-). Actress. This Chicago-born actress came to prominence as welder by day, dancer by night lead character in the hit movie *Flashdance*, 1983, while she was a freshman at Yale University. She graduated and continued acting in films like *The Bride*, 1985; *Vampire's Kiss*, 1988; and *Devil in a Blue Dress*, 1995. Her made-for-TV-movies include *A House Divided*, 2000, and *The Feast of All Saints*, 2001. Her roles on TV series include *2000 Malibu Road*, and *The L Word*.

Filmography: *My Bodyguard*, 1980; *Flashdance*, 1983; *The Bride*, 1985; *Vampire's Kiss*, 1988; *Indecency*, 1992; *Day of*

Atonement, 1993; *Dead on Sight*, 1994; *Devil in a Blue Dress*, 1995; *The Prophecy 2: Ashtown*, 1997; *Body and Soul*, 1998; *A House Divided*, 2000; *Roger Dodger*, 2002, *Catch That Kid*, 2003.

BEAUTY SHOP. 2005. (PG-13). Comedy. A cutting-edge hair stylist with a posh Chicago salon quits to open up her own shop in Atlanta. She buys a fixer-up salon and hires a batch of talkative employees who are not afraid to speak their minds. Her customers also have a lot to say, and it all comes out in the wash. Cast: **Queen Latifah**, Alicia Silverstone, Andie MacDowell, **Alfre Woodard**, Mena Suvari, Kevin Bacon, **Djimon Hounsou**, **Della Reese**, Golden Brooks. Director: Bille Woodruff. Writers: Elizabeth Hunter, Kate Lanier.

BEAVERS, LOUISE (1902-1962). Actress. She was born in Cincinnati, Ohio, and spent her teenage years in California. She was a real-life maid for actress Leatrice Joy before playing the role of a domestic many times on the screen. A talented actress, her break out performance was as Delilah Johnson in *Imitation of Life*, 1934. She was once again a domestic, but this was a rare role in Hollywood, where a black female character's background and social life was as prominent on the screen as the white co-star's was. Beavers has a long list of film credits that include *She Done Him Wrong*, 1933; *Bullets or Ballots*, 1938; and *The Jackie Robinson Story*, 1950. On **television**, she appeared on *The Danny Thomas Show*, and assumed the title role in the popular series *Beulah*, for the third and final season.

Filmography: *Coquette*, 1929; *She Done Him Wrong*, 1933; *Imitation of Life*, 1934; *Bullets or Ballots*, 1938; *Reap the Wild Wind*, 1942; *Dixie Jamboree*, 1944; *Delightfully Dangerous*, 1945; *Mr. Blandings Builds His Dream House*, 1948; *Tell It to the Judge*, 1949; *The Jackie Robinson Story*, 1950; *Goodbye, My Lady*, 1956; *Tammy and the Bachelor*, 1957.

BEBE'S KIDS. 1992. (PG-13) 74 min. Comedy/Animation. A comedy skit performed by stand-up comedian **Robin Harris** inspired this animated film. A young man who considers himself a ladies man gets played when he shows up to take his date and her son to an amusement park. She brings along three other unruly kids who leave their first date and the amusement park in a shambles. This was originally conceived as a live-action motion picture with Harris in the lead role. Upon Harris' premature death, producer's **Warrington** and **Reginald Hudlin** paid tribute to his memory by making the first ever feature-length cartoon. Voices: **Faizon Love**,

Vanessa Bell Calloway, Wayne Collins, Jonell Green, Marquis Houston, Tone Loc, Myra J., Nell Carter. Director: Bruce Smith. Writer: Reginald Hudlin. Music: John Barnes.

BELAFONTE, HARRY (1927-). Singer, actor, civil rights activist. Harry Belafonte was born in New York City and spent time growing up in his parent's homeland of Jamaica. He returned to New York to go to high school, and soon after, he joined the U. S. Navy in 1944. After his discharge, Belafonte became a maintenance man for an apartment building and began to study acting. He studied at the Stanley Kubrick Dramatic Workshop, and at the New School for Social Research, but a successful singing engagement at The Royal Roost, a Broadway jazz club, inspired him to change his focus. He began singing folk music at the Village Vangard and the Blue Angel and helped to give it a mass appeal, especially calypso. Belafonte appeared in his first movie in 1953, *Bright Road*, opposite another newcomer named **Dorothy Dandridge**. The on-screen fire between the two inspired Hollywood to team them up again in Otto Preminger's *Carmen Jones*, 1954. They became the first African American romantic duo. Belafonte became the first African American performer to have his own **television** special, which won him two **Emmy Awards**, but a national furor erupted when white British singer Petula Clark touched his arm during a musical number. A devoted civil rights activist, Belafonte marched with Dr. Martin Luther King Jr., on Montgomery, Alabama, and brought a contingent of other high-profile Hollywood celebrities to the 1968 March on Washington. With many record albums, films, and television appearances to his credit, he has received numerous awards and honors, including the 1982 MLK Jr. Nonviolent Peace Prize, three honorary doctorates, the Thurgood Marshall Lifetime Achievement Award in 1993, and the National Medal of Arts in 1994. He continues to work in film, television, and stage, and remains an active advocate for civil rights.

Filmography: *Bright Road*, 1952; *Carmen Jones*, 1954; *Island in the Sun*, 1957; *Odds Against Tomorrow*, 1959; *The Angel Levine*, 1970; ***Buck and the Preacher***, 1972; ***Uptown Saturday Night***, 1974; *Grambling's White Tiger*, 1981; *The Player*, 1992; *Ready to Wear*, 1994; ***White Man's Burden***, 1995; *Kansas City*, 1995.

BELAFONTE, SHARI (1954-). She was born in New York City and for a time followed in the footsteps of her famous father, **Harry Belafonte**. She worked on television in series like *Hotel*, *Grave-*

dale High, Beyond Reality, and *Hey Arnold.* She made her film debut in *If You Could See What I Hear,* 1982.

Filmography: *If You Could See What I Hear,* 1982; *Overnight Sensation,* 1983; *The Midnight Hour,* 1986; *Speed Zone,* 1988; *Murder by Numbers,* 1989; *Fire, Ice and Dynamite,* 1991; *The Player,* 1992; *French Silk,* 1994; *The Heidi Chronicles,* 1995; *Mars,* 1996; *Babylon 5: Third Space,* 1998; *Loving Evangeline,* 1998.

BELLAMY, BILL (1965-). Comedian, actor. This Newark, New Jersey-born actor began as a stand-up comic and was a frequent performer on *Def Comedy Jam.* He became a veejay on *I Want My MTV,* and hosted *MTV Beach House.* He also had his own series, *The Bill Bellamy Show.* His film appearances include roles in *Fled,* 1996; *Love Jones,* 1997; and *Any Given Sunday,* 1999.
  Filmography: *Who's the Man?* 1993; *Joey Breaker,* 1993; *Fled,* 1996; *Love Jones,* 1996; *How to Be a Player,* 1997; *Love Stinks,* 1999; *Any Given Sunday,* 1999; *The Brothers,* 2001; *Buying the Cow,* 2002; *Neverwas,* 2005; *Getting Played,* 2005.

BELLY. 1998. (R) 95 min. Urban Drama. Two childhood friends become successful drug dealers. One decides to go straight, while the other falls deeper into his life of crime. Once caught, he is forced to implicate a popular black leader in order to bring him down. Cast: Nas, **DMX,** Taral Hicks, Tionne "T-Boz" Watkins, Method Man, Tyrin Turner, Hassan Johnson, Power, Louie Rankin, Minister Benjamin F. Muhammed. Director: Hype Williams. Writers: Nas, Hype Williams, Anthony Bodden. Music: Stephan Cullo.

BELOVED. 1998. (R) 172 min. Drama. This was **Oprah Winfrey's** pet project and star vehicle based on Tony Morrison's Pulitzer Prize-winning novel. A former enslaved woman in rural Ohio is haunted by her former life as someone else's property, and the apparent reincarnation of her child she killed years before to keep her from having to endure the same degrading fate. Help arrives when an old friend from the same Kentucky plantation knocks on her door. Cast: **Oprah Winfrey, Thandie Newton, Danny Glover, Kimberly Elise, Lisa Gay Hamilton, Beah Richards, Albert Hall, Irma P. Hall.** Director: Jonathan Demme. Writers: **Akosua Busia,** Richard LaGravenese, Adam Brooks. Cinematographer: Tak Fujimoto. Music: Rachel Portman.

BERRY, HALLE (1968-). Actress. Born to an interracial family in Cleveland, Ohio, she grew up to win the Miss Teen Ohio beauty pageant. She studied broadcast journalism at Cleveland's Cuyahoga Community College before moving to Chicago to work as a model and study acting. Relocating to New York in 1988, she was cast in *Paper Dolls*, her first television series. Her film break came in 1991 when **Spike Lee** cast the former beauty queen in the role of a crack addict for his film *Jungle Fever*, 1991. Roles in the social satire *Strictly Business*, 1991, the action-packed *Executive Decision*, 1996, and the comedy *B*A*P*S*, 1997, followed. On television, Berry portrayed the Queen of Sheba in *Solomon and Sheba*, and **Dorothy Dandridge** in HBO's *Introducing Dorothy Dandridge*. Her performance in *Monster's Ball*, 2001, won her an **Academy Award**. She was the first African American actress to win the Best Actress **Oscar**.

Filmography: *Strictly Business*, 1991; *The Last Boy Scout*, 1991; *Jungle Fever*, 1991; *Boomerang*, 1992; *Queen*, 1993; *The Program*, 1993; *Father Hood*, 1993; *Losing Isaiah*, 1994; *The Flintstones*, 1994; *The Rich Man's Wife*, 1996; *Executive Decision*, 1996; *B*A*P*S*, 1997; *Why Do Fools Fall in Love?* 1998; *Bullworth*, 1998; *Introducing Dorothy Dandridge*, 1999; *X-Men*, 2000; *Swordfish*, 2001; *Monster's Ball*, 2001: *Die Another Day*, 2002: *X2: X-Men United*, 2003; *Cat Woman*, 2004.

BEST MAN, THE. 2000. (R) 120 min. Urban Romance. An up-and-coming writer arrives in New York City to be the best man at his best friend's wedding. A galley copy of his first novel has made the rounds between the rest of the wedding party, who all happen to be old college friends. They each see themselves, as characters in his book, which makes a secret affair between the protagonist and the bride-to-be, appear not as fiction, but an admission of fact. There will be hell to pay if the overly jealous, pro-football playing groom reads it the same way. Cast: **Taye Diggs**, **Monica Calhoun**, **Morris Chestnut**, **Nia Long**, **Melissa DeSousa**, **Harold Perrineau Jr.**, **Terrence Howard**, **Sanaa Lathan**, **Victoria Dillard**. Writer/Director: **Malcolm Lee**. Cinematographer: Frank Prinzi. Music: **Stanley Clarke**.

BEST, WILLIE (1916-1962). Actor. He was born in Sunflower, Mississippi, and began his entertainment career with a traveling show in California. Despite his natural talent for comedy, he mostly played bug-eyed, slurred-speaking, dimwitted characters and, for a while, went by the stage name "Sleep n' Eat." In Hollywood, he worked with comedy's best; Bob Hope, the Marx Brothers, and Laurel & Hardy. He made his film debut in *Deep South*, 1930, and played opposite child star Shirley Temple in *Little Miss Marker*,

1934, and *The Littlest Rebel*, 1935. His final film was *South of Caliente*, 1951. On **television**, he was a regular on *My Little Margie*, 1952-1955, and *The Stu Erwin Show*, 1950-1955. Civil rights groups often criticized his work, but Best never let that deter him.

Filmography: *Deep South*, 1930; *The Monster Walks*, 1932; *Kentucky Kernels*, 1934; *Little Miss Marker*, 1934; *The Littlest Rebel*, 1935; *The Bride Walks Out*, 1936; *The Ghost Breakers*, 1940; *South of Caliente*, 1951.

BET PICTURES. This is the film production arm of Black Entertainment Television (BET). Its role is to develop original films and acquire outside works to enhance its cinematic programming. They acquired the popular *Arabesque Books* label of African American-themed romance novels in 1998 to be adapted into made-for-television movies in a variety of genres.

BEWARE. 1946. 64 min. Musical. A jazz musician puts together a benefit concert to save a black college, his alma mater, from bankruptcy and falls for the gym teacher in the process. Cast: **Louis Jordan**, Frank Wilson, Emory Richardson, Valarie Black, Milton Woods. Director: Bud Pollard.

BEYER, TROY (1964-). Actress, writer, director. She was born in New York City and first appeared on the screen as Jacqueline "Jackie" Deveraux, 1986-1987, in the TV series *Dynasty*. Her other notable guest appearances include *Knots Landing*, *A Different World*, *The Cosby Show*, and *Diagnosis Murder*. Her film roles include *The White Girl*, 1990; *Good Advice*, 2001; and *John Q*, 2002. She wrote and directed *Let's Talk about Sex*, 1998, and *Love Don't Cost a Thing*, 2003.

Filmography: *Uncle Tom's Cabin*, 1987; *Disorderlies*, 1987; *Rooftops*, 1989; *The White Girl*, 1990; *The Five Heartbeats*, 1991; *Weekend at Bernie's II*, 1993; *The Little Death*, 1995; *Alien Avengers*, 1996; *Eddie*, 1996; *B*A*P*S*, 1997; *The Gingerbread Man*, 1998; *Let's Talk About Sex*, 1998; *Good Advice*, 2001; *John Q*, 2002; *A Light in the Darkness*, 2002; *Malevollent*, 2002.

BEYONCÉ (1981-). Singer, actress. She was born Beyoncé Knowles in Houston, Texas, and began working toward a career in entertainment at an early age. Her singing group, Destiny's Child, is at the top of the charts and her acting and solo career is off the charts. She has commercial contracts to endorse soft drink companies and beauty products, and has composed songs for movie soundtracks, such as *Romeo Must Die*, 2000, **Bad Boys II**, 2003, and **The Fighting Temptations**, 2003, in which she also stars. Filmography: **Carmen: A Hip Hopera**, 2001; *Austin Powers in Goldmember*, 2002; **The Fighting Temptations**, 2003; *The Pink Panther*, 2005.

BIG DIS, THE. 1989. (NR) 88 min. Comedy. A black soldier gets a weekend pass and spends his time trying to get laid, but a series of rejections shatters both his ego and his self-confidence. Cast: Gordon Eriksen, James Haig, Heather Johnston, Monica Sparrow, Kevin Haig. Writers/directors: Gordon Eriksen, John O'Brien.

BIKER BOYZ. 2003. (PG-13) 111 min. Urban Drama. After his father is killed as a bystander in a deadly motorcycle accident, a young hotshot motorcycle racer sets out to make a name for himself. He starts his own club and eventually challenges the top racer on the street-racing circuit. He soon learns they have more in common than just two wheels and speed. Cast: **Derek Luke, Laurence Fishburne, Orlando Jones, Djimon Hounsou, Lisa Bonet**, Brendan Fehr, **Larenz Tate**, Kid Rock, Rick Gonzalez, Meagan Good, **Salli Richardson, Vanessa Bell Calloway, Eriq La Salle**, Titus Welliver, **Kadeem Hardison, Terrence Howard**, Tyson Beckford. Director: **Reggie Rock Bythewood**. Writers: Reggie Rock Bythewood, Craig Fernandez. Cinematographer: Greg Gardiner. Music: Camara Kambon.

BILL COSBY: HIMSELF. 1983. (PG) 105 min. Comedy. This is a concert film presenting one of the self-titled comedian's hilarious routines. Shot in Ontario, Canada, Cosby pontificates about drugs, being drunk, and going to the dentist. He is well known for situational humor and his material on the often-noxious antics of family life as well. Cast: Bill Cosby. Writer/Director: Bill Cosby.

BINGO LONG TRAVELING ALL-STARS & MOTOR KINGS. 1976. (PG) 111 min. Comedy. A star-studded, animated group of baseball all-stars from the Negro League barnstorms across the country challenging white teams from the local communities. While putting on a show, it is obvious the colored ball players skill level far exceeds that of their opponents; however, within the social culture of rural 1939 America, it was always prudent to let the white team win. Film shows the skill, camaraderie, joys, and difficult times that black ball players often had to endure to play the game they loved. Cast: **Billy Dee Williams, James Earl Jones, Richard Pryor, Stan Shaw**. Director: John Badham. Writers: Mathew

Robbins, Hal Barwood. Cinematographer: Bill Butler. Music: William Goldstein.

BIRD. 1988. (R) 160 min. Biopic. This is a biopic on the life and times of famed saxman Charlie Parker, complete with original remastered solos performed by Parker himself. Cast: **Forest Whittaker**, Diane Venora, Michael Zelniker, Samuel E. Wright, **Keith David**, Michael McGuire, James Handy, Damon Whitaker, Morgan Nagler, Peter Crook. Director: Clint Eastwood. Writer: Joel Olianski. Cinematographer: Jack N. Green. Music: Lennie Niehaus. Awards: Oscars 1988: Best Sound. Cannes 1988: Best Actor (Whitaker). Golden Globes 1989: Best Director (Eastman). New York Film Critics 1988: Best Supporting Actress (Venora).

BIRTH OF A NATION, THE. 1915. 175 min. Drama. Based on the book, *The Clansman*, by Thomas Dixon, *The Birth of a Nation* was a technical masterpiece and the first feature-length silent film ever made. It set the standard for future production techniques and virtually invented film grammar. However, as monumental as the release of this film may have been, it distorted the public's perception of African Americans; glorified a racist organization based on terror, death, and hate; and ultimately undermined race relations around the world. A Civil War epic, the story follows the devastation raged upon the genteel South and predicts a catastrophic future if former slaves are allowed the right to live among whites, hold government office, and seek revenge on those who once oppressed them. However, all is saved with the birth of the Ku Klux Klan, a cavalry of sheet-wearing vigilantes who ride to the rescue, putting everyone and everything back in place. White actors in dark make-up portrayed the lead black characters. Cast: Lillian Gish, Mae Marsh, Henry B. Walthall, Ralph Lewis, Bobbie Harron, George Siegmann, Joseph Henabery, Spottiswoode Aitken, George Beranger, Mary Alden, Josephine Crowell, Elmer Clifton, Walter Long. Director: D. W. Griffith. Writer: D. W. Griffith, Frank E. Woods. Cinematographer: Billy Bitzer. Music: D. W. Griffith. Awards: AFI 1998 Top 100, National Film Registry 1992.

BIRTH OF A RACE, THE. 1918. Silent. 12 Reels. Originally titled *Lincoln's Dream*, this film was intended to be a direct response to the negative portrayals of negroes, as seen in D. W. Griffith's film ***The Birth of a Nation***, 1915. Spearheaded by Emmett J. Scott, it was to be a rectifying film statement, but lack of production funds caused Scott to take on white investors. When they came in, not only was the film's title changed, but also much of the footage already shot was left on the cutting room floor and the story took on a more universal theme. The final film took over two years to make and cost of over $1 million dollars. Considered several films in one, it became a collage of biblical and historical milestones that merged into a synthesis of the Gospels, preaching equality and tolerance. It was labeled a disaster upon its release. Cast: Marie Russell, Jane Gray, George LeGuere. Directors: William Selig, John W. Noble. Writers: Emmett J. Scott, Elaine Sterne.

BLACK AMERICAN CINEMA SOCIETY (BACS). BACS was founded by Dr. Mayme Clayton in 1976, and serves as the Film Archives of the Western States Black Research and Educational Center (WSBREC), which maintains one of the largest collections of vintage black films and research materials in the United States. The WSBREC exists to preserve and disseminate the unique history and cultural history of Americans of African descent. Black Talkies on Parade is BACS weeklong film festival and celebration of past and present contributions by black Americans to the motion picture industry. This includes an independent and student filmmaker competition with the award-winning films screened at the festival. Cash grants are awarded to the first-, second-, and third-place winners, as well as three honorable mentions. This provides tangible support and encouragement to young filmmakers. Black Talkies on Parade pays tribute to some of Hollywood's biggest stars by bestowing the Phoenix Award for lifetime achievement, and two Paul Robeson Pioneer Awards to those who have made noteworthy contributions to the film and entertainment industry. The ultimate goal of BACS and WSBREC is to aid in the promotion of pride, dignity, and intercultural understanding.

BLACK BELT JONES. 1974. (R) 87 min. Blaxploitation. A karate expert fights to keep a self-defense school in Watts, California, from being taken over by the mob. Cast: **Jim Kelly, Gloria Hendry, Scatman Crothers, Marla Gibbs.** Director: Robert Clouse. Writers: Alex Ross, Fred Weintraub, Oscar Williams. Music: Dennis Coffey, Luchi DeJesus.

BLACK BIKERS FROM HELL. 1970. (R) 87 min. Blaxploitation. An unstoppable black motorcycle gang wreaks havoc on its rivals and the community. Cast: John King III, Des Roberts, Linda Jackson, James Whitworth. James Young-EI, Clancy Syrko, Beverly Gardner. Writer/Director: Lawrence Merrick.

BLACK BRIGADE. 1969. 90 min. War. An all-black military unit takes on a dangerous suicide mission behind Nazi lines during World War II. Cast: **Billy Dee Williams, Richard Pryor,** Stephen Boyd, **Robert Hooks,** Susan Oliver, **Roosevelt "Rosey" Grier, Moses Gunn.** Director: George McCowan. Writer: Aaron Spelling. Music: Fred Steiner.

BLACK CAESAR. 1973. (R) 92 min. Blaxploitation. A small-time crook works his way up the crime chain to become head of a Harlem mob. It spawned the sequel *Hell Up in Harlem*, 1973. Cast: **Fred Williamson, Julius W. Harris,** Val Avery, Art Lund, **Gloria Hendry,** James Dixon. Writer/Director: Larry Cohen, Cinematographers: Fenton Hamilton, James Signorelli. Music: James Brown.

BLACKENSTEIN. 1973. (R) 87 min. Horror. A mad scientist starts out to replace a man's arms and legs, but a wrong injection causes the patient to become a black killing machine. Cast: John Hart, Ivory Stone, Andrea King, Liz Renay, Joe DeSue, Roosevelt Jackson, Nick Bolin. Director: William A. Levey. Writer: Frank R. Saletri. Cinematographer: Cardella Demilo. Music: Cardella Demilo, Lou Frohman.

BLACKFACE. A practice passed down from the minstrel stage show where white performers and entertainers would blacken their face with burnt cork to portray despicable characterizations of African Americans. African American vaudeville performers would eventually employ the same technique and take to the stage as well. **Bert Williams** is perhaps the best-known colored vaudevillian to perform in blackface. The practice raised much controversy when Al Jolson smeared burnt cork on his face for the "Mammy" musical number in *The Jazz Singer*, 1929, the first sound film ever made. **Spike Lee**'s film *Bamboozled*, 2000, again raised controversy when he modernized the practice to make his point.

BLACK FILM CENTER/ARCHIVE (BFC/A). Housed at the Indiana University Department of African American and African Diaspora Studies, the Black Film Center/Archive is a repository of films and related materials by and about African Americans. Included are films that have substantial participation by African Americans as writers, actors, producers, directors, musicians, and consultants as well as those that depict some aspect of black experience. It is a research facility where students and scholars can view films and have access to auxiliary research facilities on the Indiana University Bloomington campus. *Black Camera* is the micro-journal of the

BFC/A and serves as an academic, professional, and community resource.

BLACK FILMMAKERS FOUNDATION (BFF). BFF is a product of the political and artistic consciousness that developed in the early 1970s. It was founded as an organization to redress the institutional disenfranchisement of black filmmakers and black audiences. It was originally structured as a distribution cooperative of two dozen New York City-based filmmakers that has grown into a national arts service organization with one of the largest collections of black independent films and videotapes available for rental or sale to educational and cultural institutions. A nonprofit component was established in 1978 to develop and administer programs that assist emerging and independent filmmakers. It has assisted in the emergence of the contemporary black film movement by curating the annual Acapulco Black Film Festival, hosting the annual BFF summit, and providing information and contacts to the film and television industries. Co-founder **Warrington Hudlin**'s socially concerned, entertainment-driven website *DvRepublic.com* is also a project of the BFF.

BLACK FILMMAKERS HALL OF FAME (BFHF). The Cultural and Ethnic Affairs Guild of the Oakland Museum in Oakland, California, created the BFHF in February 1974 as one of 40 programs documenting the contributions of racial and ethnic minorities to the history and culture of California. It was inspired by a course on Blacks in Film by Dr. Roy Thomas, Lecturer in Afro-American Studies, University of California, Berkeley. Credit for the Hall of Fame idea goes to Sonny Buxton, whose award-winning television program *Blacks 'n Film: Some History* was used as a model for the initial program in 1974. The organization's purpose is to acknowledge the often-overlooked presence of African Americans in the cinema and to chronicle their influence on the thinking and customs of the periods in which they have contributed their talents.

BLACK GESTAPO. 1975. (R) 89 min. Blaxploitation. A vigilante force rises up in a Los Angeles ghetto to help the people, but it eventually begins to abuse its power, and the people it sought to protect. Cast: Rod Perry, Charles Robinson, Phil Hoover, Edward Cross, Angela Brent, Wes Bishop, Lee Frost, Charles Howerton, Uschi Digart. Director: Lee Frost. Writers: Wes Bishop, Lee Frost. Cinematographer: Derek Scott.

BLACK GODFATHER. 1974. (R) 90 min. Blaxploitation. A local crook works his way to the top of a drug-selling ring. Cast: Rod Perry, Damu King, Don Chastain, Jimmy Witherspoon, Diane Summerfield. Writer/Director: John Evans. Cinematographer: Jack Steely.

BLACK GOLD, 1928. Drama. Silent. This early all-black-cast film takes place during Oklahoma's oil boom days and is a story of "oil, greed, love, and heroism." It was produced by the **Norman Film Manufacturing Company**. Cast: Lawrence Criner, Kathryn Boyd, Steve Reynolds, Alfred Norcom, L. B. Tatums.

BLACK HOLLYWOOD EDUCATION AND RESOURCE CENTER (BHERC). This is a nonprofit, public benefit organization designed to advocate, educate, research, develop, and preserve the history and the future of blacks in the film and television industries. The BHERC strives to highlight the important roles that African Americans have played, and continue to play, in film and **television**. To that end, the BHERC celebrates and promotes black history and culture through a series of annual film festivals that recognize black film and television pioneers through showcasing historic films and promoting young filmmakers. Its premier event is the S. E. Manly Film Festival held each November in Los Angeles.

BLACK JESUS. 1968. (R) 93 min. Drama. In this film, an African leader uses passive resistance against a cruel and dictatorial regime backed by European colonialists to make a better life for his people. When he is betrayed and arrested, he is imprisoned with a common thief who becomes enlightened by the leader and becomes a devoted follower. It is loosely based on the history of Zaire. Cast: **Woody Strode**, Jean Servais. Director: Valerio Zurlini.

BLACK KING, THE (a.k.a. *Harlem Hotshot*). 1932. 70 min. Comedy. A con man organizes a fake back-to-Africa movement to fleece the unsuspecting people and get rich. When he takes another man's girlfriend, her jilted lover seeks his revenge by proving he is a phony. Cast: A. B. Comethiere, Vivianne Baber, Knolly Mitchell, Dan Michaels, Mike Jackson. Director: Bud Pollard.

BLACK KLANSMAN, THE (a.k.a. *I Crossed the Color Line*). 1966. 88 min. Drama. A black man infiltrates the Ku Klux Klan to avenge his daughter's murder. In the process, he sleeps with the Klan leader's daughter, and wreaks havoc amongst the ranks. Cast:

Richard Gilden, Rima Kutner, Harry Lovejoy. Director: Ted V. Mikels.

BLACK KNIGHT. 2001. (PG-13) 95 min. Comedy. A minimum-wage employee at a Medieval World theme park is transported back to the real medieval world of 14th-century England. While there, he learns some life lessons about not being selfish, and leads a revolt against the evil king. Cast: **Martin Lawrence**, Tom Wilkinson, Vincent Regan, Marsha Thomason, Kevin Conway, Daryl Mitchell, Jeannette Weegar, Michael Burgess, Isabell Monk, Helen Carey. Director: Gil Junger. Writers: Darryl Quarles, Peter Gaulke, Gerry Swallow. Cinematographer: Ueli Steiger. Music: Randy Edelman.

BLACK LIKE ME. 1964. 107 min. Drama. This film is based on the novel by journalist John Howard Griffin. For purposes of research, he used a drug to darken his skin and then traveled the South to experience racism firsthand. As a black man, he is discriminated against in employment, disrespected in social situations, and chased by white youths who want to harm him. He learns that being black in America is a trying existence that no one should have to bear. Cast: James Whitmore, **Roscoe Lee Browne, Al Freeman Jr.**, Will Geer, Walter Mason, John Marriot, Clifton James, Dan Priest, **Richard Ward**. Director: Carl Lerner. Writers: Carl Lerner, Gerda Lerner. Cinematographers: Victor Lukens, Henry Mueller. Music: Meyer Kupfeman.

BLACK SISTER'S REVENGE (a.k.a *Emma Mae*). 1976. 100 min. Drama. A young woman moves to the city from the rural South and must learn to make her way in a different world. Cast: Jerri Hayes, Ernest Williams II, Charles D. Brook III, Eddie Allen. Writer/Director: **Jamaa Fanaka**.

BLACK SIX, THE. 1974. 94 min. Drama. A black high school student is beaten and killed by the brother of a white girl he is dating. The dead boy's brother and his black biker gang show up to avenge his brother's death. The film contains lots of big, bad, professional football players on motorcycles. Cast: Robert Howard, Gene Washington, Cynthia Daly, Carl Eller. Mikel Angel, Lem Barney, John Isenberger, Mercury Morris, Joe Green, Willie Lanier, Garnett Higgens, Bill King, Marilyn McArthur, Doug Carrol, Jefferson Richard. Director: Matt Cimber. Writer: George Theakos.

BLACKULA. 1972. (PG) 92 min. Horror. African Prince Mamuwalde travels to Transylvania to discuss ending the slave trade with Count

Dracula. After Dracula makes an offer to buy his beautiful wife from him, Mamuwalde becomes irate with his host and is condemned not to die, but to live as one of the undead. One hundred years later, Mamuwalde's coffin is purchased in an estate auction and ends up in Los Angeles. After gorging himself on his unwary benefactors, he seeks out fresh blood, and discovers his beautiful reincarnate wife. The film was a melding of the horror genre with contemporary **blaxsploitation** themes. A sequel was made, *Scream Blackula Scream*, 1973. Cast: **William Marshall, Thalmus Rasulala, Denise Nicholas, Vonetta McGee**, Gordon Pinsent, Emily Yancy, Charles Mcaulay, Ted Harris. Director: **William Crain**. Writer: Raymond Koenig, Joan Torres. Cinematographer: John Stevens. Music: Gene Page.

BLADE. 1998. (R) 91 min. Horror. This is a story adaptation from the comic book character about a half-vampire/half-human who must stop an evil vampire apocalypse from taking over the world. The film is action-packed and bloody with a pulsating soundtrack. It spawned the sequel *Blade 2*. Cast: **Wesley Snipes**, Stephen Dorff, Kris Kristofferson, **N'Bushe Wright**, Donal Logue, Udo Kier, Traci Lords, Tim Guinee, Arly Jover, **Sanaa Lathan**. Director: Stephen Norrington. Writer: David S. Goyer. Cinematographer: Theo van de Sande. Music: Mark Isham.

BLADE 2. 2002. (R) 116 min. Horror. This is the gory, action-packed sequel to *Blade*, 1998. The half-human/half-vampire hero is offered a truce by the vampire overlord and asked to help fight a common enemy. The deadly Reapers eat both humans and vampires and are a threat to life itself. Blade takes up the challenge but finds the situation and the alliance is not all that it seems. Cast: **Wesley Snipes**, Kris Kristofferson, Ron Pearlman, Leonor Varela, Norman Reedus, Thomas Kretschmann, Luke Gross, Matt Schulze, Donnie Yen, Danny John Jules, Daz Crawford, Karel Roden, Tony Curran, Santiago Segura, Marit Velle Kile. Director: Guillermo del Toro. Writer: David S. Goyer. Cinematographer: Gabriel Beristain. Music: Marco Beltrami, Danny Saber.

BLADE: TRINITY. 2004. (R) 113 min. Horror. As the third film in the *Blade* series, the Daywalker must stop an apocalyptic event that would undermine humanity and leave control of the earth in the jaws of vampires. The vampire leaders frame Blade to turn the humans against him, and he becomes a hunted man. Cast: **Wesley Snipes**, Kris Kristofferson, Dominic Purcell, Jessica Biel, Ryan Reynolds, Parker Posey, Mark Berry, John Michael Higgins,

Callum Keith Rennie, Paul Michael Levesque, Paul Anthony, Francoise Yip, Michael Ralins, James Remar, Natasha Lyonne. Director: David S. Goyer. Writers: Marv Wolfman, Gene Colan. Cinematographer: Gabriel Beristain. Music: Ramin Djawadi, RZA.

BLANCHARD, TERENCE (1962-). Composer. This native of New Orleans, Louisiana, is a renowned trumpeter, jazz musician, and one of the most prolific composers to ever work in **television** and film. He studied music with Wynton Marsalis at the New Orleans Center for the Creative Arts and received a scholarship to Rutgers University. He has worked extensively on soundtracks for filmmaker **Spike Lee**, and ghosted **Denzel Washington**'s trumpet playing in the film *Mo' Better Blues*, 1990.

Filmography: *Mo' Better Blues*, 1990; *Jungle Fever*, 1991; *Malcolm X*, 1992; *Sugar Hill*, 1994; *The Inkwell*, 1994; *Crooklyn*, 1994; *Trial by Jury*, 1994; *Clockers*, 1995; *Get on the Bus*, 1996; *'Til There Was You*, 1997; *4 Little Girls*, 1997; *Eve's Bayou*, 1997; *Summer of Sam*, 1999; *Next Friday*, 2000; *Love & Basketball*, 2000; *Bamboozled*, 2000; *The Caveman's Valentine*, 2001; *Original Sin*, 2001; *Glitter*, 2001; *Barbershop*, 2002; *Dark Blue*, 2002; *25th Hour*, 2002; *She Hate Me*, 2004; *Their Eyes Were Watching God*, 2005.

BLANKMAN. 1994. (PG-13) 96 min. Comedy. This is an expanded comedy skit by **Damon Wayans** from his brother **Keenon Ivory Wayan**'s hit comedy series *In Living Color*. The story is about a wannabe superhero who fights crime in undershorts and his grandma's bathrobe. Cast: **Damon Wayans, Robbin Givens, David Allen Grier**, Jason Alexander, Jon Polito, Nicky Corello. Director: Mike Binder. Writers: J. F. Lawton, Damon Wayans. Cinematographer: Newton Thomas Sigel. Music: Miles Goodman.

BLAXPLOITATION. The Blaxploitation Era was firmly launched in the early 1970s by the films *Sweet Sweetback's Baadasssss Song*, 1971; *Shaft*, 1971; and *Superfly*, 1972. Coming out of the Civil Rights movement of the 1960s, the subject matter of these motion pictures caused an industry shift and ushered in a series of heroes and sheroes on the silver screen. Aptly named for exploiting the black image, most of these films were raw, tense, and often controversial in nature. Films that have the main character fighting against the system and "The Man" mainly define the genre itself. Many expressed the hardcore elements of inner-city street life. Films like *Black Caesar*, 1972; *Coffy*, 1973; and *The Mack*, 1973, dealt with drugs, pimps and prostitutes, graft and corruption, taking on the system, and getting paid. Regardless of how heroic or offensive these films may have been perceived to be, the black audience could not get enough of these onscreen images. Financially waning from the technical advent of television, the huge profits from these films saved many Hollywood studios from going bankrupt. Several sensitive and more family-oriented films appeared as well. These included *Sounder*, 1972; *Lady Sings the Blues*, 1972; *Claudine*, 1974; and *Sparkle*, 1976, but by 1977 the era had been phased out.

BLIND FAITH. 1998. (R) 122 min. Drama. Made for cable movie. It is 1957 and the son of the first black police sergeant in New York City is accused of killing a white boy during an attempted robbery. Racial tensions are high and many believe that a confession was beat out of him. An uncle, who is an attorney, makes plans to defend him, but soon becomes leery of his nephew's side of the story. Cast: **Courney B. Vance, Charles S. Dutton,** Garland Whitt, **Kadeem Hardison, Lonette McKee,** Karen Glave, Dan Lett. Director: **Ernest R. Dickerson.** Writer: Frank Military. Cinematographer: Rodney Charters. Music: Ron Carter.

BLOOD BROTHERS. 1997. (R) 91 min. Urban Drama. A "brother's keeper" flick about a young man who sees his gang-banging older brother take part in a brutal murder, and is pressured by the district attorney to speak up about what he saw, before the gang silences him permanently. Both brothers are torn between doing what is right and honoring the love and duty they have to protect one another. Cast: **Clark Johnson,** Richard Chevolleau, Mia Korf, Richard Yearwood, Ron White, Amir Williams, Ndehru Roberts, Timothy Stickney, **Bill Nunn.** Director: Bruce Pittman. Writer: Paris Qualles. Music: Harold Wheeler.

BLUE COLLAR. 1978. (R) 114 min. Drama. This is a powerful look at how big business and corporate America often exploit the working class, divide the races, and kill the human spirit. Three struggling and underappreciated Detroit auto assembly-line workers devise a plan to rob a safe in their corrupt union office. They do not get much, but the union uses the break-in to its own advantage, and begins to take out its revenge on those it believes are responsible. This is a serious dramatic statement with many humorous moments. Cast: **Richard Pryor, Yaphet Kotto,** Harvey Keitel, Ed Begley Jr., Lane Smith, Cliff DeYoung. Director: Paul Schrader. Writers: Paul Schrader, Leonard Schrader. Cinematographer: Bobby Byrne. Music: Jack Natzsche.

BLUE HILL AVENUE. 2001. (R) 128 min. Urban Drama. This film tells the story of Tristan, a young man from a middle-class family, who is lured into a dangerous world of crime, drugs, and corruption. Cast: **Alan Payne**, Angelle Brooks, Michael Taliferro, William L. Johnson, Aaron D. Spears, Andrew Divoff, **Richard Lawson**, Marlon Young, Dee Freeman, Gail Fulton Ross, Veronica Redd, Anthony Sherwood, Myquan Jackson, Latamra Smith, Brandon Hammond. Writer/Director: Craig Ross Jr.

BOARDINGHOUSE BLUES. 1948. 90 min. Musical. A troubled boardinghouse is home to many entertainers who live there and also perform. Cast: Dusty Fletcher, Jackie "Moms" Mabley. Performers: Lucky Millinder, Bull Moose Jackson, Uma Mae Carlisle, Stumpy and Stumpy. Director: Josh Binney.

BOATMAN, MICHAEL (1964-). Actor. He was born in Colorado Springs, Colorado, and made his film debut in *Hamburger Hill*, 1987. He landed the lead role in **Charles Burnette**'s race-based police drama *The Glass Shield*, 1994, and he has guest starred in the television series *Law & Order: Special Victims Unit, CSI: Miami*, and *Scrubs*. Boatman was also a participant in the reality series *Celebrity Mole: Hawaii*.

Filmography: *Hamburger Hill*, 1987; *China Beach*, 1988; *Running on Empty*, 1988; *Unbecoming Age*, 1992; *Urban Crossfire*, 1994; *The Glass Shield*, 1995; *The Peacemaker*, 1997; *Walking to the Waterline*, 1998; *Woman Thou Art Loosed*, 2004; *Kalamazoo?* 2005.

BODY AND SOUL. 1924. 102 min. Drama. Silent. An escaped convict posing as a man of God takes advantage of the people in his congregation and a beautiful young girl. A real-life wolf in pastor's clothing, he drinks, gambles, and consorts with common criminals until an old jail mate threatens to blow his cover. The negative portrayal of a man of God raised protests by the motion-picture censors board and several story changes were made. This was **Paul Robeson**'s first film appearance and one of director **Oscar Micheaux**'s best. Cast: Paul Robeson, Julia Theresa Russell, Mercedes Gilbert. Director: Oscar Micheaux.

BODY AND SOUL. 1981. (R) 109 min. Drama. A prizefighter is sent to prison, where he has to literally fight to survive. Cast: **Leon Isaac Kennedy, Jayne Kennedy**, Perry Lang, Nikki Swasey, Michael V. Gazzo, Kim Hamilton, **Muhammad Ali**, Peter Lawford, Gilbert Lewis, Chris Wallace, Robbie Epps, J. B. Williamson, Mel

Welles, Danny Wells, Johnny Brown. Director: George Bowers.
Writer: Leon Isaac Kennedy.

BOESMAN & LENA. 2000. (TV) 86 min. Drama. This film is based
on the play by South African playwright Athol Fugard about a
black couple living in apartheid-era Cape Town. Their shanty home
is bulldozed to the ground by the government, so they take to the
road with what little they managed to salvage. When they camp for
the night, they meet an old man with even less than they have left,
and the wife invites the old man to stay with them, much to her
husband's chagrin. Cast: **Danny Glover, Angela Bassett**, Willie
Johah. Writer/Director: John Berry. Cinematographer: Alain Cho-
quart. Music: Wally Badatou.

BOGLE, DONALD (1944-). Author. This preeminent writer and film
historian is a graduate of the prestigious Lincoln University in
southeastern Pennsylvania. He has written numerous books, including *Brown Sugar: Eighty Years of America's Black Female Superstars*, which was produced as a four-part documentary for PBS in
1986. His book *Toms, Coons, Mulattoes, Mammies & Bucks* studies the history of black images in film, and his book *Primetime
Blues: African Americans on Network Television* explores African
American roles and images on the small screen. He also wrote the
biographical book on film legend **Dorothy Dandridge** that became
the basis for the biopic ***Introducing Dorothy Dandridge***, 1999. He
teaches at The University of Pennsylvania and at New York University's Tisch School of the Arts.

BOND, JAMES, III. He began his career as a child actor in the film
The Fish That Saved Pittsburgh, 1979, and in the telepic ***Go Tell
It on the Mountain***, 1984. He went on to write, produce, direct,
and star in the horror flick ***Def by Temptation***, 1990.
    Filmography: *The Fish That Saved Pittsburgh*, 1979; *Go Tell
It on the Mountain*, 1984; ***School Daze***, 1988; *Def by Temptation*,
1990.

BONDS, DE'AUNDRE (1976-). Actor. He was born in Los Angeles,
California, and began his acting career as a teen in the TV series
Picket Fences, 1994. His other television appearances include roles
in *Chicago Hope, Touched by an Angel, The Parent Hood*, and
NYPD Blue. He made his film debut in ***Tales from the Hood***,
1995.
    Filmography: *Tales from the Hood*, 1995; *Sunset Park*, 1996;
Get on the Bus, 1996; *Kaos on Warrick Avenue*, 1997; *Ill Gotten*

Gains, 1997; *The Heist*, 1999; *The Wood*, 1999; *3 Strikes*, 2000; *Lockdown*, 2000; *Flossin*, 2001; *Black Ball*, 2003.

BONES. 2001. (R) 94 min. Horror. This is a modern-day story of terror with **blaxploitation**-style flashbacks that depict the murder of Jimmy Bones, a flashy pimp, who was killed back in the 1970s for refusing to expand his business interests into crack cocaine. His body is wrapped in his girlfriend's bloodstained dress and hidden away in a secret room on the premises. Twenty-two years later, the ambitious son of one of the men responsible for the pimp's death turns the building into a hip-hop dancehall and Jimmy Bones is resurrected to seek his revenge. Cast: **Snoop Dogg, Pam Grier,** Michael T. Weiss, **Clifton Powell,** Ricky Harris, Bianca Lawson, Khalil Kain, Katherine Isabelle, Merwin Mondesir, Sean Armstrong. Director: **Ernest R. Dickerson.** Writer: Adam Simon. Cinematographer: Flavio Labiano. Music: Elia Cmiral.

BONET, LISA (1967-). Actress, writer, director. She was born in San Francisco, and grew up in New York and Los Angeles. She attended Reseda High School and the Celluloid Actor's Studio. She began acting in commercials at age 11, and landed her breakout role as Denise Huxtable in the hit sitcom *The Cosby Show* when she was 16. She was at one time married to musician Lenny Kravitz, and was active in his career, co-writing songs for his first album, and directing the music video to his first hit song, "Let Love Rule." She took a big gamble with her first film role which included her appearing stark naked in a violent sex scene. It was a major departure from her "Cosby Daughter" image. Her character left the show soon after to star as a student at a black college on the spin-off series *A Different World*, where she worked for only one season. Other notable film roles include *Enemy of the State*, 1998, and *Biker Boyz*, 2003.

    Filmography: *Angel Heart*, 1987; *Bank Robber*, 1993; *Dead Connection*, 1994; *Enemy of the State*, 1998; *High Fidelity*, 1998; *Biker Boyz*, 2003; *Whitepaddy*, 2005.

BOOK OF NUMBERS. 1973. (R) 81 min. Drama. This is a film based on the novel by Robert Deane Pharr. A couple of Depression-era waiters make it to the big time when they become involved in the Arkansas numbers racket in the 1930s. Their success brings out a sleazy white mobster who tries to take over their turf, and the fight is on. Cast: **Raymond St. Jacques, Philip Michael Thomas,** Freda Payne, **D'Urville Martin,** Sterling St. Jacques, Gilbert Green, **Irma P. Hall,** Doug Finell, Willie Washington Jr., Hope

Clark, **Reginald T. Dorsey**, David Magnunson. Director: Raymond St. Jacques. Writer: Larry Spiegel.

BOOMERANG. 1992. (R) 118 min. Comedy. A brash and confident advertising executive for a black-owned cosmetics company is also a ruthless womanizer. He falls hard for a new colleague who is just like him...vain, aloof, and sexually provocative. He gets a taste of his own medicine and crawls sheepishly back to the good girl he left behind. A virtual all-star cast of talent, both past and present. Cast: **Eddie Murphy, Halle Berry, Robin Givens, David Allen Grier, Martin Lawrence, Grace Jones, Geoffrey Holder, Eartha Kitt, Chris Rock, Tisha Campbell, John Witherspoon, Melvin Van Peebles.** Director: **Reginald Hudlin.** Writers: Barry W. Blaustein, David Sheffield.

BOW WOW (1987-). Rapper, actor. He was born in Columbus, Ohio, as Shad Gregory Moss, and began his career rapping at an early age as "Lil' Bow Wow." He made his film debut in the rap-musical *Carmen: A Hip Hopera*, 2001, and went on to act in *All about the Benjamins*, with fellow rapper turned actor **Ice Cube.** As he grew up, Bow Wow starred in the films *Like Mike*, 2002, *Johnson Family Vacation*, 2004, and composed songs for *Big Momma's House*, 2000, and *Like Mike*, 2002.

Filmography: *Carmen: A Hip Hopera*, 2001; *All about the Benjamins*, 2002; *Like Mike*, 2002; *Johnson Family Vacation*, 2004; *Roll Bounce*, 2005; *Mr. Prez*, 2005.

BOYCOTT. 2002. (PG) 112 min. HBO Docudrama. It chronicles the birth of the Civil Rights movement. From Rosa Parks standing up to segregation and refusing to give up her seat on a Montgomery, Alabama, bus, to the subsequent bus boycott, to the full-fledged organization of a movement by Dr. Martin Luther King Jr., Ralph Abernathy, Jo Anne Robinson, and others. They face violence, jail, further oppression, and many hardships while forcing America rise up and be in practice all that it stands for in principle. Cast: **Jeffrey Wright, Terrence Howard, CCH Pounder,** Carmen Ejogo, Reg E. Cathey, Brent Jennings, Shawn Michael Howard, Eric Todd Dellums, Iris Little Thomas, **Whitman Mayo,** E. Roger Mitchell, Mike Hodge, **Clark Johnson.** Director: Clark Johnson. Writers: Timothy J. Sexton, Herman Daniel Farrell III. Cinematographer: David Hennings. Music: Stephen James Taylor.

BOYZ N THE HOOD. 1991. (R) 112 min. Urban Drama. This is a hard-hitting, coming-of-age story about growing up in the drug-infested, gang-ridden, often-violent streets of south central Los Angeles. A rebellious 10-year-old Trey is sent to live with his strict, disciplinarian father and further bonds with Ricky and Doboy, two very different brothers, sired by different fathers, who live across the street. As they grow to maturity, each seeks a different path in life based on individual abilities, opportunities, and past personal experience until one tragic event leads them to a crucial crossroads. For this film, first-time writer/director John Singleton became the youngest director ever nominated for an **Academy Award**. He was also nominated for Best Screenplay. Cast: **Cuba Gooding Jr.**, **Laurence Fishburne, Ice Cube, Nia Long, Morris Chestnut, Tyra Ferrell, Angela Bassett, Whitman Mayo**. Writer/Director: **John Singleton**. Cinematographer: **Charles Mills**. Music: Stanley Clarke. Awards: MTV Movie Awards 1992: Best New Filmmaker (Singleton). National Film Registry 2002.

BRAUGHER, ANDRE (1962-). Actor. A native of Chicago, Illinois, he earned his BA degree at Stanford University and a MFA degree from the Juilliard School. After numerous performances with the New York Shakespeare Festival and the Joseph Papp Public Theater, he landed a role on the serial drama *Homicide: Life on the Street* as Detective Frank Pembleton, and won an **Emmy Award**.

Filmography: *Glory*, 1989; *The Court-Martial of Jackie Robinson*, 1990; *The Class of '61*, 1992; *Striking Distance*, 1993; *The Tuskegee Airman*, 1995; *Primal Fear*, 1996; *Get on the Bus*, 1996; *City of Angels*, 1998; *Thick as Thieves*, 1999; *Passing Glory*, 1999; *It's the Rage*, 1999; *Homicide: The Movie*, 2000; *Frequency*, 2000; *Duets*, 2000; *A Better Way to Die*, 2000.

BREAKIN' ALL THE RULES. 2004. (PG-13) 85 min. Urban Romance. An unemployed man writes a "how to break-up" handbook after his girlfriend dumps him. He finds fame, money, and a new girl. Cast: **Jamie Foxx, Gabrielle Union, Morris Chestnut**, Peter MacNicol, Jennifer Esposito, Bianca Lawson, Jill Ritchie, Samantha Nagel, Grace Chan, Danny Comden, Octavia Spencer, Heather Headley, Patrick Cranshaw. Writer/director: Daniel Taplitz.

BRIGHT ROAD. 1953. 68 min. Drama. A Southern fourth-grade teacher befriends one of her troubled students in the hope of turning him around. It is based on "See How They Run," an award-winning story by Mary Elizabeth Vroman in the June 1951 issue of *Ladies Home Journal*. Cast: **Dorothy Dandridge**, Philip Hepburn, **Harry Belafonte**, Barbara Ann Sanders, Robert Horton, **Maidie Norman**, Rene Beard, Howard McNeeley, Robert McNeeley, Patti

Marie Ellis, Joy Jackson, Fred Moultrie, James Moultrie, Vivian Dandridge, Janet Heard. Director: Gerald Mayer. Writer: Emmet Lavery. Cinematographer: Alfred Gilks. Music: Sidney Homer.

BROKEN STRINGS. 1940. 50 min. Drama. When a concert violinist loses partial use of his left hand in a car accident, he transfers his professional dreams and desires into making his son the virtuoso that he once was. When the boy is caught playing swing music in a local juke joint, he is punished severely and made to practice the classics day and night. The father eventually comes to terms with his son and himself after his hand miraculously recovers. Written and produced by **Clarence Muse**. Cast: Clarence Muse, Sybil Lewis, William Washington, Mathew "Stymie" Beard. Director: Bernard B. Ray.

BRONZE BUCKEROO, THE. 1939. 57 min. Western. This third film in the trilogy that includes ***Two-Gun Man From Harlem***, 1939, and ***Harlem Rides the Range***, 1939. Singing cowboy Bob Blake heads across the prairie to help a friend seek justice and revenge against a murdering neighbor who killed the friend's father. Cast: **Herbert Jeffrey**, Artie Young, Rellie Hardin, **Spencer Williams Jr.**, **Clarence Brooks**, **Flournoy Miller**. Writer/Director: Richard C. Kahn.

BROOKS, AVERY (1948-). Actor, director. With his rich, deep voice and distinctive baldhead, this native of Evansville, Illinois, became well-known as Capt. Benjamin Sisko on the sci-fi television series *Star Trek: Deep Space Nine*. He was first seen on the series *Spencer For Hire*, and had his own spin-off series, *A Man Called Hawk*. He has acted in many made-for-TV movies, including ***Solomon Northup's Odyssey***, 1985; ***Uncle Tom's Cabin***, 1987; *and* ***Roots: The Gift***. He has also directed episodes of *Deep Space Nine*.

    Filmography: ***Solomon Northup's Odyssey***, 1985; *Uncle Tom's Cabin*, 1987; *Roots: The Gift*, 1988; ***The Ernest Green Story***, 1993; *The Big Hit*, 1998; *American History X*, 1998; *15 Minutes*, 2001.

BROOKS, CLARENCE. (1896-1969). Actor. He was a co-founder of the Los Angeles–based **Lincoln Motion Picture Company** in 1915, and co-starred in the company's debut film, ***Realization of a Negro's Ambition***, 1916. He also played the lead role in the company's fourth and final film, ***By Right of Birth***, 1922.

Filmography: *Realization of a Negro's Ambition*, 1916; *By Right of Birth*, 1922; **Harlem Rides the Range**, 1939; **The Bronze Buckeroo**, 1939.

BROOKS, RICHARD (1962-). Actor. Born in Cleveland, Ohio, this soft-spoken actor has become a notable presence in television and film. Filmography: *Teen Wolf*, 1985; *Good to Go*, 1986; *The Hidden*, 1987; *Short Fuse*, 1988; *Off Limits*, 1988; *Shakedown*, 1988; *Shocker*, 1989; *To Sleep With Anger*, 1990; *Memphis*, 1991; *Machine Gun Blues*, 1995; *Wolverine*, 1996; *The Substitute*, 1996; *The Crow 2: City of Angels*, 1996. *Johnny B Good*, 1998; *The Adventures of Ragtime*, 1998; *Acid Rain*, 1998; *In Too Deep*, 1999; *Lexie*, 2004.

BROTHER FROM ANOTHER PLANET, THE. 1984. (R) 109 min. Drama. An alien escapes from his home planet and is pursued to Harlem by two alien slave catchers. He blends in with the dark skinned peoples in the community and discovers that many are just like him. Cast: **Joe Morton**, Dee Dee Bridgewater, **Ren Woods**, **Steve James**, Maggie Renzie, David Strathaim. Writer/Director: John Sayles. Cinematographer: **Ernest R. Dickerson**. Music: Mason Daring.

BROTHER FUTURE. 1991. (TV) 110 min. Science Fiction. A streetsmart, inner-city kid believes that attending school and learning his history is a waste of time, until an accident transports him back in time, before the Civil War to experience his life as a slave. Cast: Phill Lewis, Frank Converse, **Carl Lumbly**, **Vonetta McGee**, **Moses Gunn**, William Bender, **Akosua Busia**, O'Neal Compton, William Crumby, Michael Flippo, Gene Jones. Writer/Director: **Roy Campanella**.

BROTHER JOHN. 1970. (PG-13) 94 min. Drama. Racial tensions and labor problems run high in a small Alabama town until a mysterious mild-mannered former citizen returns home to calm fears and give advice. Cast: **Sidney Poitier**, Will Geer, Bradford Dillman, **Beverly Todd**, **Paul Winfield**. Director: James Goldstone. Music: **Quincy Jones.**

BROTHER ON THE RUN. 1973. (R) 90 min. Drama A concerned teacher attempts to help one of his students who is in trouble with the law. Cast: **Terry Carter**, Diana Eden, **Kyle Johnson**, Art

Lund, Gwenn Mitchell, James Sikking. Writers/Directors: Edward J. Lakso, Herbert L. Strock.

BROTHERS, THE. 2001. (R) 101 min. Comedy. Four diverse, professional young men living in Los Angeles must juggle their careers and personal relationships while navigating through the modern politics of sex. Cast: **Morris Chestnut, D. L. Hughley, Bill Bellamy, Shemar Moore, Gabrielle Union, Tamala Jones**, Susan Dalian, Angelle Brooks, **Jenifer Lewis, Clifton Powell, Marla Gibbs**, Tatyana Ali, Julie Benz. Writer/Director: **Gary Hardwick**. Cinematographer: Alexander Grusynski.

BROWN, BOBBY (1969-). Singer, actor. This native of Boston, Massachusetts, began his entertainment career as a youngster in the popular singing group New Edition. He moved on to a successful solo singing career by turning out hit songs like "Every Little Step," "Don't Be Cruel," and "My Prerogative." He performed on television music and award shows, such as *Bandstand*, *Soul Train*, and *The Annual American Music Awards*. He moved into acting with roles in *Ghostbusters 2*, 1989; *A Thin Line Between Love and Hate*, 1996; and *Nora's Hair Salon*, 2004. Brown had his own reality-based television show called *Being Bobby Brown*.

Filmography: *Ghostbusters 2*, 1989; *Panther*, 1995; *A Thin Line Between Love and Hate*, 1996; ***Two Can Play That Game***, 2001; *Go for Broke*, 2002; *Gang of Roses*, 2003; *Nora's Hair Salon*, 2004.

BROWN, GEORG STANFORD (1943-). Actor, director. Born in Havana, Cuba, Brown began his acting career in *The Comedians*, 1967. He landed a starring role as a cop on the 1972 TV series *The Rookies*. He then began directing for television.

Filmography: *Dayton's Devils*, 1968; ***Roots***, 1977; ***Roots: Next Generation***, 1979; *The Night the City Screamed*, 1980; ***The Jesse Owens Story***, 1984; *Alone in the Neon Jungle*, 1987; ***House Party 2: The Pajama Jam***, 1991; *Murder without Motive*, 1992; *Ava's Magical Adventure*, 1994; ***Tyson***, 1995.

BROWN, JAMES (1933-2006). Singer. Brown was born in Barnwell, South Carolina, and was voted the 7th Greatest Rock and Roll Artist of all time. He and his band, The Famous Flames, excited audiences in the 1960s with its unique musical sound and Brown's spastic, energetic dance moves. He remained at the top of the charts for the next four decades with such songs as "Say It Loud, I'm Black and I'm Proud," and "Living in America." He and his music have appeared on **television** and numerous films and film soundtracks.

Filmography: *Mean Johnny Barrows*, 1976; *The Blues Brothers*, 1980; *Doctor Detroit*, 1983; *Rocky IV*, 1985; *Blues Brothers 2000*, 1998; **Undercover Brother**, 2002.

BROWN, JIM (1936-). Football player, athlete, actor. He was born on St. Simons Island off the southern coast of Georgia. Before graduating from Manhasset High School, he earned 13 letters in football, basketball, baseball, lacrosse, and track and field. Brown played nine seasons as a fullback in the NFL for the Cleveland Browns. As Cleveland's first-round draft pick at No. 6 overall, he was voted Rookie of the Year for the 1957 season and was named MVP the following year, leading the league in rushing with 1,527 yards and 18 touchdowns. Brown never missed a game and when he retired at age 30 after the 1965 season, he had run for 12,312 yards and scored 126 touchdowns, a record unmatched at that time. He set his sights on Hollywood and went on to appear in over 30 movies, including *The Dirty Dozen*, 1967, and *Ice Station Zebra*, 1968. Brown became an action icon during the **blaxploitation**-era films of the early 1970s. He was a country sheriff in *...tick...tick...tick*, 1970; portrayed the title character in **Slaughter**, 1972, and **Slaughter's Big Rip-off**, 1973; and one part of a super bad trio in **Three the Hard Way**, 1974. During the 1980s, he had a short stint as head of **Richard Pryor**'s production company, Indigo Productions, backed by Columbia Pictures, and he has spearheaded community work to help turn gang members and prison inmates into more productive members of society through his Amer-I-Can program. He returned to his football roots as a coach in the gridiron-based film, *Any Given Sunday*, 1999.

Filmography: *Rio Conchos*, 1964; *The Dirty Dozen*, 1967; *Ice Station Zebra*, 1968; *Dark of the Sun*, 1968; *Riot*, 1969; *100 Rifles*, 1969; *...tick...tick...tick*, 1970; *El Condor*, 1970; *Slaughter*, 1972; *Slaughter's Big Rip Off*, 1973; *Three the Hard Way*, 1974; *Fingers*, 1978; **One Down, Two to Go!** 1982; *The Running Man*, 1987; **I'm Gonna Git You Sucka**, 1988; *L. A. Vice*, 1989; **Original Gangstas**, 1996; *Mars Attacks!* 1996; **He Got Game**, 1998; *Any Given Sunday*, 1999.

BROWN, ROSCOE LEE (1925-). Actor. He is a veteran character actor with a balding head and deep velvet voice. Before taking to the stage, he taught French and literature at Lincoln University, and set a world record for the 800-meter run in 1951. His film roles include *The Comedians*, 1967; **The Liberation of L. B. Jones**, 1970;

and *Uptown Saturday Night*, 1974. He has toured with Anthony Zerbe, in *Behind the Broken Words*, a reading of lyric and dramatic verse. He was a regular on the **television** series *Falcon Crest*, and earned a Tony Award nomination for his work in August Wilson's stage play *Two Trains Running*. Filmography: *The Connection*, 1961; *Black Like Me*, 1964; *The Liberation of L. B. Jones*, 1970; *The Cowboys*, 1972; *Superfly T. N. T.*, 1973; *Uptown Saturday Night*, 1974; *Logan's Run*, 1976; *King*, 1978; *Nothing Personal*, 1980; *Legal Eagles*, 1986; *Jumpin' Jack Flash*, 1986; *For Us The Living*, 1988; *The Mambo Kings*, 1992; *Forest Warrior*, 1995; *Babe*, 1995; *Last Summer in the Hamptons*, 1996; *Dear God*, 1996; *Babe: Pig in the City*, 1998; *Hamlet*, 2001; *Treasure Planet*, 2002.

BROWN SUGAR. 2002. (PG-13) 109 min. Urban Romance. As childhood friends, Dre and Sidney shared many things together, including a love for music. Now grown up and immersed in the hip-hop music culture, Dre is a record producer while Sydney writes for a music magazine. They still share their friendship and their love for music, while suppressing their simmering love for each other. After Dre gets engaged, Sidney must decide to speak now, or forever hold her peace. Cast: **Taye Diggs**, **Sanaa Lathan**, **Mos Def**, Nicole Ari Parker, **Queen Latifah**, **Wendell Pierce**, Boris Kodjoe, Erik Weiner, Reggi Wyns. Director: Rick Famuyiwa. Writers: Rick Famuyiwa, Michael Elliot. Cinematographer: Enrique Chediak. Music: Robert Hurst.

BUCK AND THE PREACHER. 1972. (PG) 102 min. Western. A trail guide and former Buffalo soldier teams up with a traveling preacher and con man to get a wagon train of former enslaved Africans to their homestead land out West. After conflicts with the original director, **Sidney Poitier** stepped in and made his directing debut. Cast: Sidney Poitier, **Harry Belafonte**, **Ruby Dee**, Cameron Mitchell, Denny Miller. Director: Sidney Poitier.

BUCKTOWN. 1975. (R) 95 min. Blaxploitation. A man decides to reopen his murdered brother's bar in a small Southern town and runs into racism, intimidation, and police corruption. Cast: **Fred Williamson**, **Pam Grier**, **Bernie Hamilton**, **Thalmus Rasulala**, Art Lund. Director: Arthur Marks. Writer: Bob Ellison. Cinematographer: Robert Birchall. Music: Johnny Pate.

BUCKWHEAT (1931-1980). He was born William Thomas Jr., but as a child star, he became best known as Buckwheat in the *Little Rascals* series. He became a film lab technician in his later years. Filmography: *Three Men in a Tub*, 1938; *Aladdin's Lantern*, 1938; *Dog Daze*, 1939; *Good Bad Boys*, 1940; *Fightin' Fools*, 1941; *Don't Lie*, 1942; *Whistling in Dixie*, 1942; *Family Troubles*, 1943; *Radio Bugs*, 1944; *Colorado Pioneers*, 1945.

BUFFALO SOLDIERS. 1997. (G) 120 min. Western. This is a made-for-cable movie about the all-black Calvary units Congress created after the Civil War to fight Indians and patrol the West. Sgt. Washington is a former slave who, although risking his life and fighting to protect the country that once enslaved him, must still endure the spite, resentment, and degradation from his white superior officers. When his unit is sent to track down and apprehend a band of renegade Apache Indians across the New Mexico Territories, he and his men show a strength and honor not afforded to them by their racist superiors to go against their orders and do the right thing. Cast: **Danny Glover**, **Carl Lumbly**, Bob Gunton, Tom Bower, Harrison Lowe, **Glenn Turman**, **Michael Warren**, **Mykelti Williamson**, Timothy Busfield, Gabrielle Casseus. Director: Charles Haid. Writers: Frank Military, Susan Rhinehart. Cinematographer: William Wages. Music: Joel McNeely.

BUGGED! 1996. (PG-13) 90 min. Horror. A team of inept, but dedicated exterminators, fight off a hoard of flesh-eating crickets that they inadvertently helped to create. Instead of pesticide, a canister of Klemal C-38, a top-secret mutanagenic chemical is delivered to Dead and Buried Exterminators, Inc. When called to address a bug problem at the lakefront home of a beautiful author, their spray only makes the situation worse. The insects grow into giant carnivorous creatures that eat everyone and everything in sight. When the bug sprayers are called back to finish the job, the job almost finishes them. Cast: Ronald K. Armstrong, Priscilla Basque, Jeff Lee, Derek Johnson, Billy Graham. Writer/Director: Ronald K. Armstrong. Cinematographer: S. Torriano Berry. Music: Boris Elkis.

BURNING CROSS, THE. 1947. 77 min. Drama. A World War II veteran returns to his hometown but has a hard time fitting in until he is seduced by the rhetoric of a Ku Klux Klan organizer. Cast: Hank Daniels, Virginia Patton, Dick Rich, Betty Roadman, Raymond Bond, Matt Willis, John Doucette, Alexander Pope, **Joel Fluellen**, Giovanni Fostini, Walden Boyle, Dick Bailey, Jack Shutta, Ross

Elliott, Herb Vigran. Director: Walter Colmes. Writer: Aubrey Wisberg. Cinematographer: Walter Strenge. Music: Ralph Stanley.

BURTON, LeVAR (1957-). Actor, director. He was born in Landstuhl, West Germany, and starred as Kunta Kinte in the groundbreaking TV miniseries, *Roots*, 1977. He is the host of the children's television series *The Reading Rainbow*, and became well known as Lt. Commander Geordi La Forge on the sci-fi series *Star Trek: The Next Generation*. He also directed episodes of all of the *Star Trek* spin-offs, including *The Next Generation, Deep Space Nine, Voyager*, and *Enterprise*.

Filmography: *Roots*, 1977; *One in a Million: The Ron LeFlore Story*, 1978; *The Hunter*, 1980; *The Guyana Tragedy: The Story of Jim Jones*, 1980; *Grambling's White Tiger*, 1981; *The Jesse Owens Story*, 1984; *Roots: The Gift*, 1988; *Star Trek: Generations*, 1994; *Parallel Lives*, 1994; *Star Trek: First Contact*, 1996; *Yesterday's Target*, 1996; Star *Trek: Insurrection*, 1998; *Dancing in September*, 2000; *Ali*, 2001; *Star Trek: Nemesis*, 2002.

BUSH, ANITA (1883-1974). Singer, actress. She became known as the "mother of drama" in New York among colored people. As a child, Anita Bush helped her father in the costume department at the Bijou Theater in Brooklyn, NY. Moving from backstage, she became a chorus girl with the Williams and Walker Company in 1903, where she performed in the hit shows *In Dahomey* and *Abyssinia*, both at home and on the highly praised European Tour. In 1909, she organized the Anita Bush Stock Company with her own group of chorus girls, as well as popular actors **Charles Gilpin** and **Dooley Wilson**. They made their debut at the New Lincoln Theater in Harlem with the production of *The Girl at the Fort*. They would eventually come together to form the well-known **Lafayette Players**. Bush starred in *The Crimson Skull*, 1922, and *The Flying Ace*, 1926, two silent films produced by **The Norman Film Manufacturing Company**.

Filmography: *The Bulldogger*, 1921; *The Crimson Skull*, 1922; *The Flying Ace*, 1926.

BUSH, GRAND L. (1955-). Actor. He was born in Los Angeles, California, and began acting at an early age. With his ability to memorize large passages of text, he was cast as Prince Charming in his fourth-grade play, *Sleeping Beauty*. He enrolled in drama at Fairfax High School in his junior year, and attended the Theater Academy at Los Angeles City College. Upon graduation, he studied film and theater at the University of Southern California and scene acting at the Strasberg Academy in Hollywood. He began his professional career playing a role on the sitcom *Good Times*, then followed with a string of guest appearances on **television** shows and bit parts in films, such as *Stir Crazy*, 1980; *Night Shift*, 1982; and *Brewster's Millions*, 1985. His acting opportunities increased after he appeared in **Robert Townsend**'s *Hollywood Shuffle*, 1987.

Filmography: *Stir Crazy*, 1980; *Night Shift*, 1982; *Streets of Fire*, 1984; *Hollywood Shuffle*, 1987; *Die Hard*, 1988; *Colors*, 1988; *Blind Vengeance*, 1990; *Freejack*, 1992; *Demolition Man*, 1993; *Extreme Honor*, 2001; *Boa*, 2002.

BUSIA, AKOSUA (1968-). Actress, writer. Her **television** appearances include the telefilms *Warp Speed*, 1981; *Badge of the Assassin*, 1985; and *Brother Future*, 1991. Film roles include *The Color Purple*, 1985; *Rosewood*, 1997; and *Tears of the Sun*, 2003. She has written the novel, *The Seasons of Beento Blackbird* (Little Brown, 1996), and the screenplay for *Beloved*, 1998.

Filmography: *Ashanti*, 1979; *Warp Speed*, 1981; *The Final Terror*, 1983; *The Color Purple*, 1985; *Badge of the Assassin*, 1985; *Native Son*, 1986; *Hard Lessons*, 1986; *Low Blow*, 1986; *The Seventh Sign*, 1988; and *Brother Future*, 1991; *Rosewood*, 1996; *Dead Man's Walk*, 1996; *Mad City*, 1997; *Ill Gotten Gains*, 1997; *Tears of the Sun*, 2003.

BUSTIN' LOOSE. 1981. (R) 94 min. Comedy. In this film an ex-con is given a second chance at freedom after violating his probation. He is forced to drive a schoolteacher and a group of homeless, problem kids across country from Philadelphia, Pennsylvania, to a farm in Washington State. Along the way, animosity turns to mutual care and respect as he begins to understand the children and their dilemmas, and love the teacher who is working hard on their behalf. Cast: **Richard Pryor**, **Cicely Tyson**, Angel Ramirez, Jimmy Hughes, Edwin DeLeon, Edwin Kinter, Tami Luchuv, Janet Wong, Alphonso Alexander, Kia Cooper, Robert Christian, George Coe, Bill Quinn, Roy Jenson, Fred Carney. Director: Oz Scott. Writers: **Lonne Elder III**, Richard Pryor.

BYRD, THOMAS JEFFERSON (1960-). Actor. He was born in Georgia and holds a Bachelor of Science degree in education. He began his film career acting in several **Spike Lee** films, including *Clockers*, 1995; *Girl 6*, 1996; and *Get on the Bus*, 1996. His television appearances include *I'll Fly Away*, 1993; *Mama Flora's Family*, 1998; *Passing Glory*, 1999; and *Boycott*, 2001.

Filmography: *Girls of the White Orchid*, 1985; *Clockers*, 1995; *Girl 6*, 1996; *Get on the Bus*, 1996; **Set It Off**, 1996; **He Got Game**, 1998; *Bulworth*, 1998; **Bamboozled**, 2000; **Trios**, 2000; **Ray**, 2004.

BY RIGHT OF BIRTH, 1921. Silent. Drama. This is a middle-class success story about life in America under the pressures of racism. A light-skinned black person passes for white in hopes of experiencing the American dream. It was the fourth and final film produced by **Lincoln Motion Picture Company**. Cast: **Clarence Brooks**, Anita Thompson, Webb King, Leo Bates, Lester Bates, Helen Childers, Minnie Devereaux, Grace Ellenwood, Beatrice George, Baby Ruth Kimbrough, W. E. Stanley Kimbrough, Lew Meehan, Dora Mitchell, Booker T. Washington. Director: Harry A. Gant. Writers: **George Johnson**, Dora Mitchell.

BYTHEWOOD, JINA PRINCE (1969-). Writer, director. This graduate of the UCLA film school began her career writing for numerous television series, including NBC's *A Different World*, and the Warner Brother network's *Felicity*. She served as story editor of Fox's *South Central*, executive story editor of NBC's *Sweet Justice*, and became a writer and co-producer on the CBS series *Courthouse*, in 1995. Bythewood made her television-directing debut with the CBS Schoolbreak Special Presentation *What about Your Friends?*, 1995. Her feature film debut, **Love & Basketball**, 1998, was screened at the 2000 Sundance Film Festival and received rave reviews. After this success and notoriety, Bythewood was selected to direct the film adaptation of Terry McMillan's highly successful novel **Disappearing Acts**, 2000, for HBO. She is married to writer, director **Reggie "Rock" Bythewood**.
Filmography: *Stitches*, 1991; *What about Your Friends*, 1995; *Bowl of Pork*, 1997; *Progress*, 1997; *Damn Whitey*, 1997; *Love & Basketball*, 2000; *Disappearing Acts*, 2000; *I Know This Much Is True*, 2008.

BYTHEWOOD, REGGIE "ROCK" (1965-). Actor, writer, director. Bythwood began his career as a teen actor on the NBC soap opera *Another World* in the early 1980s. On the big screen, he was featured in **The Brother from Another Planet**, 1984, and *Exterminator 2*, 1984, along with roles in *The Beat*, 1987, and *Vampire's Kiss*, 1988. He segued into writing with a stint on *A Different World* from 1991-1993, where he met his wife, fellow writer/director **Jina Prince Bythewood**. National acclaim came after he penned the script for **Spike Lee**'s tribute to the Million Man

March, *Get on the Bus*, 1996. He served as a writer producer on Fox's cop drama *New York Undercover* from 1994-1997, and created the NBC action series *Players*, 1997-1998. His first feature film, *Dancing in September*, 2001, received much attention at the Sundance Film Festival and was later aired on HBO. Riding high on his many successes, Bythewood wrote and directed the action-packed *Biker Boys*, 2003.

Filmography: *Dancing in September*, 2000; *Biker Boyz*, 2003.

C

CABIN IN THE SKY. 1943. 99 min. Musical. This film is based on the highly successful Broadway play. The film took most of its theatrical cast to the screen, except for **Dooley Wilson**, who played the character of Little Joe on the stage. The film tells the story of sin and redemption. Little Joe, a hapless sinner, continually avoids what he calls his "appointment with repentance." When he is nearly killed in a crooked crap game, his wife Petunia continues to pray as emissaries of the Lord and the devil compete for his eternal soul. The film contains powerful music and dance numbers, including "Cabin in the Sky," "Life's Full of Consequence," and "Happiness is Just a Thing Called Joe." Cast: **Ethel Waters, Eddie Anderson, Lena Horne, Rex Ingram, Louis Armstrong**, Duke Ellington. Director: Vincente Minnelli. Music: Duke Ellington, Harold Arlen, E. Y. Harburg, George Bassman.

CALHOUN, MONICA (1971-). Actress. She began her acting career on **television** as Wanda in telepic *Children of the Night*, 1985. Appearances in many more made-for-TV movies followed, such as *Heart and Soul*, 1989; *The Jacksons: An American Dream*, 1992; *The Ernest Green Story*, 1993; and *The Ditchdigger's Daughters*, 1997. Her breakout film role was as bride to be Mia Morgan, in **Malcolm Lee**'s *The Best Man*, 1999.

Filmography: *Children of the Night*, 1985, *Bagdad Café*, 1988; *Jack the Bear*, 1993; *Sister Act 2: Back in the Habit*, 1993; *Rebound: The Legend of Earl "The Goat" Manigault*, 1996; *Sprung*, 1997; *The Players Club*, 1998; *The Best Man*, 1999; *Intimate Betrayal*, 1999; *Love and Basketball*, 2000; *Civil Brand*, 2002; *Pandora's Box*, 2002; *Love Chronicles*, 2003; *Gang of Roses*, 2003; *Justice*, 2004; *The Salon*, 2005.

CALLOWAY, CAB (1907-1994). Bandleader, singer, actor. As one of the premiere entertainers of all time, Cab Calloway rose to prominence during the 1930s. Born in Rochester, New York, on Christmas Day, he was performing at the world famous Cotton Club by the age of 22. His band alternated with the Duke Ellington Orchestra, and it was during this time that he wrote and recorded his signature song, "Minnie the Moocher." Calloway was featured with his band in such musical films as *Hi-De-Ho*, 1935; *The Big Broadcast*, 1932; *International House*, 1933; and *Stormy Weather*, 1943. As an actor, Calloway portrayed the character of Blade the nightclub owner in *St. Louis Blues*, 1958, with **Nat King Cole** and **Eartha Kitt**. His last film performance was in *The Blues Brothers*, 1980. On the Broadway stage, he played Sportin' Life in a revival of *Porgy and Bess*, and appeared with **Pearl Bailey** in a revival of *Hello, Dolly*. Other songs written and composed by Calloway include "Hi De Ho Man," "Lady with the Fan," "Geechie Joe," "The Jumpin' Jive," and "Are You Hep to that Jive?"

Filmography: *International House*, 1933; *Hi-De-Ho*, 1935; *Manhattan Merry-Go-Round*, 1937; *Stormy Weather*, 1943; *Sensations of 1945*, 1944; *St. Louis Blues*, 1958; The *Cincinnati Kid*, 1965; *The Littlest Angel*, 1969; *The Blues Brothers*, 1980.

CALLOWAY, VANESSA BELL (1957-). Actress. This stage, screen, and **television** star was born in Cleveland, Ohio. She received her BFA degree with a concentration in dance from Ohio University. She later danced with Alvin Ailey, Otis Sallid, and George Faison. She has guest starred in the television series *In the Heat of the Night, A Different World, The Division*, and *The Parkers*. Her recurring roles include *Dream On, Boston Public, The District*, and she co-hosted the **Black Entertainment Television** talk show *Oh, Drama*. She also starred in the daytime soap operas *Days of Our Lives* and *All My Children*. Calloway's film roles include *Coming to America*, 1988; *Crimson Tide*, 1995; and *Biker Boyz*, 2002.

Filmography: *Number One with a Bullet*, 1987; *Coming to America*, 1988; *Memphis*, 1991; *Bebe's Kids*, 1992; *What's Love Got to Do with It?* 1993; *Crimson Tide*, 1995; *America's Dream*, 1995; *Daylight*, 1996; *The Temptations*, 1998; *Love Song*, 2000; *The Red Sneakers*, 2001; *Biker Boyz*, 2003.

CAMBRIDGE, GODFREY (1933-1976). Comedian, actor. The New York-born Cambridge was educated at Hofstra University and City College of New York, 1954. He made his Broadway debut in *Nature's Way*, and was in both the stage and film versions of *Purlie*

Victorious, for which he received a Tony Award nomination. He appeared in the off-Broadway productions of *Lost In the Stars*, *Take A Giant Step*, *Detective Story*, and he won an Obie award in 1961 for his performance in *The Blacks*. As a comedian, his routines often addressed the country's racial problems and his candid style has been praised and emulated. He released four comedy albums on Epic Records, including *Those Cotton-Pickin Days Are Over* and *Godfrey Cambridge Toys with the World*. On **television**, he has appeared on numerous variety hours, including *The Jack Paar Show*, *The David Frost Show*, and *The Johnny Carson Show*. He has also made guest appearances on various dramatic television series, including *Naked City*, *Daktari*, *Night Gallery*, and *Police Story*. On the big screen, Cambridge played the lead in **Watermelon Man**, 1970, and portrayed the character of Grave-digger Jones in the films **Cotton Comes to Harlem**, 1970, and its sequel, **Come Back, Charleston Blue**, 1973. He made a cameo appearance in the horror film *Beware! The Blob*, 1972.

   Filmography: **Purlie Victorious**, 1963; *Gone Are the Days*, 1963; *The President's Analyst*, 1967; *Watermelon Man*, 1970; *Cotton Comes to Harlem*, 1970; *Beware! The Blob*, 1972; *Come Back Charleston Blue*, 1973; *Whiffs*, 1975; **Friday Foster**, 1975.

CAMPANELLA, ROY II (1948-). Director, producer. He is the son of baseball great Roy Campanella, and a sought-after **television** and film producer/director who has helmed numerous telepics and countless episodes of a variety of popular TV series. He also executive produced the initial **Black Entertainment Television** series of films based on the Arabesque line of romance novels.

   Filmography: *Incognito*, 1999; *Rendezvous*, 1999; *Intimate Betrayal*, 1999; *After All*, 1999; *Hidden Blessings*, 2000; *A Private Affair*, 2000; *Masquerade*, 2000; *Rhapsody*, 2000; *Playing with Fire*, 2000; *Midnight Blue*, 2000.

CAMPBELL, TISHA (1968-). Actress, singer. She was born in Oklahoma City, Oklahoma, and graduated from the Newark School for the Performing Arts in New Jersey. She entered show business early, appearing in children's programs like *Unicorn Tales*, *Big Blue Marble*, and *Wonderama* throughout the late 1970s and early 1980s. She appeared in the stage productions of *Betsy Brown*, *Really Rosie*, and *Mama, I Want to Sing*. Campbell landed the role of a back-up singer in the off-Broadway production of *Little Shop of Horrors*, and appeared in the film version. She starred in the telefilm *Rags to Riches*, 1986, as well as the TV series. Guest appearances include *The Fresh Prince of Bel-Air*, *A Different World*, and *Roc.* She has been a regular on *Linc's*, *Martin*, and the ABC series *My Life & Kids.* Her film roles include *School Daze*, 1988; *House Party*, 1990; and *Sprung*, 1997.

Filmography: *Little Shop of Horrors*, 1986; *Rags to Riches*, 1987; *School Daze*, 1988; *Rooftops*, 1989; *Another 48 Hrs.*, 1989; *House Party*, 1990; *House Party 2*, 1991; *Boomerang*, 1992; *House Party 3*, 1994; *Snitch*, 1996; *Sprung*, 1997; *The Sweetest Gift*, 1998; *Last Place On Earth*, 2002.

CANDYMAN. 1992. (R) 98 min. Horror. While researching urban folklore for her dissertation, a graduate student discovers the frightening urban myth of The Candyman at an inner-city Chicago housing complex. He was the son of a former slave who was unjustly lynched, and now seeks his revenge, killing his victims with his hook of a hand. It spawned two sequels: *Candyman 2: Farewell to the Flesh*, 1995, and *Candyman 3: Day of the Dead*, 1998. Cast: Virginia Madsen, **Tony Todd**, Xander Berkeley, **Kasi Lemmons**, **Vanessa Williams**, DeJuan Guy, Michael Culkin, Gilbert Lewis, Stanley DeSantis. Writer/Director: Bernard Rose. Cinematographer: Anthony B. Richmond. Music: Philip Glass.

CANNON, NICK (1980-). Actor. He was born in San Diego, California, and graduated from Monte Vista High School in Spring Valley, California, class of 1998. He became a regular performer on the **television** series *All That*, 1998-2000, and landed the lead role in *Drumline*, 2002. Other important rolls soon followed and he has also embarked on a singing career.

Filmography: *Whatever It Takes*, 2000; *Men in Black II*, 2002; *Drumline*, 2002; *Love Don't Cost a Thing*, 2003; *Garfield*, 2004; *Shall We Dance*, 2004; *The Underclassman*, 2005; *Roll Bounce*, 2005; *Jump Shot*, 2005; *The Beltway*, 2005; *Monster House*, 2006.

CANNON, REUBEN (1946-). Producer, casting director. The Chicago-born Cannon attended Southeast City College before relocating to Los Angeles to pursue a career in the entertainment industry. He landed a job in the mailroom at Universal Studios in 1970 and quickly learned the ropes. From 1977 to 1978, he became the head of television casting for Warner Brothers and started his own casting agency, Reuben Cannon & Associates, a year later. He cast for the television shows *Moonlighting* and *Touched by an Angel*, and the feature films *The Color Purple*, 1985; *Desperado*, 1995; and *What's Love Got to Do with It?* 1993. Cannon's **television** producing credits include *The Women of Brewster Place*, 1989, and the popular television sitcom *Amen*. His film-producing credits include **Spike Lee**'s *Get on the Bus*, 1996; **Maya Angelou**'s *Down in the Delta*, 1998; **Reggie "Rock" Bythewood**'s *Dancing in September*, 2001; and *Woman Thou Art Loosed*, 2004, based on the self-help book by **Rev. T. D. Jakes**. He is also working with gospel playwriter **Tyler Perry** to produce films and the original sitcom *House of Payne*.

CAPERS, VIRGINIA (1925-2004). Actress. She was born in Sumpter, South Carolina, and attended Howard University in Washington, D.C., before studying voice at Juilliard in New York City. She first sang with bandleader Abe Lyman, appearing on his radio show and on-the-road tours. She appeared on Broadway in the late 1950s in the productions of *Jamaica* and *Saratoga*, and she earned a Tony Award for her role as matriarch Lena Younger in the 1974 musical *Raisin*. She was a founding member of the Lafayette Players in Los Angeles. On **television**, she guest appeared in the series *Daniel Boone*, *Mannix*, *Knots Landing*, *ER*, *The Fresh Prince of Bel-Air*, and *The Hughleys*. Her film roles include *Lady Sings the Blues*, 1972; *Five on the Black Hand Side*, 1973; and *Ferris Bueller's Day Off*, 1986.

Filmography: *House of Women*, 1962; *Ride to Hangman's Tree*, 1967; *The Lost Man*, 1969; *The Great White Hope*, 1970; *Norwood*, 1970; *Support Your Local Gunfighter*, 1971; *Big Jake*, 1971; *Lady Sings the Blues*, 1972; *Trouble Man*, 1972; *The World's Greatest Athlete*, 1973; *Five on the Black Hand Side*, 1973; *White Mama*, 1980; *The Toy*, 1982; *Bayou Romance*, 1982; *Teachers*, 1984; *Jo Jo Dancer, Your Life Is Calling*, 1986; *Ferris Bueller's Day Off*, 1986; *Howard the Duck*, 1986; *Off the Mark*, 1986; *Backfire*, 1987; *Pacific Palisades*, 1990; *What's Love Got to Do with It?*, 1993; *Beethoven's 2nd*, 1993; *The Feminine Touch*, 1994; *Everybody Can Float*, 1995; *Bad City Blues*, 1999; *Move*, 2002.

CARA, IRENE. Actor, singer, songwriter. She was born with a musical gift and instinctively began playing piano by ear at age five. Taking her budding talent seriously, she studied music, acting, and dance, and made her stage debut in the Broadway musical "Maggie Flynn." Cara recorded her first record in Spanish for the Latin market at age eight, and followed with a Christmas album in English. On **television**, as a member of the rock group The Short Circus, she delivered musical grammar lessons on the nationally syndicated educational program *The Electric Company*. Moving to film, she starred in the title role of *Aaron Loves Angela*, 1975, and followed that success with a starring role in the family-based musical drama

Sparkle, 1976. The film that brought all of her talents together and made Cara a star was the performing arts high school-based mega-hit *Fame*, 1980. In addition to her acting, she contributed to the multi-platinum soundtrack by singing both the title song and the film's second hit single "Out Here on My Own." Both songs were nominated for **Oscars** that year, and the theme song from *Fame* took home the prize. It was the first time that two songs from one film had ever been nominated in the same category, and Cara became the only performer to ever sing two **Academy Award**-nominated songs. Many more award nominations followed, including a Grammy nomination for Best New Female Artist and Best New Pop Artist, and a **Golden Globe** nomination for Best Motion Picture Actress in a Musical. *Billboard* magazine named her Top New Single Artist and *Cashbox* gave her its Most Promising Female Vocalist and Top Female Vocalist awards. In 1982, she received the National Association for the Advancement of Colored People **Image Award** for her work in the NBC Movie of the Week, *Sister, Sister*. As the songwriter of the title song for *Flashdance*, 1983, Cara received another Academy Award, two Grammys, a Golden Globe, and a People's Choice Award.

Filmography: *Aaron Loves Angela*, 1975; *Sparkle*, 1976; ***Roots: The Next Generation***, 1979; *Fame*, 1980; *D. C. Cab*, 1984; *City Heat*, 1984; *Killing 'Em Softly*, 1985; *Certain Fury*, 1985; *Busted Up*, 1986; ***For Us the Living***, 1988; *Caged in Paradiso*, 1989; *The Magic Voyage*, 1993; *Happily Ever After*, 1993.

CAREW, TOPPER (1943-). Producer, director, writer. He was born in Boston, Massachusetts, and has written, produced, and directed for film and **television**. His first television series was *The Righteous Apples*, 1981, and he also produced *And the Children Shall Lead*, 1985, for Wonderworks. His feature films include *D. C. Cab*, 1983, and ***Talkin' Dirty After Dark***, 1991. Carew is creator and executive producer of the hit sitcom *Martin*, starring **Martin Lawrence**.

Filmography: *The Righteous Apples*, 1981; *D. C. Cab*, 1983; *Be Somebody or Be Somebody's Fool!*, 1984; *And the Children Shall Lead*, 1985; *Talkin' Dirty after Dark*, 1991.

CARMEN: A HIP HOPERA. 2001. (PG-13) 88 min. Musical. This made-for-cable movie is an urban contemporary update based on the tragic opera *Carmen* by Georges Bizet, as well as a novelty adaptation of ***Carmen Jones***, 1954, starring **Dorothy Dandridge**. In this modern version, Carmen is a wannabe singer, who seduces a New York police officer into throwing away his career and accompanying her to Los Angeles, where she plans to become a star. He makes the sacrifice, but the fickle singer quickly tires of his jealous devotion. When Carmen takes a fancy to an established rapper who could help her career, she ditches the lawman for her chance at fame and fortune, only to secure her chances of becoming a femme fatale. The project is full of musical artists of the hip-hop generation, and rappers turned actors. Cast: **Beyoncé, Mekhi Pfifer, Mos Def**, Rah Digga, **Bow Wow**, Wyclef Jean, Troy Winbush. Director: **Robert Townsend**. Writer: Michael Elliott. Cinematographer: Geary McLeod. Music: Kip Collins. Narrator: Da Brat.

CARMEN JONES. 1954. 106 min. Musical. This is a film based on Georges Bizet's opera of *Carmen*. A parachute factory worker during World War II entices an American soldier sent to arrest her for fighting to go absent without leave. She soon tires of their boring, "never leave the house" existence and runs off to Chicago with a charismatic prizefighter. The soldier tracks her down for the tragic ending. This film is a major musical with such songs as "Dat's Love," "Beat Out Dat Rhythm on a Drum," "Stand Up and Fight," and "My Joe." Cast: **Dorothy Dandridge, Harry Belafonte, Pearl Bailey, Roy Glen, Diahann Carroll, Brock Peters**. Director: Otto Preminger. Writer: Harry Kleiner. Cinematographer: Sam Leavitt. Music: Oscar Hammerstein, Georges Bizet. Awards: Golden Globe 1955 best film musical/comedy, National Film Registry 1992.

CARROLL, DIAHANN (1935-). Actress, singer. As the first African American actress to star in a network **television** series, Diahann Carroll's career has also included film, stage, and nightclub performances. She was born in the Bronx, New York, and sang in the church choir as a child. At the age of 10, she won a scholarship from the Metropolitan Opera. She attended the High School of Music and Art, and later enrolled at New York University as a sociology student. After winning a television talent show, entertainment became her career focus. One of her first stage roles was in *House of Flowers* in 1954, and she later won a Tony Award for her performance in *No Strings* on Broadway, and made her big-screen debut in *Carmen Jones*, 1954. Other film roles include *Porgy and Bess*, 1959, with **Dorothy Dandridge**; and *Paris Blues*, 1961, with **Sydney Poitier**. Carroll landed the groundbreaking lead role in the 1960s television series *Julia*, and later portrayed the title role in *Claudine*, 1974, for which she received an **Academy Award** nomination for Best Actress. On television, she has been featured in the dramatic series *Dynasty*, and on the sitcom *A Different*

World. She was a 1976 inductee into the **Black Filmmakers Hall of Fame.**

Filmography: *Carmen Jones*, 1954; *Porgy and Bess*, 1959; *Goodbye Again*, 1961; *Paris Blues*, 1961; *Hurry Sundown*, 1967; *The Split*, 1968; *Claudine*, 1974.

CARROLL, ROCKY (1963-). Actor. He was born in Cincinnati, Ohio, and plays the trumpet as well as acts. After small parts in the telepic *Money, Power, Murder*, 1989, and the theatrical release *Born on the Fourth of July*, 1989, he landed the role of Joey Emerson on the TV series *Roc.* He has also played in recurring roles on the **television** series *Chicago Hope* and *The Agency.* His film roles include *Crimson Tide*, 1995; *The Great White Hype*, 1996; and *The Ladies Man*, 2000. He provides the voice for Derek Maza in the animated film *Gargoyles: The Force of Goliath*, 1998.

Filmography: *Born on the Fourth of July*, 1989; *Prelude to a Kiss*, 1992; *Fathers & Sons*, 1992; *The Chase*, 1994; *Crimson Tide*, 1995; *The Great White Hype*, 1996; *Best Laid Plans*, 1999; *The Ladies Man*, 2000.

CARSON, LISA NICOLE (1969-). Actress. She was born in Brooklyn, New York, and spent her teenage years in Gainesville, Florida. After graduating from Buchholz High School class of 1987, she returned to New York to live with her grandmother and begin her acting career. By 1992 she was performing on the television series *Uptown Comedy Club* and *The Apollo Comedy Hour*, and made her film debut in *Let's Get Bizzee*, 1993. She later landed key roles in *Jason's Lyric*, 1994; *Devil in a Blue Dress*, 1995; and *Eve's Bayou*, 1997. Her big television break came when she was cast as District Attorney Renee Radick on the popular series *Ally McBeal.*

Filmography: *Let's Get Bizzee*, 1993; *Jason's Lyric*, 1994; *Devil in a Blue Dress*, 1995; *Love Jones*, 1997; *Eve's Bayou*, 1997; *Life*, 1999.

CARSON, TERRENCE T. C. (1969-) Actor. This Chicago-born actor always dreamed of being a professional performer. He began working in plays and musicals, such as *The Wiz*, *Dreamgirls*, and *Ain't Misbehavin.* His big film break came as the lead in *Livin' Large*, 1991. **Television** soon called and he was cast as Kyle Baker in the hit sitcom *Living Single.* His deep and distinctive voice has been used in several animation series, including *Clifford the Big Red Dog*, *Forgotten Realms: Icewind Dale II*, and *The Animatrix.*

Filmography: *Livin' Large*, 1991; *Gang Related*, 1997; *Relax...It's Just Sex*, 1998; *Her Married Lover*, 1999; *U-571*, 2000;

Proximity, 2001; *Forgotten Realms: Icewind Dale II*, 2002; *The Animatrix*, 2003.

CARTER, BEN (1911-1946). Actor. Carter was born in Fairfield, Iowa. He became a theatrical agent for black performers and once partnered with **Mantan Moreland** in a vaudeville comedy act. He shifted his sights to acting during the 1930s and 1940s. His film roles include *The Green Pastures*, 1936; *Tin Pan Alley*, 1940; and *Dark Alibi*, 1946. He was also active in radio with the *Happy-Go-Lucky* series and the *Bob Burns Show*, 1944-1945. He won an International Film and Radio Guild award for *Crash Dive*, 1943.

Filmography: *Kentucky Blue Streak*, 1935; *The Green Pastures*, 1936; *Tin Pan Alley*, 1940, *Reap the Wild Wind*, 1942, *Crash Dive*, 1943; *The Scarlet Clue*, 1945, and *Dark Alibi*, 1946.

CARTER, TERRY (1928-). Actor, producer. This native of Brooklyn, New York, graduated from Stuyvesant High School, class of 1946. He continued his education by attending Hunter College, Boston University, and UCLA, before earning his Bachelor of Science degree in Communications from Northeastern University, in 1983. While working for WBZ-TV Eyewitness News in Boston, Massachusetts, Carter became the first African American TV anchor newscaster in 1965. His **television** career took off in 1955 when he was cast as Pvt. Sugarman on *The Phil Silvers Show*. Other early television appearances include *Playhouse 90, Naked City, Dr. Kildare,* and *Mannix*. Carter's most memorable television role is perhaps as Col. Tigh on the long-running sci-fi series *Battlestar Galactica*. His film roles include *Foxy Brown*, 1974; *Abby*, 1974; and he starred in the film *Brother on the Run*, 1973.

Filmography: *Parrish*, 1961; *Nerosubianco*, 1969; *Brother on the Run*, 1973; *Foxy Brown*, 1974; *Benji*, 1974; *Abby*, 1974; *Man on the Run*, 1975; *Hamilton*, 1998; *Battlestar Galactica: The Second Coming*, 1999.

CARTER, THOMAS (1953-). Actor, producer, director. He began his career as a young actor in the 1970s **television** series, *The White Shadow*. Carter was always interested in what went on behind the camera and often shadowed the director while on the set. He was eventually given a chance to direct an episode and has since made his living as a director in both television and film, often producing his projects as well. Other television shows he has directed include *Hill Street Blues, Fame, Remington Steele, Amazing Stories,* and the pilot episode of the hit series *Miami Vice*. His roles in made-for-TV movies include *Call to Glory*, 1984; *Heart of the*

City, 1986; *Hack*, 2002; and the miniseries *A Year in the Life*, 1986. He made the jump to directing feature films with *Swing Kids*, 1993, and followed with *Save the Last Dance*, 2001, and **Coach Carter**, 2005.

Filmography: *Call to Glory*, 1984; *Heart of the City*, 1986; *Under the Influence*, 1986; *Equal Justice*, 1990; *Swing Kids*, 1993; *Divas*, 1995; *Metro*, 1997; *Bronx County*, 1998; *Save the Last Dance*, 2001; *Hack*, 2002; *Partners and Crime*, 2003; *Coach Carter*, 2005; *Company Town*, 2006; *Freedom House*, 2006; *Marcus Dixon*, 2007.

CAR WASH. 1976. (PG) 97 min. Comedy. This film depicts antics at a Los Angeles car wash. Filmed during the Disco Era, it is a series of loosely related comic bits ranging from a lovesick scrubber in pursuit of the woman of his dreams, to the serious subplot of a disgruntled worker's more criminal intent. It is packed with cameos and rather unknown talent at that time, a few of which have now become major stars. Cast: **Franklin Ajaye**, Sully Boyer, Richard Brestoff, George Carlin, **Richard Pryor**, Melanie Mayron, **Ivan Dixon**, **Antonio Fargas**, **Bill Duke**, Danny Devito. Director: **Michael Schultz**. Writer: Joel Schumacher. Cinematographer: Frank Stanley. Music: Norman Whitfield.

CASEY, BERNIE (1939-). Athlete, actor. Casey was born in Wyco, West Virginia, and graduated from Columbus East High School in Columbus, Ohio. He played professional football for the San Francisco 49ers, 1961-1966, and for the Los Angeles Rams, 1967-1968. He made his big-screen acting debut in *Guns of the Magnificent Seven*, 1969, and gained prominence during the 1970s film boom with starring roles in *Hit Man*, 1972; *Cleopatra Jones*, 1975; and *Dr. Black, Mr. Hyde*, 1976. His television movies include *Brian's Song*, 1971; *The Martian Chronicles*, 1980; *The Sophisticated Gents*, 1981; and *The Last Brickmaker in America*, 2001. Later film roles include *Sharky's Machine*, 1981; *I'm Gonna Git You Sucka*, 1988; and *Once Upon a Time in America*, 1995.

Filmography: *Guns of the Magnificent Seven*, 1969; *Brian's Song*, 1971; *Boxcar Bertha*, 1972; *Hit Man*, 1972; *Cleopatra Jones*, 1973; *Big Mo*, 1973; *Cornbread, Earl & Me*, 1975; *The Man Who Fell to Earth*, 1976; *Dr. Black, Mr. Hyde*, 1976; *The Martian Chronicles*, 1979; *Sophisticated Gents*, 1981; *Sharky's Machine*, 1981; *Never Say Never Again*, 1983; *Revenge of the Nerds*, 1984; *Spies Like Us*, 1985; *Rent-A-Cop*, 1988; *I'm Gonna Git You Sucka*, 1988; *Backfire*, 1988; *Another 48 Hours*, 1990;

Chains of Gold, 1992; *Street Knight*, 1993; *The Cemetery Club*, 1993; *In the Mouth of Madness*, 1995; *Tomcats*, 2001.

CASH, ROSALIND (1938-1995). Actress. Born in Atlantic City, New Jersey, she was known for refusing to play stereotypical roles. Cash attended City College of New York and worked with the Negro Ensemble Company, the YMCA Little Theater, and at one time, she sang with the Clark Terry band. She appeared on stage in numerous productions, including *Dark of the Moon*, *No Strings*, *Ceremonies in Dark Old Men*, and *Boesman and Lena*. She was nominated for an **Emmy** award for her work in the PBS production of ***Go Tell It On the Mountain***, 1985, and guest starred on the **television** series *Good Times*, *Starsky and Hutch*, *Righteous Apples*, and *The Cosby Show*. Her film roles include ***Cornbread, Earl & Me***, 1975; ***Melinda***, 1971; and *The Omega Man*, 1971. She continued to work consistently on television in such shows as *Barney Miller*, *Kojak*, *Cagney & Lacey*, *Police Story*, and *Hill Street Blues*.

Filmography: *Omega Man*, 1971; *Amazing Grace*, 1974; *Cornbread, Earl & Me*, 1975; ***Dr. Black, Mr. Hyde***, 1976; *Monkey Hustle*, 1977; ***Sophisticated Gents***, 1981; *Keeping on*, 1981; *Wrong Is Right*, 1982; *Go Tell It on the Mountain*, 1984; *The Adventures of Buckaroo Banzai*, 1984; *The Offspring*, 1987; *The Mighty Pawns*, 1987; ***Tales from the Hood***, 1995.

CAUGHT UP. 1998. (R) 95 min. Urban Drama. An ex-con is released from prison after serving a five-year sentence for a bank robbery and becomes tangled in a sticky web of violence and deceit. He becomes involved with a girl with a shady past who has ripped off some dangerous people. She gets him a job driving a limousine for drug dealers and thieves, but he soon discovers the job description requires so much more. Cast: **Bokeem Woodbine**, **Cynda Williams**, **Snoop Dogg**, Joseph Lindsey, **Clifton Powell**, Basil Wallace, Tony Todd, **L.L. Cool J**, Jeffery Combs, Damon Saleem, Shedrick Hunter Jr. Writer/Director: Darin Scott. Cinematographer: Thomas Calloway. Music: Marc Bonilla.

CB4: THE MOVIE. 1993. (R) 83 min. Comedy. This film was intended to be a "Saturday Night Livesque" parody of a "rockumentary" (ala *This is Spinal Tap*). A couple of gangsta rappers take on the identity of a jailed local nightclub owner to further their careers. Cast: **Chris Rock**, **Allen Payne**, Deezer D, Phil Hartman, Charlie Murphy, **Khandi Alexander**, **Art Evans**, Chris Elliot,

Willard Pugh, Theresa Randle. Director: Tamra Davis. Writers: Chris Rock, Nelson George, Robert Locash. Music: John Barnes.

CEDRIC THE ENTERTAINER (1964-). Actor, comedian, producer. He was born Cedric Kyles in Jefferson City, Missouri, and came to comedic prominence on **television**'s *Def Comedy Jam*. He later landed a starring role on *The Steve Harvey Show* and has made appearances on numerous award shows as host, co-host, or presenter. His TV comedy variety show *Cedric the Entertainer Presents* had a short run in 2002. His film roles include *Big Momma's House*, 2000; *Kingdom Come*, 2001; and the controversial *Barbershop*, 2002, and its sequel. He has provided the voice for many animated characters, including Zoo Bear #1 in *Dr. Dolittle*, 2001; Bobby Proud in *The Proud Family*, 2001; and Rhino in *Ice Age*, 2002. He was producer and star of *Johnson Family Vacation*, 2004.

Filmography: *Ride*, 1998; *Big Momma's House*, 2000; *Kingdom Come*, 2001; *Serving Sara*, 2002; *Ice Age*, 2002; *Barbershop*, 2002; *Barbershop 2*; 2004, *The Honeymooners*, 2005.

CHAMELEON STREET. 1989. (R) 95 min. Drama. This film is based on a true story about William Douglas Street, a Detroit man who impersonated several professional career positions, including a reporter and a surgeon. He is sent to jail for his actions but escapes. He forges an identity as a student at Yale University, and then impersonates a Detroit Human Rights Commission attorney. Wendell B. Harris is the writer, director, and star. Cast: Wendell B. Harris Jr., Angela Leslie, Amina Fakir, Paula McGee, Mano Breckenridge, David Kileyu, Anthony Ennis. Cinematographer: Daniel S. Noga. Music: Peter S. Moore. Awards: Sundance 1990 Grand Jury Prize.

CHAPPELLE, DAVID (1973-). Comedian, actor, writer, producer. He was born in Washington, D.C., and grew up in Silver Spring, Maryland. He appeared on comedy specials, such as *Def Comedy Jam*, *Comic Relief VIII*, and *Dave Chappelle: Killin' Them Softly*. He made his film-acting debut in *Robin Hood: Men in Tights*, 1993. Chappelle is the writer, executive producer, and star of his own cable **television** series *Chappelle's Show*.

Filmography: *Robin Hood: Men in Tights*, 1993; *Undercover Blues*, 1993; *Getting In*, 1994; *The Nutty Professor*, 1996; *Joe's Apartment*. 1996; *Con Air*, 1997; *The Real Blonde*, 1997; *Damn Whitey*, 1997; *Bowl of Pork*, 1997; *Half Baked*, 1998; *Woo*, 1998; *You've Got Mail*, 1998; *200 Cigarettes*, 1999; *Blue Streak*, 1999; *Screwed*, 2000; *Undercover Brother*, 2002.

CHEADLE, DON (1964-). Actor. Born in Kansas City, Missouri, Cheadle graduated from East High School in Denver, Colorado. He earned his BA degree in Fine Arts from CalArts and began auditioning for stage, television, and film. He first gained notoriety for his role as Mouse in *Devil in a Blue Dress*, 1995, which won him a best supporting actor award from the Los Angeles Film Critics, and he received rave reviews for his portrayal of veteran performer **Sammy Davis Jr.** in *The Rat Pack*, 1998. With an eye for unique roles and opportunities not often available in Hollywood, Cheadle was instrumental in getting two powerful independent films made in 2005. These films were the African genocide-based *Hotel Rwanda*, for which he received an **Academy Award** nomination, and the contemporary race-relations-based *Crash*.

Filmography: *Hamburger Hill*, 1987; *Colors*, 1988; *Lush Life*, 1994; *Devil in a Blue Dress*, 1995; *Rosewood*, 1996; *Rebound*, 1996; *Volcano*, 1997; *The Rat Pack*, 1998; *Out of Sight*, 1998; *Bulworth*, 1998; *A Lesson Before Dying*, 1999; *Traffic*, 2000; *Mission to Mars*, 2000; *Things Behind the Sun*, 2001; *Swordfish*, 2001; *Rush Hour 2*, 2001; *Ocean's Eleven*, 2001; *Hotel Rwanda*, 2005; *Crash*, 2005.

CHENAULT, LAWRENCE. (1877-?) Actor. He made his film debut during the **silent era** in **Oscar Micheaux's** *The Brute*, 1920, and appeared in a dozen Micheaux films, including *Body and Soul*, 1924; *The Conjure Woman*, 1926; and *Ten Minutes to Live*, 1932. He worked with all of the top **race movie** companies of that time, including **Reol Pictures**, **The Norman Film Manufacturing Company**, and **The Colored Players Film Corporation**.

Filmography: *The Brute*, 1920; *The Symbol of the Unconquered*, 1920; *The Gunsaulus Mystery*, 1921; *The Crimson Skull*, 1921; *The Sport of the Gods*, 1921; *Secret Sorrow*, 1921; *The Burden of Race*, 1921; *The Call of His People*, 1922; *Ghost of Tolston's Manor*, 1923; *Birthright*, 1924; *Body and Soul*, 1924; *The Devil's Disciple*, 1926; *The Conjure Woman*, 1926; *A Prince of His Race*, 1926; *Ten Nights in a Barroom*, 1926; *The Scar of Shame*, 1927; *The House Behind the Cedars*, 1927; *Children of Fate*, 1928; *Veiled Aristocrats*, 1932; *Ten Minutes to Kill*, 1932; *Harlem after Midnight*, 1934.

CHESTER, ALFRED "SLICK" (1900-1978). Born in New York City, Chester became an early black actor in silent films. On stage he was in *Seven Eleven*, *Watermelons*, *Chocolate Dandies 1924*, and *The Trial of Mary Dugan*. He also performed with the Ida

Anderson Dramatic Players. He became known as "The Colored Cagney" after appearing in several **Oscar Micheaux** films, including *Temptation*, 1936; and *Underworld*, 1937. He was inducted into the **Black Filmmakers Hall of Fame** in 1976.

Filmography: *Harlem after Midnight*, 1934; *Murder in Harlem*, 1935; *Temptation*, 1936; *Underworld*, 1937; *Miracle in Harlem*, 1948.

CHESTNUT, MORRIS (1969-). Actor. Born in Cerritos, California, Chestnut made his feature-film debut in **John Singleton**'s *Boyz N the Hood*, 1991. He made television guest appearances on *ER* and *Living Single*, and starred in the short-lived series *Out All Night* with Patti LaBelle. Moving back into motion pictures, Morris co-starred in a series of relationship-driven projects, such as *The Best Man*, 1999; *The Brothers*, 2001; and *Two Can Play That Game*, 2001, which all helped to make him a bona fide leading man.

Filmography: *Boyz N the Hood*, 1991; *The Last Boy Scout*, 1991; *The Ernest Green Story*, 1993; *The Inkwell*, 1993; *Under Siege 2: Dark Territory* 1995; *G. I. Jane*, 1997; *Firehouse*, 1997; *The Best Man*, 1999; *The Brothers*, 2001; *Two Can Play That Game*, 2001; *Scenes of the Crime*, 2001; *Like Mike*, 2002; *Half Past Dead*, 2002; *Confidence*, 2003; *Breakin' All the Rules*, 2003.

CHONG, RAE DAWN (1961-). Actress. She was born in Edmonton, Alberta, Canada, and is the daughter of actor/comedian Tommy Chong of Cheech & Chong fame. After acting on several telefilms, she made her feature film debut in *Quest For Fire*, 1981. Larger roles followed in films, such as *Beat Street*, 1984; *The Color Purple*, 1985; *Soul Man*, 1986; and *The Visit*, 2000. Her television guest appearances include *St. Elsewhere*, *Melrose Place*, *Judging Amy*, and *Highlander*. She has starred in the television series *Mysterious Ways*, and the Lifetime series *Wildcard*. She is the writer, producer, and director of the film *Cursed Part 3*.

Filmography: *Quest for Fire*, 1982; *Choose Me*, 1984; *Beat Street*, 1984; *Commando*, 1985; *The Color Purple*, 1985; *American Flyers*, 1985; *Soul Man*, 1986; *The Squeeze*, 1987; *The Principal*, 1987; *The Borrower*, 1989; *Tales from the Darkside: The Movie*, 1990; *Amazon*, 1990; *Common Bonds*, 1991; *Time Runner*, 1992; *Dangerous Relations*, 1993; *Power of Attorney*, 1994; *Hideaway*, 1994; *Boulevard*, 1994; *Boca*, 1994; *The Break*, 1995; *Starlight*, 1997; *Mask of Death*, 1997; *Smalltime*, 1999; *The Visit*, 2000, *Constellation*, 2005.

CIVIL BRAND. 2002. (R) 95 min. Drama. This is a serious look at how the prison industrial complex affects female inmates. A young law student who works part-time as a prison guard befriends a group of female prisoners who are forced to work under slave labor conditions. When they discover a big corporation is profiting from this plantation-like environment, they organize a protest and take over the joint. Cast: **LisaRaye, N'Bushe Wright, Mos Def**, Da Brat, **Monica Calhoun, Clifton Powell**, Reed R. McCants, Tichina Arnold, Lark Voorhies, MC Lyte, Robert Archer Lynn. Director: **Neema Barnette**. Writer: Preston A. Whitmore II.

CLARKE, STANLEY (1951-). Musician, film composer. This native of Philadelphia, Pennsylvania, is an expert player on both acoustic and electric basses. His unique style brought the bass guitar out of the background and into the forefront, making it a lead instrument. In the 1970s, he played with Chick Corea's band, Return to Forever. He had a successful solo career and also performed with his group, The Stanley Clarke Trio. His rock anthem "School Days" has become a classic. In the 1980s, he began to compose and orchestrate musical scores for film and television productions. Filmography: *The Court-Martial of Jackie Robinson*, 1990; *Book of Love*, 1990; *The Five Heartbeats*, 1991; *Boyz N the Hood*, 1991; *Passenger 57*, 1992; *Boy Meets Girl*, 1993; *What's Love Got to Do with It?*, 1993; *Poetic Justice*, 1993; *Higher Learning*, 1995; *Panther*, 1995; *Eddie*, 1996; *B*A*P*S*, 1997; *Sprung*, 1997; *Down in the Delta*, 1998; *Funny Valentine*, 1999; *The Best Man*, 1999; *Romeo Must Die*, 2000; *Undercover Brother*, 2002; *The Transporter*, 2002; *Into the Sun*, 2005; *The Boys & Girls Guide to Getting Down*, 2006.

CLASS ACT. 1992. (PG-13) 98 min. Comedy. The identification and student records of a party-minded bully get switched with a study-minded nerd when they register at a new school in this role reversal comedy. Cast: **Christopher Reid, Christopher Martin, Meshach Taylor**, Karyn Parsons, **Doug E. Doug**, Rick Ducommun, Lamont Jackson, Rhea Perlman. Director: Randall Miller. Music: Vassal Benford.

CLAUDINE. 1974. (PG) 92 min. Comedy/Drama. This film tells a touching story of a hard-working single mother on welfare, struggling to raise and provide for her six children in the harsh environment of the inner city. While working as a domestic in the suburbs, she meets a garbage man on his route, and he asks her out. As their relationship grows, he must not only court her, but her six children as well, while not being able to pay alimony or child support to his own ex-wife. Life intensifies as they all try to hide the financial benefits of having a working man around from the social worker who seems eager to boot the family off the state payroll. Cast: **Diahann Carroll, James Earl Jones, Lawrence Hilton-Jacobs**, Tamu Blackwell, David Kruger, Yvette Curtis, Eric Jones, Socorro Stephens, Adam Wade, C. Harrison Avery, Mordecai Lawner, Elisa Loti, Roxie Roker, Jay Van Leer, Judy Mills. Director: John Berry. Writers: Lester Pine, Tina Pine.

CLEOPATRA JONES. 1973. (PG) 89 min. **Blaxploitation**. A lean and mean female government agent takes on a deadly drug cartel with fast cars, big guns, and karate. It spawned the sequel *Cleopatra Jones and the Casino of Gold*, 1975. Cast: **Tamara Dobson**, Shelley Winters, **Bernie Casey, Brenda Sykes**, Albert "Poppy" Popwell. Director: Jack Starrett. Writers: **Max Julien** and Sheldon Keller. Cinematographer: David M. Walsh. Music: J. J. Johnson.

CLOCKERS. 1995. (R) 128 min. Urban Drama. This is an inner-city street drama about a drug dealer in conflict with his supplier, his do-good brother, and his own guilty conscious. He is being pursued for a murder he did not commit by an overzealous narco-cop, and must come to terms with his actions and his future. Cast: **Mekhi Phifer**, Harvey Keitel, **Delroy Lindo, Isaiah Washington**, John Turturro, **Keith David**. Director: **Spike Lee**. Cinematographer: **Malik Sayeed**. Music: **Terence Blanchard**.

COACH CARTER. 2005. (PG-13). 136 min. Drama. This film is based on a true story about a high school basketball coach who padlocks the gym and benches his entire undefeated, championship-bound team due to their failing grades. He receives both praise and criticism for his drastic actions, but the players, the school, and the entire community pull together to overcome these obstacles and all benefit in the end. It was inspired by the life of Ken Carter. Cast: **Samuel L. Jackson**, Robert Richard, Rob Brown, Ashanti, **Debbie Morgan**. Director: **Thomas Carter**. Writers: Mark Schwahn, John Gatins.

COBBS, BILL (1935-). Actor. He was born and raised in Cleveland, Ohio, and began acting as a young man in the play *Purlie Victorious*, produced at the community Karamu House Theater. He joined the U.S. Air Force as a radar technician for eight years, worked for IBM selling office products, and sold cars at a Cleveland dealership before heading to New York City to pursue an acting career in

1970. After working at a series of odd jobs, Cobbs landed his first professional acting role in the Negro Ensemble Company's production of *Ride a Black Horse*. He made his feature debut in *The Taking of Pelham One Two Three*, 1974, and his first **television** appearance was in the New York public television educational series *Vegetable Soup*, 1976.
Filmography: *The Taking of Pelham One Two Three*, 1974; **Greased Lightning**, 1977; ***A Hero Ain't Nothing but a Sandwich***, 1978; *The Hitter*, 1979; *Trading Places*, 1983; *Silkwood*, 1983; ***The Brother from Another Planet***, 1984; *The Cotton Club*, 1984; *Compromising Positions*, 1985; *The Color of Money*, 1986; *Five Corners*, 1987; *Suspect*, 1987; *Bird*, 1988; *January Man*, 1989; *Moe's World*, 1990; *Exiled in America*, 1990; **New Jack City**, 1991; *The Hard Way*, 1991; *The People Under the Stairs*, 1991; *The Bodyguard*, 1992; *Demolition Man*, 1993; *Tuesday Morning Ride*, 1995; *Goldilocks and the Three Bears*, 1995; *Fluke*, 1995; *Ed*, 1996; *First Kid*, 1996; *That Thing You Do!*, 1996; *Ghosts of Mississippi*, 1996; *Soulmates*, 1997; *Air Bud*, 1997; **Always Out Numbered, Always Outgunned**, 1998; *Pauli*, 1998; *Hope Floats*, 1998; *Random Hearts*, 1999; *Sweet Deadly Dreams*, 2002; *Enough*, 2002; *Duck*, 2004; *Special Ed*, 2005; *Squirrel Man*, 2005; *Return to Sender*, 2005; *Retirement*, 2006.

COFFY. 1973. (R) 91 min. **Blaxploitation.** A hard-working nurse fakes drug addiction to seek revenge on the addicts and dealers she believes are responsible for her younger sister's drug overdose. Cast: **Pam Grier**, William Elliott, Sid Haig, Booker Bradshaw, **Robert DoQui**, Allan Arbus. Writer/Director: Jack Hill. Cinematographer: Paul Lohmann. Music: Roy Ayers.

COLE, NAT KING (1919-1965). Singer, actor. He was born Nathaniel Adams Coles in Montgomery, Alabama. He is hailed as one of the best all-around entertainers of the century, and his smooth, velvet voice, and classic style of playing piano has him on a short list of best baritone singers of all time. He has recorded countless award-winning singles and record albums and his music has graced innumerable film and television production soundtracks over the years. His more popular tunes include *Unforgettable*, *The Christmas Song*, *For Sentimental Reasons*, and *Nature Boy*. He performed extensively with his band, The Nat King Cole Trio, and they performed in several films, including *Pistol Packin' Mama*, 1943, *Stars on Parade*, 1944, and *See My Lawyer*, 1945. He also portrayed the role of W. C. Handy, the father of jazz music in the biographical film *St. Louis Blues*, 1958. His final film role was as

Shouter, a roaming minstrel in *Cat Ballou*, 1965. Cole became the first African American to host his own television variety series, *The Nat King Cole Show*, 1957, but it was cancelled due to racist threats and protests from the network's Southern sponsors. He is the father of singer Natalie Cole.

Filmography: *Citizen Cane*, 1941; *Pistol Packin' Mama*, 1943; *Pin Up Girl*, 1944; *Stars on Parade*, 1944; *See My Lawyer*, 1945; *Istanbul*, 1957; *China Gate*, 1957; *St. Louis Blues*, 1958; *Night of the Quarter Moon*, 1959; *Cat Ballou*, 1965.

COLEMAN, GARY (1968-). Actor. He was born in Zion, Illinois, and later adopted. He was discovered by a talent scout for TV producer Norman Lear and signed for a part in a never-produced television revival of *The Little Rascals*. He became a child star when he was cast as Arnold Jackson in the hit sitcom *Different Strokes*. He starred in several telepics, including *The Kid with the Broken Halo*, 1982; and *The Kid with the 200 I. Q.*, 1983. At the height of his career, Coleman sued his adoptive parents/managers over misappropriation of his trust fund. In 2003, Coleman unsuccessfully ran for governor of California in the recall election of Governor Gray Davis.

Filmography: *The Kid from Left Field*, 1979; *Scout's Honor*, 1980; *On the Right Track*, 1981; *The Kid with the Broken Halo*, 1982; *Jimmy the Kid*, 1982; *The Kid with the 200 I. Q.*, 1983; *The Fantastic World of D. C. Collins*, 1984; *Playing with Fire*, 1985; *Party*, 1994; *Fox Hunt*, 1996; *Dirty Work*, 1998; *Shafted*, 2000; *The Flunky*, 2000; *A Carol Christmas*, 2003; *A Christmas Too Many*, 2005.

COLES, KIM (1966-). Actress. She is a Brooklyn, New York, native with a natural comic streak. She began on the comedy TV series *In Living Color* and landed a role in the film **Strictly Business**, 1991. Her breakout **television** role was as Synclaire James on the sitcom *Living Single*, and she was seen on *The Geena Davis Show*. She hosted the series *New Attitude*, and appeared on the TV reality shows *Celebrity Mole: Hawaii*, 2000, and *Celebrity Fit Club*, 2005. She has appeared as herself on *Sinbad and Friends: All the Way Live...Almost!*; *Coming to the Stage*; and *The BET Comedy Awards*. She is author of the book, *I'm Free, But It Will Cost You.*

Filmography: *Strictly Business*, 1991; *Kids in America*, 2004.

COLOR ADJUSTMENT. 1991. (TV) 86 min. Documentary. This film analyzes 40 years of television's negative portrayals of African Americans from 1948 through 1988. Looks at the interplay between the network's primetime programming and America's racial consciousness, and allows viewers to examine America's and their personal attitudes about race. Cast: **Diahann Carroll**, Steven Bochco, **Ruby Dee**, Norman Lear, **Denise Nicholas**, **Tim Reid**, **Esther Rolle**, David L. Wolper.

COLORED PLAYERS FILM CORPORATION. This Philadelphia-based company was organized in 1926 by European-American Jewish producers David Starkman and Louis Groner specifically to make **race films** for African American audiences. Well-known for interracial and interethnic collaborations, their first three feature-length films were directed by company co-founder Roy Calnek. They were A *Prince of His Race*, 1926; *Ten Nights in a Barroom*, 1926; and *Children of Fate*, 1927. In the summer of 1927, African American show promoter and theater owner Sherman H. Dudley was named company president. He worked with Italian director Frank Perugini and cameraman Al Liguori to make the company's fourth and final film, *The Scar of Shame*, 1929.

COLOR OF COURAGE, THE. 1998. (PG) 92 min. Drama. This made-for-cable movie is based on the landmark civil rights case of Sipes vs. McGhee. The story takes place in Detroit, Michigan, in 1944. The McGhee family moves into an integrated neighborhood. Only one woman is happy they are there, while the rest of the community rises up to try and force this black family's eviction. Cast: **Lynn Whitfield**, Linda Hamilton, Bruce Greenwood, **Roger Guenveur Smith**. Director: Lee Rose. Writer: Kathleen McGhee-Anderson. Cinematographer: Eric Van Haren Norman. Music: **Terence Blanchard**.

COLOR PURPLE, THE. 1985. (PG-13) 154 min. Drama. This film is based on Alice Walker's best-selling novel about a poor Negro girl growing up in the rural South. She is separated from her sister and forced into an abusive marriage. The movie goes from 1909 to 1947, chronicling her life, her strained marriage, and the people she comes into contact with. Cast: **Whoopi Goldberg, Danny Glover, Oprah Winfrey, Margaret Avery, Adolph Ceasar, Rae Dawn Chong, Willard Pugh, Akosua Busia**. Director: Steven Spielberg. Writer: Menno Meyjes. Cinematographer: Allen Daviau. Music: Chris Boardman, **Quincy Jones**. Awards: Director's Guild Award (Spielberg). Golden Globe Award for Best Actress-Drama (Goldberg). National Board of Review Best Actress Award (Goldberg).

COMBS, SEAN PUFFY, P. DIDDY (1969-). He was born in Harlem, New York, and became a major player in the entertainment world of rap and hip-hop music. He began as an intern at Uptown Records and appeared as a dancer in Father MC's "Treat Them Like They Want to be Treated" video, 1991. He made a name for himself by making rap-remixes of popular tunes and beats from the 1980s. He has his own urban clothing line called Sean John and his record company, Bad Boy Records, is worth an estimated $500,000,000. On **television**, Combs headed the music-based reality show *Making the Band*, and he has appeared in the films *Monster's Ball*, 2001; *Made*, 2001; and *Carlito's Way: Rise to Power*, 2005. He made his Broadway stage debut as Walter Lee Younger in the 2004 revival of **Lorraine Hansberry**'s *A Raisin in the Sun*.

   Filmography: *Monster's Ball*, 2001; *Made*, 2001; *Death of a Dynasty*, 2003; *Carlito's Way: Rise to Power*, 2005; *Love in Vain*, 2005.

COMING TO AMERICA. 1988. (R) 116 min. Comedy. An African prince comes to America in search of a bride. He begins looking in Queens, New York, and learns that finding an American mate is more difficult than he ever imagined. **Eddie Murphy** plays several roles with make-up and disguises by Rick Baker. A major lawsuit resulted in columnist Art Buchwald receiving story credit but little money. Cast: Eddie Murphy, **Arsenio Hall, James Earl Jones, John Amos, Madge Sinclair, Shari Headly**, Don Ameche, Louie Anderson, Paul Bates, Allison Dean, **Eriq LaSalle, Calvin Lockhart, Samuel L. Jackson, Cuba Gooding Jr., Vanessa Bell Calloway**, Frankie Faison, **Vondie Curtis-Hall, Calvin Lockhart**. Director: John Landis. Writer: David Sheffield, Barry W. Blaustein. Cinematographer: Woody Omens. Music: Nile Rogers.

COMPENSATION. 1999. (NR) 95 min. Drama. This rich and complex modern-day silent film simultaneously tells two parallel stories involving young black couples from different periods of time. One is a turn of the century examination of the issues of race and the ravages of tuberculosis; the other is a contemporary tale that explores the social differences between a deaf girl and her male suitor in this trying era of AIDS. Cast: **John Jelks**, Michelle A. Banks, Nirvana Cobb, Kevin L. Davis, Christopher Smith, K. Lynn Stephens, Edith McLoud Armstrong, Crystal Barnes, Lisa Brock, Iverson White. Director: Zeinabu irene Davis. Writer: Marc Chery.

CONSTELLATION. 2005. 96 min. Drama. This film explores the lives and loves of a black family in the deep South who must confront the dark secret of a past interracial affair, in the midst of changing social attitudes and in an evolved racial landscape. Cast: Ever Carradine, David Clennon, **Rae Dawn Chong, Melissa De Sousa, Hill Harper,** Alec Newman, Zoe Saldana, **Billy Dee Williams, Gabrielle Union,** Daniel Bess, Howie Dorough, Shin Koyamada, Lesley Ann Warren, **Glenn Plummer.** Writer/Director: Jordan Walker-Pearlman.

COOKOUT, THE. 2004. (PG-13). 97 min. Comedy. After signing a $30 million contract with the New Jersey Nets, a basketball player throws the annual family cookout at his new mansion in the suburbs, surrounded by neighbors who do not look like him. Once his family arrives, it is a cultural clash from beginning to end, with many embarassing stereotypes on both sides of the color line. Cast: Ja Rule, **Tim Meadows, Jenifer Lewis, Meagan Good, Queen Latifah,** Quran Pender, Jonathan Silverman, Farrah Fawcett, Ruperto Vanderpool, Frankie Faison, Vincent Pastore, Kevin Phillips, Gerry Bamman, Carl Wright, Reg E. Cathey, Rita Owens. Director: Lance Rivera. Writers: Queen Latifa, Shakim Compere.

COOLEY HIGH. 1975. (PG) 107 min. Comedy/Drama. This film has become a black male coming-of-age anthem. A group of high school seniors skip school to chase girls, fight, party, and joy ride in a stolen car during their last year in school. It was shot in Chicago and blessed with a Motown soundtrack. It provided inspiration for the TV series *What's Happening.* Cast: **Glynn Turman, Lawrence-Hilton Jacobs, Garrett Morris,** Cynthia Davis. Director: **Michael Schultz.** Writer: **Eric Monte.**

COOL BREEZE. 1972. (R) 101 min. Drama. This film was adapted from the novel by W. R. Burnett, about a group of Los Angeles criminals who rob a bank in order to get the money to start a bank of their own. Cast: **Thalmus Raulala, Judy Pace,** Jim Watkins, **Lincoln Kilpatrick,** Sam Laws, **Margaret Avery, Pam Grier, Paula Kelly,** Wally Taylor, Rudy Challenger, Stewart Bradley, Ed Cambridge, Royce Wallace, Stack Pierce, John Lupton. Writer/Director: Barry Pollack.

COOL RUNNINGS. 1993. (PG) 98 min. Comedy. This film is based on a true story about a Jamaican bobsled team that enters the 1988 Winter Olympics in Calgary. The four unlikely athletes meet with ridicule and disbelief, but find the courage and determination to see it through. Cast: **Leon, Doug E. Doug,** John Candy, Marco Brambilla, **Malik Yoba,** Rawle Lewis, Raymond J. Barry, Peter Outerbridge, Larry Gilman, Paul Coeur. Director: John Turtteltaub. Writer: Tommy Swerdlow, Lynn Siefert, Michael Goldberg. Cinematographer: Phedon Papamichael. Music: Hans Zimmer.

COOL WORLD, THE. 1963. (NR) 107 min. Docudrama. A tough, 15-year-old gang member wants nothing more than to get a gun, run the streets, and hang with his gang in this Harlem, New York-based film. Cast: **Gloria Foster**, Hampton Clanton, **Carl Lee, Clarence Williams III**. Director: Shirley Clark. Awards: National Film Registry.

COOPER, RALPH (1908-1992). Actor, dancer, producer. This New York City native became known as "The Dark Gable," after Clark Gable, because of his charm, good looks, and quick wit. He began his career as an emcee at the famed **Apollo Theater**, and is credited with creating the original Amateur Night at the Apollo. After choreographing the Shirley Temple movie *Poor Little Rich Girl*, 1936, the film bug bit Cooper and while on the set as he watched and studied the filmmaking process. Cooper then helped to organize Million Dollar Productions with producer/director Harry Popkins. Their company made several successful gangster films starring Cooper, including **Dark Manhattan**, 1937; **Bargain with Bullets**, 1937; and **Gang War**, 1940. Cooper is perhaps best known for starring with **Lena Horne** in *The Duke is Tops*, 1938.
Filmography: *Lloyd's of London*, 1936; *White Hunter*, 1936; *Dark Manhattan*, 1937; *Bargain with Bullets*, 1937; *The Duke is Tops*, 1938; *Gang War*, 1940; *Am I Guilty?*, 1940.

CORA UNASHAMED. 2000. (NR) 95 min. Drama. This made-for-TV movie explores racism in a small Iowa town back in the 1930s. Cora and her mother are the only blacks in town. As a housekeeper for a wealthy white family, Cora bonds with the family's daughter, but their relationship is strongly resented by the family matriarch whose drastic actions bring about a tragedy. Cast: **Regina Taylor, CCH Pounder**, Cherry Jones, Michael Gaston, Arlen Dean Snyder, Molly Graham, Ellen Muth, Kohl Sudduth. Director: Deborah Pratt. Writer: Ann Peacock. Cinematographer: Ernest Holzman. Music: Patrice Rushen.

CORNBREAD, EARL & ME. 1975. (R) 95 min. Drama. When the police mistakenly shoot down a popular high school basketball star, racial tensions flare in a climate of protest and hate. Cast: **Moses Gunn, Rosalind Cash, Bernie Casey**, Tierre Turner, **Madge Sinclair**, Keith Wilkes, **Antonio Fargas, Laurence Fishburne**. Director: Joseph Manduke. Writer: Leonard Lamensdorf. Cinematographer: Jules Brenner. Music: Donald Byrd.

CORRUPT. 1999. (R) 72 min. Urban Drama. A drug lord who holds sway over the South Bronx gets some unwanted competition from a rival gang. One gang member wants out of the game, but his former friends and gangbangers will not let him. Cast: **Ice T, Ernie Hudson**, Silkk the Shocker, Karen Dyer. Director: Albert Pyun.

COSBY, BILL (1937-). Actor, comedian, philanthropist. Cosby dropped out of high school in Philadelphia and became a medic in the Navy. He earned his diploma while in the service and attended Temple University once he was discharged, where he played football and also worked as a bartender. He began his career in entertainment in 1962 as a comedian playing small Philadelphia and Greenwich Village nightclubs. After **television** appearances on the Johnny Carson, Jack Paar, and Andy Williams shows, he rapidly became one of the top nightclub acts in the country. Cosby made television history in 1965, when he became the first African American actor to star in a network television series. The name of the show was *I Spy,* and he was also the first to win an **Emmy Award** for his role. He landed his own television series, *The Bill Cosby Show,* in 1969. His film roles include ***Uptown Saturday Night,*** 1974; ***Let's Do It Again,*** 1975; and ***A Piece of the Action,*** 1977, all with **Sidney Poitier**. Continuing on with his education, Cosby earned his doctorate in education from the University of Massachusetts in 1977. After a short stint of playing a high school guidance counselor on his TV series *The Bill Cosby Show,* he later became Dr. Heathcliff Huxtable on the long-running *The Cosby Show,* considered one of the most-watched shows of all time. Throughout his career, Cosby has lent his comedic talents to over 20 record albums and won numerous awards, including Emmy Awards, Grammy awards, and seven gold albums. He has authored several books, including *Fatherhood,* 1986, and *Time Flies,* 1987. He is also the television commercial spokesman for Jello Pudding. He has shared his fortune with various social causes and educational institutions, including a $20 million gift to Spellman College in 1988.

Filmography: *To All My Friends on Shore,* 1971; ***Man & Boy,*** 1971; *Uptown Saturday Night,* 1974; *Let's Do It Again,* 1975; *Mother, Jugs and Speed,* 1976; *Piece of the Action,* 1977; *California Suite,* 1978; *The Devil & Max Devlin,* 1981; ***Leonard Part 6,*** 1987; ***Ghost Dad,*** 1990; ***The Meteor Man,*** 1993; *Jack,* 1996; ***Fat Albert,*** 2004.

COSMIC SLOP. 1994. (R) 87 min. Science Fiction. This is a three-part anthology on the order of *The Twilight Zone* or *The Outer Limits*. "Space Traders" is based on a Derick Bell short story about space aliens who want to swap information that will cure all the country's social problems in return for taking the country's black population back with them. "The First Commandment" pits a Catholic priest in a Latino parish against the community's belief in Santeria. The final short, "Tang," is taken from a Chester Himes story about an unhappily married inner-city couple plotting what to do to each other with a mysterious rifle left at their door. Cast: **Robert Guillaume**, Jason Bernard, Nicholas Turturro, Richard Herd, Paula Jai Parker, Chi McBride. Directors: **Reginald Hudlin, Warrington Hudlin, Kevin Rodney Sullivan**. Writers: Warrington Hudlin, Trey Ellis, Kyle Baker. Cinematographer: Peter Deming.

COTTON COMES TO HARLEM. 1970. (R) 97 min. Comedy. Based on the Chester Himes novel, two Harlem detectives investigate a suspicious back-to-Africa movement being run by a shady preacher. They think it is a scam and a missing Mississippi cotton bale full of money could prove it. This spawned the sequel *Come Back, Charleston Blue*, 1971. Cast: **Godfrey Cambridge**, **Raymond St. Jacques**, **Calvin Lockhart**, **Judy Pace**, **Redd Foxx**, John Anderson, Emily Yancy, J. D. Cannon, Teddy Wilson, Eugene Roche, **Cleavon Little**, Lou Jacobi. Writer/Director: **Ossie Davis**. Cinematographer: Gerald Hirshfeld. Music: Galt McDermot.

COURT-MARTIAL OF JACKIE ROBINSON, THE. 1990. (R) 100 min. Biopic. This is a film based on the early life of baseball star Jackie Robinson when he was drafted into the U.S. Army. He is assigned to a Texas training camp deep in the racist South and faces a court-martial for insubordination when he refuses to go to the back of the bus when the white civilian driver of the military bus orders him to. Cast: **Andre Braugher**, Daniel Stern, **Ruby Dee, Stan Shaw**, Paul Dooley, **Kasi Lemmons, J. A. Preston**, Michael Green, Dale Dye, **Steve Williams**, Noble Willingham, Gary Grubbs, Bruce Dern, Don Hood, Howard French. Director: Larry Peerce. Writers: L. Travis Clark, Steve Duncan.

CRAIN, WILLIAM (1949-). Director, writer, producer. Born in Columbus, Ohio, Crain entered the cinema department at the University of California, Los Angeles, and began his directing career on the television series *The Mod Squad*. He has also directed episodes of *The Rookies*, *S. W. A. T.*, *The Dukes of Hazzard*, and *Designing*

Women. His feature films include ***Blackula***, 1972; ***Dr. Black, Mr. Hyde***, 1976; and *Midnight Fear*, 1990.

Filmography: *Blackula*, 1972; *Greenhouse*, 1973; *Joy Ride: An Auto Theft*, 1976; *Dr. Black, Mr. Hyde*, 1976; *The Kid from Not-So-Big*, 1978; *Lifetime Contract*, 1986; *Midnight Fear*, 1990.

CRASH, 2004. (R) 113 min. Drama. This film deftly explores the often subtle, sometimes hidden, but very real underlying tensions of a multi-racial Los Angeles, California. As a virtual melting pot of people from various cultures, the lives of otherwise isolated characters are skillfully woven together to tell a story of mistrust, contempt, and the power of race as a serious social issue in modern-day America. The cast of characters includes a police detective, a pair of car thieves, the district attorney and his pampered wife, a racist cop and his idealist young partner, a Middle-Eastern shop keeper, a black social worker, a Hispanic locksmith, and a Hollywood director and his spouse. They all collide at one point or another to cause a chain reaction of death, conflict, and personal introspection. Cast: **Don Cheadle**, Sandra Bullock, Matt Dillon, Jennifer Esposito, William Fitchtner, Brendan Fraser, **Terrence Howard**, Ludacris, **Thandie Newton**, Ryan Phillippe, **Larenz Tate**, Tony Danza, **Keith David**, Shaun Toub, **Loretta Devine**. Writer/Director: Paul Haggis. Awards: 2005 Oscars, Best Picture, Best Editing, Best Screenplay written directly for the screen.

CRIMSON SKULL, THE. 1921. Mystery/Western. Silent. The **Norman Film Manufacturing Company** of Jacksonville, Florida, produced this early all-black-cast Western. It was shot in the all-black town of Boley, Oklahoma. Producer Richard E. Norman intended to make a film titled *A Rodeo Star* that featured the talents of black cowboy Bill Pickett, who invented the rodeo event "bulldogging." Pickett worked as a hand on the Miller's Bros. 101 Ranch. Norman was so disappointed that the rodeo legend was now well into his fifties and past his prime that he fashioned a broader story line to inter-cut with the rodeo footage and cast well-known stage actress **Anita Bush** in the lead role. Bush plays a cattleman's daughter in this baffling Western mystery photoplay. A shorter version was also released as *The Bull-Dogger*, featuring Bill Pickett. Cast: Anita Bush, Lawrence Chenault, Bill Pickett, Steve "Peg" Reynolds. Director: Richard E. Norman.

CRINER, LAWRENCE (1898-1965). Actor. Criner was a pioneer actor who began in the silent era. He made his film debut in the **Norman Film Manufacturing Company**'s ***The Flying Ace***,

1926, and *Black Gold*, 1928. **Oscar Micheaux** cast him in *The Millionaire*, 1927, and he worked with **Ralph Cooper** in *Bargain with Bullets*, 1937; *The Duke Is Tops*, 1938; and *Gang War*, 1940. His final film role was as the minister in *The Jackie Robinson Story*, 1950.

Filmography: *The Flying Ace*, 1926; *Black Gold*, 1928; *The Millionaire*, 1927; *Bargain with Bullets*, 1937; *The Duke Is Tops*, 1938; *Gang War*, 1940; *Miracle in Harlem*, 1948, *The Jackie Robinson Story*, 1950.

CROOKLYN. 1994. (PG-13) 112 min. Urban Drama. This is a coming-of-age story about a young girl growing up with four hardheaded brothers in 1970s Brooklyn. Things get tough when the mother becomes ill and the daughter is sent away to stay with a relative in the rural South. Not fitting in with this distorted world, she returns to New York and the hectic sights and sounds that she knows. Cast: **Alfre Woodard, Delroy Lindo**, Zelda Harris, David Patrick Kelly, Carlton Williams, Sharif Rashed, Tse-March Washington, Christopher Knowings, Jose Zuniga, **Isaiah Washington**, Ivelka Reyes, N. Jeremi Duru, Francis Foster, Norman Matlock, Patriece Nelson, Joie Lee, **Vondie Curtis-Hall**, Tiasha Reyes, **Spike Lee**. Director: Spike Lee. Writers: Joie Lee, Cinque Lee. Cinematographer: **Arthur Jaffa**. Music: **Terence Blanchard**.

CROSSOVER. 2006. (PG-13) 95 min. Drama/sports. A gifted basketball player resists an offer from an ex-sports agent to shop his ball-handling abilities to the NBA and sets his sights on going to college to become a doctor. When an old friend asks for his help to win a major underground streetball game against an ego-driven rival, a prior debt will not let him say no. Cast: Tamer Werfali, Gavin J. Behrman, Michael Lamone Bivins, Shelli Boone, Wayne Brady, Philip Champion, Allan Cunningham, Alecia Jai Fears, Dana Gamarra, Nicholas Harvell, Little JJ, William L. Johnson, Wesley Jonathan. Director: Writer/director: Preston A. Whitmore. Cinematographer: Christian Sebaldt. Editors: Stuart Acher, Anthony Adler.

CROSSOVER ACTORS. Many actors have previously gained fame and notoriety by excelling in other fields of endeavor, usually either sports, or in some form of entertainment before crossing over to the silver screen. Many popular athletes and entertainers generate fans and followings just like movie stars. Because name and face recognition is crucial to the marketing and success of a film, Hollywood often attempts to capitalize on their prior celebrity status by casting them in movie roles hoping to entice their loyal fan base to come and ante up at the box office. Several categories in which these multitalented performers reside are:

Athlete Actors. The hue and cry of sports is charged with conflict and drama, and athletes are often cast in a variety of roles on television and in fiction films. Former Los Angeles Ram Woody Strode portrayed the title role in *Sergeant Rutledge*, 1961, and was cast as a gladiator in *Spartacus*, 1961. Many other football heroes, such as **O. J. Simpson, Jim Brown, Bernie Casey,** and **Fred Williamson** moved easily from the gridiron to the silver screen. Karate expert and tournament fighter **Jim Kelly** displayed his "kick butt" talents in *Enter the Dragon*, 1973, and was cast in the title role of *Black Belt Jones*, 1974. From basketball, star center **Kareem Abdul-Jabbar** has appeared in many films, including a fight scene with Bruce Lee in the martial arts flick *Game of Death*, 1979, and as the co-pilot in the comedy spoof *Airplane*, 1980. Shaquille O'Neal has acted on the big screen and appears on **television** in numerous commercials and product endorsements. Hoopster Michael Jordan starred opposite the entire Looney Toon gang in the live-action/animated film *Space Jam*, 2000. Boxing great Joe Lewis was cast as a prizefighter in *Spirit of Youth*, 1938, and again in *The Fight Never Ends*, 1949. However, in his own biopic *The Joe Lewis Story*, 1954, actor Coley Wallace portrayed Lewis. Pugilist **Muhammad Ali** starred in *The Greatest*, 1977, the biopic on his life and career. He also played a dramatic role as a Negro politician in *Freedom Road*, 1979. Other biopics on black athletes include *The Jackie Robinson Story*, 1950 (baseball), in which Jackie Robinson portrays himself, and *The Jesse Owens Story*, 1984 (track), starring Dorian Harewood.

Dancer Actors. Dance is a popular form of entertainment that was perfect for film. Capturing the movements from different angles or manipulating the film speed can give dance a whole different look and feel from a live performance. Many of the early images of African Americans on film were of dance numbers from the vaudeville stage. One of the most famous and noteworthy dancers to cross over to the silver screen was **Bill "Bojangles" Robinson,** who not only danced, but also starred in films like *Stormy Weather*, 1943, and perhaps became mostly known for his film dance numbers with little Shirley Temple. The world-famous **Nicholas Brothers,** who began dancing as kids, were relegated to just the dance numbers in films like *Kid Millions*, 1934, *Orchestra Wives*, 1942, and *Stormy Weather*, 1943, with very little opportunity to interact with other characters in a dramatic way. In their later years, Fayard Nicholas landed a small dramatic role in the film *The Liberation of L. B. Jones*, 1970, and Harold played a bit part in the hit comedy film *Let's Do It Again*, 1975. **John "Bubbles" Sublett** is perhaps best remembered for his portrayal of the hot-tempered gambler Domino Johnson in the hit musical *Cabin in the Sky*, 1943, but he made earlier film appearances in *High Tones*, 1929, and *Dark Town Follies*, 1929, performing with a partner as Buck and Bubbles. Years later, **Gregory Hines** danced with his brother Maurice in *The Cotton Club*, 1984, and went on to a stellar acting career in such films as *White Nights*, 1985, and *Tap*, 1989. Modern-day tap sensation **Savion Glover** showed off his fancy footwork in *Bamboozled*, 2000, and female dancer/choreographer **Debbie Allen** has enjoyed a long career in film and television that began with *The Fish that Saved Pittsburgh*, 1979.

Rapper Actors. The 1980s ushered in a new style of music where performers rhythmically spoke the words to songs instead of singing them. A popular and powerful hip-hop culture soon emerged that crossed racial barriers, influenced dress and social attitudes, and made a lot of money for the artists and the entertainment industry. Successful rappers that made the transition to film include **Ice Cube**, *Boyz N the Hood*, 1991; **Ice T**, *New Jack City*, 1991; **Tupac Shakur**, *Poetic Justice*, 1993; **Queen Latifah**, *Bringing Down the House*, 2003; **Will Smith**, *I-Robot*, 2004; **L. L. Cool J**, *Kingdom Come*, 2001; **Mos Def**, *Something the Lord Made*, 2004; Ludicris, *Crash*, 2005.

Singer Actors. Many film genres, specifically musicals, often require the talents of already established vocalists, or singers who can also act. **Paul Robeson** was well known for his deep, baritone voice long before it was utilized for his classic rendition of "Old Man River" in *Showboat*, 1936. Big band crooner Herb Jeffries became known as "The Bronze Buckeroo," a singing cowboy in *Harlem on the Prairie*, 1938. Lena Horne's lovely voice and exceptional beauty were prominent in the films *Cabin in the Sky*, 1943, and *Stormy Weather*, 1943. **Pearl Bailey** sang, danced, and "beat out that rhythm on a drum" in **Carmen Jones**, 1954. Well-known jazz vocalist Abby Lincoln left her singing voice at home and only acted in the films *Nothing but a Man*, 1964, and *For Love of Ivy*, 1968. Popular singing star Whitney Houston's powerful voice burst onto the screen in *The Bodyguard*, 1992, and as *The Preacher's Wife*, 1996.

Stand-Up Comic Actors. The dawn of the crossover comedians was ushered in during the 1970s when the brash and controversial stylings of stand-up comic **Richard Pryor** became a top box-office draw in films like *Silver Streak*, 1976; *Which Way Is Up?* 1977; and *Stir Crazy*, 1980. Comedian **Bill Cosby** was already popular from the hit 1960s television series *I Spy* when he teamed up with straight man **Sidney Poitier** to make the comedy film trilogy *Uptown Saturday Night*, 1974; *Let's Do It Again*, 1975; and *Piece of the Action*, 1977. The box-office success of these established funnymen opened the door for a flurry of popular comics to follow their path to the big screen. **Eddie Murphy** transitioned from his featured spot on NBC's *Saturday Night Live*, to film roles in *48 HRS*, 1982, and the highly successful *Beverly Hills Cop* trilogy of films. **Whoopi Goldberg**'s comic genius was another beneficiary of this time of funny-filmed entertainment. She first appeared on the big screen in the dramatic film *The Color Purple*, 1985, and followed with comedies like *Jumpin' Jack Flash*, 1986; *Fatal Beauty*, 1987; and *Burglar*, 1987. Many of these were mainstream films with the popular black lead intended to help draw the African American audience into the theaters. In the 1990s, a new crop of comedians gained popularity and their film careers continued to grow into the new millennium. They include **Martin Lawrence,** *Talkin' Dirty After Dark*, 1991; **Chris Rock,** *CB4: The Movie*, 1993; **Joe Torre,** *Tales From the Hood*, 1995; **Chris Tucker,** *Rush Hour*, 1998; **Eddie Griffin,** *Foolish*, 1999; and **Dave Chapelle,** *Screwed*, 2000. Three generations of film stand-up comics were brought together in one film when **Redd Foxx**, Richard Pryor, and Eddie Murphy starred in the comedy/crime/drama *Harlem Nights*, 1989.

CROTHERS, SCATMAN (1910-1986). Actor, singer, songwriter. He was born in Terre Haute, Indiana, as Benjamin Sherman Crothers, and after high school, he traveled across the Midwest with his band performing in hotels and nightclubs. His first film role was as Billie Holiday's jilted lover in the one-reel musical with Duke Ellington, *Symphony in Black*, 1936. In 1948, he traveled with his band to Los Angeles and later appeared in the Hollywood films *Yes Sir, Mr. Bones*, 1951, and *Meet Me at the Fair*, 1953, for which he also provided some of the music. Crothers recorded many of his original tunes , including "The Gal Looks Good," "I Was There," and "A Man's Gotta Eat," and he took his nickname "Scatman" from the scat style of singing he did.

Filmography: *Symphony in Black*, 1936; *Yes Sir, Mr. Bones*, 1951; *Meet Me at the Fair*, 1953; *East of Sumatra*, 1953; *Walking My Baby Back Home*, 1953; *Tarzan and the Trappers*, 1958; *The Sins of Rachel Cade*, 1961; *Lady in a Cage*, 1964; *The Patsy*, 1964; *Three on a Couch*, 1966; *Chandler*, 1971; *Lady Sings the Blues*, 1972; *Slaughter's Big Rip-Off*, 1973; *Detroit 9000*, 1973; *Black Belt Jones*, 1974; *Truck Turner*, 1974; *Friday Foster*,

1975; *Coonskin*, 1975; *One Flew Over the Cuckoo's Nest*, 1975; *Stay Hungry*, 1976; *The Shootist*, 1976; *Silver Streak*, 1976; **Roots**, 1977; *Mean Dog Blues*, 1977; *The Cheap Detective*, 1978; *Scavenger Hunt*, 1979; *The Shining*, 1980; *Billy Bronco*, 1980; *Zapped!*, 1982; *Deadly Eyes*, 1982; *Two of a Kind*, 1983; *Twilight Zone: The Movie*, 1983; *The Journey of Natty Gann*, 1985; *The Wonderful World of Johnathan Winters*, 1986.

CRY FREEDOM. 1987. (PG) 157 min. Drama. This film is based on the death of South African activist Steven Biko, and the subsequent harassment of Donald Woods, a white newspaper editor who takes up the slain leader's cause. Cast: Kevin Kline, **Denzel Washington**, Penelope Wilton, Kevin McNally, John Thaw, Timothy West, John Hargreaves, Alec McCowan, **Zakes Mokae**, Ian Richardson, Juanita Waterman. Director: Richard Attenborough. Writer: John Briley. Cinematographer: Ronnie Taylor. Music: George Fenton, Jonas Gwangwa.

CRY, THE BELOVED COUNTRY. 1951. (PG) 111 min. Drama. This motion picture is based on the novel by Alan Paton about a black youth accused of killing a white man in South Africa. The boy's father, a Zulu minister, travels to Johannesburg for his son's trial, and the horror and brutality of the apartheid system is revealed. It was remade in 1995 with **James Earl Jones** and Richard Harris. Cast: **Canada Lee**, Charles Carson, **Sidney Poitier**, Joyce Carey, Geoffrey Keen. Director: Zoltan Korda. Writer: John Howard Lawson, Alan Paton. Cinematographer: Robert Krasker.

CUNDIEFF, RUSTY (1965-). Actor, writer, director. He was born in Pittsburgh, Pennsylvania, and began his acting career in 1985 on the daytime soap opera *Days of Our Lives*, and the TV sitcom *What's Happening Now*. He moved on to writing, directing, and acting in the films ***Fear of a Black Hat***, 1994; ***Tales From the Hood***, 1995; and ***Sprung***, 1997. He has also worked in cable television on comedian **David Chappelle**'s *Chappelle's Show*.
Filmography: ***Hollywood Shuffle***, 1987; ***School Daze***, 1988; *Eddie Presley*, 1993; *Fear of a Black Hat*, 1994; *Tales From the Hood*, 1995; *Sprung*, 1997.

CURTIS-HALL, VONDIE (1956-). Actor, director. He was born in Detroit, Michigan, and made his film debut as a basketball game vendor in ***Coming to America***, 1988. He has since graced both the big and small screen in telepics, such as *Murder Without Motive: The Edmond Perry Story*, 1992; ***Don King: Only in America***,

1997; and *Ali: An American Hero*, 2000. His television series work includes *Cop Rock*, and *Chicago Hope*. He directed the feature films *Gridlock'd*, 1997; *Glitter*, 2001; and the made-for-TV movie *Redemption: The Stan Tookie Williams Story*, 2004. Filmography: *Coming to America*, 1988; *Mystery Train*, 1989; *Black Rain*, 1989; *Die Hard 2*, 1990; *One Good Cop*, 1991; *The Mambo Kings*, 1992; *Passion Fish*, 1992; *Falling Down*, 1993; *Sugar Hill*, 1994; *Crooklyn*, 1994; *Clear and Present Danger*, 1994; *Drop Squad*, 1994; *Tuesday Morning Ride*, 1995; *Broken Arrow*, 1996; *Heaven's Prisoners*, 1996; *Romeo + Juliet*, 1996; *Gridlock'd*, 1997; *Eve's Bayou*, 1997; *Dr. Hugo*, 1998; *Turn It Up*, 2000; *Glitter*, 2001; *Redemption: The Stan Tookie Williams Story*, 2004.

D

DANCING IN SEPTEMBER. 2000. (R) 106 min. Drama. An out-of-work sitcom writer, an ambitious TV executive, and an ex-gangbanger create a controversial TV show that draws resentment from the black community. This causes them to question who they are, what they are doing, and to rethink their goals and aspirations. Cast: Nicole Ari Parker, **Isaiah Washington**, Vicellous Reon Shannon, Malinda Williams, Jay Underwood, Michael Cavanaugh, Chi McBride, James Avery, **LeVar Burton**, **Anna Maria Horsford**, Peter Onorati, **Jenifer Lewis**, **Kadeem Hardison**. Writer/Director: **Reggie "Rock" Bythewood**. Cinematographer: Bill Dill.

DANDRIDGE, DOROTHY (1922-1965). Actress. The daughter of actress Ruby Dandridge, Dorothy grew up in Cleveland, Ohio, and began entertaining at an early age. She performed with her sister, Vivian, as The Wonder Kids. With the addition of Etta Jones, the group became a trio, and they performed as The Dandridge Sisters and appeared in the movies *It Can't Last Forever*, 1937, and *Irene*, 1940. In the 1940s, Dandridge went solo and worked in numerous musical shorts, including *Easy Street, Jungle Jig, Cow Cow Boogie*, and *Paper Doll*. She had a brief marriage to dancer **Harold Nicholas**, from 1944-1951. After her divorce, Dandridge began a successful career as a nightclub singer. She moved into acting in the 1950s, starring in *Bright Road*, 1953, with **Harry Belafonte**, and she later became the first African American actress to receive an **Academy Award** nomination for Best Actress, for her performance in the title role as *Carmen Jones*, 1954. Despite her immense talent and beauty, racism hampered her career opportunities and she would only appear in seven other films, including *Island In the Sun*, 1957, and **Porgy and Bess**, 1959. She married Jack Denison in 1959, and they divorced three years later. She wrote her autobiography, *Everything and Nothing: The Dorothy Dandridge Tragedy*, with Earl Conrad. Donald Bogle wrote the book *Dorothy Dandridge: A Biography*. HBO produced a biopic on her life, **Introducing Dorothy Dandridge**, 1999, starring **Halle Berry**. Dandridge was the first African American woman to appear on the cover of *Life* magazine.

Filmography: *Teacher's Beau*, 1935; *The Big Broadcast of 1936*, 1936; *A Day at the Races*, 1937; *It Can't Last Forever*, 1937; *Irene*, 1940; *Four Shall Die*, 1940; *Lady From Louisiana*, 1941; *Sundown*, 1941; *Sun Valley Serenade*, 1941; *Drums of the Congo*, 1942; *Lucky Jordan*, 1942; *Since You Went Away*, 1944; *Atlantic City*, 1944; *Pillow to Post*, 1945; *Ebony Parade*, 1947; *Tarzan's Peril*, 1951; *Harlem Globetrotters*, 1951; *Bright Road*, 1953; *Carmen Jones*, 1954; *Island In the Sun*, 1957; *Tamango*, 1957, *The Happy Road*, 1957; *The Decks Ran Red*, 1958; *Porgy and Bess*, 1959; *Moment of Danger*, 1960; *The Murder Men*, 1961.

DANIELS, LEE. Producer, director. Daniels began his career as an actor but decided he liked producing better. He is responsible for *Monster's Ball*, 2001, the film in which **Halle Berry** became the first African American actress to receive a Best Actress **Oscar**. His follow-up productions are *The Woodsman*, 2004, and *Shadowboxer*, 2005. He also directed *Shadowboxer*, and has plans to direct *Iced*, 2007.

Filmography: *Monster's Ball*, 2001; *The Woodsman*, 2004; *Shadowboxer*, 2005; *Tennessee*, 2007; *Iced*, 2007.

DARK MANHATTAN. 1937. 70 min. Drama. A low-level mobster sets out to take over the numbers rackets in Harlem. Cast: **Ralph Cooper**, Cleo Hernndon, **Clarence Brooks**, Jess Lee Brooks, Sam McDaniel, Corny Anderson, Rubeline Glover, James Adamson, Everett Brown, **Joel Fluellen**, **Roy Glenn**, Jack Lincy, Clinton Rosemond, **Nick Stewart**. Director: Harry L. Fraser. Writer: George Randol. Cinematographer: Arthur Reed. Music: Harvey Brooks, Ben Ellison.

DARKTOWN STRUTTERS. 1975 (PG) 85 min. Blaxploitation. This is a satirical tale of a black female motorcycle gang that sets out to rescue the kidnapped mother of one of its members. Cast: Trina

Parks, **Roger E. Mosley**, Shirley Washington. Director: William Witney.

DASH, JULIE (1952-). Writer, director. A native of New York, Dash became the first African American woman to receive a general theatrical release for her feature-length film *Daughters of the Dust*, 1991. Dash began her film studies in 1969 at the Studio Museum of Harlem. She studied psychology at the City College of New York before entering the film studies program at the Leonard Davis Center for Performing Arts, in the David Picker Film Institute. After earning her BA degree in Film Production, she headed west to Los Angeles to attend the Center for Advanced Film Studies at the American Film Institute. From there, she enrolled in the graduate film program at the University of California, Los Angeles, and earned her MFA degree in Film and Television Production. While a student at UCLA, Dash made her critically acclaimed film *Illusions*, 1983, which received the 1989 Jury Prize for Best Film of the Decade from the **Black Filmmakers Foundation**. She has directed the MTV original movie *Love Song*, and the romantic thriller *Incognito*, for **Black Entertainment Television**'s Arabesque Films. Her made-for-TV film *Funny Valentines*, was the first BET/ENCORE/StarZ3 original movie. Her other cable credits include writing and directing episodes of *Women* for Showtime, and a segment of HBO's *Subway Stories*. Dash has directed music videos for the singing group Tony, Toni, Tone's "Thinking of You," and Tracy Chapman's "Give Me One Reason," which was nominated for MTV's best video of a female vocalist in 1996.

Filmography: *Four Women*, 1975; *Diary of an African Nun*, 1977; *Illusions*, 1982; *Daughters of the Dust*, 1991; *Praise House*, 1991; *SUBWAY Stories: Tales from the Underground*, 1997; *Funny Valentines*, 1999; *Incognito*, 1999; *Love Song*, 2000; *The Rosa Parks Story*, 2002; *Brothers of the Borderland*, 2004; *Making Angels*, 2007.

DASH, STACEY (1966-). This Bronx, New York, native began doing commercials as a child and quickly moved up to TV guest appearances on shows like *St. Elsewhere*, *The Cosby Show*, and *The Fresh Prince of Bel-Air*. Her film debut came in the comedy *Moving*, 1988, with **Richard Pryor**. Bigger roles followed in *Mo' Money*, 1992; and *Renaissance Man*, 1994; but her break-out role came as a Beverly Hills valley girl in *Clueless*, 1995. She reprised her role on the *Clueless* television series, 1996-1999. Her independent film work includes *Personals*, 1998, and she has appeared in *The Painting*, 2002, and *Paper Soldiers*, 2002.

Filmography: *Moving*, 1988; *Mo' Money*, 1992; *Renaissance Man*, 1994; *Black Water*, 1994; *Illegal in Blue*, 1995; *Clueless*, 1999; *Cold Around the Heart*, 1997; *Personals*, 2000; *The Painting*, 2002; *Paper Soldiers*, 2002; **Getting Played**, 2005.

DAUGHTERS OF THE DUST. 1991. (NR) 113 min. Drama. The year is 1902, the members of a Gullah family on one of the Sea Islands, off the coast of Georgia, hold a family reunion to discuss the clan's relocation to the mainland. As the descendants of escaped West African slaves, their relative isolation has allowed them to retain their culture and unique dialect, and some family members feel it would all be lost. Family ties and memories may be all that remains in such a move. Cast: Cora Lee Day, Barbara O, Alva Rogers, Kaycee Moore, Cheryl Lynn Bruce, Adisa Anderson, Eartha D. Robinson, Bahni Turpin, Tommy Redmond Hicks, Malik Farrakhan, Cornell Royal, Vertamae Crosvenor, Umar Abdurrahman, Sherry Jackson, Rev. Ervin Green. Writer/Director: **Julie Dash**. Cinematographer: **Arthur Jafa**. Music: John Barnes. Awards: Sundance 1991 Best Cinematography.

DAVID, KEITH (1956-). Actor. He was born and raised in New York City and attended the High School of the Performing Arts. He continued his studies at Juilliard, and later received a Tony Award nomination for Best Supporting Actor for his role in the Broadway musical *Jelly's Last Jam*. His deep and distinguished voice has been lent to numerous voiceovers, cartoon characters, and commercial advertisements. His made-for-TV movie roles include **Don King: Only in America**, 1997, and **The Tiger Woods Story**, 1998. His major film roles include *Platoon*, 1986; *The Quick and the Dead*, 1994; **Dead Presidents**, 1995; and **Barbershop**, 2002.
   Filmography: *The Thing*, 1982; *Platoon*, 1986; *Off Limits*, 1987; *Bird*, 1988; *They Live*, 1988; *Marked for Death*, 1990; *Final Analysis*, 1992; *Article 99*, 1992; *The Last Outlaw*, 1993; *The Quick and the Dead*, 1994; *Dead Presidents*, 1995; **Clockers**, 1995; *Larger Than Life*, 1996; *Volcano*, 1997; **Spawn**, 1997; *Executive Target*, 1997; *There's Something about Mary*, 1998; *Armageddon*, 1998; *Where the Heart Is*, 2000; *The Replacements*, 2000; *Pitch Black*, 2000; *Novocaine*, 2002; *Barbershop*, 2002; *Hollywood Homicide*, 2003; **Head of State**, 2003; *Agent Cody Banks*, 2003, **Crash**, 2005.

DAVIDSON, TOMMY (1965-). Actor, comedian. Davidson grew up in Washington, D.C., and became one of the original cast members of **Keenen Wayans**'s edgy, hit comedy television series *In Living*

Color. He began his career as a stand-up comic and became known for his impressions of **Sammy Davis, Jr.**, and **Michael Jackson**. His performances at local comedy showcases led to opening act appearances for musical artists, such as Patti LaBelle, Kenny G., and Luther Vandross. While performing at the Comedy Act Theater in Los Angeles, Davidson met fellow comedian **Robert Townsend**, who cast him in his nationally televised special, *Robert Townsend and His Partners in Crime*. Three comedy specials on Showtime followed, along with a host of lead and co-starring roles in such films as *Strictly Business*, 1992; *Booty Call*, 1997; and *Woo*, 1998.

Filmography: *Strictly Business*, 1991; *Ace Ventura: When Nature Calls*, 1995; *Booty Call*, 1996; *Woo*, 1997; *Plump Fiction*, 1997; *Bamboozled*, 2000; *Juwanna Mann*, 2002.

DAVIS, CLIFTON (1945-). Actor, singer, songwriter. This native of Chicago, Illinois, had already made a name for himself in music when he moved into **television** and film. He wrote the hit song "Never Can Say Goodbye" recorded by The Jackson Five, and was co-host of the popular variety show *The Melba Moore–Clifton Davis Show*, 1972. His other television work includes roles in the sitcoms *That's My Mama*, 1974, and *Amen*, 1986. Davis's film appearances include *Scott Joplin*, 1977; *Any Given Sunday*, 1999; and *Kingdom Come*, 2001.

Filmography: *Together for Days*, 1972; *Lost in the Stars*, 1974; *Scott Joplin*, 1977; *Don't Look Back: The Story of Leroy "Satchel" Paige*, 1981; *Any Given Sunday*, 1999; *Kingdom Come*, 2001; *Max Keeble's Big Movie*, 2001; *The Painting*, 2001; *The Climb*, 2002.

DAVIS, OSSIE (1917-2005). Actor, writer, producer, director. Originally from Waycross, Georgia, Davis attended Howard University in Washington, D.C., but left the school before graduating. After a stint in the U.S. Army, he pursued an acting career in New York and landed his first role in the 1946 stage production of *Jeb*. His first film role was in the movie *No Way Out*, 1950, and he continued on the Broadway stage in *No Time for Sergeants*, *A Raisin in the Sun*, and *Jamaica*. Davis wrote and starred in the stage play *Purlie Victorious,* along with his actress wife, **Ruby Dee**. They would reprise their roles in the movie version titled *Gone Are the Days!* His other early film credits include *The Cardinal*, 1963, *Shock Treatment*, 1964, and *A Man Called Adam*, 1966. Davis became a director with *Cotton Comes to Harlem*, 1970; *Black Girl*, 1972; and *Countdown at Kusini*, 1976. He has played countless

TV roles in television series, such as *The Defenders*, *The Nurses*, and *East Side, West Side*. In 1974, an educational television program called *The Ruby Dee/Ossie Davis Story Hour* was produced. The arts education series *With Ossie and Ruby* was aired in 1981. The duo also started the Institute of New Cinema Artists and the Recording Industry Training Program. Later film roles include *Let's Do It Again*, 1975; *Nothing Personal*, 1979; and a quartet of Spike Lee films: *School Daze*, 1988; *Do the Right Thing*, 1989; *Jungle Fever*, 1991; and *Get on the Bus*, 1996. Davis also starred in the TV miniseries *Queen*, 1993, another sequel to the popular miniseries *Roots*. He is author of the young adult novel *Just Like Martin*.

Filmography: *No Way Out*, 1950; *Purlie Victorious*, 1963; *Gone Are the Days!*, 1963; *The Hill*, 1965; *A Man Called Adam*, 1966; *The Scalphunters*, 1968; *Let's Do It Again*, 1975; *Roots*, 1977; *King*, 1978; *All God's Children*, 1980; *Don't Look Back: The Story of Leroy "Satchel" Paige*, 1981; *Avenging Angel*, 1985; *School Daze*, 1985; *Do the Right Thing*, 1989; *Jungle Fever*, 1991; *Queen*, 1993; *Grumpy Old Men*, 1993; *The Ernest Green Story*, 1993; *The Stand*, 1994; *The Client*, 1994; *I'm Not Rappaport*, 1996; *Get on the Bus*, 1996; *Twelve Angry Men*, 1997; *Miss Evers' Boys*, 1997; *Dr. Dolittle*, 1998; *Dinosaur*, 2000.

DAVIS, SAMMY, JR. (1925-1990). Singer, dancer, actor. Known as the World's Greatest Entertainer, Davis was born in New York City and was performing with his father and uncle on the vaudeville stage by age four as part of the Will Mastin Trio. He appeared in the film *Rufus Jones for President*, 1931, with **Ethel Waters**. Davis served two years in the U.S. Army, in which he produced camp shows until his discharge. As a vocalist, Davis's hits include "Hey There," "Mr. Wonderful," and "Too Close for Comfort." His first Broadway show, *Mr Wonderful*, was a big hit in 1956, and he followed that stage success with *Golden Boy*. On film, he played the character Sportin' Life in *Porgy and Bess*, 1959. His other films include *Oceans 11*, 1960, and *Robin and the Seven Hoods*, 1964. His career spanned television, film, and nightclubs.

Filmography: *Oceans 11*, 1960; *Robin and the Seven Hoods*, 1964; *A Man Called Adam*, 1966; *Sweet Charity*, 1969; *The Trackers*, 1971; *Gone with the West*, 1972; *Cannonball Run*, 1981; *Cracking Up*, 1983; *Cannonball Run 2*, 1984; *Moon over Parador*, 1988; *Tap*, 1989; *The Kid Who Loved Christmas*, 1990.

DAWSON, ROSARIO (1979-). Actress. She was born in New York City and made her screen debut in the film *Kids*, 1995. Her career took off after she was cast in **Spike Lee**'s *He's Got Game*, 1998. Dawson gained critical acclaim for her role in *Men In Black II*, 2002, opposite **Will Smith**, and in *The Rundown*, 2003, opposite **The Rock**. She portrayed the role of Mimi Marquez in the film version of the hit musical play *Rent*, 2005.

Filmography: *Kids*, 1995; *Girls Night Out*, 1997; *He Got Game*, 1998; *Light it Up*, 1999; *Down to You*, 2000; *Sidewalks of New York*, 2001; *King of the Jungle*, 2001; *Josie and the Pussycats*, 2001; *Men in Black II*, 2002; *Ash Wednesday*, 2002; *The Adventures of Pluto Nash*, 2002; *The 25th Hour*, 2002; *The Rundown*, 2003; *This Girl's Life*, 2003; *Shattered Glass*, 2003; *Alexander*, 2004; *This Revolution*, 2004; *The Devil's Rejects*, 2005; *Sin City*, 2005; *Little Black Dress*, 2005; *Rent*, 2005; *Descent*, 2006; *Killshot*, 2006; *Grind House*, 2007; *Sin City 2*, 2007.

DAY, MORRIS (1957-). Singer, actor. He began his music career as the frontman for the Minniapolis-based band, The Time. His suave, arrogant, over-the-top persona was featured in the films *Purple Rain*, 1984, and *Graffiti Bridge*, 1990.

Filmography: *Purple Rain*, 1984; *Graffiti Bridge*, 1990; *The Adventures of Ford Fairlane*, 1990.

D. C. CAB. 1984. (R) 100 min. Comedy. A zany group of cab drivers must pull together to gain their self-respect and figure out a way to save the company. Cast: **Mr. T**, Leif Erickson, Adam Baldwin, Charlie Barnett, **Irene Cara**, Anne DeSalvo, Max Gail, Gloria Gifford, Gary Busey, Jill Schoellen, Marsha Warfield. Director: Joel Schumacher. Writers: Joel Schumacher, **Topper Carew**. Cinematographer: Dean Cundy.

DEAD PRESIDENTS. 1995. (R) 120 min. Urban Drama. A desperate Vietnam War veteran helps to pull off an armored car robbery. Trust, greed, and deceit make it hard for the thieves to get away. Cast: **Larenz Tate**, **Keith David**, **Chris Tucker**, Freddy Rodriguez, **N'Bushe Wright**, **Bokeem Woodbine**, Rose Jackson, **Clifton Powell**. Director: **Albert** and **Allen Hughes**. Writer: Michael Henry Brown. Cinematographer: Lisa Rinzler. Music: Danny Ellfman.

DE ANDA, PETER (1940-). Actor. He was born in Pittsburgh, Pennsylvania, and began his theatrical career working at the Pittsburgh Playhouse. He studied at the Actor's Workshop and performed on stage in *The Blacks*, *The Dutchman*, *The Guide*, and *The House of Leather*. His **television** work includes roles in the daytime drama

One Life to Live, and he portrayed the title role in the detective series *Cutter*. His film work includes roles in *Lady Liberty*, 1971; *The New Centurions*, 1972, and he portrayed the title character in *Come Back, Charleston Blue*, 1972.

Filmography: *The Cool World*, 1964; *Cutter*, 1972; *Come Back, Charleston Blue*, 1972; *The New Centurions*, 1972; *Advice to the Lovelorn*, 1981.

DEE, RUBY (1923-). Actress. Born in Cleveland and raised in Harlem, Dee attended Hunter College in New York and landed her first major stage role in the 1942 production of *South Pacific* with **Canada Lee**. After meeting during the stage production of *Jeb*, she and **Ossie Davis** would marry two years later and become a well-known and productive creative team. Her early film roles include *No Way Out*, 1950; *Edge of the City*, 1957; *A Raisin in the Sun*, 1964; and *The Balcony*, 1963. She was the first African American actress to play major roles for the American Shakespeare Festival in Stratford, Connecticut. Other film roles include *The Incident*, 1967; *Up Tight!*, 1968; *Buck and the Preacher*, 1972; and *Countdown at Kusini*, 1976, independently produced by the women's social organization Delta Sigma Theta Sorority, Inc.

Filmography: *No Way Out*, 1950; *The Jackie Robinson Story*, 1950; *A Raisin in thee Sun*, 1961; *Purlie Victorious*, 1963; *Gone Are the Days!*, 1963; *The Balcony*, 1963; *The Incident*, 1967; *Up Tight!*, 1968; *Buck and the Preacher*, 1972; *Countdown at Kusini*, 1976; *Roots: The Next Generation*, 1979; *I Know Why the Caged Bird Sings*, 1979; *Cat People*, 1982; *Go Tell It on the Mountain*, 1984; *Love at Large*, 1989; *Do the Right Thing*, 1989; *Zora Is My Name!* 1990; *Decoration Day*, 1990; *The Court-Martial of Jackie Robinson*, 1990; *Jungle Fever*, 1991; *The Ernest Green Story*, 1993; *The Stand*, 1994; *Just Cause*, 1994; *A Simple Wish*, 1997; *Baby Geniuses*, 1998; *The Wall*, 1999; *Having Our Say: The Delany Sisters' First 100 Years*, 1999; *Finding Buck Henry*, 2000.

DEEP COVER. 1992. (R) 107 min. Drama. An undercover cop infiltrates the drug world and becomes caught up in the game, until the death of another cop causes him to rethink his loyalties and his priorities. Cast: **Laurence Fishburne**, Jeff Goldblum, **Victoria Dillard**, Charles Martin Smith, Sydney Lassick, **Clarence Williams III**, Gregory Sierra, **Roger Guenveur Smith**, Cory Curtis, **Glynn Turman**, Def Jef. Director: **Bill Duke**. Writers: Michael Tolkin, Henry Bean. Cinematographer: Bojan Bazelli. Music: Michel Colombier.

DEF BY TEMPTATION. 1990. (R) 95 min. Horror. A theology student from the South goes to visit a cousin in New York City. While there, he meets a beautiful succubus, who tries to seduce him and causes him to question his faith. Cast: **James Bond III, Kadeem Hardison, Bill Nunn, Samuel L. Jackson**, Minnie Gentry, Rony Clanton, Cynthia Bond, **John Canada Terrell**. Writer/Director: James Bond III, Cinematographer: **Ernest R. Dickerson**. Music: Paul Lawrence.

DEFIANT ONES, THE. 1958. 97 min. Drama. Two escapees from a chain gang, one black and one white, must overcome their own prejudice and racial hatred toward each other in order to survive and stay free in the rural South. Cast: **Sidney Poitier**, Tony Curtis, Theodore Bikel, Lon Chaney Jr., Charles McGraw, Cara Williams. Director: Stanley Kramer. Writers: Nedrick Young, Harold Jacob Smith. Cinematographer: Sam Leavitt. Music: Steve Dorff. Awards: 1958 Oscars: Cinematography, Story & Screenplay. 1958 British Academy Awards: Best Actor (Poitier), 1959 Golden Globes: Best Drama. NY Film Critics, Best Director (Kramer), Best Film, Best Screenplay.

DELIVER US FROM EVA. 2003. (R) 105 min. Comedy/Romance. This is an urban spin on William Shakespeare's tale of *The Taming of the Shrew*. A known ladies' man is hired by four desperate men to seduce and mellow out their rude and overbearing sister-in-law, who spends far too much time interfering in their relationships with her four sisters. The job becomes more complicated when the player truly falls for his mark. Cast: **Gabrielle Union, L. L. Cool J, Duane Martin, Essence Atkins**, Robbine Lee, **Meagan Good, Mel Jackson**, Dartanyan Edmonds, Kym E. Whitley, Royale Watkins, Matt Winston, Ruben Paul, Dorian Gregory. Director: **Gary Hardwick**. Writers: Gary Hardwick, James Iver Mattson, B. E. Brauner. Cinematographer: Alexander Grusynski. Music: Marcus Miller.

DEMPS, JOHN L. Cinematographer. This Los Angeles-based director of photography has a long line of film credits, including features, commercials, industrial films, and documentaries.

Filmography: *The Three Muscatels*, 1991; ***Street Wars***, 1992; *No Saving Grace*, 1992; ***The Inkwell***, 1994; ***Fear of a Black Hat***, 1994; *The Walking Dead*, 1995; *The Show*, 1995; *The Annihilation of Fish*, 1999; *Cursed Part 3*, 2000; ***The Visit***, 2000; *Sacred is the Flesh*, 2001; *Nat Turner: A Troublesome Property*, 2003; *"The Blues"*, 2003; ***Constellation***, 2005.

DE PASSE, SUZANNE (1948-). Producer, writer. Born in Harlem, New York, she attended Manhattan High School and Syracuse University. She was a booking agent for a New York theater when Motown Records founder Berry Gordy offered her a job as his creative assistant. Having a keen eye for talent, she is credited with bringing The Jackson 5 and the Commodores to the label. De Passe received an Oscar nomination for best script for co-writing *Lady Sings the Blues*, 1972. She became the head of the film and television division of Motown Productions and her effort garnered many awards. Her *Motown 25: Yesterday, Today, Forever*, 1983, won several **Emmy** Awards, and the 1989 miniseries *Lonesome Dove*, won a total of seven Emmy Awards, a **Golden Globe**, and a Peabody Award. She also produced biopics, such as *The Jacksons: An American Dream*, 1992, and the docudrama based on the famed Motown singing group *The Temptations*, 1999. She runs her own company, de Passe Entertainment, which produced the Warner Brothers shows *Sister, Sister*, and *The Smart Guy*. Her company also produces *Showtime at the Apollo*, and the *NAACP Image Awards* telecasts, and the *Essence Awards*. She is a former Time/Warner endowed chair at Howard University's Department of Radio, Television, and Film.

Filmography: *Lonesome Dove*, 1989; *Bridesmaids*, 1989; *Class Act*, 1992; *The Jacksons: An American Dream*, 1992; *Someone Else's Child*, 1994; *Buffalo Girls*, 1995; *Streets of Laredo*, 1995; *Dead Man's Walk*, 1996; *The Temptations*, 1998; *Chains*, 1999; *Zenon: Girl of the 21st Century*, 1999; *The Loretta Clairborne Story*, 2000; *Cheaters*, 2000; *Zenon: The Zequel*, 2001; *Zenon: Z3*, 2004.

DESMOND, CLEO (1880-1958). Actress. She was born in Philadelphia, Pennsylvania, and began her acting career during the **silent era** in *The Easiest Way*, 1917. She worked in **Oscar Micheaux's** *The Millionaire*, 1927, with **Clarence Muse** in *Spirit of Youth*, 1938, and with **Ralph Cooper** in *Am I Guilty?*, 1940.

Filmography: *The Easiest Way*, 1917; *Deceit*, 1923; *The Millionaire*, 1927; *Spirit of Youth*, 1938; *Am I Guilty?* 1940; *Mr. Washington Goes to Town*, 1941; *The Vanishing Virginian*, 1942; *Mokey*, 1942.

DE SOUSA, MELISSA (1967-). Actress. She was born in New York City and began her **television** acting career guest starring on such series as *Living Single*, *Silk Stalkings*, and *Valley of the Dolls*. She

was the star of the films *Ride*, 1998, and *30 Years to Life*, 2001, co-starred in the hit ensemble cast film *The Best Man*, 1999.
Filmography: *Spark*, 1996; *Ride*, 1998; *The Best Man*, 1999; *Lockdown*, 2000; *Miss Congeniality*, 2000; *30 Years to Life*, 2001; *I Shaved My Legs for This*, 2001; *Laurel Canyon*, 2002; *Biker Boyz*, 2003; *Constellation*, 2004.

DEVIL IN A BLUE DRESS. 1995. (R) 102 min. Drama. This film is based on the **Walter Mosley** novel about an out-of-work factory worker turned private eye named Easy Rawlins. In 1948 Los Angeles, Rawlins has lots of time, a new house, and bills to pay. He is hired to find a woman who has ties to a white political candidate and a set of mysterious photos that could crush his opponent. He finds that in this line of work, people lie and people die, and he soon finds that he is a suspect wanted by the police. Rawlins must find the girl and the photos to clear his name and stay alive in the process. Cast: **Denzel Washington, Jennifer Beals, Don Cheadle**, Tom Sizemore, Maury Chayukin, Terry Kinney, Mel Winkler, **Albert Hall**, Renee Humphrey, **Lisa Nicole Carson**, John Roselius, Beau Starr. Writer/Director: **Carl Franklin**. Cinematographer: Tak Fujimoto. Music: Elmer Bernstein. Awards: LA Film Critics 1995: Best Supporting Actor (Cheadle). National Society of Film Critics 1995: Best Cinematography, Best Supporting Actor (Cheadle).

DEVIL'S DAUGHTER, THE. 1939. 60 min. Horror. A sister's jealousy leads to hatred, envy, and a voodoo spell to get what she wants. Cast: **Nina Mae McKinney**, Jack Carter, Ida James, Hamtree Harrington. Director: Arthur Leonard. Cinematographer: Jay Rescher.

DEVINE, LORETTA (1949-). Born in Houston, Texas, she graduated from the University of Houston and earned her Master's degree from Brandeis University. She moved to New York and landed a role in the stage production of *Coming Uptown*. She followed with a role in *Big Deal*, a Bob Fosse Broadway production, and created the Lorell character in the hit Broadway play *Dreamgirls*. Devine has guest starred on the **television** series *Amen*, *Roc*, and *Touched by an Angel*, and starred in the Fox network series *Boston Public*. Her film roles include *Waiting to Exhale*, 1995; *Down in the Delta*, 1998; and *Woman Thou Art Loosed*, 2004.
Filmography: *Stanley and Iris*, 1990; *Caged Fear*, 1992; *Waiting to Exhale*, 1995; *Rebound*, 1996; *The Preacher's Wife*, 1996; *Hoodlum*, 1996; *Lover Girl*, 1997; *Don King: Only in America*, 1997; *Urban Legend*, 1998; *Down in the Delta*, 1998; *Introducing*

Dorothy Dandridge, 1999; *The Breaks*, 1999; *What Women Want*, 2000; *Urban Legends 2: Final Cut*, 2000; *Freedom Song*, 2000; *Kingdom Come*, 2001; *I Am Sam*, 2001; *Book of Love*, 2002; *The Script*, 2002; *Baby of the Family*, 2002; *Crash*, 2004; *Woman Thou Art Loosed*, 2004; *King's Ransom*, 2005.

DIARY OF A MAD BLACK WOMAN. 2005. (PG-13) Comedy. This is a film version of one of **Tyler Perry**'s popular stage plays featuring his "Madea" character. The perfect married couple with money, a mansion, and everything they have ever wanted in life are about to celebrate their 20th wedding anniversary, when one asks for a divorce. Cast: **Kimberly Elise**, Steve Harris, Tyler Perry, **Shemar Moore**, Vic Aviles, Sho Dixon, Mablean Ephriam, Wilbur Fitzgerald, Tamela J. Mann, Lisa Marcos, Judge Greg Mathis, Donnie McClurkin, **Cicely Tyson**, Steve Warren, Tamara Taylor. Director: Darren Grant. Writer: Tyler Perry. Cinematographer: David Claessen.

DICKERSON, ERNEST (1951-). Writer, director, cinematographer. Dickerson first came to prominence as the cinematographer for **Spike Lee**'s award-winning New York University student film *Joe's Bed-Stuy Barbershop: We Cut Heads*, 1980. He was tapped by director John Sayles to shoot his urban-based *The Brother from Another Planet*, 1984. He also lensed the rap music vehicle *Krush Groove*, 1985, for director **Michael Shultz**, and the stand-up comedy concert film *Eddie Murphy Raw*, 1987, for director **Robert Townsend**. Dickerson continued to work with Spike Lee, shooting Lee's first six films before transitioning into his own directing career with the harsh, urban gang drama *Juice*, 1992. Dickerson has worked in television as a director of photography on the first season of the horror anthology series *Tales from the Darkside*, and on the series *Law & Order*. His television directing credits include *ER*, *Criminal Minds*, *CSI: Miami*, and *The Wire*. He also directed the action film *Surviving the Game*, 1994, starring rapper **Ice T**, and the horror film from the hood, *Bones*, 2001, starring rapper **Snoop Dogg**.
    Filmography: *Juice*, 1992; *Surviving the Game*, 1994; *Demon Knight*, 1995; *Bulletproof*, 1996; *Blind Faith*, 1998; *Ambushed*, 1998; *Futuresport*, 1998; *Strange Justice*, 1999; *Bones*, 2001; *Monday Night Mayhem*, 2002; *Big Shot*, 2002; *Good Fences*, 2003; *Never Die Alone*, 2004; *For One Night*, 2006.

DIESEL, VIN (1967-). Actor, producer, director. He was born in New York City and dropped out of college to direct his short film *Multi-*

Facial, 1994. It was screened at the 1995 Cannes Film Festival, where it came to the attention of director Steven Spielberg, who cast Diesel in his war epic *Saving Private Ryan*, 1998. He has since become a top action star in such films as *Pitch Black*, 2000; *The Fast and the Furious*, 2001; *XXX*, 2002; and *The Chronicles of Riddick*, 2004. He has produced *Strays*, 1997; *A Man Apart*, 2003; *Find Me Guilty*, 2005; and *Hannibal*, 2005.

Filmography: *Multi-Facial*, 1994; *Strays*, 1997; *Saving Private Ryan*, 1998; *Boiler Room*, 2000; *Pitch Black*, 2000; *The Fast and the Furious*, 2001; *Knockaround Guys*, 2001; *XXX*, 2002; *A Man Apart*, 2003; *The Chronicles of Riddick*, 2004; *The Pacifier*, 2005; *Find Me Guilty*, 2005; *Hannibal*, 2005.

DIGGS, TAYE (1972-). Actor. Diggs attended a fine arts high school in Rochester, New York, before earning his BFA in Musical Theater. He has performed on Broadway in productions of *Carousel* and *Rent*, and portrayed his stage character in the film version of *Rent*, 2005. On **television**, he portrayed the recurring role of Adrian "Sugar" Hill in the daytime soap opera *Guiding Light*. National acclaim came to Diggs when he costarred in the film adaptation of Terry McMillan's popular novel *How Stella Got Her Groove Back*, 1998. Many more film and television roles followed, including a guest stint on the TV series *Ally McBeal*. He also starred in his own comedy series *Kevin Hill*.

Filmography: *How Stella Got Her Groove Back*, 1998; *The Wood*, 1999; *Go*, 1999; *The Best Man*, 1999; *House on Haunted Hill*, 1999; *The Way of the Gun*, 2000; *Equilibrium*, 2001; *New Best Friend*, 2002; *Media Whore*, 2002; *Just a Kiss*, 2002; *Cross the Line*, 2002; *Brown Sugar*, 2002; *A Midsummer Night's Rave*, 2002; *Chicago*, 2002; *Basic*, 2002; *Malibu's Most Wanted*, 2003; *Rent*, 2005.

DILLARD, VICTORIA (1969-). Actress. She was born in New York City and made her film debut in *Coming to America*, 1988. Her other feature film work includes roles in *Deep Cover*, 1992; *The Glass Shield*, 1994; and *Out-of-Sync*, 1995. Her notable **television** appearances include roles as Dr. Nadine Winslow in the dramatic series *Chicago Hope*, and as Janelle Cooper in the sitcom *Spin City*.

Filmography: *Coming to America*, 1988; *Internal Affairs*, 1990; *Ricochet*, 1991; *Deep Cover*, 1992; *Killing Obsession*, 1994; *The Glass Shield*, 1994; *Statistically Speaking*, 1995; *Out-of-Sync*, 1995; *The Ditch Digger's Daughters*, 1997; *The Best Man*, 1999; *Ali*, 2001.

DIRTY GERTIE FROM HARLEM U.S.A. 1946. 60 min. Drama. A troubled woman runs off to Trinidad to get away from her jilted boyfriend. Cast: Francine Everett, Katherine Moore, **Spencer Williams Jr.**, Alfred Hawkins. Director: Spencer Williams Jr.

DISAPPEARING ACTS. 2000. (R) 115 min. Drama. Based on the novel by Terry McMillan, a college-educated music teacher with dreams of becoming a singer meets a high school drop out, who is working in construction, and a relationship ensues. All is fine until a series of unexpected complications test the man's loyalty and commitment. Cast: **Sanaa Lathan, Wesley Snipes, Regina Hall, Clark Johnson, John Amos, CCH Pounder**, Aunjanue Ellis, Lisa Arrindell Anderson, Kamaal Fareed, Michael Imperioli. Director: **Gina Prince-Bythewood**. Writer: Lisa Jones. Cinematographer: Tami Reiker.

DISORDERLIES. 1987. (PG) 86 min. Comedy. Members of the rap group The Fat Boys, are bumbling hospital orderlies assigned to care for a wealthy and cantankerous old patient. Cast: The Fat Boys, Ralph Bellamy. Director: **Michael Schultz**. Music: Jerry Goldsmith.

DISPLACED PERSON. 1985. (TV) 60 min. Drama. After World War II, a black German boy, who is also an orphan, has never seen his father or any other black person in his life. He sees some American soldiers and instantly thinks the black sergeant in charge is his father. Cast: **Stan Shaw**, Rosemary Leach, Ricco Ross, Neville Aurelius, Kate Saunders, Julius Gordon, Jason Smart, Jeremy Osborn, Tom Espiner, David Bartlett, Richard Humphreys, John J. Carney, Jerome Flynn, David Pinner, Joseph Mydell. Director: Alan Bridges. Writers: Fred Barron, Kurt Vonnegut Jr.

DISTINGUISHED GENTLEMAN, THE. 1992. (R) 122 min. Comedy. A con man scams his way into the U. S. Congress and discovers a much larger and more illegal system of graft and corruption. Cast: **Eddie Murphy**, Lane Smith, **Sheryl Lee Ralph**, Joe Don Baker, Victoria Rowell, Grant Shaud, Kevin McCarthy, **Charles S. Dutton**, James Garner. Director: Johnathan Lynn. Writer: Marty Kaplan. Cinematographer: Gabriel Beristain. Music: Randy Edelman.

DIXON, IVAN (1931-). Actor, producer, director. Dixon was born in New York City and graduated from the famed Lincoln Academy boarding school in North Carolina. He studied history at North Carolina College with a minor in drama and political science. He pursued an acting career and appeared on Broadway in the original cast of *A Raisin in the Sun*, and *The Cave Dwellers*. His many film roles include *Something of Value*, 1957; *Porgy and Bess*, 1959; *The Murder Men*, 1961; *A Raisin in the Sun*, 1961; and *The Battle at Bloody Beach*, 1961. He is perhaps best known for two roles, as Duff Anderson in *Nothing But a Man*, 1964, and as Sergeant James Kinchloe on the **television** series *Hogan's Heroes*. Dixon began directing with the **blaxploitation**-era film *Trouble Man*, 1972, and followed it by producing and directing the revolutionary film adaptation of Sam Greenlee's novel, *The Spook Who Sat By the Door*, 1973. For television, Dixon directed episodes of *Palmerstown, U. S. A.*, *Magnum P. I.*, and the television movie *Percy & Thunder*, 1993.

Filmography: *Something of Value*, 1957; *Porgy and Bess*, 1959; *The Murder Men*, 1961; *A Raisin in the Sun*, 1961; *The Battle at Bloody Beach*, 1961; *Nothing but a Man*, 1964; *A Patch of Blue*, 1965; *Suppose They Gave a War and Nobody Came*, 1970; *Fer-De-Lance*, 1974; *Car Wash*, 1976.

DMX (1970-). Actor, rapper, producer. Born Earl Simmons, in Baltimore, Maryland, DMX moved to New York to live with an aunt and built a reputation for himself as a deejay and developed his skills as a rapper. His stage name has two possible origins. One is that he took it from the DMX digital sounds machines he used at the time; the other is that it is an acronym for Dark Man X. He signed with Columbia Records in the early 1990s and released his first single "Born Loser." He went on to appear on albums by rappers **L. L. Cool J**, Mase, and Lox, before signing with Ruff Ryders/Def Jam Records. He released his successful single, "Get At Me Dog," and his number one debuting solo album in 1998, *It's Dark and Hell is Hot*. His first four albums debuted at number one on the *Billboard* charts. After appearing in the movies *Belly*, 1998, and *Romeo Must Die*, 2000, DMX became an action star in his own right, landing a roll opposite Steven Seagal in *Exit Wounds*, 2001. He followed with the action-packed *Cradle 2 the Grave*, 2003, with karate man Jet Li, and played the lead in *Never Die Alone*, 2004.

Filmography: *Belly*, 1998; *Romeo Must Die*, 2000; *Exit Wounds*, 2001; *Cradle 2 the Grave*, 2003; *Never Die Alone*, 2004.

DOBSON, TAMARA. (1947-). Actress. The Baltimore, Maryland-born Dobson was a licensed beautician when she earned a degree in fashion illustration at the Maryland Institute of Art. Standing at a statuesque 6'2" she went to New York and was chosen for a fashion show, then became a *Vogue* model, appearing in a number of **television** commercials. Moving to films, Dobson had small roles in *Come Back, Charleston Blue*, 1972, and *Fuzz*, 1972. Her big screen success came when she landed the title role in *Cleopatra Jones*, 1973. Television appearances include *Jason of Star Command*, as Samantha, during the 1980-81 season, and an episode of *Buck Rogers in the 25th Century*, 1980.

Filmography: *Fuzz*, 1972; *Come Back, Charleston Blue*, 1972; *Cleopatra Jones*, 1973; *Cleopatra Jones and the Casino of Gold*, 1975; *Norman...Is That You?* 1976; *Murder at the World Series*, 1977; *Chained Heat*, 1983; *Amazons*, 1984.

DOCUMENTARY FILMS. These films represent a historical, realistic, or factual record of people, events, and places, often recording or commenting on the human condition. They are often documents of life that are generally devoid of a narrative structure. Noted African American documentary films and filmmakers include: *From These Roots*, by **William Greaves**; *Let the Church Say Amen*, by **St. Clair Bourne**; **Henry Hampton**'s civil rights series, *Eyes on the Prize*; **Stanley Nelson**'s *Two Dollars and a Dream*; Michele Parkerson's *But Then, She's Betty Carter*; **Marlon Riggs**'s *Ethnic Notions*; Debra Robinson's *I Be Done Been Was Is*; and Zeinabu irene Davis' *Trumpetically: That's Clora Bryant*.

DOLEMITE. 1975. (R) 88 min. Blaxploitation. Action and comedy come together in this now classic film by stand-up comic **Rudy Ray Moore**. Falsely accused on trumped-up charges, a convict and his madam friend assemble a team of beautiful and deadly kung fu ladies to break him out of jail, so they can seek revenge on his archenemy and the crooked cops who framed him. It spawned the sequel *Dolemite 2: The Human Tornado*, 1976. Cast: Rudy Ray Moore, **D'Urville Martin**, Jerry Jones, Lady Reeds. Director: D'Urville Martin. Writer: Jerry Jones. Cinematographer: Nicholas Josef von Sternberg. Music: Arthur Wright.

DON'T BE A MENACE TO SOUTH CENTRAL WHILE DRINKING YOUR JUICE IN THE HOOD. 1995. (R) 88 min. Urban Comedy. A parody on the urban based "In-the-Hood" films, such as *Boyz N the Hood*, 1991, *South Central*, 1992, *Juice*, 1992, and *Menace II Society*, 1993. A troublesome young man is sent to live with his father in South Central Los Angeles and starts hanging out with an overzealous, beer-swigging, gun-toting homeboy from around the way. For the sake of comedy, there are plenty of intentional stereotypes and negative representations of what life is like in the hood. Cast: **Shawn Wayans, Marlon Wayans,** Tracey Cherelle Jones, Chris Spencer, Suli McCullough, Darrell Heath, Helen Martin, Isaiah Barnes, Lahmard Tate, **Keenen Ivory Wayans.** Director: **Paris Barclay.** Writers: Shawn Wayans, Marlon Wayans, Phil Beauman. Cinematographer: Russ Brandt. Music: John Barnes.

DOQUI, ROBERT (1934-). Actor. He was born in Stillwater, Oklahoma, and has amassed an impressive list of screen credits, but is perhaps most remembered as the flashy pimp King George from the **blaxploitation**-era film *Coffy*, 1973. He could be seen on the **television** series *Felony Squad, Up and Coming,* and the miniseries *Centennial.* Other notable film roles include *Nashville,* 1975, *Almos' a Man,* 1976, *Short Cuts,* 1993, and the *Robocop* series of films.

　　Filmography: *Clarence the Cross-Eyed Lion,* 1965; *Up Tight!,* 1968; *The Devil's 8,* 1968; *Tarzan's Deadly Silence,* 1970; *The Red, White, and Black,* 1970; *The Man,* 1972; *Coffy,* 1973; *Nashville,* 1975; *Walking Tall Part II,* 1975; *How the West Was Won,* 1978; *I'm Dancing as Fast as I Can,* 1982; *Cloak and Dagger,* 1984; *Fast Forward,* 1985; *My Science Project,* 1985; *Good to Go,* 1986; *RoboCop,* 1987; *Paramedics,* 1987; *Mercenary Fighters,* 1987; *Miracle Mile,* 1988; *Robocop 2,* 1990; *The Court-Martial of Jackie Robinson,* 1990; *Diplomatic Immunity,* 1991; *Original Intent,* 1992; *Robocop 3,* 1993; *Short Cuts,* 1993; *Walking Thunder,* 1997; *A Hollow Place,* 1998; *Glam,* 2001.

DORSEY, REGINALD T. He made his film-acting debut as Junebug in *Book of Numbers,* 1973, and portrayed the role of Cowboy Graham in the western telemovie *The Cherokee Kid,* 1996. His **television** guest appearances include the series *Good Times, Hill Street Blues, The A-Team, Magnum P. I., 21 Jump Street, Renegade,* and *Pacific Blue.*

　　Filmography: *Book of Numbers,* 1974; *Miracle of the Heart: A Boys Town Story,* 1986; *South Central,* 1992; *Why Colors,* 1992; *Return to Lonesome Dove,* 1993; *The Black Man's Guide to Understanding Black Women,* 2005.

DO THE RIGHT THING. 1989. (R) 120 min. Drama. Racial tensions erupt at a white-owned pizza parlor located in a black section of Brooklyn after an unruly patron is brutalized and killed by the police. Cast: Danny Aiello, **Spike Lee,** Richard Edson, **Ruby Dee,**

Ossie Davis, Giancarlo Esposito, Bill Nunn, John Turturro, John Savage, **Rosie Perez,** Frankie Faison. Writer/Director: Spike Lee. Cinematographer: **Ernest R. Dickerson.** Music: Bill Lee. Awards: 1989 Film Critics, Best Director (Lee), Best Film, Best Supporting Actor (Aiello). 1999 National Film Registry. 1989 NY Film Critics, Best Cinematography.

DOUBLE DEAL. 1939. 60 min. Gangster/Drama. A gangster and a good guy bump heads over the same woman. When the gangster robs a jewelry store, he frames his competition for the crime. Cast: **Monte Hawley,** Jeni Le Gon, Edward Thompson, Florence O'Brien. Director: Arthur Dreifuss.

DOUBLE TAKE. 2001. (PG-13) 88 min. Urban Drama. A street hustler and a businessman framed for laundering drug money switch places to get to the bottom of things. Cast: **Orlando Jones, Eddie Griffin,** Gary Grubbs, Daniel Roebuck, Sterling Macer, Garcelle Beauvais, Edward Hermann, Benny Nieves, Shawn Elliott, Brent Briscoe, Carlos Carasco. Writer/Director: George Gallo. Cinematographer: Theo Van de Sande. Music: Graeme Revell.

DOUG, DOUG E. (1970-). Actor, comedian. This Brooklyn, New York, native began his entertainment career at age 17 as a stand-up comic. He made his film debut in **Spike Lee's** *Mo' Better Blues,* 1990. His other notable film appearances include *Jungle Fever,* 1991, *Cool Runnings,* 1993, and *Citizen James,* 2000, which he also wrote, produced, and directed. His **television** guest appearances include roles in *Touched by an Angel, Law & Order: Special Victims Unit,* and *Cosby.*

Filmography: *Mo' Better Blues,* 1990; *Hangin' with the Homeboys,* 1991; *Jungle Fever,* 1991; *Class Act,* 1992; *Dr. Giggles,* 1992; *Cool Runnings,* 1993; *Operation Dumbo Drop,* 1995; *That Darn Cat,* 1997; *Rusty: A Dog's Tale,* 1998; *Everything's Jake,* 2000; *Citizen James,* 2000; *Eight Legged Freaks,* 2002; *Shark Tale,* 2004.

DOUGLASS, SUZZANNE (1957-). Actress. Born in Chicago, Illinois, and made her film debut in *Tap,* 1989. On **television,** she appeared in *Against the Law, Condition Critical,* the miniseries *Story of a People,* and she was a regular on *The Parent Hood.*

Filmography: *Tap,* 1989; *Chain of Desire,* 1992; *I'll Do Anything,* 1994; *The Inkwell,* 1994; *Jason's Lyric,* 1994; *How Stella Got Her Groove Back,* 1998; *The Last Weekend,* 1998; *Alyson's Closet,* 1998; *The School of Rock,* 2003.

DOWN IN THE DELTA. 1998. (PG-13) 111 min. Drama. A trouble-some daughter and her two young children are sent from Chicago to live with relatives in the Mississippi Delta. Once acquainted with a life of drugs and other inner-city temptations, she finds it hard to fit in, but eventually becomes involved in local struggles, and with the love and support of her Southern family, finds her self-respect. Cast: **Alfre Woodard, Al Freeman Jr.**, **Mary Alice, Wesley Snipes, Esther Rolle, Loretta Devine, Anne-Marie Johnson**, Mpho Koaho, Kulani Hassen, Richard Blackburn. Director: **Maya Angelou**. Writer: Myron Goble. Cinematographer: William Wages. Music: **Stanley Clarke**.

DOWN TO EARTH. 2001. (PG-13) 87 min. Comedy/Romance. This is a remake of a remake, à la *Heaven Can Wait*, 1978, or *Here Comes Mr. Jordan*, 1941. A young man dies before his time and arrives in heaven. When the mistake is discovered, he is returned to earth in the body of an older, wealthy, white businessman. He meets a young girl, falls in love, but must now give up the body and the life he has come to know. Cast: **Chris Rock, Regina King**, Chazz Palmenteri, Eugene Levy, Frankie Faison, Mark Addy, Greg Germann, Jennifer Coolidge. Directors: Chris Weitz, Paul Weitz. Writers: Chris Rock, Lance Crouther, Ali LeRoi, Louis CK. Cinematographer: Richard Crudo. Music: Jamshield Sharifi.

DR. BLACK, MR. HYDE. 1976. (R) 88 min. Horror. A black scientist takes a potion that turns him into a white monster. Cast: **Bernie Casey, Rosalind Cash, Stu Gilliam**, Marie O'Henry. Director: **William Crain**.

DR. DOLITTLE. 1998. (PG-13). 85 min. Comedy. A veterinarian gets an increase in business when he learns that he can communicate with animals. However, communicating with his wife and kids becomes a bit more difficult. Cast: **Eddie Murphy, Ossie Davis**, Oliver Platt, Peter Boyle, Richard Schiff, Kristen Wilson, Jeffrey Tambor, Kyla Pratt, Raven Symone, Steven Gilborn, Erik Dellums, June Christopher, Cherie Franklin, Mark Adair-Rios, Don Calfa. Director: Betty Thomas. Writer: Nat Mauldin.

DR. DOLITTLE 2. 2001. (PG) 87 min. Comedy. The man who can talk to the animals sets out to save a forest from being cut down, and preserve an endangered bear species, while trying to maintain a relationship with his own family, including a daughter who is developing powers of her own. Cast: **Eddie Murphy**, Kristen Wilson,

Raven Symone, Kyla Pratt, Lil' Zane, Denise Dowse, James Avery, Elayn Taylor, Andy Richter, Kevin Pollak, Victor Raider-Wexler, Jeffrey Jones, Mark Griffin, Ken Hudson Campbell, Anne Stedman. Director: Steve Carr. Writer: Hugh Lofting, Larry Levin.

DREAMGIRLS. 2006. (PG-13) Music/Drama. Based on the Broadway musical. Three female friends from Chicago in the early 1960s form a singing group called The Dreamettes. They compete in a talent show at the famed **Apollo Theater** in New York and an ambitious but unscrupulous manager devises a plan to take the soulful R&B group to the pop charts. As The Dreams, they rise to international stardom, but their success comes at a price they eventually refuse to pay. Cast: **Beyoncé, Jamie Foxx, Eddie Murphy**, Jennifer Hudson, Keith Robinson, Hinton Battle, Sharon Leal, Anika Noni Rose, **Danny Glover**, Jordan Belfi, Gilbert Glenn Brown, Robert Curtis Brown, Yvette Nicole Brown, Laura Bell Bundy, E.J. Callahan, Yvette Cason, John Centatiempo, Robert Cicchini, Michael Cline, **Loretta Devine**, Colvon Collins, Thomas Crawford. Writer/director: Bill Condon. Cinematographer: Tobias A. Schliessler. Editor: Virginia Katz.

DROP SQUAD. 1994. (R) 88 min. Drama. A vigilante group known as Deprogramming and Restoration of Pride (D. R. O. P.) kidnaps a black advertising executive for pushing questionable products in the black community using cultural stereotypes, and attempts to restore his sense of heritage. Cast: **Eriq LaSalle, Vondie Curtis-Hall, Ving Rhames, Kasi Lemmons, Vanessa Williams**, Nicole Powell, Afemo Omilami, **Spike Lee**. Director: David Johnson. Writers: David Johnson, Butch Robinson, David Taylor. Cinematographer: Ken Kelsch. Music: Michael Bearden.

DRUM. 1976. (R) 110 min. Drama. This is the sequel to the successful slave drama ***Mandingo***, 1975. It is a story of incest, torture, castration, and the blatant mistreatment of black slaves in early 19th-century America. Cast: Ken Norton, **Pam Grier**, Warren Oates, Isela Vega, **Yaphet Kotto**, John Colicos, Fiona Lewis, **Paula Kelly**, Royal Dano, Lillian Hayman, Cheryl Smith, Alain Patrick, **Brenda Sykes**, Clay Tanner, Lila Finn. Director: Steve Carter. Writer: Norman Wexler.

DRUMLINE. 2002. (PG-13) 118 min. Drama. A naturally talented hip-hop drummer from Harlem, New York, receives a full music scholarship to Atlanta A&T University. Known for its dynamic marching band, musicians must earn a spot on line through a pledge routine that requires hard work, discipline, and a respect of authority. These are three qualities the drummer does not have. As a show-off who likes to do his own thing, he butts heads with the section leader and upsets the band leader, but the school president likes what he sees and wants more of it. Mounting school pressures and conflicting attitudes lead to his expulsion from the band, but he eventually gets over his selfishness and works for the good of the band. Cast: **Nick Cannon**, Zoe Saldana, **Orlando Jones**, Leonard Roberts, GQ, Jason Weaver, Earl C. Poitier, Candace Carey, Afemo Omilami, Shay Roundtree, Miguel A. Gaetan, J. Anthony Brown. Director: Charles Stone III. Writers: Shawn Schepps, Tina Gordon Chism. Cinematograher: Shane Hurlbut. Music: John Powell.

DRUMS O'VOODOO (a.k.a *Louisiana She Devil*). 1934. 70 min. Drama. The town villain finds that his days are numbered when a voodoo princess confronts him about his criminal ways. Cast: Laura Bowman, Augustus Smith, Edna Barr, Morris McKenny, Lionel Monagas, Fred Bonny, James Davis. Director: Arthur Hoerl. Writer: Augustus Smith.

DRY WHITE SEASON, A. 1989. (R) 105 min. Drama. This film is a striking indictment on the horror of the apartheid system in South Africa. A white Afrikaner is made aware of the cruelty being unleashed upon blacks when his gardener's son is arrested and killed by police. He takes up the cause to find out what happened and make the guilty parties pay in a court of law, but all does not end well. Cast: Donald Southerland, Marlon Brando, Susan Sarandon, **Zakes Mokae**, Janet Suzzman, Juergen Prochnow, Winston Ntshona, Susannah Harker, Thoko Ntshinga, Rowan Elmes. Director: **Euzhan Palcy**. Writer: Colin Welland, Euzhan Palcy. Music: Dave Grusin.

DUBOIS, JA'NET (1945-). Actress, singer. This native of Philadelphia, Pennsylvania, is perhaps best remembered as Willona, the nosey neighbor on the 1970s sitcom *Good Times*. Other notable TV roles include Grandma Ellington on *The Wayans Bros.*, and she provided the voice of Mrs. Avery on the animated series *The PJ's*. DuBois also co-wrote and performed the theme song to the hit television sitcom *The Jeffersons*.

Filmography: *Sophie & the Moonhanger*, 1996; *Don't Look Back*, 1996; *Best Friends for Life*, 1998; *Hard Time*, 1998; *Waterproof*, 1999; *Charlie's Angels: Full Throttle*, 2003.

DUKE, BILL (1943-). Actor, producer, director. A native of Pough-keepsie, New York, Duke graduated from Boston University with a B. A. degree in 1964, and received an M. A. degree in 1968 from New York University. He began his career as a director of off-Broadway plays and won an Adelco Award for his direction of *Unfinished Business* in 1974. As an actor, he debuted in *American Gigolo*, 1979, and has worked both in front of and behind the camera ever since. Acting jobs include *Predator*, 1987; *Commando*, 1985; and *Action Jackson*, 1988. As a director, he has helmed *A Rage In Harlem*, 1991; *Deep Cover*, 1992; *The Cemetery Club*, 1992; and *Hoodlum*, 1997. He is a former Time/Warner endowed chair at Howard University's Department of Radio, Television, and Film.

Filmography: *American Gigolo*, 1979; *Commando*, 1985; *Predator*, 1987; *Action Jackson*, 1988; *Bird on a Wire*, 1990; *Menace II Society*, 1992; *Payback*, 1998; *Dying to Get Rich*, 1998; *Foolish*, 1999; *Fever*, 1999; *Never Again*, 2001; *Exit Wounds*, 2001; *Red Dragon*, 2002; *National Security*, 2003.

DUKE IS TOPS, THE. 1938. 80 min. Musical. A singer and song-writer team who have worked the vaudeville circuit for years have fallen in love. When a big-time New York talent scout wants to sign up the girl singer as a solo, the smitten songwriter will not stand in her way. Both experience successes and failures, and real-ize in the end that they need each other and are more effective as a team. The film was also released as *Bronze Venus* to take advan-tage of **Lena Horne**'s later stardom. Cast: **Ralph Cooper, Lena Horne, Lawrence Criner, Monte Hawley**, Willie Covan, Neva Peoples, Vernon McCalla, Edward Thompson, Johnny Taylor, Ray Martin, Guernsey Morrow, Charles Hawkins, Marie Bryant, Basin Street Boys, Rubberneck Holmes, Cats and the Fiddle.

DUNBAR HOTEL, THE. This was a home-away-from-home for Afri-can American stars in the 1920s to 1940s, and was the only hotel in Los Angeles that accepted blacks. It was located on Central Ave-nue and built by entrepreneur James Nelson to be a gathering place for local and visiting artists. The Negro Actors Protective League held an organizational meeting at the Dunbar Hotel to protest race bias of Hollywood producers and to address the boycott of black cast films by the Central Avenue district theater owners. Several scenes from the musical film *Georgia Rose*, 1930, about a minister trying to save his daughter from the corruption of cabaret life were shot at this location.

DUPOIS, STARLETTA. Actress. This UCLA Theater Department-trained actress received a Tony Award nomination for Best Featured Actress in a Play for a 1978 production of Richard Wesley's *The Mighty Gents*. She made her film debut in *The Gambler*, 1974, and has made guest appearances on the **television** series *The Jeffersons, Hill Street Blues, St. Elsewhere, Knots Landing, City of Angels,* and *Crossing Jordan*. Her other notable film roles include *Dark Exodus*, 1985; *Hollywood Shuffle*, 1987; *Waiting to Exhale*, 1995; and *The Black Man's Guide to Understanding Black Women*, 2005.

    Filmography: *The Gambler*, 1974; *The Torture of Mothers*, 1980; *Odd Jobs*, 1984; *Pee-Wee's Big Adventure*, 1985; *Dark Exodus*, 1985; *Hollywood Shuffle*, 1987; *Convicts*, 1990; *Ricochet*, 1991; *Last Breeze of Summer*, 1991; *Frogs!* 1991; *The Waterdance*, 1992; *South Central*, 1992; *Let's Get Bizzee*, 1993; *The Thing Called Love*, 1993; *Strapped*, 1993; *Wolf*, 1994; *Waiting to Exhale*, 1995; *The Maker*, 1997; *3 Strikes*, 2000; *Big Momma's House*, 2000; *Friday After Next*, 2003; *The Notebook*, 2004; *Duck*, 2004; *The Black Man's Guide to Understanding Black Women*, 2005.

DUTCHMAN. 1966. 55 min. Drama. This film is based on Amiri Baraka's controversial stage play about white society's blatant contempt for the black race. A white woman befriends a black man on the subway and the results are disastrous. Cast: **Al Freeman Jr.**, Shirley Knight, Frank Lieberman, Robert Calvert, Howard Bennett, Sandy McDonald, Dennis Alaba Peters, Keith James, Devon Hall. Director: Anthony Harvey. Writer: Amiri Baraka.

DUTTON, CHARLES (1951-). Actor, director, producer. After a serious brush with the law, this native of Baltimore, Maryland, attended Yale Drama School and Towson University. He became well known with his own successful **television** sitcom, *Roc*, 1991, which ran for several seasons on Fox. In order to challenge his cast and push the ratings, Dutton chose to broadcast the last season live. He has also played powerful, indomitable characters in films, such as *The Distinguished Gentleman*, 1992; *Surviving the Game*, 1994; and *The Piano Lesson*, 1994. He has directed the films *Against the Ropes*, 2004, and *Mama Black Widow*, 2002, as well as the TV miniseries *The Corner*, 2000. He was executive producer on the TV series *Laurel Avenue*, 1993.

    Filmography: *Cat's Eye*, 1985; *Crocodile Dundee 2*, 1988; *Jacknife*, 1989; *Q&A*, 1990; *Mississippi Masala*, 1992; *The Distinguished Gentleman*, 1992; *Alien 3*, 1992; *Menace II Society*,

1992; *Rudy*, 1993; *Surviving the Game*, 1994; *The Piano Lesson*, 1994; *A Low Down Dirty Shame*, 1994; *Zooman*, 1995; *Cry, the Beloved Country*, 1995; *A Time to Kill*, 1996; *Get on the Bus*, 1996; *Mimic*, 1997; *Blind Faith*, 1998; *Black Dog*, 1998; *Cookie's Fortune*, 1999; *Aftershock: Earthquake in New York*, 1999; *For Love or Country: The Arturo Sandoval Story*, 2000; *Deadlocked*, 2000; *Eye See You*, 2001; *10,000 Black Men Named George*, 2002; *Against the Ropes*, 2004; *Secret Window*, 2004.

E

EALY, MICHAEL (1973-). Actor. He was born in Silver Spring, Maryland, and made his film debut as Isaac Youngblood in *The Lush Life*, 2000. He portrayed the character of Calvin McDade in the TV series *Metropolis*, and was Tea Cake in the telepic *Their Eyes Were Watching God*, 2005. Other film roles include *Barbershop*, 2002, *2 Fast 2 Furious*, 2003, and *Never Die Alone*, 2004.
   Filmography: *The Lush Life*, 2000; *Kissing Jessica Stein*, 2001; *Bad Company*, 2002; *Barbershop*, 2002; *Justice*, 2003; *2 Fast 2 Furious*, 2003; *Never Die Alone*, 2004; *Barbershop 2: Back in Business*, 2004; *Their Eyes Were Watching God*, 2005.

EDMONDS, KENNETH "BABYFACE" (1959-). Singer, songwriter, music and film producer. Edmonds was born into a musically talented family in Indianapolis, Indiana. He started writing songs at an early age and decided to pursue a music career after he performed at a high school dance in his brother's band. After graduating from North Central High School Class of 1976, he eagerly pursued his musical interests by joining several bands leading up to The Deele in the 1980s. After three albums and several pop and R&B hits, he signed with Solar Records to begin his solo career. Teaming up with former The Deele drummer, Antonia "L. A." Reid, the two became the powerhouse producing team behind **Bobby Brown**, **Whitney Houston**, and Paula Abdul. In 1989, they formed the record label LaFace and signed such artists as Toni Braxton and TLC. As a multi-faceted award-winning artist, Babyface has continued his solo career while writing, producing, and helping to shepherd others to stardom. He has won Grammy Awards for his album *For the Cool in You*, as writer for the hit song "End of the Road," performed by Boys II Men, and a Grammy for Producer of the Year. In film, he has produced the music soundtrack for *Waiting to Exhale*, 1995; co-distributed the independent film *Hav Plenty*, 1997; and produced the hit film *Soulfood*, 1997, with his wife, **Tracey Edmonds**.

Filmography: *Hav Plenty*, 1997; *Soul Food*, 1997; *Light It Up*, 1999; *Punks*, 2000; *Josie and the Pussycats*, 2001.

EDMONDS, TRACEY (1967-). Producer. The Los Angeles-born Edmonds is the president and CEO of Edmonds Entertainment Group, and former wife of **Kenneth "Babyface" Edmonds**. She began producing independent films with *Hav Plenty*, 1997, in which she also had a cameo role. She produced *Soulfood*, 1997, and was executive producer on the cable spin-off series. In 2006 she teamed with media magnate Bob Johnson to create Our Story Studio, the first black-owned movie studio in Hollywood history.

Filmography: *Hav Plenty*, 1997; *Soul Food*, 1997; *Light It Up*, 1999; *Punks*, 2000; *Josie and the Pussycats*, 2001, *Robbin Hoods*, 2005.

EDUCATION OF SONNY CARSON, THE. 1974. (R) 104 min. Drama. Drugs, prostitution, and crime surround a young man's life growing up in a Brooklyn ghetto. Cast: Rony Clanton, Don Gordon, Paul Benjamin, Joyce Walker, Thomas Hicks, **Mary Alice**, Ram John Holder, Jerry Bell. Director: Michael Campus. Writers: Sonny Carson, Fred Hudson.

EDWARDS, JAMES (1918-1970). Actor. One of the early actors to raise the status of black male roles out of mere comic buffoonery and away from the **Stepin Fetchit** stereotype. He brought strength, power, and dignity to his roles and is perhaps best known for his leading role in producer Stanley Kramer's war-torn **Problem Picture**, *Home of the Brave*, 1949.

Filmography: *The Set-Up*, 1949; *Home of the Brave*, 1949; *The Steel Helmet*, 1951; *The Member of the Wedding*, 1952; *The Killing*, 1956; *Men in War*, 1957; *Pork Chop Hill*, 1959; *The Manchurian Candidate*, 1962; *Patton*, 1970.

ELDER, LONNE, III (1927-1996). Born in Americus, Georgia, Elder became the first African American screenwriter to be nominated for an **Academy Award** for Best Screenplay based on material from another medium for *Sounder*, 1972. William H. Armstrong shared the writing credit, but was not a co-nominee. Elder began writing for **television** in the 1950s and has written episodes for the series *N. Y. P. D.* and *McCloud*. For the stage, he wrote the play *Ceremonies in Dark Old Men*, and adapted it for television. His feature film writing credits include *Melinda*, 1972; *Sounder: Part 2*, 1976; and *Bustin' Loose*, 1981.

Filmography: *Sounder*, 1972; *Melinda*, 1972; *Sounder: Part 2*, 1976; *Bustin' Loose*, 1981.

ELISE, KIMBERLY (1971-). Actress. This native of Minneapolis, Minnesota, graduated from the University of Minnesota with a degree in communications. She performed in local theater before enrolling at the American Film Institute in Los Angeles, graduating in 1995. Since making her film debut in *Set It Off*, 1996, Elise has costarred in *Bait*, 2000, and two films opposite **Denzel Washington**: *John Q*, 2002, and *The Manchurian Candidate*, 2004. She won the Chicago Film Critic's Award for Most Promising Actress and a Golden Satellite Award for Best Supporting Actress for her performance in *Beloved*, 1998, and a Cable Ace Award for her performance in the telefilm *The Ditchdigger's Daughter*, 1997. Her other telefilms include *The Loretta Clairborne Story*, 2000, and *Bojangles*, 2001. She has been awarded a $25,000 grant from the Minnesota Independent Film Fund to direct *Snow in April*, based on her original screenplay. She was also selected to receive an emerging artists grant from the **Academy of Motion Picture Arts and Sciences** for her film *Cornroll*.

Filmography: *Set It Off*, 1996; *Beloved*, 1998; *Bait*, 2000; *John Q*, 2002; *Woman Thou Art Loosed*, 2004; *The Manchurian Candidate*, 2004.

EMBALMER. 1996. (NR) 87:30 min. Horror. This film is based on an urban legend about a deranged mortician who slaughtered his own family with his scalpel, and now seeks fresh blood and body fluids to bring them back to life. Four runaway friends decide to hide out at Undertaker Zach's abandoned funeral parlor and discover that the neighborhood myth is in fact a reality. Cast: Jennifer T. Kelly, Kenneth Mullen, Myron Creek, Tracy Lynn Owens, Dexter K. Tennie, Cynthia Webb, Andre M. Manly, Alena V. Joseph, Anita Cooper, Henry Joseph III. Writer/director/cinematographer/editor: S. Torriano Berry. Music: Andre Epps.

EMMY AWARDS. The Emmy Awards are administered by three sister organizations, the Academy of Television Arts and Sciences, the National Academy of Television Arts and Sciences, and the International Academy of Television Arts and Sciences, to recognize excellence within various areas of the television industry. The awards are a symbol of peer recognition from over 12,000 members of the Academy, each of whom casts a ballot for the category of competition in his/her field of expertise. Prominent areas of competition include the Primetime Awards, Daytime Awards, the Los Angeles Area Awards, as well as categories for sports, news, and documentary programming.

EMPEROR JONES, THE. 1933. 72 min. Drama. Based on the stage play by Eugene O'Neil, an ambitious Pullman porter gets into a fight after a crooked crap game and receives a life sentence for murder. He escapes from the chain gang and takes a job as a stoker on a steam ship sailing to Haiti. He jumps ship and uses tricks and superstition to take control of a remote Caribbean island. Having everything he ever wanted, he becomes a tyrant and the people rise up in revolt. Cast: **Paul Robeson**, Dudley Digges, Frank Wilson, **Fredi Washington**, Ruby Elzy. Director: Dudley Murphy. Awards: National Film Registry 1999.

EPPS, OMAR (1973-). Actor. This Brooklyn, New York, native made his big-screen debut in ***Juice***, 1992, and continued his rise to stardom with a string of hit films, including ***Higher Learning***, 1995; ***Love and Basketball***, 2000; and *Against the Ropes*, 2004. On **television**, he portrays Dr. Eric Foreman on the medical drama series *House*.

Filmography: ***Perfume***, 1990; *Juice*, 1992; *The Program*, 1993; *Major League II*, 1994; *Higher Learning*, 1995; *Scream II*, 1997; *The Mod Squad*, 1999; ***The Wood***, 1999; *In Too Deep*, 1999; *Breakfast of Champions*, 1999; *Love and Basketball*, 2000; *Dracula 2000*, 2000; *Brother*, 2001; *Big Trouble*, 2002; *Against the Ropes*, 2004; *Alfie*, 2004.

ERNEST GREEN STORY, THE. 1993. (TV-G) 92 min. Biopic. The film is based on the integration of Central High School in Little Rock, Arkansas, in 1957. Nine black students face racism and verbal and physical abuse from the white students, and unfair academic treatment from the teachers. Ernest Green, the only senior in the group, is determined to graduate. Cast: Sonny Shroyer, **Morris Chestnut**, **CCH Pounder**, Gary Grubbs, Tina Lifford, **Avery Brooks**, **Ruby Dee**, **Ossie Davis**. Director: **Eric Laneuville**.

ESPOSITO, GIANCARLO (1958-). Actor. Born in Copenhagen, Denmark, Esposito is a stage-trained actor who has played supporting roles in many films and **television** programs. He played Broadway at age eight in the 1966 run of *Maggie Flynn*, with Shirley Jones. His other stage work includes *Miss Moffatt*, with Betty Davis, *Balm in Gilead*, directed by John Malkovich, and

Zooman and the Sign. On the big screen, Esposito has kept very busy and has been a featured player in many **Spike Lee** films. Filmography: *The Cotton Club*, 1984; *Desperately Seeking Susan*, 1985; *Maximum Overdrive*, 1986; *Sweet Lorraine*, 1987; **School Daze**, 1988; **Do the Right Thing**, 1989, *Mo' Better Blues*, 1990; *King of New York*, 1990; *Harley Davidson and the Marlboro Man*, 1991; *Night on Earth*, 1992; *Bob Roberts*, 1992; *Malcolm X*, 1992; *Amos and Andrew*, 1993; *Fresh*, 1994; *Smoke*, 1995; *The Usual Suspects*, 1995; *Blue in the Face*, 1995; *Reckless*, 1995; *Nothing to Lose*, 1997; *The Keeper*, 1997; *Twilight*, 1998; *Phoenix*, 1998; *Trouble on the Corner*, 1998; *Monkeybone*, 2001; *Pinero*, 2001; *Ali*, 2001.

ETHNIC NOTIONS. 1986. (TV) 57 min. Documentary. This **Emmy Award**–winning documentary explores the images and deep-rooted **stereotypes** in society that perpetrate racism and anti-black prejudice. It is a survey of the dehumanizing caricatures and practices that permeated popular culture from the 1820s through the Civil Rights era with commentary by respected scholars. It presents a context in which viewers can begin to understand the evolution of America's racial consciousness. Cast: Barbera T. Christian. Narrator: **Esther Rolle**. Writer/Director: **Marlon Riggs**.

EVANS, ART (1942-). Actor. This native of Berkeley, California, has amassed a long list of credits on stage, **television**, and film. His first notable film role was a Blind Lemon Jefferson in the film *Leadbelly*, 1976. He portrayed the character of Private Wilkie in the stage and screen versions of *A Soldier's Story*, 1984, and portrayed A. D. King in the TV miniseries *King*, 1978. His **television** work includes appearances in the series *Hill Street Blues*, *In the Heat of the Night*, *A Different World*, *Mad About You*, *Walker: Texas Ranger*, *City of Angels*, and *The X Files*. He teaches acting classes and is an acting coach in Los Angeles, California.

Filmography: *Amazing Grace*, 1974; *Claudine*, 1974; *Leadbelly*, 1976; *Fun with Dick and Jane*, 1977; *Big Time*, 1977; *Youngblood*, 1978; *I Know Why the Caged Bird Sings*, 1979; *The In-Laws*, 1979; *The Main Event*, 1979; *The Apple Dumpling Gang Rides Again*, 1979; *Wright is Wrong*, 1982; *Class Reunion*, 1982; *A Soldier's Story*, 1984; *Tuff Turf*, 1985; *Into the Night*, 1985; *Fright Night*, 1985; *Jo Jo Dancer, Your Life Is Calling*, 1986; *Ruthless People*, 1986; *Native Son*, 1986; *School Daze*, 1988; *The Mighty Quinn*, 1989; *Downtown,* 1990; *Die Hard 2*, 1990; *Mom*, 1990; *Moe's World*, 1990; *Trespass*, 1992; *CB4*, 1993; *Bitter Harvest*, 1993; *Tales from the Hood*, 1995; *The Great White Hype*,

1996; *Metro*, 1997; ***Always Outnumbered, Always Outgunned***, 1998; *The Breaks*, 1999; *Deadly Rhapsody*, 2001; *Sonny Listening*, 2002; *Interstate 60*, 2002; *Gas*, 2004; *Anderson's Cross*, 2004; *The Black Man's Guide to Understanding Black Women*, 2005.

EVE'S BAYOU. 1997. (R) 109 min. Drama. Set in 1962 and told in flashback, a 10-year-old girl sets in motion the events that would get her womanizing father killed. Cast: **Samuel L. Jackson, Lynn Whitfield, Debbi Morgan, Diahann Carroll, Jurnee Smollett, Meagan Good, Vondie Curtis-Hall, Lisa Nicole Carson**, Jake Smollett, Ethel Ayler. Writer/Director: **Kasi Lemmons**. Cinematographer: Amy Vincent. Music: **Terence Blanchard**. Narrator: Tamara Tunie. Awards: 1998 Independent Spirit First Feature Award, Best Supporting Actress (Morgan).

F

FALANA, LOLA (1942-). Actress, dancer, singer. She was born Loletha Elaine Falana and began dancing in nightclubs while she was still in junior high school. Determined and ambitious, she relocated to New York City to begin her career in show business, but it did not happen overnight and she often fell on hard times. Her big break came when entertainer extraodinaire **Sammy Davis Jr.** saw her in an Atlantic City chorus line and hired her as the lead dancer in his Broadway show, *Golden Boy*, in 1964. As a singer, Falana released her first single called "My Baby" and was invited to perform on the popular television variety show *Hullabaloo*. Moving to film, she had a small part in **A Man Called Adam**, 1966, with Sammy Davis Jr., **Ossie Davis**, and Frank Sinatra. The world of Las Vegas welcomed her with an opening spot for comedian Don Adams. In 1967, Falana began making movies in Italy, where she was hailed as the Black Venus. Her first Italian film was the spaghetti western *Lola Colt: Face to Face with the Devil*. The following year she made two more, *Stasera Mi Butto* and *Quando Dico Che Ti Amo*, 1968. Her **television** acting career began in 1969 in *The FBI*, and appearances on *Hollywood Palace* and the *Joey Bishop Show*. Her first starring role in an American film was in famed director William Wyler's ***The Liberation of L. B. Jones***, 1970. She also portrayed the title role in ***Lady Cocoa***, 1975. She continued to act throughout the 1970s on both stage and screen, winning numerous awards. She moved into advertising with a series of highly successful ads for Faberge Tigress perfume. Falana also hosted her own variety series.

Filmography: *A Man Called Adam*, 1956; *The Liberation of L. B. Jones*, 1970; *The Klansman*, 1974; *Lady Cocoa*, 1975.

FANAKA, JAMAA (1942-). Writer, producer, director. He was born in Jackson, Mississippi, and studied his craft as one of the **UCLA Rebellion** film students in the 1970s. He has remained an independent filmmaker writing, producing, and directing with six films to his credit, including the *Penitentiary* series of urban dramas starring **Leon Isaac Kennedy**.

Filmography: *Soul Vengeance*, 1975; *Black Sister's Revenge*, 1976; *Penitentiary*, 1979; *Penitentiary 2*, 1982; *Penitentiary 3*, 1987; *Street Wars*, 1992.

FARGAS, ANTONIO (1946-). Actor. He was born in New York City and is perhaps best remembered as Huggy Bear in the **television** series *Starsky and Hutch*. He appeared in several **blaxploitation** films, including *Shaft*, 1971; *Cleopatra Jones*, 1973; and *Foxy Brown*, 1974, as well as the comedy spoof *I'm Gonna Git You Sucka*, 1988. His television guest appearances include roles in *The Bill Cosby Show*, *Sanford and Son*, *The Fresh Prince of Bel-Air*, *Martin*, and *Living Single*.

Filmography: *The Cool World*, 1964; *Three*, 1969; *Putney Swope*, 1969; *Pound*, 1970; *Shaft*, 1971; *Believe in Me*, 1971; *Cisco Pike*, 1972; *Across 110th Street*, 1972; *Cleopatra Jones*, 1973; *Busting*, 1974; *Foxy Brown*, 1974; *Conrack*, 1974; *The Gambler*, 1974; *Cornbread, Earl & Me*, 1975; *Car Wash*, 1976; *Pretty Baby*, 1978; *Up the Academy*, 1980; *Streetwalkin'*, 1984; *Firestarter*, 1984; *Shakedown*, 1988; *I'm Gonna Git You Sucka*, 1988; *Percy & Thunder*, 1993; *Three Strikes*, 2000; *Extreme Honor*, 2001; *Lesser of Three Evils*, 2005.

FARINA (1920-1980). Actor. He was born Allen Hoskins in Boston, Massachusetts, and became the highest-paid child actor on the *Our Gang* series of films during the 1930s.

Filmography: *Seeing the World*, 1927; *Spook Spoofing*, 1928; *Rainy Days*, 1928; *The Holy Terror*, 1929; *The First Seven Years*, 1930; *Teacher's Pet*, 1930; *Helping Grandma*, 1931; *Fly My Kite*, 1931; *You Said a Mouthful*, 1932, *Fish Hooky*, 1933; *The Life of Jimmy Dolan*, 1933; *The Mayor of Hell*, 1933; *Reckless*, 1935; *Winterset*, 1936; *Krakatoa, East of Java*, 1969.

FAT ALBERT, 2004. (PG) 93 min. Comedy. This film is derived from the successful animated series based on a comedy routine by **Bill Cosby**. In this live-action version, a teen girl is sad that she has no friends. When a tear hits her TV remote control, Fat Albert and the Cosby Kids tumble out of the TV set and into the real world. As they wait for the next day's broadcast to return to their animated world, they spend the day with the girl and help her to make new friends. Cast: **Kenan Thompson**, Kyla Pratt, Shedrack Anderson III, Jermaine Williams, Keith Robinson, Alphonso McAuley, Aaron Frazier, Marques Houston, Dania Ramirez, Omarion Grandberry, J. Mack Slaughter, Rick Overton, Keri Lynn Pratt, Alice Greczyn, Farnsworth Bentley. Director: Joel Zwick. Writers: Bill Cosby, Charles Kipps.

FEAR OF A BLACK HAT. 1994. (R) 87 min. Comedy. This is a behind-the-music spoof about a trio of out-of-sync rappers, Ice Cold, Tone-Def, and Tasty-Taste, who call themselves NWH (Niggaz With Hats). On tour promoting their new album, a female filmmaker questions their hard-core image, causing the group to be a lot more of what they are not. Cast: **Larry B. Scott**, Mark Christopher Lawrence, **Rusty Cundieff, Kasi Lemmons**. Writer/Director: Rusty Cundieff. Cinematographer: **John L. Demps**.

FEAST OF ALL SAINTS, THE. 2001. (R) 100 min. Romance/Drama. This film is based on the novel by Anne Rice and is the complicated story of life and the conflicting lifestyles of a higher class of free blacks living in New Orleans during the 19th century. They are caught within a pre-Civil War world of passion and power, but find they are still trapped and controlled by white privilege and black oppression. Cast: Robert Richard, Peter Gallagher, Gloria Reuben, **Jennifer Beals, Ossie Davis, Ruby Dee, Pam Grier, Jasmine Guy, James Earl Jones, Eartha Kitt, Ben Vereen, Forest Whitaker**, Jenny Levine, Bianca Lawson, Nicole Lyn. Director: Peter Medak. Writer: John Wilder. Cinematographer: Edward J. Pei. Music: Patrick Seymour.

FEGAN, ROY (1961-). Actor. He was born in Los Angeles, California, and began his acting career in two UCLA graduate student productions, Gay Abel-Bey's *Fragrance*, 1981; and Nancy Jones's *Mothers and Daughters*, 1981. He landed his first Hollywood film role in *They Call Me Bruce?* 1982, and was cast in three films directed by **Robert Townsend, Hollywood Shuffle**, 1987; **The Five Heartbeats**, 1991; and **The Meteor Man**, 1993. Fegan also appeared on the HBO special *The Best of Robert Townsend & His*

Partners in Crime, 1991. Other television credits include *Sisters*, *227, Hangin' With Mr. Cooper, Murphy Brown, Martin, The Jamie Foxx Show, Will & Grace*, and *The Shield*.

Filmography: *Fragrance*, 1981; *Mothers and Daughters*, 1981; *They Call Me Bruce*, 1982; *Hollywood Shuffle*, 1987; ***I'm Gonna Git You Sucka***, 1988; *Syngenor*, 1990; *The Three Muscatels*, 1991; *The Five Heartbeats*, 1991; *The Meteor Man*, 1993; ***House Party 3***, 1994; *The Cherokee Kid*, 1996; *The Cheapest Movie Ever Made*, 2000; *Midnight Blue*, 2000, *Thug Life*, 2001.

FERRELL, TYRA. Actress. Born in Houston, Texas, her stage credits include Broadway's *Lena Horne: The Lady and Her Music*. She made her **television** debut in the series *Moonlighting*, and made guest appearances on *Hunter, Full House, The Shield*, and *Soul Food*. She had recurring roles on *Thirtysomething*, and *ER*, and she was a regular on *The Cape*. Her film roles include ***Boyz N the Hood***, 1991, ***White Men Can't Jump***, 1992, and the HBO miniseries *The Corner*, 2000.

Filmography: *So Fine*, 1981; *Gimme an 'F'*, 1984; *Nuts*, 1987; ***School Daze***, 1988; *Tapeheads*, 1988; ***The Mighty Quinn***, 1989; *The Exorcist III*, 1990; *Boyz N the Hood*, 1991; ***Jungle Fever***, 1991; *White Men Can't Jump*, 1992; *Equinox*, 1992; *Ulterior Motives*, 1992; ***Poetic Justice***, 1993; *The Corner*, 2000.

FETCHIT, STEPIN (1902-1985). Actor. Born in Key West, Florida, Lincoln Theodore Monroe Andrew Perry became a controversial character archetype in early sound films. At one time, he was among the highest-paid actors in Hollywood for playing a slow-minded, lazy, slurred-talking character who was all the time serving and cowtowing to whites. He began his show business career in the Royal American Shows plantation reviews, performing with his partner, Ed Lee, under the names "Step 'n' Fetchit: Two Dancing Fools from Dixie." Fetchit appeared in many films, including *Old Kentucky*, 1927; ***Hearts in Dixie***, 1929; *Swing High*, 1930; and *One More Spring*, 1936. His role in *Hearts in Dixie* was actually expanded once production began and producers realized his comedic potential. Known on the street as "The High Steppin' Fetchit," he spent the money he made on an extravagant lifestyle, and filed for bankruptcy in the 1930s. Later film appearances include ***Miracle in Harlem***, 1949; *Amazing Grace*, 1974; and *Won Ton Ton, The Dog Who Saved Hollywood*, 1976.

Filmography: *Old Kentucky*, 1927; *Hearts in Dixie*, 1929; *Swing High*, 1930; *Wild Horse*, 1931; *Stand Up and Cheer*, 1934; *Judge Priest*, 1934; *One More Spring*, 1936; *On the Avenue*, 1937;

Miracle in Harlem, 1938; *Miracle in Harlem*, 1949; *The Sun Shines Bright*, 1953; *Amazing Grace*, 1974; *Won Ton Ton, The Dog Who Saved Hollywood*, 1976.

FIGHTING TEMPTATIONS, THE. 2003. (PG-13) 123 min. Music/Comedy. An up-and-coming New York advertising agent receives an inheritance, but he must return to the small Georgia town where he grew up for the reading of the will. He learns that to receive the money, he must first take on his dead aunt's choir; prepare them for a national choir competition...and win. Cast: **Cuba Gooding Jr.**, **Beyoncé**, Nigel Washington, Chloe Bailey, Demetress Long, Ann Nesby, Faith Hill, **Melba Moore**, LaTanya Washington, Ricky Dillard, Larry John Meyers, Shirley Caesar, LaTanya Richardson, **Wendell Pierce**, Lou Myers, Lourdes Benedicto. Director: Johnathan Lynn. Writer: Elizabeth Hunter.

FILM GENRES. A genre is a recognizable type of movie with a ready-made narrative form that is characterized by specific character types and pre-established conventions, such as comedy, drama, science fiction, or suspense. Genre films exclusive to African American cinema include Blaxploitation, Urban Drama, and Urban Romance films.

Blaxploitation: African Americans were fresh off the Civil Rights Movement of the 1960s and fired up when maverick filmmaker **Melvin Van Peebles**'s stark, anti-hero flick *Sweet Sweetback's Baadasssss Song*, 1971, ushered in a series of hard-hitting films that depicted black people taking it to "the Man" and fighting the system. These films often dealt with the seedier side of black life and emphasized ghetto environments teeming with the aftereffects of drugs, illicit sex, and violence. This was one of the most productive periods of black film production lasting from 1971-1976. It became a new film genre and created a fresh crop of on-screen heroes, including **Richard Roundtree**: *Shaft*; **Ron O'Neil**: *Superfly*; **Max Julien**: *The Mack*; **Jim Brown**: *Slaughter*; **Robert Hooks**: *Trouble Man*; **Bernie Casey**: *Hit Man*; **Fred Williamson**: *Hammer*, and *Nigger Charley*. Popular female character icons of this period were **Pam Grier**: *Coffy* and *Friday Foster*; **Lola Falana**: *Lady Coco*; and **Tamara Dobson**: *Cleopatra Jones*.

Comedy: African Americans often bore the brunt end of jokes, or were used to make people laugh in mainstream society and on the vaudeville stage. Many early films continued to exploit this comic persona, often to the detriment of the entire race. Several degrading examples, such as *The Wooing and Wedding of a Coon*, 1905, featured white actors in **blackface** portraying racially offensive characters. Vaudeville performer **Bert Williams** was the first African American to be featured as a star, in the motion picture *Darktown Jubilee*, 1914. Other popular vaudeville performers who made successful transitions to the big screen include **Mantan Moreland**, in *Mantan Messes Up*, 1946; **Dewey "Pigmeat" Markham**, in *House-Rent Party*, 1946; and **Eddie Green** in *The Devil's Parade*, 1930; and *Mr. Adam's Bomb*, 1949. The 1970s became the Dawn of the Crossover Comedians as stand-up comic **Richard Pryor** ushered in a host of highly successful comedy films such as *Silver Streak*, 1976; *Car Wash*, 1976; *Which Way Is Up*, 1977; and *Stir Crazy*, 1980. He paved the way for a flurry of other comedian-turned-actor activity that included **Eddie Murphy** and **Whoopi Goldberg**, both often appearing as the sole black lead of a mainstream film. Live concert films included Richard Pryor: *Live on the Sunset Strip*; Eddie Murphy: *Delirious*; and *Bill Cosby: Himself*. Urban Comedy has evolved from a focus on the ghetto or inner-city urban lifestyle. A number of films portray this element, such as *Friday*, 1995; *Next Friday*, 2000; *Friday After Next*, 2002; and *Don't Be a Menace to South Central While Drinking Your Juice in the Hood*, 1996.

Gangster Films: Inspired by the highly successful mobster movies of the 1930s with film stars such as George Raft and James Cagney, famed Apollo Theater emcee-turned-actor **Ralph Cooper** teamed up with producer Harry Popkin to create Million Dollar Productions. Their company produced the gangster films *Dark Manhattan*, 1937; *Bargain with Bullets*, 1937; and *Gang War*, 1940. These films paralleled the basic constructs of focusing on the criminal element in society with mob shootouts, racketeering, turf battles, and tough crime bosses fighting to maintain their own lucrative, though illegal spoils. **Oscar Micheaux** touched on the gangster genus with his films *Easy Street*, 1930, and *Underworld*, 1937. Popular actors of the genre include **Alfred "Slick" Chester**, known as "the Colored Cagney," and **Lorenzo "The Black Valentino" Tucker**. More contemporary versions of this genre or gangsta films include *Hoodlum*, 1986; *King of New York*, 1990; and *A Rage in Harlem*, 1991.

Drama: There are two main parts to dramatic narrative structure: The story, or what happens and to whom, and the discourse, or how the story unfolds. Conflict is the essence of drama, and the purpose of a dramatic story line is to move or touch the audience in some emotional way. There is usually a struggle going on that is wrought with hardships, difficulty, and pain: *Sounder*, 1974. Or, someone has an important goal to reach and someone else says no: *The Jackie Robinson Story*, 1950. Dramas are generally serious stories depicting life situations in a realistic way with characters behaving at their worst and their best. These heart-wrenching tales of trouble and woe can take on many forms: Man against man: *The Defiant Ones*, 1958. Man against society: *Sweet Sweetback's Baadasssss Song*, 1971. Man against nature: *Cast Away*, 2000. Man against machine: *I-Robot*, 2005. By the 1980s, some areas of the inner cities of American had become virtual war zones caused by an influx of illegal drugs and the gang violence that erupted due to the harsh turf battles that followed. One of the first films to reflect this state of urban strife in an honest way was **John Singleton**'s, *Boyz N the Hood*, 1991. Many other Urban Dramas soon exploited this newfound reality and created a popular new genre characterized by guns, drugs, violence, and revenge. Such films as *New Jack City*, 1991; *Juice*, 1992; *South Central*, 1992; and *Menace II Society*, 1993, were "keeping it real." They were also keeping an audience in the theater seats. There were also softer tales from the hood that explored life's hardships and interpersonal relationships, such as *The Women of Brewster Place*, 1989; *There Are No Children Here*, 1993; and *Lackawanna Blues*, 2005.

Horror: These scary movies with dark and macabre plots and characters often ooze with blood and gore. Audiences witness murder, death, and mayhem vicariously while munching popcorn from the safety of their seat in a crowded movie theater. Early black horror movies include *Son of Ingagi*, 1940; *Professor Creeps*, 1941; and the horror/comedy *Fight That Ghost*, 1946. The **blaxploitation** boom of the 1970s included the horror films *Blackula*, 1972; *The Thing With Two Heads*, 1972; and *Dr. Black, Mr. Hyde*, 1976. The black film renaissance of the 1990s provided the independently produced *Def by Temptation*, 1990, and *Tales from the Hood*, 1995. Straight-to-video releases in this genre include Ron Armstrong's *Bugged!*, 1996, and S. Torriano Berry's *Embalmer*, 1996.

Romance: Love stories are always ripe with passion, tension, betrayal, forgiveness, revenge, conflict, and lots of controversy...which all makes for good cinema. Some films focus on the search, *Waiting to Exhale*, 1995; others on the journey, *No Time for Romance*, 1948; and many explore the break-ups, *A Thin Line Between Love & Hate*, 1996. Two early relationship pictures from the 1960s with African American leads were the interracial *A Patch of Blue*, 1965, and *For Love of Ivy*, 1968, both of which starred screen idol **Sidney Poitier**. The 1970s brought *Aaron Loves Angela*, 1975; *Claudine*, 1975; and *Sparkle*, 1976. In the 1990s, the focus shifted to inner-city love themes, which brought about a string of urban romance movies, including *Poetic Justice*, 1993; *Jason's Lyric*, 1994; *Love Jones*, 1996; *The Wood*, 1999; *The Best Man*, 2000;

and *Brown Sugar*, 2002. In 2000, **Black Entertainment Television** purchased the Arabesque line of romance novels from Kensington Publishing and turned many of these books into films.

Westerns: These movies usually take place in the Wild West or out on the lawless prairie during America's formative years circa the 1800s. Horse riding, fistfights, and "shoot'em up" shootouts are common staples of these exciting films. Ten-gallon hats, cowboy boots, chaps, and spurs are common wardrobe. Two early Westerns of the silent era were *The Crimson Skull*, 1922, and *The Bull-Dogger*, 1921. Both featured the rodeo talents of famed cowboy Bill Pickett. In the late 1930s, popular big band vocalist **Herbert Jeffrey**, who would later become known as Herb Jeffries, became a singing cowboy known as "The Bronze Buckeroo," in a series of films beginning with *Harlem on the Prairie*, 1938. Scat-musician **Louis Jordan** starred in *Look-Out Sister*, 1946; funnyman **Mantan Moreland** rides tall in *Come On, Cowboy*, 1948; and former UCLA football star **Woody Strode** portrayed the title role in *Sergeant Rutledge*, 1961. Blaxploitation-era films of this genre include *Buck and the Preacher*, 1972, and *Thomasine and Bushrod*, 1974. The solo offering to come out of the black film renaissance era of the 1990s is *Posse*, 1999, the action-packed Spanish-American War drama starring and directed by **Mario Van Peebles**.

FILM LIFE PICTURES. Entrepreneur and Acapulco Black Film Festival organizer Jeff Friday founded this New York-based film distribution company in January 2001. As part of a new breed of African American-owned distribution companies, Friday devised novel ways to collect crucial marketing data and generate a buzz in hopes of enticing theaters to carry their first film, *One Week*, 2001. He created a "micro-cinema" arm, known as Black Cinema Café (BCC), to hold free screenings of the film on college campuses, and at restaurants and bars. Major companies, such as Grand Marnier and the Ford Motor Company, sponsored the BCC events, and audiences filled out surveys on what they thought of the film. Friday then used these high ratings to get the film booked into theaters and continued to use this novel approach to help crack what was once considered the last celluloid barrier.

FINAL COMEDOWN, THE. 1972. (R) 84 min. Drama. When a black revolutionary fails to get white radicals to support his fight against racism, a race war ensues. Cast: **Billy Dee Williams, D'Urville Martin**, Celia Kaye, **Raymond St. Jaques**, Pamela Jones, R. G. Armstrong. Director: Oscar Williams.

FINAL EXAM. 1998. (NR) 93 min. Drama. An inner-city high-school basketball star takes his English teacher hostage after he fails the course and loses his chance at a college scholarship. He believes it was his only chance to escape his ghetto environment and that racism has played a factor in it all. Cast: Alvin O. McCray, John Mollica, Mario Valasquez, Gregor Manns, Augustina Montesino. Writer/Director: John Mollica. Cinematographer: Mike Dolgetta.

FISHBURNE, LAURENCE (1961-). Actor, writer, director. Fishburne was apparently born to act in Augusta, Georgia. He made his stage debut with the Negro Ensemble Theater at age 10. He was also cast as part of the first African American family on a daytime television drama *One Life to Live*. He first appeared on the big screen at age 12 in *Cornbread, Earl & Me*, 1975. He followed with a co-starring role as a teenage soldier in Francis Ford Coppola's *Apocalypse Now*, 1979. Other film roles include *Rumble Fish*, 1983; *The Cotton Club*, 1984; *King of New York*, 1990; and *Deep Cover*, 1992. His breakout film was as a concerned single father in *Boyz N the Hood*, 1991, and he received an **Academy Award** nomination for his portrayal of pop icon Ike Turner in the film *What's Love Got to Do with It?*, 1993. He also became the first African American to play *Othello* on screen in a 1995 film version of the Shakespeare classic. He returned to the stage and received rave reviews in August Wilson's *Two Trains Running*. Recent film projects include *Fled*, 1996; *Hoodlum*, 1997; *Event Horizon*, 1998; and *The Matrix Trilogy*, 1999 and 2003. He has also directed several independent film projects.

Filmography: *Cornbread, Earl & Me*, 1975; *Apocalypse Now*, 1979; *Willie & Phil*, 1980; *A Rumor of War*, 1980; *Quicksilver*, 1986; *A Nightmare on Elm Street 3: Dream Warriors*, 1987; *Gardens of Stone*, 1987; *School Daze*, 1988; *Red Heat*, 1988; *For Us the Living*, 1988; *Cadence*, 1989; *King of New York*, 1990; *Class Action*, 1991; *Boyz N the Hood*, 1991; *Deep Cover*, 1992; *What's Love Got to Do with It?*, 1993; *Searching for Bobby Fischer*, 1993; *Just Cause*, 1994; *Higher Learning*, 1994; *Bad Company*, 1994; *The Tuskegee Airmen*, 1995; *Othello*, 1995; *Hoodlum*, 1996; *Fled*, 1996; *Miss Evers' Boys*, 1997; *Event Horizon*, 1997; *Always Outnumbered, Always Outgunned*, 1998; *The Matrix*, 1999; *The Matrix Reloaded*, 2003; *The Matrix Revolutions*, 2003; *Biker Boyz*, 2003.

FISH THAT SAVED PITTSBURGH, THE. 1979. (PG) 102 min. Comedy/Sports. When it comes to basketball, the Pittsburgh Pythons are "the Pits." As the worst team in the NBA, morale is low, while fan support is even lower. When the team walks out over the perceived ball hogging and spotlight-grabbing antics of their star player, the towel boy consults with an astrologist on a way to pull the team together. They hold open tryouts in search of players born under the same zodiac sign as their star player, Pisces. They find some interesting characters who can really play ball. When the new players go on a winning streak, the team name is changed to the Pittsburgh Pisces. Cast: Julius Erving, Jonathan Winters, Meadowlark Lemon, Jack Kehoe, **Kareem Abdul-Jabbar**, **Margaret Avery**, **James Bond III**, Michael V. Gazzo, Peter Isacksen, Nicholas Pryor, M. Emmet Walsh, Stockard Channing, Flip Wilson, Marv Albert, **Debbie Allen**. Director: Gilbert Moses. Writer: David Dashev.

FIVE HEARTBEATS, THE. 1991. (R) 122 min. Music/Drama. A 1960s soul-singing group goes through the joys and pains of success, industry pressure, and personal failures throughout 30 years of their own changing interpersonal relationships. The story was inspired by and features vocal performances by the R&B group The Dells. Cast: **Robert Townsend**, Tressa Thomas, **Michael Wright**, **Harry J. Lennix**, **Diahann Carroll**, **Leon**, Hawthorne James, Chuck Patterson, **Roy Fegan**, Chico Wells, **John Canada Terrell**, **Harold Nicholas**, Paul Benjamin, Norma Donaldson, Eugene Glazer. Director: Robert Townsend. Writers: Robert Townsend, **Keenen Ivory Wayans**. Cinematographer: Bill Dill. Music: **Stanley Clarke**.

FLUELLEN, JOEL (1911-1991). Actor, activist. This renowned character actor of stage and screen was born in Monroe, Louisiana. When a racial incident in town jeopardized his safety, a young Fluellen hopped a freight train to Chicago, and eventually migrated to New York. After becoming involved in the theater, he was invited out to Hollywood by **Louise Beavers** who was impressed after seeing his stage work. As a member of the Screen Actor's Guild (S. A. G.) beginning in 1937, he started out as an extra earning $7.50 a day. He later became a member of the Actor's Lab in Los Angeles. After 10 years with the Actor's Lab, he formed the Negro Art Theater. Fluellen drafted one of the first resolutions at S. A. G. that demanded better treatment and more opportunities for its black members and was later labeled "guilty by association" and placed on the infamous Hollywood Blacklist during the 1950s McCarthy Era. To get through this difficult time, he supported himself by making and selling ceramic pottery and custom-made hats, doing interior decorating, and running his own catering business. Fluellen also served as **Paul Robeson**'s personal driver whenever he came to town. His major film work includes roles in *Porgy and Bess*, 1958; *A Raisin in the Sun*, 1961; *The Learning Tree*, 1969; and *The Great White Hope*, 1970. He spearheaded the push to get his good friend Dorothy Dandridge a star on the Hollywood Walk of Fame and succeeded with the help and support of **Sidney Poitier** and **Harry Belafonte**. Fluellen was at one time married to early screen icon **Nina Mae McKinney**.

Filmography: *The Jackie Robinson Story*, 1950; *Porgy and Bess*, 1958; *Run Silent, Run Deep*, 1958; *A Raisin in the Sun*, 1961; *The Learning Tree*, 1969; *The Great White Hope*, 1970; *A Dream for Christmas*, 1973; *Man Friday*, 1975.

FLY BY NIGHT. 1993. (PG-13) 93 min. Music/Drama. Two New York rappers crawl out of obscurity to climb the gangsta-rap charts, but the pressures of their success creates personal and professional animosities that drive them apart. Cast: Jeffrey D. Sams, Ron Brice, Daryl Mitchell, Todd Graff, Leo Burmester, Soulfood Jed, Larry Gilliard Jr., Omar Carter, Maura Tierney, Yul Vazquez, M.C. Lyte, Christopher-Michael Gerrard, Ebony Jo-Ann. Director: Steve Gomer. Writer: Todd Graff. Cinematographer: Larry Banks. Music: Kris Parker. Awards: Sundance 1993: Filmmaker's Trophy.

FLYING ACE, THE. 1926. 65 min. Silent. Adventure. In this film, a World War I flyer-hero is hired to solve the mystery of a missing paymaster and the $25,000 payroll he was carrying. It was produced by the **Norman Film Manufacturing Company** and promoted as "The Greatest Airplane Thriller Ever Filmed, Six Smashing Reels of Action!" Cast: **Lawrence Criner**, Kathryn Boyd, George Colvin, Boise De Legge, Lions Daniels, Sam Jordan, Steve Reynolds, Dr. R. L. Brown, Harold Platts. Director: Richard E. Norman.

FOOLISH. 1999. (R) 96 min. Comedy. A struggling, stand-up comedian and his manager/brother fight the industry together to establish and build his career, but they bump heads when one falls for the other's former girlfriend. Cast: **Eddie Griffin, Master P**, Frank Silvero, Amy Petersen, Jonathan Banks, Andrew Dice Clay, **Marla Gibbs**, Daphnee Lynn Duplaix, Sven-Ole Thorsen, **Bill Nunn, Bill Duke**. Director: Dave Meyers. Writer: Master P. Cinematographer: Steve Gainer. Music: Wendy Melvoin, Lisa Coleman.

FOR US THE LIVING. 1988. (TV) 84 min. Biopic. Based on the bi-ography of Medgar Evers, written by his wife, this PBS *American Playhouse* production chronicles the life achievements of this prominent civil rights leader and his brutal assassination. Cast: **Howard E. Rollins Jr.**, Rocky Aoki, **Paul Winfield, Irene Cara, Margaret Avery, Roscoe Lee Brown, Laurence Fishburne, Janet MacLachlan, Dick Anthony Williams**. Director: **Michael Schultz**.

FOR LOVE OF IVY. 1968. (G) 101 min. Romance. Based on a story by **Sidney Poitier** about a gambler who falls for a white family friend's maid. Cast: Sidney Poitier, **Abby Lincoln**, Beau Bridges, Leon Bibb, Nan Martin, Lauri Peters, Lester Mack, Carroll O'Connor, Mae Crane, **Gloria Hendry**. Director: Daniel Mann. Writer: Robert Alan Aurthur. Cinematographer: Joseph F. Coffey. Music: **Quincy Jones**.

FOSTER, GLORIA (1936-2003). Actress. She was born in Chicago, Illinois, and raised by her grandmother. She attended Illinois State University and taught school for two years before studying acting at the Goodman Theater School of Drama. Foster made her profes-sional stage debut with the University of Chicago's County Thea-ter. In 1963, she moved to New York City. She won an Obie Award in 1963 for her performance in *In White America*, and re-ceived a Theater World Award for her title role portrayal in *Madea*. Her first Broadway role was in *A Raisin in the Sun*. Her film debut came in director Shirley Clark's independent film *The Cool World*, 1963. Other film roles include *Nothing But a Man*, 1964, with **Ivan Dixon**, and *To All My Friends on Shore*, 1971, with **Bill Cosby**. Foster made many guest **television** appearances, including *I Spy*, *The Mod Squad*, where she acted with her husband and *The Cool World* co-star, **Clarence Williams III**.

Filmography: *The Cool World*, 1964; *Nothing But a Man*, 1964; *The Comedians*, 1967; *The Angel Levine*, 1970; *To All My Friends on Shore*, 1972; *Man & Boy*, 1972; *Leonard Part 6*, 1987; *Separate But Equal*, 1991; *City of Hope*, 1991; *The Matrix*, 1999; *The Matrix Reloaded*, 2003.

FOSTER PHOTOPLAY COMPANY. Former performer turned vaudeville booking agent William "Bill" Foster established Foster Photoplay Company in 1910. It was the first African American-owned company to produce all-black-cast films. The company turned out one reelers, including two comedies, *The Railroad Por-*

ter, 1912, and *The Fall Guy*, 1913, plus a detective story, *The Butler*, 1913, and *The Grafter and the Maid*, 1913, a melodrama.

FOUR-WALLING. Four-walling was an early and basic method of film distribution. It consisted of someone personally taking a single film print from theater to theater for screening purposes.

FOX, VIVICA A. (1964-). Actress. A native of Indianapolis, Indiana, Fox earned an Associate Art degree in Social Sciences from Golden West College in Huntington Beach, California. Turning to acting, she landed a major **television** role in the short-lived series *Out All Night*, with Patti LaBelle and Morris Chestnut. Her guest-starring roles include *Living Single, Family Matters, Matlock, Beverly Hills 90210, The Fresh Prince of Bel-Air,* and *China Beach*. She was later cast in a starring role for the hospital medical drama *City of Angels*. Her big break in film came when she portrayed **Will Smith**'s exotic dancing girlfriend in *Independence Day*, 1996. Her other notable films include *Set It Off*, 1996; *Soul Food*, 1997; *Two Can Play That Game*, 2001; and *Kill Bill*, 2004.

Filmography: *Born on the Fourth of July*, 1989; *The Tuskegee Airmen*, 1995; *Set It Off*, 1996; *Independence Day*, 1996; *Booty Call*, 1996; *Soul Food*, 1997; *Batman and Robin*, 1997; *Why Do Fools Fall in Love?* 1998; *Solomon*, 1998; *Idle Hands*, 1999; *Hendrix*, 2000; *Two Can Play That Game*, 2001; *Kingdom Come*, 2001; *Juwanna Mann*, 2002; *Boat Trip*, 2003; *Kill Bill*, 2004.

FOXX, JAMIE (1967-). Actor, singer, musician. Born Eric Morlon Bishop in Terrell, Texas, Foxx began playing piano at age three, played football in high school, and attended United States International University in San Diego on a music scholarship. He also studied classical piano at Juilliard and released a 1994 music album, *Peep This*. He liked to tell jokes and accepted a friend's challenge to perform during an open-mic night at a comedy club, and his career began. He was cast in the television sitcom *Roc*, 1991, and *In Living Color*, 1990. He later starred in his own sitcom, *The Jamie Foxx Show*, on the Warner Bros.' Network. His music training came in handy when he landed the title role in *Ray*, 2004, a film based on the life and times of blind soul singer Ray Charles.

Filmography: *Toys*, 1992; *The Truth about Cats and Dogs*, 1996; *The Great White Hype*, 1996; *Booty Call*, 1997; *The Players Club*, 1998; *Held Up*, 1999; *Any Given Sunday*, 1999; *Bait*, 2000; *Date from Hell*, 2001; *Ali*, 2001; *Shade*, 2003; *Breakin' All the Rules*, 2004; *Collateral*, 2004; *Ray*, 2004; *Stealth*, 2005; *Jarhead*, 2005; *Miami Vice*, 2006.

FOXX, REDD (1922-1991). Comedian, actor. He was born John Elroy Sanford and began performing comedy on the "chitlin circuit" of black theaters and nightclubs while he was still in his teens. For a stage name, he combined his old nickname of Red, due to his light complexion, with the surname of his favorite baseball player, Jimmie Foxx. He recorded a series of explicit blues records in the mid-1940s before teaming up with fellow comic Slappy White to tour the club circuit. He cut a variety of comedy record albums that were so raunchy they often had to be sold under-the-counter. These controversial and groundbreaking records included *Laff of the Party*, *Sly Sex*, *Laff Your Ass Off*, *Mr. Hot Pants*, and *Foxx A Delic*. Foxx was one of the first comics to use four-letter words and blatant profanity on his major label releases. As his popularity grew and his audience expanded, he began to make **television** appearances, and landed his first film role in *Cotton Comes to Harlem*, 1970. He signed to do the television sitcom *Sanford and Son*, a concept reworked from the hit British TV show *Steptoe and Son*. It became very popular in 1972 and ran for five seasons. Other Foxx-based shows include *Sanford*, *The Redd Foxx Show*, and *The Red Foxx Comedy Hour*. In his live recording taped at the **Apollo Theater** in 1976, *You Gotta Wash Your Ass*, he continued to blend vulgarity with comedy, and again, it was a huge hit. After starring in *Norman, Is That You?*, 1976, he became a headliner in Las Vegas. Despite a dip in his popularity during the 1980s, Foxx has been a major influence on a whole new generation of African American comedians. Comic and mega-star **Eddie Murphy** cast Foxx and comedian **Richard Pryor** to co-star in his crime-noir film *Harlem Nights*, 1989, bringing three generations of top comic talent to the screen. With his career renewed, Foxx signed on to do the sitcom, *The Royal Family*, in 1991, shortly before he passed away.
   Filmography: *Cotton Comes to Harlem*, 1970; *Norman, Is That You?* 1976; *Harlem Nights*, 1989.

FOXY BROWN. 1974. (R) 92 min. Blaxploitation. A grieving woman fakes being a prostitute to seek revenge on the mobsters who killed her brother and her boyfriend. Cast: **Pam Grier**, **Terry Carter**, **Antonio Fargas**, Kathryn Loder, Peter Brown, Sid Haig, Juanita Brown. Writer/Director: Jack Hill. Cinematographer: Brick Marquard. Music: Willie Hutch.

FRANKLIN, CARL (1949-). Actor, writer, director. A native of Richmond, California, Franklin received a scholarship and studied history at the University of California at Berkeley, where he began to act. He moved to New York after graduation and began a stage career at the New York Shakespeare Festival, performing in *Cymbeline, Timon of Athens*, and *Twelfth Night*. He made his film debut in *Five on the Black Hand Side*, 1973, and worked steadily on **television**, guest starring on *The Streets of San Francisco, Good Times, The Incredible Hulk*, and *The Rockford Files*. After working for two seasons as a regular on *The A-Team* from 1983 to 1985, Franklin entered the directing program at the American Film Institute. After graduation, Franklin was hired as an apprentice at Concorde Films, the production company of fast-paced, low-budget filmmaking guru Roger Corman. While there, Franklin wrote, produced, directed, and often acted in three straight-to-video films: *Nowhere to Run*, 1989; *Eye of the Eagle 2: Inside the Enemy*, 1989; and *Full Fathom Five*, 1990. He moved on the write and direct **One False Move**, 1991, his critically acclaimed independent crime thriller, for which he won a New Generation Award from the Los Angeles Film Critics Association, Independent Award for Best Director, and an MTV Movie Award for Best New Filmmaker. His other directing credits include the HBO miniseries **Laurel Avenue**, 1993, and the movie adaptation of Walter Mosley's novel **Devil in a Blue Dress**.

Filmography: *Punk*, 1986; *Nowhere to Run*, 1989; *Eye of the Eagle 2: Inside the Enemy*, 1989. *Full Fathom Five*, 1990; *One False Move*, 1992; *Laurel Avenue*, 1993; *Devil in a Blue Dress*, 1995; *One True Thing*, 1998; *High Crime*, 2002; **Out of Time**, 2003; *The Senator's Wife*, 2007.

FRAZIER, SHEILA (1948-). Actress, producer. This New York City-born actress began her career with the Negro Ensemble Company and is perhaps best known as "Priest's woman" in the hit **blaxploitation**-era film **Superfly**, 1972. It was her first feature film role after doing commercials and industrial films. She reprised her role in the sequel, **Superfly T. N. T.**, 1973; as well as **Three the Hard Way**, 1974; *Uomini Duri*, 1974; and *California Suite*, 1978. On **television**, she costarred with Louis Gossett Jr. in *The Lazarus Syndrome*, 1979. She now heads Frazier MultiMedia Group, a television, talent acquisition, and special events company.

Filmography: *Superfly*, 1970; *Firehouse*, 1972; *Superfly T. N. T.*, 1973; *Three the Hard Way*, 1974; *The Hitter*, 1979.

FREDERICK DOUGLASS FILM COMPANY. This early black film company produced *The Colored American Winning His Suit*, 1916.

FREEMAN, AL, JR. (1934-). Actor, professor. A consummate actor in both stage and film, Freeman was born in San Antonio, Texas. He attended school in Ohio and later studied law at Los Angeles City College. After a tour of duty in the Army, Freeman returned to college to pursue a degree in theater arts. While in Los Angeles, he acted in local plays and also did radio shows before landing his first Broadway play, *The Long Dream*. Other Broadway performances include *Golden Boy*, *Blues for Mr. Charley*, *The Dozens*, and *Conversation at Midnight*. His off-Broadway credits include *The Premise*, *Trumpets of the Lord*, and *The Slave*. He was also active in the New York Shakespeare Festival. He was prominent on the big screen in such feature films as ***Black Like Me***, 1964; ***The Dutchman***, 1967; *Finian's Rainbow*, 1968; *The Detective*, 1968; and *The Lost Man*, 1969. Freeman has been in many **television** series, including *The Defenders*, *The FBI*, and *Naked City*. He portrayed Lt. Ed Hall in the daytime drama *One Life to Live* on ABC. He was nominated for an **Emmy Award** for his role in the television film *My Sweet Charlie*, 1970. He also co-wrote the screenplay and was the original lead actor for ***Countdown at Kusini***, 1976, but had to drop out of the project due to production setbacks. He is perhaps best remembered for his portrayal of the Honorable Elijah Muhammad in ***Malcolm X***, 1992. Freeman teaches acting at Howard University's School of Fine Arts and had a long stint as chair of the Theater Arts Department.

Filmography: *Ensign Pulver*, 1964; *Black Like Me*, 1964; *The Dutchman*, 1967; *Finian's Rainbow*, 1968; *The Detective*, 1968; *The Lost Man*, 1969; *My Sweet Charlie*, 1970; ***Roots: The Next Generation***, 1979; *Seven Hours to Judgment*, 1988; *Malcolm X*, 1992; ***Once Upon a Time When We Were Colored***, 1995; ***Down in the Delta***, 1998.

FREEMAN, BEE (1899-1986). Actress. This one-time Broadway chorus line dancer became known as "the sepia Mae West" for her sexy voice and strong knack for innuendo. She starred in several of **Oscar Micheaux**'s films and the two were once married. She often played a cigarette-smoking femme fatale.

Filmography: *Harlem after Midnight*, 1934; *Temptation*, 1935; *Murder in Harlem*, 1935; *Underworld*, 1937.

FREEMAN, MORGAN (1937-). Actor. Freeman was born in Memphis, Tennessee, and raised in Greenwood, Mississippi. He enlisted in the U.S. Air Force in 1955, and left the military service to pursue his acting career in Los Angeles. He relocated to New York City and got his first important role in the 1967 off-Broadway production of *The Nigger-Lovers*, and later acted in an all–African American revival production of the Broadway musical *Hello, Dolly*. Freeman appeared in the PBS series *The Electric Company* as the hip, Easy Reader from 1971 to 1976. He won an Obie Award for his role in the Broadway play *Driving Miss Daisy*, and received an **Academy Award** nomination for Best Actor for his role in the 1989 film version. Other powerful roles include *Glory*, 1989; *Lean on Me*, 1989; *Unforgiven*, 1993; *Outbreak*, 1995; and *Seven*, 1995. He directed the 1993 film on South Africa, *Bopha*, and was again nominated for an Academy Award for his role in *The Shawshank Redemption*, 1994. He won the best supporting actor **Oscar** for his role in *Million Dollar Baby*, 2004.

Filmography: *Roll of Thunder, Hear My Cry*, 1978; *Brubaker*, 1980; *Eyewitness*, 1981; *Marie*, 1985; *Street Smart*, 1987; *Clean and Sober*, 1988; *Lean on Me*, 1989; *Johnny Handsom*, 1989; *Glory*, 1989; *Driving Miss Daisy*, 1989; *The Bonfire of the Vanities*, 1990; *Robin Hood: Prince of Thieves*, 1991; *Unforgiven*, 1992; *The Shawshank Redemption*, 1994; *Outbreak*, 1994; *Seven*, 1995; *Chain Reaction*, 1996; *Kiss the Girls*, 1997; *Amistad*, 1997; *Deep Impact*, 1998; *Under Suspicion*, 2000; *Along Came a Spider*, 2001; *The Sum of All Fears*, 2002; *High Crimes*, 2002; *Levity*, 2003; *Dream Catcher*, 2003; *Bruce Almighty*, 2003; *Million Dollar Baby*, 2004; *Batman Begins*, 2005.

FRESH. 1994. (R) 114 min. Drama. A streetwise 12-year-old boy skillfully manipulates the people in his life like pieces in a chess game in order to save his crack-addicted sister from her drug-dealing boyfriend and get them both out of the game. Cast: **Sean Nelson, Samuel L. Jackson, Giancarlo Esposito, N'Bushe Wright**, Ron Brice, Jean LaMarre, Louis Lantiqua, Yul Vazquez, Cheryl Freeman. Writer/Director: Boaz Yakin. Cinematographer: Adam Holender. Awards: Independent Spirit 1995, Debut Performance (Nelson). Sundance 1994: Special Jury Prize, Filmmaker's Trophy.

FRIDAY. 1995. (R) 91 min. Urban Comedy. An unemployed man and his equally worthless homeboy spend most of their time sitting on the front porch smoking pot, but occasionally, they get into some crazy antics involving their neighbors and family members. There is a running feud with the neighborhood bully, a crass uncle who is full of gas and proud of it, and a host of other off-the-wall characters. Cast: **Ice Cube, Chris Tucker, Bernie Mac, John Witherspoon, Regina King, Nia Long**, Tommy "Tiny" Lister, **Anna Maria Horsford, LaWanda Page**. Director: **F. Gary Gray**.

Writers: DJ Pooh, Ice Cube. Cinematographer: Gerry Lively. Music: Frank Fitzpatrick.

FRIDAY AFTER NEXT. 2002. (R) 85 min. Urban Comedy. Sequel to *Next Friday*, 2000, and third film of the series. It is Christmas time. Chris and Day-Day are forced to take jobs as security guards after their rent money and presents are ripped off by a thief in a Santa Claus outfit. Cast: **Ice Cube, Mike Epps, John Witherspoon**, Don Curry, **Anna Maria Horsford, Clifton Powell**, Terry Crews, BeBe Drake, Sommore, **Starletta DuPois**, K.D. Aubert, Katt Micah Williams, Rickey Smiley, Joel McKinnon Miller, Reggie Gaskins. Director: Marcus Raboy. Writer: Ice Cube. Cinematographer: Glenn McPherson. Music: John Murphy.

FRIDAY FOSTER. 1975. (R) 90 min. Blaxploitation. This film is based on the *Chicago Tribune* comic strip. While investigating an attempted assassination, a female photojournalist puts her own life in danger when she discovers a conspiracy to undermine black politicians. Cast: **Pam Grier, Yaphet Kotto, Thalmus Rasulala, Carl Weathers, Godfrey Cambridge**. Director: Arhur Marks. Writer: Orville H. Hampton. Cinematographer: Harry J. May. Music: Luchi De Jesus.

FULLER, CHARLES (1939-). Writer. He was born in Philadelphia, Pennsylvania, and is a prolific writer of stage, **television**, and film.
    Filmography: *The Sky Is Gray*, 1980; *A Soldier's Story*, 1984; *A Gathering of Old Men*, 1987; *Zooman*, 1995; *The Wall*, 1998; *Love Songs*, 1999.

FUQUA, ANTOINE (1966-). Director. He was born in Pittsburgh, Pennsylvania, and transitioned from directing commercials for Reebok and Toyota, and award-winning music videos for Arrested Development and Toni Braxton, to directing mainstream feature films. His feature debut was the stylized action flick *The Replacement Killers*, 1998, and he is credited with directing **Denzel Wasington** to an **Oscar** in *Training Day*, 2001. Fuqua also directed the war-torn *Tears of the Sun*, 2003, and the big-budget epic *King Arthur*, 2004. He also directed the blues music documentary *Lightning in a Bottle*, 2004. Fuqua is married to actress **Lela Rochon**.
    Filmography: *The Replacement Killers*, 1998; *Bait*, 2000; *Training Day*, 2001; *Tears of the Sun*, 2003; *Lightning in a Bottle*, 2004; *King Arthur*, 2004; *Murder Book*, 2006; *The Call*, 2006; *Shooter*, 2007; *By Any Means Necessary*, 2007.

G

GANG SMASHERS. 1938. 70 min. Gangster/Drama/Music. A police-woman goes undercover as a nightclub singer to nail the big boss of the Harlem racketeers. She sings songs and breaks hearts as she gathers her clues, while two men fall for her. Cast: **Nina Mae McKinney, Lawrence Criner, Monte Hawley,** Reginald Fenderson, **Mantan Moreland,** Edward Thompson, Vernon McCalla, Charles Hawkins, Everett Brown, Lester Wilkins, Neva Peoples, Arthur Ray, Bo Jinkins, John Criner, Margaret Flemmings. Director: Leo C. Popkin. Writers: Hazel Barsworth, **Ralph Cooper.**

GANG WAR. 1940. 60 min. Gangster/Drama. A gangster film about rival gangs fighting to control the Harlem jukebox trade. Cast: **Ralph Cooper,** Gladys Snyder, Reggie Fenderson, **Lawrence Criner, Monte Hawley,** Jesse C. Brooks, Maceo B. Sheffield. Director: Leo C. Popkin.

GANJA AND HESS. 1973. (R) 110 min. Horror/Thriller. An archaeologist conducting an excavation of an ancient African culture is stabbed with a primeval artifact that turns him into a vampire. Cast: Duane Jones, Marlene Clark, Bill Gunn, Sam Waymon, Leonard Jackson, Candice Tarpley, Mabel King. Writer/Director: **Bill Gunn.** Cinematographer: James E. Hinton. Music: Sam Waymon.

GANT, RICHARD E. (1940-). Actor. A native of San Francisco, California, Gant spent his early years living with grandparents in Muskogee, Oklahoma. He is an alum of the Negro Ensemble Company and has many Broadway and Off-Broadway credits, including *The Mighty Gents*, *Playboy of the West Indies*, and appeared in the Los Angeles workshop production of Yrneh Brown's *Portrait of a Poet*, at the Ivar Theater. His numerous **television** credits include appearances in series, such as *The Bonnie Hunt Show*, *Special Unit II*, *NYPD Blue, Eve, Raven,* and *Deadwood*. His film work includes roles in *Rocky V*, 1990; *Posse*, 1993; *Kingdom Come*, 2001; and *Hood of Horror*, 2006.

   Filmography: *Death of a Prophet*, 1981; *Krush Groove*, 1985; *Suspect*, 1987; *Collision Course*, 1989; *Love or Money*, 1990; *The Freshman*, 1990; *Rocky V*, 1990; *Last Breeze of Summer*, 1991; *CB4*, 1993; *Posse*, 1993; *Jason Goes to Hell: The Final Friday*, 1993; *City Hall*, 1996; *Ed*, 1996; *The Glimmer Man*, 1996; *Mr. Bean*, 1997; *Johnny B Good*, 1998; *The Big Lebowski*, 1998; *Sour Grapes*, 1998; *Godzilla*, 1998; *Divorcing Jack*, 1998; *Nutty Pro-*

fessor II: The Klumps, 2000; *Kingdom Come*, 2001; *Lesser of Three Evils*, 2005; *Hood of Horror*, 2006.

GATHERING OF OLD MEN, A. 1987. (PG) 91 min. Drama. This is a film based on the novel by Ernest J. Gains about race relations in the old American South. When a white man is shot to death in a black man's yard, a group of old men gather and each one takes the blame. White retaliation is a constant threat as the sheriff conducts his investigation. At the end of the day, some of the circumstances and some of the people have changed. Cast: **Louis Gossett Jr.**, Richard Widmark, **Julius Harris**, **Woody Strode**, **Joe Seneca**, James Michael Bailey, Lenore Banks, Walter Breaux, Rosanna Carter, Papa John Creach, Stocker Fontelieu, Tiger Haynes, Holly Hunter, Will Patton, Al Shannon, Adam Storke, Dave Petitjean. Director: Volker Schlondorff. Writer: **Charles Fuller**.

GAYE, NONA (1974-). Singer, actress. This multi-talented native of Los Angeles, California, is the daughter of famed R&B singer Marvin Gaye. She released her first CD, *Love for the Future*, in 1992, featuring the hit singles "I'm Overjoyed" and "The Things That We All Do For Love." She made her film debut with a small part in *Harlem Nights*, 1989, portrayed **Muhammad Ali**'s first wife in his biopic *Ali*, 2001, and also appeared in both sequels to *The Matrix*.

    Filmography: *Harlem Nights*, 1989; *Ali*, 2001; *The Matrix Reloaded*, 2003; *The Matrix Revolutions*, 2003; *The Polar Express*, 2004; *XXX: State of the Union*, 2005; *Crash*, 2005.

GERIMA, HAILE (1946-). Writer, producer, director, professor. A native of Gondar, Ethiopia, Gerima came to the United States to study acting and directing at The Goodman Theater in Chicago, Illinois. He transferred to the Theater Arts Department at UCLA, and earned his Master's Degree in Film. Upon graduation, he became a professor at Howard University's newly established School of Communications, Department of Radio, Television, and Film. Gerima perhaps became best known for his independently produced film *Sankofa*, 1993. When he could not come to terms with a major distributor to release his film on the cruelty of slavery and the hope of rebellion, Gerima **"four-walled"** the film to over 35 cities, grossing over $3 million. He has established his own production company, Myphedu Films, and opened Sankofa Books and Tapes, a bookstore and video rental house in Washington, D. C. He has completed principal photography on his newest film, *Teza*, scheduled for release in 2006.

Filmography: *Hour Glass*, 1971; *Child of Resistance*, 1972; *Harvest: 3,000 Years*, 1975; *Bush Mama*, 1979; *Wilmington 10-U.S.A. 10,000*, 1979; *After Winter: Sterling Brown*, 1985; *Sankofa*, 1993; *Adwa*, 1999; *Teza*, 2006.

GET CHRISTIE LOVE! 1974. (TV) 95 min. Action/Crime. Based on a detective novel by Dorothy Uhnak, a policewoman goes undercover to infiltrate and bust a drug cartel. The film spawned a TV series of the same name. Cast: Teresa Graves, Harry Guardino, Louise Sorel, Paul Stevens, Andy Romano, Debbie Dozier. Director: William A. Graham.

GET ON THE BUS. 1996. (R) 122 min. Drama. A group of men take a chartered bus ride from South Central Los Angeles to Washington, D.C., for the Million Man March. Each has his very own story, background, and reason for wanting or needing to be there. In the spirit of the movie, the $2.4 million budget was independently raised from 12 black men. Cast: **Andre Braugher, Ossie Davis, Charles S. Dutton, De'Aundre Bonds**, Gabriel Casseus, **Albert Hall, Hill Harper, Harry J. Lennix, Bernie Mac, Wendell Pierce, Roger Guenveur Smith, Isaiah Washington**, Steve White, **Thomas Jefferson Byrd**, Richard Belzer, Randy Quaid. Director: **Spike Lee**. Writer: **Reggie "Rock" Bythewood**. Cinematography: Elliot Davis. Music: **Terence Blanchard**.

GETTING PLAYED. 2005. (PG-13) 79 min. Comedy/Romance. Three beautiful women who have each been hurt in the game of love decide to turn the tables. They randomly select a total stranger for each of them to seduce and videotape their conquests. Their plan is to use these tapes of his multiple encounters to embarrass him and to prove that men are unfaithful. But things do not work out as planned. Cast: **Vivica A. Fox**, Carmen Electra, **Bill Bellamy, Stacey Dash, Joe Torry, Tichina Arnold**, Earthquake, Dorian Gregory, Kathy Najimy, Joseph C. Phillips, **Larry B. Scott**, Mindy Sterling, Sheryl Underwood, **Michael Jai White**. Writer/Director: David Silberg.

GHOST DAD. 1990. (PG) 84 min. Comedy/Drama. A hard-working single father is accidentally killed. He had little time for his children while he was alive, but returns as a ghost to look after them until they are ready to handle the future. Cast: **Bill Cosby, Denise Nicholas**, Ian Bannen, Christine Ebersole, Dana Ashbrook, Arnold Stang. Director: **Sidney Poitier**. Writer: S. S. Wilson, Brent Maddock. Music: Henry Mancini.

GIBBS, MARLA (1931-). Actress. She was born in Chicago, Illinois, graduated from Wendell Phillips High School, worked for United Airlines, and acted in her spare time before landing her breakout role as Florence Johnson on the hit sitcom *The Jeffersons*. She appeared in the telepics *Checking In*, 1981; *Menu for Murder*, 1990; and *Lily in Winter*, 1994. She also starred in her own series as Mary Jenkins in *227*. Some of her key film roles include *Passing Through*, 1977; *The Meteor Man*, 1993; *The Visit*, 2000; and *The Brothers*, 2001. In 1990, she opened the Vision Theater Complex and Marla's Memory Lane jazz supper club in Los Angeles.

Filmography: *Sweet Jesus Preacher Man*, 1973; *Black Belt Jones*, 1974; *Passing Through*, 1977; *Up Against the Wall*, 1991; *Last Breeze of Summer*, 1991; *The Meteor Man*, 1993; *Border to Border*, 1998; *Foolish*, 1999; *Lost & Found*, 1999; *The Visit*, 2000; *Stanley's Gig*, 2000; *The Brothers*, 2001.

GILPIN, CHARLES (1879-1930). Actor. This native of Richmond, Virginia, became a founding member of the **Lafayette Players**. He was famed for originating the role of The Emperor Jones on the stage and was at one time slated for the film version. He has an impressive list of stage credits but missed out on several high-profile film roles and is only credited with one: *Ten Nights in a Barroom*, 1926.

GIRL FROM CHICAGO. 1932. 69 min. Romance. A secret service agent meets and falls in love with a beautiful woman while on an assignment in Mississippi. Cast: Starr Calloway, Grace Smith, Eugene Brooks, Frank Wilson. Director: **Oscar Micheaux**.

GIRL 6. 1996. (R) 107 min. Drama. A telephone sex operator becomes entangled in her work and loses sight of reality. The entire film is underscored with wall-to-wall music by **Prince**. Cast: **Theresa Randle**, **Isaiah Washington**, Ron Silver, John Turturro, Naomi Campbell, **Halle Berry**, Madonna, Quentin Tarantino, Debbie Mazar, Peter Berg, Richard Belzer, **Spike Lee**, **Jenifer Lewis**, Michael Imperioli, Kristen Wilson, Dina Pearlman, Maggie Rush, Desi Moreno, Susan Batson. Director: Spike Lee. Writer: Susan-Lori Parks. Cinematography: **Malik Hassan Sayeed**. Music: Prince.

GIST, JAMES and ELOYCE (1892-1974). Filmmakers, evangelists. This husband and wife evangelistic team was responsible for the religion-based films *Hellbound Train*, 1929, and *Verdict Not Guilty*,

1933. James had already completed his silent film *Hellbound Train* when they married, and Eloyce is credited with helping to rewrite the title cards and reediting his production into a stronger presentation. The film is a string of morality plays pointing out what lies in store for the un-righteous and the un-godly. They would screen their film at churches and for civic organizations. A graduate of Howard University's School of Music, Eloyce would play the piano and lead the audience in a hymn before the screening, and after, James would preach a sermonette. They would then take up an offering and split it with the church or organization. The Gists' film footage was donated to the Library of Congress in disjointed fragments and is now being restructured and reedited.

Filmography: *Hellbound Train*, 1929; *Verdict Not Guilty*, 1933.

GIVENS, ROBIN (1964-). Actress. She was born in New York City and began taking acting classes at the American Academy of Dramatic Arts. She entered Sarah Lawrence College to study pre-med at age 15, but decided to use her looks and her talent in another way. She landed roles on the daytime soap operas *The Guiding Light*, and *Loving*. Many television roles followed, including *The Cosby Show*, *Different Strokes*, and *Moesha*. She had a recurring role in *In the House*, and was a series regular on *Head of the Class*, *Sparks*, and *Courthouse*. She was also the host of *Forgive Or Forget*, a daytime talk show. She has appeared in many feature films and television movies, including **The Women of Brewster's Place**, 1989; *A Rage in Harlem*, 1991; and **Boomerang**, 1992. She had a short but highly publicized marriage to boxer Mike Tyson.

Filmography: *The Women of Brewster Place*, 1989; *A Rage in Harlem*, 1991; *Boomerang*, 1992; *Foreign Student*, 1994; **Blankman**, 1994; *Dangerous Intentions*, 1995; *Secrets*, 1997; *Everything's Jake*, 2000; *Elite*, 2000; *Book of Love*, 2002; **Head of State**, 2003; *A Good Night to Die*, 2003.

GLASS, RON (1945-). Actor. He is a native of Evansville, Indiana, and made his acting TV debut in *Beg, Borrow, or Steal*, 1973. He was later cast as Detective Ron Harris in the popular cop sitcom *Barney Miller*, and portrayed Felix Unger in the TV series *The New Odd Couple*. He appeared in many telepictures, including *Gus Brown and the Midnight Brewster*, 1985; *Perry Mason: The Case of the Shooting Star*, 1986; and *Incognito*, 1999.

Filmography: *The Crazy World of Julius Vrooder*, 1974; *Deep Space*, 1987; *Houseguest*, 1995; *It's My Party*, 1996; *Back in Business*, 1997; *Unbowed*, 1999.

The Dictionary

131

GLASS SHIELD, THE. 1995. (PG-13) 109 min. Drama. A black rookie cop experiences racism from the other officers in his precinct. He tries to fit in by lying under oath at the trial of a black motorist being framed by corrupt white cops and might end up taking the fall. Cast: **Michael Boatman**, Lori Petty, Michael Ironside, M. Emmet Walsh, **Ice Cube**, Richard Anderson, Elliot Gould. Writer/Director: **Charles Burnett**. Cinematographer: Elliot Davis. Music: Stephen James Taylor.

GLENN, ROY (1914-1971). Actor. Glenn spent a major part of his life acting in film and **television**. He began with an uncredited bit part in *Dark Manhattan*, 1937, and worked constantly in bit and supporting roles ever since. Some of his most notable roles are in *Carmen Jones*, 1954; *A Raisin in the Sun*, 1961; and as Mr. Prentice, **Sidney Poitier**'s father in *Guess Who's Coming to Dinner*, 1967. On television, he appeared in many episodes of *Amos 'n' Andy*, and provided the original voice for Tony the Tiger in the Kellogg's Sugar Frosted Flakes TV commercials.
Filmography: *Jungle Drums of Africa*, 1953; *Carmen Jones*, 1954; *A Raisin in the Sun*, 1961; *Guess Who's Coming to Dinner*, 1967.

GLOVER, DANNY (1947-). Actor. The San Francisco native went to San Francisco State University and attended the Black Actors Workshop of the American Conservatory Theater. On stage, he appeared in *Macbeth*, *Island*, and *Sizwe Banzi is Dead*. He relocated to New York and took to the stage in *Suicide in B Flat*, *The Blood Knot*, and *Master Harold and the Boys*, for which he received a Theater World Award. His film credits include *Witness*, 1985; *Places in the Heart*, 1985; *The Color Purple*, 1985; *Mandela*, 1987; *To Sleep With Anger*, 1990; and the *Lethal Weapon series 1-4*. His **television** appearances include the popular series *Hill Street Blues*, the TV miniseries *Chiefs*, *Lonesome Dove*, and a TV remake of *A Raisin in the Sun*.
Filmography: *Escape from Alcatraz*, 1979; *Keeping On*, 1981; *Places in the Heart*, 1984; *Iceman*, 1984; *Witness*, 1985; *Silverado*, 1985; *The Color Purple*, 1985; *Mandela*, 1987; *Lethal Weapon*, 1987; *Bat 21*, 1988; *A Raisin in the Sun*, 1989; *Lonesome Dove*, 1989; *Lethal Weapon 2*, 1989; *To Sleep With Anger*, 1990; *Predator 2*, 1990; *Flight of the Intruder*, 1990; *A Rage in Harlem*, 1991; *Grand Canyon*, 1991; *Lethal Weapon 3*, 1992; *Queen*, 1993; *Bopha*, 1993; *Angels in the Outfield*, 1994; *Operation Dumbo Drop*, 1995; *America's Dream*, 1995; *Gone Fishin'*, 1997; *Buf-*

falo Soldiers, 1997; *Lethal Weapon 4*, 1998; *Beloved*, 1998; *Freedom Song*, 2000; *Boesman & Lena*, 2000; *3 A. M.* 2001; *The Royal Tenenbaums*, 2001.

GLOVER, SAVION (1973-). Dancer, choreographer, actor. This Newark, New Jersey-born dancing phenomenon won a Tony Award for Best Choreography for the musical *Bring in 'da Noise, Bring in 'Da Funk*. He began dancing at an early age and made his film debut in the film *Tap*, 1989. His only other film appearance has been as a street-dancer-turned-star in the **Spike Lee** film *Bamboozled*, 2000. On **television**, he appeared on numerous episodes of *Sesame Street*, and in the TV movies *The Wall*, and *Bojangles*, 2001.

Filmography: *Tap*, 1989; *The Wall*, 1998; *Bamboozled*, 2000; *Bojangles*, 2001.

GO DOWN DEATH. 1941. 63 min. Drama. A devout preacher man becomes entangled in a moral dilemma that has him trapped between heaven and hell. Cast: Myra D. Hemmings, Samuel H. James, Eddy L. Houston, **Spencer Williams Jr.**, Amos Droughan. Director: Spencer Williams Jr.

GOD'S STEP CHILDREN. 1938. 105 min. Drama. An adopted light-skinned child struggles to find her place in both the black and white worlds. Cast: Jacqueline Lewis, **Ethel Moses**, **Alice B. Russell**, Trixie Smith, Charles Thompson, Carman Newsome, Gloria Press, Alec Lovejoy, Columbus Jackson, Laura Bowman, Sam Patterson, Charles R. Moore, Consuelo Harris, Sammy Gardiner, Leon Gross. Director/Writer: **Oscar Micheaux**. Cinematographer: Lester Lang.

GOLDBERG, WHOOPI (1950-). Actress, comedian, producer. She was born Caryn Johnson in New York City and grew up in a Manhattan housing project. She made her performing debut when she was eight years old with the Helena Rubinstein Children's Theater at the Hudson Guild. She dropped out of high school and worked as a summer camp counselor before appearing on Broadway in the choruses of shows, such as *Hair*, *Jesus Christ Superstar*, and *Pippin*. She moved to California, where she co-founded the San Diego Repertory Theater and performed with the improvisational theater group Spontaneous Combustion. At this time, she adopted her stage name of Whoopi Goldberg. She moved to the San Francisco Bay area and joined the improvisational group The Blake Street Hawkeyes Theater in Berkeley. Goldberg further developed her stand-up routine and toured the U. S. and Europe with her one-woman production, *The Spook Show.* She returned to Broadway in another one-woman performance of her original work at the Lyceum Theater, which was taped for an HBO special titled *Whoopi Goldberg: Direct From Broadway.* The record album of the show won a Grammy Award as Best Comedy Recording of the Year. She was later cast in the lead role of **The Color Purple**, 1986, for which she was nominated for an **Oscar** and won both a **Golden Globe** and an NAACP **Image Award**. After a number of back-to-back hit films, such as *Jumpin' Jack Flash*, 1986; *Burglar*, 1987; and *Fatal Beauty*, 1987, her big-screen career was set. She won an **Academy Award** for her performance as an unwitting psychic in the smash hit *Ghost*, 1990, and received critical acclaim for her performances in *Sister Act*, 1992, and *Sister Act 2*, 1993. Goldberg has also hosted her own talk show, starred in her own sitcom, produced and guest starred on the TV game show *Hollywood Squares*, and hosted the 66th annual Academy Awards telecast. With fellow comedians Billy Crystal and Robin Williams, she co-hosted HBO's *Comic Relief*, a series of cable shows that raised over $40 million to benefit America's homeless population. Numerous awards, movie roles, and **television** appearances followed, and she is currently one of the most sought-after entertainers in the industry.

Filmography: *The Color Purple*, 1985; *Jumpin' Jack Flash*, 1986; *The Telephone*, 1987; *Fatal Beauty*, 1987; *Burglar*, 1987; *Clara's Heart*, 1988; **The Long Walk Home**, 1989; *Kiss Shot*, 1989; *Homer and Eddie*, 1989; *Ghost*, 1990; *Soapdish*, 1991; *Sister Act*, 1992; **Sarafina**, 1992; *The Player*, 1992; *Sister Act 2: Back in the Habit*, 1993; *Naked in New York*, 1993; *Made in America*, 1993; *Star Trek: Generations*, 1994; *The Little Rascals*, 1994; *The Lion King*, 1994; *Corina, Corina*, 1994; *Boys on the Side*, 1994; *Ghosts of Mississippi*, 1996; *Eddie*, 1996; *The Associate*, 1996; *Cinderella*, 1997; *A Knight in Camelot*, 1998; **How Stella Got Her Groove Back**, 1998; *The Deep End of the Ocean*, 1998; *Jackie's Back*, 1999; *Girl Interrupted*, 1999; *Alice in Wonderland*, 1999; *The Adventures of Rocky & Bullwinkle*, 2000; *Rat Race*, 2001; *Monkeybone*, 2001; **Kingdom Come**, 2001; *Call Me Claus*, 2001.

GOLDEN CHILD, THE. 1986. (PG-13) 94 min. Drama/Thriller. A professional "finder of lost children" comes to the rescue of a kidnapped Tibetan child with magical powers from an evil force out to destroy him. A beautiful woman joins him on his quest, and the fate of the world is in their hands. Cast: **Eddie Murphy**, Charlotte Lewis, Charles Dance, Victor Wong, Randall "Tex" Cobb, James

Hong. Director: Michael Ritchie. Writer: Dennis Feldman. Cinematographer: Donald E. Thorin. Music: Michel Colombier.

GOLDEN GLOBE AWARDS, THE. This annual award is given each January by the Hollywood Foreign Press Association to honor excellence in film and television. Its members are foreign correspondents that cover Hollywood for publications outside the U. S. The award ceremony is a highly anticipated, star-studded event that is televised around the world. Past African American winners include: **Sidney Poitier**, actor in leading role, *Lilies of the Field*, 1963. **James Earl Jones**, new male star of the year, *The Great White Hope*, 1970. **Isaac Hayes**, original score, *Shaft*, 1971. **Diana Ross**, new female star of the year, *Lady Sings the Blues*, 1972. **Louis Gossett Jr.**, actor in supporting role, *An Officer and a Gentleman*, 1982. Stevie Wonder, original song, "I Just Called to Say I Love You," *Woman in Red*, 1984. Lionel Richie, original song, "Say You, Say Me," *White Nights*, 1985. **Whoopi Goldberg**, actress in leading role, *The Color Purple*, 1985. **Denzel Washington**, actor in supporting role, *Glory*, 1989. **Morgan Freeman**, actor in leading role: musical/comedy, *Driving Miss Daisy*, 1989. Whoopi Goldberg, actress in supporting role, *Ghost*, 1990. **Angela Bassett**, actress in leading role: musical/comedy, *What's Love Got to Do with It?* 1993. Denzel Washington, actor in leading role: drama, *The Hurricane*, 1999. **Jamie Foxx**, actor in leading role: musical/comedy, *Ray*, 2005.

GOOD, MEAGAN (1981-). Actress, singer. She was born Meagan Monique Good in Panorama, California, and appeared in commercials when she was only four years old. She was once a member of the singing group Isyss, and began her acting career on **television** in series, such as *Moesha, Touched by an Angel, The Steve Harvey Show*, and *The Parent Hood*. She also portrayed the roles of Vanessa in *My Wife and Kids*, and Melanie in the series *Kevin Hill*. Her notable film appearances include *Eve's Bayou*, 1997; *Biker Boyz*, 2003; and *The Cookout*, 2004.

  Filmography: *House Party 3*, 1994; *Friday*, 1995; *Make a Wish, Molly*, 1995; *Eve's Bayou*, 1997; *The Secret Life of Girls*, 1999; *Three Strikes*, 2000; *Biker Boyz*, 2003; *Deliver Us from Eva*, 2003; *Ride or Die*, 2003; *You Got Served*, 2004; *The Cookout*, 2004; *Brick*, 2005; *Roll Bounce*, 2005; *Crenshaw Blvd.*, 2005.

GOODING JR., CUBA (1968-). Actor. Gooding was born in Bronx, New York, but moved with his family to Los Angeles in the 1970s when his father's career in entertainment took off. Cuba Gooding, his father, was lead singer for the popular singing group The Main Ingredient. Gooding liked to dance and his first professional performance was as a break-dancer for Lionel Ritchie's performance at the 1986 Olympics in Los Angeles. His acting potential was noticed when he appeared in a high school production of *Li'l Abner* when a friend's parent, who was a talent agent, offered to represent him. He worked in commercials and landed a spot on the TV series *Hill Street Blues*. His first feature role was in **Coming to America**, 1988, but a star was born when he received the lead role in **John Singleton**'s **Boyz N the Hood**, 1991. Gooding worked consistently from then on, landing the crucial part of a pro football player in director Cameron Crowe's mega-hit *Jerry Maquire*, 1996, which earned him an **Oscar** for Best Supporting Actor.

Filmography: *Coming to America*, 1988; *Boyz N the Hood*, 1991; *Murder without Motive*, 1992; *Hitz*, 1992; *Gladiator*, 1992; *A Few Good Men*, 1992; *Judgment Night*, 1993; *Daybreak*, 1993; *Outbreak*, 1994; **Losing Isaiah**, 1994; *Lightning Jack*, 1994; **The Tuskegee Airmen**, 1995; *Jerry Maguire*, 1996; *As Good as It Gets*, 1997; *What Dreams May Come*, 1998; *Instinct*, 1999; *Men of Honor*, 2000; *Rat Race*, 2001; *Pearl Harbor*, 2001; *In the Shadows*, 2001; *Snow Dogs*, 2002; **The Fighting Temptations**, 2003; *Boat Trip*, 2003.

GORDON'S WAR. 1973. (R) 89 min. Drama. A Vietnam veteran returns home to find that Harlem is infested with drugs and that his wife is an addict. When all else fails, he forms a vigilante group to address the problem. Cast: **Paul Winfield**, **Carl Lee**, David Downing, Tony King, **Grace Jones**. Director: **Ossie Davis**. Music: Angelo Badalamenti.

GORDY, BERRY (1929-). Businessman, songwriter, music and film producer. Starting out as a professional boxer, Gordy began to write songs and, in 1959, borrowed $700 to start Motown Records. Nearly 30 years later, the company was sold to MCA Records for $61 million. Gordy's winning concept was for a music company that turned out hit records like the Detroit car factories turned out cars...on an assembly line. He signed mostly unknown artists to his label and developed their talent to produce a string of back-to-back hits that included "Get a Job," "Fingertips," "How Sweet It Is to Be Loved by You," "Can't Hurry Love," and "My Girl." He made big stars out of Smokey Robinson and the Miracles, Little Stevie Wonder, Marvin Gaye, Tammy Terrell, The Supremes, The Temptations, and many others. He insisted on quality, hard work, and 110% dedication to the cause. His efforts established Motown as one of the most successful black-owned businesses of all time. Motown ventured into film in the 1970s with **Mahogany**, 1975, starring **Diana Ross** and **Billy Dee Williams**, with Gordy credited as director. Other films include the Billie Holiday biopic *Lady Sings the Blues*, 1972, and *The Last Dragon*, 1985, an urban, musical martial arts flick starring karateka Taimak, and pop music icon Appolonia. An independently produced docudrama titled *Standing in the Shadows of Motown*, 2002, documents the rise of the Motown Sound and focuses on The Funk Brothers, Motown's non-compensated and previously overlooked contracted band of studio musicians who actually created the Motown sound of music.

Filmography: *Lady Sings the Blues*, 1972; *Mahogany*, 1975; **Bingo Long Traveling All-Stars & Motor Kings**, 1976; **The Wiz**, 1978; *The Last Dragon*, 1985.

GOSSETT, LOUIS, JR. (1936-). Actor. Gossett was born in Brooklyn, New York, and began his acting career at the age of 17 when a leg injury kept him from playing basketball. He received a Donaldson Award for Best Newcomer of the year for his role in the stage play *Take A Giant Step*. In 1958, while performing on stage in *The Desk Set*, Gossett was drafted by the New York Knicks to play professional basketball, but chose to stay involved with the theater instead, appearing in more than 60 plays, including *Lost in the Stars*, *A Raisin in the Sun*, and *The Blacks*. On **television**, Gossett acted in several series, including *The Nurses*, *The Defenders*, and *East Side, West Side*. He won an **Emmy Award** in 1977 for his portrayal of Fiddler in the miniseries **Roots**. He brilliantly portrayed Egyptian leader Anwar Sadat in a television biopic on his life and accomplishments, and later starred as *Gideon Oliver* in his own dramatic television series. Gossett was seen on the big screen in such films as *Skin Game*, 1971; *The Deep*, 1977; *Iron Eagle 1 & 2*, 1986 and 1988; and *Diggstown*, 1993. He won an **Academy Award** for Best Supporting Actor for his portrayal of the hard-core drill sergeant in *An Officer and a Gentleman*, 1983.

Filmography: *A Raisin in the Sun*, 1961; *The Bushbaby*, 1970; *Skin Game*, 1971; *It's Good to Be Alive*, 1974; *The White Dawn*, 1975; *J. D.'s Revenge*, 1976; *The Deep*, 1977; *The Choirboys*, 1977; *He Who Walks Alone*, 1978; *The Lazarus Syndrome*, 1989; *Don't Look Back: The Story of Satchel Paige*, 1981; *An Officer and a Gentleman*, 1982; *Sadat*, 1983; *Jaws 3*, 1983; *The Guardian*, 1984; *Finders Keepers*, 1984; *Enemy Mine*, 1985; *Iron Eagle*, 1986; *Firewalker*, 1986; *The Principal*, 1987; **Roots: The Gift**, 1988; *Iron Eagle 2*, 1988; **Zora Is My Name**, 1990; *Straight Up*, 1990; **The Josephine Baker Story**, 1990; *El Diablo*, 1990

Cover-Up, 1991; *Keeper of the City*, 1992; *Diggstown*, 1992; *Aces: Iron Eagle 3*, 1992; *Return to Lonesome Dove*, 1993; *Dangerous Relations*, 1993; *Flashfire*, 1994; *Zooman*, 1995; *Iron Eagle 4*, 1995; **Run for the Dream: The Gail Devers Story**, 1996; *Inside*, 1996; *Managua*, 1997; *Bram Stroker's The Mummy*, 1997; *The Inspectors*, 1998; *Y2K*, 1999; **Strange Justice: The Clarence Thomas and Anita Hill Story**, 1999; *Love Songs*, 1999; *The Highway Man*, 1999.

GO TELL IT ON THE MOUNTAIN. 1984. (TV) 100 min. Drama. A PBS American Playhouse production based on the semiautobiographical novel by James Baldwin about a young man wanting to earn the love and respect of his strict stepfather in the 1930s. Cast: **Paul Winfield**, Olivia Cole, **Ruby Dee**, **Alfre Woodard**, **James Bond III**, **Rosalind Cash**, Linda Hopkins. Director: **Stan Lathan**.

GRAFFITI BRIDGE. 1990. (PG-13) 95 min. Music/Drama. The sequel to **Purple Rain**, 1984. Two Minneapolis nightclub owners are in a power struggle. They make a bet about which can write the best song and put their establishments on the line. Cast: **Prince**, **Morris Day**, Jerome Benton, Jill Jones, Mavis Staples, George Clinton, Ingrid Chavez, Michael Bland, Phillip C, Rosie Gaines, Levi Seacer Jr., Damon Dixon, Kirk Johnson, Tony Mosely, Miko Weaver, Garry Johnson, Jesse Johnson, Jimmy Jam, Tevin Campbell. Writer/Director: Prince. Cinematographer: Bill Butler.

GRAY, F. GARY (1970-). Director, producer. Raised in South Central Los Angeles, Gray began his filmmaking career working for **Black Entertainment Television** and directing music videos for artists, such as TLC's "Waterfalls," Coolio's "Fantastic Voyage," and **Ice Cube**'s "It was a Good Day." Recognizing Gray's talent, rapper turned actor/producer Ice Cube insisted he direct his hit urban comedy *Friday*, 1995. He now directs mainstream films.
    Filmography: *Friday*, 1995; **Set It Off**, 1996; *The Negotiator*, 1998; *Ryan Caulfield: One Year*, 1999; *A Man Apart*, 2003; *The Italian Job*, 2004; *Be Cool*, 2005.

GREASED LIGHTNING. 1977. (PG) 95 min. Comedy/Drama. This is a film based on the life of Wendell Scott, the first black auto-racing champion who faced racism and rejection in his quest to obtain his professional goals. Cast: **Richard Pryor**, **Pam Grier**, Beau Bridges, **Cleavon Little**, Vincent Gardenia. Director: **Michael Schultz**. Writer: Leon Capetanos, **Melvin Van Peebles**.

GREAT WHITE HOPE, THE. 1970. (PG-13) 103 min. Drama. Inspired by the stage play based on the life of Jack Johnson, who became the first African American world heavyweight-boxing champion in 1910. Cast: **James Earl Jones**, Jane Alexander, Lou Gilbert, **Joel Fluellen**, Chester Morris, Robert Webber, Hal Holbrook, R. G. Armstrong, **Moses Gunn, Scatman Crothers**. Director: Martin Ritt. Cinematography: Burnett Guffey.

GREAT WHITE HYPE, THE. 1996. (R) 95 min. Comedy. This film satire explores the comical and corrupt side of the boxing world. In hopes of boosting pay-per-view revenues for his dwindling championship fights on cable TV, a slick promoter seeks out a white boxer to create a "great white hope." Cast: **Samuel L. Jackson, Damon Wayans**, Peter Berg, Jeff Goldblum, Jon Lovitz, Corbin Bernsen, Richard "Cheech" Marin, John Rhys-Davies, **Salli Richardson, Rocky Carroll, Jamie Foxx**, Michael Jace. Director: **Reginald Hudlin**. Writers: Ron Shelton, Tony Hendra. Cinematography: Ron Garcia. Music: Marcus Miller.

GREATEST, THE. 1977. (PG) 100 min. Biopic. This is an autobiography film on world heavyweight boxing champion **Muhammad Ali**. It follows his rise to stardom, his family life, his many fights, and his involvement with the Nation of Islam. Cast: **Muhammad Ali**, Robert Duvall, Ernest Borgnine, **James Earl Jones**, John Marley, **Roger E. Mosley**, Dina Merrill, **Paul Winfield**. Director: Tom Gries. Writer: Ring Lardner Jr. Cinematographer: Harry Stradling Jr. Music: Michael Masser.

GREAVES, WILLIAM (1926-). Documentary filmmaker, director, editor, actor. The New York-born Greaves began his long career as an actor in films like *Miracle in Harlem*, 1948, *Lost Bounderies*, 1949, and *The Fight Never Ends*, 1949. He later enrolled at City College of New York and studied at the Actor's Studio with Lee Strasberg and Elia Kazan. He was also a dancer at one time with the Sierra Leonian Asadata Dafora Dance Company. He later joined the Pearl Primus Dance Troupe and was a member of the American Negro Theater. Greaves moved to Canada in the 1950s and recorded sound on many film productions, and became director of the Canadian National Film Board, 1952-1960. He returned to the United States and began to produce television and documentaries. He was executive producer on *Black Journal* in 1968, a program that became *Tony Brown's Journal*. His work has received numerous national and international awards.

Filmography: *Putting It Straight*, 1957; *Smoke and Weather*, 1958; *Emergency Ward*, 1959; *Four Religions*, 1960; *Symbiopsychotaxiplasm: Take One*, 1968; *Ali, the Fighter*, 1971; *The Voice of La Raza*, 1972; *From These Roots*, 1974; *That's Black Entertainment*, 1990; *The Deep North*, 1990; *Ralph Bunch: An American Odyssey*, 2001; *Symbiopsychotaxiplasm: Take 2 ½*, 2005.

GREEN, EDDIE (1896-1950). Comedian, actor, producer, director. Green began his career on the vaudeville stage, received acclaim on radio with *Duffy's Tavern*, and made his film debut in *The Devil's Parade*, 1930. He produced and starred in *Dress Rehearsal*, 1939, which was the first all-black cast film to have a **television** broadcast, on NBC in March 1940. As head of the production company Sepia Arts, he wrote, produced, and directed several comedy shorts, including *One Round Jones*, 1946, and *Eddie's Laugh Jamboree*, 1947, distributed by **Ted Toddy**. Green was director and star of *Mr. Adam's Bomb*, 1949.

Filmography: *The Devil's Parade*, 1930; *What Goes Up*, 1939; *Dress Rehearsal*, 1939; *Comes Midnight*, 1940; *Mantan Messes Up*, 1946; *Mr. Adam's Bomb*, 1949.

GREEN PASTURES. 1936. 93 min. Drama. This film was inspired by the Pulitzer Prize-winning play by Marc Connelly and recounts Old Testament stories from the Bible with an African American slant. It received criticism for its **stereotypical** broken-English dialect and some theaters in the South refused to screen the film because it depicted biblical characters as black. Cast: **Rex Ingram, Oscar Polk, Eddie Anderson**, George Reed, Abraham Graves, Myrtle Anderson, Frank Wilson. Director: William Keighley, Marc Connelly. Cinematographer: Hal Mohr.

GRIDLOCK'D. 1997. (R) 91 min. Urban Drama. A couple of New York heroine addicts are motivated to kick their drug habits when a friend overdoses. Their day is spent in the endless red tape required to enroll in a government detox program while avoiding the police and being chased by drug dealers to whom they still own money. Cast: **Tupac Shakur**, Tim Roth, **Thandie Newton**, Charles Fleischer, Howard Hesseman, James Pickens Jr., John Sayles, Eric Payne, Tom Towles, Tom Wright, James Shanta, Jim O'Malley, George Poulos, Debbie Zaricor, Mike Scriba. Writer/Director: **Vondie Curtis-Hall**.

GRIER, DAVID ALAN (1955-). Comedian, actor. This Detroit, Michigan-born actor earned his Master of Fine Arts Degree from

Yale University, School of Drama in 1981, and received a Tony Award nomination for his portrayal of baseball great Jackie Robinson in the Broadway musical *The First*. He has an impressive list of film and **television** appearances, including *Streamers*, 1983; *Boomerang*, 1992; and *The Woodsman*, 2004. He was a regular on the comedy series *In Living Color*, and provided the voice for Red the Alley Cat in *Stuart Little*, 1999.

Filmography: *Streamers*, 1983; *A Soldier's Story*, 1984; *Beer*, 1985; *From the Hip*, 1987; *Amazon Women on the Moon*, 1987; *Off Limits*, 1988; *I'm Gonna Git You Sucka*, 1988; *Loose Cannons*, 1990; *In the Army Now*, 1994; *Blankman*, 1994; *Tales From the Hood*, 1995; *Jumanji*, 1995; *McHale's Navy*, 1997; *Top of the World*, 1997; *Stuart Little*, 1999; *Damned if You Do*, 1999; *Three Strikes*, 2000; *Return to Me*, 2000; *The Adventures of Rocky and Bullwinkle*, 2000; *15 Minutes*, 2001; *Baadasssss!* 2003; *Tiptoes*, 2003; *The Woodsman*, 2004; *Bewitched*, 2005.

GRIER, PAM (1949-). Actress. Born into a military family in Winston-Salem, North Carolina, and spent her developing years in Europe. She returned to the United States at age 14 and lived in Denver, Colorado. Planning for a career in medicine she attended Metropolitan State College. As the runner-up in the 1967 Miss Colorado Universe contest, Grier signed with a Hollywood agent and relocated to Los Angeles to pursue an acting career. She took acting classes while working at the Agency of Performing Arts switchboard, when she was finally cast in *The Birdcage*, 1969. From there, she became the reigning queen over an onslaught of black-cast Hollywood movies in the 1970s that became known as the **blaxploitation** era. She was cast as the first black action shero in films like *Coffy*, 1973; *Foxy Brown*, 1974; and *Friday Foster*, 1975, but found the often-**stereotypical** character range to be constricting. She took some time off and did not act again until 1981, with a co-starring role in *Fort Apache: The Bronx*, 1981. Grier has since acted on stage and **television**, and portrayed the title role in Quentin Tarrentino's *Jackie Brown*, 1997. Grier has been honored with numerous awards, including an NAACP **Image Award** for Best Actress, a National Black Theater Festival Award, and the African American Film Society Award.

Filmography: *The Birdcage*, 1969; *Beyond the Valley of the Dolls*, 1970; *The Big Doll House*, 1971; *Twilight People*, 1972; *The Big Bird Cage*, 1972; *Scream Blackula Scream*, 1973; *Coffy*, 1973; *The Arena*, 1973; *Foxy Brown*, 1974; *Sheba Baby*, 1975; *Friday Foster*, 1975; *Bucktown*, 1975; *Drum*, 1976; *Greased Lightning*, 1977; *Fort Apache, the Bronx*, 1981; *Something*

Wicked This Way Comes, 1993; *Above the Law*, 1988; *Class of 1999*, 1990; **Posse**, 1993; **Original Gangstas**, 1996; *Mars Attacks*, 1996; *Escape from L. A.*, 1996; **Woo**, 1997; *Jackie Brown*, 1997; *In Too Deep*, 1999; *Holy Smoke*, 1999; *Snow Day*, 2000; *Ghosts of Mars*, 2001; **Bones**, 2001; **The Adventures of Pluto Nash**, 2002.

GRIER, ROOSEVELT "ROSEY" (1932-). Actor, athlete, minister. This All-Pro player for the Los Angeles Rams football team during the 1960s was born in Linden, New Jersey. He made guest appearances in **television** series, such as *The Man from U. N. C. L. E.*; *The Wild, Wild West*; *Daniel Boone*; and *Kojak*. Grier hosted his variety show, *The Rosey Grier Show*, in 1969. His film work includes roles in **The Thing with Two Heads**, 1972; **Roots: The Next Generation**, 1979; and **Sophisticated Gents**, 1981.

Filmography: *Skyjacked*, 1972; *The Thing with Two Heads*, 1972; *Timber Tramps*, 1975; *Evil in the Deep*, 1976; *Rabbit Test*, 1978; *Roots: The Next Generation*, 1979; *The Seekers*, 1979; *The Glove*, 1979; *The Sophisticated Gents*, 1981; *Reggie's Prayer*, 1996.

GRIFFIN, EDDIE (1968-). Comedian, actor. He was born in Kansas City, Missouri, and attended Lincoln High School, where he was voted class clown three times. Griffin used his gift to make people laugh and became a stand-up comedian before moving into **television** and film. His film work includes the lead roles in **Foolish**, 1999, and **Undercover Brother**, 2002. On television, he portrayed the title character of Eddie Sherman in the sitcom *Malcolm & Eddie*, 1996, and starred in his own stand-up comedy special *Dys-Funktional Family*, 2003. He also wrote and produced *My Baby's Daddy*, 2004.

Filmography: **The Five Heartbeats**, 1991; *The Last Boy Scout*, 1991; *Brain Donors*, 1992; *Coneheads*, 1993; **The Meteor Man**, 1993; **House Party 3**, 1994; **Jason's Lyric**, 1994; *The Walking Dead*, 1995; *Armageddon*, 1998; *Deuce Bigalow: Male Gigolo*, 1999; *The Mod Squad*, 1999; *Foolish*, 1999; *Picking Up the Pieces*, 2000; *Double Take*, 2001; **John Q**, 2002; *The New Guy*, 2002; *Undercover Brother*, 2002; *Scary Movie 3*, 2003; *Pryor Offenses*, 2004; *My Baby's Daddy*, 2004; *Who Made the Potato Salad?*, 2005; *The Wendell Baker Story*, 2005; *Deuce Bigalow: European Gigolo*, 2005; *Irish Jam*, 2005; *Bunyan and Babe*, 2005.

GUESS WHO'S COMING TO DINNER. 1967. (NR) 108 min. Drama. A white graduate student returns from holiday with her new African American fiancé in tow. Although he is a successful doctor, the color barrier is raised when she brings him home for parental approval. His father is also color struck over the news and rejects his son's choice. Although the mothers are much more supportive, both families must cross the color line and come to terms over a family dinner. Cast: **Sidney Poitier**, Katharine Hepburn, Spencer Tracy, Katharine Houghton, Cecil Kellaway, **Beah Richards**. Director: Stanley Kramer. Writer: William Rose. Cinematography: Sam Leavitt. Music: Frank Devol. Awards: 1967 **Oscars**, Best Actress (Hepburn), Best Story & Screenplay; 1968 British Academy Awards, Best Actor (Tracy), Best Actress (Hepburn). The AFI Top 100 Films List.

GUILLAUME, ROBERT (1927-). Actor, singer, producer. He was raised by his maternal grandmother in the poor section of St. Louis, Missouri, and became a celebrated actor of stage, film, and **television**. He spent time in the U.S. Army before enrolling at St. Louis University to study business administration. He took on menial jobs as a cook and a streetcar conductor to support himself and began training his voice. His plan was to someday sing tenor at the Metropolitan Opera, and he would eventually spend eight months starring in the Los Angeles production of *Phantom of the Opera*. Guillaume received a scholarship to the Aspen Music Festival and his performance there gained him an apprenticeship at the Karamu Theater in Cleveland, where he made his semi-professional debuts in opera and musical comedy. He moved to New York and appeared in many stage productions, including *Othello*, *Porgy and Bess*, *Golden Boy*, and he received a Tony Award nomination for his performance as Nathan Detroit in *Guys and Dolls*. His big television break came in 1977 when he was cast as Benson DuBois, the outspoken butler in the daytime-drama parody series *Soap*, for which he won an **Emmy Award**. His own series followed, where his upwardly mobile character goes from being a butler, to state budget director, to lieutenant governor in the series *Benson*, for which he won another Emmy Award. Other notable television performances include *The Robert Guillaume Show*, *Sports Night*, and numerous made-for-TV movies. He produced and starred in the PBS drama *You Must Remember This*, and the ethnically diverse fairy-tale series *Happily Ever After*, for Home Box Office. He also wrote, directed, and starred in *John Grin's Christmas*. His film roles include *Lean on Me*, 1989; *Death Warrant*, 1990; and he provided the voice of Rafiki in *The Lion King*, 1994.

Filmography: *Seems Like Old Times*, 1980; *Purlie*, 1981; *Prince Jack*, 1984; *Wanted: Dead or Alive*, 1987; *They Still Call Me Bruce*, 1987; *Lean on Me*, 1989; *Death Warrant*, 1990; *The*

Meteor Man, 1993; *The Lion King*, 1994; *Spy Hard*, 1996; *Run for the Dream: The Gail Devers Story*, 1996; *First Kid*, 1996; *The Lion King II: Simba's Pride*, 1998; *Silicon Towers*, 1999; *13th Child*, 2002; *Big Fish*, 2003; *The Lion King III*, 2004; *Tough Like Wearing Dreadlocks*, 2005; *Jack Satin*, 2005.

GUNN, BILL (1934-1989). Director, writer, actor. He was born in Philadelphia, Pennsylvania, and began his acting career in an episode of *Route 66*, 1961. His other **television** guest appearances include roles in *Naked City*, *The Outer Limits*, *The Fugitive*, and *The Cosby Show*. As a writer Gunn penned the scripts for *The Landlord*, 1970, and *The Angel Levine*, 1970. He also wrote, directed, and appeared in *Ganja & Hess*, 1973.

Filmography: *The Interns*, 1962; *The Spy with My Face*, 1965; *Penelope*, 1966; *Ganja & Hess*, 1973; *Losing Ground*, 1982.

GUNN, MOSES (1929-1993). Actor. A native of St. Louis, Missouri, Gunn graduated from Tennessee State University before making a name for himself on the New York stage, winning an Obie Award for his work in Leslie Lee II's *The First Breeze of Summer*. He also appeared off-Broadway in Jean Genet's *The Blacks*, and as Joe Mott in *The Iceman Cometh*. He has also been nominated for a Tony and an *Emmy Award* and was a founder of the Negro Ensemble Company in New York. His film roles include *Shaft*, 1971, and *The Great White Hope*, 1970, and he was seen on **television** in the miniseries *Roots*, 1977, the sitcom *Good Times*, and he was a regular on the series *A Man Called Hawk*. He wrote the stage play *The Promised Land: A Musical Drama*, and won an NAACP **Image Award** for his portrayal of Booker T. Washington in the film *Ragtime*, 1981.

Filmography: *Black Brigade*, 1969; *The Hot Rock*, 1970; *The Great White Hope*, 1970; *Shaft*, 1971; *Shaft's Big Score*, 1972; *Amazing Grace*, 1974; *Rollerball*, 1975; *Cornbread, Earl & Me*, 1975; *Aaron Loves Angela*, 1975; *Ragtime*, 1981; *Amityville 2: The Possession*, 1982; *The Never Ending Story*, 1984; *Firestarter*, 1984; *Killing Floor*, 1985; *Charlotte Forten's Mission: Experiment in Freedom*, 1985; *Certain Fury*, 1985; *Heartbreak Ridge*, 1986; *The House of Dies Drear*, 1988; *The Women of Brewster Place*, 1989; *Perfect Harmony*, 1991; *Memphis*, 1991.

GUY, JASMINE (1964-). Actress, dancer, singer. The daughter of a Baptist minister, Guy was born in Boston, Massachusetts, and raised in Atlanta, Georgia. She moved to New York City at age 16 to study dance with famed choreographer Alvin Ailey. Her dance training led to work in revival and road company tours of the Broadway shows *The Wiz* and *Leader of the Pack*. She was a dancer on several episodes of the television series *Fame*, which brought her to the attention of show's director and choreographer **Debbie Allen**. Allen cast Guy in the role of a spoiled Southern belle named Whitley Gilbert, in the black college-based sitcom, *A Different World*. As a spin-off from the mega hit series *The Cosby Show*, it too was a big hit, and ran for six seasons on NBC. Her television guest-starring appearances include *Touched by an Angel*, *Living Single*, and *The Parkers*. She had a recurring role on *Melrose Place*, and stars in the Showtime cable series *Dead Like Me*. Guy made her feature film debut in **Spike Lee**'s *School Daze*, 1988, and played opposite **Eddie Murphy** in *Harlem Nights*, 1989. Her made for TV movies include *Stompin' at the Savoy*, 1992, *Queen*, 1993, *The Feast of All Saints*, 2001, and *Carrie*, 2002. Her recent stage work includes *Grease*, and *Chicago: The Musical*.

Filmography: *School Daze*, 1988; *Harlem Nights*, 1989; *Queen*, 1993; *America's Dream*, 1995; *Perfect Crime*, 1997; *Cats Don't Dance*, 1997; *Guinevere*, 1999; *Diamond Men*, 2001.

H

HALEY, ALEX (1921-1992). Author, scriptwriter. Haley was born in Tennessee and joined the U.S. Coast Guard at the age of 17. While deployed on ship during World War II, he wrote stories to relax and pass the time. Haley became a full-time writer when he retired from the Coast Guard at age 37. A major break came when he interviewed Muslim leader Malcolm X for *Playboy* magazine, an encounter that lead to his writing of *The Autobiography of Malcolm X*, published in 1965. Filmmaker **Spike Lee** produced a film version of the book in 1992, starring **Denzel Washington**. Inspired by stories of his family history, Haley traced his bloodline back to an African man named Kunta Kinte. His research and experience became the book *Roots* that received the 1976 National Book Award and a Pulitzer Prize in 1977. After selling millions of copies, it was turned into a 12-hour TV miniseries in 1977. The sequel *Roots: The Next Generation* was aired in 1979.

HALL, ALBERT (1937-). Actor. He was born in Boothton, Alabama, and began his entertainment career performing with the Richmond Sheppard Mime Troup. He made his TV debut in the 1973 season of the daytime soap opera *One Life to Live*, and his film debut was as a background detective in *Cotton Comes to Harlem*, 1970. His major screen roles include *Apocalypse Now*, 1979; *Malcolm X*, 1992; and *Ali*, 2001. On **television**, he portrayed baseball great Hank Aaron in *The Tiger Woods Story*, 1998; NAACP leader Roy Wilkins in *Path to War*, 2002; and had recurring roles on the series *Ally McBeal* and *24*.

Filmography: *Cotton Comes to Harlem*, 1970; **Willie Dynamite** 1974; **Leadbelly**, 1976; *The Bermuda Triangle*, 1979; *Apocalypse Now*, 1979; *Ryan's Four*, 1983; *Trouble in Miami*, 1985; *Betrayed*, 1988; *The Fabulous Baker Boys*, 1989; *Music Box*, 1989; **Malcolm X**, 1992; *Rookie of the Year*, 1993; *Major Payne*, 1995; **Devil in a Blue Dress**, 1995; **The Great White Hype**, 1996; *Courage under Fire*, 1996; **Get on the Bus**, 1996; **Beloved**, 1998; *Ali*, 2001.

HALL, ARSENIO (1955-). Comedian, actor. Born in Cleveland, Ohio, Hall began his career as a stand-up comic and emcee at the Sheba Lounge in Chicago in the late 1970s. He took his comedy routine to Los Angeles and was soon on **television** hosting *The 1/2 Hour Comedy Hour* and *Solid Gold*, and he later hosted his own late-night talk show, *The Arsenio Hall Show*. He also hosted *Star Search*, and was a regular on the series *Martial Law*. His film appearances include roles in **Coming to America**, 1988, and **Harlem Nights**, 1989.

Filmography: *Amazon Women on the Moon*, 1987; *Coming to America*, 1988, *Harlem Nights*, 1989; *The Proud Family Movie*, 2005.

HALL, IRMA P. (1937-). Actress. She was born in Beaumont, Texas, and attended Briar Cliff College before transferring to Texas College while studying to become a language teacher. An interest in acting developed after she met actor-director **Raymond St. Jacques** while she was working as a volunteer reporter for a Dallas newspaper. He hired her to do publicity for his film **Book of Numbers**, 1972, and also cast her in a small role after hearing her read some of her poetry while on the set. She went on to help form the Dallas Minority Regional Theater and made her stage debut in their production of *Happy Endings*. She retired from teaching in 1984. Moving to Chicago, Illinois, Hall stayed in the theater, appearing in many productions, including *Member of the Wedding*, *Black Girl*, and *Gentle Fire*, which earned her a local Chicago theater prize, the Joseph Jefferson Award. She landed guest-starring roles in **television** shows, such as *Dallas*, *Touched by an Angel*, *Judging Amy*, and *The Bernie Mac Show*, and appeared in many made-for-

TV movies. Her breakthrough role came as Aunt T in *A Family Thing*, 1996, with **James Earl Jones**, and she won a Chicago Critics Award for Best Supporting Actress for her performance. Other film work includes roles in *Backdraft*, 1991; *Midnight in the Garden of Good and Evil*, 1997; *Beloved*, 1998; and *Ladykillers*, 2004, with Tom Hanks. She won an NAACP **Image Award** for her performance in *Soul Food*, 1997.

Filmography: *Book of Numbers*, 1973; *Split Image*, 1982; *On Valentine's Day*, 1986; *Square Dance*, 1987; *They Still Call Me Bruce*, 1987; *Backdraft*, 1991; *Straight Talk*, 1992; *Babe*, 1992; *Mo' Money*, 1992; *A Family Thing*, 1996; *Buddy*, 1997; *Nothing to Lose*, 1997; *Steel*, 1997; *Soul Food*, 1997; *Midnight in the Garden of Good and Evil*, 1997; *The Love Letter*, 1998; *Beloved*, 1998; *Patch Adams*, 1998; *A Slipping Down Life*, 1999; *A Lesson Before Dying*, 1999; *Something to Sing About*, 2000; *Our America*, 2002; *Don't Let Go*, 2002; *Bad Company*, 2002; *Ladykillers*, 2004; *Collateral*, 2004.

HALL, REGINA (1971-). Actress. She was born in Washington, D.C., and earned a master's degree in journalism from New York University. She appeared in several commercials after graduation and made her film debut in *The Best Man*, 1999. She had a recurring role as Coretta Lipp in the TV series *Ally McBeal*, and she has guest starred on *NYPD Blue* and *New York Undercover*.

Filmography: *The Best Man*, 1999; *Love and Basketball*, 2000; *Scary Movie*, 2000; *Disappearing Acts*, 2000; *Scary Movie 2*, 2001; *The Other Brother*, 2002; *Paid in Full*, 2002; *Malibu's Most Wanted*, 2003; *Scary Movie 3*, 2003.

HALLELUJAH! 1929. 90 min. Silent. Drama. A Southern cotton picker becomes a traveling preacher, only to be lured off the righteous path by a beautiful vixen. This was the second Hollywood sound film ever made, and there was also a silent version. Cast: **Daniel L. Haynes**, **Nina Mae McKinney**, William Fountaine, Harry Gray, Fannie Bell DeKnight, Everett McGarrity. Director: King Vidor. Music: Irving Berlin.

HAMILTON, BERNIE (1928-). This Los Angeles-born actor became well known as Captain Dobey on the hit 1970s TV series *Starsky and Hutch*. Before that, he had a long run of playing various TV roles, such as *Ramar of the Jungle*, 1953; *Twilight Zone*, 1961; *The Virginian*, 1969; and *Police Story*, 1973. His film roles include *The Jackie Robinson Story*, 1950; *One Potato, Two Potato*, 1964; and *Scream Blacula Scream*, 1973.

Filmography: *The Jackie Robinson Story*, 1950; *The Young One*, 1961; *Captain Sinbad*, 1963; *One Potato, Two Potato*, 1964; *The Lost Man*, 1969; *The Losers*, 1970; *Scream Blackula Scream*, 1973; *Bucktown*, 1975.

HAMILTON, LISA GAY (1964-). Actress, director. She was born in Los Angeles, California, and began acting at an early age. She took private acting lessons in junior high school and attended summer drama camps. She graduated from New York University and received a master's degree from Julliard. Her notable **television** roles include Dr. Laura Reed, 1996, in the daytime drama *One Life to Live*, and Rebecca Washington, 1997-2003, in the law series *The Practice*. Her major film work includes roles in *Jackie Brown*, 1997; *Beloved*, 1998; and *The Sum of All Fears*, 2002. Hamilton produced and directed the award-winning **documentary**, *Beah: A Black Woman Speaks*, 2003.

Filmography: *Krush Groove*, 1985; *Reversal of Fortune*, 1990; *Naked in New York*, 1993; *Drunks*, 1995; *Palookaville*, 1995; *Twelve Monkeys*, 1995; *Nick and Jane*, 1997; *Lifebreath*, 1997; *Jackie Brown*, 1997; *Beloved*, 1998; *True Crime*, 1999; *A House Divided*, 2000; *Ten Tiny Love Stories*, 2001; *The Sum of All Fears*, 2002; *The Truth about Charlie*, 2002; *Nine Lives*, 2005.

HAMPTON, HENRY (1940–1998). Documentary filmmaker. A native of St. Louis, Missouri, Hampton founded Blackside Inc. to produce documentary and industrial films focusing on projects that would inform, educate, and address social change. The company has produced *Malcolm X: Make It Plain*, 1995, for The American Experience. Other productions include *America's War on Poverty*, *Code Blue*, *The Great Depression*, and the award-winning, 14-hour documentary series covering the civil rights movement, *Eyes on the Prize*. Hampton has received six **Emmy Awards**, an **Academy Award** nomination, and a Dupont/Columbia Award for excellence in journalism. His final project was, *I'll Make Me a World*, a six-hour PBS series on African American artists.

Filmography: *Eyes on the Prize*, 1987; *Eyes on the Prize II*, 1990; *The Great Depression*, 1993; *The Land of Four Winds*, 1995; *America's War on Poverty*, 1995; *Malcolm X: Make It Plain*, 1995; *Breakthrough: The Changing Face of Science in America*, 1996; *I'll Make Me a World*, 1999.

HANCOCK, HERBIE (1940-). Jazz musician, composer. This Chicago, Illinois-born jazz keyboard player is renowned in the field of music and has compiled an awesome list of musical scores and soundtracks, including *The Spook Who Sat by the Door*, 1973; *A Soldier's Story*, 1984; *Round Midnight*, 1986; and *Harlem Nights*, 1989. Hancock was inducted into the Big Band and Jazz Hall of Fame in 1995, and he received a Jazz Masters Award from the National Endowment for the Arts in 2004.

Filmography: *Herbie*, 1966; *Blowup*, 1966; *The Spook Who Sat by the Door*, 1973; *Death Wish*, 1974; *A Soldier's Story*, 1984; *The George McKenna Story*, 1986; *Jo Jo Dancer, Your Life is Calling*, 1986; *'Round Midnight*, 1986; *Action Jackson*, 1988; *Colors*, 1988; *Harlem Nights*, 1989; *Livin' Large*, 1991.

HANGING WITH THE HOMEBOYS. 1991. (R) 89 min. Urban Comedy. Four young men from the Bronx discuss and complain about their lives and lack of opportunity one night while hanging out. Cast: Mario Joyner, **Doug E. Doug**, John Leguizamo, Nestor Serrano, Kimberly Russell, Mary B. Ward, Christine Claravall, Rosemark Jackson, Reggie Montgomery. Writer/Director: Joseph B. Vasquez. Cinematographer: Anghel Decca. Awards: Sundance 1991: Best Screenplay.

HANK AARON: CHASING THE DREAM. 1995. (TV) 120 min. Docudrama. The story chronicles the life and sports career of Hank Aaron, the Hall of Fame outfielder for the Milwaukee and Atlanta Braves baseball team. Dramatic reenactments, interviews, and archival footage are combined to give a comprehensive look at Aaron's involvement in the struggle for civil rights as well as his accomplishments on the baseball field. Narration: Dorian Harewood.

HANSBERRY, LORRAINE (1930-1965). Author, playwright. She was the first African American woman to have a play produced on Broadway. Based on her family's actual experience years before, *A Raisin in the Sun* focused on the Younger family's plans to move out of their crowded tenement apartment and into an all-white neighborhood in Chicago. After initially raising the $100,000 to produce the play, it ran for 19 months with **Sidney Poitier** in the lead role, and took its entire cast to the big screen when a movie version was filmed in 1961. Her stage play, turned TV program, *To Be Young, Gifted and Black*, was inspired by Hansberry's life, her writings, and other biographical information.

HARDISON, KADEEM (1965-). Actor. He was born in New York City and first came to America's attention as Dewayne Wayne in the **television** sitcom *A Different World*. His other TV series include *Between Brothers, Static Shock, Abby*, and he was the host of *Livin' Large*. His film roles include **Def by Temptation**, 1990; **Vampire in Brooklyn**, 1995; and **Biker Boyz**, 2003.

Filmography: *Rappin'*, 1985; **School Daze**, 1988; **I'm Gonna Git You Sucka**, 1988; *Def by Temptation*, 1990; **White Men Can't Jump**, 1992; *Gunmen*, 1994; *Renaissance Man*, 1994; *Vampire in Brooklyn*, 1995; **Panther**, 1995; *The Sixth Man*, 1997; *Drive*, 1997; *Blind Faith*, 1998; **Dancing in September**, 2000; **30 Years to Life**, 2001; *Instinct To Kill*, 2001; *Thank Heaven*, 2001; *Showtime*, 2002; *Biker Boyz*, 2003; *Dunsmore*, 2003; *Face of Terror*, 2003.

HARDWICK, GARY. Writer, director. He was born the 10th of 12 children in Detroit, Michigan, and is now one of the foremost filmmakers of the hip-hop generation. He majored in English at the University of Michigan in Ann Arbor, and received his law degree from Wayne State Law School in Detroit. He worked his way through law school doing stand-up comedy and continued this sideline while practicing law at various corporations and the United States Department of Justice. After writing his first novel, *Cold Medina*, Hardwick was selected as a Walt Disney Writing Fellow and relocated to California. He worked on the **television** shows *Where I Live, South Central*, and *In the House*, also serving as executive producer. After publication of his first novel in 1996, he followed with two more: *Double Dead* in 1997, which was bought by Warner Brothers for a feature film; and *Supreme Justice*, 1998. His first produced screenplay was **Trippin'**, 1999, and he made his directorial debut with **The Brothers**, 2001. Other directing projects include **Deliver Us from Eva**, 2003, and *Radio*, 2004. His fourth novel, *Color of Justice*, was published in 2002.

Filmography: *The Brothers*, 2001; *Deliver Us from Eva*, 2003; *Radio*, 2004; *Universal Remote*, 2007.

HARDY, ROB. Director. He began making films as a college student in Florida while working on a degree in engineering. He teamed with fellow student William Packer to create Rainforest Productions to make their first film, *Chocolate City*, 1994. After a successful straight-to-video release, the duo independently raised the budget for their next film, **Trois**, 2000, which grossed over $1.3 million in theatrical distribution. They followed with a sequel, *Trois 2: Pandora's Box*.

Filmography: *Chocolate City*, 1994; *Trois*, 2000; *Pandora's Box*, 2002; *The Gospel*, 2005.

HAREWOOD, DORIAN (1950-). Actor. This native of Dayton, Ohio, made his **television** debut in the telepic *Foster and Laurie*, 1975, and his film debut in ***Sparkle***, 1976. He portrayed Olympic sprinter Jesse Owens in the biopic ***The Jesse Owens Story***, 1984; Lenell Geter in *Guilty of Innocence: The Lenell Geter Story*, 1987, and has guest appeared in TV series, such as *Trauma Center, I'll Fly Away*, and *Viper*. He has provided his voice for numerous animated productions, including *Johnny Quest*, 1986; *Teenage Mutant Ninja Turtles*, 1987; *Sonic the Hedgehog*, 1993; *Biker Mice from Mars*, 1993; and *Mortal Kombat: The Animated Series*, 1995. Other notable film and telepic roles include ***Roots: The Next Generation***, 1979; ***Beulah Land***, 1980; ***Hendrix***, 2000; *Hollywood Wives: The New Generation*, 2003; and *Assault on Precinct 13*, 2005.

Filmography: *Sparkle*, 1976; *Gray Lady Down*, 1978; *Looker*, 1981; *Against All Odds*, 1984; *Tank*, 1984; *The Falcon and the Snowman*, 1985; *Full Metal Jacket*, 1987; *Solar Crisis*, 1990; *Pacific Heights*, 1990; *Sudden Death*, 1995; *Evasive Action*, 1998; *Glitter*, 2001; *Gothika*, 2003; *Assault on Precinct 13*, 2005.

HARLEM NIGHTS. 1989. (R) 118 min. Comedy. This is a gangster tale about two Harlem nightclub owners in the 1930s who must protect their territory from crooked cops and the white mob. Cast: **Eddie Murphy, Richard Pryor, Redd Foxx**, Danny Aiello, **Jasmine Guy**, Michael Lerner, **Arsenio Hall, Della Reese**, Eugene Glazer. Writer/Director: Eddie Murphy. Cinematographer: Woody Omens. Music: Herbie Hancock.

HARLEM ON THE PRAIRIE (a.k.a. *Bad Man of Harlem*). 1938. 54 min. Western. Singing cowboy Jeff Kincaid helps a young woman find a stash of gold hidden by her murdered father and protect her from the villains that killed him. Cast: **Herbert Jeffery, Mantan Moreland, F. E. Miller**, Connie Harris, Maceo B. Sheffield, **Spencer Williams, Jr**. Director: Sam Newfield.

HARLEM RIDES THE RANGE. 1939. 58 min. Western. This is the sequel to *Harlem on the Prairie*, 1938, but with a new name for the hero. Singing cowboy Bob Blake and his trusty horse Stardusk, fight to keep a greedy neighbor from stealing a uranium mine from its rightful owners. Cast: **Herbert Jeffrey**, Lucius Brooks, Artie Young, **F. E. Miller, Spencer Williams Jr., Clarence Brooks**, Tom Southern, Wade Dumas, Leonard Christmas. Director: Richard C. Kahn. Writers: F. E. Miller, Spencer Williams Jr.

HARPER, HILL (1966-). Actor. Hill was born in Iowa City, Iowa, and graduated magna cum laude from Brown University with a BA degree and from Harvard Law School, cum laude, with a JD degree. He is now an accomplished actor of stage, **television** and film. He guest starred in TV series, such as *NYPD Blue, ER, Soul Food, The Sopranos,* and had a recurring role as Aaron in *Married . . . with Children.* He also portrayed Dr. Wesley Williams in *City of Angels* and Dr. Sheldon Hawkes in *CSI: NY.* His notable film roles include *Get on the Bus,* 1996; *In Too Deep,* 1999; *The Visit,* 2000; and *Lackawanna Blues,* 2005. Harper's first starring role was in the independent short film *One Red Rose,* 1995, directed by his cousin, Charlie Jordan. In 2004, he was selected as one of *People* magazine's "Sexiest Men Alive."

Filmography: *Confessions of a Dog,* 1993; *Pumpkinhead II: Blood Wings,* 1994; *One Red Rose,* 1995; *Drifting School,* 1995; *Get on the Bus,* 1996; *Hoover Park,* 1997; *Steel,* 1997; *Hav Plenty,* 1997; *He Got Game,* 1998; *Park Day,* 1998; *The Nephew,* 1998; *Beloved,* 1998; *Mama Flora's Family,* 1998; *Slaves of Hollywood,* 1999; *Loving Jezabel,* 1999; *In Too Deep,* 1999; *The Skulls,* 2000; *The Visit,* 2000; *Higher Ed,* 2001; *The Badge,* 2002; *America Brown,* 2004; *Lackawanna Blues,* 2005; *Constellation,* 2005; *Cross the Line,* 2005; *Whitepaddy,* 2005; *The Breed,* 2006; *Premium,* 2006.

HARRINGTON, CHERYL FRANCIS. Actress. She began her acting career in W. O. Garrett's USC student film *The Deluxe,* 1983. She landed guest-starring roles in numerous television series, such as *L.A. Law, Babylon 5, Living Single, Philly, The District, Boston Public, Without a Trace,* and *Commander in Chief.* She provided the voice of Haiti Lady in the animated comedy series *The PJ's.* Her notable film roles include *Perfume,* 1991, and the TV movie *Run for the Dream: The Gail Devers Story,* 1996.

Filmography: *The Deluxe,* 1983; *Perfume,* 1991; *Fire: Trapped on the 37th Floor,* 1991; *The Heroes of Desert Storm,* 1991; *Sgt. Bilko,* 1996; *Run for the Dream,* 1996; *Tital Wave: No Escape,* 1997; *Legal Deceit,* 1997; *Kartenspieler,* 1999; *He's the One,* 2000; *The Stepdaughter,* 2000; *American Tragedy,* 2000; *Spring Break Lawyer,* 2001; *Lucky,* 2002; *Domino,* 2005; *Surf School,* 2006; *The Candy Shop,* 2006.

HARRIS, JULIUS (1923-2004). Actor. Harris was born in Philadelphia, Pennsylvania, and became an Army medic during World War II. He was a hard-working character actor in **television** and films with memorable roles in *Nothing but a Man*, 1964; and *Shaft's Big Score*, 1972.

Filmography: *Nothing but a Man*, 1964; *Slaves*, 1969; *Shaft's Big Score*, 1972; *Superfly*, 1972; *Trouble Man*, 1972; *Hell Up in Harlem*, 1973; *Black Caesar*, 1973; *Live and Let Die*, 1973; *Let's Do It Again*, 1975; *Friday Foster*, 1975; *A Cry for Help*, 1975; *Rich Man, Poor Man*, 1976; *King Kong*, 1976; *Looking for Mr. Goodbar*, 1977; *Delta Fox*, 1979; *First Family*, 1980; *The Blue and the Gray*, 1982; *Circle of Power*, 1983; *Going Berserk*, 1983; *Crimewave*, 1985; *Hollywood Vice Squad*, 1986; *A Gathering of Old Men*, 1987; *To Sleep with Anger*, 1990; *Darkman*, 1990; *Harley Davidson and the Marlboro Man*, 1991; *Maniac Cop 3*, 1993; *Shrunken Heads*, 1994.

HARRIS, ROBIN (1953-1990). Comedian, actor. This popular stand-up comic turned actor was born in Chicago, Illinois. His popular film work includes roles in *Do the Right Thing*, 1989, and *House Party*, 1990. His career was cut short by a massive heart attack at age 36. The animated cartoon *Bebe's Kids*, 1992 was inspired by one of Harris' comedy routines and made as a tribute to him.

Filmography: *I'm Gonna Git You Sucka*, 1988; *Do the Right Thing*, 1989; *Harlem Nights*, 1989; *House Party*, 1990; *Mo' Better Blues*, 1990.

HARRIS, THERESA (1909-1985). Actress, A true but often-overlooked star of Hollywood's Golden Era, Harris could sing, dance, and act with the best of them, but was mostly relegated to playing maid roles, which she did with dignity and grace. As one of the most popular actresses in Hollywood, she appeared in over 60 films between 1930 and 1958, working at every major studio with some of their biggest stars. She is perhaps best remembered for her role in *Professional Sweetheart*, 1933, with Ginger Rogers. Other movie roles include *Drums o'Voodoo*, 1934, *Bargain with Bullets*, 1937, *Jezebel*, 1938, and *Miracle on 34th Street*, 1947.

Filmography: *Merrily We Go to Hell*, 1932; *Private Detective 62*, 1933; *Baby Face*, 1933; *Blood Money*, 1933; *Drums o'Voodoo*, 1934; *Black Moon*, 1934; *Bargain with Bullets*, 1937; *Jezebel*, 1938; *Tell No Tales*, 1939; *One Hour to Live*, 1939; *Buck Benny Rides Again*, 1940; *Our Wife*, 1941; *Blossoms in the Dust*, 1941; *Tough as They Come*, 1942; *I Walked with a Zombie*, 1943; *Smooth as Silk*, 1946; *The Velvet Touch*, 1948; *The File on Thelma Jordon*, 1950; *Grounds for Marriage*, 1951; *Angel Face*, 1952; *Back From Eternity*, 1956; *The Gift of Love*, 1958.

HARRY, JACKEE (1956-). Actress. This native of Winston-Salem, North Carolina, got her big break when she was cast as Sandra Clark, the high, squeaky-voiced neighbor in the sitcom *227*. Her made-for-TV movies include *Crash Course*, 1988; *The Women of Brewster Place*, 1989; *Double Your Pleasure*, 1989; and *We'll Take Manhattan*, 1990. Other TV series include *The Royal Family*, and *Sister, Sister*.

Filmography: *Ladybugs*, 1992; *You Got Served*, 2004.

HARVEY, STEVE (1956-). Comedian, actor. He was born in Welch, West Virginia, and got his big comedy start as the host of the television series *It's Showtime at the Apollo*, 1993-2000. He has appeared on many award shows and comedy specials, including the *31st NAACP Image Awards*, *1st Annual Black Entertainment Television Awards*, *Heroes of Black Comedy*, and *Def Comedy Jam*. He was co-host of the 2nd Annual BET Awards, and hosted the 2003 Essence Awards. He portrays vice-principal Steve Hightower on his own sitcom *The Steve Harvey Show*, and executive produced the TV series *Steve Harvey's Big Time*, 2003. He currently hosts the BET Comedy Awards. On film, he was one of the *Original Kings of Comedy*, 2000, and appeared in *Love Don't Cost a Thing*, 2003, and *Johnson Family Vacation*, 2004.

Filmography: *The Original Kings of Comedy*, 2000; *The Fighting Temptations*, 2003; *Love Don't Cost a Thing*, 2003; *You Got Served*, 2004; *Johnson Family Vacation*, 2004; *Racing Stripes*, 2005.

HAUSER, FAY. Actress. She began her acting career with roles in sitcoms, such as *What's Happening*, *Good Times*, *Taxi*, and *Benson*. Her notable film work includes roles in *Roots: The Next Generation*, 1979; *Jo Jo Dancer, Your Life is Calling*, 1986; and *The Hot Chick*, 2002. She also portrayed Detective Sallena Wiley, 1997, on the daytime drama *The Young and the Restless*.

Filmography: *Roots: The Next Generation*, 1979; *Christmas Lilies of the Field*, 1979; *Seems Like Old Times*, 1980; *Marvin and Tige*, 1983; *Jimmy the Kid*, 1983; *Jo Jo Dancer, Your Life Is Calling*, 1986; *The Waterdance*, 1992; *Candyman: Farewell to the Flesh*, 1995; *The Hot Chick*, 2002.

HAVING OUR SAY: THE DELANY SISTERS' FIRST 100 YEARS. 1999. (TV) 90 min. Drama. This film is based on the book and Broadway play of the Delany Sisters, 103-year-old Sadie, and 101-year-old Bessie, as they share their wealth of life experiences with a *New York Times* reporter. Cast: **Diahann Carroll, Ruby Dee,**

Bill and Peggy Walker at home with Joel Fluellen. Bill and Joel appeared in No Time for Romance, *the first all-black cast musical shot on color film. Peggy was a child film star in Europe. Photo: Steve T. Berry*

Theatrical head shot of actress Marla Gibbs, who appeared in the films Black Belt Jones *and* The Meteor Man, *and the TV sitcoms* The Jeffersons *and* 227. *Courtesy of Marla Gibbs*

Lloyd Kaufman &
Michael Herz
Present A
Troma Team
Release

Publicity photo from the independent horror/sci-fi film Bugged, *featuring writer, producer, director, and star bug exterminator Ronald K. Armstrong with co-star/damsel in distress Pricilla Basque, whom he rescues from a hoard of flesh-eating insects. Courtesy of Troma Films*

A church congregation makes the trek to the river to perform baptisms in this production still from Blood of Jesus, directed by and starring Spencer Williams. Courtesy of James E. Wheeler

The life of a newborn child is saved and protected by enslaved Africans after the mother dies from an overseer's cruel whipping in this production still from the independent film Sankofa. Written and directed by Haile Gerima. Courtesy of Mypheduh Films

Runaway high school students Kenneth Mullins and Jennifer Kelly are in the grips of Undertaker Zach (Dexter K. Tennie) in this publicity photo from the independent horror flick Embalmer. *The debut feature film of S. Torriano Berry. Photo: Steve T. Berry*

Tracy Williams and Caron Tate are rival stage actresses pursuing the same role while the play's unscrupulous producer pursues the both of them in this production still from Uptown Angel. *The debut feature film by Joy Shannon. Photo: Steve T. Berry*

Lucia Lynn Moses contemplates her uncertain future in this production still from the 1927 silent film Scar of Shame. *Produced by the Colored Players of Philadelphia.*

Eugene Jackson and Madie Norman at Black Filmmakers Hall of Fame panel. Photo: Steve T. Berry

Screen stars Vonetta McGhee, Carol Speed, and Joan Pringle at the 1984 Black Filmmakers Hall of Fame weekend in Oakland, California. Photo: Steve T. Berry

Producer/director Stan Lathan and wife Marguerite at the 1984 Black Filmmakers Hall of Fame weekend in Oakland, California. Photo: Steve T. Berry

Loretta Devine, star of the films Waiting to Exhale *and* Down in the Delta, *and the TV series* Boston Public. *Photo: Steve T. Berry*

Veteran actor, direct, activist Ossie Davis, star of numerous stage and screen productions. Photo: Steve T. Berry

Venerable actor James Earl Jones, star of the films The Great White Hope, Claudine, *the TV mini-series* Roots: The Next Generation, *and the voice of Darth Vader in* Star Wars. *Photo: Steve T. Berry*

Bill Duke, actor/director, appeared in the films Predator *and* Action Jackson, *and director of the films* A Rage in Harlem, Deep Cover, *and* Hoodlum. *Photo: Steve T. Berry*

Sage actor/director Ivan Dixon, star of the film Nothing but a Man, *and director of the films* Trouble Man *and* The Spook Who Sat by the Door. *He was also a featured player in the popular TV series* Hogan's Heroes. *Photo: Steve T. Berry*

Mykelti **Williamson**, **Lonetta McKee**, Lisa Anderson, Audra McDonald, **Richard Roundtree**, **Della Reese**. Director: Lynne Littman. Writer: Emily Mann. Cinematographer: Frank Byers.

HAV PLENTY. 1997. (R) 87 min. Comedy/Drama. An unemployed writer accepts an invitation to spend New Year's Eve at a party given by a jilted, female friend from college. Once there, hormones go wild. Several women, including his friend's newlywed sister court him, and her muscle-bound husband does not appreciate this. Cast: Christopher Scott Cherot, Chenoa Maxwell, **Hill Harper**, Tammi Katherine Jones, Robbine Lee, Betty Vaughn, Reginald James, **Kenneth "Babyface" Edmonds**. Writer/Director: Christopher Scott Cherot. Cinematographer: Kerwin Devonish. Music: Wendy Melvoin, Lisa Coleman.

HAWLEY, MONTE (1901-1950). Actor. This native of Chicago, Illinois, was a top actor of the 1930s and 1940s. He began acting as a teen and became a member of the famous Lafayette Players. He was in the stage productions of *Shuffle Along* and *Runnin' Wild*, and traveled with several road shows. He broke into silent films and became known as "one-shot Monte" for his ability to never need to do a retake. He worked the vaudeville stage with **Eddie Anderson** and **Mantan Moreland**, and often worked for Million Dollar Productions, the company organized by **Ralph Cooper** and Harry Popkin, to make a series of gangster films, such as *Gang War*, 1940, and *Am I Guilty?*, 1940. His other notable film roles include *The Duke is Tops*, 1938, with **Lena Horne**, and *Gang Smashers*, 1938, with **Nina Mae McKinney**.

Filmography: *Ghost of Tolston's Manor*, 1923; *Life Goes On*, 1938; *The Duke is Tops*, 1938; *Gang Smashers*, 1938; *Reform School*, 1939; *One Dark Night*, 1939; *Double Deal*, 1939; *What a Guy*, 1939; *Prison Bait*, 1939; *Gang War*, 1940; *While Thousands Cheer*, 1940; *Am I Guilty?* 1940; *Four Shall Die*, 1940; *Mystery in Swing*, 1940; *Mr. Smith Goes Ghost*, 1940; *Mr. Washington Goes to Town*, 1941; *Lucky Ghost*, 1941; *Take My Life*, 1942; *Tall, Tan, and Terrific*, 1946; *Mantan Messes Up*, 1946; *Look Out Sister*, 1947; *Miracle in Harlem*, 1948.

HAYES, ISAAC (1942-). Musician, film composer, actor. Hayes was born in Covington, Tennessee, and raised by his sharecropping grandparents who moved to Memphis when he was a teen. He sang in the church and learned to play piano and saxophone, which led him to working with the Memphis-based Stax Records house band, recording on more than 200 tunes, including "Soul Man" and

"Hold On, I'm Coming," both co-written by Hayes and lyricist David Porter. He began recording his own records in 1967 and his 1969 *Hot Buttered Soul* album was a huge hit. Hayes carved out his own image of wearing massive gold chains and sporting a shaved head, and became known as the Black Moses. His soundtrack for **Gordon Parks'** film *Shaft*, 1970, won a Grammy Award and went platinum. It also made Hayes the first African American film composer to win an **Academy Award** in a music category (Best Original Score). Originally considered for the lead role in *Shaft*, Hayes was later cast in the title role as a bounty hunter in *Truck Turner*, 1974. Other film roles followed, including *Escape From New York*, 1981; *Dead Aim*, 1987; *I'm Gonna Git You Sucka*, 1988; and *Posse*, 1993. He also provided the voice for Chef in the animated cable TV series *South Park*. He was inducted into the Rock and Roll Hall of Fame in 2002.

Filmography: *Truck Turner*, 1974; *Escape From New York*, 1981; *Nightstick*, 1987; *Dead Aim*, 1987; *I'm Gonna Git You Sucka*, 1988; *Prime Target*, 1991; *Guilty as Charged*, 1992; *Final Judgment*, 1992; *Robin Hood: Men in Tights*, 1993; *Posse*, 1993; *Acting on Impulse*, 1993; *Oblivion*, 1994; *Backlash Oblivion 2*, 1995; *Illtown*, 1996; *Flipper*, 1996; *Woo*, 1997; *South Park: Bigger, Longer, and Uncut*, 1999; *Six Ways to Sunday*, 1999; *Shaft 2000*, 2000; *Reindeer Games*, 2000; *Dr. Dolittle 2*, 2001.

HAYNES, DANIEL (1894-1954). Actor. Born in Atlanta, Georgia, Haynes was educated at Atlanta University, the University of Chicago, Turner Theological Seminary, and City College of New York. He performed on stage in *Brother Elijah in Earth*, *Rang Tang*, and he was an understudy in a 1929 production of *Show Boat*. He made his film debut as a gangster in the silent film *John Smith*, 1922, and he landed the lead role of Zeke in the film *Hallelujah*, 1929, one of the first all-black sound films.

Filmography: *Can This Be Dixie?* 1936; *Fury*, 1936; *The Invisible Ray*, 1936; *Escape from Devil's Island*, 1935; *Mary Burns, Fugitive*, 1935; *So Red the Rose*, 1935; *The Last Mile*, 1932; *Hallelujah*, 1929; *John Smith*, 1922.

HAYSBERT, DENNIS (1955-). Actor. He was born in San Mateo, California, and began his acting career in the made-for-TV movies *Code Red*, 1981; *Grambling's White Tiger*, 1981; and *The Return of Marcus Welby, MD*, 1984. He had a recurring role on the series *Code Red*, and *Just the Ten of Us*, and was a regular as president of the United States on the series *24*. He appeared in the TV miniseries *Queen*, 1993; *Return to Lonesome Dove*, 1993; and *Empire*,

2004. Haysbert's notable film roles include *Waiting to Exhale*, 1995; *Random Hearts*, 1999; and *Far From Heaven*, 2002.

Filmography: *Major League*, 1989; *Navy SEALS*, 1990; *Love Field*, 1991; *Mr. Baseball*, 1992; *Suture*, 1993; *Return to Lonesome Dove*, 1993; *Widow's Kiss*, 1994; *Major League 2*, 1994; *Waiting to Exhale*, 1995; *Heat*, 1995; *Standoff*, 1997; *Absolute Power*, 1997; *Major League 3: Back to the Minors*, 1998; *The Thirteenth Floor*, 1999; *Random Hearts*, 1999; *The Minus Man*, 1999; *What's Cooking*, 2000; **Love and Basketball**, 2000; *Far From Heaven*, 2002; *Sinbad: Legend of the Seven Seas*, 2003.

HEADLEY, SHARI (1964-). Actress. This native of Queens, New York, made her film debut as a possible queen-to-be with **Eddie Murphy** in *Coming to America*, 1988. Her notable **television** roles include Carla Royce in *Matlock*, Dawn in *The Wayans Brothers*, and Heather in *The Bold and the Beautiful*. Headley also appeared as Officer Mimi Reed Frye, 1991-1995, in the popular daytime drama *All My Children*, and as Felicia Boudreaux #1, 2001-2002, in *The Guiding Light*.

Filmography: *Coming to America*, 1988; **The Preacher's Wife**, 1996; *A Woman Like That*, 1997; **Johnson Family Vacation**, 2004.

HEAD OF STATE. 2003. (PG-13) 95 min. Comedy. A Washington, D. C., alderman runs for president of the United States when his party's candidate is killed in a plane crash. Not expected to win, his party just wants to play the diversity card, to set them up for the next election. Taking his bid for office seriously, the candidate must fight his handlers to develop his own identity and set his own standards for the campaign. Cast: **Chris Rock**, **Bernie Mac**, Dylan Baker, Nick Searcy, **Lynn Whitfield**, **Robin Givens**, **Tamala Jones**, Stephanie March, James Rebhorn, **Keith David**, Tracy Morgan, Robert Stanton, Jude Ciccolella, Nate Dogg. Director: Chris Rock. Writers: Chris Rock, Ali LeRoi. Cinematographer: Donald E. Thorin. Music: Marcus Miller, David "DJ Quik" Blake.

HEARTS IN DIXIE. 1929. 71 min. Music/Drama. A musical drama set in the Old South. It was advertised as Hollywood's first all-black all-talking-and-singing musical. Set after the Civil War, an aging tenant farmer works his land and wants a better life for his family. When his daughter dies, he decides that his grandson should go north to study medicine, and some day, return to help his people. The film has been criticized for perpetuating happy-go-lucky negroes content with their lower standard of life, working the fields all day, and singing and dancing all night. This is the movie that made **Stepin Fetchit** a star. Cast: **Clarence Muse, Stepin Fetchit, Mildred Washington, Eugene Jackson**, Vivian Smith, Zach Williams, Dorothy Morrison, Bernice Pilot, Gertrude Howard, A. C. H. Billbrew, Richard Carlysle, Clifford Ingram, Robert Brooks, and the Billbrew Chorus.

HE GOT GAME. 1998. (R) 134 min. Drama. A prison inmate is given a one-week furlough to try and convince his estranged high school basketball star son to attend the prison warden's alma mater. Cast: **Denzel Washington**, Ray Allen, Milla Jovovich, **Rosario Dawson, Hill Harper**, Zelda Harris, **Jim Brown**, Ned Beatty, **Lonette McKee**, John Turturro, Michele Shay, **Bill Nunn, Thomas Jefferson Byrd**. Writer/Director: **Spike Lee**. Cinematographer: **Malik Hassan Sayeed**.

HELL UP IN HARLEM. 1973. (R) 98 min. Blaxploitation. This is the sequel to *Black Caesar*, 1972. After recovering from an attempted assassination, a Harlem crime lord sets out to regain his power. Cast: **Fred Williamson, Julius W. Harris, Margaret Avery**, Gerald Gordon, **Gloria Hendry**. Writer/Director: Larry Cohen. Cinematographer: Fenton Hamilton. Music: Fonce Mizell, Freddie Perren.

HENDRIX. 2000. (R) 103 min. Biopic. The life and times of legendary rock guitarist Jimi Hendrix are chronicled in this made-for-cable production. The story goes from his first band in Seattle, Washington, through his notable performances at the 1967 Monterey Pop Festival and Woodstock, to his drug overdose in 1970 while performing in England. Cast: Wood Harris, **Vivica A. Fox**, Billy Zane, Christian Potenza, **Dorian Harewood**, Kris Holdenried, Christopher Ralph, Michie Mee. Director: Leon Ichaso. Writers: Art Washington, Hal Roberts, Butch Stein. Cinematographer: Claudio Chea. Music: Daniel Licht.

HENDRY, GLORIA (1949-). Actress. She was born in Winter Haven, Florida, and grew up in Newark, New Jersey. She became a model and landed her first acting role in the film *For Love of Ivy*, 1968, while working as a Playboy Bunny. And striking screen presence, this bronze bombshell quickly became a visual mainstay in a string of what became known as **Blaxploitation** Films produced in the early 1970s. Her exposure in action-packed dramas, such as *Across 110th Street*, 1972; *Black Ceasar*, 1973; and *Slaughter's Big Rip-Off*, 1973, led to her being cast as the first black "Bond Girl." She played the role of Rosie Carver, Sean Connery's love interest/nemesis in the James Bond 007-spy drama *Live and Let Die*, 1973. Hendry also portrayed karate man **Jim Kelly**'s high-kicking co-star in *Black Belt Jones*, 1973.

Filmography: *For Love of Ivy*, 1968; *The Landlord*, 1970; *Across 110th Street*, 1972; *Black Caesar*, 1973; *Slaughter's Big Rip-Off*, 1973; *Live and Let Die*, 1973; **Hell Up in Harlem**, 1973; *Black Belt Jones*, 1974; *Savage Sisters*, 1974; *Doin' Time on Planet Earth*, 1988; *Seeds of Tragedy*, 1991; *Pumpkinhead II: Blood Wings*, 1994; *South Bureau Homicide*, 1996; *Lookin' Italian*, 1998; *Seven Swans*, 2005; *Black Kissinger*, 2006.

HERNANDEZ, JUANO (1901-1970). Actor. Born in San Juan, Puerto Rico, Hernandez was the son of a seaman, and experienced many diverse careers. He began his entertainment career on the streets of Rio de Janeiro, Brazil, singing to raise money for food. He joined the circus as part of an acrobatic act, and later lived in the Caribbean and worked as a professional boxer under the name Kid Curley. He eventually worked as a radio scriptwriter and also performed on the vaudeville stage. Hernandez made his Broadway debut in the chorus of the 1927 stage production of the musical *Showboat*. As an actor, he played bit parts in several early **race movies**, including **Oscar Micheaux**'s *The Girl from Chicago*, 1932, and *Lying Lips*, 1939. He received critical acclaim for his lead role in *Intruder in the Dust*, 1949. Hernandez continued to play sensitive, dignified roles that helped to pave the way for actors like **Sidney Poitier**. Hernandez delivered notable performances in such films as *St. Louis Blues*, 1958; *Sergeant Rutledge*, 1960; and *They Call Me Mister Tibbs!* 1970. On **television**, his guest appearances include *Studio One*, *Alfred Hitchcock Presents*, *Route 66*, *The Dick Powell Show*, and *Naked City*.

Filmography: *The Girl from Chicago*, 1932; *Lying Lips*, 1939; *Intruder in the Dust*, 1949; *Stars in My Crown*, 1950; **Something of Value**, 1957; **Mark of the Hawk**, 1957; *St. Louis Blues*, 1958; *Sergeant Rutledge*, 1960; *They Call Me Mr. Tibbs!* 1970.

HERO AIN'T NOTHIN' BUT A SANDWICH, A. 1978. (PG) 107 min. Urbana Drama. This is a film based on Alice Childress' novel about an inner-city youth who is saved from a life of drugs and violence. Cast: **Cicely Tyson, Paul Winfield, Larry B. Scott**, Helen Martin, **Glynn Turman**, David Groh. Director: Ralph Nelson.

HI-DE-HO. 1935. 60 min. Musical. A jazz band is caught between rival gangsters. Cast: **Cab Calloway**, Ida James. Director: Josh Binney.

HIGHER LEARNING. 1994. (R) 127 min. Drama. This is a look at the freshman year of three college students as they experience racism, a change of ideals, and their own self-identity. A black track star questions the school's exploitation of athletes, a girl from the suburbs questions her sexuality, and an introverted Caucasian questions the survival of the white race and joins a group of skinheads to do something about it. Cast: **Omar Epps**, Kristy Swanson, Michael Rapaport, **Laurence Fishburne**, Jennifer Connelly, **Ice Cube**, **Tyra Banks**, Jason Wiles, Cole Hauser, **Regina King**, Colleen Fitzpatrick. Writer/Director: **John Singleton**. Cinematographer: Peter Lyons Collister.

HILTON-JACOBS, LAWRENCE (1953-). Actor. He was born in the Virgin Islands and went to high school in New York City. He studied acting at Al Fann's Theatrical School and with the Negro Ensemble Company performing in such plays as *Cora's Second Cousin*, and *What the Wine Sellers Buy*. He landed his first film role as Charles, the militant son in *Claudine*, 1974. His breakthrough role came as the ill-fated college bound basketball star, Cochise, in *Cooley High*, 1975. This film helped land him the role of Freddie "Boom Boom" Washington in the hit **television** sitcom, *Welcome Back, Kotter.*

Filmography: *Claudine*, 1974; *Death Wish*, 1974; *Cooley High*, 1975; *Youngblood*, 1978; *The Comedy Company*, 1978; *For the Love of it*, 1980; *The Annihilators*, 1985; *Paramedics*, 1988; *Angels of the City*, 1990; *Chance*, 1990; *The Jacksons: An American Dream*, 1992; *Tuesday Never Comes*, 1993; *Indecent Behavior*, 1993; *Southlander*, 2001; *Hip, Edgy, Sexy, Cool*, 2002; *The Streetsweeper*, 2002; *30 Miles*, 2004; *Don't Give Me the Finger*, 2005; *Sublime*, 2007.

HINES, GREGORY (1946-2004). Dancer, actor, director. Hines was born in New York City and began dancing professionally at age five with his brother Maurice. He was performing on Broadway by age eight, and his extraordinary feet would light up stages for years to come. He was nominated three years in a row for a Tony Award for *Eubie*, 1979; *Comin' Uptown*, 1980; and *Sophisticated Ladies*, 1981; and finally won for his performance in *Jelly's Last Jam*, 1993. Hines moved easily from the stage to the big screen in a variety of films from comedies, to musicals, to dramas. He often starred in films that highlighted his dancing abilities, such as *The Cotton Club*, 1984; *Tap*, 1989; and as his dancing idol **Bill "Bojangles" Robinson** in the Showtime cable biopic *Bojangles*, 2001. On television, he performed in his own short-lived CBS sitcom *The Gregory Hines Show*, 1997-98. As a director, he helmed the independent film *Bleeding Hearts*, 1994, and made his cable-directing debut with *The Red Sneakers*, 2001, on Showtime.

Filmography: *History of the World Part I*, 1981; *Wolfen*, 1981; *Deal of the Century*, 1983; *The Muppets Take Manhattan*, 1984; *The Cotton Club*, 1984; *White Nights*, 1985; *Running Scared*, 1986; *Off Limits*, 1988; *Tap*, 1989; *Eve of Destruction*, 1991; *A Rage in Harlem*, 1991; *Renaissance Man*, 1994; *Waiting to Exhale*, 1995; *Mad Dog Time*, 1996; *The Preacher's Wife*, 1996; *Good Luck*, 1997; *Color of Justice*, 1997; *The Tic Code*, 2000; *Once in a Life*, 2000; *Things You Can Tell Just by Looking at Her*, 2001; *Bojangles*, 2001.

HIT. 1973. (R) 135 min. Drama. A government agent hires his own vigilante force and seeks his revenge on French drug traffickers after his daughter dies from a heroin overdose. Cast: **Billy Dee Williams**, **Richard Pryor**, Gwen Welles, Paul Hampton, Warren Kemmerling, Sid Melton. Director: Sidney J. Furie. Writers: Alan R. Trustman, David M. Wolf. Music: Lalo Schifrin.

HOLDER, GEOFFREY (1930-). Choreographer, actor. He was born in Port-of-Spain, Trinidad, and perhaps is best known as the "Uncola Man," from a series of 7-Up soft drink commercials. Well recognized for his bald head and deep voice, he also gained recognition as a choreographer and costume designer. His film appearances include *Live and Let Die*, 1973; *Annie*, 1982; and *Boomerang*, 1992.

Filmography: *Carib Gold*, 1957; *Doctor Dolittle*, 1967; *Krakatoa, East of Java*, 1969; *Everything You Always Wanted to Know About Sex But Were Afraid to Ask*, 1972; *Live and Let Die*, 1973; *Swashbuckler*, 1976; *Annie*, 1982; *Boomerang*, 1992; *Goosed*, 1999.

HOLLYWOOD SHUFFLE. 1987. (R) 81 min. Comedy. An out-of-work actor must choose between playing a degrading role and maintaining his dignity. The film is a satire on the **stereotypical** roles that perpetuate false industry perceptions of African Americans. Cast: **Robert Townsend, Anne-Marie Johnson, Starletta DuPois**, Helen Martin, **Keenen Ivory Wayans, Damon Wayans**, Craigus R. Johnson, Eugene Glazer. Director: Robert Townsend.

Writers: Robert Townsend, Keenen Ivory Wayans. Cinematographer: Peter Deming. Music: Patrice Rushen, Udi Harpaz.

HOME OF THE BRAVE. 1949. 86 min. War/Drama. A black GI faces racism from others in his unit as well as the threat from the enemy on a Japanese-held island during World War II. He returns home paralyzed with no sign of physical injury. His doctor discovers his problem is not only psychological, but also more universal than his patient would imagine. The first in a series of "**Problem Pictures**" Hollywood made to address the race issue in America. Cast: **James Edwards**, Lloyd Bridges, Frank Lovejoy, Jeff Corey, Douglas Dick, Steve Brodie, Cliff Clark. Director: Mark Robson. Writer: Carl Foreman. Cinematographer: Robert DeGrasse. Music: Dimitri Tiomkin.

HONEYBABY, HONEYBABY. 1974. (PG) 94 min. Blaxploitation. A beautiful American interpreter and a soldier of fortune must rescue a politician kidnapped by Mid-East terrorists. Cast: **Calvin Lockhart, Diana Sands**. Director: **Michael Schultz**.

HONEYMOONERS, THE. 2005. (PG-13) 85 min. Comedy. A New York City bus driver and his best friend come up with a get-rich-quick scheme to augment their menial savings for a down payment on a Brooklyn duplex. In the process, they lose all of their money, which spoils their plans to move and their marriages. It was intended to be a remake of the popular 1950s **television** series starring Jackie Gleason. Cast: **Cedric the Entertainer, Mike Epps**, **Gabrielle Union, Regina Hall**, Eric Stoltz, Jon Polito, John Leguizamo, Carol Woods, Ajay Naidu, Arnell Powell, Leticia Castillo, Doreen Keogh, Camile Donegan, Joanna Dickens, Kim Chan. Director: John Shultz. Writers: Barry W. Blaustein, Danny Jacobson.

HOODLUM. 1996. (R) 130 min. Gagster/Urban Drama. This is a fictional account of Harlem gangster "Bumpy" Johnson and his fight to defend his numbers racket from mobsters Dutch Schultz and Lucky Luciano. Cast: **Laurence Fishburne**, Tim Roth, Andy Garcia, **Vanessa L. Williams, Cicely Tyson, Clarence Williams III**, William Atherton, **Chi McBride**, Richard Bradford, **Loretta Devine, Queen Latifah**, Paul Benjamin, Mike Starr, Beau Starr, Joe Guzaldo, Ed O'Ross. Director: **Bill Duke**. Writer: Chris Brancato. Cinematographer: Frank Tidy. Music: Elmer Bernstein.

HOOKS, KEVIN (1958-). Actor, director. Born in Philadelphia, Pennsylvania, he is the son of actor **Robert Hooks**, and began his own acting career at age 14 in the sentimental drama *Sounder*, 1972, for which he received a **Golden Globe** nomination for Best Newcomer. He landed the title role in *Aaron Loves Angela*, 1974, which also featured his dad. On **television**, Hooks played four seasons on the high school basketball-themed series *The White Shadow*, 1978-81, and played the young mayor of an urban city in *He's the Mayor*, 1986. Moving on to direct, he helmed made-for-TV movies like *Heat Wave*, 1990; *Murder Without Motive: The Edmund Perry Story*, 1992; and the theatrical releases *Passenger 57*, 1994; and *Fled*, 1996.

Filmography: *Sounder*, 1972; *Aaron Loves Angela*, 1975; *Take Down*, 1975; *The Story of Freddie Prinze*, 1979; *Innerspace*, 1987.

HOOKS, ROBERT (1937-). A native of Washington, D. C., Hooks graduated from Temple University in Philadelphia, Pennsylvania, and moved to New York City. He made his Broadway debut in the 1962 production of *Tiger Tiger Burning Bright*, and became a co-founder of the Negro Ensemble Company. In film, Hooks was cast in the independently produced *Sweet Love, Bitter*, 1966, but his big break came from his role in *Hurry Sundown*, 1967. During the **blaxploitation** era of the 1970s, he portrayed the title role in the hard-hitting *Trouble Man*, 1972. On **television**, Hooks co-starred in the New York-based cop series *NYPD*, and starred in the military-based series *Supercarrier*, 1988. He is the father of actor/director **Kevin Hooks**.

Filmography: *Sweet Love Bitter*, 1967; *Black Brigade*, 1969; *Aaron Loves Angela*, 1975; *A Woman Called Moses*, 1978; *Sophisticated Gents*, 1981; *Fast Walking*, 1982; *Words by Heart*, 1984; *The Execution*, 1985; *Heat Wave*, 1990; *Passenger 57*, 1992; *Posse*, 1993; *Free of Eden*, 1998; *Seventeen Again*, 2000.

HOOP DREAMS. 1994. (PG-13) 169 min. Sports. This is a **documentary** about two urban high school basketball players who receive scholarships to attend a Catholic school and continue on with their dreams of playing professional ball in the National Basketball Association. There is plenty of game footage and lots of scenes of the players at home with their families. Regardless of their talent on the court, the odds of them making it are still extreme. Cast: Arthur Agee, William Gates. Director: Steve James. Cinematographer: Peter Gilbert. Awards: Directors Guild 1995: Best Feature Documentary. L.A. Film Critics 1994: Best Feature Documentary. MTV

Movie Awards 1995: Best New Filmmaker. National Board of Review 1994: Best Feature Documentary. N.Y. Film Critics 1994: Best Feature Documentary. National Society of Film Critics 1994: Best Feature Documentary. Sundance 1994: Audience Award.

HORNE, LENA (1917-). Singer, actress. At one time known as "the most beautiful woman in the world," Lena Horne, enjoyed a successful career in the entertainment industry. Born in Brooklyn, she was hired at age 16 as a chorus girl in 1933 at the world-famous Cotton Club. She toured with the Noble Sissle Orchestra. In 1939, she landed the lead role in the stage production of *Blackbirds*. She began her singing career with the Charlie Barnett band and recorded her first records with Barnett, including "Haunted Town." Other recordings include "Stormy Weather," "Blues in the Night," "The Lady Is a Tramp," and "Mad about the Boy." She could be heard on the radio shows *Strictly from Dixie*, 1941, and *The Cats n' Jammers Show*, 1941. Horne went to Hollywood to act in films like ***The Duke is Tops***, 1940; *Panama Hattie*, 1942; ***Cabin in the Sky***, 1943; and ***Stormy Weather***, 1943. She became the first African American actress to sign a long-term contract with a major studio, MGM. After continuing her nightclub career, she took a break to star in *Jamaica*, her first Broadway musical, and closed out her dynamic career with her one-woman show, *Lena Horne: The Lady and Her Music*, 1981-1982, at the Pantages Theater in Los Angeles. She later took the production on a cross-country tour, and the soundtrack won two Grammy Awards.

Filmography: *The Duke Is Tops*, 1938; *Panama Hattie*, 1942; *Thousands Cheer*, 1943; *Stormy Weather*, 1943; *I Dood It*, 1943; *Cabin in the Sky*, 1943; *Two Girls and a Sailor*, 1944; *Broadway Rhythm*, 1944; *Ziegfeld Follies*, 1946; *Till the Clouds Roll By*, 1946; *Words and Music*, 1948; *The Duchess of Idaho*, 1950; *Death of a Gunfighter*, 1969; *The Wiz*, 1978.

HORSFORD, ANNA MARIA (1948-). Actress. This New York City-born actress has been active on stage, television, and film. She guest starred on television shows like *L. A. Law*, *Moesha*, and *The Fresh Prince of Bel-Air*. She was a regular on *The Wayans Bros.*, *Tall Hopes*, *Method & Red*, and portrayed the role of Thelma Frye on the NBC series *Amen*. Her stage credits include *Peep*, *For Colored Girls*, and *Les Femmes Noire*. Horsford's notable film roles include *Street Smart*, 1987; ***Friday***, 1995; and ***Once Upon a Time When We Were Colored***, 1996.

Filmography: *An Almost Perfect Affair*, 1979; *Times Square*, 1980; *The Fan*, 1981; *Love Child*, 1982; *Class*, 1983; *Crackers*,

1984; *St. Elmo's Fire*, 1985; *Heartburn*, 1986; *Street Smart*, 1987; *Presumed Innocent*, 1990; *Mr. Jones*, 1993; *Friday*, 1995; *Once upon a Time When We Were Colored*, 1996; *Dear God*, 1996; *Set It Off*, 1996; *One Fine Day*, 1996; *Kiss the Girls*, 1997; *At Face Value*, 1999; *Dancing in September*, 2000; *Nutty Professor II: The Klumps*, 2000; *Lockdown*, 2000; *Along Came a Spider*, 2001; *Jacked*, 2001; *How High*, 2001; *Minority Report*, 2002; *Friday After Next*, 2002.

HOTEL RWANDA. 2004. (PG-13) 110 min. Drama. This film is based on the true-life story of Paul Rusesabagina, a hotel manager who saved over a thousand Tutsi refugees from genocide during their struggle against the Hutu militia in Rwanda. It is a powerful portrayal of one man's refusal to give up hope in the midst of brutal violence and the countless atrocities committed during the Rwandan holocaust of 1994. **Don Cheadle** received an **Academy Award** nomination for his portrayal of Rusesabagina. Cast: Don Cheadle, Sophie Okonedo, Nick Nolte, Joaquin Phoenix, Desmond Dube, David O'Hara, Cara Seymour, Fana Mokoena, Hakeem Kae-Kazim, Tony Kgoroge, Mosa Kaiser.

HOT POTATO. 1976. (PG) 87 min. Blaxploitation. This is the sequel to ***Black Belt Jones***, who uses his karate skills to rescue a senator's daughter from a crazy general out to pull a coup d'etat. Cast: **Jim Kelly**, George Memmoli, Geoffrey Binney. Director: Oscar Williams.

HOUSE DIVIDED, A. 2000. (R) 99 min. Drama. This film is based on the book *Woman of Color, Daughter of Privilege* by Kent Anderson Leslie. This is a true story about the only child of a wealthy plantation owner in 1870s Georgia who inherits her father's vast estate. Her uncle, who claims that she is not entitled to the estate because her mother was a slave, contests the will. Cast: Sam Waterston, **Jennifer Beals**, **Lisa Gay Hamilton**, Timothy Daly, Ron White, Shirley Douglas, Sean McCann, Gerard Parkes, Colin Fox. Director: John Kent Harrison. Writer: Paris Qualles. Cinematographer: Kees Van Oostrum. Music: Lawrence Shragge.

HOUSE PARTY. 1990. (R) 100 min. Comedy. Rap artists turned actors Kid 'n' Play star as high school students in a serious party mode. After his strict, disciplinarian father grounds Play, he sneaks out of the house to attend Kid's wild party. All is well with girls, music, and dancing, until Play's father crashes the festivities in search of his disobedient son. This spawned two sequels. Cast: **Christopher**

Reid, Christopher Martin, Martin Lawrence, Tisha Campbell, Paul Anthony, A. J. Johnson, Robin Harris. Writer/Director: **Reginald Hudlin.** Cinematographer: Peter Deming. Music: Marcus Miller. Awards: Sundance 1990: Best Cinematography.

HOUSE PARTY 2: THE PAJAMA JAM. 1991. (R) 94 min. Comedy. This is the sequel to *House Party.* Rappers Kid 'n' Play return as college freshmen who try to raise their tuition money by holding a school dance that must be attended in pajamas. Cast: **Christopher Reid, Christopher Martin, Tisha Campbell,** Iman, **Queen Latifah, Georg Stanford Brown, Martin Lawrence,** Eugene Allen, George Anthony Bell, Kamron, Tony Burton, Helen Martin, William Schallert. Directors: **George Jackson, Doug McHenry.** Writers: **Rusty Cundeiff,** Daryl G. Nickens. Music: Vassai Benford.

HOUSE PARTY 3. 1994. (R) 93 min. Comedy. This is the third film in the *House Party* series. Kid, now all grown up is about to get married and Play sets about organizing his bachelor party. They also try to sign the female rap group TLC to their fledgling record label. Cast: **Christopher Martin, Christopher Reid,** Angela Means, **Tisha Campbell, Bernie Mac,** Michael Colyar, David Edwards, Betty Lester, **Chris Tucker.** Director: Eric Meza. Writer: Takashi Bufford. Music: David Allen Jones.

HOUSTON, WHITNEY (1963-). Singer, actress. As an international superstar in music, Houston seamlessly moved onto the big screen in the blockbuster film *The Bodyguard,* 1992, and performed on what became the biggest-selling motion picture soundtrack, selling more than 33 million copies worldwide. Her second movie, *Waiting to Exhale,* 1995, was also a huge success and Houston had three top selling tracks on the soundtrack album as well. Her vocal talents were again exploited on the screen during her title role as *The Preacher's Wife,* 1996.
　　Filmography: *The Bodyguard,* 1992; *Waiting to Exhale,* 1995; *The Preacher's Wife,* 1996; *Cinderella,* 1997.

HOWARD, TERRENCE DASHON (1969-). Actor, producer. He was born in Chicago, Illinois, and began acting in the early 1990s. His made-for-television movie roles include *The Jacksons: An American Dream,* 1992; *The O. J. Simpson Story,* 1995; and *Mama Flora's Family,* 1998, and he guest appeared on the sitcom *Sparks.* He gained the public's attention as Quentin, the wise cracking, no-holds-barred voice of truth in the film *The Best Man,* 1999, and he starred in and executive produced *Love Beat the Hell Outta Me*, 2000. Filmography: *Who's the Man*, 1993; *Lotto Land*, 1995; *Dead Presidents*, 1995; *Mr. Holland's Opus*, 1995; *Sunset Park*, 1996; *Johns*, 1996; *Double Tap*, 1997; *Spark*, 1998; *The Players Club*, 1998; *Butter*, 1998; *Best Laid Plans*, 1999; *The Best Man*, 1999; *Big Momma's House*, 2000; *Love Beat the Hell Outta Me*, 2000; *Angel Eyes*, 2001; *Glitter*, 2001; *Hart's War*, 2002; *Biker Boyz*, 2003; *Love Chronicles*, 2003; *Crash*, 2004; *Ray*, 2004; *The Salon*, 2005; *Hustle & Flow*, 2005; *Their Eyes Were Watching God*, 2005; *Animal*, 2005.

HOW HIGH. 2001. (R) 93 min. Comedy. Rappers Method Man and Redman star as a pair of pot-smoking homeboys who toke on some miraculous "smart" ganja that inadvertently gets them accepted into very preppy Harvard University. While there, the two fish-out-of-water do more dope smoking and chasing women than studying, but manage to shine a light on an element of institutional corruption and earn the appreciation of the administration and faculty. Cast: Redman, Method Man, **Obba Babatunde**, Chuck Davis, **Anna Maria Horsford**, Fred Willard, Lark Voorhies, **Essence Atkins**, Jeffrey Jones, **Mike Epps**, Hector Elizondo, Chris Elwood, Spalding Gray, Tracey Walter. Director: Jesse Dylan. Writer: Dustin Lee Abraham. Cinematographer: Francis Kenny. Music: Rockwilder.

HOW STELLA GOT HER GROOVE BACK. 1998. (R) 124 min. Drama/Romance. This film is based on the novel by Terry McMillan, about a fortyish, overworked single mother who takes a vacation to the beautiful island of Jamaica. While there, she meets and falls for an island man half her age. More than just a fling, she brings him back to the United States to meet her family, and fill a void she has endured for far too long. Cast: **Angela Bassett**, **Whoopi Goldberg**, **Taye Diggs**, **Regina King**, Suzanne Douglas, **Richard Lawson**, Michael J. Pagan, Barry Henley, Sicily. Director: **Kevin Rodney Sullivan**. Writers: Ronald Bass, Terry McMillian. Cinematographer: Jeffrey Jur. Music: Michel Colombier.

HOW YOU LIKE ME NOW? 1992. (R) 109 min. Urban Drama. This is a relationship flick set on the south side of Chicago. A guy with menial skills and employment opportunities has a hard time holding on to his ostentatious girlfriend who wants more than he can deliver. Cast: Darnell Williams, **Salli Richardson**, Daniel Gardner, Raymond Whitefield, Debra Crable, Jonelle Kennedy, Byron

Stewart, Charnele Brown, Daryll Roberts. Writer/Director: Daryll Roberts. Music: Kahil El Zabar, Chuck Webb.

HUDLIN, REGINALD (1961-). Director, producer, screenwriter. This East St. Louis, Illinois, native was at the forefront of the black independent cinema movement of the 1980s and 1990s. A graduate of Harvard University, his award-winning thesis film *House Party*, 1983, was successfully expanded into a feature film in 1990, produced by brother **Warrington Hudlin**. Now on Hollywood's A-List, The Hudlin Brothers followed up with the romantic comedy *Boomerang*, 1992, featuring **Eddie Murphy** and **Halle Berry**, and then transferred the late comedian Robin Harris' comic skit about *Bebe's Kids*, 1992, into the first African American feature-length cartoon. On **television**, the brothers produced and each directed a segment of the HBO sci-fi anthology *Cosmic Slop*, 1994. Reggie also provided the voice of Rodney Roach in the offbeat comedy *Joe's Apartment*, 1996. In 2005, he was named President of Entertainment for the **Black Entertainment Television** Network.

Filmography: *House Party*, 1990; *Boomerang*, 1992; *Cosmic Slop*, 1994; *The Great White Hype*, 1996; *The Ladies Man*, 2000; *Serving Sara*, 2002.

HUDLIN, WARRINGTON (1952-). Producer, director. A native of East St. Louis, Illinois, Hudlin was educated at Yale University, where he directed his film *Black at Yale*, 1974. He is the brother of director **Reginald Hudlin** and together they are known as "The Hudlin Brothers." They made the hit films *House Party*, 1990; *Boomerang*, 1992; and *Bebe's Kids*, 1992. Warrington also directed a segment of their HBO sci-fi anthology *Cosmic Slop*, 1994. He was the curator of the Acapulco Black Film Festival, cofounder of the **Black Filmmakers Foundation**, and is creator of the film and entertainment-based website *DVRepublic*.

HUDSON, ERNIE (1945-). Actor. Born and raised in Benton Harbor, Michigan, Hudson is an actor with an impressive list of credits in both **television** and film. He wrote short stories as a child and envisioned them being performed on a stage. After spending time in the U. S. Marine Corps, he moved to Detroit and became the resident playwright at the vintage black theater Concepts East. He attended Wayne State University and, upon graduation, was given a full scholarship to study acting in the MFA program at the Yale School of Drama. He received his first film role in *Leadbelly*, 1976, after meeting **Gordon Parks**, the film's director. When additional acting opportunities failed to materialize, Hudson enrolled in the PhD program at the University of Minnesota. While there, he played the starring role in the Minneapolis Theater In The Round's production of *The Great White Hope*, and his career finally kicked into gear. A string of television appearances followed, including *Fantasy Island*, *Little House on the Prairie*, *Taxi*, *The A-Team*, and *The Incredible Hulk*. He also accepted a host of film roles, including **Roots: The Next Generation**, 1979; *Spacehunter*, 1983; and as Winston Zeddemore in the *Ghostbusters* series of films. He more recently portrayed the prison warden in the HBO series *Oz*.

Filmography: **Dolemite 2: The Human Tornado**, 1976; *The Jazz Singer*, 1980; **Penitentiary 2**, 1982; *Spacehunter: Adventures in the Forbidden Zone*, 1983; *Joy of Sex*, 1984; *Ghostbusters*, 1984; *The Wrong Guys*, 1988; *Leviathan*, 1989; *Ghostbusters 2*, 1989; *The Hand That Rocks the Cradle*, 1992; *The Crow*, 1993; **Sugar Hill**, 1994; *No Escape*, 1994; *In the Army Now*, 1994; *The Basketball Diaries*, 1994; *Congo*, 1995; *Tornado*, 1996; *The Substitute*, 1996; *Operation Delta Force*, 1997; *Mr. Magoo*, 1997; *Never 2 Big*, 1998; *Urban Menace*, 1999; *Stealth Fighter*, 1999; *Interceptor Force*, 1999; *Corrupt*, 1999; *The Watcher*, 2000; *Red Letters*, 2000; *Nowhere to Land*, 2000; *Miss Congeniality*, 2000.

HUGHES, ALBERT and ALLEN (1972-). Writers, producers, directors. These twin brothers were born in Detroit, Michigan, and started making movies at age 12. While in high school, Allen took a TV production class and they made their short film *How to be a Burglar*, and their next project, *Uncensored Videos*, was shown on a local cable channel. Albert attended film school at Los Angeles Community College and continued to create innovative productions. Continually co-writing, co-producing, and co-directing, their first feature film was the hood flick **Menace II Society**, 1993, and they followed with the robbery-driven **Dead Presidents**, 1995. Their documentary *American Pimp*, 1999, took a hard look at the lives of prostitutes and the men who pimp them. They produced and directed the mainstream Jack the Ripper-based *From Hell*, 2001, as well as the **television** series *Touching Evil*.

Filmography: *Menace II Society*, 1993; *Dead Presidents*, 1995; *American Pimp*, 1999; *From Hell*, 2001; *Art Con*, 2005.

HUGHLEY, D. L. (1963-). Actor, comedian. This Los Angeles, California-born comedian got his big break on **television** shows like *Def Comedy Jam* and *Black Entertainment Television's Comicview*. His comedy special, *D. L. Hughley: Goin' Home*, 1999, was well received and a year later he was chosen to be one of the **Original Kings of Comedy**, 2000. He starred in his own family-oriented sitcom, *The Hughleys*, 1998, and guest hosted *The Late Late Show with Craig Kilborn*, 2004.

Filmography: *Inspector Gadget*, 1999; **The Brothers**, 2001; *Inspector Gadget II*, 2003; *Chasing Papi*, 2003; *Scary Movie 3*, 2003; **Soul Plane**, 2004; *Shackles*, 2005.

HURD, MICHELLE (1966-). Actress. This New York City-born actress is the daughter of actor Hugh Hurd. She graduated from Boston University's Acting School and has performed with the National Theater of Great Britain. She made her Broadway debut in *Getting Away with Murder*, and has also appeared in *Othello, Hot Keys*, and *Hamlet*. Her TV guest appearances include *Law & Order, The Cosby Mysteries*, and *Single Life*. She had recurring roles on *New York Undercover, The Practice*, and *Law & Order: SVU*. She also starred in the Showtime series *Leap Years*, and the daytime soap opera *Another World*.

Filmography: *Wilbur Galls*, 1998; **Personals**, 1999; *Random Hearts*, 1999; *Double Parked*, 2000; *April Showers*, 2005.

HURRICANE, THE. 1999. (R) 125 min. Sports/Drama. This film is based on the book *Lazurus and the Hurricane* about middleweight boxing champion Reuben "Hurricane" Carter who is convicted of a murder he did not commit and sentenced to 20 years in prison. After reading Carter's book *The Sixteenth Round*, a young boy motivates members of a legal rights group to fight to get his sentence overturned. Cast: **Denzel Washington**, Vicellous Reon Shannon, Deborah Kara Unger, Liev Schreiber, John Hannah, David Paymer, Dan Hedaya, **Debbi Morgan**, Clancy Brown, Harris Yulin, Vincent Pastore, Rod Steiger. Director: Norman Jewison. Writers: Armyan Bernstein, Dan Gordon. Cinematographer: Roger Deakins. Music: Christopher Young. Awards: **Golden Globes** 2000: Best Actor-Drama (Washington).

HURSTON, ZORA NEALE (1891-1960). Author, anthropologist, folklorist. She was born in Notasulga, Alabama, educated at Barnard College and Columbia University, and is one of the most famous writers to come out of the Harlem Renaissance era of the 1920s. Several of her books were optioned and turned into films, including *The Gilded Six Bits*, 2001, and **Their Eyes Were Watching God**, 2005. As an anthropologist, she filmed African American life in the rural South and used this ethnographic record as a research methodology, capturing folk life as it was, and incorporating her observations into her creative and scholarly writings. The recently discovered 16mm film footage is now housed at the Library of Congress. Hurston was pictured on a 37-cent USA commemorative postage stamp as part of the 2003 Literary Arts series.

HUSTLE AND FLOW. 2005. (R) 114 min. Music/Drama. In this film, a Memphis pimp experiences a midlife crisis and begins to question the path he has taken and tries his hand at rap music, dirty South style. When a successful dirty South rapper returns home for a visit, the former pimp launches a scheme to get him and his music noticed. Cast: **Terrence Deshon Howard, Anthony Johnson,** Taryn Manning, Taraji P. Henson, Paula Jai Parker, **Elise Neal,** DJ Qualls, Ludacris, **Isaac Hayes.** Writer/Director: Craig Brewer. Awards: 2006 **Oscars:** Best Original Song, "It's Hard Out Here for a Pimp."

I

ICE CUBE. (1969-). Rapper, actor, writer, producer. Born O'Shea Jackson in Los Angeles, California, this controversial hardcore rapper was one of the best-known hip-hop artists in the recording industry before he moved into a film career. Along with rappers Eazy-E and Dr. Dre, they formed the rap group N.W.A. (Niggas with Attitude), to produce the groundbreaking album *Straight Out of Compton*. He went solo in 1989 and garnered two double-platinum albums. His portrayal of Doboy, a troubled inner-city youth in director **John Singleton**'s *Boyz N the Hood*, 1991, impressed fans and critics, and led to many more subsequent roles. He wrote, produced, and starred in the cult hit *Friday*, 1995, which garnered two successful sequels. He made his director's debut with *The Player's Club*, 1998, and starred in and executive produced the controversial comedy *Barbershop*, 2002, which received criticism for lambasting several popular civil rights leaders.

Filmography: *Boyz N the Hood*, 1991; *Trespass*, 1992; *Higher Learning*, 1994; *The Glass Shield*, 1995; *Friday*, 1995; *Dangerous Ground*, 1996; *Anaconda*, 1996; *The Players Club*, 1998; *I Got the Hook-Up*, 1998; *Three Kings*, 1999; *Next Friday*, 2000; *Ghosts of Mars*, 2001; *Friday after Next*, 2002; *Barbershop*, 2002; *All about the Benjamins*, 2002; *Barbershop 2*, 2004; *Are We There Yet?*, 2005.

ICE T (1969-). Rapper, actor. He was born Tracy Morrow in Newark, New Jersey, and raised in the troubled streets of South Central Los Angeles. He showed a talent for music at an early age and pursued his career with a vengeance. He has had his share of controversy and criticism with his hard-core, streetwise lyrics and used the exposure to further his career in music, **television**, and film. In music, his major label debut *Rhyme Pays*, and the follow-up *Power*, both went gold, and his 1990 hit single "New Jack Hustler," was nominated for a **Grammy Award**. In 1992, his song "Cop Killer" incited angry protests from conservatives and numerous police groups, prompting Ice T to schedule a college lecture tour to discuss the state of first amendment rights and civil liberties in America. His 1989 book, *The Iceberg/Freedom of Speech...Just Watch What You Say*, was a literary protest against music censorship. While making headlines with the politics of his music, Hollywood responded by offering him roles in the urban-based films *New Jack City*, 1991; *Ricochet*, 1991; and *Trespass*, 1992. After playing several guest spots on the NBC urban cop series *New York Undercover*, Ice T was cast as a regular on NBC's *Law & Order: SVU*.

Filmography: *Ricochet*, 1991; *New Jack City*, 1991; *Trespass*, 1992; *Who's the Man?* 1993; *Tank Girl*, 1994; ***Surviving the Game***, 1994; *Johnny Mnemonic*, 1995; *Man Guns*, 1997; *The Deli*, 1997; *Body Count*, 1997; *Crazy Six*, 1998; *Urban Menace*, 1999; *Stealth Fighter*, 1999; *Judgment Day*, 1999; *Leprechaun 5: In the Hood*, 1999; ***Corrupt***, 1999; *Agent of Death*, 1999; *The Guardian*, 2000.

IDLEWILD. 2006. (R) 121 min. Music/Drama. The story takes place during the Prohibition Era in the deep South. In the town of Idlewild, Georgia, a speakeasy performer and the manager of the club where he works resist being taken over by gangsters. Several big stage musical productions accent the jazz, blues, and swinging hip-hop music of the movie's stars, Big Boi and André 3000, of the rap group Outcast. The plot also weaves together a love story with a murder mystery. Cast: André Benjamin, Big Boi, Paula Patton, **Terrence Howard**, **Faizon Love**, Malinda Williams, **Cicely Tyson**, Macy Gray, **Ben Vereen**, Paula Jai Parker, Bobb'e J. Thompson, Pattie Labelle, **Ving Rhames**, Jackie Long, Oscar Dillon. Writer/director: Bryan Barber. Cinematographer: Pascal Rabaud. Editor: Anne Goursaud.

I GOT THE HOOK-UP. 1998. (R) 93 min. Urban Comedy. Two hustlers who sell hot or stolen goods out of the trunk of their car go into a new business when they get hold of a load of cell phones. But the phones are defective and begin to cause problems for the sellers and the users. Cast: **Master P**, **Anthony Johnson**, Gretchen Palmer, Frantz Turner, Tommy "Tiny" Lister, Helen Martin, **John Witherspoon**, Harrison White, **Ice Cube**, Anthony Bosell, **Snoop**

Dogg, Lola Mae. Director: Michael Martin. Writer: Master P. Cinematographer: Antonio Calvache. Music: Tommy Coster, Brad Fairman.

I KNOW WHY THE CAGED BIRD SINGS. 1979. (TV) 100 min. Drama. Film is based on the novel by **Maya Angelou** and chronicles one woman's memory of growing up down South in the 1930s. Cast: **Diahann Carroll, Ruby Dee, Esther Rolle, Roger E. Mosley**, Paul Benjamin, Constance Good. Director: Fielder Cook.

IDENTITY CRISIS. 1989. (R) 98 min. Comedy. A fashion designer and a rap star switch identities. This film was produced by the father-and-son team **Melvin** and **Mario Van Peebles**. Cast: Mario Van Peebles, Ilan Mitchell-Smith, Nicholas Kepros, Shelly Burch, Richard Clarke. Director: Melvin Van Peebles.

IMAGE AWARD. This award is given by the civil rights organization National Association for the Advancement of Colored People (NAACP) to celebrate outstanding achievements and performances of people of color in the arts, as well as those individuals or groups who promote social justice. The annual awards ceremony is a star-studded salute to the best in entertainment. There are 36 competitive categories in the fields of motion picture, **television**, music, and literature, and there are several honorary awards. The festivities have been shown in primetime on the Fox network since 1996.

I'M GONNA GET YOU SUCKA. 1988. (R) 89 min. Comedy. This parody on the **blaxploitation** films of the 1970s features appearances by many of the period's black action heroes themselves. Cast: **Keenen Ivory Wayans, Bernie Casey, Steve James, Isaac Hayes, Jim Brown, Ja'net DuBois**, Dawn Lewis, **Anne-Marie Johnson**, John Vernon, **Antonio Fargas**, Eve Plumb, Clu Gulager, **Kadeem Hardison, Damon Wayans**, Gary Owens, **Clarence Williams III, David Allen Grier, Kim Wayans, Robin Harris, Chris Rock**, Jester Hairston, Eugene Glazer, Peggy Lipton, **Robert Townsend**. Writer/Director: Keenen Ivory Wayans. Cinematographer: Tom Richmond. Music: David Michael Frank.

IMITATION OF LIFE. 1934. 106 min. Drama. A white widow markets her black maid's pancake recipe and makes a fortune. The two live and raise their daughters together. For added drama, the light-skinned daughter of a domestic worker rejects her to pass for white, and the white daughter falls in love with her mother's fiancé. Cast: Claudette Colbert, **Louise Beavers**, Rochelle Hudson, **Fredi**

Washington, Warren William, Ned Sparks, Alan Hale. Director: John M. Stahl. Writers: Preston Sturges, William Hurlbut. Cinematographer: Merritt B. Gerstad.

IMITATION OF LIFE. 1959. 124 min. Drama. This is the successful remake of the 1934 version with a few story changes. A single white mother puts more time into becoming a successful actress than into raising her own daughter. Her black helper and roommate possesses more than enough mothering instincts to fill the void, but loses her own daughter who decides to pass for white. Cast: Lana Turner, **Juanita Moore**, John Gavin, Troy Donahue, Sandra Dee, Susan Kohner. Director: Douglas Sirk. Cinematographer: Russell Metty. Awards: 1960 **Golden Globes**, Best Supporting Actress (Kohner).

INGRAM, REX (1895-1969). Actor. Rex Ingram was born aboard a Mississippi riverboat and went on to become a major personality on radio and film during the 1930s and 1940s. After attending military school, he developed an interest in acting and decided to pursue it as a career. In 1919, after working as a cook for the Union Pacific Railroad, Ingram went to Hollywood, where he appeared in the very first *Tarzan* film in 1918. He followed with roles in a few Hollywood classics, such as *Lord Jim* 1925, *Beau Geste*, 1926, *King Kong*, 1933, **Green Pastures**, 1936, and *Huckleberry Finn*, 1939. He was also active in legitimate theater in San Francisco. By the late 1930s, Ingram was starring in daytime radio dramas and in Work Projects Administration (WPA) Theater, which led to numerous New York stage productions. In **television**, he played Pozzo in the 1957 production of *Waiting for Godot*. He also continued his film career with films like *Elmer Gantry*, 1960; *Your Cheating Heart*, 1964; *Hurry Sundown*, 1967; and *Journey to Shiloh*, 1968. Ingram also had an impressive theatrical career.

Filmography: *Green Pastures*, 1936; *The Adventures of Huckleberry Finn*, 1939; *The Thief of Baghdad*, 1940; *Talk of the Town*, 1942; *Sahara*, 1943; *Cabin in the Sky*, 1943; *Dark Waters*, 1944; *A Thousand and One Nights*, 1945; *Moonrise*, 1948; *Elmer Gantry*, 1960; *Your Cheating Heart*, 1964; *Hurry Sundown*, 1967; and *Journey to Shiloh*, 1968.

IN THE HEAT OF THE NIGHT. 1967. 109 min. Drama. A black homicide detective from Philadelphia is sent to a small Mississippi town to help solve a murder. Resented by the local sheriff and the townsfolk, he faces racism and threats but maintains his dignity throughout. Cast: **Sidney Poitier**, Rod Steiger, Warren Oates, Lee

Grant. Director: Norman Jewison. Writer: Stirling Silliphant. Cinematographer: Haskell Wexler. Music: **Quincy Jones**. Awards: 1967 **Oscars**, Best Picture, Best Actor (Steiger), Best Adapted Screenplay, Film Editing, Picture, Sound. 1967 British Academy Awards, Best Actor (Steiger). 1968 **Golden Globes**, Best Actor (Steiger), Best Film—Drama, Best Screenplay.

INKWELL, THE. 1994. (R) 112 min. Drama/Romance. A nerdy inner-city boy spends his 1976 summer break with family on Martha's Vineyard, where he meets his first love. As a fish-out-of-water, he has a hard time fitting in with the upscale inhabitants and faces major competition from his girl's well-bred, upper-class boyfriend. Cast: **Larenze Tate, Joe Morton**, Phyllis Stickney, **Jada Pinkett**. Director: **Matty Rich**. Writers: Paris Qualles, Tom Ricostronza. Cinematographer: **John L. Demps Jr.** Music: **Terence Blanchard**.

INTRODUCING DOROTHY DANDRIDGE. 1999. (R) 115 min. Biopic. The film is based on the remarkable but often-tragic life of actress **Dorothy Dandridge**. Taken from the book by former husband Earl Mills, the film chronicles her turbulent childhood, failed marriages, her success, and career struggles. Cast: **Halle Berry**, Brent Spiner, **Obba Babatunde, Loretta Devine, Cynda Williams**, Latanya Richardson, Tamara Taylor, Klaus Maria Brandauer, D. B. Sweeney, William Atherton. Director: Martha Coolidge. Writers: Scott Abbott, Shonda Rhimes. Cinematography: Robbie Greenberg. Music: Elmer Bernstein.

INTRUDER IN THE DUST. 1949. 87 min. Drama. This film is adapted from the William Faulkner novel about a black man who is falsely accused of killing a white man in a small Southern town. The majority of the population wants to address the issue with a rope. Cast: David Brian, Claude Jarman Jr., **Juano Hernandez**, Porter Hall, Elizabeth Patterson. Director: Clarence Brown. Cinematography: Robert L. Surtees.

ISLAND IN THE SUN. 1957. 119 min. Drama. Based on the novel by Alec Waugh, this film explores race issues and interracial relationships that disrupt lives on a Caribbean island. Cast: **Dorothy Dandridge, Harry Belafonte**, James Mason, Joan Fontaine, John Williams. Director: Robert Rossen. Cinematographer: Frederick A. Young. Music: Malcolm Arnold.

J

JACKIE ROBINSON STORY, THE. 1950. 76 min. Biopic. This is a film autobiography on the life and times of famed baseball player Jackie Robinson, who plays himself. It goes from his college days at the University of California, Los Angeles, to breaking the color line to become the first African American to play modern-day major league baseball. He faces racism from the fans and his teammates but weathers it all to become a true hero of all people. Cast: Jackie Robinson, **Ruby Dee**, Minor Watson, **Joel Fluellen, Louise Beavers**, Richard Lane, Harry Shannon, Ben Lessy. Director: Alfred E. Green. Writers: Arthur Mann, Lawrence Taylor. Cinematographer: Ernest Laslo. Music: David Chudnow.

JACKSON, EUGENE (1916-2001). Actor. As a six-year-old child star, Jackson portrayed **Farina**'s older brother, Pineapple, in Hal Roach's 1920s series *Our Gang*, and made his feature film debut in *Hearts in Dixie*, 1929. He later sang and danced on the vaudeville circuit billed as "Hollywood's Most Famous Colored Kid Star." He continued to act, mostly in uncredited bit parts, but appeared on television as **Diahann Carroll**'s Uncle Lou on her series *Julia*, and as a friend of **Redd Foxx** on his series *Sanford and Son*. Jackson taught dance at his own studios in Compton and Pasadena, California, and his choreography was featured in a dance retrospective for the 1993 Los Angeles Festival.

Filmography: *Hearts in Dixie*, 1929; *Red River Valley*, 1936; *Shenandoah Valley*, 1965.

JACKSON, FAY M. (1902-1979). She was the first Hollywood press correspondent for the Associated Negro Press in the 1930s, and wrote many articles on politics and the entertainment industry for the *California News* and the *California Eagle*. Jackson founded and published *Flash Magazine* in 1928, directed at the economic, social, and political needs of the African American community. It was the only Negro newsmagazine with a regular publishing schedule at that time. The 23 September 1929 issue included an article on "The Dilemma of the Negro Actor," written by **Clarence Muse**.

JACKSON, GEORGE (1958-2000). Producer, director. A media executive in both music and film, Jackson ran **Motown** Records for a while, as well as **Richard Pryor**'s production company, Indigo Productions. He partnered with **Doug McHenry** to produce more than a dozen films, including *New Jack City*, 1991; *A Thin Line*

Between Love and Hate, 1996; and the sequel to *House Party*, *House Party 2: The Pajama Jam*, 1991, which he also directed. He was co-executive producer of the TV comedy series *Malcolm & Eddie*.

Filmography: *Krush Groove*, 1985; *Disorderlies*, 1987; *New Jack City*, 1991; *House Party 2*, 1991; *House Party 3*, 1994; *Scenes for the Soul*, 1995; *The Walking Dead*, 1995; *A Thin Line Between Love and Hate*, 1996; *Body Count*, 1998; *Mr. Murder*, 1998.

JACKSON, JANET (1966-). Singer, actress. Jackson is the youngest child born to the multi-talented family from Gary, Indiana, which produced the mega-successful singing group The Jackson 5. She performed with her brothers in Las Vegas, Nevada, when she was seven, and appeared on their **television** special two years later. Recognizing her immense talent, she was cast in the television sitcom *Good Times*, 1977-79, and *Different Strokes*, 1981-82. She signed her first record deal with A&M Records in 1982, but her musical breakout came in 1986 with her album *Control*, which went quadruple platinum and sold more than four million copies. Her *Rhythm Nation 1814* album was also very successful. Moving to film, she starred as the title character in director **John Singleton**'s *Poetic Justice*, 1993, opposite rapper **Tupac Shakur**.

Filmography: *Poetic Justice*, 1993; *Nutty Professor 2: The Klumps*, 2000.

JACKSON, MEL (1970-). Actor. This Chicago, Illinois, native toured with the 2003 production of David E. Talbert's stage play *Love on Layaway*. He made his television debut on the TV sitcom *Living Single*, and his film debut in *Soul Food*, 1997. His telepic performances include *To Sir with Love II*, 1996; *The Temptations*, 1998; *Little Richard*, 2000; and *Playing with Fire*, 2000. He also toured with the stage play *Friends and Lovers*.

Filmography: *Soul Food*, 1997; *Carmen's Choice*, 1998; *An Uninvited Guest*, 1999; *Dancing in September*, 2000; *Little Richard*, 2000; *Deliver Us from Eva*, 2003; *Motives*, 2004; *The Black Man's Guide to Understanding Black Women*, 2005.

JACKSON, MICHAEL (1958-). Singer, songwriter, actor. Jackson became a child star with his four brothers as the lead singer of The Jackson 5. After signing with **Motown** Records in 1969, the group put out 13 top-20 hits in just six years. As a solo artist, Jackson teamed with producer Quincy Jones to release his *Off the Wall*, album in 1979, followed by *Thriller* in 1981, which became the best-selling album of all time. Other albums include *Bad*, *Victory*, *Dangerous*, and *HIStory*. Jackson is known for his innovative dance moves and made film history with music videos that set the standard. The visual representations of his songs "I'm Bad," "Billy Jean," "Scream," and especially "Thriller,' complete with make-up and visual effects by Rick Baker, have been praised, awarded, and emulated. He produced and stared in the short film *Captain EO*, which experimented with the latest in visual effects. Jackson also portrayed the scarecrow in the big budget musical film *The Wiz*, 1978.

Filmography: *The Wiz*, 1978; *Captain EO*, 1998; *Men in Black 2*, 2002.

JACKSON, MO'NIQUE (1967-). Comedienne, actress. Born in Baltimore, Maryland, this full-figured funny lady has her own line of clothing called Mo'Nique's Big Beautiful and Loving It. She began her entertainment career doing stand-up, and landed a coveted spot on the *Queens of Comedy*, 2001, movie and tour. She has hosted *It's Showtime at the Apollo*, the *3rd and 4th Annual BET Awards*, appeared on the TV series *Last Comic Standing*, and numerous other comedy specials. She also stars as Nicole "Nikki" Parker in the sitcom *The Parkers*. Her film roles include **Three Strikes**, 2000; **Two Can Play That Game**, 2001; and **Hair Show**, 2004.

Filmography: *Three Strikes*, 2000; **Baby Boy**, 2001; *Two Can Play That Game*, 2001; *Half Past Dead*, 2002; **Soul Plane**, 2004; *Hair Show*, 2004; *Shadow Boxer*, 2005; *Domino*, 2005.

JACKSON, SAMUEL L. (1949-). Actor. Born in Chattanooga, Tennessee, Jackson studied drama at Morehouse College in Atlanta. He moved to New York City after graduation and began to work on stage and in film. He was cast in three **Spike Lee** films, including **School Daze**, 1988; **Mo' Better Blues**, 1990; and **Jungle Fever**, 1994, for which he received the Cannes Film Festival's Best Supporting Actor Award. Jackson also appeared in *Patriot Games*, 1992, and *Jurassic Park*, 1993. His standout performance was as a hit man in Quentin Tarrentino's *Pulp Fiction*, 1994. Now a bankable star, he followed his success with key roles in *Die Hard: With a Vengeance*, 1995; **The Great White Hype**, 1996; **The Caveman's Valentine**, 2001; and as a Jedi Knight in *Star Wars: Episode 1—The Phantom Menace*, 1999; and *Episode 2—Attack of the Clones*, 2002.

Filmography: *School Daze*, 1988; **Coming to America**, 1988; *Mo' Better Blues*, 1990; *Goodfellas*, 1990; **Def By Temptation**, 1990; *Jungle Fever*, 1991; *White Sands*, 1992; *Patriot Games*,

1992; *Juice*, 1992; *Fathers and Sons*, 1992; *True Romance*, 1993; *Loaded Weapon 1*, 1993; *Menace II Society*, 1993; *Jurassic Park*, 1993; *Pulp Fiction*, 1994; *Losing Isaiah*, 1994; *Fresh*, 1994; *Against the Wall*, 1994; *Die Hard: With a Vengeance*, 1995; *A Time to Kill*, 1996; *The Long Kiss Goodnight*, 1996; *Hard Eight*, 1996; *The Great White Hype*, 1996; *Sphere*, 1997; *Jackie Brown*, 1997; *Eve's Bayou*, 1997; *The Red Violin*, 1998; *Out of Sight*, 1998; *The Negotiator*, 1998; *Star Wars: Episode 1—The Phantom Menace*, 1999; *Deep Blue Sea*, 1999; *Unbreakable*, 2000; *Shaft 2000*, 2000; *Rules of Engagement*, 2000: *The Caveman's Valentine*, 2001; *XXX*, 2002; *Star Wars: Episode 2—Attack of the Clones*, 2002; *Changing Lanes*, 2002; *S. W. A. T.*, 2003; *Basic*, 2003; *Coach Carter*, 2005.

JACKSON, STONEY (1960-). Actor. He was born in Richmond, Virginia, and moved to California with his family when he was 16. He began acting on **television** in the 1980-81 season of the TV series *The White Shadow*, and played several student roles before being cast as Phones in *Roller Boogie*, 1979. He starred as the title character in the telepic *The 100 Lives of Black Jack Savage*, 1991, and has consistently worked in both film and television.

Filmography: *Roller Boogie*, 1979; *Streets of Fire*, 1984; *Knights of the City*, 1985; *Sweet Perfection*, 1990; *Up Against the Wall*, 1991; *Trespass*, 1992; *The Disappearance of Kevin Johnson*, 1995; *Wild Bill*, 1995; *The Fan*, 1996; *Black Scorpion 2: Ground Zero*, 1996; *Trippin'*, 1999; *At Face Value*, 1999; *Footprints*, 2002; *Black Ball*, 2003.

JAFA, ARTHUR (1960-). Cinematographer. He was born in Tupelo, Mississippi. Jafa married filmmaker **Julie Dash** and lensed her groundbreaking film *Daughters of the Dust*, 1991, for which he won the Best Cinematography prize at the Sundance Film Festival. He went on to work with director **Spike Lee** on his films *Malcolm X*, 1992, and *Crooklyn*, 1994.

Filmography: *Daughters of the Dust*, 1991; *Malcolm X*, 1992; *The Darker Side of Black*, 1993; *Seven Songs for Malcolm X*, 1993; *Crooklyn*, 1994; *Rouch in Reverse*, 1995; *A Litany for Survival: The Life and Work of Audre Lorde*, 1995; *W. E. B. Debois: A Biography in Four Voices*, 1996.

JAKES, T. D. (1957-) Pastor, writer, producer, actor. He was born in South Charleston, West Virginia, and went on to become a well-known and highly respected bishop in the Christian church. He has a large **television** ministry through his series *Get Ready with T. D.*

Jakes, and videotapes of his preaching have sold in the millions. He is the author of the self-help novel *Woman Thou Art Loosed,* and also appears in the film version of his work.

Filmography: *Tell the Devil I Changed My Mind,* 1994; *Get Ready: The Best of T. D. Jakes,* 2000; *Left Behind,* 2000; **Woman Thou Art Loosed,** 2004.

JAMES, STEVE (1952-1993). A native of New York City, James studied art and film at C. W. Post College. After graduation, he did stage work and TV commercials, and entered the film industry as a stuntman on *The Wiz,* 1978; *Wolfen,* 1981; and *Ragtime,* 1981. With his buff build and a knack for the martial arts, he was soon being cast as the sidekick in action films, such as *The Exterminator,* 1980, and *The Delta Force,* 1986. He was also featured in the *American Ninja* series of karate films. Other notable appearances include roles in **The Brother from Another Planet,** 1984, and **I'm Gonna Git You Sucka,** 1988.

Filmography: *The Land That Time Forgot,* 1975; *Exterminator,* 1980; **The Brother from Another Planet,** 1984; *American Ninja,* 1985; *Stalking Danger,* 1986; *The P. O. W. Escape,* 1986; *Avenging Force,* 1986; *American Ninja 2: The Confrontation,* 1987; *Python Wolf,* 1988; *Johnny Be Good,* 1988; *I'm Gonna Git You Sucka,* 1988; *River Bend,* 1989; *American Ninja 3: Blood Hunt,* 1989; *Street Hunter,* 1990; *McBain,* 1991; *The Player,* 1992; *Weekend at Bernie's 2,* 1993; *Bloodfist 5: Human Target,* 1993.

JASON'S LYRIC. 1994. (R) 119 min. Urban Drama. Love and romance try to survive amid the stress and gang-motivated violence of Houston's inner city. A hardworking young man falls in love with a soul-food waitress. They make plans to move away together but rivalries and family ties are pulling them apart. Cast: **Allen Payne, Bokeem Woodbine, Jada Pinkett, Suzzanne Douglass, Forest Whitaker,** Treach. Director: **Doug McHenry.** Writer: Bobby Smith Jr. Music: Matt Noble.

JEAN-BAPTISTE, MARIANNE (1967-). Actress. This London, England-born actress graduated from the Royal Academy of Dramatic Arts and made her film debut in *London Kills Me,* 1991. She received **Golden Globe** and **Academy Award** Best Supporting Actress nominations for her performance in *Secrets & Lies,* 1996. She has appeared on stage in *It's a Great Big Shame, Measure for Measure, Running Dream,* and she wrote and performed in *Ave Africa.* She stars as a regular on the CBS **television** series *Without a Trace.*

Filmography: *London Kills Me*, 1991; *Secrets & Lies*, 1996; *Mr. Jealousy*, 1997; *How to Make the Cruelest Month*, 1998; ***The Wedding***, 1998; *Nowhere to Go*, 1998; *The 24 Hour Woman*, 1999; *A Murder of Crows*, 1999; *28 Days*, 2000; *The Cell*, 2000; *New Year's Day*, 2000; *Women in Film*, 2001; *Men Only*. 2001; *Spy Game*, 2001; *Don't Explain*, 2002; *Loving You*, 2003.

J. D.'S REVENGE. 1976. (R) 95 min. Blaxploitation. While participating in a hypnotist's nightclub act, a man becomes possessed by the spirit of a murdered gangster from the 1940s who commandeers his new form to seek his revenge. Cast: **Glynn Turman, Louis Gossett Jr., Joan Pringle**, David McNight, James L.Watkins. Director: Arthur Marks. Writer: Jaison Starkes. Cinematographer: Harry J. May.

JEFFRIES, HERB (1911-). Actor, singer. He is credited on the screen as Herbert Jeffrey, and became known as "The Bronze Buckeroo," the hard-riding, fast-shooting hero in a string of black musical Westerns from the late 1930s. The Michigan native began his singing career with a trio as a teenager in Detroit. While performing in a speakeasy, **Lewis Armstrong** recommended Jeffries to bandleader Erskine Tate at the Savoy Ballroom in Chicago, where he performed for only two nights before being hired away by the Earl Hines Big Band. He also sang with **Duke Ellington's** band. Motivated by the multitude of segregated movie theaters in the 1930s showing mostly white movies, Jeffries set out to produce a black cowboy film to give children who had no hero on the big screen someone to identify with. Born of mixed parentage, the film producers darkened his skin with makeup for his first lead role as singing cowboy Jeff Kincaid in ***Harlem on the Prairie***, 1937. He then worked with another producer on a trio of films, starring as ranch hand Bob Blake, and introducing his trusty horse "Stardusk." In his later years, Jeffries joined the military service, owned a jazz club in Paris, and earned doctorate degrees in psychology in 1972, and divinity in 1979. He has made guest appearances on television shows such as *Hawaii Five-O*, *The Virginian*, and *Name of the Game*. He is still singing and writing his autobiography, *Skin Deep*.

Filmography: *Harlem on the Prairie*, 1937; ***Two-Gun Man from Harlem***, 1938; ***Harlem Rides the Range***, 1938; ***The Bronze Buckaroo***, 1939; *Disc Jockey*, 1951; *Calypso Joe*, 1957; *Chrome and Hot Leather*, 1971; *Portrait of a Hitman*, 1977.

JELKS, JOHN. Actor. This theatrically trained actor is perhaps best known for his roles in independent films, such as Iverson White's

Dark Exodus, 1985, and several works by independent filmmaker Zeinabu Irene Davis, including *A Powerful Thang*, 1991, and *Compensation*, 1999. He has played the lead role in playwright August Wilson's *Joe Turner's Dead and Gone* and appeared on the New York stage in Wilson's play, *Gem of the Ocean*. Filmography: *Dark Exodus*, 1983; *Crocodile Conspiracy*, 1986; *A Powerful Thang*, 1991; *Magic Love*, 1992; *Compensation*, 1999.

JESSE OWENS STORY, THE. 1984. (TV) 174 min. Biopic. This is a film based on the life of four-time Olympic Gold medal winner Jesse Owens. It follows his rise to fame at the 1936 Olympic Games in Germany, and his often-honored but disappointing career path afterward. Cast: **Dorian Harewood, Debbie Morgan, Georg Stanford Brown, LeVar Burton**, George Kennedy, Tom Bosley, **Ben Vereen**. Director: Richard Irving.

JOE LEWIS STORY, THE. 1953. 88 min. Biopic. This is a film based on the life of world heavyweight boxing champion Joe Lewis. Cast: Coley Wallace, Paul Stewart, Hilda Simms, Albert "Poppy" Popwell. Director: Robert Gordon. Writer: Robert Sylvester. Cinematographer: Joseph Brun. Music: George Bassman.

JOE'S BED-STUY BARBERSHOP: WE CUT HEADS. 1983. 60 min. Drama. This is **Spike Lee**'s student film project while at New York University. A desperate barbershop owner tries to rip off a local numbers man but gets caught. The film is packed with humor, political issues, and social awareness. Cast: Monty Ross, Donna Bailey, Stuart Smith, Tommy Redmond Hicks, Horace Long, LaVern Summer, Africanus Rocius, Robert Delbert, Alphonzo Lewis, William Badgett, Herbert Burks, Vanita Taylor, Lynn Dummett, Loretta Cragett, Curtis Brown. Writer/Director: Spike Lee. Cinematographer: **Ernest R. Dickerson**.

JOHN Q. 2002. (PG-13) 118 min. Drama. An everyday working man takes over a hospital emergency room after his son is denied an expensive medical treatment he needs to live by the father's Health Maintainance Organization. Cast: **Denzel Washington**, Robert Duval, James Woods, Anne Heche, **Eddie Griffin, Kimberly Elise**, Shawn Hatosy, Ray Liotta, Daniel E. Smith, David Thornton, Ethan Suplee, Kevin Connolly, Paul Johansson, **Troy Beyer, Obba Babatunde**, Laura Harring. Director: Nick Cassavetes. Writer: James Keams. Cinematographer: Roger Stoffers. Music: Aaron Zigman.

JOHNSON, A. J. (1967-). Actress. This New Jersey native was born Adrienne-Joi Johnson and became an actress during the hip-hop era of the 1990s. She made her screen debut in **Spike Lee's** *School Daze*, 1988, and danced her way into **Reginald Hudlin's** *House Party*, 1990. Other notable film performances include *Sister Act*, 1992; *Baby Boy*, 2001; and *Skin Deep*, 2003. She has made guest appearances on **television** series, such as *In the Heat of the Night*, *Amen*, *Chicago Hope*, and *Touched by an Angel*.

Filmography: *School Daze*, 1988; *House Party*, 1990; *Dying Young*, 1991; *Double Trouble*, 1992; *Sister Act*, 1992; *The Inkwell*, 1994; *High Frequency*, 1998; *Two Shades of Blue*, 2000; *Baby Boy*, 2001; *Tara*, 2001; *Skin Deep*, 2003.

JOHNSON, A. J. (ANTHONY). Actor. He is a loud-mouthed, quick-witted, character actor often cast as a modern-day comedic sidekick to the strong male lead in such films as *How to Be a Player*, 1997; *The Players Club*, 1998; *Two Can Play That Game*, 2001; and *Hustle and Flow*, 2005. His **television** guest appearances include *The Parent Hood*, *Martin*, *Malcolm & Eddie*, *Moesha*, and *The Jamie Foxx Show*.

Filmography: *House Party*, 1990; *Ninja Academy*, 1990; *True Identity*, 1991; *Menace II Society*, 1993; *House Party 3*, 1994; *Friday*, 1995; *Panther*, 1995; *The Great White Hype*, 1996; *How to Be a Player*, 1997; *B*A*P*S*, 1997; *Hoover Park*, 1997; *The Players Club*, 1997; *Woo*, 1998; *I Got the Hook-Up*, 1998; *Rising to the Top*, 1999; *Hot Boyz*, 1999; *Sweet Hideaway*, 2003; *Hittin' It!* 2004; *Hustle and Flow*, 2005.

JOHNSON, ANNE-MARIE (1960-). She was born in Los Angeles, California, and graduated from the UCLA Theater Department. She has worked on **television** as Aletha Tibbs in *In the Heat of the Night*, 1988-1993, as Representative Bobbi Lathan in *JAG*, 2002, and as Sharon Upton Farley in *Girlfriends*, 2003-2004. Her film roles include *Hollywood Shuffle*, 1987; *I'm Gonna Git You Sucka*, 1988; *The Five Heartbeats*, 1991; and *Down in the Delta*, 1998.

Filmography: *Hollywood Shuffle*, 1987; *I'm Gonna Git You Sucka*, 1988; *Robert Jox*, 1990; *The Five Heartbeats*, 1991; *True Identity*, 1991; *Strictly Business*, 1991; *Why Colors?* 1992; *Down in the Delta*, 1998; *Pursuit of Happiness*, 2001; *Life Drawing*, 2001.

JOHNSON, BEVERLY (1952-). Supermodel, actress, writer. Born in Buffalo, New York, Johnson's face has been on more than 500 magazine covers and has launched hundreds of advertising campaigns around the world. She broke the color barrier in August 1974, when she became the first African American to grace the cover of *Vogue* magazine, and the following year, became the first on the cover of the French magazine *Elle*. She expanded her image to film and television with film roles in *The Baron*, 1977; *Ashanti*, 1979; *Meteor Man*, 1993; and *How to Be a Player*, 1997. Her appearances in made-for-TV movies include *Crisis in Sun Valley*, 1978; *The Sky is Gray*, 1980; and *The Cover Girl Murders*, 1993. Johnson's **television** guest appearances include *Hunter*, *Law & Order*, *3rd Rock from the Sun*, and *Girlfriends*.

Filmography: *Ashanti: Land of No Mercy*, 1979; *The Cover Girl Murders*, 1993; *Meteor Man*, 1993; *True Vengeance*, 1997; *How to Be a Player*, 1997; *Crossroads*, 2002.

JOHNSON, CLARK (1954-). Actor, director. Johnson played football while attending film school in Canada. He started acting in bit roles on Canadian productions while also serving as camera assistant, special effects, and doing stunts. His Hollywood career began in 1987 with roles in *Wild Thing*, 1987; *Adventures in Babysitting*, 1987; and *Nowhere to Hide*, 1987. He also supplied a voice for the ABC animated children's adventure and music series, *Hammerman*, 1991. Since his impressive run as Detective Meldrick Lewis on the NBC series *Homicide: Life on the* Streets, Johnson has effectively transitioned into directing. His directing efforts began with an episode of *Homicide*, and he has since helmed shows like HBO's *The Wire*. He received an **Emmy Award** nomination for Outstanding Directing for a Drama Series for his work on the pilot for the F/X series *The Shield*. He landed the directing job on the HBO film *Boycott*, 2001, about the Montgomery Bus Boycott in the 1960s, and made his theatrical directing debut with the action-packed police drama *S. W. A. T.*, 2003.

Filmography: *Colors*, 1988; *Personals*, 1990; *The Finishing Touch*, 1992; *Final Round*, 1993; *Soul Survivor*, 1995; *Rude*, 1996; *Junior's Groove*, 1997; *Blood Brothers*, 1997; *Love Come Down*, 2000; *Homicide: The Movie*, 2000; *Disappearing Acts*, 2000; *Deliberate Intent*, 2001; *Boycott*, 2002.

JOHNSON, GEORGE (1887-1939). He was born in Colorado Springs, Colorado, and became a postman in Omaha, Nebraska. He joined his brother **Noble Johnson**'s company, **Lincoln Motion Picture Company**, after the success of their first film and became general booking manager. He is also credited with writing the company's final production, *By Right of Birth*, 1921. He ran the company once Noble returned to acting until financial pressures forced him to close the doors in 1922.

Filmography: *Trooper of Company K*, 1918; *A Man's Duty*, 1919; *By Right of Birth*, 1921.

JOHNSON, HALL (1888-1970). Choir director, composer. This son of a church pastor from Athens, Georgia, organized his first choir while living in Harlem and developed his own distinct sound. Warner Brothers studio brought Johnson and his choir to Hollywood from the Broadway stage in New York to provide the music for *Green Pastures*, 1935. **Sound films** were relatively new and the music he provided became a sought-after staple in many additional films, including *Lost Horizon*, 1937; *Way Down South*, 1939; and *Cabin in the Sky*, 1943. He was posthumously inducted into the **Black Filmmakers Hall of Fame** in 1975.

JOHNSON, KYLE (1951-) Actor. Child actor and son of actress Nichelle Nichols from the TV series *Star Trek*. He starred in the coming-of-age film based on photographer **Gordon Parks'** autobiographical book, *The Learning Tree*, 1969. His **television** guest appearances include *Dr. Kildare*, *The Mod Squad*, and *McCloud*.

Filmography: *The Learning Tree*, 1969; *Pretty Maids All in a Row*, 1971; *Brother on the Run*, 1973; *Man on the Run*, 1975; *Woman in the Rain*, 1978; *The Paraclete*, 1996.

JOHNSON, NOBLE (1881-1978). Actor, producer. Often noted as being the first black actor, Johnson is perhaps best remembered for his part in organizing the **Lincoln Motion Picture Company** in 1915, along with fellow actor **Clarence Brooks**. Johnson was born in Marshall, Missouri, and left school at 15 to work and travel with his father who was an expert horse trainer. Before turning to acting, Johnson was a cowboy, a rancher, a horse trainer, and a miner for a time in 1909, until he was hired by the Lubin Company to play an Indian in a silent film it was shooting in Colorado. After doing more film work with the company back in Philadelphia, he migrated to Los Angeles and continued his acting career. Johnson was a light-skinned Negro but the roles he played were mostly racial exotics. He has portrayed a Chinese man, a Cossack, a Persian prince, a Cuban zombie, a dusky weather-beaten cowboy, and numerous Indian chiefs. His first starring role came in Lincoln Picture Company's *Realization of a Negro's Ambition*, 1916. His Los Angeles-based production company was established to produce and distribute motion pictures exclusively for the black community. Once their first film was a success, Noble's brother, **George Johnson** joined the company and they produced three additional films, *Trooper of Company K*, 1918; *A Man's Duty*, 1919 (their first feature film); and *By Right of Birth*, 1921. Noble left the company in 1918 for a steady paycheck at Universal Pictures and continued to work as an actor until 1950.

Filmography: *Realization of a Negro's Ambition*, 1916; *The Navigator*, 1924; *Murders in the Rue Morgue*, 1932; *The Mummy*, 1932; *The Most Dangerous Game*, 1932; *King Kong*, 1933; *The Lives of Bengai Lancer*, 1935; *The Ghost Breakers*, 1940; *She Wore a Yellow Ribbon*, 1949; *North of the Great Divide*, 1950.

JOHNSON'S FAMILY VACATION, THE. 2004. (PG-13) 97 min. Comedy. Complications arise on the road when a family goes on vacation. Lots of wrong turns, car troubles, and the police almost keep them from reaching their destination. Cast: **Cedric the Entertainer, Vanessa L. Williams**, Solange Knowles, **Bow Wow**, Gabby Soleil, Shannon Elizabeth, **Steve Harvey**, Aloma Wright, **Shari Headley**, Jennifer Freeman, Philip Bolden, Rodney Perry, Christopher B. Duncan, Lorna Scott, Kevin P. Farley. Director: Christopher Erskin. Writers: Todd R. Jones, Earl Richey Jones. Cinematographer: Shawn Maurer. Music: Al Eaton, Richard Gibbs.

JOHNSON vs. JEFFRIES FIGHT FILM. 1910. On 4 July, 1910, in 100-degree heat at an outdoor boxing ring near Reno, Nevada, film cameras recorded what was supposed to be the fight of the century. Former heavyweight champion Jim Jeffries was reluctantly brought out of retirement to fight Jack Johnson, a black man. The film begins with the master of ceremonies inviting a few former champs into the ring for perfunctory applause and accolades from the thousands of fight fans in attendance. Then, the referee motions for the opening bell. The fight lasts for 14 grueling rounds, and when it is over, the fallen Great White Hope is on the mat receiving the ten-count. The referee raises Johnson's fists high into the air and, for the first time in history, there was a black heavyweight champion of the world. At least 10 people lost their lives because of Johnson's victory and hundreds more were injured due to white retaliation and wild celebrations in the streets. Public screenings received instantaneous protests and hundreds of cities barred the film from being shown. The United States Congress passed a law making it a federal offense to transport moving pictures of prizefights across a state line, and the most powerful portrayal of a black man ever recorded on film was made virtually invisible. Many years later, a

Broadway play and a film version of Jack Johnson's life made it to the stage and the big screen as *The Great White Hope*, 1970.

JO JO DANCER, YOUR LIFE IS CALLING. 1986. (R) 97 min. Biopic. This is the semi-autobiographical story of comedian **Richard Pryor**, who begins to reevaluate his life after an attempted drug-related accident/suicide. Told mostly in flashback, it follows his life from childhood, to fame and fortune, to almost losing his life. Pryor stars as himself and also co-wrote and directed. Cast: Richard Pryor, **Debbie Allen**, **Art Evans**, **Fay Hauser**, Barbara Williams, **Paula Kelly**, Wings Hauser, Carmen McRae, Diahnne Abbott, Scoey Mitchell, Billy Eckstine, **Virginia Capers**, Dennis Farina. Director: Richard Pryor. Writers: Richard Pryor, Rocco Urbisci. Cinematographer: John A. Alonzo. Music: **Herbie Hancock**.

JONES, GRACE (1948-). Model, singer, actress. Jones was born in Spanish Town, Jamaica, and was already known as a singer and fashion model when she appeared in **television** and film. Jones signed with Island Records and released her debut album *Portfolio* in 1977. Her androgynous look, statuesque style, and outrageous stage shows made her a cult favorite. She ranked #82 on VH1's 100 Greatest Women of Rock and Roll.
  Filmography: *Gordon's War*, 1973; *Deadly Vengeance*, 1981; *Conan the Destroyer*, 1984; *A View to a Kill*, 1985; *Vamp*, 1986; *Straight to Hell*, 1987; *Siesta*, 1987; *Boomerang*, 1992; *Cyber Bandits*, 1995; *McCinsey's Island*, 1998; *Palmer's Pick Up*, 1999; *Shaka Zulu: The Citadel*, 2001.

JONES, JAMES EARL (1931-). Actor. The son of actor Robert Earl Jones, James Earl Jones was born in Tate County, Mississippi, and raised on his grandparent's farm near Jackson, Michigan. He has had a distinguished career on stage, **television**, and film. Highly praised for his numerous Shakespearean roles, including *Othello*, he also embraced a number of contemporary and avant-garde stage productions. After a short time as a University of Michigan premedical student, and a stint in the military, Jones gravitated to New York and studied at the American Theater Wing. His off-Broadway debut came in 1957 in *Wedding in Japan*. Other notable stage performances include *The Cool World*, *The Blood Knot*, and *The Blacks*. He has won numerous awards, including an Obie Award in 1961, and the 1961-62 Daniel Blum Theater World Award. Jones' career took off in 1969 after portraying Jack Jefferson in the smash Broadway hit *The Great White Hope*, based on the life of the first black heavyweight, boxing champion Jack Johnson. He received a Tony Award for best dramatic actor in a Broadway play, and a Drama Desk best-performance award. He also starred in the film version and received an **Academy Award** nomination for his on-screen portrayal of the pugilist. He received numerous stage roles in the 1970s that had mostly gone to white actors, including the title role in *King Lear*, and the portrayal of Lenny in *Of Mice and Men*. In 1987, Jones won another Tony Award for the lead in *Fences*, August Wilson's Pulitzer Prize-winning play. His powerful **television** appearances include *Roots: The Next Generation*, *Gabriel's Fire*, *Percy and Thunder*, and the CBS series *Under One Roof*. The University of Michigan honored Jones with an honorary Doctorate of Humane Letters in 1971. New York gave him their Man of the Year Award in 1976. He was elected to the Board of Governors of the Academy of Motion Picture Arts and Sciences that same year, and he was inducted into the Theater Hall of Fame in 1985. Perhaps one of his most notable accomplishments of his career is that Jones was the voice of Darth Vader in the *Star Wars Trilogy*. He is currently the national television spokesperson for Verizon Communications.

Filmography: *Dr. Strangelove*, 1964; *The Great White Hope*, 1970; *End of the Road*, 1970; *Deadly Hero*, 1975; *Swashbuckler*, 1976; *The River Niger*, 1976; *Bingo Long Traveling All-Stars and Motor Kings*, 1976; *Star Wars*, 1977; *A Piece of the Action*, 1977; *Paul Robeson*, 1977; *The Greatest*, 1977; *The Exorcist II*, 1977; *Roots: The Next Generation*, 1979; *The Empire Strikes Back*, 1980; *Flight of the Dragons*, 1982; *Conan the Barbarian*, 1982; *Blood Tide*, 1982; *Return of the Jedi*, 1983; *Soul Man*, 1986; *My Little Girl*, 1987; *Matewan*, 1987; *Gardens of Stone*, 1987; *Coming to America*, 1988; *Field of Dreams*, 1989; *Best of the Best*, 1989; *Ivory Hunters*, 1990; *The Hunt for Red October*, 1990; *Heatwave*, 1990; *Sneakers*, 1992; *Patriot Games*, 1992; *The Sandlot*, 1993; *Percy and Thunder*, 1993; *The Meteor Man*, 1993; *Naked Gun 33 1/3: The Final Insult*, 1994; *The Lion King*, 1994; *Clear and Present Danger*, 1994; *Cry the Beloved Country*, 1995; *Gang Related*, 1996; *A Family Thing*, 1996; *Horton's Foot*, 1997; *Merlin*, 1998; *Undercover Angel*, 1999; *Summer's End*, 1999; *The Annihilation of Fish*, 2003.

JONES, ORLANDO (1968-). Actor, comedian. He was born in Mobile, Alabama, and went on to graduate from Mauldin High School in Mauldin, South Carolina, and from the College of Charleston. He became the original spokesman for an ad campaign of commercials for the soft drink 7-Up, and he was a cast member of the comedy skit series *Mad TV*, 1995-1997. His notable film roles include, **Double Take**, 2001; *The Time Machine*, 2002; and **Drumline**, 2002.

Filmography: *In Harm's Way*, 1997; *Sour Grapes*, 1998; **Woo**, 1998; *Waterproof*, 1999; *New Jersey Turnpikes*, 1999; *Office Space*, 1999; *Liberty Heights*, 1999; *Magnolia*, 1999; *The Replacements*, 2000; *Chain of Fools*, 2000; *Bedazzled*, 2000; *Double Take*, 2001; *Evolution*, 2001; *The Time Machine*, 2002; *Drumline*, 2002; **Biker Boyz**, 2003; *Run Away Jury*, 2003; *House of D*, 2004; *The Evidence*, 2006.

JONES, QUINCY (1933-). Composer, arranger, producer. Jones began playing the trumpet while attending grade school in Seattle, Washington. By his early teens, he had met and worked with Count Basie and Ray Charles, and received a scholarship to attend Boston's Berklee School of Music. Oscar Pettiford invited Jones to New York, where he met Charlie Parker, Miles Davis, and Thelonious Monk. Shortly after, he toured Europe with the Lionel Hampton Orchestra, and later with Dizzy Gillespie. After studying classical composition in Paris with Nadia Boulanger, Jones returned to New York as vice-president of Mercury Records. He scored his first film, *The Pawnbroker*, 1965. His other film scores include *In the Heat of the Night*, 1967; *The Wiz*, 1978; and *The Color Purple*, 1985, on which he was also associate producer. In 1980, he established his own label, Quest Records, and was a key player in a cable TV venture. Jones organized the famine relief project for Africa, "We Are the World." The documentary film *Listen Up: The Lives of Quincy Jones*, explores his life and career.

Filmography: *The Pawnbroker,* 1965; *In the Heat of the Night*, 1967; *The Wiz*, 1978; *The Color Purple*, 1985; **Their Eyes Were Watching God**, 2005.

JONES, ROBERT EARL (1904-2006). Actor. He was born in Coldwater, Mississippi, and trained at the Actors Studio in New York City. He performed off-Broadway in the title role in the 1936 productions of both *Othello* and *The Emperor Jones*, and he continued working on stage into the mid-1980s. First film work was in two **Oscar Micheaux** films: **Lying Lips**, 1939, and *The Notorious Elinor Lee*, 1940. His **television** guest appearances include roles in *Kojak*, 1976, *Lou Grant*, 1978, and the telepic **The Sophisticated Gents**, 1981. Father of actor **James Earl Jones,** he taught at Wesleyan University and The City University of New York.

Filmography: *Lying Lips*, 1939; *The Notorious Elinor Lee*, 1940; *Odds Against Tomorrow*, 1959; *Wild River*, 1960; **One Po-**

tato, Two Potato, 1964; *Terror in the City*, 1966; *Mississippi Summer*, 1971; *The Sting*, 1974; **Willie Dynamite**, 1974; *Tuskegee Subject #626*, 1980; *Trading Places*, 1983; *Cotton Club*, 1984; *Witness*, 1985.

JONES, TAMALA (1974-). Actress. Born and raised in Los Angeles, Jones took an early interest in entertainment. She performed in backyard skits with her cousin and started acting lessons in the sixth grade. She began her career as a model and after appearing in magazine ads and **television** commercials. She was cast on an episode of the preteen sitcom *California Dreams* and continued to guest star on comedy and dramatic series, such as *The Fresh Prince of Bel-Air*, *The Wayans Bros.*, *ER*, and *The Parent 'Hood*. Her first regular role on television was as a student on ABC network's *Dangerous Minds*. Her first film role was in *How to Make an American Quilt*, 1995, and her first major supporting film role was in **Booty Call**, 1997.

   Filmography: *Booty Call*, 1976; **The Wood**, 1999; *Blue Streak*, 1999; **Turn It Up**, 2000; **Next Friday**, 2000; **Little Richard**, 2000; **The Ladies Man**, 2000; **Two Can Play That Game**, 2001; *On the Line*, 2001; **The Brothers**, 2001; **Head of State**, 2003.

JORDAN, LOUIS (1908-1975). Singer, actor. Jordan was born in Brinkley, Arkansas, and became known as the vocalist of his popular swing band The Tympani Five. He began acting in musical films, such as *Meet Miss Bobby Socks*, 1944, and the Western musical **Look-Out Sister**, 1947, which he also directed.

   Filmography: *Meet Miss Bobby Socks*, 1944; *Beware*, 1946; *Look-Out Sister*, 1947; **Reet, Petite, and Gone**, 1947.

JOSEPHINE BAKER STORY, THE. 1990. (R) 129 min. Biopic. The rise and fall of **Josephine Baker**, a poor girl from St. Louis who became an exotic entertainer and the toast of pre-World War II Europe, only to return to face racism and career blocks at home. Cast: **Lynn Whitfield**, Ruben Blades, David Dukes, Craig T. Nelson, **Louis Gossett Jr.**, Kene Holiday, Vivian Bonnell. Director: Brian Gibson. Music: Ralph Burns.

JUICE. 1992. (R) 95 min. Urban Drama. This film tells a gritty story about life, death, and the importance of gaining respect in the inner city. Four Harlem friends plan to rob a corner grocery store, but it all goes astray once a gun is introduced and one becomes seduced by the power it brings. Cast: **Omar Epps**, **Tupac Shakur**, Jermaine Huggy Hopkins, Khalil Kain, Cindy Herron, Vincent Laresca, **Samuel L. Jackson**, George Gore II, Grace Garland, **Queen Latifah**, Bruklin Harris, Victor Campos, Eric Payne, Sharon Cook, Darien Berry. Director: **Ernest R. Dickerson**. Writers: Ernest R. Dickerson, Gerard Brown.

JUKE JOINT. 1947. 60 min. Comedy. Two men from the South arrive in Hollywood to seek their fame and fortune with only a quarter between them. They take a room with a local family and are taken to a nearby juke joint, where they make an important contact. Cast: **Spencer Williams Jr.**, Judy Jones, **Mantan Moreland**. Director: Spencer Williams Jr.

JULIEN, MAX (1945-) Actor. After playing small film roles in *The Black Klansman*; 1966; *Up Tight!*, 1968; and *Getting Straight*, 1970, Julien achieved star status for his portrayal of Goldie the top pimp in the **blaxploitation**-era film *The Mack*, 1973. The following year he wrote, produced, and starred in the period crime drama *Thomasine & Bushrod*, 1974, costarring with his then real-life girlfriend, **Vonetta McGhee**. His screen icon status was revisited with a cameo role as Uncle Fred in *How to Be a Player*, 1997. Julien's **television** guest appearances include roles in *The Mod Squad*, 1968; *The Name of the Game*, 1970; and *One on One*, 2005.

   Filmography: *The Black Klansman*, 1966; *Psyche-Out*, 1968; *The Savage Seven*, 1968; *Up Tight!*, 1968; *Deadlock*, 1969; *Getting Straight*, 1970; *The Mack*, 1973; *Thomasine & Bushrod*, 1974; *How to Be a Player*, 1997.

JUNGLE FEVER. 1991. (R) 131 min. Drama. An interracial office affair causes hardship and remorse for a black architect and his white assistant. Both are ridiculed and estranged from family and friends, and although they try to make it work, they find that society will not allow their union to be. A subplot involves the architect's crack-head brother and the strain it places on family bonds. Cast: **Wesley Snipes**, Annabella Sciorra, John Turturro, **Samuel L. Jackson**, **Ossie Davis**, **Ruby Dee**, **Lonette McKee**, Anthony Quinn, **Spike Lee**, **Halle Berry**, **Tyra Ferrell**, Veronica Webb, Frank Vincent, Tim Robbins, Brad Dourif, Richard Edison. Director: Writer/Director: Spike Lee. Cinematographer: **Ernest R. Dickerson**. Music: **Terence Blanchard**. Awards: 1991 Film Critic's Award, Best Supporting Actor (Jackson).

JUST ANOTHER GIRL ON THE I. R. T. 1993. (R) 96 min. Drama. A 17-year-old girl has her life all planned out until an unplanned pregnancy puts her life in disarray. Cast: Ariyal Johnson, Kevin Thigpen, Ebony Jerido, Jerard Washington, Chequita Jackson, William Badget. Writer/Director: Leslie Harris. Cinematographer: Richard Conners. Awards: 1993 Sundance, Special Jury Prize.

JUWANNA MANN, 2002. (PG-13) 91 min. Comedy. A hot-tempered pro basketball player is kicked out of the league for mooning a referee after what he considered a bad call. Still needing to make a living and basketball his only skill, he dresses in drag and joins a professional woman's league. Cast: **Miguel A. Nunez Jr., Vivica A. Fox**, Kevin Pollack, **Tommy Davidson, Kim Wayans, Jenifer Lewis**, Lil' Kim, Annie Corley, Ginuwine. Director: Jesse Vaughan. Writer: Bradley Allenstein. Cinematographer: Reynaldo Villalobos. Music: Lisa Coleman, Wendy Melvoin.

K

KEEPER, THE. 1996. (NR) 97 min. Drama. A Brooklyn correction officer who is also working on a law degree befriends a Haitian inmate who claims he was falsely accused of rape. The officer helps him to make bail and invites the man home to meet his wife, which becomes a big mistake. Cast: **Giancarlo Esposito, Regina Taylor**, Isaach de Bankole. Writer/Director: Joe Brewster. Cinematographer: Igor Sunara. Music: John Peterson.

KEEP PUNCHING. 1939. 80 min. Drama. A talented boxer must navigate his way through the fast life of gambling, shady promoters, and seductive women while fighting his way to the top. Cast: Henry Armstrong, Mae Johnson, **Canada Lee**. Director: John Clein.

KELLY, JIM (1946-). Actor, martial arts champion. Born in Paris, Kentucky, Kelly became the International Middleweight Karate Champion in 1971, and quickly became a top martial arts film star. His big film break came opposite karate master Bruce Lee in *Enter the Dragon*, 1973, and he kicked his way into **blaxploitation** films, such as *Black Belt Jones*, 1974, and *Three the Hard Way*, 1974. A talented athlete, Kelly was also highly ranked in tennis.

Filmography: *Enter the Dragon*, 1972; *Three the Hard Way*, 1974; *Black Belt Jones*, **Take a Hard Ride**, 1975; *Hot Potato*, 1976; *Black Samurai*, 1977; *Kill Factor*, 1978; *Black Eliminator*, 1978; *One Down, Two to Go*, 1982.

KELLY, PAULA (1943-). Actress. Born in Jacksonville, Florida, Kelly became a notable actress in **television** and film. She made her film debut in *Sweet Charity*, 1969, and worked throughout the early 1970s in films like *Cool Breeze*, 1972; *Soylent Green*, 1973; *The Spook Who Sat by the Door*, 1973; and *Uptown Saturday Night*, 1974. Kelly's television appearances include *Peter Pan*, 1976; *Uncle Tom's Cabin*, 1987; and *The Women of Brewster Place*, 1989.

Filmography: *Sweet Charity*, 1969; *The Andromeda Strain*, 1971; *Cool Breeze*, 1972; *Top of the Heap*, 1972; *Trouble Man*, 1972; *Soylent Green*, 1973; *The Spook Who Sat by the Door*, 1973; *Uptown Saturday Night*, 1974; *Lost in the Stars*, 1974; *Drum*, 1976; *Jo Jo Dancer, Your Life is Calling*, 1986; *Bank Robber*, 1993; *Drop Squad*, 1994; *Once Upon a Time When We Were Colored*, 1995.

KENNEDY, JANE (1951-). Actress. This former Miss Ohio beauty queen was born in Wickliffe, Ohio. She made her film debut in *Lady Sings the Blues*, 1972. Her other notable roles include the made-for-TV movies *Cover Girls*, 1977, and *Mysterious Island of Beautiful Women*, 1979. She married radio personality Leon Issac, who took on her last name, and they combined their careers and made several films together. She made guest appearances on the **television** shows *The Love Boat*, *Different Strokes*, *Benson*, and *227*.

Filmography: *Lady Sings the Blues*, 1972; *Group Marriage*, 1973; *Let's Do It Again*, 1975; *The Muthers*, 1976; *Cover Girls*, 1977; *Big Time*, 1977; *Death Force* 1978; *Mysterious Island of Beautiful Women*, 1979; *Ms. 45*, 1981; *Body and Soul*, 1981; *Night Trap*, 1993.

KENNEDY, LEON ISSAC (1949-). Actor, writer, producer. Born in Cleveland, Ohio, Kennedy was a radio disc jockey before moving into films. He gained national attention when he married actress Jane Kennedy and took on her last name. They made several films together, including *Death Force*, 1978, and *Body and Soul*, 1981, for which he also wrote the screenplay. He guest starred on **television** in the series *ChiPs*, and *The Hitchhiker*, and starred in the *Penitentiary* series of boxing films directed by **Jamaa Fanaka**.

Filmography: *Mean Johnny Barrows*, 1976; *Death Force*, 1978; *Penitentiary*, 1980; *Body and Soul*, 1981; *Penitentiary II*, 1982; *Lone Wolf McQuade*, 1983; *Too Scared to Scream*, 1985; *Hollywood Vice Squad*, 1986; *Knights of the City*, 1986; *Skeleton Coast*, 1987; *Penitentiary III*, 1987.

KILLER OF SHEEP. 1977. (NR) 83 min. Drama. This is a gritty, realistic portrait of daily life and the constant struggle that goes on just to survive in the inner cities of America. A slaughterhouse butcher works hard to provide for his family, maintain his secrets, and stay above the urban decay that surrounds him every day. This film is considered a classic and was chosen for the American Film Institute's Film Registry. Cast: Henry G. Sanders, Kaycee Moore, Charles Bracy, Angela Burnett, Eugene Cherry, Jack Drummond. Writer/Director: **Charles Burnett**.

KILLING FLOOR. 1985. (PG) 118 min. Drama. This film is based on the factors that led to the bloody race riots the summer of 1919. A Southern sharecropper relocates to Chicago and takes a job at the stockyards, where he becomes involved in starting a union. Tensions rise and the fighting begins. Cast: Damien Leake, **Alfre Woodard**, **Moses Gunn**, Clarence Felder, **Mary Alice**. Director: **Bill Duke**. Writer: Leslie Lee. Music: Elizabeth Swados.

KILPATRICK, LINCOLN (1932-2004). Actor. He was born in St. Louis, Missouri, and made his film debut as Detective Dave Foster in *Cop Hater*, 1958. He worked consistently in **television** and film mostly in bit and character roles that include *The Lost Man*, 1969; *Cool Breeze*, 1972; *Soylent Green*, 1973; *Uptown Saturday Night*, 1974; and *The Stoneman*, 2002. He made guest appearances on the TV series *Mannix*, *Baretta*, *Hunter*, *The Jeffersons*, *Hill Street Blues*, *Amen*, *NYPD Blue*, *Sisters*, *Melrose Place*, and *ER*.

Filmography: *Cop Hater*, 1958; *Madigan*, 1968; *A Lovely Way to Die*, 1968; *The Lost Man*, 1969; *Stiletto*, 1969; *Generation*, 1969; *The Red, White, and Black*, 1970; *Brother John*, 1971; *The Omega Man*, 1971; *Honky*; 1971; *Cool Breeze*, 1972; *Soylent Green*, 1973; *Chosen Survivors*, 1974; *Uptown Saturday Night*, 1974; *Together Brothers*, 1974; *The Master Gunfighter*, 1975; *King*, 1978; *Deadly Force*, 1983; *Flicks*, 1987; *Prison*, 1988; *Bulletproof*, 1988; *Hollywood Cop*, 1988; *Fortress*, 1993; *The Stoneman*, 2002.

KING. 1978. (TV) 272 min. Docudrama. The story is about the life of civil rights leader Dr. Martin Luther King Jr. Cast: **Paul Winfield**, **Cicely Tyson**, **Roscoe Lee Brown**, **Ossie Davis**, **Art Evans**, **Howard E. Rollins Jr.**, Ernie Banks, William Jordan, Cliff DeYoung. Writer/Director: Abby Mann. Music: Billy Goldenberg.

KING, REGINA (1971-). Actress. This Los Angeles, California-born actress made her television-acting debut in the comedy series *227*, while she was still in high school. She later guest starred in *Northern Lights*, *New York Undercover*, and *Living Single*. King was a regular on the series *Leap of Faith*. She made her film debut in *Boyz N the Hood*, 1991, and costarred in *Rituals*, 1998; *Down to Earth*, 2001; and *Ray*, 2004.

Filmography: *Boyz N the Hood*, 1991; *Poetic Justice*, 1993; *Higher Learning*, 1995; *Friday*, 1995; *A Thin Line Between Love and Hate*, 1996; *Jerry McGuire*, 1996; *Rituals*, 1998; *How Stella Got Her Groove Back*, 1998; *Enemy of the State*, 1998; *Mighty Joe Young*, 1998; *Love and Action in Chicago*, 1999; *Quest for Atlantis*, 1999; *The Acting Class*, 2000; *Down to Earth*, 2001; *Final Breakdown*, 2002; *Daddy Daycare*, 2003; *Legally Blonde 2: Red, White & Blonde*, 2003; *A Cinderella Story*, 2004; *Ray*, 2004; *Miss Congeniality 2*, 2005.

KINGDOM COME. 2001. (PG) 89 min. Comedy. The funeral of a family patriarch brings a dysfunctional family together. Cast: **L. L. Cool J**, **Jada Pinkett Smith**, **Vivica A. Fox**, **Loretta Devine**, **Anthony Anderson**, **Cedric the Entertainer**, Darius McCray, **Whoopi Goldberg**, Toni Braxton, Masasa, **Clifton Davis**, Richard Gant, Doug McHenry. Director: **Doug McHenry**. Writer: Jessie Jones, David Bottrell. Cinematographer: Francis Kenny. Music: Tyler Bates.

KITT, EARTHA (1927-). Actress, singer. She was born in the cotton fields of South Carolina to become a true diva of stage, television, and film. Her mother was a black Cherokee Indian, her father a white sharecropper, but neither had much to do with her upbringing. She was sent to live with an aunt in Harlem, where she took piano lessons and sang in the choir at church. She attended the high school for the performance arts, but an argument with her aunt left her with nowhere to live, so she left school at age 15 to work in a factory as a seamstress. She lived with friends and was even homeless for a time, before using her immense talent to rise out of her despair. In 1943, she auditioned for the famed Katherine Dunham dance troupe, and eventually toured with it through Europe, South America, and Mexico as a featured dancer. In the 1950s, she sang at nightclubs in Paris, London, and Turkey, building her solo career. She starred in the Broadway musical *New Faces of 1952*, and made several musical recordings. She received her first Tony award nomination for her performance in *Timbuktu!* She made her film debut in *The Mark of the Hawk*, 1958, and followed with *St.*

Louis Blues, 1958, and *Anna Lucasta*, 1959. She received national acclaim as The Catwoman on the popular 1960s television series *Batman*. Famed actor and director Orson Welles once referred to her as "the most exciting woman in the world." Her career took a turn for the worse after she spoke out against the Vietnam War. The CIA developed a file on her and she was blacklisted, so she moved to Europe to live and work for the next 10 years. She has written three autobiographies, *Thursday's Child*, *Alone with Me*, and *I'm Still Here: Confessions of a Kitten*.

Filmography: *The Mark of the Hawk*, 1958; *St. Louis Blues*, 1958; *Anna Lucasta*, 1959; *Saint of Devil's Island*, 1961; *Friday Foster*, 1975; *The Serpent Warriors*, 1985; *Dragonard*, 1987; *Master of Dragonard Hill*, 1989; *Living Doll*, 1990; *Boomerang*, 1992; *Fatal Instinct*, 1993; *Feast of All Saints*, 2001; *Holes*, 2003; *On the One*, 2004; *Instant Karma*, 2005.

KOTTO, YAPHET (1937-). Actor. Born in New York City, Kotto has a long and distinguished career in television and film. He made his film debut in *4 for Texas*, 1963, and followed with a role in *Nothing But a Man*, 1964. He received worldwide attention as Secret Agent 007's deadly foil in *Live and Let Die*, 1973. He was also featured in several **blaxploitation** films during the 1970s, including *Across 110th Street*, 1972; *Truck Turner*, 1974; and *Friday Foster*, 1975. Many mainstream roles followed in films like *Blue Collar*, 1978; *Alien*, 1979; and *The Running Man*, 1987. He made guest appearances on numerous **television** shows, including *Homicide: Life on the Street*.

Filmography: *4 for Texas*, 1963; *Nothing But a Man*, 1964; *The Thomas Crown Affair*, 1968; *The Liberation of L. B. Jones*, 1970; *Man and Boy*, 1972; *Across 110th Street*, 1972; *Live and Let Die*, 1973; *Truck Turner*, 1974; *Shark's Treasure*, 1975; *Friday Foster*, 1975; *Drum*, 1976; *The Monkey Hustle*, 1976; *Roots*, 1977; *Blue Collar*, 1978; *Alien*, 1979; *Brubaker*, 1980; *The Star Chamber*, 1983; *Warning Sign*, 1985; *Eye of the Tiger*, 1986; *Terminal Entry*, 1986; *The Running Man*, 1987; *Midnight Run*, 1988; *Tripwire*, 1990; *Freddy's Dead: The Final Nightmare*, 1991; *Almost Blue*, 1992; *Extreme Justice*, 1993; *The Puppet Masters*, 1994; *Out-of-Sync*, 1995; *Dead Badge*, 1995; *Two If by Sea*, 1996; *Homicide: The Movie*, 2000.

KRUSH GROOVE. 1985. (R) 95 min. Music/Comedy. Inspired by the early days of rap music mogul Russell Simmons, a young music producer accepts money from a greedy loan shark to start a record label and gets in over his head. Success brings about strained relationships as a rival label tries to steal his stable of new stars. Relatively unknown at the time, this film showcases some of the biggest names in rap music today. Cast: **Blair Underwood**, Eron Tabor, Kurtis Blow, Sheila E. Director: **Michael Schultz**.

L

L. L. COOL J (1968-). Rapper, actor. He was born James Todd Smith in St. Albans, Queens, New York, and is a two-time Grammy Award-winning rapper. He appeared on the music scene in 1985 and became the first rap artist to release a single on the Def Jam Records Label. He has since amassed eight consecutive platinum-plus selling albums. His first on-screen appearance was in the hip-hop based movie *Krush Groove*, 1985. He starred on the NBC television series *In the House*, and his first starring film role was in *Out-of-Sync*, 1995. His autobiography, *I Make My Own Rules* (St. Martin's Press/Ilion Books), chronicles his early life and career.

Filmography: *Krush Groove*, 1985; *Out-of-Sync*, 1985; *The Hard Way*, 1991; *Toys*, 1994; *B*A*P*S*, 1997; *Halloween 5*, 1998; *Deep Blue Sea*, 1999; *In Too Deep*, 1999; *Any Given Sunday*, 2000; *Charlie's Angels*, 2000; *Kingdom Come*, 2001; *Rollerball*, 2002; *Crazy School*, 2001; *Mind Hunters*, 2003.

LACKAWANNA BLUES. 2005. (PG-13) 95 min. Drama. As a young boy grows up amid the culture of rhythm and blues music, he is inspired by the love and encouragement he receives from the varied occupants of the boarding house where he lives. Cast: S. Epatha Merkerson, **Louis Gossett Jr.**, Carmen Ejogo, Jimmy Smits, **Mos Def**, Marcus Carl Franklin, Macy Gray, **Terrence Dashon Howard**, **Ernie Hudson**, **Delroy Lindo**, Roxanne Mayweather, **Rosie Perez**, Ruben Santiago-Hudson, Liev Schreiber, Henry Simmons, Patricia Wettig, Michael K. Williams, Charlayne Woodard, **Jefffrey Wright**. Director: George C. Wolfe. Writer: Ruben Santiago-Hudson.

LADIES MAN, THE. 2000. (R) 84 min. Comedy. In this extended version of a *Saturday Night Live* TV show skit, a late-night radio talk show host who dispenses questionable romantic advice loses his job and starts using his own advice to seduce married women. It eventually backfires and he is forced to reevaluate his ways. Cast: **Tim Meadows**, Will Ferrell, Tiffani-Amber Thiessen, **Billy Dee Williams**, Karyn Parsons, Lee Evans, **John Witherspoon**, Eugene Levy, **Tamala Jones**, Julianne Moore, Sean Thibodeau. Director:

Reginald Hudlin. Writers: Tim Meadows, Dennis McNicholas, Andrew Steele. Cinematographer: Johnny E. Jensen. Music: Marcus Miller.

LADY COCOA. 1975. (R) 93 min. Drama. In this film, a falsely accused woman gets a 24-hour reprieve from jail to find the man who framed her. Cast: **Lola Falana,** Joe "Mean Joe" Green, Gene Washington, Alex Dreier. Director: Matt Cimber.

LADY SINGS THE BLUES. 1972. (R) 144 min. Music/Drama. This musical drama is based on the life of jazz singer Billie Holiday, who struggles against racism, sexism, and drug addiction in her quest for love and fame. **Diana Ross** received an **Academy Award** nomination for her portrayal of the famed singer. Cast: Diana Ross, **Billy Dee Williams, Richard Pryor,** James Callahan, Paul Hampton, Sid Melton. Director: Sidney J. Furie. Cinematographer: John A. Alonzo.

LAFAYETTE PLAYERS, THE (1915-1932). This early theater company was founded on 15 November 1915 as the Anita Bush Stock Company. The five original members consisted of **Anita Bush, Charles S. Gilpin, Arthur "Dooley" Wilson,** Carlotta Freeman, and Andrew Bishop. As one of the first professional black stock companies in America, it performed legitimate dramas that began to create black roles and images that far exceeded the degrading minstrel-show caricatures that were prevalent at that time. It initially performed at Harlem's Lincoln Theater, but soon moved to the Lafayette Theater, where the troop took its name and quickly grew as a training platform for African American actors of stage and film.

LANE, CHARLES (1953-). Director, actor. This New York City native received rave reviews as the writer, director, and star of his independent film *Sidewalk Stories,* 1989. He went on to direct the Hollywood feature film *True Identity,* 1991, and the telepic *Hallelujah,* 1993. His acting credits also include *Posse,* 1993.

Filmography: *A Place in Time,* 1976; *Sidewalk Stories,* 1989; *True Identity,* 1991; *Hallelujah,* 1993; *Posse,* 1993.

LANEUVILLE, ERIC (1952-). Actor, director, producer. Born in New Orleans, Louisiana, he became a child star with roles in films like *The Omega Man,* 1971; *Black Belt Jones,* 1972; and *Foster and Laurie,* 1975. He began directing on the television series *St. Elsewhere,* and directed episodes of *Quantum Leap, M. A. N. T. I.*

S., *ER*, and *The Gilmore Girls.* He has directed the made-for-TV movies **The Ernest Green Story**, 1993; *Pandora's Clock*, 1996; *America's Prince: The John F. Kennedy Jr. Story*, 2003; and *Naughty or Nice*, 2004.

Filmography: *Death Wish*, 1994; *Shoot It Black, Shoot It Blue*, 1974; *Black Belt Jones*, 1974; *A Piece of the Action*, 1977; *Love at First Bite*, 1979; *A Force of One*, 1979; *The Baltimore Bullet*, 1980; *Back Roads*, 1981; *Paramedics*, 1987; *Fear of a Black Hat*, 1994.

LANGE, TED (1948-). Actor, director. He was born in Oakland, California, and is perhaps best remembered as the jovial bartender on the popular series *The Love Boat.* He began his acting career during the **blaxploitation** films of the 1970s with minor roles in *Trick Baby*, 1973; *Black Belt Jones*, 1974; and *Friday Foster*, 1975. After his run on *The Love Boat*, Lange began directing television shows, such as *Fantasy Island*, *Mike Hammer*, *The Wayans Brothers*, *Moesha*, and *The Love Boat: The Next Wave.*

Filmography: *Trick Baby*, 1973; *Blade*, 1973; *Black Belt Jones*, 1974; *Record City*, 1977; *Terminal Exposure*, 1987; *Glitch!* 1988; *Othello*, 1989; *Penny Ante: The Motion Picture*, 1990; *Perfume*, 1991; *The Naked Truth*, 1992; *Sandman*, 1998; *The Redemption*, 2000; *Is This Your Mother?*, 2002; *Gang of Roses*, 2003; *Banana Moon*, 2003.

LaSALLE, ERIQ (1962-). Actor, director. He was born and raised in Hartford, Connecticut, and made his film debut in *Straight to Hell*, 1985. More roles followed, including a stint on the daytime soap opera *Another World*, as Charles Thompson. His breakthrough role was as Dr. Peter Benton on the long-running TV series *ER.* He has branched off into directing and helmed episodes of *Soul Food*, and *The Twilight Zone.* He directed the telepicture *Rebound: The Legend of Earl "The Goat" Manigault*, 1996. He also produced, directed, and starred in *Crazy as Hell*, 2002.

Filmography: *Straight to Hell*, 1985; *Rappin'*, 1985; *Where Are the Children*, 1986; *Five Corners*, 1987; *Coming to America*, 1988; *Jacob's Ladder*, 1990; *Color of Night*, 1994; *Drop Squad*, 1994; *One Hour Photo*, 2002; *Crazy as Hell*, 2002; *Biker Boyz*, 2003; *Inside Out*, 2004.

LAST DRAGON, THE. 1985. (PG-13) 108 min. Comedy. A Harlem karate master is hired as a bodyguard to a beautiful woman and they end up falling in love. He must also fight off a rival karateka who challenges him, intent on taking over his dojo. Cast: Taimak,

Vanity, Christopher Murney, Julius J. Carry III, Faith Prince. Director: **Michael Schultz**. Writer: Louis Venosta. Cinematographer: James A. Contner. Music: Misha Segal.

LATHAN, SANAA (1971-). Actress. Born in New York, Lathan studied English at University of California at Berkeley and graduated from the master's program at the Yale School of Drama. She is the daughter of **television** director **Stan Lathan** and professional dancer Eleanor McCoy, and as a part of this entertainment-based family, Lathan was destined to be a star. She began performing in off-Broadway productions until moving to Los Angeles to find work in television. She appeared in such TV shows as *NYPD Blue*, *In the House*, *Moesha*, *Family Matters*, and also in *Miracle In the Woods*, a made-for-TV movie. After a series of engaging ensemble roles she starred in writer/director **Gina Prince Bythewood**'s independent film *Love and Basketball*, 2000 and was firmly on her way.

Filmography: *Blade*, 1998; *Life*, 1999; *The Wood*, 1999; *The Best Man*, 1999; *Love and Basketball*, 2000; *Catfish in Black Bean Sauce*, 2000; *Disappearing Acts*, 2000; *Brown Sugar*, 2002; *Out of Time*, 2003; *Alien vs. Predator*, 2004.

LATHAN, STAN (1945-). Director, producer. He is a notable director of **television** and film with an impressive list of credits who began his career working on *Sesame Street* in 1969. He quickly became a sought-after director working on such series as *Say Brother*, *Sanford and Son*, and *Barney Miller*. His early film productions include *Save the Children*, 1973, and *Amazing Grace*, 1974. He worked mostly in television throughout the 1980s and 1990s with credits on shows like *Hill Street Blues*, *Miami Vice*, *A Man Called Hawk*, *Roc*, *Martin*, *Moesha*, and *The Steve Harvey Show*. He teamed with rap music mogul Russell Simmons to produce *Def Poetry Jam* and various other television movies and specials. He is the father of actress **Sanaa Lathan**.

Filmography: *Statues Hardly Ever Smile*, 1971; *Save the Children*, 1973; *Amazing Grace*, 1974; *Almos' A Man*, 1976; *The Cotton Club*, 1982; *A House Divided: Denmark Vessey's Rebellion*, 1982; *Beat Street*, 1984; *Go Tell It On the Mountain*, 1985; *The Child Saver*, 1988; *Heart and Soul*, 1989; *It's Black Entertainment*, 2002.

LAUREL AVENUE. 1993. (R) 156 min. Miniseries. Trouble erupts when a diverse and dysfunctional family comes together for a Sunday dinner party. Cast: **Mary Alice**, Mel Winkler, Scott Lawrence,

Malinda Williams, Jay Brooks, Juanita Jennings, Rhonda Stubbins White, Monte Russell, Vonte Sweet. Director: **Carl Franklin**. Writers: Michael Henry Brown, Paul Aaron.

LAWRENCE, MARTIN (1965-). Comedian, actor. Born in Frankfurt, Germany, and raised in Maryland, Lawrence had a knack for comedy and developed his early routines while attending Eleanor Roosevelt High School in Landover, Maryland. A performance on the **television** talent show *Star Search* led to a role in *What's Happening Now!* After a supporting role in director **Spike Lee**'s *Do the Right Thing*, 1989, he gained national exposure as the emcee of HBO's *Def Comedy Jam*. A few big-screen roles followed and, in 1992, he landed his own Fox television sitcom, *Martin*, which ran for five seasons. His vulgarity-laced comedy concert film *You So Crazy*, 1994, was a huge success, and became one of the highest grossing concert films ever. Lawrence made his film directorial debut with *A Thin Line Between Love and Hate*, 1996, in which he also starred. He has continued on the big screen in several blockbuster hits, including *Bad Boys* and *Bad Boys II*, 1995 and 2003, and *Big Mamma's House*, 2000. In his second concert film, *Martin Lawrence Live: Runteldat*, 2003, Lawrence revealed a humorous side to his many past problems with drugs, the law, and his personal life.

Filmography: *House Party*, 1990; *Talkin' Dirty After Dark*, 1991; *House Party II*, 1991; *Boomerang*, 1992; *You So Crazy*, 1994; *Bad Boys*, 1995; *A Thin Line Between Love and Hate*, 1996; *Nothing to Lose*, 1996; *Life*, 1999; *Blue Streak*, 1999; *Big Momma's House*, 2000; *What's the Worst That Could Happen*, 2001; *Black Knight*, 2001; *National Security*, 2003; *Bad Boys II*, 2003.

LAWSON, RICHARD (1947-). Actor. He was born in Loma Linda, California, and teaches acting and directing at The Beverly Hills Playhouse. He began his film acting career in the early 1970s with small roles in *Dirty Harry*, 1971; *Scream Blackula Scream*, 1973; *Sugar Hill*, 1974; and *Willie Dynamite*, 1974. His **television** appearances include *Hotel Story*, *Chicago Story*, *T. J. Hooker*, *Sister, Sister*, and *The Days and Nights of Molly Dodd*. He had a recurring role as Nick Kimball on *Dynasty*, and portrayed Lucas Barnes on *All My Children*.

Filmography: *Dirty Harry*, 1971; *Scream Blackula Scream*, 1973; *Sugar Hill*, 1974; *Willie Dynamite*, 1974; *Black Fist*, 1975; *Audrey Rose*, 1977; *Coming Home*, 1978; *The Main Event*, 1979; *Poltergeist*, 1982; *Streets of Fire*, 1984; *Stick*, 1985; *Wag the Dog*,

1997; *How Stella Got Her Groove Back*, 1998; *Mars and Beyond*, 2000; *Blue Hill Avenue*, 2001; *Out of the Rain*, 2003.

LEAN ON ME. 1989. (PG-13) 109 min. Drama. This film is based on the life and controversial methods of Joe Clark, a New Jersey principal who used strict discipline and hard-line tactics to turn a troubled high school around. Cast: **Morgan Freeman, Robert Guillaume, Beverly Todd**, Alan North, **Lynne Thigpen**, Robin Bartlett, **Michael Beach**, Ethan Phillips, **Regina Taylor**. Director: John G. Avildson. Writer: Michael Schiffer. Cinematographer: Victor Hammer. Music: Bill Conti.

LEARNING TREE, THE. 1969. (PG) 107 min. Drama. This film is based on Gordon Parks's autobiographical novel about a young boy's life, loves, and coming of age in a small, racist Kansas town. With this film, Parks became the first African American to direct a major motion picture for a Hollywood studio. Cast: **Kyle Johnson**, Alex Clarke, Estelle Evans, **Joel Fluellen**, Dana Elcar, **Saundra Sharp**. Writer/Director/Music: **Gordon Parks**. Cinematographer: Burnett Guffey. Awards: 1989 National Film Registry.

LEADBELLY. 1976. (PG) 126 min. Biopic. This is a film based on the life and times of blues singer Huddie Ledbetter. Cast: **Roger E. Mosley**, Paul Benjamin, **Madge Sinclair**, Alan Manson, **Albert Hall, Art Evans**, James Brodhead, John Henry Faulk, Vivian Bonnell, Dana Manno, Lynn Hamilton, Loretta Greene, Valerie Odell, Rozaa Jean. Director: **Gordon Parks**. Writer: Ernest Kinoy. Cinematographer: Bruce Surtees. Music: Fred Karlin.

LEE, CANADA (1907-1951). Actor, civil rights activist. Born in Manhattan, New York, as Leonard Corneliou Caneagata, he studied violin as a boy but always longed to be a jockey. He became a prizefighter instead, winning 90 out of 100 fights, which included the national amateur lightweight title. He turned professional in 1926, winning 175 out of 200 fights, until a detached retina brought his successful ring career to an end. Lee struggled along as a musician until he landed his first acting role in the Work Projects Administration stage play *Brother Moses* in 1934. A major career break came in 1941, when Orson Welles cast him to play Bigger Thomas in the stage version of *Native Son*, based on the **Richard Wright** novel. Lee's voice narrated the landmark radio series *New World A-Comin'* in 1944, which addressed the question of race in America. That same year, he appeared in Alfred Hitchcock's film *Lifeboat*, 1944, the Broadway play *Anna Lucasta*, and worked as master of ceremonies for several war-related programs on NBC radio. Lee was blacklisted for speaking out against racism and discrimination in the industry after he was labeled as being a communist agent. He would later star in *Cry, the Beloved Country*, 1951, a British production, and the first film to address the deplorable conditions of apartheid in South Africa.

Filmography: *Keep Punching*, 1939; *Lifeboat*, 1944; *Body and Soul*, 1947; *Lost Boundaries*, 1949; *Cry, the Beloved Country*, 1951.

LEE, CARL (1926-1986). Actor. He was the son of actor **Canada Lee** and studied acting with noted instructor Stella Adler. He worked primarily on the New York stage and earned an Obie Award for his performance in *The Connection*. He was also cast in the film version. One of his most notable film roles was as the drug dealing, back-stabbing partner in *Superfly*, 1972.

Filmography: *The Connection*, 1961; *The Cool World*, 1963; *Superfly*, 1972; *Gordon's War*, 1973; *Keeping On*, 1981.

LEE, MALCOLM (1970-). Director, writer. He is the cousin of film director **Spike Lee** and received much of his early training on the sets of *Malcolm X*, 1992, and *Crooklyn*, 1995. His big break came when he wrote and directed the trend setting out-of-the-hood flick *The Best Man*, 1999. He has since directed *Undercover Brother*, 2002, and *Roll Bounce*, 2005.

Filmography: *The Best Man*, 1999; *Undercover Brother*, 2002; *Roll Bounce*, 2005; *The Champions*, 2007.

LEE, SHELDON "SPIKE" (1957-). Filmmaker, actor. Born in Atlanta, Georgia, Lee's family moved to Chicago before relocating to New York. He returned to Atlanta to attend Morehouse College and went back to New York for graduate school at New York University's Institute of Film and Television. Lee became a household name in the area of independent film production and ushered in a new wave of black theme productions. His New York University student film *Joe's Bed-Sty Barbershop: We Cut Heads* won the 1982 Student Academy award. His 1986 hit film *She's Gotta Have It*, 1986, won the LA Film Critics New Generation award and the Prix de Jeunesse at the Cannes Film Festival. Lee would then roll out a film a year for the next 12 years, including *School Daze*, 1988; *Do the Right Thing*, 1989; *Mo Better Blues*, 1990; *Jungle Fever*, 1991; *Malcolm X*, 1992; *Clockers*, 1994; *Girl 6*, 1996; *Get on the Bus*, 1996; and *The 25th Hour*, 2003. Well-known for taking on controversial subjects in his films to help garner press and word-of-mouth publicity, Lee has positioned himself as a top director in the field. He not only insists on maintaining control over his projects, but he also fights to make sure there is a fair representation of African Americans and minorities in front of and behind the camera. His production company is aptly named Forty Acres and a Mule Filmworks, referencing a crucial broken promise the United States government made to the freed African descendents after the Civil War.

Filmography: *She's Gotta Have It*, 1986; *School Daze*, 1988; *Do the Right Thing*, 1989; *Mo' Better Blues*, 1990; *Jungle Fever*, 1991; *Malcolm X*, 1992; *Drop Squad*, 1994; *Clockers*, 1994; ***Crooklyn***, 1994; *Girl 6*, 1996; *Get on the Bus*, 1996; *Summer of Sam*, 1999; ***Bamboozled***, 2000; *The 25th Hour*, 2003; ***She Hate Me***, 2004; *Inside Man*, 2006.

LEGEND OF NIGGER CHARLIE, THE. 1972. (PG) 98 min. Western. Three escaped slaves become Wild West outlaws, evading a bounty hunter, while helping others along the way. It spawned the sequel ***The Soul of Nigger Charlie***, 1973. Cast: **Fred Williamson**, **D'Urville Martin**, Don Pedro Colley, Gertrude Jeannette, Marcia McBroom, Alan Gifford, John P. Ryan, Will Hussing, Bill Moor, Thomas Anderson, Jerry Gatlin, Tricia O'Neil, Douglas Rowe, Keith Prentice, Tom Pemberton. Director: Martin Goldman. Writers: James Warner Bellah, Martin Goldman, Larry G. Spangler. Cinematographer: Peter Eco. Music: John Bennings, Lloyd Price.

LEMMONS, KASI (1959-). Director, actress, writer. She studied acting before going on to write and direct her acclaimed independent feature film ***Eve's Bayou***, 1997. She received her education at The Lee Strasburg Institute, UCLA, and NYU, and appeared off-Broadway in the 1984 production of *Balm in Gilead*. Her first film role was playing a hostage in the TV movie *11th Victim*, 1979, and she guest starred on the **television** series *Spencer for Hire, A Man Called Hawk, Walker, Texas Ranger*, and *ER*. Other notable acting credits include the films *The Silence of the Lambs*, 1991; ***The Five Heartbeats***, 1991; and ***Candyman***, 1992. A string of film roles followed before Lemmons moved into the director's chair. She followed up *Eve's Bayou* with ***Caveman's Valentine***, 2001.

Filmography: ***School Daze***, 1988; *Vampire's Kiss*, 1989; *The Silence of the Lambs*, 1991; *The Five Heartbeats*, 1991; *Candyman*, 1992; *Hard Target*, 1993; ***Fear of a Black Hat***, 1994; ***Drop Squad***, 1994; ***Gridlock'd***, 1997; *Eve's Bayou*, 1997; *'Til There Was You*, 1997; *Liars Dice*, 1998; *Caveman's Valentine*, 2001.

LENNIX, HARRY J. (1965-). Actor. Before becoming an actor, Lennix taught in the public school system of his hometown, Chicago, Illinois. After landing roles on several TV movies, he was cast in **Robert Townsend**'s *The Five Heartbeats*, 1991. More film roles followed, such as *Mo' Money*, 1992; *Get on the Bus*, 1996; and *Love and Basketball*, 2000. He has guest starred on many TV series, including *The Parent Hood, ER, Diagnosis Murder, Ally McBeal, Girlfriends, The Practice*, and *The Handler*. His recent film roles include *The Matrix Reloaded*, 2003, *The Human Stain*, 2003; *Barbershop 2: Back in Business*, 2004, and *Ray*, 2004. He portrayed the lead role of Adam Clayton Powell Jr., in the biopic *Keep the Faith, Baby*, 2002.

Filmography: *The Package*, 1989; *The Five Heartbeats*, 1991; *Mo' Money*, 1992; *Bob Roberts*, 1992; *Guarding Tess*, 1994; *Notes in a Minor Key*, 1994; *Clockers*, 1995; *Comfortably Numb*, 1995; *Get on the Bus*, 1996; *Chicago Cab*, 1998; *Titus*, 1999; *The Unspoken*, 1999; *Love and Basketball*, 2000; *All or Nothing*, 2001; *Home Invaders*, 2001; *Pumpkin*, 2002; *Collateral Damage*, 2002; *Don't Explain*, 2002; *Never Get Out of the Boat*, 2002; *Black Listed*, 2003; *The Matrix Reloaded*, 2003; *The Human Stain*, 2003; *The Matrix Revolutions*, 2003; *Chrystal*, 2004; *Barbershop 2: Back in Business*, 2004; *Suspect Zero*, 2004; *Ray*, 2004.

LEON (1962-). Actor. This Bronx, New York-born actor has portrayed three legendary singers: Little Richard, Jackie Wilson, and David Ruffin of the Temptations. He also portrayed a singer in **Robert Townsend**'s *The Five Heartbeats*, inspired by the soul group The Dells. His **television** guest-starring appearances include *Hunter, L. A. Law, Central Park West, Oz*, and *Crossing Jordan*, and he portrayed the Jesus character in Madonna's controversial "Like a Prayer" music video.

Filmography: *All the Right Moves*, 1983; *Sole Survivor*, 1983; *Streetwalkin'*, 1984; *The Flamingo Kid*, 1984; *Band of the Hand*, 1986; *The Lawless Land*, 1988; *Colors*, 1988; *The Women of Brewster Place*, 1989; *The Five Heartbeats*, 1991; *Cliffhanger*, 1993; *Cool Runnings*, 1993; *Above the Rim*, 1994; *Once Upon a Time When We Were Colored*, 1995; *Waiting to Exhale*, 1995; *Spirit Lost*, 1996; *Pure Danger*, 1996; *The Price of Kissing*, 1997; *Side Streets*, 1998; *The Temptations*, 1998; *Friends & Lovers*, 1999; *Bats*, 1999; *Mr. Rock and Roll*, 1999; *Little Richard*, 2000; *Buffalo Soldiers*, 2001; *Four Faces of God*, 2002.

LEONARD PART 6. 1987. (PG) 83 min. Comedy. Despite trying to sort out a lot of personal problems, a secret agent comes out of retirement to help stop a series of attacks being perpetrated by animals on other agents. Cast: **Bill Cosby, Gloria Foster**, Tom Courtenay, Joe Don Baker, Director: Paul Weiland. Writers: Bill Cosby, Johnathan Reynolds. Cinematographer: Jan De Bont. Music: Elmer Bernstein.

LESSON BEFORE DYING, A. 1999. (PG-13) 100 min. Drama. Based on the novel by Ernest J. Gains, an idealistic teacher in 1948 befriends a death row inmate awaiting execution for a crime he did not commit. Cast: **Don Cheadle, Cicely Tyson, Mekhi Phifer, Irma P. Hall**, Brent Jennings, Lisa Arrindell Anderson, Frank Hoyt Taylor. Director: Joseph Sargent. Writer: Ann Peacock. Cinematographer: Donald M. Morgan.

LET'S DO IT AGAIN. 1975. (PG) 113 min. Comedy. As the sequel to *Uptown Saturday Night*, 1974, two middle-class working men devise a wild scheme to con a couple of notorious gamblers out of the money to build a fraternal lodge meeting hall. Cast: **Sidney Poitier, Bill Cosby, John Amos, Calvin Lockhart, Jimmy Walker, Ossie Davis, Denise Nicholas**. Director: Sidney Poitier. Writer: **Richard Wesley**.

LEWIS, DAWNN (1961-). Actress. She first made her mark as college student Jalessa Vinson on the hit television sitcom *A Different World*, and later joined the cast of *Hangin' with Mr. Cooper* as Robin Dumars. Her other television credits include work on *Any Day Now*, *Girlfriends*, *The Parent Hood*, and *The Jamie Foxx Show*. She began doing voice-over work providing character voices in animated series, such as *Spider Man*; *Futurama*; *X-Men Legends II: Rise of the Apocalyse*; and *The Boondocks*. Her film roles include *I'm Gonna Git You Sucka*, 1988; *Stompin' at the Savoy*, 1992; and *Dreamgirls*, 2006.
    Filmography: *I'm Gonna Git You Sucka*, 1988; *Stompin' at the Savoy*, 1992; *Race to Freedom: The Undergroung Railroad*, 1994; *The Cherokee Kid*, 1996; *The Wood*, 1999; *The Poof Point*, 2001; *Nicolas*, 2001; *Before Now*, 2002; *Dreamgirls*, 2006.

LEWIS, JENIFER (1957-). Actress. She was born in Kinloch, Missouri, and began her showbiz career in a 1979 production of the Broadway musical *Eubie*. She once sang background as one of Bette Midler's Harlettes, and she co-wrote and starred in the one-woman show *The Diva is Dismissed*, which earned her two NAACP **Image Awards**. She has worked extensively in both film and television, often portraying motherly characters, such as Dean

Dorothy Dandridge on *A Different World*; Aunt Hellen on *The Fresh Prince of Bel-Air*; and Veretta Childs on *Girlfriends*. She provided the voice of Bebe Ho in the animated series *The PJs*, the voice of Motown Turtle in *Shark Tale*, and the voice of Flo in the animated feature film *Cars*. Her notable film appearances include supporting roles in **The Temptations**, 1998; **Little Richard**, 2000; **The Brothers**, 2001; and *Nora's Hair Salon*, 2004.

Filmography: *Red Heat*, 1988; *Beaches*, 1988; *Sister Act*, 1992; *Frozen Assets*, 1992; **What's Love Got to Do with It?** 1993; **Poetic Justice**, 1993; **The Meteor Man**, 1993; *Undercover Blues*, 1993; *Sister Act 2: Back in the Habit*, 1993; *Renaissance Man*, 1994; *Corrina, Corrina*, 1994; **Panther**, 1995; **Dead Presidents**, 1995; **Girl 6**, 1996; **The Preacher's Wife**, 1996; *Rituals*, 1998; *The Mighty*, 1998; *The Temptations*, 1998; *Blast from the Past*, 1999; *Mystery Men*, 1999; *Little Richard*, 2000; **Dancing in September**, 2000; *Cast Away*, 2000; *Partners*, 2000; *The Brothers*, 2001; **Juwanna Mann**, 2003; **Antwone Fisher**, 2002; *Sunday Morning Stripper*, 2003; **The Cookout**, 2004; *Shark Tale*, 2004; *Nora's Hair Salon*, 2004; *Madea's Family Reunion*, 2006; *Cars*, 2006; *Dirty Laundry*, 2006; *Redrum*, 2007.

LEWIS, JOE (1914-1981). Boxing champion, actor. After an impressive slate of wins, 48 of 54 by knockouts, as an amateur light heavyweight, Lewis took the heavyweight crown in 1937 by defeating James Braddock. He held the crown for 11 years and eight months and was only defeated three times out of 71 professional fights. Lewis starred in *Spirit of Youth*, 1938, with **Clarence Muse**, and **The Fight Never Ends**, 1949, with **Ruby Dee**. His biopic film, **The Joe Lewis Story**, 1954, was made on his life and career with actor Coley Wallace portraying the boxer.

LIBERATION OF L. B. JONES, THE. 1970. (R) 101 min. Drama. A wealthy mortician in a small Southern town must cope with racism, his wife's infidelity with a disrespectful white police officer, and his dwindling self-esteem as he navigates his way through a world that seems to be pitted against him. Cast: **Roscoe Lee Brown, Lola Falana**, Lee J. Cobb, Barbera Hershey, Fayard Nicholas, Anthony Zerbe. Director: William Wilder. Writer: Stirling Silliphant. Music: Elmer Bernstein.

LIFE. 1999. (R) 108 min. Comedy/Drama. Two New York hoods make a moonshine run down South in the 1940s. They are framed for a murder and given life sentences in a Mississippi prison. They adjust to prison life until the truth is revealed. Cast: **Eddie Mur-**

phy, **Martin Lawrence**, Ned Beatty, **Cicely Tyson**, **Clarence Williams III**, **Obba Babatunde**, **Bernie Mac**, Michael Taliferro, **Miguel Nunez**, **Bokeem Woodbine**, Barry Henley, Guy Torry, **Lisa Nicole Carson**, Nick Cassavetes, **Anthony Anderson**, Rick James. Director: Ted Demme. Writers: Robert Ramsey, Matthew Stone. Cinematographer: Geoffrey Simpson. Music: Wyclef Jean.

LIGHT IT UP. 1999. (R) 99 min. Drama. High school students protest after a popular teacher is unfairly suspended. Tensions rise until a security guard is shot, leading to a hostage situation and full-blown rebellion. Cast: **Forest Whitaker**, Judd Nelson, Sara Gilbert, **Rosario Dawson**, Usher Raymond, Robert Ri'chard, Fredro Starr, **Glynn Turman**, Clifton Collins Jr., Vic Polizos, **Vanessa L. Williams**. Writer/Director: Craig Bolotin. Cinematographer: Elliot Davis. Music: Harry Gregson-Williams.

LIKE MIKE. 2002. (PG) 99 min. Sports/Comedy. A teenage orphan finds a pair of Air Jordan sneakers with seemingly magical powers. The shoes are adorned with the initials M. J. (for Michael Jordan), and when the little orphan puts them on, he can play ball just like his basketball idol. He is signed to a professional basketball team as a publicity stunt, but there are forces out to get him and the magic shoes. Cast: **Bow Wow**, Johnathan Lipnicki, **Morris Chestnut**, Eugene Levy, Crispin Glover, Reggie Theus. Special appearances by NBA players Gary Payton, Alonzo Mourning, Rasheed Wallace, and Jason Kidd. Director: John Schultz. Writers: Jordon Moffet, Mike Elliot.

LINCOLN, ABBEY (1930-). Actress, singer. Born in Chicago, Illinois, she became a popular jazz singer before starring in *Nothing But a Man*, 1964, with **Ivan Dixon**, and *For Love of Ivy*, 1968, with **Sidney Poitier**. Her television guest appearances include *The Name of the Game*, *Mission Impossible*, and *All in the Family*.

Filmography: *Nothing But a Man*, 1964; *For Love of Ivy*, 1968; *Short Walk to Daylight*, 1972; *Mo' Better Blues*, 1990.

LINCOLN MOTION PICTURE COMPANY, THE (1915-1923). This Los Angeles-based production company was established in 1915 to produce and distribute motion pictures made exclusively for the black community. In the wake of the release of D. W. Griffith's controversial and racist film *The Birth of a Nation*, 1915, popular sentiment in the African American community was that another film was needed to counteract the stereotypical portrayals of blacks, as seen in *The Birth of a Nation*. Character actors Noble

Johnson and Clarence Brooks teamed with Dr. James T. Smith, a local druggist, and a white Universal Studios cameraman named Harry Gant to do just that. With a production office on Central Avenue, and a filming stage located on Tennessee Avenue in West Los Angeles, their first film was *The Realization of a Negro's Ambition*, 1916. Once their first film was a success, Noble Johnson's brother, **George Johnson** joined the company and they produced three additional films, *Trooper of Company K*, 1918; *A Man's Duty*, 1919 (their first feature film); and *By Right of Birth*, 1921.

LINDO, DELROY (1952-). Actor. This London, England-born actor exudes a powerful presence on stage and screen. He was born to Jamaican parents and moved to Toronto, Canada, with his mother as a teen, and later to the United States, where he graduated from the American Conservatory Theater in San Francisco. His first notable film role was in *More American Graffiti*, 1979, and he spent the next 10 years on the stage. He made his Broadway debut in a 1982 production of *Master Harold and the Boys*, directed by the play's author, Athol Fugard. He received a Tony Award nomination for portraying Harold Loomis in August Wilson's play *Joe Turner's Come and Gone*. He received national acclaim as numbers boss West Indian Archie in *Malcolm X*, 1992, and won an NAACP **Image Award** for his work. He portrayed baseball great Satchel Paige in the film *Soul of the Game*, 1996.

Filmography: *Find the Lady*, 1976; *Voice of the Fugitive*, 1978; *More American Graffiti*, 1979; *Perfect Witness*, 1989; *The Blood of Heroes*, 1990; *Mountains of the Moon*, 1990; *Bright Angel*, 1991; *Malcolm X*, 1992; *Bound by Honor*, 1993; *Crooklyn*, 1994; *Congo*, 1995; *Clockers*, 1995; *Get Shorty*, 1995; *Soul of the Game*, 1996; *Ransom*, 1996; *Glory and Honor*, 1998; *Strange Justice*, 1999; *The Cider House Rules*, 1999; *Romeo Must Die*, 2000; *Gone in Sixty Seconds*, 2000; *Heist*, 2001; *The One*, 2001; *The Core*, 2003; *Sahara*, 2005; *Domino*, 2005; *Hounddog*, 2006.

LISARAYE (1966-). Actress. This native of Chicago, Illinois, made her film debut in *Reasons*, 1996, and followed with roles in *The Players Club*, 1998, and *The Wood*, 1999. Her notable TV guest appearances include *In the House*, *The Parent Hood*, and *Faking It*. She is a regular on the TV sitcom *All of Us*.

Filmography: *Reasons*, 1996; *The Players Club*, 1998; *The Wood*, 1999; *The Cheapest Movie Ever Made*, 2000; *Date from Hell*, 2001; *All About You*, 2001; *Civil Brand*, 2002; *Go for Broke*,

2002; *Gang of Roses*, 2003; *The Black Man's Guide to Understanding Black Women*, 2005.

LITTLE, CLEAVON (1939-1992). Actor. He was born in Chickasha, Oklahoma, and raised in California, where he attended San Diego College. He received a scholarship to Juilliard in New York City, and also trained at the American Academy of Dramatic Art. Little was soon appearing off-Broadway and he won a Tony Award for his work in the stage musical *Purlie*. Film offers lured him to Hollywood, where he is possibly best remembered for his work in producer/director Mel Brooks' Western spoof *Blazing Saddles*, 1974. Filmography: *What's So Bad about Feeling Good*, 1964; *John and Mary*, 1969; **Cotton Comes to Harlem**, 1970; *Vanishing Point*, 1971; *Blazing Saddles*, 1974; **Greased Lightning**, 1977; *FM*, 1978; *Scavenger Hunt*, 1979; *The Salamander*, 1981; *High Risk*, 1981; *Double Exposure*, 1982; *Jimmy the Kid*, 1983; *Toy Soldiers*, 1984; *Surf II*, 1984; *The Gig*, 1985; *Once Bitten*, 1985; *Fletch Lives*, 1989; *Murder by Numbers*, 1990; *Goin' to Chicago*, 1991; **Separate But Equal**, 1991.

LITTLE RICHARD. 2000. (TV) 120 min. Biopic. This is a made-for-TV movie about the life and times of rock-and-roll legend "Little Richard" Penniman. The story goes from his humble beginnings as a girly little boy in 1940s Georgia, to being encouraged to sing in church, to a successful secular career in the 1950s. He helped to define rock 'n' roll before returning to the church and ascending to the pulpit, with all the ups and downs in between. Cast: **Leon, Jenifer Lewis, Carl Lumbly, Tamala Jones, Mel Jackson, Garrett Morris**. Director: **Robert Townsend**. Writer: Daniel Taplitz. Cinematographer: Edward Pei.

LIVIN' FOR LOVE: THE NATALIE COLE STORY. 2000. (TV) 120 min. Biopic. This is a made-for-TV movie based on Natalie Cole's own autobiography. She plays herself as an adult in this biopic that goes from her childhood as the daughter of the legendary singer **Nat King Cole**, to her attempts to find love as she grows, and her battles with drug addiction. Cast: Natalie Cole, **Theresa Randle**, James McDaniel, **Diahann Carroll**. Director: **Robert Townsend**.

LIVIN' LARGE. 1991. (R) 96 min. Comedy. A delivery boy gets a chance of a lifetime when he picks up the microphone from a downed TV reporter at a crime scene and continues the live report. He is hired by the news station and begins to live a whole new life, but he loses himself in the process. Cast: **Terrence T. C. Carson**,

Lisa Arrindell Anderson, Blanche Baker, Nathanial Hall, Julia Campbell. Director: **Michael Schultz**. Cinematographer: Peter Lyons Collister. Music: **Herbie Hancock**.

LOCKHART, CALVIN (1934-). Actor. Born in Nassau, Bahamas, Lockhart was in construction and wanted to be a civil engineer. He studied with acting coach Uta Hagen and was discovered while driving a taxicab in New York City by playwright Ketti Frings, who cast him in the play *The Cool World*, in 1960. He later starred opposite Angela Lansbury in the race-based love story, *A Taste of Honey*. He moved to England to appear with the Royal Shakespeare Company at Stratford-on-Avon, and appeared in several British movies. His film career took off during the **blaxploitation** era of the 1970s with strong roles in films like *Cotton Comes to Harlem*, 1970; *Halls of Anger*, 1970; *Melinda*, 1972; and *Honeybaby, Honeybaby*, 1974. His television appearances include *Good Times*, *Get Christie Love*, and *Dynasty*.

Filmography: *Venere Creola*, 1961; *Family Christmas*, 1965; *A Dandy in Aspic*, 1968; *The Mercenaries*, 1968; *Only When I Laugh*, 1968; *Salt and Pepper*, 1968; *Nobody Runs Forever*, 1968; *Joanna*, 1968; *Le Grabuge*, 1968; *Halls of Anger*, 1970; *Leo the Last*, 1970; *Cotton Comes to Harlem*, 1970; *Myra Breckenridge*, 1970; *Melinda*, 1972; *The Beast Must Die*, 1974; *Uptown Saturday Night*, 1974; *Honeybaby, Honeybaby*, 1974; *Let's Do It Again*, 1975; *The Baron*, 1977; *The Baltimore Bullet*, 1980; *Coming to America*, 1988; *Wild at Heart*, 1990; *Predator 2*, 1990; *Twin Peaks: Fire Walk with Me*, 1992.

LONG, NIA (1970-). Actress. A native of Brooklyn, New York, Long developed a love for acting at an early age and after gaining experience on the daytime soap opera *Guiding Light*, made her bigscreen breakout in director **John Singleton**'s *Boyz N the Hood*, 1991. After two years on the television sitcom *The Fresh Prince of Bel Air*, she returned to the big screen in a string of ensemble cast films, including *Soul Food*, 1997, and *The Best Man*, 1999. Her first lead role was in *Love Jones*, 1996.

Filmography: *Boyz N the Hood*, 1991; *Maid in America*, 1993; *Friday*, 1995; *Love Jones*, 1996; *Soul Food*, 1997; *Never 2 Big*, 1998; *Stigmata*, 1999; *In Too Deep*, 1999; *The Best Man*, 1999; *If These Walls Could Talk*, 2000; *Held Up*, 2000; *The Broken Hearts Club*, 2000; *Boiler Room*, 2000; *Big Momma's House*, 2000.

LONG WALK HOME, THE. 1989. (PG) 95 min. Drama. The question of racial and gender equality come together in this sympathetic look at the personal impact of the Montgomery, Alabama, bus boycott during the 1950s. A black maid who chooses to walk to work receives help and compassion from the lady of the house, which antagonizes her conservative-minded husband. Cast: **Whoopi Goldberg**, Sissy Spacek, Dan E. Butler, Dwight Schultz, **Ving Rhames**, Dylan Baker. Director: Richard Pearce. Writer: John Cook. Cinematographer: Roger Deakins. Music: George Fenton. Narrator: Mary Steenburgen.

LOOK OUT SISTER. 1948. 64 min. Musical/Western. Music man **Louis Jordan** saves a dude ranch from foreclosure in this satire on musical Westerns. Tagline: "When he's not singin', he's shootin'. When he's not shootin', he's lovin'!" Cast: Louis Jordan, Suzette Harbin, **Monte Hawley**, Bob Scott, Maceo B. Sheffield, Glen Allen, Ania Clark, Louise Franklin. Directors: Louis Jordan, Bud Pollard. Writer: John E. Gordon.

LOSING ISAIAH. 1994. (R) 108 min. Drama. This is a film based on the novel by Seth Margolis, a social worker adopts an abandoned "crack baby" and raises him for four years, until his birth mother sobers up, tracks her child down, and sues to regain custody. Cast: **Halle Berry**, Jessica Lang, David Strathaim, **Samuel L. Jackson**, **Cuba Gooding, Jr.**, LaTanya Richardson. Director: Stephen Gyllenhaal. Writer: Naomi Foner. Cinematographer: Andrzej Bartkowiak. Music: Mark Isham.

LOST BOUNDERIES. 1949. 99 min. Drama. This film is based on a true story about a light-skinned black family passing for white in a segregated New Hampshire town. Consequences ensue once the truth is revealed. Cast: Mel Ferrer, **Canada Lee**, Betrice Pearson, Richard Hylton, Susan Douglas, Carleton Carpenter, Seth Arnold, Wendell Holmes. Director: Alfred Werker. Writers: Virginia Shaler, Eugene Ling, Charles A. Palmer, Furland de Kay. Cinematographer: William J. Miller. Music: Louis Applebaum.

LOST MAN, THE. 1969. (PG-13) 122 min. Drama. Black militants pull off a robbery to help finance a civil rights organization. Two are killed in a shoot-out with police. The leader escapes and tries to flee the country with the help of a white social worker. Cast: **Sidney Poitier**, Joanna Shimkus, **Al Freeman Jr.**, Michael Tolan, Richard Dysart, **Paul Winfield**, **Bernie Hamilton**, Dolph Sweet, David Steinberg. Writer/Director: Robert Arthur. Cinematographer: Gerald Perry Finnerman. Music: **Quincy Jones**.

LOUIS ARMSTRONG: CHICAGO STYLE. 1976. (TV) 74 min. Music/Drama. This is a film based on the life and career path of jazz trumpeter Louis Armstrong. It tells how he began playing the clubs in Chicago to his European tours, his ups and downs, and how he and his music gained international fame. Cast: **Ben Vereen**, Red Buttons, **Margaret Avery, Janet MacLachlan**, Lee de Broux, Karen Jensen, Albert Paulsen, Bill Henderson, Ketty Lester, Stack Pierce, Richard X. Slattery, Wallace Rooney, Jason Wingreen, Jerry Fogel, Britt Leach. Director: Lee Philips. Writer: James Lee.

LOVE AND BASKETBALL. 2000. (R) 124 min. Romance. Basketball plays an important part in the lives of two childhood friends and neighbors who grow up with the dream of playing professionally. One is a boy, the other a girl, and their love-hate relationship continues throughout their schooling until one day they pursue the game and each other. Cast: **Sanaa Lathan, Omar Epps, Alfre Woodard, Dennis Haysbert, Debbie Morgan, Harry J. Lennix**, Kyla Pratt, Glenndon Chatman. Writer/Director: **Gina Prince Blythewood**. Cinematographer: Reynaldo Villalobos. Music: **Terence Blanchard**. Editor: **Terilyn Shropshire**.

LOVE BEAT THE HELL OUTTA ME. 2000. (R) 89 min. Drama. A friendly evening of drinks and dominoes goes astray when four male friends, each going through a painful breakup, start talking about women. The hostilities they are feeling toward women get turned toward each other, and before the night ends, they must come to terms with their actions, their manhood, and whatever friendship may remain. Cast: **Glenn Plummer, Terrence Howard**, Clyde Jones, Charles R. Penland, Kristen Andreotti, Shay Best, Latricia Cruz, Somalia Goldsby, Jay King, Julissa Marquez, Phoenix Rivera, Raven Williams, AlexSandra Wright. Director/Writer: Kennedy Goldsby.

LOVE DON'T COST A THING. 2003. (PG-13) 100 min. Comedy/Romance. This is a remake of the 1980s film *Can't Buy Me Love*, 1987. A nerdy high school pool boy pays a popular cheerleader to date him so he can join the "cool crowd" at school. It works for a while, and he even gets the big head and turns his back on his nerd friends, until he is forced to be true to himself. Cast: **Nick Cannon, Steve Harvey**, Jordan Burg, Jackie Benoit, George Cedar, Gay Thomas Wilson, Al Thompson, Sam Sarprong, Nichole Mercedes Robinson, Melissa Schuman, Imani Parks, Ian Chidlaw, J. B. Ghuman Jr., Christina Milian, Russell Howard, Elimu Nelson,

LOVE, FAIZON (1968-). Actor. He was born in Santiago de Cuba, Cuba, and began his Hollywood career providing the voice of Robin Harris in *Bebe's Kids*, 1992. This hefty actor was later seen on the screen in numerous films, such as *The Meteor Man*, 1993; *Friday*, 1995; *3 Strikes*, 2000; and *Idlewild*, 2006. His television work includes appearances on comedy series, such as *The Parent Hood*, *The Wayans Bros.*, and *That's So Raven*.

Filmography: *Bebe's Kids*, 1992; *The Meteor Man*, 1993; *Fear of a Black Hat*, 1994; *Friday*, 1995; *A Thin Line Between Love and Hate*, 1996; *B*A*P*S*, 1997; *Money Talks*, 1997; *The Players Club*, 1998; *3 Strikes*, 2000; *The Replacements*, 2000; *Mr. Bones*, 2001; *Blue Crush*, 2002; *Wonderland*, 2003; *The Fighting Temptations*, 2003; *Elf*, 2003; *Ride or Die*, 2003; *Torque*, 2004; *Just My Luck*, 2006; *All You've Got*, 2006; *Idlewild*, 2006; *Perfect Christmas*, 2006; *A Day in the Life*, 2006.

LOVE JONES. 1996. (R) 105 min. Urban Romance. A modern looks at love and urban relationships. An affair between a photographer's assistant and a writer/poet becomes much more than either had intended. They both frequent a poetry club to perform their written thoughts on open-mic night, but their words and their feelings for each other grow too strong and eventually out of control. Cast: **Larenz Tate, Nia Long, Isaiah Washington, Lisa Nicole Carson**, Khalil Kain, **Bill Bellamy**, Leonard Roberts, Bernardette L. Clarke. Writer/Director: Theodore Witcher. Cinematographer: Ernest Holzman. Music: Darryl Jones. Awards: 1997 Sundance Audience Award.

LOW DOWN DIRTY SHAME, A. 1994. (R) 100 min. Comedy. A down-and-out private detective is hired to track down a drug dealer, a beautiful woman, and $20 million in cash. Cast: **Keenen Ivory Wayans, Jada Pinkett Smith, Salli Richardson, Charles S. Dutton**, Andrew Divoff, Corwin Hawkins. Writer/Director: Keenen Ivory Wayans.

LUMBLY, CARL (1952-). Actor. This focused and versatile actor was born in Jamaica, West Indies, and attended McAlester College in St. Paul, Minnesota. He made his film debut as an inmate in *Escape From Alcatraz*, 1979, and his career has accelerated. He has starred and guest appeared on many television series, including *Cagney & Lacey*, *L. A. Law*, *EZ Streets*, *Alias*, and portrayed the title role of Dr. Miles Hawkins in the sci-fi series *M. A. N. T. I. S.* His notable telepicture and film roles include *To Sleep with Anger*, 1990; *Brother Future*, 1991; *Nightjohn*, 1976; *Buffalo Soldiers*,

1997; and *Little Richard*, 2000. He is married to actress **Vonetta McGhee.**

Filmography: *Escape from Alcatraz*, 1979; *Lifepod*, 1980; *Caveman*, 1981; *The Adventures of Buckaroo Banzai across the 8th Dimension*, 1984; *The Bedroom Window*, 1987; *Judgment in Berlin*, 1988; *Everybody's All American*, 1988; *To Sleep With Anger*, 1990; *Pacific Heights*, 1990; *Moe's World*, 1990; ***South Central***, 1992; ***How Stella Got Her Groove Back***, 1998; *Men of Honor*, 2000; *9mm of Love*, 2000; *Just a Dream*, 2002.

LYING LIPS. 1939. 60 min. Drama. A beautiful nightclub singer is framed for murder and her boyfriend sets out to clear her name. Cast: Edna Mae Harris, Carmen Newsome, **Robert Earl Jones**, **Frances E. Williams**, Cherokee Thornton, Slim Thompson, **Juano Hernandez**, Don De Leo, George Reynolds, Charles La Torre, Robert Paquin, Henry Gines, Teddy Hall, Gladys Williams, Amanda Randolph. Director: **Oscar Micheaux**. Cinematographer: Lester Lang. Music: Jack Shilkret.

M

MAC, BERNIE (1958-). Comedian, actor, producer. He was born Bernard Jeffrey McCollough in Chicago, Illinois. He started his comedy career in 1977 at age 19 and struggled for years while playing the local comedy circuit. He made his film debut in *Mo' Money*, 1992, which led to a string of small comic parts in films like *Who's the Man*, 1993; *House Party 3*, 1994; and *Friday*, 1995. His Home Box Office (HBO) comedy special, *Midnight Mac*, 1985, proved a turning point in his career. He landed a recurring role on the television sitcom *Moesha,* and he stood out and got noticed in the film *Life*, 1999. His breakout opportunity came as one of four featured comics on *The Original Kings of Comedy*, 2000. Bernie Mac became a household name and his own sitcom was soon to follow. *The Bernie Mac Show* debuted in 2001, which he also produces. He was the star of the film *Mr. 3,000*, 2004, and one part of the star-studded remake film *Ocean's Eleven*, 2001, and the sequel *Ocean's Twelve*, 2004.

Filmography: *Mo' Money*, 1992; *Who's the Man*, 1993; *House Party 3*, 1994; *Above the Rim*, 1994; *The Walking Dead*, 1995; *Friday*, 1995; ***Don't Be a Menace to South Central While Drinking Your Juice in the Hood***, 1996; ***Get on the Bus***, 1996; *Reasons*, 1996; ***Booty Call***, 1997; ***B*A*P*S***, 1997; ***How to Be a Player***, 1997; ***The Players Club***, 1998; ***Life***, 1999; *What's the*

Worst That Could Happen? 2001; *Ocean's Eleven*, 2001; **Head of State**, 2003; *Charlie's Angel's: Full Throttle*, 2003; *Bad Santa*, 2003; *Mr. 3000*, 2004; *Ocean's Twelve*, 2004; *Guess Who?* 2005.

MACK, THE. 1973. (R) 110 min. Blaxploitation. A pimp gets out of prison after five years. He sets out to regain his territory and win a competition for biggest ladies' man in Oakland, California. His efforts are thwarted by two corrupt white cops who set out to stop him. Cast: **Max Julien, Richard Pryor**, Don Gordon, **Roger E. Mosley, Carol Speed**, William Watson, George Murdock, Juanita Moore, Paul Harris, Kai Hernandez, Annazette Chase, Junero Jennings, Lee Duncan, Stu Gilliam, Sandra Brown, Christopher Brooks, Fritz Ford, John Vick, Norma McClure, David Mauro, Allen Van, Willie Redman, Frank Ward, Ted Ward. Director: Michael Campus. Cinematographer: Ralph Woolsey. Music: Willie Hutch.

MACLACHLAN, JANET (1933-). Actress. She began her acting career in socially relevant films, such as *Up Tight!*, 1968, and *...tick...tick...tick*, 1970. Costarring roles on **television** soon followed in the sitcoms *Love Thy Neighbor* and *Friends*. Other film roles include **The Sophisticated Gents**, 1981; *The 13th Floor*, 1999; and *A Private Affair*, 2000.

    Filmography: *Up Tight!*, 1968; *Darker than Amber*, 1970; *...tick...tick...tick*, 1970; **Sounder**, 1972; **Big Mo**, 1973; **Roll of Thunder, Hear My Cry**, 1978; *Sophisticated Gents*, 1981; *She's in the Army Now*, 1981; *Murphy's Law*, 1986; **For Us the Living**, 1988.

MAHOGANY. 1975. (PG) 109 min. Drama/Romance. An ambitious inner-city fashion designer becomes a professional model in Rome and leaves her politically minded boyfriend behind. She finds that success is nothing without someone you love to share it with and returns home to stand by her man. Cast: **Diana Ross, Billy Dee Williams**, Jean-Pierre Aumont, Anthony Perkins, Nina Foch. Director: **Berry Gordy**. Writer: John Byrum. Cinematographer: David Watkin.

MALCOLM X. 1992. (PG-13) 201 min. Docudrama. This film is based on **Alex Haley**'s book *The Autobiography of Malcolm X*. A small-time Harlem thug goes from committing crimes, to jail, to a high-ranking position with the Nation of Islam, to the most powerful civil rights leader in the country. Cast: **Denzel Washington, Angela Bassett, Albert Hall, Al Freeman Jr., Delroy Lindo, Spike**

Lee, **Theresa Randle**, Kate Vernon, **Lonette McKee**, Tommy Hollis, James McDaniel, Ernest Thompson, Jean LaMarre, **Giancarlo Esposito**, Craig Wasson, John Ottavino, David Patrick Kelly, Shirley Stoler. Director: Spike Lee. Writers: Spike Lee, Arnold Perl, James Baldwin. Music: **Terence Blanchard**.

MALCOLM X: MAKE IT PLAIN. 1995. (TV) 136 min. Biography. This is a documentary on the life of Malcolm Little (El Malik Shabazz), as told by close friends and those who knew, loved, and worked with him. It includes footage from his speeches and interviews. Speakers: **Maya Angelou, Ossie Davis, Alex Haley,** Mike Wallace, various family members.

MAMA FLORA'S FAMILY. 1998. (TV) 175 min. Drama. This film is based on **Alex Haley**'s book about his maternal family, and how a concerned mother's strength and love holds her family together through tragedy, death, discrimination, and hardships. Cast: **Cicely Tyson, Mario Van Peebles, Blair Underwood, Queen Latifah, Hill Harper, Shemar Moore, Della Reese**. Director: Peter Werner. Writers: David Stevens, Carol Schreder. Cinematographer: Neil Roach.

MAN & BOY. 1971. (G) 98 min. Drama. A former Buffalo Soldier faces racism and discrimination when he sets up a homestead on a piece of land in Arizona. Cast: **Bill Cosby, Gloria Foster**, George Spell, Henry Silva, **Yaphet Kotto**. Director: E. W. Swackhamer. Music: **Quincy Jones**.

MAN CALLED ADAM, A. 1966. 103 min. Music/Drama. Haunted by the guilt of having accidentally killed his family, a jazz musician faces hardships and race prejudice while pursuing his life and career goals. Cast: **Sammy Davis Jr., Louis Armstrong, Ossie Davis, Cicely Tyson**, Frank Sinatra Jr., **Lola Falana**, Mel Torme, Peter Lawford. Director: Leonard Penn. Cinematographer: Jack Priestley.

MANDELA. 1994. (R) 135 min. Biopic. This film is based on the real-life trials and tribulations of Nelson and Winnie Mandela and their struggle against the South Africa apartheid system. Cast: **Danny Glover, Alfre Woodard**, John Matshikiza, Warren Clarke, Allan Corduner, Julian Glover. Director: Phillip Saville.

MANDINGO. 1975. (R) 127 min. Drama. In this film, deep South slavery is addressed, circa 1840, with focus on the inter-love and intermingling between the masters and their slaves. This was the screen debut for heavyweight boxing champion Ken Norton, who makes his master money with his boxing skills. It spawned the sequel *Drum*, 1975. Cast: Ken Norton, **Brenda Sykes**, James Mason, Susan George, Perry King, **Richard Ward**, Ben Masters, Paul Benedict, Jio-Tu Cumbuka. Director: Richard Fleischer. Writers: Richard H. Kline, Norman Wexler. Music: Maurice Jarre.

MANTAN MESSES UP. 1946. Comedy/Musical. **Mantan Moreland** stars in this tale of musical high jinks. Produced by **Ted Toddy**. Cast: Mantan Moreland, Doryce Bradley, The Four Tones, **Eddie Green**, Monte Hawley, **Lena Horne**, Bo Jinkins, Ford Washington Lee, **Nina Mae McKinney**, Neva Peoples, The Redcaps, John William Sublett. Director: Sam Newfield.

MARKHAM, DEWEY "PIGMEAT" (1904-1981). Vaudeville performer, actor. He was born in Durham, North Carolina, and left home in his teens after joining a carnival that passed through town. Markham later performed on the vaudeville stage, often in **blackface**, and he received his nickname from a comedy sketch in which he proclaims himself "Sweet Poppa Pigmeat." He also performed as part of the comedy team, Judge Pigmeat Markham and Shorty. In film, he worked with producer **Ted Toddy** in *House-Rent Party*, 1946, and *Fight That Ghost*, 1946. His **television** appearances include *Toast of the Town*, 1953-1962; *ABC Stage 67*, 1967; and he is possibly best remembered as "The Judge" on the hit comedy series *Rowen & Martin's Laugh-In*, 1968. The residential street his family lived on in Durham was renamed Markham Street in his honor.
    Filmography: *Swanee Showboat*, 1940; *One Big Mistake*, 1940; *Mr. Smith Goes Ghost*, 1940; *Am I Guilty*, 1940; *That's My Baby*, 1944; *House-Rent Party*, 1946; *Fight That Ghost*, 1946; *Junction 88*, 1947.

MARTIN, CHRISTOPHER (1962-). Singer, actor. This Queens, New York-born rapper came to prominence as Christopher "Play" Martin of the hip-hop group Kid 'N Play. His film work includes roles in the *House Party* series of films.
    Filmography: *House Party*, 1990; *House Party 2*, 1991; *Class Act*, 1992; *House Party 3*, 1994; *Rising to the Top*, 1999.

MARTIN, DARNELL (1964-). Director, writer. She was born in Bronx, New York, and is credited with being the first African American woman to direct a feature film for a Hollywood studio for her film *I Like It Like That*, 1994. She has directed such **television** series as *Homicide: Life on the Streets*, *ER*, *Oz*, *Law & Order: Criminal Intent*, and *Dragnet*. She wrote and produced *Prison Song*, 2001.

Filmography: *Suspect*, 1992; *I Like It Like That*, 1994; *Prison Song*, 2001; *Their Eyes Were Watching God*, 2005.

MARTIN, DUANE (1970-). Actor, producer, writer. He was born in Hollywood, California, and played professional basketball with the New York Knicks before returning home to act. He used his on-the-court skills in basketball-heavy films like *White Men Can't Jump*, 1992, and *Above the Rim*, 1994. His TV guest appearances include *The Fresh Prince of Bel Air*, *Living Single*, *Between Brothers*, *Girlfriends*, *One on One*, and he stars in the TV sitcom *All of Us*. Other notable film roles include *Woo*, 1998; *Deliver Us from Eva*, 2003; *Ride or Die*, 2003; and *The Seat Filler*, 2004, which he also wrote and produced. Martin is married to actress Tisha Campbell.

Filmography: *Moe's World*, 1990; *White Men Can't Jump*, 1992; *Above the Rim*, 1994; *The Inkwell*, 1994; *Down Periscope*, 1996; *Scream 2*, 1997; *Fakin' Da Funk*, 1997; *Woo*, 1998; *The Faculty*, 1998; *Any Given Sunday*, 1999; *The Groomsmen*, 2001; *Deliver Us from Eva*, 2003; *Ride or Die*, 2003; *The Seat Filler*, 2004.

MARTIN, D'URVILLE (1938-1984). Actor, director. Martin was a mover and shaker in the 1970s **blaxploitation** boom in films like *The Final Comedown*, 1972; *Sheba, Baby*, 1975; and *Blind Rage*, 1978. He also directed and costarred in **Rudy Ray Moore**'s cult classic *Dolemite*, 1974.

Filmography: *Watermelon Man*, 1970; *The Final Comedown*, 1972; *Boss*, 1974; *Sheba, Baby*, 1975; *Dolemite*, 1975; *Death Journey*, 1976; *Blind Rage*, 1978; *Big Score*, 1983.

MASTER P. (1970-). Rapper, actor, producer. The New Orleans, Louisiana, native helped to usher in the gangsta rap genre of music with his underground hip-hop label No Limit Records. His music stressed hardcore rap records with street beats, lifted hook lines, and funk-riffed backing. Staying underground and independent, his hit 1994 solo debut, *Ghetto's Tryin' to Kill Me!* ushered in a musical formula that quickly found commercial success. He self-produced and self-financed the film, *I'm Bout It*, 1997, an autobiographical movie that showcased his record label's gangsta rap tunes. His second film was *I Got the Hook-Up*, 1998. In addition to his music and film interests, he has a clothing line and a sports management agency. Filmography: *I'm Bout It*, 1997; *I Got the Hook-Up*, 1998; *Foolish*, 1999; *Lockdown*, 2000; *Hollywood Homicide*, 2003; *Dark Blue*, 2003.

MAURICE FILM COMPANY, THE (1920-1929). This early film-production company made only one short and two feature-films in its 10-year history. The company was located in Detroit, Michigan, and was founded by Richard D. Maurice, who wrote, produced, directed, and starred in his movies: *Home Brew*, 1920; *Nobody's Children*, 1920; and *Eleven P. M.*, 1929.

MAYFIELD, CURTIS (1942-1999). Singer, songwriter, film composer, producer. This rhythm-and-blues legend helped to define the Chicago sound in the 1960s that rivaled Detroit's **Motown** sound. He wrote hit songs for local artists, such as Jerry Butler, Major Lance, Gene Chandler, and Walter Jackson, and his unique style of music is still an influence in the hip-hop culture of today. He began singing at age seven and taught himself how to play the guitar. After years of writing and composing music, much of it containing serious social commentary, Mayfield became a driving force with his gospel-soul group, The Impressions. They released songs like "Gypsy Woman," "He Will Break Your Heart," and the classics "It's All Right," and "People Get Ready." He went solo in 1970 and wrote and produced the music for the hit film *Superfly*, 1972. The soundtrack album sold more than a million copies and received four Grammy nominations. His other hit film soundtracks include *Claudine*, 1975; *Sparkle*, 1976; and *A Piece of the Action*, 1978. He also wrote the music and had an acting role in the film *Short Eyes*, 1979. In 1990, he was paralyzed from the neck down when part of a public address rig collapsed on top of him during a concert. Confined to a wheelchair, he recorded his critically acclaimed *New World Order* album while suspended by a harness. Mayfield was inducted into the Rock and Roll Hall of Fame twice; the first time, with his gospel-soul group The Impressions in 1991; and again for his solo career in 1999.

MAYO, WHITMAN (1930-2001). Actor. He was born and raised in Harlem and Queens, New York, but moved to Southern California with his family when he was 17. He joined the U. S. Army and served from 1951-1953, before going on to study at Chaffey College, Los Angeles City College, and UCLA, while doing a little acting. He worked at various careers and odd jobs before joining

The New Lafayette Theater repertory company in New York City. He was cast for a single episode of the **Redd Foxx** sitcom *Sanford and Son*, and remained for the duration of the show. Mayo is perhaps best known as that character, which enjoyed a brief spin-off series, *Grady*, in 1975. He opened a travel agency in Inglewood, California, in the 1980s, and left Los Angeles for Georgia in 1994, where he taught drama at Clark Atlanta University in Atlanta.

Filmography: *The Black Klansman*, 1966; *The Main Event*, 1979; *D. C. Cab*, 1983; *The Old Man*, 1990; **Boyz 'N the Hood**, 1991; *The Seventh Coin*, 1993; *Waterproof*, 1999; **Boycott**, 2000.

McBRIDE, CHI (1961-). Actor. He was born in Chicago, Illinois, and embarked upon his acting career at the age of 30. He got on the fast track with **television** guest appearances in *The Fresh Prince of Bel-Air*, *Married...with Children*, and *Nash Bridges*. He later costarred as principal Steven Harper in the series *Boston Public*, and in the recurring role of Edward Vogler in *House, M. D.* He was cast earlier in the title role of the short-lived, controversial slave series *The Secret Diary of Desmond Pfeiffer*, 1998.

Filmography: **The Distinguished Gentleman**, 1992; **What's Love Got to Do with It?** 1993; **Cosmic Slop**, 1994; *The Frighteners*, 1996; **Hoodlum**, 1997; **Mercury Rising**, 1998; *Magicians*, 2000; **Dancing in September**, 2000; *Gone in 60 Seconds*, 2000; *The Kid*, 2000; *Narc*, 2002; **Undercover Brother**, 2002; *Paid in Full*, 2002; *Cradle 2 the Grave*, 2003; *Delusion*, 2003; *The Terminal*, 2004; *I, Robot*, 2004; *The Gate*, 2005; *Waiting*, 2005; **Roll Bounce**, 2005; *Annapolis*, 2006; *You Are Going to Prison*, 2006.

McDANIEL, HATTIE (1895-1952). Actress. Born in Wichita, Kansas, Hattie McDaniel started her showbiz career in Denver, Colorado, at age 13, performing in school plays and black minstrel shows. After winning a local talent award, she quit school to become a vaudeville performer, touring the West Coast circuit with the Henry McDaniel Minstrel Show, a troupe organized by her father. She toured with the Melody Hounds, led by George Morrison in 1920, and made her radio debut in 1924, while they were performing in Denver. McDaniel also wrote and recorded many of her own songs on the Okeh and Paramount Labels in Chicago, and became a headliner on the Pantages Theater circuit. She made her way to Hollywood in 1931 and supported herself as a washerwoman and maid until she began to land movie roles in films, such as *Judge Priest*, 1934; *The Little Colonel*, 1935; and *Showboat*, 1936. She also revived her radio career while in Los Angeles and performed weekly as Hi-Hat Hatie. In 1940, she became the first

African American to win an **Academy Award** for her portrayal of Mammy in *Gone with the Wind*, 1939. Despite this achievement, the National Associatgion for the Advancement of Colored People (NAACP), often criticized McDaniel for perpetuating the "Mammy" stereotype. Another first came in 1947, when she became the first black actress to play a black character on *The Beulah Show*, a nationally syndicated radio program. She later replaced **Ethel Waters** in the television version of the series.

Filmography: *Impatient Maiden*, 1932; *Crooner*, 1932; *Blonde Venus*, 1932; *The Boiling Point*, 1932; *Hello, Sister*, 1933; *I'm No Angel*, 1933; *Judge Priest*, 1934; *Imitation of Life*, 1934; *Flirtation*, 1934; *Okay Toots!*, 1935; *Little Men*, 1935; *China Seas*, 1935; *Alice Adams*, 1935; *Music is Magic*, 1935; *Our Gang*, 1935; *The Singing Kid*, 1936; *Show Boat*, 1936; *Star for a Night*, 1936; *Reunion*, 1936; *Racing Lady*, 1936; *Can This Be Dixie?* 1936; *The Bride Walks Out*, 1936; *Don't Tell the Wife*, 1937; *Saratoga*, 1937; *Nothing Sacred*, 1937; *True Confessions*, 1937; *Battle of Broadway*, 1938; *Carefree*, 1938; *Everybody's Baby*, 1939; *Zenobia*, 1939; *Gone with the Wind*, 1939; *They Died with Their Boots on*, 1941; *Thank Your Lucky Stars*, 1943; *Since You Went Away*, 1944; *Three is a Family*, 1944; *Janie Gets Married*, 1946; *Song of the South*, 1946; *Never Say Goodbye*, 1946; *The Flame*, 1947; *Mickey*, 1948; *Family Honeymoon*, 1948; *The Big Wheel*, 1949.

McGEE, VONETTA (1940-). Actress. While attending San Francisco State University, McGee joined the socially conscious theater troupe Aldridge Player's West, and began her training on stage. After winning the Miss Bronze California beauty contest, she was offered small parts in several independent European films. She returned to the States during the **blaxploitation** film boom and landed a part in *The Lost Man*, 1969. Her talent and beauty led to larger roles in *Melinda*, 1972; *Blackula*, 1972; *Hammer*, 1972; and *Shaft in Africa*, 1973. She shared the title role in *Thomasine & Bushrod*, 1974, with then-boyfriend **Max Julien**. She guest starred on numerous television shows, such as *Different Strokes*, *Magnum P. I.*, and *Amen*, and had a recurring role on *Cagney & Lacey*. She is married to actor **Carl Lumbly**, and they played a married couple in **Charles Burnett**'s *To Sleep With Anger*, 1990.

Filmography: *The Big Silence*, 1968; *Faustina*, 1968; *The Lost Man*, 1969; *The Kremlin Letter*, 1970; *Melinda*, 1972; *Blackula*, 1972; *Hammer*, 1972; *Shaft in Africa*, 1973; *Detroit 9000*, 1973; *Thomasine & Bushrod*, 1974; *The Eiger Sanction*, 1975; *Brothers*, 1977; *Repo Man*, 1984; *To Sleep with Anger*, 1990; *Brother Future*, 1991; *You Must Remember This*, 1992; *Johnny B.*, 1998.

McHENRY, DOUG. Producer, director. He is co-founder of Elephant Walk Entertainment with **George Jackson**. As a co-producing team, they made more than a dozen films, including *Krush Groove*, 1985; *Disorderlies*, 1987; and *Jason's Lyric*, 1994, which he also directed. Other directing credits include *House Party 2*, 1991, and *Kingdom Come*, 2001.

Filmography: *Krush Groove*, 1985; *Disorderlies*, 1987; *New Jack City*, 1991; *House Party 2*, 1991; *House Party 3*, 1994; *Jason's Lyric*, 1994; *The Walking Dead*, 1995; *Scenes for the Soul*, 1995; *A Thin Line Between Love and Hate*, 1996; *Body Count*, 1998; *The Brothers*, 2001; *Two Can Play That Game*, 2001.

McKEE, LONETTE (1954-). Actress. This Detroit, Michigan-born actress appeared for two years on the daytime soap opera *As the World Turns*, and has guest starred on **television** shows, such as *The Equalizer*, *Amen*, and *Law & Order: Special Victims Unit*. She had a recurring role on the series *Third Watch*. She was nominated for a Tony Award for her performance in the stage play **Show Boat**, and she appeared in *Lady Day at Emerson's Bar and Grill*, as songstress Billie Holiday. Her first feature film was *Sparkle*, 1976. Other film roles include *Which Way is Up*, 1977; *Jungle Fever*, 1991; and *She Hate Me*, 2004. She studied film directing at The New School in New York City, and teaches a master actor's workshop at Cetenary College. She also writes and produces music with several CDs to her credit, including *Natural Love*.

Filmography: *Sparkle*, 1976; *Which Way Is Up?* 1977; *Cuba*, 1979; *Illusions*, 1982; *The Cotton Club*, 1984; *Brewster's Millions*, 1985; *'Round Midnight*, 1986; *Gardens of Stone*, 1987; *The Women of Brewster Place*, 1989; *Dangerous Passion*, 1990; *Jungle Fever*, 1991; *Malcolm X*, 1992; *Queen*, 1993; *He Got Game*, 1998; *Having Our Say: The Delaney Sisters' First 100 Years*, 1999; *A Day in Black and White*, 1999; *Fast Food, Fast Women*, 2000; *Men of Honor*, 2000; *Lift*, 2001; *The Paper Mache Chase*, 2003; *Honey*, 2003; *She Hate Me*, 2004.

McKINNEY, NINA MAE (1912-1967). Actress, singer, dancer. A native of Lancaster, South Carolina, Nannie Mayme McKinney performed in school plays at the all-black Lancaster Industrial School while living with an aunt. She left school at age 13 and moved to New York City to live with her mother. She took on the stage name of Nina Mae McKinney and was soon performing in Harlem nightclubs, and landed a role as a dancer in Lew Leslie's 1928 Broadway musical *Blackbirds*. Film director King Vidor was impressed by her lively performance on stage and took the sultry 16-year-old to Hollywood to star in his upcoming sound film *Hallelujah*, 1929. As Chick, the half-girl, half-woman temptress, McKinney received a five-year contract with MGM studios and became the **talkies'** first black love goddess and tragic mulatto character. A sexy African American leading lady was not the norm in the 1930s and she only did two pictures under her lengthy contract, *Safe in Hell*, 1931, and her singing voice was overdubbed for a Jean Harlow song in *Reckless*, 1935. She also starred in the musical short, *Pie Pie Blackbird*, 1932, where she danced with the very young **Nicholas Brothers**. Despite her big breakout, opportunities in America were rather slim. McKinney toured Europe billed as the "Black Garbo," and was referred to as the dusky "Clara Bow" when she returned to the United States. While in England, she starred in *Sanders of the River*, 1935, with **Paul Robeson**. The onset of World War II brought her back to New York, where she married jazz musician Jimmy Monroe, organized a band, and toured the country. Her additional film roles include *The Devil's Daughter*, 1939; **Mantan Messes Up**, 1946; and *Pinky*, 1949. McKinney also lived and performed in Athens, Greece, during the 1950s and 1960s, when she was known as "Queen of the Night Life." She would later marry character actor **Joel Fluellen** in a Mexican wedding ceremony in Caliente, but their union would be short-lived.

Filmography: *Hallelujah*, 1929; *Safe in Hell*, 1931; *Reckless*, 1935; *Sanders of the River*, 1935; *The Devil's Daughter*, 1939; *Mantan Messes Up*, 1946; *Pinky*, 1949.

McNEIL, CLAUDIA (1917-1993). Actress. She was born in Baltimore, Maryland, and became a librarian before beginning a career in show business. As a vaudeville singer, she also performed in nightclubs and on the radio. On stage, she was nominated for Tony awards for *A Raisin in the Sun*, in 1959, and *Tiger, Tiger Burning Bright*, in 1962. She became well known for her roles as the strong matriarch in films like *A Raisin in the Sun*, 1961, and *Black Girl*, 1972.

Filmography: *The Last Angry Man*, 1959; *A Raisin in the Sun*, 1961; *There Was a Crooked Man*, 1970; *Black Girl*, 1972; *To Be Young, Gifted, and Black*, 1972; *Roll of Thunder, Hear My Cry*, 1978; *Roots: The Next Generation*, 1979.

McQUEEN, BUTTERFLY (1911-1995). Actress. Born as Thelma McQueen in Tampa, Florida, she began her career as a radio actress in the 1930s on such shows as *The Goldbergs*, *The Danny Kaye Show*, *The Jack Benny Show*, and *The Beulah Show*. On stage she appeared in *Brown Sugar*, 1937; *Brother Rat*, 1937; and *What a Life*, 1938. In motion pictures, she was cast as Prissy in the epic film *Gone with the Wind*, 1937. Her other screen performances include *I Dood It*, 1943; *Mildred Pierce*, 1945; and *Duel in the Sun*, 1947. She appeared on the *Give Us Our Dream* episode of *Studio One*, and was Oriole on the **television** series *The Beulah Show*.

Filmography: *The Women*, 1939; *Gone with the Wind*, 1939; *Affectionately Yours*, 1941; *Cabin in the Sky*, 1943; *I Dood It*, 1943; *Flame of Barbery Coast*, 1945; *Mildred Pierce*, 1945; *Duel in the Sun*, 1946; *Killer Diller*, 1948; *The Green Pastures*, 1957; *Amazing Grace*, 1974; *The Mosquito Coast*, 1986; *Polly*, 1989.

MEADOWS, TIM (1961-). Comedian, actor. He was born in Highland Park, Michigan, and graduated from Wayne State University in Detroit, Michigan. He received his early training in comedy with Chicago's Improv Olympic improvisation troupe, and the Second City Improv Company in Chicago. He is perhaps best known as a regular on the long-running NBC comedy series *Saturday Night Live*. He also appeared on the television series *The Michael Richards Show*, and *Leap of Faith*. He has starred in the films *The Ladies Man*, 2000, which he also wrote, and *The Cookout*, 2004.

Filmography: Coneheads, 1993; *Wayne's World 2*, 1993; *It's Pat*, 1994; *The Ladies Man*, 2000; *Wasabi Tuna*, 2003; *Nobody Knows Anything*, 2003; *Mean Girls*, 2004; *The Cookout*, 2004.

MELINDA. 1972. (R) 109 min. Drama. This is a revenge tale of lies, greed, and political corruption. Cast: **Calvin Lockhart**, **Rosalind Cash**, **Vonetta McGee**, Raul Stevens, Rockne Tarkington, Ross Hagen, Renny Roker, Judyann Elder, **Jim Kelly**, Jan Tice, **Lonne Elder III**, Ed Cambridge, Allen Pinson, Joe Hooker, Jack Manning. Director: **Hugh A. Robinson**. Writers: Raymond Cistheri, Lonne Elder III.

MENACE II SOCIETY. 1993. (R) 104 min. Urban Drama. This haunting tale explores a world of inner-city drugs, violence, and hopelessness. A small-time drug dealer plans to escape from the hood when he graduates from high school but his environment and circumstances beyond his control have other plans. Cast: Tyrin Turner, **Larenze Tate**, **Samuel L. Jackson**, **Glenn Plummer**, Julian Roy Doster, **Bill Duke**, **Charles S. Dutton**, **Jada Pinkett**, Vonte Sweet, Ryan Williams. Directors: **Allen Hughes**, **Albert Hughes**. Writer: Tyger Williams, Cinematographer: Lisa Rinzler. Awards: Independent Spirit Awards 1994: Best Cinematography. MTV Movie Awards 1994: Best Film.

METEOR MAN, THE. 1993. (PG) 100 min. Comedy. This film is a comedy satire on superhero movies. A concerned schoolteacher develops super powers when a meteor strikes him. He uses these powers to confront the neighborhood gang and tries to bring peace to his troubled community. Cast: **Robert Townsend, Robert Guillaume, Marla Gibbs, James Earl Jones**, Frank Gorshin. Cameo appearances by **Bill Cosby**, Luther Vandross, **Sinbad**, and **LaWanda Page**. Writer/Director: **Robert Townsend**. Cinematographer: John A. Alonzo.

MICHEAUX, OSCAR (1884-1951). Filmmaker, author. The most prolific independent filmmaker of his time, Micheaux was born in Metropolis, Illinois, and left home to work as a Pullman porter at age 17. He became a homesteader in Gregory County, South Dakota, in 1904, and wrote and self-published *The Conquest: Story of a Negro Pioneer* in 1917, a novel based loosely on his experience. His other novels, *Forged Note: Romance of the Darker Races*, and *The Homesteader*, soon followed. Micheaux entered filmmaking after the **Lincoln Motion Picture Company** expressed an interest in turning *The Homesteader* novel into a film, but refused to let him direct. He organized the Oscar Micheaux Corporation and produced over 30 films between 1919 and 1948. An effective self-promoter, he would personally take the film prints around the theater circuit and talk the owners into investing a portion of the money made from the screening into his next film. Due to the added expense of talking pictures and the effects of the Great Depression, Micheaux was forced to file bankruptcy in 1928. In 1931, he partnered with Leo Brecher and Frank Schiffman, two white Harlem theater owners and began to produce a series of "soundies," including *The Exile*, 1931, and *Veiled Aristocrats*, 1932. He wrote four more novels between 1941 and 1943, including *Wind from Nowhere* and *Masquerade*. His final film, *The Betrayal*, was released in 1948.

Filmography: *The Homesteader*, 1919; *8th Regiment in Chicago*, 1919; *Within Our Gates*, 1920; *The Brute*, 1920; *The Symbol of the Unconquered*, 1920; *The Gunsaulus Mystery*, 1921; *The Dungeon*, 1922; *The Virgin of Seminole*, 1922; *Deceit*, 1923; *Birthright*, 1924; *A Son of Satan*, 1924; *The House Behind the Cedars*, 1925; *The Devil'a Desciple*, 1925; *Body and Soul*, 1925; *The Conjure Woman*, 1926; *The Spider's Web*, 1926; *The Millionaire*, 1927; *Thirty Years Later*, 1928; *The Broken Violin*, 1928; *The Wages of Sin*, 1929; *When Men Betray*, 1929; *A Daughter of the Congo*, 1930; *Easy Street*, 1930; *The Exile*, 1931; *The Darktown*

Revue, 1931; *Veiled Aristocrats*, 1932; *Ten Minutes to Live*, 1932; **The Girl from Chicago**, 1932; *Harlem after Midnight*, 1934; **Murder in Harlem**, 1935; *Temptation*, 1936; *Underworld*, 1937; **God's Step Children**, 1938; *Birthright*, 1938; *Swing!* 1938; **Lying Lips**, 1939; *The Notorious Elinor Lee*, 1940; *The Betrayal*, 1948.

MICHELE, MICHAEL (1966-). Actress. She was born Michael Michele Williams in Evansville, Indiana. A natural athlete, she played basketball in high school for a top-ranked Indiana team. She moved to New York City after graduation and appeared in several commercials. She made her film debut in the independent horror film **Def by Temptation**, 1990, and later landed roles in **New Jack City**, 1991; *The Sixth Man*, 1997; and *Ali*, 2001. Her television guest appearances include *1st & Ten*, *Players*, and *Law & Order*. Michele landed recurring roles on the series *New York Undercover*, *Homicide: Life on the Street*, and *ER*. She starred in the UPN series *Kevin Hill*. Michele has appeared in the stage productions of *A Raisin in the Sun*, *Purlie Victorious*, and *The Owl & the Pussycat*.

Filmography: *Def by Temptation*, 1990; *New Jack City*, 1991; *The Sixth Man*, 1997; *Homicide: The Movie*, 2000; *Ali*, 2001; *Dark Blue*, 2002; *How to Lose a Guy in 10 Days*, 2003.

MIGHTY QUINN, THE. 1989. (R) 98 min. Drama. The Caribbean Island of Jamaica is used as a location where the local police chief comes to believe that a murder suspect is completely innocent. The fact that it is a childhood friend raises concern about his effort and his judgment. Cast: **Denzel Washington**, **Robert Townsend**, James Fox, Mimi Rogers, M. Emmet Walsh, **Sheryl Lee Ralph**, **Esther Rolle**, **Art Evans**, Norman Beaton, Keye Luke. Director: Carl Schenkel. Writer: Hampton Fancher. Cinematographer: Jacques Steyn. Music: Anne Dudley.

MILLER, FLOURNOY (1887-1971). Comedian, actor, writer, composer. Miller was born in Nashville, Tennessee, and attended Fisk University. He wrote songs for the Pekin Theater Company in Chicago, Illinois, and worked the vaudeville stage in comedy teams with Aubrey Lyles and Mantan Moreland. He appeared in the series of all-black Westerns in the late 1930s—**Harlem on the Prairie**, 1938; **Two-Gun Man from Harlem**, 1939; **Harlem Rides the Range**, 1939; which he also co-wrote, and the final film of the series, **The Bronze Buckeroo**, 1939. In radio, Miller wrote scripts for Amos 'n' Andy, and penned many works for the stage, including *The Oyster Man*, and *Shuffle Along of 1933*.

Filmography: *That's the Spirit*, 1932; *Harlem on the Prairie*, 1938; *Two-Gun Man from Harlem*, 1939; *Harlem Rides the Range*, 1939; *The Bronze Buckeroo*, 1939; ***Double Deal***, 1939; *Lady Luck*, 1940; *Mystery in Swing*, 1940; *Professor Creeps*, 1941; ***Stormy Weather***, 1943; *Mantan Runs for Mayor*, 1946; *She's Too Mean for Me*, 1948; *Yes, Sir, Mr. Bones*, 1951.

MILLS, CHARLES. Cinematographer, director. Mills began his cinematic career as second camera operator on the hit film *Animal House*, 1978. He has since shot dramatic **television** series, such as *In the Heat of the Night*, *City of Angels*, and many made-for-TV movies. Mills has also directed episodes of *In the Heat of the Night*. His feature film work includes the lensing of director **John Singleton**'s ***Boyz N the Hood***, 1991.

Filmography: ***Secret Agent 00 Soul***, 1990; *Boyz N the Hood*, 1991; *How I Spent My Summer Vacation*, 1997; *Body Count*, 1998; ***Trois***, 2000; ***Baby Boy***, 2001; *Black Listed*, 2003; *Deadly*, 2005.

MIRACLE IN HARLEM. 1948. 69 min. Drama. In this film, a young woman becomes a murder suspect when the leader of a local gang who tried to take over her father's candy store is found dead. Cast: Sheila Guyse, **Stepin Fetchit**, Hilda Offley, **Lawrence Criner**, **Monte Hawley**. Director: Jack Kemp.

MISS EVERS' BOYS. 1997. (PG) 120 min. Drama. This is a docudrama based on a play by David Feldshuh about a group of African American men in a medical study started in the 1930s by the U. S. Public Health Service. They were purposely infected with syphilis and then lied to about their disease after funding was cut, and monitored with the painful disease for 40 years with no treatment. Cast: **Alfre Woodard**, **Laurence Fishburne**, **Joe Morton**, Craig Sheffer, **Obba Babatunde**, **Ossie Davis**, E. G. Marshall. Director: Joseph Sargent. Writer: Walter Bernstein. Cinematographer: Donald M. Morgan. Music: Charles Bernstein.

MISS MELODY JONES. 1973. (PG) 86 min. Drama. A beautiful young girl's dreams of stardom begin to fall apart when she is paid to take off her clothes in public. Cast: Philomena Nowlin, Ronald Warren, Jacqueline Dalya, Peter Jacob. Writer/Director: Bill Brame.

MISSISSIPPI BURNING. 1988. (R) 127 min. Drama. Forceful social drama about two FBI agents sent to Mississippi to investigate the mysterious disappearance of three civil rights workers in 1964. This is basically a mainstream film with a black backdrop, but it does point out America's often-erroneous national values of freedom and democracy, especially when juxtaposed to the active practice of racial hatred and bigotry. Cast: Gene Hackman, Willem Defoe, Francis McDormand, Brad Dourif, R. Lee Ermey, Gailard Sartain, Stephen Tobolowski, Michael Rooker, Pruitt Taylor Vince, Badja Djola, Kevin Dunn, Frankie Faison, Tom Mason, Park Overall. Director: Alan Parker. Writer: Chris Gerolmo. Cinematographer: Peter Biziou. Music: Trevor Jones. Awards: Oscars 1988: Best Cinematography. Berlin International Film Festival 1988: Best Actor (Hackman). National Board of Review 1988: Best Actor (Hackman), Best Director (Parker), Best Supporting Actress (McDormand).

MISSISSIPPI MASALA. 1992. (R) 118 min. Drama/Romance. Two cultures collide when an interracial romance causes tension in a small Southern town. Just like masala, the Indian seasoning that mixes different colored spices, a woman of East Indian descent falls in love with a hard-working young black man, but many people, including her father, find their mixture to be in bad taste. Cast: **Denzel Washington**, Sarita Choudhury, Roshan Seth, Shamila Tagore, **Charles S. Dutton, Joe Seneca**, Ranjit Chowdhry, Mira Nair. Director: Mira Nair. Writer: Sooni Taraporevala. Music: L. Subramaniam.

MO' BETTER BLUES. 1990. (R) 129 min. Music/Drama. Set to a jazz music backdrop, a dedicated horn player divides what little spare time he has between two women. Most of his time is spent practicing and trying to maintain his band, which, between the group's manager who has a serious gambling problem, and his overly ambitious saxophone player, is a real challenge. His music and his two lovers soon mix and blend into a strained way of life that begins to play off key. The Branford Marsalas Quartet provides music. Cast: **Denzel Washington, Spike Lee**, Joie Lee, **Wesley Snipes, Cynda Williams, Giancarlo Esposito, Robin Harris, Bill Nunn**, John Turturro, **Dick Anthony Williams**, Ruben Blades, Nicholas Turturro, **Samuel L. Jackson, Abby Lincoln**, Tracy C. Johns, **Joe Seneca**. Writer/Director: Spike Lee. Cinematographer: **Ernest R. Dickerson**. Music: Bill Lee, Branford Marsalis.

MOKAE, ZAKES (1935-). Actor. He was born in Johannesburg, South Africa, and attended the Royal Academy of Dramatic Arts. He is one of a few actors to bridge the South African racial divide by working with white writer Athol Fugard. In the 1950s, they organized the radical theater group The Rehearsal Room, and produced work that exposed the injustices going on in the country. Their productions of *The Blood Knot, Boesman and Lena, A Lesson from Aloes,* and *Master Harold and the Boys,* have been performed universally and are still being produced today. After being stifled by the oppressive racial policies of apartheid, he went to London, England, in 1961, and moved to the United States in 1969. He co-founded the Black Actors Theater in San Francisco with actor **Danny Glover** in 1980, and later won a Tony Award for a 1982 production of *Master Harold and the Boys.* His films include *Cry Freedom,* 1987; *The Serpent and the Rainbow,* 1988; and *A Dry White Season,* 1989. On television, he has guest starred on *Starsky and Hutch, Knight Rider, A Different World, Law & Order, The X Files, The West Wing,* and *Monk.* He is currently directing for the stage.

Filmography: *Dilemma,* 1962; *Darling,* 1965; *The Comedians,* 1967; *The River Niger,* 1976; *The Island,* 1980; *Cry Freedom,* 1987; *The Serpent and the Rainbow,* 1988; *A Dry White Season,* 1989; *Gross Anatomy,* 1989; *Dad,* 1989; *A Rage in Harlem,* 1991; *Body Parts,* 1991; *Dust Devil,* 1992; *Slaughter of the Innocents,* 1994; *Vampire in Brooklyn,* 1995; *Outbreak,* 1995; *Waterworld,* 1995; *Krippendorf's Tribe,* 1998.

MO' MONEY. 1992. (R) 97 min. Comedy. A small-time con artist tries to go straight when he takes a job at a credit card company. Despite the nurturing support of a beautiful co-worker, the temptation of having access to all that credit causes him to backslide and he is soon back to old tricks, including an even bigger scam being run by the company's own head of security. Cast: **Damon Wayans, Marlon Wayans, Stacey Dash,** Joe Santos, John Diehl, **Harry J. Lennix,** Mark Beltzman, Quincy Wong, Larry Brandenburg, Almayvonne. Director: Peter Macdonald. Writer: Damon Wayans. Cinematographer: Don Burgess. Music: Jay Gruska.

MONEY TALKS. 1997. (R) 97 min. Comedy. A small-time hustler somehow gets the credit for helping a criminal mastermind escape from prison. Now sought by the police, and rival mobsters, he makes a deal with a TV reporter to tell his story and stay alive and free. Cast: **Chris Tucker,** Charlie Sheen, Larry Hankin, Robertson Dean, Marty Levy, David Lee McLain, Mark Benninghoffen, Nathan Anderson, Victor Ferrerira, Gary Briggs, Richard Noyce, Damian Chapa, Kevin Lowe, **Faizon Love,** Gerard Ismeal. Director: Brett Ratner. Writers: Joel Cohen, Alec Sokolow.

MONKEY HUSTLE, THE. 1977. (PG) 90 min. Comedy/Drama. Both the good and bad elements of an inner-city community come together to stop a planned super freeway from coming through and destroying their neighborhood. Cast: **Yaphet Kotto, Rudy Ray Moore, Rosalind Cash, Debbie Morgan, Thomas Carter.** Director: Arthur Marks.

MONTE, ERIC. Writer. He began his career as a staff writer on the sitcom *All in the Family*, and became writer and co-creator of the series *Good Times.* He wrote the screenplay for the hit film *Cooley High*, 1975, and created the sitcom inspired by that movie, *What's Happening!*

Filmography: *All in the Family*, 1971; *Good Times*, 1974; *The Nine Lives of Fritz the Cat*, 1974; *Cooley High*, 1975; *What's Happening!* 1976; *The Wayans Bros.*, 1995; *Moesha*, 1996.

MOODY, LYNNE (1950-) Actress. She studied acting at the Pasadena Playhouse and her film credits include *Scream Blacula Scream*, 1973; *The Evil*, 1978; and *Some Kind of Hero*, 1982. Her **television** guest-starring roles include *All in the Family, The White Shadow, The Jeffersons, 21 Jumpstreet,* and *MacGyver.* She had recurring roles in *Soap, Hill Street Blues,* and *Chicago Hope.* She was a series regular on *ER, Knots Landing,* and the daytime soap opera *General Hospital.*

Filmography: *Scream Blackula Scream*, 1973; *Nightmare in Badham County*, 1976; *The Las Vegas Lady*, 1976; *The Evil*, 1978; **Roots: The Next Generation**, 1979; *Some Kind of Hero*, 1982; *Wait Till Your Mother Gets Home*, 1983; *A Fight for Jenny*, 1990; *Last Light*, 1993; *Ellen Foster*, 1997.

MOONEY, PAUL. Comedian, writer, actor. He was born in Louisiana and raised in Oakland, California. He wrote comedy material for comics **Redd Foxx** and **Richard Pryor**, and his own routines often focus on race and social issues. On **television**, he appeared on *The Richard Pryor Show, Def Comedy Jam,* and in his own stand-up performance show *Paul Mooney Live: Analyzing White America*, 2002. His film work includes bit parts in *Which Way is Up?* 1977; *Bustin' Loose*, 1981; and *Hollywood Shuffle*, 1987. He has written extensively for television and sitcoms, such as *Sanford and Son, Good Times, Saturday Night Live,* and *In Living Color.*

Filmography: *Carter's Army*, 1970; *Which Way is Up?* 1977; *The Buddy Holly Story*, 1978; *Bustin' Loose*, 1981; *Hollywood Shuffle*, 1987; *In the Army Now*, 1994; *High Frequency*, 1998;

Bamboozled, 2000; *The Old Settler*, 2001; *The Ketchup King*, 2002.

MOON OVER HARLEM. 1939. 67 min. Music/Drama. A lonely widow marries a smooth-talking gangster who, unbeknownst to her, makes his money in the numbers racket. They live the high life in this musical melodrama that includes a full-piece orchestra, a church choir, and plenty of dancing girls. Cast: Bud Harris, Cora Green, Alec Lovejoy, Sidney Bechet. Director: Edgar G. Ulmer.

MOORE, JUANITA (1922-). Actress. Moore was born in Los Angeles, California, and became a Cotton Club chorus girl before starting her film career as an extra. Her feature film debut was in *Pinky*, 1949, and she went on to play a variety of domestic's roles in films like *Affair in Trinidad*, 1952; *Queen Bee*, 1955; and *Band of Angels*, 1957. Her role as Annie Johnson in the remake of *Imitation of Life*, 1959, earned her **Academy Award** and **Golden Globe** nominations for Best Supporting Actress and brought her national acclaim. Her television guest appearances include *Wagon Train*, *Mannix*, *Marcus Welby, M. D.*, and *Judging Amy*. She continues to work in film and television with recent appearances in *The Kid*, 2000, and *8 Mile*, 2002.

Filmography: *Pinky*, 1949; *Affair in Trinidad*, 1952; *Queen Bee*, 1956; *The Girl Can't Help It*, 1956; *Band of Angels*, 1957; *Imitation of Life*, 1959; *The Singing Nun*, 1966; *Foxstyle*, 1973; *A Dream for Christmas*, 1973.

MOORE, MELBA (1945-). Singer, actress. This native of New York City studied piano and voice at the High School for Performing Arts, and earned her BA degree in music education from Montclair State College. She first came to prominence on the Broadway stage in 1969 when she replaced actress Diane Keaton in a production of the stage musical *Hair*. She was the first black actress to replace a white actress on Broadway and later became the first black actress to play the role of Fantine in *Les Miserables* in 1996. Her Tony award for best supporting actress with *Purlie* led to her **television** and recording career. She was often a performance guest on *The Tonight Show Starring Johnny Carson*, as well as *The Flip Wilson Show* and *Top of the Pops*. A string of other appearances and guest-hosting opportunities led to her co-hosting the variety show *The Melba Moore-Clifton Davis Show* in 1972. Moore recorded "Lift Every Voice and Sing," which became the official African American National Anthem.

Filmography: ***Cotton Comes to Harlem***, 1970; *Pigeons*, 1971; *Lost in the Stars*, 1974; *Hair*, 1979; *Charlotte Forten's Mission: Experiment in Freedom*, 1985; ***Def by Temptation***, 1990; ***The Fighting Temptations***, 2003.

MOORE, RUDY RAY (1937-). Comedian, producer, singer, actor. Moore began his singing and comedy career while in the U. S. Army and later moved to Los Angeles to test his singing chops. He wrote and recorded a number of R&B songs released on Norton Records, but did not have the money to get them played. While working in a local record store, he was inspired by a tale being told by the neighborhood wino about a bad rascal named Dolemite. Moore incorporated this raunchy character into his comedy material and the story immediately took off. He spent his own money to make his first X-rated party record *Dolemite for President*, which despite industry skepticism became a huge hit. His follow-up recordings include *Eat-Out More Often* and *I Can't Believe I Ate the Whole Thing*. The story of Dolemite was a prime candidate to join the **blaxploitation** film boom of the 1970s, with Moore in the title role, delivering his lines in rhythm and rhyme. The film ***Dolemite***, 1974, was both loved and criticized for its campy content and poor production values and is now a cult classic. It is packed with comedy, nudity, wild music, evil white folks, and beautiful women either dancing or performing butt-kicking karate moves. It spawned the sequel ***Dolemite II: The Human Tornado***, 1976. Moore's other films include ***Petey Wheatstraw, The Devil's Son-in-Law***, 1977, and ***The Avenging Disco Godfather***, 1977. He is often credited with being first to use explicit four-letter words in his comedy material, which influenced the work of **Richard Pryor** and **Eddie Murphy**. Now recognized as the Godfather of Rap for the way he delivered his material in rhymes, rap and hip-hop artists, such as 2 Live Crew and NWA, have used samples from Moore's albums. He has also worked in the studio with Big Daddy Kane. He continues to sing his R&B songs and perform his x-rated comedy routines on stage, often at cult movie film conventions around the world. Still acting and on the move, Moore also played a bounty hunter named Dangerous Dan in the science fiction flick, *It Came From Trafalo*. He is also working on the final edit on his new film *The Dolemite Explosion*, formerly known as *Return of Dolemite*, and plans to release, *Let Me Sing To You*, his new singing album by 2005.

Filmography: *Dolemite*, 1974; *Dolemite II*, 1976; *Petey Wheatstraw, The Devil's Son in Law*, 1977; *The Avenging Disco Godfather*, 1977.

MOORE, SHAMAR (1970-). Actor. This native of Oakland, California has become a popular actor of stage, **television**, and film. He graduated from Santa Clara University, where he studied communications and played varsity basketball. He is perhaps best known as Malcolm Winters in the daytime drama *The Young and the Restless*, or as the host of *Soul Train*, 1999-2003. His notable film work includes roles in *Mama Flora's Family*, 1998; *The Brothers*, 2001; and *Diary of a Mad Black Woman*, 2005.

Filmography: *Hav Plenty*, 1997; *Butter*, 1998; *Mama Flora's Family*, 1998; *Box Marley*, 2000; *The Brothers*, 2001; *Motives*, 2004; *The Seat Filler*, 2004; *Greener*, 2004; *Diary of a Mad Black Woman*, 2005.

MORELAND, MANTAN (1902-1973). Actor, comedian. Moreland was born in Monroe, Louisiana, and worked the vaudeville stage with Tim Moore and **Flournoy Miller**. He also worked on the Broadway stage in comedy and musical reviews, such as *Blackbirds of 1928*, *Singin' the Blues*, *Yeah Man*, and *Shuffle Along*. He made his film debut in *That's the Spirit*, 1933, and appeared as singing cowboy Herb Jeffries' sidekick in *Harlem on the Prairie*, 1937, and *Two-Gun Man from Harlem*, 1938. Known for spastic body movements and his bug-eyed style of comedy, Moreland became highly recognized during the 1940s as Birmingham Brown, the chauffeur in the *Charlie Chan* series of detective films. Television guest appearances include *Adam 12*, *Love, American Style*, and the *Bill Cosby Show*. On stage, he played the character of Estragon in the 1957 production of *Waiting for Godot*.

Filmography: *The Spirit of Youth*, 1937; *Harlem on the Prairie*, 1938; *Two-Gun Man from Harlem*, 1938; *Next Time I Marry*, 1938; *Frontier Scout*, 1938; *Mr. Washington Goes to Town*, 1940; *Up in the Air, 1940; The Gang's All Here, 1940; King of the Zombies, 1941; Phantom Killer*, 1942; *Law of the Jungle*, 1942; *Footlight Serenade*, 1942; *Revenge of the Zombies*, 1943; *The Pin-Up Girl*, 1944; *Meeting at Midnight*, 1944; *The Chinese Cat*, 1944; *Charlie Chan in the Secret Service*, 1944; *The Shanghai Cobra*, 1945; *The Scarlet Clue*, 1945; *The Jade Mask*, 1945; *Tall, Tan, and Terrific*, 1946; *Mantan Messes Up*, 1946; *Juke Joint*, 1947; *Spider Baby*, 1964; *The Young Nurses*, 1973.

MORGAN, DEBBIE (1956-). Actress. This Dunn, North Carolina-born actress made a name for herself in **television** before moving to film. She played notable roles in the TV series, such as *Behind the Screen*, *Generations*, and *Port Charles*, and she portrayed the character of Dr. Angela Baxter on the daytime drama *All My Chil-*

dren. Notable film roles include *Eve's Bayou*, 1997, and *Love and Basketball*, 2000.

Filmography: *Eve's Bayou*, 1997; *Asunder*, 1998; *She's All That*, 1999; *The Hurricane*, 1999; *Love and Basketball*, 2000: *Woman Thou Art Loosed*, 2004; *Coach Carter*, 2005; *Relative Strangers*, 2005; *The Blackman's Guide to Understanding Black Women*, 2005; *Once in a Wifetime*, 2006.

MORRIS, GREG (1933-1996). Actor. This accomplished actor was born in Cleveland, Ohio, and moved to Hollywood in the early 1960s after a few minor roles on the Seattle stage. He worked in the **television** series *The Dick Van Dyke Show* and *The Twilight Zone*, and was then cast as electronics expert Barney Collier on *Mission Impossible*. His other TV regular role was as Lt. George Nelson on the series *Vega$*, in 1978. His film roles include *The Sword of Ali Baba*, 1965; *Countdown at Kusini*, 1976; and the miniseries *Roots: The Next Generation*, 1979. He is the father of actors Iona and Phil Morris.

Filmography: *The New Interns*, 1964; *The Lively Set*, 1964; *The Sword of Ali Baba*, 1965; *Blade Rider, Revenge of the Indian Nations*, 1966; *Countdown at Kusini*, 1976; *S. T. A. B.*, 1976; *The Jesse Owens Story*, 1984; *Tropical Gamble*, 1990.

MORTON, JOE (1947-). Actor. Born in New York City, Morton made his Broadway debut in a production of *Hair*, and received a Tony Award nomination for his performance in *Raisin*. His big-screen break came with portraying the title role in director John Sayles' *The Brother from Another Planet*, 1984. He has since stayed busy working in both television and film.

Filmography: *The Brother from Another Planet*, 1984; *Trouble in Mind*, 1986; *Crossroads*, 1986; *Alone in the Neon Jungle*, 1987; *Zelly and Me*, 1988; *The Good Mother*, 1988; *Tap*, 1989; *Skin*, 1989; *Terminator 2: Judgment Day*, 1991; *City of Hope*, 1991; *Of Mice and Men*, 1992; *The Legacy of Lies*, 1992; *Forever Young*, 1992; *The Walking Dead*, 1994; *Speed*, 1994; *The Inkwell*, 1994; *Lone Star*, 1995; *The Pest*, 1996; *Executive Decision*, 1996; *Speed 2: Cruise Control*, 1997; *Miss Ever's Boys*, 1997; *The Apt Pupil*, 1997; *Blues Brothers 2000*, 1998; *Mutiny*, 1999; *The Astronaught's Wife*, 1999; *What Lies Beneath*, 2000; *Bounce*, 2000; *Ali*, 2001; *Dragonfly*, 2002.

MOS DEF (1973-). Hip-hop artist, actor. Born Dante Terrell Smith in Brooklyn, New York, he made a name for himself on the underground hip-hop circuit by working with such artists as De La Soul and the Bush Babees. He released the single "Body Rock" with Q-Tip from A Tribe Called Quest, and was on the Lyricist Lounge tour with Company Flow and The Roots. He has since evolved into a fresh and conscientious voice on the new school hip-hop scene. He made his TV acting debut in *God Bless the Child*, 1988, and worked on *The Cosby Mysteries* TV series, 1994. His breakout big-screen role was in ***Brown Sugar***, 2002, and he was cast as the lead in the TV movie *Something the Lord Made*, 2004.

Filmography: *The Hard Way*, 1991; *Ghosts*, 1997; *Where's Marlowe?* 1998; *Island of the Dead*, 2000; ***Bamboozled***, 2000; *Monster's Ball*, 2001; *Showtime*, 2002; ***Civil Brand***, 2002; *Brown Sugar*, 2002; *The Italian Job*, 2003; *The Woodsman*, 2004; *The Hitchhiker's Guide to the Galaxy*, 2005; *The Italian Job II*, 2006.

MOSES, ETHEL. Actress, dancer. Nicknamed the Black Jean Harlow, Moses was a popular actress and dancer during Harlem's golden Era in the 1930s. Before appearing in movies, she danced and entertained at the Cotton Club and the Ubangi Club, and later starred in several of **Oscar Micheaux**'s films, including *Birthright*, 1924; *Underworld*, 1937; and *God's Stepchildren*, 1938. Her acting was natural and charismatic, and she was once called one of the most beautiful women in America.

Filmography: *Birthright*, 1924; *Temptation*, 1935; *Underworld*, 1937; *God's Step Children*, 1938; *Gone Harlem*, 1939; *Birthright*, 1939.

MOSLEY, ROGER E. (1938-). Actor. He was born in Los Angeles, California, and is perhaps best known as T. C. Calvin on the TV series *Magnum P. I.* He began his acting career during the **blaxploitation** era of the early 1970s in such films as ***Hit Man***, 1972; ***Sweet Jesus Preacher Man***, 1973; ***The Mack***, 1973; and ***The River Niger***, 1976. He was cast in the title role as blues singer Huddie Ledbetter in the biopic ***Leadbelly***, 1976. Other television appearances include the miniseries ***Roots: The Next Generation***, 1979, the telepic ***I Know Why the Caged Bird Sings***, 1979, and the series *You Take the Kids*, *Hangin' With Mr. Cooper*, and *Rude Awakening*. He portrayed the role of Sgt. James Hammer in the film *Hammerlock*, 2000.

Filmography: *The New Centurions*, 1972; *Hickey & Boggs*, 1972; *Hit Man*, 1972; *Sweet Jesus Preacher Man*, 1973; *Terminal Island*, 1973; *The Mack*, 1973; *McQ*, 1974; ***Darktown Strutters***, 1975; *Stay Hungry*, 1976; ***Drum***, 1976; *The River Niger*, 1976; *Leadbelly*, 1976; ***The Greatest***, 1977; *Semi-Tough*, 1977; *Big Time*, 1977; *Steel*, 1980; *Pray TV*, 1980; *The White Lions*, 1981;

Heart Condition, 1990; *Pentathlon*, 1994; ***A Thin Line Between Love & Hate***, 1996; *Letters from a Killer*, 1998; *Hammerlock*, 2000.

MOSLEY, WALTER (1952-). Writer. He was born in Los Angeles, California, and wrote his popular series of novels based on the character of 1940s private eye, Easy Rawlins, who was portrayed by **Denzel Washington** in the book-based film *Devil in a Blue Dress*, 1995. Mosley made a rare cameo appearance in the role of Congressman Rawlins in the political thriller *The Manchurian Candidate*, 2004, which starred Denzel Washington.

  Filmography: *Devil in a Blue Dress*, 1995; ***Always Outnumbered, Always Outgunned***, 1998; *The Henry Lee Project*, 2003.

MOSS, CARLTON (1909-1997). Writer, producer, director. Born in Newark, New Jersey, Moss was a well-known documentary filmmaker during the 1940s and 1950s. He is best known for his productions *The Negro Soldier*, 1944, and *Frederick Douglass: The House on Cedar Hill*, 1953.

  Filmography: *The Negro Soldier*, 1944; *Frederick Douglass: The House on Cedar Hill*, 1953.

MOTEN, ETTA (1901-2004). Singer, actress. Born in Weimer, Texas, Moten graduated from the University of Kansas and became a star of stage and screen. Her singing voice was overdubbed in several early films, including *Gold Diggers of 1933* (song, "Remember My Forgotten Man), and she was the uncredited singing voice for Theresa Harris in *Professional Sweetheart*, 1933. She appeared in the film *Flying Down to Rio*, 1933, as the Carioca Singer. On stage, Moten played the role of Bess in a 1942 revival of *Porgy and Bess*, but refused to sing the "N" word, which writer George Gershwin eventually wrote out of the libretto. Other stage performances include *Lysistrata* and *Sugar Hill*. At the invitation of President and Mrs. Franklin D. Roosevelt, she became the first African American stage and screen star to perform at the White House in 1933. For many years, she conducted her own radio show for WMAQ/NBC in Chicago.

  Filmography: *Gold Diggers of 1933*; *Bombshell*, 1933; *Flying Down to Rio*, 1933.

MOTOWN. *See* **GORDY, BERRY.**

MOVING. 1988. (R) 89 min. Comedy. In order to accept the job of his dreams, an eccentric engineer packs up his family and moves them from New Jersey to Idaho. Not surprisingly, the move, his new job, and his family life become a nightmare. Cast: **Richard Pryor, Randy Quaid, Dana Carvey, Dave Thomas, Rodney Dangerfield, Stacy Dash**. Director: Alan Metter. Writer: Andy Breckman. Music: Howard Shore.

MR. T. (1952-). Professional wrestler, actor. He was born in Chicago, Illinois, and became well known for his partially shaved head and "Mohawk" hairdo. This muscular, one-time night club bouncer came to national prominence when he was cast as Sylvester Stallone's main boxing opponent in *Rocky III*, 1982. He was later cast as Sgt. B. A. Baracus on the TV series *The A-Team*, and starred in the short-lived series *T. and T.*

Filmography: *Penitentiary II*, 1982; *Rocky III*, 1982; *D. C. Cab*, 1983; *The Toughest Man in the World*, 1984; *Freaked*; 1993; *The Magic of the Golden Bear: Goldy III*, 1994; *Spy Hard*, 1996; *Not Another Teen Movie*, 2001; *Judgment*, 2001.

MR. WASHINGTON GOES TO TOWN. 1940. Comedy. This story line follows the exploits of a bellhop in a hotel filled with strange guests and a gorilla. It was **Mantan Moreland**'s first starring role and was advertised as "the first sound comedy feature with an all-colored cast." Cast: Mantan Moreland, **Flournoy Miller, Monte Hawley**, Arthur Ray, Florence O'Brien, DeForrest Coven, **Cleo Desmond**, Maceo Sheffield. Director: Jed Buell.

MURDER IN HARLEM. 1935. Drama. The film is based on the **Oscar Micheaux** novel, *The Story of Dorothy Stanfield*. A night watchman at a chemical factor discovers the body of a murdered white woman and becomes the prime suspect. Oscar Micheaux makes a rare cameo appearance as a detective. Cast: **Clarence Brooks**, Dorothy Van Engle, Andrew Bishop, Alec Lovejoy, Laura Bowman, **Bee Freeman**, Lionel Monagas, **Alice B. Russell**, Sandy Burns, Lea Morris, Joe Brown Jr., Eunice Wilson, Henrietta Loveless, Lorenzo McClane, Helen Lawrence. Director/Writer: Oscar Micheaux. Cinematographer: Charles Levine. Music: Clarence Williams.

MURDER ON LENOX AVENUE. 1941. 60 min. Drama. An angry man vows revenge after he is ousted as head of Harlem's Better Business Bureau. Cast: Alec Lovejoy, Mamie Smith, Norman Astwood, Augustus Smith, Alberta Perkins, Edna Mae Harris. Flo Lee. Director: Arthur Dreifuss. Writers: Frank Wilson, Vincent Valentini.

MURPHY, EDDIE (1961-). Actor, comedian. Born in Brooklyn, New York, Murphy's talent to make people laugh began early, and he was a stand-up comic by age 15. He landed a prestigious spot on NBC's *Saturday Night Live*, seasons 1980-84, and was a powerful mainstay of those years. His feature film debut came in the highly successful *48 Hrs.*, 1982, and he quickly became a major box office draw. He went on to star in several high-grossing films, including *Another 48 Hrs.*, 1990, and the *Beverly Hill Cop* series of films. Murphy made his directorial debut with **Harlem Nights**, 1989, and through Eddie Murphy Productions he has produced several sitcom pilots, the made-for-TV movie *The Kid Who Loved Christmas*, 1990, and the CBS sitcom *The Royal Family* starring vintage comedian **Redd Foxx**.

Filmography: *48 Hrs.*, 1982; *Trading Places*, 1983; *Beverly Hills Cop*, 1984; *Best Defense*, 1984; *The Golden Child*, 1986; *Beverly Hills Cop 2*, 1987; *Coming to America*, 1988; *Harlem Nights*, 1989; *Another 48 Hrs.*, 1990; *The Distinguished Gentleman*, 1992; *Boomerang*, 1992; *Beverly Hills Cop 3*, 1994; *Vampire in Brooklyn*, 1995; *The Nutty Professor*, 1996; *Metro*, 1996; *Mulan*, 1998; *Holy Man*, 1998; *Dr. Dolittle*, 1998; *Life*, 1999; *Bowfinger*, 1999; *Nutty Professor 2: The Klumps*, 2000; *Shrek*, 2001; *Dr. Doolittle 2*, 2001; *Showtime*, 2002; *I Spy*, 2002; *The Adventures of Pluto Nash*, 2002; *Daddy Daycare*, 2003; *The Haunted House*, 2004.

MUSE, CLARENCE (1889-1979). Actor, director, playwright. Born in Baltimore, Maryland, Clarence Muse was destined for the arts. He studied law at Dickenson University in Pennsylvania, performed with a hotel quartet in Palm Beach, Florida, and toured the South with a stock company for a while. From there, he returned to New York and performed on the vaudeville stage, which led to several plays with the now-famous Lincoln Theater and **Lafayette Players** in Harlem. On Broadway, Muse apeared in *Dr. Jekyll and Mr. Hyde*, a controversial production where the white roles were portrayed by blacks in white face, and he became known as an actor and a singer. His first film role was in Fox Studio's **Hearts in Dixie**, 1929, where he portrayed the character of Nappus, a 90-year-old tenant farmer who wanted a better life for his family. It was promoted as the first all-black, all-talking, all-singing musical. Muse was chosen to direct the Federal Theater Project's Los Angeles run of Hal Johnson's *Run Little Chillun*, which ran for two years. He would later adapt the stage play for the screen as *Way Down South*, 1939. He went on to play many more roles in films like *So Red the Rose*, 1935; *Tales of Manhattan*, 1942; and ***Buck and the Preacher***, 1971. He also performed in concerts and on radio programs. His last film role was in *The Black Stallion*, 1979. Muse was once one of the highest-paid actors in Hollywood. He wrote, produced, directed, and starred in ***Broken Strings***, 1940, about a classic violinist, and he also wrote the screenplay. Muse devoted much of his life to gaining more roles for African Americans and altering the **stereotypical** images so often depicted in Hollywood films.

Filmography: *The White Zombie*, 1932; *So Red the Rose*, 1935; *Prison Train*, 1938; *Way Down South*, 1939; *The Gang of Mine*, 1940; *Broken Strings*, 1940; *The Invisible Ghost*, 1941; *The Gentleman From Dixie*, 1941; *Tales of Manhattan*, 1942; *Watch on the Rhine*, 1943; *A Dream for Christmas*, 1973; ***Buck and the Preacher***, 1974; *The Black Stallion*, 1979.

MY BROTHER'S WEDDING. 1983. 115 min. Drama. A man must choose between being the best man at his brother's wedding, whom he despises for his pretentiousness, or attending his best friend's funeral. Cast: Everett Silas, Jessie Holmes, Gaye Shannon-Burnett, Ronnie Bell, Dennis Kemper, Sally Easter, Frances E. Nealy, **Sy Richardson**. Director/writer/cinematographer: **Charles Burnett**.

N

NATIONAL BLACK PROGRAMMING CONSORTIUM (NBPC). This non-profit national media arts organization was created in 1979, in response to the lack of African American programming on the Public Broadcasting System (PBS). The NBPC is committed to the preservation, funding, promotion, and distribution of positive images of African Americans and the African Diaspora. The organization has a long-standing history of providing on-going workshops and training to emerging, mid-level, and seasoned producers. Their goal is to enhance producer skills while keeping them updated on the latest developments in media and public television. The NBPC supports insightful outreach programs targeted for the national PBS schedule. In the spirit of healthy competition, it presents a bi-annual international film festival called Prized Pieces. Since 1990, NBPC has awarded over $6 million in grants to producers and directors of African American film and video projects.

NATIVE SON. 1951. 91 min. Urban Drama. This film is based on the novel by **Richard Wright**. A young man from a Chicago slum is hired by a rich family to be a chauffeur for their daughter. He unintentionally kills her and burns the body to cover his crime, but is eventually brought to justice. Cast: Richard Wright, Willa Pearl Curtis, Ruth Robert, George D. Green, Jean Wallace, Nicholas Joy, Gloria Madison, Charles Cain. Writer/Director: Pierre Chenal. Cinematographer: Antonio Merayo. Music: Juan Ehlert.

NATIVE SON. 1986. (R) 111 min. Urban Drama. This is a toned-down remake of **Richard Wright**'s classic novel about a poor black kid who unintentionally kills a rich white girl and attempts to hide his crime, but is eventually convicted of murder. Cast: Victor Love, Geraldine Page, **Oprah Winfrey**, Matt Dillon, John Karlen, Elizabeth McGovern, **Akosua Busia**, John McMartin, **Art Evans**, **Willard Pugh**, David Rasche. Director: Jerrold Freedman. Writer: **Richard Wesley**. Cinematographer: Thomas Burstyn. Music: James Mtume.

NEAL, ELISE (1970-). Actress. She was born in Memphis, Tennessee, and studied at the Philadelphia College of Performing Arts before moving to New York City. Her **television** guest appearances include shows, such as *Law & Order, Family Matters, Living Single,* and *The Wayans Bros.* She was a regular on the daytime soap opera *Loving,* the TV series *Sea Quest DSV,* and the sitcoms *The Hughleys* and *All of Us.* Her film appearances include *How to Be a Player,* 1997; *Scream 2,* 1997; and *Playas Ball,* 2003.

Filmography: *Malcolm X,* 1992; *Let It Be Me,* 1995; *Rosewood,* 1997; *How to Be a Player,* 1997; *Money Talks,* 1997; *Scream 2,* 1997; *Restaurant,* 1998; *Mission to Mars,* 2000; *Sacred Is the Flesh,* 2001; *The Rising Place,* 2001; *Paid in Full,* 2002; *Playas Ball,* 2003; *Holla,* 2004.

NEGOTIATOR, THE. 1998. (R) 115 min. Drama. Officers from his own unit frame a police hostage negotiator for murder and theft. In a fit of desperation, he takes the Internal Affairs Bureau hostage and demands that a negotiator from another precinct be brought in to discuss the release of his prisoners. Together, they expose the real culprits. Cast: **Samuel L. Jackson**, Kevin Spacey, David Morse, Ron Rifkin, John Spencer, **Regina Taylor**, J. T. Walsh, Siobhan Fallon, Paul Giamatti, Paul Guilfoyle, Carlos Gomez, Nestor Serrano. Director: **F. Gary Gray**. Writers: James DeMonaco, Kevin Fox. Cinematographer: Russell Carpenter. Music: Graeme Revell.

NELSON, SEAN (1981-). Actor. Nelson began his acting career at an early age and first starred in the title role of *Fresh*, 1994. His numerous **television** guest appearances include *Law & Order*, *Homicide: Life on the Streets*, and *New York Undercover*, and he costarred as DeAndre McCullough in the urban-based miniseries *The Corner*, 2000.

Filmography: *Fresh*, 1994; *American Buffalo*, 1996; *Stranger in the Kingdom*, 1998; *The Wood*, 1998; *The Corner*, 2000; *The Year That Trembled*, 2002; *Date*, 2004; *The Orphan King*, 2005; *Their Eyes Were Watching God*, 2005.

NEW JACK CITY. 1991. (R) 101 min. Urban Drama. This is a drama about an inner-city drug lord who takes over a housing project to sell his wares. Business is good until an undercover cop infiltrates his organization to bring him down. Cast: **Wesley Snipes, Ice T, Mario Van Peebles, Chris Rock**, Judd Nelson, **Allen Payne**, Tracy C. Johns, Kim Park, **Vanessa Williams**, Nick Ashford, **Thalmus Rasulala, Michael Michele, Bill Nunn**, Russell Wong. Director: Mario Van Peebles. Writers: Keith Critchlow, Barry Michael Cooper. Cinematographer: Francis Kenny. Music: Roger Mourland, Michel Colombier.

NEW JERSEY DRIVE. 1995. (R) 98 min. Urban Drama. Inspired by a series of *New York Times* articles by Michel Marriott, an ambitious young man gets bored with his Newark surroundings and starts stealing cars to joyride with his friends, which puts the cops on his trail and his future in jeopardy. Cast: Sharon Corley, Gabriel Casseus, Saul Stein, Andre Moore, Donald Adeosun, Conrad Martin, Jr., Deven Eggleston, Gwen McGee, Koran C. Thomas, Samantha Brown, Christine Baranski, Robert Jason Jackson, Roscoe Orman, Dwight Errington Myers, Gary DeWitt Marshall. Director: Nick Gomez. Writers: Nick Gomez, Michel Marriott. Cinematographer: Adam Kimmel. Music: Wendy Blackstone.

NEWTON, THANDIE (1972-). Actress. She was born in Zambia and raised in England. She made her acting debut in *Flirting*, 1991, and continued to act while earning her anthropology degree at Cambridge University. Her big break came working opposite Tom Cruise in *Mission Impossible II*, 2000, and she was cast in the title role of *Beloved*, 1998. On **television**, she landed a recurring role on the NBC medical series *ER*.

Filmography: *Flirting*, 1991; *The Young Americans*, 1993; *Interview with a Vampire: The Vampire Chronicles*, 1994; *Loaded*, 1994; *Jefferson in Paris*; 1995; *The Journey of August King*, 1995;

The Leading Man, 1996; ***Gridlock'd***, 1997; *Besieged*, 1998; ***Beloved***, 1998; *Mission Impossible II*, 2000; *It Was an Accident*, 2000; *The Truth about Charlie*, 2002; *Shade*, 2003; *The Chronicles of Riddick*, 2004; ***Crash***, 2004.

NEXT FRIDAY. 2000. (R) 93 min. Urban Comedy. This is the sequel to the film **Friday**. The neighborhood bully is out of jail and out for revenge, so Craig flees to safety in the suburbs at the home of his lottery-winning uncle. While there, he spurns the lurid advances of his would-be aunt, and keeps himself busy by ripping off some drug-dealing neighbors. Cast: **Ice Cube**, Tommy "Tiny" Lister, **John Witherspoon**, Justin Pierce, Jacob Vargas, Lobo Sebastian, Rolando Molina, **Tamala Jones**, **Mike Epps**, Don Curry, Lisa Rodriquez, Kym E. Whitley, Amy Hill, Robin Allen. Director: Steve Carr. Writer: Ice Cube. Cinematographer: Christopher Baffa. Music: **Terence Blanchard**.

NICHOLAS BROTHERS, THE. Fayard (1914-2006), Harold (1921-2000). Dancers. Even as children (age 13 and 7), they were one of the greatest dance teams ever. Their parents were musicians and ran the orchestra at the Standard Theater in Philadelphia. Once they saw what their little boys could do, the proud parents got them a job at the club. Word quickly spread and they were soon performing at the world-famous Cotton Club in New York City. Always sharply dressed and exuding class and style, they excited audiences around the world for more than 60 years with their unique style, brilliant choreography, and acrobatic excellence. Whether on the vaudeville stage, in nightclubs, theaters, or on film and television, they were more than impressive with their smooth mix of tap, jazz, and ballet. Their first film appearance was in the musical short, ***Pie, Pie Blackbird***, 1932, with Eubie Blake and **Nina Mae McKinney**. Movie mogul Samuel Goldwyn invited them to Hollywood to appear in their first feature film, *Kid Millions*, 1943, with Eddie Cantor. They danced and sometimes sang in a total of six films for 20th Century Fox, but their most memorable dance number was perhaps in ***Stormy Weather***, 1943, where they concluded with an awesome routine in which they leapfrogged over each other down a curved staircase. Their first Broadway show was the *Ziegfeld Follies* with Bob Hope, Eve Arden, and **Josephine Baker**. They starred in the London production of Lew Leslie's *Blackbirds of 1936*, and made many more international appearances. In their later years, both Harold and Fayard continued to perform individually on and off-Broadway, and in many theatrical productions, including *St Louis Woman*, *Stompin' at the Savoy*, in San Francisco (Harold), and *So-*

phisticated Ladies in Los Angeles (Harold). When it came to acting, Fayard played a bit part in *The Liberation of L. B. Jones*, 1970, and Harold was cast in small but comedic roles in, *Uptown Saturday Night*, 1974, and *The Five Heartbeats*, 1991. They have received numerous awards and accolades for their lifetime of quality entertainment, including a star on the Hollywood Walk of Fame, 1994. The documentary *We Sing, We Dance: The Nicholas Brothers*, contains interviews and film clips of their performances, and has aired on Public Broadcasting Stations (PBS).

Filmography: *Pie, Pie Blackbird*, 1932; *Kid Millions*, 1934; *An All Colored Vaudeville Show*, 1935; *The Big Broadcast of 1936*, 1935; *Down Argentine Way*, 1940; *Sun Valley Serenade*, 1941; *Orchestra Wives*, 1942; *Stormy Weather*, 1943; *The Pirate*, 1948; *Bonjour Kathrin*, 1956; *The Liberation of L. B. Jones*, 1970 (Fayard); *Uptown Saturday Night*, 1974 (Harold); *Tap*, 1989 (Harold).

NICHOLAS, DENISE (1946-). Actress, writer. She received her B. A. degree from the University of Michigan, then studied acting with Paul Mann and dance with Louis Johnson. She is a seasoned actress on stage, film, and **television** with a long list of cast credits dating back to the 1960s. Her first off-Broadway appearance was in the 1966 revue *Viet Rock*. She was also in the productions of *Ceremonies in Dark Old Men*, and *Dame Lorraine*. She was a member of the famed Negro Ensemble Company, and also active with the New Federal Theater, and the Free Southern Theater in Mississippi and Louisiana. She first became well known as Liz McIntyre, a high school teacher on the television series *Room 222*. Other TV credits include *Police Story*, *Baby, I'm Back*, *Magnum P. I.*, and *In the Heat of the Night*, a show in which she was also a writer. Nicholas received two L. A. Emmy Awards for the local television special *Voices of Our People*. She has received five NAACP **Image Awards** and appeared in several telefilms, including *Ring of Passion*, 1978, and *The Children Shall Lead*, 1985. She has toured with the stage productions of *In White America*, *Purlie Victorious*, *Waiting for Godot*, and *Three Boards and a Passion*. Her feature film debut was in *Blackula*, 1972. Nicholas is the former wife of director Gil Moses, then soul singer Bill Withers, and is now married to CBS sportscaster Jim Hill.

Filmography: *Blackula*, 1972; *The Soul of Nigger Charley*, 1973; *Mr. Rocco*, 1975; *Let's Do It Again*, 1995; *A Piece of the Action*, 1977; *Capricorn One*, 1978; *Sophisticated Gents*, 1981; *Marvin & Tige*, 1983; *Ghost Dad*, 1990; *Ritual*, 2000.

NIGHTJOHN. 1996. (PG-13) 96 min. Drama. This is a made-for-cable movie shot on location in Sumpter, South Carolina, at Rip Raps Plantation. A newly bought slave who can read and write arrives on the Walker Plantation, and a 12-year-old cabin mate is determined to be his student, even though learning to read and write is against the law for slaves. Cast: **Carl Lumbly**, Allison Jones, Beau Bridges, Lorraine Toussaint, **Bill Cobbs**, Kathleen York, Gabriel Casseus, Tom Nowicki, Monica Ford, Joel Thomas Traywick. Director: **Charles Burnett**. Writer: Bill Cain. Cinematographer: Elliot Davis. Music: Stephen James Taylor.

NORMAN FILM MANUFACTURING COMPANY. Richard Edward Norman founded this company in 1912 with his brother Kenneth Bruce Norman. They were two white producers from Middleburg, Florida, who made and distributed several "all-black-cast" films during the silent years of cinema. Norman began by traveling through the Midwest, filming local events and writing scenarios as he went along. He cast local townsfolk in the character roles and would sell tickets to screenings in churches, schools, or at the local theater, offering a 60–40% split of the receipts. His movies were usually love stories using the same situation over and over while adapting the basic concept to each town's unique locations. In 1916, Norman returned to Jacksonville, Florida, to make feature-length films for national distribution. His first was the all-white cast, *The Green-Eyed Monster*, 1916, a romantic melodrama that he remade in 1919 with an all-black cast. Norman's other notable African American films include *The Crimson Skull*, 1921; *The Flying Ace*, 1926; and *Black Gold*, 1926. In later years, Norman distributed sound versions of the **Oscar Micheaux** films *The Millionaire*, 1927; *The Exile*, 1931; and *The Girl from Chicago*, 1932.

NORMAN...IS THAT YOU? 1976. (PG) 91 min. Comedy. A man finds out his son is gay and goes about trying to straighten him out. Cast: **Redd Foxx**, **Pearl Bailey**, **Michael Warren**, Dennis Dugan, **Tamara Dobson**, Vernee Watson-Johnson, Jane Meadows, Wayland Flowers. Director: George Schlatter. Writers: Sam Bobrick, Ron Clark.

NORMAN, MAIDIE (1912-1998). Actress. She was born in Lima, Ohio. At the urging of one of her teachers, her father enrolled her in drama school and by the time she was 10, Norman was acting in Shakespearean plays. By the age of 12, she had committed her life to the stage. After receiving four scholarship offers in her senior year in high school, she decided to attend Bennett College, where she started an in-depth study of black theater history. After earning her B.A. degree from Bennett, she received her M.A. in theater at Columbia University. Norman moved to Hollywood in 1943, but her first major role was in *The Burning Cross*, 1948, and she followed with roles in *The Well*, 1951, and *Bright Road*, 1953. Determined to bring dignity to her characters, she often clashed with directors over role interpretations and managed to portray a strong and dignified maid in *Whatever Happened to Baby Jane*, 1962. On stage, she has played Odessa in *The Amen Corner* and Mama in *A Raisin in the Sun*. She was appointed as artist in residence at Stanford University in the 1968-1969 school year, when she taught acting classes and performed with the Stanford Repertory Company, and later taught black theater history at UCLA. Her **television** guest appearances include roles in *The Jeffersons*, *Goodtimes*, and *Cannon*. She was a member of the Actor's Lab, the Negro Arts Theater, and a 1977 inductee into the **Black Filmmakers Hall of Fame**.

Filmography: *The Burning Cross*, 1948; *The Well*, 1951; *Bright Road*, 1953; *Torch Song*, 1953; *About Mrs. Leslie*, 1954; *Susan Slept Here*, 1954; *Tarzan's Hidden Jungle*, 1955; *The Opposite Sex*, 1956; *Written on the Wind*, 1957; *Whatever Happened to Baby Jane*, 1962; *The Final Come Down*, 1972; *Maurie*, 1973; *A Star Is Born*, 1976; *Airport '77*, 1977; *Movie Movie*, 1979.

NOTHING BUT A MAN. 1964. 95 min. Drama. A roaming railroad worker marries a schoolteacher and tries to settle down in a small and bigoted Southern town. He takes a job at the local sawmill but is soon fired and labeled a trouble-maker for speaking up about injustices on the job. Life becomes complicated and he begins to question his decisions. Cast: **Ivan Dixon**, **Abbey Lincoln**, **Gloria Foster**, **Julius W. Harris**, Martin Priest, **Yaphet Kotto**, Leonard Parker, Stanley Greene, Helen Lounck, Helene Arrindell. Director: Michael Roemer. Writers: Michael Roemer, Robert M. Young. Cinematographer: Robert M. Young. Awards: National Film Registry 1993.

NO TIME FOR ROMANCE, 1948. Musical/Romance. This was the first all-black cast musical to be filmed in color. A shy composer discovers a singing star and together they make music that expands their careers. On their rise to the top, they must overcome a jealous rival's plan to ruin them. Features the bebop/jazz music of Austin McCoy. Cast: Eunice Wilson, **Bill Walker**, Austin McCoy, Shirley Haven, **Joel Fluellen**, DeForest Coven.

NO WAY BACK, 1974. (R) 92 min. **Blaxploitation**. Former pro-football-star-turned-actor **Fred Williamson** wrote, produced, and directed this action-packed battle against the white establishment. As mercenary Jess Crowder, he takes the fight to "the man," demanding his rights and respect. Cast: Fred Williamson, Tracy Reed, Charles Woolf, Virginia Gregg, Don Cornelius. Writer/Director: Fred Williamson.

NO WAY OUT. 1950. 105 min. Drama. Two racists are shot while doing wrong and taken to the hospital. When one dies, the other blames his death on the black doctor who could not save his brother's life and has his bigoted friends make trouble. Cast: **Sidney Poitier**, Richard Widmark, Stephen McNally, Linda Darnell, Harry Bellaver, Stanley Ridges, **Ruby Dee, Ossie Davis**. Director: Joseph L. Mankiewicz. Writers: Joseph L. Mankiewicz, Lesser Samuels. Cinematographer: Milton Krasner. Music: Alfred Newman.

NUNEZ, MIGUEL A., JR. (1964-). Actor. This New York City-born actor has amassed an impressive list of **television** and film credits. He is perhaps best remembered as attorney Maxie Sparks on the TV series *Sparks*, and he portrayed the title role in the film *Juwanna Mann*, 2002.

Filmography: *Joy of Sex*, 1984; *Friday the 13th: A New Beginning*, 1985; *The Return of the Living Dead*, 1985; *Dangerously Close*, 1986; *Jumpin' Jack Flash*, 1986; *Action Jackson*, 1988; **Harlem Nights**, 1989; *Shadowzone*, 1990; *Lethal Weapon 3*, 1992; *Round Trip to Heaven*, 1992; *Hard Vice*, 1994; *There Goes My Baby*, 1994; *Street Fighter*, 1994; *Slam Dunk Ernest*, 1995; *Carnosaur 2*, 1995; **A Thin Line Between Love and Hate**, 1996; *For Richer or Poorer*, 1997; **Why Do Fools Fall in Love?**, 1998; **Life**, 1999; *If You Only Knew*, 2000; **Nutty Professor II: The Klumps**, 2000; *MacArthur Park*, 2001; *Flossin*, 2001; *ZigZag*, 2002; *Scooby-Doo*, 2002; *Juwanna Mann*, 2002; *The Adventures of Pluto Nash*, 2002; *Clean Up Men*, 2005.

NUNN, BILL (1953-). Actor. He was born in Pittsburgh, Pennsylvania, and graduated from Morehouse College in Atlanta, Georgia. He first came to prominence in the role of Radio Raheem, the silent, boom-box-toting thug in director **Spike Lee's** *Do the Right Thing*, 1989. Nunn has appeared in many of Lee's later films, including *Mo' Better Blues*, 1990, and *He Got Game*, 1998. He was trained on the Atlanta stage and has played a wide spectrum of characters on film, and appeared in three **television** pilots and several series.

Filmography: *Sharky's Machine*, 1981; **School Daze**, 1988; *Do the Right Thing*, 1989; **Glory**, 1989; **Def by Temptation**, 1990; *Cadillac Man*, 1990; *Mo' Better Blues*, 1990; **New Jack City**, 1991; *Regarding Henry*, 1991; *Sister Act*, 1992; *Save Me*, 1993; *Blood Brothers*, 1993; *Loaded Weapon 1*, 1993; *Dangerous Heart*, 1994; *The Last Seduction*, 1994; *Candyman: Farewell to the Flesh*, 1995; *Things to Do in Denver When You're Dead*, 1995; *Canadian Bacon*, 1995; *Money Train*, 1995; *True Crime*, 1996; *Bulletproof*, 1996; *Extreme Measures*, 1996; *Kiss the Girls*, 1997; **Always Outnumbered, Always Outgunned**, 1998; *He Got Game*, 1998; *Ambushed*, 1998; *The Tic Code*, 1999; **Foolish**, 1999; *Lockdown*, 2000; *Spider-Man*, 2002; *People I Know*, 2002; *Runaway Jury*, 2003; *Spider-Man 2*, 2004.

NUTTY PROFESSOR, THE. 1996. (PG-13) 95 min. Comedy. This film is a remake of the 1963 version starring Jerry Lewis, with lots of new and original plot twists. Professor Sherman Klump is an overweight, good-hearted college professor who is very unhappy with his size. When he meets and falls in love with a beautiful new teacher, his low self-esteem tells him she would never be interested in a clumsy fat man. He is conducting research on a weight-loss formula involving DNA restructuring that has been very effective on lab rats. In a fit of desperation, he tries the formula on himself and turns into a slim, suave, egomaniac with far too much testosterone for anyone to put up with. He is rude, callous, and insensitive, and this threatens all the professor has worked for, including the love of his life. **Eddie Murphy** plays multiple roles. Cast: Eddie Murphy, **Jada Pinkett Smith**, James Coburn, Larry Miller, **David Chappelle**, John Ales, Patricia Wilson, Jamal Mixon, Nichole McAuley, Hamilton von Watts, Chao Li Chi, Tony Carlin, Quinn Duffy, Montell Jordan, Doug Williams. Director: Tom Shadyac. Writers: Jerry Lewis, Bill Richmond.

NUTTY PROFESSOR II: THE KLUMPS. 2000. (PG-13) 106 min. Comedy. Professor Klump is getting married, but his drug-induced alter ego keeps resurfacing, and threatens to destroy his plans. This is the sequel to *The Nutty Professor*, 1996. Cast: **Eddie Murphy**, **Janet Jackson**, Larry Miller, John Ales, Richard Gant, **Anna Maria Horsford**, Melinda McGraw, Gabriel Williams, Chris Elliot, Duffy Taylor, Earl Boen, Nikki Cox, Freda Payne, Sylvester Jenkins. Director: Peter Segal. Writers: Jerry Lewis, Steve Oedekerk.

O

OLD SETTLER, THE. 2001. (TV) 90 min. Drama. This film is based on the stage play by John Henry Redwood, about a middle-aged old maid who rents a spare room to a Southern boy just arrived in Harlem from South Carolina. Her live-in sister takes a liking to the boy, but his romantic interests are swayed toward his much older landlady. Cast: **Phylicia Rashad, Debbie Allen,** Bumper Robinson, Eartha D. Robinson, Crystal Fox, Randy J. Gooodwin. Director: Debbie Allen. Cinematographer: **Johnny Simmons.** Writer: Shaunelle Perry.

ONCE UPON A TIME WHEN WE WERE COLORED. 1995. (PG) 112 min. Drama. This is a film adaptation based on the autobiographical novel by Clifton Taulbert. A young boy being raised by his grandparents in the 1950s learns how to survive being black in a small, racist Mississippi town. From learning the difference between the meaning of a "C" or "W" on a restroom door, to watching the Ku Klux Klan boldly march down the town's main street, he learns that he is different and hated, but also loved. The film is the directorial debut of actor **Tim Reid.** Cast: **Al Freeman, Jr., Paula Kelly, Phylicia Rashad,** Polly Bergen, **Richard Roundtree,** Charles Taylor, Willie Norwood, Jr., Damon Hines, **Leon.** Director: Tim Reid. Writer: Paul Cooper. Cinematographer: **Johnny Simmons.** Music: Steve Tyrell. Narrator: Phil Lewis.

O'NEIL, RON (1937-2004). Actor, director. Born in Utica, New York, O'Neil came to prominence during the **blaxploitation** era of films when he starred in the title role as *Superfly*, 1972, and the sequel *Superfly T. N. T.*, 1973, which he also directed. He continued to portray powerful film roles in *A Force of One*, 1979; *Sophisticated Gents*, 1981; and *Red Dawn*, 1984. He also teamed with other 1970s film icons **Jim Brown, Fred Williamson,** and **Pam Grier** for the retro-exploitation film *Original Gangstas*, 1996. His work in **television** includes *Hill Street Blues, Knight Rider, Frank's Place, A Different World, Living Single,* and *The Wayans Brothers.*

Filmography: *Superfly*, 1972; *Superfly T. N. T.*, 1973; *When a Stranger Calls*, 1979; *The Hitter*, 1979; *Freedom Road*, 1979; *Sophisticated Gents*, 1981; *Red Dawn*, 1984; *As Summers Die*, 1986; *Trained to Kill*, 1988; *Mercenary Fighters*, 1988; *Hyper Space*, 1989; *Up Against the Wall*, 1991; *Original Gangstas*, 1996.

ONE DOWN, TWO TO GO! 1972. (R) 84 min. Blaxploitation. Two karate tournament fighters team up to stop the mob from rigging a championship fight. Cast: **Jim Brown, Fred Williamson, Jim Kelly, Richard Roundtree,** Tom Signorelli, Joe Spinell, Paula Sills, Laura Loftus. Director: Fred Williamson. Writer: Jeff Williamson. Cinematographer: James Lemmo. Music: Herb Hetzer, Joe Trunzo.

ONE FALSE MOVE. 1991. (R) 105 min. Urban Drama. A murderous trio, on the run from the police, leaves Los Angeles and heads for the supposed safety of a small Arkansas town. As the body count grows, the local sheriff and two L.A. cops join forces to capture the fugitives and bring them to justice. Cast: Bill Paxton, **Cynda Williams, Michael Beach,** Billy Bob Thornton, Jim Metzler, Earl Billings, Natalie Canerday, Robert Ginnaven, Robert Anthony Bell, Kevin Hunter. Director: **Carl Franklin.** Writers: Billy Bob Thornton, Tom Epperson. Cinematographer: James L. Carter. Music: Peter Haycock, Derek Holt. Awards: Independent Spirit Award 1993: Best Director, MTV Movie Awards 1993: Best New Filmmaker Award.

ONE POTATO, TWO POTATO. 1964. 83 min. Drama. This film was made when the volatile issue of inter-racial marriage was not in sync with the social-sexual mores of the time. Problems erupt when a divorced white mother marries a black man. Cast: **Bernie Hamilton,** Barbara Barrie, Harry Bellaver, Faith Burwell, Vinnette Carroll, **Robert Earl Jones,** Marti Mericka, Richard Mulligan, Paul S. Orgill, Michael Shane, Anthony Spinelli, Jack Stamberger. Director: Larry Peerce. Writers: Orville H. Hampton, Raphael Hayes.

ONE WEEK, 2000. (R) 97 min. Drama. All is going well for a soon-to-be-groom who was raised in the foster-care system after his drug-addicted parents abandoned him. He is about to receive a promotion at work and start a new family with the woman he loves. A week before the wedding, he learns that a former sexual partner who tested positive for the AIDS virus included him on her list of contacts and he must now be tested himself. His life and career plans begin to unravel as he waits the seven days for the results, and attempts to discover which of his old flames has put his name on the list. Cast: Kenny Young, Saadiqa Muhammad, Eric Lane, Milauna Jemai, Pam Mack, Gwen Carter, Cynthia Maddox, Charles Moore, Malik Middleton, J. J. McCormick, James T. Alfred, P. Francois Battiste, Rhonda Bedgood, Sharyn Grose, Don Adams. Director: Carl Seaton. Writers: Carl Seaton, Kenny Young.

ORGANIZATION, THE. 1971. (PG) 108 min. Drama. This is the third and final film from the *In the Heat of the Night* series featuring Philadelphia detective Virgil Tibbs. This time, he teams up with a vigilante group to go up against a drug smuggling ring. It is the sequel to *They Call Me Mr. Tibbs*, 1970. Cast: Sidney Poitier, Barbara McNair, Gerald S. O'Loughlin. Sheree North, Fred Beir, Allen Garfield, Bernie Hamilton, Graham Jarvis, Raul Julia, Ron O'Neal, James A. Watson Jr., Charles H. Gray, Jarion Monroe, Daniel J. Travanti, Billy Green Bush. Director: Don Medford. Writers: John Ball, James R. Webb.

ORIGINAL GANGSTAS. 1996. (R) 98 min. Drama. A group of older, butt-kicking, **blaxploitation** heroes from the 1970s is brought together in this action-packed, return-to-the-hood film. When a former gang banger's father is shot to death by a local gang leader, he calls in his former street hoods to take back the old neighborhood from the gun-toting thugs who have run amuck. Cast: **Fred Williamson, Jim Brown, Ron O'Neil, Pam Grier, Richard Roundtree, Paul Winfield**. Director: Larry Cohen. Writer: Aubrey Rattan. Cinematographer: Carlos Gonzalez. Music: Vlaimir Horunzhy.

ORIGINAL KINGS OF COMEDY, THE. 2000. (R) 115 min. Comedy/Documentary. A comedy concert filmed in Charlotte, North Carolina, during a tour that featured four top African American stand-up comedians. Cast: **Steve Harvey, D. L. Hughley, Cedric the Entertainer, Bernie Mac**. Director: **Spike Lee**.

OSCAR, THE. A statuette awarded at the **Academy Awards** in various performance and technical categories. It was designed by art director Cedric Gibbons and fashioned by sculptor George Stanley. The figurine stands 13 1/2 inches high and depicts a man holding a sword and standing on a reel of film.

OUT-OF-SYNC. 1995. (R) 105 min. Music/Drama. A popular hip-hop deejay in Los Angeles gets into debt with his bookie, then gets into some trouble with the police, and is pressured to go undercover to help bust a club owner who also deals drugs. The pressure intensifies when the deejay falls in love with the marked club owner's girlfriend. Cast: **L. L. Cool J, Victoria Dillard**, Howard Hesseman, Ramy Zada, Don Yesso, **Yaphet Kotto**. Director: **Debbie Allen**. Writer: Robert E. Dom. Cinematographer: Isidore Mankofsky. Music: Steve Tyrell.

OUT OF TIME. 2003. (PG) 105 min. Drama. The police chief of a small Florida town must solve a double murder where all the evidence points back to him. Cast: **Denzel Washington**, Eva Mendes, **Sanaa Lathan**, Dean Cain, John Billingsly, Rober Baker, Alex Carter, Antoni Corone, Terry Loughlin, Nora Dunn, James Murtaugh, Peggy Sheeffield, Evelyn Brooks, Eric Hissom, Tom Hillmann. Director: **Carl Franklin**. Writer: David Collard.

P

PACE, JUDY (1950-). Actress. Born and raised in Los Angeles, California, Pace graduated from Dorsey High School and was a business major at Los Angeles City College. Once labeled "the most beautiful African American woman in Hollywood," by the show biz journal *Daily Variety*, she first appeared on film in *13 Frightened Girls*, 1963. Her first lead film role was as Eulice in the sexually controversial film *Three in the Attic*, 1968, a groundbreaking film told from a feminist point of view. She became a regular on *Peyton Place* in 1969, for which she received an NAACP **Image Award**, and starred in the hit movie *Cotton Comes to Harlem*, the following year. She won a second Image Award when she starred in her own series, *The Young Lawyers*. Other television work includes *Bewitched, Batman, I Spy, The Mod Squad, Sanford and Son, Good Times*, and *What's Happening*. Her first husband was actor Don Mitchell. She later married St. Louis Cardinal center fielder Curt Flood.

Filmography: *13 Frightened Girls*, 1963; *Three in the Attic*, 1968; *Three in the Cellar*, 1970; *Cotton Comes to Harlem*, 1970; *Brian's Song*, 1971; *Frogs*, 1972.

PAGE, LAWANDA (1920-2002). Actress. This Cleveland, Ohio-born actress began her career on the club circuit as a dancer and chorus girl. While dancing in St. Louis, she was billed as "The Bronze Goddess of Fire" for lighting cigarettes with her fingertips, and using flaming torches as part of her act. She started acting and doing stand-up comedy in her later years and appeared in the stage production of *Take it to the Lord...Or Else*. Her big break came when her childhood friend, comedian **Redd Foxx**, cast her as Aunt Esther, his loud-mouthed, Bible-carrying sister-in-law in his long-running 1970s sitcom *Sanford and Son*.

Filmography: *Zapped*, 1980; *Good-Bye Cruel World*, 1983; *Mausoleum*, 1983; *My Blue Heaven*, 1990; *Shakes the Clown*, 1992; **CB4**, 1993; **The Meteor Man**, 1993; **Friday**, 1995; **Don't Be a Menace to South Central While Drinking Your Juice in the Hood**, 1996; *West From North Goes South*, 2004.

PAID IN FULL. 2002. (R) 93 min. Urban Drama. The story of friendship, greed, and the desperate things the pressure of living in poverty can lead young men to do. It is the 1980s, and cocaine is the street drug of choice. Three Harlem drug dealers live the gangsta life and ride it to the top of their game. Once there, the rivalries begin as the friendship wanes, and lies, treachery, and the law brings some low. Cast: Wood Harris, **Mekhi Pfifer**, Kevin Carroll, Esai Morales, **Chi McBride**, Cynthia Martells, **Elise Neal**, Cam'ron, **Regina Hall**, Remo Greene, Anthony Clark. Director: Charles Stone III. Writers: Azie Faison Jr., Austin Phillips, Matthew Cirulnick, Thulani Davis. Cinematographer: Paul Sarossy. Music: Vernon Reid, Frank Fitzpatrick.

PALCY, EUZHAN (1958-). Director. The Martinique-born filmmaker watched and loved films from an early age. She wrote and directed the short film *The Messenger* for French television in Martinique when she was 17 years old before embarking upon her filmmaking studies. She earned a master's degree in French literature at the Sorbonne in Paris, a master's degree in theater, and a film degree from the Louis Lumiere School of Cinema. Focusing on films dealing with cultural issues and social change, Palcy shot **Sugar Cane Alley**, 1983, her feature debut for less than $1 million and won more than 17 international prizes for her work. She was handpicked by Robert Redford to attend the 1984 Sundance Director's Lab, where she was encouraged to seriously consider her options in Hollywood. Her second feature, **A Dry White Season**, 1989, is credited with helping to bring down the racist, South African system of apartheid, and she became the first female director of African descent to be produced by a major Hollywood studio.

Filmography: *Sugar Cane Alley*, 1983; *A Dry White Season*, 1989; *Ruby Bridges*, 1998; *The Killing Yard*, 2001.

PANTHER. 1995. (R) 124 min. Biopic. This film is a fictionalized account of the rise and fall of the Black Panther Party during the 1960s and 1970s. Starting with its pro-active beginnings in Oakland, California, activists Bobby Seal and Hey P. Newton forge their group into a national organization for African Americans' rights and liberties. Not afraid to use guns or force to achieve their aims, they quickly become targets of the FBI, who force a down-and-out Vietnam vet to become an informant to help bring them down. Cast: **Kadeem Hardison**, Marcus Chung, **Courtney B. Vance**, **Bokeem Woodbine**, Joe Don Baker, Anthony Griffith, Nefertiti, James Russo, Richard Dysart, M. Emmet Walsh, **Mario Van Peebles**. Director: Mario Van Peebles. Writer: **Melvin Van Peebles**. Cinematographer: Edward Pei. Music: **Stanley Clarke**.

PARADISE IN HARLEM. 1940. 83 min. Musical. This is an early all-black-cast musical. A cabaret performer is forced to consider leaving town after witnessing a gangland-style murder. Cast: Frank Wilson, Mamie Smith, Edna Mae Harris. Director: Joseph Seiden.

PARKS, GORDON (1912-2006). Photographer, director, novelist, composer. Gordon Parks was born in Fort Scott, Kansas, and attended high school in St. Paul, Minnesota. After becoming interested in photography, he moved to Chicago in 1937 and was involved with the South Side Community Art Center. A one-man exhibit of his photographs earned him a prestigious Rosenwald Fellowship. Parks accepted an assignment with the Overseas Division of the Office of War Information, and after World War II, he became a staff photographer for *Life* magazine. He has garnered many awards for his work, including Magazine Photographer of the Year in 1961, the Newhouse Award from Syracuse University, and a Springarn Award from the National Association for the Advancement of Colored People in 1972. As an award-winning writer, Parks has written several novels, including his autobiographically based books *The Learning Tree* and *A Choice of Weapons*. In 1968, he became the first African American director ever to helm a feature-length film for a major Hollywood studio with the film version of *The Learning Tree*. He also produced, and wrote the screenplay and the original music score. Parks produced and directed documentaries and feature films *Shaft*, 1971, and *Leadbelly*, 1976, based on the life of blues singer and composer Huddie "Leadbelly" Ledbetter.

Filmography: *The Learning Tree*, 1969; *Shaft*, 1971; *Shaft's Big Score*, 1972; *Leadbelly*, 1976; *Half Slave, Half Free*, 1985.

PARKS, GORDON, JR. (1934-1979). Director. Parks directed a string of films in the early 1970s. First was the drug pusher-based *Superfly*, 1972. He followed with the black Bonnie & Clyde style western, *Thomasine & Bushrod*, 1974, and the hard-hitting *Three the Hard Way*, 1974. His last film was the inner-city love tale, *Aaron Loves Angela*, 1975. He was the son of world-renowned photographer/film director **Gordon Parks**. His career was cut short when he was killed in a plane crash while filming in Africa.

Filmography: *Superfly*, 1972; *Thomasine & Bushrod*, 1974; *Three the Hard Way*, 1974; *Aaron Loves Angela*, 1975.

PARIS BLUES. 1961. 100 min. Music/Drama. A salt-and-pepper jazz duo touring Paris become intimately involved with two beautiful American tourists and are tempted to put down their instruments and come in off the road. **Louis Armstrong** makes a guest appearance and **Duke Ellington** provides the **Academy Award**-nominated music. Cast: **Sidney Poitier**, Paul Newman, **Diahann Carroll**, Joanne Woodward, **Louis Armstrong**, Barbara Lang. Director: Martin Ritt. Writers: Jack Sher, Walter Bernstein. Music: Duke Ellington.

PASSING THROUGH. 1977. (NR) 105 min. Drama. A jazz musician is released from prison and becomes involved in a revolution. Cast: Cora Lee Day, **Marla Gibbs**, Pamela Jones, George Kramer, **Clarence Muse**, Horace Tapscott, Nathaniel Taylor. Director: Larry Clark. Writers: Larry Clark, **Ted Lange**.

PATCH OF BLUE, A. 1965. 108 min. Drama. In this film, an interracial love affair between a blind white girl and a caring black man pushes the race issue to the limit. Cast: **Sidney Poitier**, Elizabeth Hartman, Shelley Winters, Wallace Ford, **Ivan Dixon**, John Qualen, Elisabeth Fraser, Kelly Flynn. Director: Guy Green. Cinematographer: Robert Burks. Music: Jerry Goldsmith. Awards: Oscar 1965, Supporting Actress (Winters).

PAYNE, ALLEN (1968-). Actor. He was born in Harlem, New York, and made his film debut in *Rooftops*, 1989. Other notable film roles include *New Jack City*, 1991; *Jason's Lyric*, 1994; *Vampire in Brooklyn*, 1995; and the telepic *The Tuskegee Airmen*, 1995.

Filmography: *Rooftops*, 1998; *Cookie*, 1998; *New Jack City*, 1991; *CB4*, 1993; *Jason's Lyric*, 1994; *Vampire in Brooklyn*, 1995; *The Walking Dead*, 1995; *A Price above Rubie*, 1998; *The Perfect Storm*, 2000; *30 Years to Life*, 2001; *Blue Hill Avenue*, 2001; *Playas Ball*, 2003.

PENITENTIARY. 1979. (R) 99 min. Action. This gritty tale of survival involves a prison inmate who spends his incarceration fighting against other prisoners in the boxing ring. He does very well and the betting on these bouts is intense, until his girlfriend is threatened if he does not lose. It spawned two sequels, *Penitentiary 2 &*

3. Cast: **Leon Isaac Kennedy, Jamaa Fanaka**, Badja Djola, Chuck "Porky" Mitchell. Writer/Director: Jamaa Fanaka. Cinematographer: Marty Ollstein.

PENITENTIARY 2. 1982. (R) 108 min. Action. When the man who murdered his girlfriend is sent to the same prison, an angry pugilist prisoner seeks his revenge. This is the sequel to *Penitentiary*, 1979. Cast: **Leon Isaac Kennedy, Mr. T**, Leif Erickson, **Ernie Hudson, Glynn Turman**. Writer/Director: **Jamaa Fanaka**. Cinematographer: Stephen Posey. Music: Jack Wheaton.

PENITENTIARY 3. 1987. (R) 91 min. Action. An incarcerated boxing inmate continues to fight in the ring and for his very survival. This is the sequel to *Penitentiary 2*, 1982. Cast: **Leon Isaac Kennedy**, Anthony Geary, Steve Antin, Ric Mancini, Kessler Raymond, Jim Bailey. Writer/Director: **Jamaa Fanaka**.

PERCY & THUNDER. 1993. (TV) 90 min. Drama. A tough, hardworking trainer discovers a talented young pugilist and has to fight with the crooked boxing promoters to give his contender a fair chance at the middleweight championship. Cast: **James Earl Jones, Billy Dee Williams, Courtney B. Vance**, Robert Wuhl, **Gloria Foster, Zakes Mokae**, Gloria Reuben. Director: **Ivan Dixon**. Writer: Art Washington. Music: Tom Scott.

PEREZ, ROSIE (1964-). Actress, dancer, producer. She was born in Brooklyn, New York, and began her entertainment career as a dancer on the television show *Soul Train*. She was later hired as a choreographer for music videos and stage shows for such performers as **Diana Ross, Bobby Brown**, and **L. L. Cool J**, and earned an **Emmy Award** nomination for her choreography on the TV series *In Living Color*. She made her film debut acting in and dancing under the opening credits of *Do the Right Thing*, 1989. She is executive producer of the TV movie *SUBWAY Stories: Tales from the Underground*.

    Filmography: *Do the Right Thing*, 1989; *Night on Earth*, 1991; *White Men Can't Jump*, 1992; *Untamed Heart*, 1993; *Fearless*, 1993; *It Could Happen to You*, 1994; *Somebody to Love*, 1994; *A Brother's Kiss*, 1997; *Perdita Durango*, 1997; *Louis & Frank*, 1998; *The 24 Hour Woman*, 1999; *Human Nature*, 2001; *Riding in Cars with Boys*, 2001; *King of the Jungle*, 2001; *Exactly*, 2004; *Lackawanna Blues*, 2005.

PERFUME. 1991. (R) 98 min. Drama. Five beautiful lifelong friends known as "The Groovy Girls" join forces in a business venture to manufacture and sell cosmetics to black women around the world. As their private lives begin to diverge and intertwine, the high pressure of the cosmetics industry begins to take its toll, and dark secrets threaten to destroy their company and their friendships. Cast: Cheryl Francis Harrington, Kathleen Bradley Overton, Shy Jefferson, Lynn Marlin, Eugina Wright, **Ted Lange**. Writer/Director: Roland S. Jefferson. Cinematographer: Nicholas Von Sternberg. Music: Willie Hutch.

PERRY, TYLER (1969-). Actor, director, writer, producer. He was born in New Orleans, Louisiana, and began writing plays when he was 18. He created and portrays the character of Madea, a gruff, grandmotherly, sharp-witted, no-nonsense, pistol-toting woman who speaks her mind with reckless abandon. He began to tour the country with a series of religious-based plays that featured this popular character and videotaped the stage productions for a straight-to-video release. After gaining notoriety and racking up hefty video and DVD sales, Perry teamed with producer **Reuben Cannon** to make more elaborate feature-film versions. They have built a production studio in Atlanta, Georgia, to achieve this task, and to produce their original **television** sitcom *House of Payne*.
Filmography: *Madea's Family Reunion*, 2002; ***Diary of a Mad Black Woman***, 2002; *I Can Do Bad All by Myself*, 2002; *Madea's Class Reunion*, 2003; *Meet the Browns*, 2004; *Madea's Family Reunion*, 2006; *Why Did I Get Married?* 2006; *Madea Goes to Jail*, 2006; *Daddy's Little Girls*, 2007.

PERSONALS. 2000. (R) 91 min. Romance/Drama. A down-and-out writer decides to write an expose on the women who answer his personal ads for dates. He meets, he talks, and he dates, and in the process, finds out more about himself than he ever planned to. Cast: **Malik Yoba, Stacy Dash, Sheryl Lee Ralph**, Rhonda Ross Kendrick, Monteria Ivey. Writer/Director: Mike Sargent.

PETERS, BROCK (1927-2005). Actor, producer. Peters was born in New York City and acted on Broadway before moving into film. His stage debut was a 1943 production of **Porgy and Bess**, and he was later cast in the film version as well. His first film role was as Sergeant Brown in the Otto Preminger musical ***Carmen Jones***, 1954. He received rave reviews for his portrayal of the falsely accused Tom Robinson in *To Kill a Mockingbird*, 1962. He was a producer on the film *Five on the Black Hand Side*, 1973. On **tele-**

vision, Peters produced *This Far by Faith*, 1975, starred in **Roots: The Next Generation**, 1979, and was a regular on the daytime soap opera *The Young and the Restless*. He continued to act on stage, television and film, and received numerable awards, including an **Image Award**, a Drama Desk Award, and an **Emmy**. Filmography: *Carmen Jones*, 1954; *To Kill a Mockingbird*, 1962; *The L-Shaped Room*, 1962; *The Pawnbroker*, 1965; *The Incident*, 1967; *Dating Game*, 1968; *Ace High*, 1968; *The McMasters*, 1970; *Soylent Green*, 1973; *Slaughter's Big Ripoff*, 1973; *Framed*, 1975; *The Adventures of Huckleberry Finn*, 1978; *Star Trek 4: The Voyage Home*, 1986; *To Heal a Nation*, 1988; *Alligator 2: The Mutation*, 1990; *Star Trek 6: The Undiscovered Country*, 1991; *The Secret*, 1993; *The Locket*, 2002.

PHAT BEACH. 1996. (R) 99 min. Comedy. A lighthearted, hip-hop filled, romp at the beach. An overweight romantic empties out his savings account, borrows the family Mercedes, and heads to southern California with his fast-talking friend in search of sun, sand, and sex. The soundtrack includes Biz Markie, Suga T featuring The Click, and E-40, with a guest appearance by Coolio. Cast: Jermaine "Huggy" Hopkins, Brian Hooks, Jennifer Lucienne, Claudia Kaleem, Gregg D. Vance, Tommy "Tiny" Lister, Erick Fleeks, Alma Collins, Candice Merideth, Sabrina De Pina, Coolio. Director: Doug Ellin. Writers: Doug Ellin, Brian E. O'Neil, Ben Morris. Cinematographer: Jurgen Baum. Music: Paul Stewart.

PIANO LESSON, THE. 1994. (PG) 99 min. Drama. This film was adapted from the 1990 Pulitzer Prize-winning play by August Wilson. Set in 1936, intra-family conflict erupts in a Pittsburgh home when a prodigal son returns from Mississippi wanting to sell the family heirloom, an ornately carved, 80-year-old upright piano. He wants to buy a plot of land their enslaved grandfather once worked on, but his sister refuses to let the prized antique go. Cast: **Alfre Woodard, Charles S. Dutton, Courtney B. Vance**, Carl Gordon, Tommy Hollis, Zelda Harris, Lou Myers, Rosalyn Coleman, Tommy La Fitte. Director: Lloyd Richards. Writer: August Wilson. Music: Stephen James Taylor, Dwight Andrews.

PIECE OF THE ACTION. 1977. (PG) 135 min. Comedy. A former police officer tricks two con men into working with troubled youths at a Chicago community center. Cast: **Sidney Poitier, Bill Cosby, James Earl Jones, Denise Nicholas**, Hope Clarke, Tracy Reed, Titos Vandis, **Ja'net Dubois**. Director: Sidney Poitier. Music: **Curtis Mayfield**.

PIERCE, WENDELL (1962-). Actor. He made his film debut as a paramedic in *The Money Pit*, 1986. Other notable film roles include *Waiting to Exhale*, 1995; *Get on the Bus*, 1996; *The Fighting Temptations*, 2003; and *Ray*, 2004. He produced and starred in *The Date*, 2002. His **television** guest-starring roles include *A Man Called Hawk*, *The Equalizer*, *I'll Fly Away*, *Law & Order*, *New York Undercover*, *Third Watch*, *My Wife and Kids*, *City of Angels*, and *Girlfriends*.

Filmography: *The Money Pit*, 1986; *Casualties of War*, 1989; *Family Business*, 1989; *A Matter of Degrees*, 1990; *A Rage in Harlem*, 1991; *Malcolm X*, 1992; *It Could Happen to You*, 1994; *Bye Bye, Love*, 1995; *Hackers*, 1995; *Waiting to Exhale*, 1995; *Get on the Bus*, 1996; *Sleepers*, 1996; *Bulworth*, 1998; *Abilene*, 1999; *The Gilded Six Bits*, 2001; *The Date*, 2002; *Brown Sugar*, 2002; *The Fighting Temptations*, 2003; *A Hole in One*, 2004; *Land of Plenty*, 2004; *Ray*, 2004.

PINKETT SMITH, JADA (1971-). Actress. The Baltimore native performed in regional theater and landed several TV show guest spots before being cast as a regular on the fifth season of the NBC sitcom *A Different World*, 1991-93. Her first big-screen role was in *Menace II Society*, 1993, and she followed with powerful performances in *The Inkwell*, 1994; *Jason's Lyric*, 1994; and *A Low Down Dirty Shame*, 1994. Now a box office draw, she has continued to pursue a distinguished acting career. She married rapper/actor **Will Smith** in 1997. Together, they produce the UPN sitcom *All of Us*.

Filmography: *Menace II Society*, 1993; *The Inkwell*, 1994; *Jason's Lyric*, 1994; *A Low Down Dirty Shame*, 1994; *Tales from the Crypt Presents Demon Knight*, 1995; *The Nutty Professor*, 1996; *Set It Off*, 1996; *Scream 2*, 1997; *Woo*, 1998; *Return to Paradise*, 1998; *Princess Mononoke*, 1999; *Bamboozled*, 2000; *Kingdom Come*, 2001; *Ali*, 2001; *The Matrix Reloaded*, 2003; *The Matrix Revolutions*, 2003; *Collateral*, 2004.

PINKY. 1948. 102 min. Drama. This is a film based on the novel *Quality* by Cyd Ricketts Sumner, about a light-skinned black girl who passes for white to enjoy a higher quality of life. In the process, she disrespects her grandmother, lies to her fiancée, and loses herself in an attempt to be someone and something she is not. Cast: Jeanne Crain, **Ethel Waters**, Ethel Barrymore, **Nina Mae McKinney**, William Lundigan. Director: Elia Kazan. Writers: Philip Dunne, Dudley Nichols. Music: Alfred Newman.

PIPE DREAMS. 1976. (PG) 89 min. Drama. A couple's marriage is put in jeopardy when the husband takes a job on an Alaskan pipeline construction crew. Cast: Gladys Knight, Barry Hankerson, Bruce French, Sally Kirkland, Sherry Bain. Director: Stephen Verona.

PLAYAS BALL. 2003. (R) Drama. After signing a lucrative shoe-endorsement deal, a young, superstar athlete defends himself from a patenity suit by a woman that he has not been involved with. *Playas Ball* was produced by the Detroit Piston's forward Dale Davis. After a three-year delay, the film premiered February 2006 in Houston, Texas, as part of the NBA All-Star festivities to benefit Habitat for Humanity and the Hurricane Katrina victims. Cast: **Allen Payne**, **Elise Neal**, **Treach**, Chelsi Smith, Tracey Cherelle Jones, MC Lyte, Jordana Spiro, Anthony C. Hall, Tasha Smith, Jackie Long, Matthew Hatchett, Pamella D'Pella, Judge Joe Brown, Chino XL, Liisa Lee. Director: Jennifer Harper. Writers: Jennifer Harper, Jason Towne.

PLAYERS CLUB, THE. 1998. (R) 103 min. Urban Drama. This film explores a series of urban dramas played out to the backdrop of a local strip club. A single mom, putting herself through college, works as a dancer at The Players Club. Despite the other dancers' games, scams, and jealousies, she maintains her self-respect and resists the pressure to turn tricks on the side, but her young and naive cousin is not so fortunate. The club's deejay falls for the dancer and eventually wants to do the right thing by her, but not before fireworks break out. Cast: **LisaRaye**, **Bernie Mac**, **Monica Calhoun**, **A. J. (Anthony) Johnson**, **Jamie Foxx**, **Ice Cube**, **Dick Anthony Williams**, Tommy "Tiny" Lister, **John Amos**, **Faizon Love**, Alex Thomas, Chrystale Wilson, Adele Givins, Larry McCoy. Writer/Director: Ice Cube. Cinematographer: **Malik Hassan Sayeed**. Music: Hidden Faces.

PLUMMER, GLENN (1961-). Actor. This Richmond, California, native made his film debut in *Who's That Girl*, 1986, and has been working in **television** and film ever since. On television, he could be seen in *The Women of Brewster Place*, 1989, the miniseries *The Corner*, 2000, and the television series *ER*. His more prominent film roles include ***South Central***, 1992; *Speed*, 1994; and *Day after Tomorrow*, 2004.

Filmography: *Color*, 1988; *Pastime*, 1991; *South Central*, 1992; ***Menace II Society***, 1993; *Speed*, 1994; *Strange Days*, 1995;

Showgirls, 1995; *Up Close and Personal*, 1996; *The Substitute*, 1996; *Speed 2: Cruise Control*, 1997; *One Night Stand*, 1997; *Spy Games*, 1999; *Smalltime*, 1999; *Interceptor Force*, 1999; *Rangers*, 2000; *Ruby's Bucket of Blood*, 2001; *Rhapsody*, 2001; *The Salton Sea*, 2002; *Poolhall Junkies*, 2002; *Day after Tomorrow*, 2004; *Roscoe's House of Chicken n Waffles*, 2004; **Constellation**, 2004; *Go for Broke 2*, 2005; *El Cortez*, 2005.

POETIC JUSTICE. 1993. (R) 109 min. Urban Drama. After her boyfriend is murdered, an inner-city hairdresser gives up her plans for college and throws herself into her work and writing poetry (provided by poet **Maya Angelou**). She meets, and after a rocky start, falls for a brash and arrogant postman, and decides to try love again. This was singer Janet Jackson's first film role. Cast: **Janet Jackson, Tupac Shakur, Tyra Ferrell, Regina King, Joe Torry**, Norma Donaldson. Writer/Director: **John Singleton**. Cinematographer: Peter Collister. Music: **Stanley Clarke**. Awards: Golden Raspberries 1993: Worst New Star (Jackson). MTV Movie Awards 1974: Best Female Performance (Jackson), Most Desirable Female (Jackson).

POITIER, SIDNEY (1927-). Actor, director. Born in Miami, Sidney Poitier spent his early years with his family in the Bahamas. He returned to Miami at age 15, hopped freight trains to New York City, and became a dishwasher. When Japan attacked Pearl Harbor, Poitier enlisted in the U.S. Army and served four years. Upon returning to New York, he tried out for the American Negro Theater but was turned away because of his diction. Poitier worked hard to make improvements and was later accepted by the theater group and his career destiny was set. His first Hollywood film was *No Way Out*, 1950, and dozens of starring roles followed. These included *Cry, the Beloved Country*, 1952; *Blackboard Jungle*, 1956; *Something of Value*, 1957; and *Porgy and Bess*, 1959. On stage, Poitier starred in the Broadway version of Lorraine Hansberry's award-winning *A Raisin in the Sun*, and repeated his character in the big screen version. He became a major box office attraction during the 1960s. He was the first African American actor nominated for an **Oscar** for his role in *The Defiant Ones*, 1958, and was the first to win a best actor **Academy Award** for his performance in *Lilies of the Field*, 1965. Later in his career, Poitier turned to directing and helmed the films *Buck and the Preacher*, 1972; *Stir Crazy*, 1980; *Hanky Panky*, 1982; and *Ghost Dad*, 1990. In 2001, he received a Lifetime Achievement Award from the **Academy of Motion Picture Arts and Sciences**.

Filmography: *No Way Out*, 1950; *Cry, the Beloved Country*, 1951; *Red Ball Express*, 1952; *Blackboard Jungle*, 1955; *Goodbye, My Lady*, 1956; *Something of Value*, 1957; *The Mark of the Hawk*, 1957; *Band of Angels*, 1957; *The Defiant Ones*, 1958; *All the Young Men*, 1960; *A Raisin in the Sun*, 1961; *Paris Blues*, 1961; *Pressure Point*, 1962; *Lilies of the Field*, 1963; *The Long Ships*, 1964; *The Slender Thread*, 1965; *A Patch of Blue*, 1965; *The Greatest Story Ever Told*, 1965; *Bedford Incident*, 1965; *Duel at Diablo*, 1966; *To Sir, with Love*, 1967; *In the Heat of the Night*, 1967; *Guess Who's Coming to Dinner*, 1967; *For Love of Ivy*, 1968; *The Lost Man*, 1969; *They Call Me Mr. Tibbs!*, 1970; *Brother John*, 1970; *The Organization*, 1971; *Buck and the Preacher*, 1972; *Uptown Saturday Night*, 1974; *Let's Do It Again*, 1975; *A Piece of the Action*, 1977; *Shoot to Kill*, 1988; *Little Nikita*, 1988; *Separate But Equal*, 1991; *Sneakers*, 1992; *A Good Day to Die*, 1995; *Mandela and de Klerk*, 1997; *The Jackal*, 1997; *Free of Eden*, 1998; *The Simple Life of Noah Dearborn*, 1999.

POLK, OSCAR (1900-1949). Actor. Born in Marianna, Arizona, Polk became an actor and often played characters with such names as "Lazy Bones," "Pork," and "Salt Meat." He also portrayed "Gabriele" in *The Green Pastures*, 1936, and "The Deacon/Fleetfoot" in *Cabin in the Sky*, 1943.

Filmography: *It's a Great Life*, 1935; *The Green Pastures*, 1936; *Underworld*, 1937; *Big Town Czar*, 1939; *Gone with the Wind*, 1939; *Birth of the Blues*, 1941; *Reap the Wild Wind*, 1942; *White Cargo*, 1942; *Cabin in the Sky*, 1943.

POOTIE TANG. 2001. (PG-13) 81 min. Comedy. This film is an expanded version of a one-joke sketch from *The Chris Rock Show*. Pootie Tang is a cool, gibberish-talking crime-fighter who gets tricked into endorsing a lifestyle of booze, cigarettes, and junk food by a crafty businessman. When he realizes the error, Pootie returns to his hometown in disgrace. Cast: Lance Crouther, Jennifer Coolidge, Robert Vaughn, **Chris Rock**, Reg E. Cathey, Wanda Sykes, Dave Attell, Mario Joyner, JB Smoove, Andy Richter. Writer/Director: Louis CK. Cinematographer: Willy Kurant.

PORGY AND BESS. 1959. 138 min. Musical/Drama. This is a film based on the opera by George Gershwin. Bess, a woman with a disreputable background lives in shame among the residents of a small fishing village in South Carolina. When her abusive lover flees and goes into hiding in the swamp after killing a man in a crap game, she has nowhere to go. She takes up with a crippled man, Porgy, who is willing to overlook her past. He gives her shelter, but their union is threatened not only by the villagers disapproval, but also by the return of her old drug supplier, Sportin' Life, and the possible return of her jealous and murderous lover. Cast: **Sidney Poitier, Dorothy Dandridge, Sammy Davis Jr.**, **Pearl Bailey, Brock Peters, Diahann Carroll**, Leslie Scott, Ruth Attaway, **Clarence Muse**, Everdinne Wilson, Earl Jackson, Moses LaMarr, Margaret Hairston, **Ivan Dixon, Joel Fluellen**, Antoine Durousseau. Director: Otto Preminger.

POSSE. 1993. (R) 113 min. Western. A Western tale about how African American cowboys helped to tame the Wild West. The story is told in flashback by an ex-Buffalo Soldier who explains how he, and his band of rebellious soldiers, came across a stash of gold while fighting in Mexico. Getting the gold back to the United States would prove a daunting task for all they had to do to protect it and themselves from another gang of outlaws. Cast: **Mario Van Peebles**, Charles Lane, Stephen Baldwin, Tommy "Tiny" Lister, Big Daddy Cane, Billy Zane, **Blair Underwood**, Tone Loc, **Salli Richardson, Reginald Hudlin**, Richard Edson, Reginald Vel Johnson, **Warrington Hudlin**. Cameos: **Melvin Van Peebles, Woody Strode, Pam Grier, Isaac Hayes, Robert Hooks**, Richard Jordon, Paul Bartel, **Nipsey Russell**, Aaron Neville, Stephen J. Cannell. Director: Mario Van Peebles. Writers: Sy Richardson, Dario Scardapane. Cinematographer: Peter Menzies, Jr., Music: Michel Colombier.

POUNDER, CCH. (1952-). Actress. Her name is Carol Christine Hilaria Pounder. Born in Guyana, South America, she graduated from Ithaca College. After performing in a few regional repertoire companies, she began working in **television** and made her film debut in *All That Jazz*, 1979. She guest starred in the TV series *Hill Street Blues, Cagney and Lacey, South Central*, and *The Cosby Show*. She had recurring roles in *L. A. Law, ER*, and *Millennium*, and stars in the FX cable series *The Shield*. She has appeared in numerous made-for-television movies, including *Go Tell It On the Mountain*, 1984; *The Atlanta Child Murders*, 1985; and *Boycott*, 2001.

Filmography: *All That Jazz*, 1979; *Union City*, 1980; *I'm Dancing as Fast as I Can*, 1982; *Prizzi's Honor*, 1985; *Bagdad Café*, 1988; *Postcards From the Edge*, 1990; *The Importance of Being Earnest*, 1992; *Benny and Joon*, 1993; *Silver*, 1993; *RoboCop 3*, 1993; *Demon Knight*, 1995; *Face Off*, 1997; *Melting Pot*, 1997; *Blossoms & Veils*, 1997; *Final Justice*, 1998; *End of Days*,

1999; *Things Behind the Sun*, 2001; *Baby of the Family*, 2002; *Tough Like Wearing Dreadlocks*, 2004.

POWELL, CLIFTON (1947-). Actor. His strong and calming screen presence has made him a highly sought after character actor. His notable film credits include *House Party*, 1990; *Bones*, 2001; *Civil Brand*, 2002; and *Ray*, 2004. His television appearances include *Roc*, *Martin*, *In the Heat of the Night*, *South Central*, *New York Undercover*, *NYPD Blue*, *Moesha*, *One on One*, and *Third Watch*. Filmography: *Alphabet City*, 1984; *House Party*, 1990; *Deep Cover*, 1992; *3 Ninjas*, 1992; *Menace II Society*, 1993; *Conflict of Interest*, 1993; *Dead Presidents*, 1995; *Buffalo Soldiers*, 1997; *Phantoms*, 1998; *Deep Rising*, 1998; *Caught Up*, 1998; *Why Do Fools Fall in Love*, 1998; *Rush Hour*, 1998; *Selma, Lord Selma*, 1999; *Safe House*, 1999; *The Breaks*, 1999; *Foolish*, 1999; *Hot Boyz*, 1999; *Next Friday*, 2000; *Lockdown*, 2000; *The Brothers*, 2001; *Bones*, 2001; *Tapped Out*, 2001; *Civil Brand*, 2002; *Friday after Next*, 2002; *Never Die Alone*, 2004; *Woman Thou Art Loosed*, 2004; *Ray*, 2004; *Roscoe's House of Chicken n Waffles*, 2004; *White Men Can't Rap*, 2005.

POWERFUL THANG, A. 1991. (NR) Romance/Drama. A single mother has been celibate since the birth of her five-year-old child. She meets and falls for a kind and considerate young man, and after months of platonic dating, she is ready to take the next step, but is he? Cast: Asma Feyijinmi, **John Jelks**, Barbara O. Director: Zeinabu irene Davis. Writer: Marc Arthur Chery. Cinematographer: S. Torriano Berry.

PREACHER'S WIFE, THE. 1996. (PG) 124 min. Music/Drama. This is a modern remake of the classic film *The Bishop's Wife*, 1947. A troubled Newark, New Jersey, minister must raise the funds to save his church from a covetous land developer. He is so bogged down with his external problems he pays little attention to his wife or the fact that it is the Christmas season. His prayers are answered when the Lord sends his angel to work things out, but may fall for the preacher's choir-leading wife in the process. This is singer Whitney Houston's first film role and there is also a song and appearance by Lionel Ritchie. Cast: **Denzel Washington, Whitney Houston, Shari Headley, Courtney B. Vance, Gregory Hines, Jennifer Lewis, Loretta Devine**, Lionel Ritchie, Paul Bates, Justin Pierre Edmund, Darvel Davis Jr., William James Stiggers Jr. Director: Penny Marshall. Writers: Nat Mauldin, Allan Scott. Cinematographer: Miroslav Ondricek. Music: Hans Zimmer.

PREER, EVELYN (1896-1932). Actress. The Vicksburg, Mississippi, native became a pioneering black actress in **race movies** and dramatic theater. As an icon in Hollywood and on the Broadway stage, Preer, with her light complexion, was a leading lady who could easily cross over. Her career began in Chicago doing minstrel shows with Charley Johnson's vaudeville troupe until maverick filmmaker **Oscar Micheaux** chose her for the lead role in *The Homesteader*, 1918, his film debut. He heavily promoted Preer into star status with personal appearance tours, and she became his premiere leading lady, starring in at least 10 of his films, including *Within Our Gates*, 1920; *Birthright*, 1924; and *The Conjure Woman*, 1926. Preer also starred in three comedy shorts produced at the Al Christie studios: *The Framing of the Shrew*, 1928; *Melancholy Dame*, 1928; and *Oft in the Silly Night*, 1928. Between films, Preer performed on stage with **The Lafayette Players**, the theatrical stock company founded by fellow pioneer actress **Anita Bush**. It was here that Preer met her husband, actor Edward Thompson. On Broadway, she was in David Belasco's 1926 production of Edward Sheldon's *Lulu Belle*, where she supported and understudied German actress Lenore Ulrich in the leading role. Preer was also a jazz singer and recording artist, often backed by the music of **Duke Ellington** and Red Nichols.

Filmography: *The Homesteader*, 1918; *Within Our Gates*, 1920; *Birthright*, 1924; *The Conjure Woman*, 1926.

PRESTON, J. A. Actor. This Washington, D.C.-born actor studied at Louise Bramwell's Stage Studio, and with Jerome Robbins's American Theater Laboratory. He made his film debut in *Mississippi Summer*, 1971, and received critical acclaim for his portrayal of Dawson in producer/director **Ivan Dixon**'s powerful *The Spook Who Sat by the Door*, 1973. He has continued to work in both film and **television** with guest-starring appearances in such TV shows as *All in the Family, Good Times, The Jeffersons, Different Strokes*, and *Little House on the Prairie*. He had recurring roles on, *Hill Street Blues* as Ozzie Cleveland and Daltry on *Dallas*. His stage work includes *The Death of Bessie Smith, King John, Comedy of Errors*, and *The Gladiator*. Recent film projects include *Sweet Deadly Dreams*, 2002, and *Old Man Music*, 2004.

Filmography: *The Spook Who Sat by the Door*, 1973; *Body Heat*, 1981; *Remo Williams: The Adventure Begins*, 1985; *Fire Birds*, 1990; *A Few Good Men*, 1992; *Harvest of Fire*, 1995.

PRINCE (1958-). Singer, musician, actor, producer. This eclectic, Minneapolis, Minnesota-based performer has been up and down the charts for the past 20 years with his unique style of musical blends. His first two albums sold well, but it was the songs and musical soundtrack from *Purple Rain*, 1984, his semi-biographical film about the Minneapolis sound in music and the local club scene, that made him a star. He followed with *Under the Cherry Moon*, 1986, and *Graffiti Bridge*, 1990, which he also wrote and directed. Prince songs were the only tunes featured in director **Spike Lee**'s *Girl 6*, 1996, and he performed on the soundtrack from *Batman*, 1989. In 1993, Prince changed his name to a cryptic symbol after his 12th album. After a contractual disagreement that tied up the performer's name, he went for a while by The Artist Formerly Known as Prince.

Filmography: *Purple Rain*, 1984; *Under the Cherry Moon*, 1986; *Graffiti Bridge*, 1990.

PRINCE OF HIS RACE, A. 1926. Drama. A man from a good family falls into disgrace when he is falsely accused and sentenced to five years in prison for manslaughter. His sweetheart tries to remain loyal and true while being courted by the man whose lies put her lover in jail. It was produced by the Philadelphia-based production company **The Colored Players Film Corporation**. Cast: Harry Henderson, Shingzie Howard, William A. Clayton Jr., Lawrence Chenault, Arline Mickey, Ethel Smith. Director: Roy Calnek.

PRINGLE, JOAN. Actress. She was born in New York City and received her B. A. degree in Drama from City College of New York. She pursued the Theater Arts at Hunter College and studied acting with Uta Hagen. Pringle performed on stage in *Operation Sidewinder*, 1970 before moving on to film and **television**. After appearances on *The Bob Crane Show*, *Marcus Welby, M. D.*, *Sanford and Son*, and *That's My Mama*, she perhaps became best known as Principle Sybil Buchanan on the hit 1970s television series *The White Shadow*. Pringle also appeared on the daytime drama *General Hospital* as Dr. Patricia Mason, 1982-1984, and later as Elizabeth Jackson during the 1994 season.

Filmography: *Double Indemnity*, 1973; *J. D.'s Revenge*, 1976; *Best Friends*, 1982; *Visions of Terror*, 1994; *Percy & Thunder*, 1993; *Incognito*, 1999; *Original Sin*, 2001.

PROBLEM PICTURES. A series of films produced in the late 1940s and early 1950s that explored the problem of race relations in

America. Such films included *Home of the Brave*, 1949; *Pinky*, 1949; *Intruder in the Dust*, 1949; and *No Way Out*, 1950.

PRYOR, RICHARD (1940-2005). Comedian, actor, director. Born Richard Franklin Lennox Thomas Pryor III, in Peoria, Illinois, he discovered his knack for comedy in the 6th grade. A real cut-up in class, his teacher would give him time at the end of class to act up and entertain in exchange for good behavior the rest of the time. Following a two-year stint in the U. S. Army, he began his career as a stand-up comic. He moved from Peoria to New York City in 1963; by 1965, he was on *The Ed Sullivan Show*. His controversial act centered on sex and racism, and profanity was seldom in short supply. Five of his 23 comedy albums have received Grammy Awards, including *That Nigga's Crazy*, and *Bicentennial Nigger*. His filmed concerts brought in high box-office grosses. As an actor, Pryor was nominated for an **Academy Award** for his role as Piano Man in *Lady Sings the Blues*, 1972, and he has dozens of other film roles to his credit. As the top black actor working at one time, Columbia Pictures gave his Indigo Productions $30 million to produce films of interest to the African American audience. He made his directorial debut in 1986 with *Jo Jo Dancer, Your Life Is Calling*, 1986, which chronicled his troubled and often drug-plagued life. Shortly thereafter, Pryor was diagnosed with multiple sclerosis and his acting and comedy career waned. His autobiography, *Pryor Convictions*, was published in 1995.

　　Filmography: *Wild in the Streets*, 1968; *Black Brigade*, 1969; *Dynamite Chicken*, 1970; *Lady Sings the Blues*, 1972; *The Mack*, 1973; *Some Call It Loving*, 1973; *Hit*, 1973; *Uptown Saturday Night*, 1974; *Adios Amigos*, 1975; *Silver Streak*, 1976; *Car Wash*, 1976; *Bingo Long Traveling All-Stars and Motor Kings*, 1976; *Which Way is Up*, 1977; *Greased Lightning*, 1977; *The Wiz*, 1978; *California Suite*, 1978; *Blue Collar*, 1978; *Wholly Moses!* 1980; *Stir Crazy*, 1980; *In God We Trust*, 1980; *Bustin' Loose*, 1981; *The Toy*, 1982; *Some Kind of Hero*, 1982; *Superman 3*, 1983; *Brewster's Millions*, 1985; *Jo Jo Dancer, Your Life Is Calling*, 1986; *Critical Condition*, 1986; *Moving*, 1988; *See No Evil, Hear No Evil*, 1989; *Harlem Nights*, 1989; *Another You*, 1991; *Trigger Happy*, 1996; *Lost Highway*, 1996.

PUGH, WILLARD E. Actor. This hard-working actor once taught broadcasting and film classes at Chaffey College in Rancho Cucamonga, California. He made his film debut as a runaway slave in *Divided We Fall*, 1982, and his **television** debut came with the role

of Lynn Tatum in *Hill Street Blues*, 1983. He is perhaps best remembered as Harpo in *The Color Purple*, 1986.
Filmography: *Divided We Fall*, 1982; *Toy Soldiers*, 1984; *Stand Alone*, 1985; *Moving Violations*, 1985; *The Hills Have Eyes: Part II*, 1985; *The Color Purple*, 1986; *Blue City*, 1986; *Native Son*, 1986; *Amazon Women on the Moon*, 1987; *Made in Heaven*, 1987; *Traxx*, 1988; *Robocop 2*, 1990; *The Guyver*, 1991; *A Rage in Harlem*, 1991; *Ambition*, 1991; *Eddie Presley*, 1993; *CB4*, 1993; *Puppet Master 5: The Final Chapter*, 1974; *Under the Hulla Moon*, 1995; *Air Force One*, 1997; *High Frequency*, 1998; *Progeny*, 1998; *Spoiler*, 1998; *Today's Life*, 2000; *Up Against Amanda*, 2000; *The Big Leaf Tobacco Company*, 2001.

PURLIE VICTORIOUS. 1963. 93 min. Drama. A film based on the award-winning Broadway play, the story deals with the pros and cons of racial integration. Cast: **Ossie Davis**, **Ruby Dee**, **Godfrey Cambridge**, Alan Alda. Director: Nicholas Webster.

PURPLE RAIN. 1984. (R) 113 min. Music/Drama. A film based on the life and struggles of **Prince** before he was who he became. The film shows his pain of growing up in an interracial, dysfunctional family, and how he had to overcome his own ego and insecurities to become accepted, recognized, and to make it in the highly competitive Minneapolis music scene. Cast: Prince, Apollonia, **Morris Day**, Olga Karlatos, **Clarence Williams III**. Director: Albert Magnoli. Writer: William Blinn. Cinematographer: Donald E. Thorin. Music: Michel Columbier. Awards: **Oscars** 1984: Original Song Score and/or Adaptation.

PUTNEY SWOPE. 1969. (R) 84 min. Comedy. A comedic look at the inside operations of a large Madison Avenue ad agency when the token African American ad executive is accidentally elected as chairman of the board. The company and their commercials will never be the same. Cast: Arnold Johnson, Laura Greene, Stanley Gottlieb, Mel Brooks. Writer/Director: Robert Downey. Cinematographer: Gerald Cotts. Music: Charles Cura.

Q

QUEEN. 1993. (TV) 282 min. Drama. A miniseries based on the writings of **Alex Haley**, author of *Roots*, which chronicles the maternal side of his family, *Queen* covers his father's side. The son of a plantation owner fathers a child with a slave girl. They name their light-skinned daughter Queen, who grows up in a post-Civil War world that refuses to accept her as she is. Often rejected by each of the two cultures that make up her heritage, she is determined to weather the storm, conquer the hate, and make her own place in the world. Cast: **Halle Berry, Ossie Davis**, Dan Biggers, Leo Bermester, Patricia Clarkson, Timothy Daly, **Danny Glover, Jasmine Guy**, Linda Hart, **Dennis Haysbert**, Tommy Hollis, Peter Malony, **Lonette McKee**, Bob Minor, Alan North, Martin Sheen, **Madge Sinclair**, Eric Ware, **Paul Winfield**, Samuel E. Wright. Director: John Erman. Writer: David Stevens.

QUEEN LATIFAH (1970-). Rapper, actress, producer. She was born Dana Elaine Owens in Newark, New Jersey, and has been called the "First Lady of Rap." She began her entertainment career with the all-female rap group Ladies Fresh, and recorded the single "Wrath of My Madness." Taking on her stage name of Queen Latifah (Arabic for delicate and sensitive), her debut album was *All Hail the Queen*, which contained the hits "Ladies First," and "Dance for Me." Her later albums include *Nature of a Sista*, and *Black Reign*, which contained the popular single "U. N. I. T. Y." that won her a Grammy Award for best rap solo performance. Her **television** credits include *The Fresh Prince of Bel-Air, Hangin' With Mr. Cooper*, and *Roc*. She starred in the series *Living Single*, hosted *The Queen Latifah Show*, her own talk show from 1999-2001, and provides the voice for a series of Pizza Hut commercials. She made her film debut in a bit part as a waitress in **Spike Lee's** *Jungle Fever*, 1991, and went on to receive an **Academy Award** nomination for Best Supporting Actress, for her work in *Chicago: The Musical*, 2002. She runs her own record label called Flavor Unit, as well as a management company.

Filmography: *Jungle Fever*, 1991; *House Party 2*, 1991; *Juice*, 1992; *Who's the Man*, 1993; *My Life*, 1993; *Set It Off*, 1996; *Hoodlum*, 1997; *Sphere*, 1998; *Living Out Loud*, 1998; *The Bone Collector*, 1999; *The Country Bears*, 2002; *Brown Sugar*, 2002; *Chicago: The Musical*, 2002; *Bringing Down the House*, 2003; *Taxi*, 2004; *Barbershop 2*, 2004; *Beauty Shop*, 2005.

QUEENS OF COMEDY. 2001. (R) 79 min. Comedy/Documentary. This is a comedy concert with four stand-up comediennes filmed at the Orpheum Theater in Memphis, Tennessee. It is a female counterpart to **Spike Lee's** *Original Kings of Comedy*, 2000. Cast: Miss Laura Hayes, Adel Givens, Mo'Nique, Sommore. Director: Steve Purcell.

R

RACE MOVIES. This is a catch phrase for the all-black-cast films that were produced between the 1920s and 1940s. They began with the use of sound films or "talkies" that saw a rise of black actors in roles dealing with a wide range of genres ranging from melodramas to light comedy, to musicals and dance. Race movies were mostly produced on low budgets and aimed at the black audiences of the segregated movie-houses in the South, and the larger black populations that dwelled in the cities of the North through "midnight rambles" and the black-owned theaters.

RACE TO FREEDOM: THE STORY OF THE UNDERGROUND RAILROAD. 1994. (PG) 90 min. Historical. This is a made-for-cable movie about the network of people and safe houses used to smuggle runaway slaves from captivity in the South to freedom in the north. In 1850, four fugitives flee from North Carolina on their way to a new life in Canada. Cast: **Courtney B. Vance**, Janet Bailey, **Glynn Turman**, **Tim Reid**, Michael Riley, Dawn Lewis, Ron White, **Alfre Woodard**. Director: Don McBrearty. Writers: Nancy Trite Botkin, Diana Braithwaite. Music: Christopher Dedrick.

RAGE IN HARLEM, A. 1991. (R) 108 min. Urban Drama. A film based on a Chester A. Himes Novel, a sexy female thief hits town with a load of stolen gold in the 1950s. She is running from a group of crooks who are after the gold, and she takes up with a virtuous man who protects her while falling in love with her. Cast: **Forest Whitaker**, **Gregory Hines**, **Robin Givens**, **Zakes Mokae**, **Danny Glover**, Tyler Collins, Ron Taylor, T. K. Carter, **Willard Pugh**, Samm-Art Williams, Screamin' Jay Hawkins, Badja Djola, John Toles-Bey, Stack Pierce. Director: **Bill Duke**. Writers: John Toles-Bey, Bobby Crawford. Music: Elmer Bernstein.

RAGTIME. 1981. (PG) 156 min. Music/Drama. A film taken from the novel by E. L. Doctorow, a middle-class African American man refuses to back down to racism in 1906. This simple act ignites hateful passions and the impending scandal involves his family in all of the turmoil and racist attacks. Cast: **Howard E. Rollins, Jr.**, Kenneth McMillan, Brad Dourif, Mary Steenburgen, James Olson, Elizabeth McGovern, Pat O'Brien, James Cagney, **Debbie Allen**, Jeff Daniels, **Moses Gunn**, Donald O'Connor, Mandy Patinkin, Norman Mailer. Director: Milos Forman. Writer: Michael Weller. Music: Randy Newman.

RAILROAD PORTER, THE. 1912. Silent. Two reels. Comedy. A short comedy about a railroad porter who leaves for work one day and returns home to find another man sitting at his dinner table eating his food. It includes a farcical chase routine that is reminiscent of the Keystone Cops comedies of that time. The film's producer, **William Foster**, is credited with being the first African American to control his own-filmed image on film.

RAISIN IN THE SUN, A. 1961. 128 min. Urban Drama. The film is based on the 1959 Broadway play by Lorraine Hansberry. An African American family living in a crowded tenement apartment on the southside of Chicago awaits the arrival of a $10,000.00 life insurance check from the recent death of the family patriarch. Tired, ambitious, and desperate, each family member has his or her own use for the money, the most appealing being a new house in an all-white neighborhood. Cast: **Sidney Poitier, Ruby Dee, Diana Sands, Claudia McNeil**, John Fiedler, **Ivan Dixon, Louis Gossett Jr.** Director: Daniel Petrie. Writer: **Lorraine Hansberry**. Cinematography: Charles Lawton Jr. Music: Laurence Rosenthal. Awards: National Board of Review 1961: Best Supporting Actress (Dee).

RAISIN IN THE SUN, A. 1989. (TV) 171 min. Urban Drama. This is a **television** remake of the 1961 film about a black family in the 1950s struggling to survive and make a better life for themselves in a brand-new neighborhood that does not want them. Cast: **Danny Glover, Esther Rolle, Starletta DuPois**. Director: **Bill Duke**.

RALPH, SHERYL LEE (1956-). Actress, singer. She was born in Waterbury, Connecticut, although her parents were from Jamaica. She won a scholarship to Rutgers University and earned a degree in English literature and theater. She earned a Tony nomination for her role as Deena Jones in the Broadway musical *Dreamgirls*, and quickly moved to **television** with guest starring roles in *The Jeffersons, Hunter, L. A. Law*, and *Amazing Stories*. She had a recurring role in the TV series *The District*, and was a regular on *Code Name: Foxfire, It's a Living, New Attitude*, and *Designing Women*, and the daytime soap opera *Search for Tomorrow*. She costarred in the sitcom *Moesha*, and has appeared in many telefilms, including *The Neighborhood*, 1982; *No Child of Mine*, 1993; and *Witch Hunt*, 1994. Ralph has also pursued a singing career and recorded several albums. She made her film debut in *A Piece of the Action*, 1977. She organizes the Jamerican Film and Music Festival in

Kingston, Jamaica. She also tours with her powerful one-woman show, *Sometimes, I Cry*, a series of monologues about women affected by and infected with HIV and AIDS.

Filmography: *A Piece of the Action*, 1977; ***The Mighty Quinn***, 1989; *Skin Deep*, 1989; ***To Sleep with Anger***, 1990; *Mistress*, 1992; ***The Distinguished Gentleman***, 1992; *Sister Act 2: Back in the Habit*, 1993; *The Flintstones*, 1994; ***White Man's Burden***, 1995; *Lover's Knot*, 1996; *Bogus*, 1996; *Secrets*, 1997; ***Personals***, 1999; *Deterrence*, 1999; *Unconditional Love*, 1999; *Lost in the Pershing Hotel*, 2000; *Baby of the Family*, 2002.

RANDLE, THERESA (1967-). Actress. She was born in Los Angeles, California, and began training in acting and dance at an early age. She appeared in music videos and TV commercials and landed her first film role in *Maid to Order*, 1987. Other film roles followed in ***King of New York***, 1990; ***The Five Heartbeats***, 1991; and ***Sugar Hill***, 1994. She won the lead role as a phone sex worker in **Spike Lee**'s ***Girl 6***, 1996. Her television guest appearances include *Seinfeld* and *A Different World*.

Filmography: *Maid to Order*, 1987; ***Jungle Fever***, 1991; *King of New York*, 1990; *The Five Heartbeats*, 1991; ***Malcolm X***, 1992; ***CB4: The Movie***, 1993; *Sugar Hill*, 1994; *Beverly Hills Cop 3*, 1994; ***Bad Boys***, 1995; *Space Jam*, 1996; ***Girl 6***, 1996; ***Spawn***, 1997; ***Livin' for Love: The Natalie Cole Story***, 2000; ***Bad Boys 2***, 2003.

RAPPIN'. 1985. (PG) 92 min. Urban Drama. An ex-convict has a hard time on the outside when he gets on the wrong side of his landlord and the leader of a local street gang. Cast: **Mario Van Peebles**, Tasia Valanza, Harry Goz, Charles Flohe. Director: Joel Silberg.

RASHAD, PHYLICIA (1948-). Actress. She was born in Houston, Texas, and graduated with a B. F. A. degree in Fine Arts from Howard University in Washington, D. C. She moved to New York and began working on stage in the productions of *The Cherry Orchard*, *Weep Not for Me*, and *Dreamgirls*. She appeared on Broadway in *Jelly's Last Jam*. Early **television** and film appearances include the TV show *Delvecchio*, and she was a Munchkin in the film ***The Wiz***, 1978. She was on the daytime soap opera *One Life to Live* from 1983 to 1984 as Courtney Wright, but her role as Clair Huxtable on *The Cosby Show* brought her worldwide attention. Rashad has appeared in numerous made-for-TV movies, including ***Uncle Tom's Cabin***, 1987; *Polly*, 1989; and ***The Old Settler***, 2001, in which she costarred with her sister, **Debbie Allen**. She was once married to sports announcer and former football player Ahmad Rashad.

Filmography: *The Wiz*, 1978; ***Once Upon a Time When We Were Colored***, 1996; *Free of Eden*, 1999; *Loving Jezebel*, 1999; ***The Visit***, 2000.

RASULALA, THALMUS (1939-1991). Actor. He was born Jack Crowder and attended the University of Redlands, where he began acting. He won a Theater World award for his role as Cornelius Hackle in the 1967 all-black revival of *Hello, Dolly*, starring **Pearl Bailey**. He hit the big screen in ***Blackula***, 1972, with his new name, and starred in ***Cool Breeze***, 1972, and ***Willy Dynamite***, 1974.

Filmography: *Blackula*, 1972; *Cool Breeze*, 1972; *Willy Dynamite*, 1974; ***Friday Foster***, 1975; ***Bucktown***, 1975; *Adios Amigos*, 1975; ***Sophisticated Gents***, 1981; *Born American*, 1986; *Bulletproof*, 1988; *Above the Law*, 1988; *The Package*, 1989; *Blind Vengeance*, 1990; ***New Jack City***, 1991; *Mom and Dad Save the World*, 1992.

RAY. 2004. (PG-13). 152 min. Biopic. This is a film based on the life and times of legendary R&B singer Ray Charles. This outstanding musical biography won numerous awards, including two **Academy Awards** for best performance by an actor and best achievement in sound, a **Golden Globe** for best actor, and four **Image Awards**. The story documents the musical genius of Ray Charles. It explores his demons, as well as his fight to overcome all obstacles in a phenomenal rise to fame. It is also known as *Unchain My Heart: The Ray Charles Story*. Cast: **Jamie Foxx, Kerry Washington, Regina King, Clifton Powell, Harry J. Lennix, Bokeem Woodbine,** Aunjanue Ellis, **Sharon Warren,** C. J. Sanders, Curtis Armstrong, Richard Schiff, **Larenze Tate, Terrence Howard,** David Krumholtz, **Wendell Pierce.** Director: Taylor Hackford. Writers: Taylor Hackford, James L. White. Cinematographer: Pawel Edelman. Music: Craig Armstrong, Ray Charles.

REALIZATION OF A NEGRO'S AMBITION. 1916. Silent. Two reels. Drama. This was the first film produced by **Lincoln Motion Picture Company**, the second African American-owned film company. A recent Tuskeegee graduate with a degree in civil engineering leaves his father's farm to seek his fortune in the world. His skin tone makes getting the job he seeks difficult, until he saves the life of a local oil magnate's daughter. To show his gratitude, the father hires him as head of oil exploration for his company. Cast:

Noble Johnson, Clarence Brooks, Webb King, G. H. Reed, A. Burns, A. Collins, Beulah Hall, Lottie Boles, Bessie Mathews, Bessie Baker, Gertrude Christmas.

REDEMPTION. 2003. (R) 120 min. Drama. A young man dreams of being a movie actor like his father. He befriends an industry insider who begins to make his dream come true. He starts getting acting jobs and dating beautiful girls as his career really takes off, until drugs enter the scene, and destroy him and his dream. Cast: Brian J. White, Tracey Stone, Dwayne Chattman, T. J. Storm, Stecy Bellew, Doron Keenan, Scottie Tate, Darrow Igus, Barry Trachten, Thi Nguyen, Samantha Elkin, Pete Walsh. Director: Sean A. Reid. Writer: Hunter Dennis.

REDEMPTION: THE STAN TOOKIE WILLIAMS STORY. 2004. (R) 95 min. Drama. This film tells a true story about murder, death row, and redemption. The founder of a notorious street gang is incarcerated and sentenced to death for his many crimes. While in prison, he begins to write children's books that promote peace and stress non-violent solutions to problems. This earns him a nomination for the Nobel Peace Prize. Cast: **Jamie Foxx, Lynn Whitfield**, Lee Thompson Young, Brenden Jefferson, Brenda Bazzinet, Wes Williams, Greg Ellwand, **CCH Pounder**, Barbara Barnes-Hopkins, Tom Barnett, Karl Campbell, Joseph Pierre, Vilbert Cobham, David Fraser, Kahmaara Armatrading. Director: **Vondie Curtis-Hall**. Writer: J. T. Allen.

RED, WHITE, AND BLACK, THE. (a.k.a. *Soul Soldier*). 1970. (PG) 103 min. Western. The story of a troop of black Buffalo Soldiers who fight and kill Indians for a white government power structure that is mistreating them both. Cast: **Robert DoQui**, Isaac Fields, Barbara Hale, Rafer Johnson, **Lincoln Kilpatrick, Isabel Sanford**, Otis Taylor, Janee Michelle, Bobby Clark, Robert Dix, Byrd Holland, Steve Drexel, Bill Collins, Russ Nannarello Jr., John J. Fox. Director: John "Bud" Cardos. Writer: Marlene Weed.

REESE, DELLA (1931-). Actress, singer, comedian. She began singing when she was six years old and left her hometown of Detroit, Michigan, as a teenager and toured with famed gospel singer Mahalia Jackson. Reese later sang with the Erskine Hawkins Orchestra and began recording her own records. She was the first to take gospel into the casinos of Las Vegas and was nominated for a Grammy award as Best Female Soloist in Gospel Music in 1987. Reese performed regularly on *The Tonight Show Starring Johnny Carson*, and as an actress, she guest starred in over two dozen **television** series, including *McCloud, Police Woman, The Rookies, Crazy Like a Fox,* and *Promised Land.* She is perhaps best known as Tess in the series *Touched by an Angel.* Her film work includes roles in **Harlem Nights,** 1989; **Mama Flora's Family,** 1998; and **Beauty Shop,** 2005.

Filmography: *Psychic Killer,* 1975; *Harlem Nights,* 1989; **You Must Remember This,** 1992; **The Distinguished Gentleman,** 1996; **A Thin Line Between Love and Hate,** 1996; *Mama Flora's Family,* 1998; **Having Our Say: The Delany Sisters' First 100 Years,** 1999; *Dinosaur,* 2000; *Beauty Shop,* 2005.

REET, PETITE AND GONE. 1947. 75 min. Music/Comedy. A sneaky lawyer tries to cheat a young woman out of her inheritance after her mother dies. Musical numbers are provided by singer **Louis Jordan** and The Tympani Five. Cast: Louis Jordan, June Richmond. Director: William Forest Crouch.

REID, CHRISTOPHER (1964-). Singer, actor. This Bronx, New York-born rapper came to prominence as Chris "Kid" Reid of the hip-hop duo Kid 'N Play. His film work includes roles in the *House Party* series of films.

Filmography: *House Party,* 1990; **House Party 2,** 1991; **Class Act,** 1992; **Sword of Honor,** 1994; **House Party 3,** 1994; **The Temptations,** 1998; **Border Line,** 1999.

REID, TIM (1944-). Actor, writer, producer, director. A native of Norfolk, Virginia, Reid received his B.S. degree in business/marketing in 1968 from Norfolk State University. After working in the marketing department at DuPont, Reid began to write comedy and decided to venture into show business. After tours with such comedians as Tom Dreesen and **Della Reese,** he landed in Hollywood and began to work in **television.** He portrayed radio deejay Venus Flytrap on the popular CBS series *WKRP in Cincinnati,* 1978-1982, and received two NAACP **Image Award** nominations for Best Actor in a Comedy. He also appeared on *Simon & Simon* and *The Richard Pryor Show.* Along with his wife, **Daphne Maxwell Reid,** they produced and costarred in the television series *Frank's Place, Snoops,* and *The Tim and Daphne Show.* His critically acclaimed feature film, **Once Upon a Time When We Were Colored,** 1995, received numerous awards, and his Family Channel/BET movie *Race to Freedom: The Underground Railroad,* was nominated for a Cable Ace Award and a Producer's Guild Award. Going where no present-day producers have gone before, Reid and wife Daphne built their own film production studio in Petersburg, Virginia. New Millennium Studios has given birth to television shows, feature films, and commercials, including *Asunder*, 1999, and the Showtime series *Link's*. He is also on the hit Warner Brothers TV series *Sister, Sister.*

Filmography: *Dead Bang*, 1989; *Stephen King's It*, 1990; *The Fourth War*, 1990; *You Must Remember This*, 1992; *Race to Freedom The Story of the Underground Railroad*, 1994.

REID, DAPHNE MAXWELL (1948-). Actress, producer. As cofounder of New Millennium Studios with her husband, **Tim Reid**, she is mostly recognized as Aunt Viv on NBC's *The Fresh Prince of Bel Air*. Born and raised in New York City, she majored in interior design and architecture at Northwestern University, and later signed a modeling contract with the Eileen Ford Agency and became the first African American woman on the cover of *Glamour* magazine. She began an acting career and has been very active in **television** roles in series, such as *Simon & Simon, Hardcastle and McCormick, Cagney and Lacey, Hill Street Blues*, and *The Cosby Show*. She has also acted with her husband in their own productions, including *Frank's Place, Snoops, Link's*, and their syndicated talk show, *The Tim and Daphne Show*. Her feature film appearances include *Protocol,* 1984, and *Once Upon a Time When We Were Colored*, 1995.

Filmography: *Protocol*, 1984; *You Must Remember This*, 1992; *Once Upon a Time When We Were Colored*, 1995; *Asunder*, 1998; *Alley Cats Strike*, 2000.

REMEMBER THE TITANS. 2000. (PG) 113 min. Drama. The true story of an African American coach appointed to a newly integrated school in Virginia. As the head football coach at T. C. Williams High School, he was hired over another highly successful white coach, which strains race relations within the school and the community. The team and his efforts become a unifying force as they all learn to trust and depend on one another, and just get along. Cast: **Denzel Washington**, Will Patton, Wood Harris, Ryan Hurst, Donald Faison, Craig Kirkwood, Ethan Suplee, Kip Pardue, Hayden Panettiere, Nicole Ari Parker, Kate Bosworth, Earl Poitier, Ryan Gosling, Burgess Jenkins, Neal Ghant. Director: Boaz Yakin. Writer: Gregory Allen Howard.

REOL PICTURES. This was an early race movie company from the 1920s founded by white producer Robert Levy to produce all-black cast films. These films were *The Burden of Race*, 1921; *The Sport* *of the Gods*, 1921; *The Call of His People*, 1921; and *Spitfire*, 1922, and all starred the popular actor **Lawrence Chenault**.

RETURN OF SUPERFLY. 1990. (R) 94 min. Blaxploitation. The sequel to the mega-**blaxploitation** hit *Superfly*, 1971. Clad with the moniker of an insect, a Harlem man harasses drug dealers and sometimes even the cops. Once again, **Curtis Mayfield** provides the music. Cast: **Margaret Avery**, Nathan Purdee, **Samuel Jackson**. Music: Curtis Mayfield, **Ice T**.

RHAMES, VING (1961-). Actor. This native of Harlem discovered a love for acting while attending the New York High School for the Performing Arts. He continued his studies at the Julliard School of Drama and worked on the New York theater circuit. He first appeared on Broadway in a 1984 production of *The Winter Boys*. His big-screen break came when Quentin Tarantino cast him as the merciless drug kingpin Marsellus Wallace in his hit film *Pulp Fiction*, 1994. He won a Golden Globe award for his portrayal of the title role in the TV biopic ***Don King: Only in America***, 1997.

Filmography: *Patty Hearst*, 1988; ***The Long Walk Home***, 1989; *Rising Son*, 1990; *Jacob's Ladder*, 1990; *Flight of the Intruder*, 1990; *The People Under the Stairs*, 1991; *Homicide*, 1991; *Pulp Fiction*, 1994; ***Drop Squad***, 1994; *Striptease*, 1996; ***Rosewood***, 1996; *Mission Impossible*, 1996; ***Don King Only In America***, 1997, *Con Air*, 1997; *Body Count*, 1997; *Out of Sight*, 1998; *Entrapment*, 1999; *Mission Impossible 2*, 2000; *Holiday Heart*, 2000; *Sins of the Father*, 2001; ***Baby Boy***, 2001; *Undisputed*, 2002; *RFK*, 2002; *Little John*, 2002; *Dark Blue*, 2003.

RICH, MATTY (1971-). Director. He was born Mathew Statisfield Richardson in Brooklyn, New York, and attended New York University film school before dropping out to make films on his own. For his feature debut, he called upon his experiences growing up in Brooklyn's Red Hook Houses to write the script for ***Straight Out of Brooklyn***, 1991, which won the Special Jury Prize at the Sundance Film Festival. His second film was ***The Inkwell***, 1994.

Filmography: *Straight Out of Brooklyn*, 1991; *The Inkwell*, 1994.

RICHARDS, BEAH (1920-2000). Actress, writer. She was born Beulah Richardson in Vicksburg, Mississippi. She graduated from Dillard University in 1948 and decided to leave the segregated South to pursue acting. Her initial training at the Old Globe Theater in San Diego helped prepare her for a 50-year career that would combine stage, movies, and **television**, while often playing feisty character roles and strong matriarchs. She moved to New York City in the early 1950s to take on the grandmother role in the stage production of *Take a Giant Step*, and reprised her role in the 1959 film version. Richard's screen debut was as a maid in *The Mugger*, 1958. She received **Emmy Awards** for her guest appearances on CBS's *Frank's Place*, 1988, and ABC's *The Practice*, 2000. She received an **Oscar** nomination for supporting actress for her role as Mrs. Prentiss in *Guess Who's Coming to Dinner*, 1968. Other film roles include *Hurry Sundown*, 1966; *In the Heat of the Night*, 1967; and *The Great White Hope*, 1970. Television guest appearances include *ER*, *The Bill Cosby Show*, and *Roots: The Next Generation*. Further stage work includes James Baldwin's *The Amen Corner*, and a Lincoln Center revival of Lillian Hellman's *The Little Foxes*. She has written three books: *One is a Crowd*, *A Black Woman Speaks*, and *A Black Woman Speaks and Other Poems*. Adapting her writings for the stage, she went on tour with *An Evening with Beah Richards*. Her last film role was in *Beloved*, 1998. Richards received the Los Angeles Pan-African Film Festival's Lifetime Achievement Award in 2000, and was once married to artist Hugh Harrell. Actress Lisa Gay Hamilton has produced and directed *Beah: A Black Woman Speaks*, 2003; a documentary on Beah Richards' life and achievements.

Filmography: *The Miracle Worker*, 1962; *Gone Are the Days!*, 1963; *Guess Who's Coming to Dinner*, 1967; *A Dream for Christmas*, 1973; *Roots: The Next Generation*, 1979; *A Christmas Without Snow*, 1980; *Sophisticated Gents*, 1981; *As Summers Die*, 1986; *Acceptable Risks*, 1986; *Drugstore Cowboy*, 1989; *Inside Out*, 1991; *Beloved*, 1998.

RICHARDSON, SALLI (1967-). Actress. She was born in Chicago, Illinois, and made her film debut in the film *Up Against the Wall*, 1991. She has made guest appearances to the **television** series *Roc*, *Between Brothers*, and *The Jamie Foxx Show*. Her recurring roles include *Rude Awakening* and *CSI Miami*, and she was a regular on the series *Mercy Point* and *Family Law*. She is married to actor Dondre Whitfield.

Filmography: *Up Against the Wall*, 1991; *Prelude to a Kiss*, 1992; *Mo' Money*, 1992; *How U Like Me Now*, 1992; *Posse*, 1993; *I Spy Returns*, 1994; *A Low Down Dirty Shame*, 1994; *Sioux City*, 1994; *Once Upon a Time When We Were Colored*, 1996; *Soul of the Game*, 1996; *The Great White Hype*, 1996; *Butter*, 1998; *Lillie*, 1999; *Book of Love*, 2002; *Antwone Fisher*,

2002; *Baby of the Family*, 2002; **Biker Boyz**, 2003; *Anacondas: The Hunt for the Blood Orchid*, 2004.

RICHARDSON, SY. Actor. He was born in Cincinnati, Ohio, and raised in Chicago, Illinois. He began singing at age 12 and recorded his first record with the group Lil June and the Januarys at 16. Richardson served two years with the U.S. Navy and graduated from the University of Colorado, Boulder, with a B.S. degree in journalism. After working for several Colorado newspapers, he joined the Heritage Square Opera House and performed for two years before moving to Hollywood. He teaches acting workshops and is a member of the International Society for Excellence in Christian Film and Television.

Filmography: *Cinderella*, 1977; *Petey Wheatstraw*, 1977; *Fairy Tales*, 1979; **My Brother's Wedding**, 1983; *Repo Man*, 1984; *Sid and Nancy*, 1986; *Medium Rare*, 1987; *Straight to Hell*, 1987; *Colors*, 1988; *Tapeheads*, 1988; *Dead Man Walking*, 1988; *They Live*, 1988; *Three Fugitives*, 1989; *Mystery Train*, 1989; **To Sleep with Anger**, 1990; *Street Asylum*, 1990; *Catchfire*, 1990; *Fragrance*, 1991; *Eye of the Stranger*, 1993; **Posse**, 1993; *Floundering*, 1994; **The Glass Shield**, 1994; *The Winner*, 1996; *Shattered Illusions*, 1998; *Beat*, 1999; *The Playaz Court*, 2000; *Human Nature*, 2001; *Extreme Honor*, 2001; *Surviving Christmas*, 2004; *South of Heaven*, 2006.

RIDE. 1998. (R) 83 min. Comedy/Drama. This is a road movie about a group of Harlem youths being transported to Miami to participate in a rap music video shoot. The trip includes lots of fights, funky attitudes, and narrow escapes from sophomoric pranks. Their arrival in Florida brings about even more distress, but love could be waiting as well. Cast: **Malik Yoba, Melissa De Sousa**, Fredro Starr, **John Witherspoon, Cedric the Entertainer**, Sticky Fingaz, Kellie Williams, Idalis de Leon, Julia Garrison, Guy Torry, Reuben Asher, The Lady of Rage, Dartanyan Edmonds, Downtown Julie Brown, **Snoop Dogg**. Writer/Director: Millicent Shelton. Cinematographer: Frank Byers. Music: Dunn Pearson Jr.

RIGGS, MARLON (1957-1994). Documentary filmmaker, educator, poet. Born in Ft. Worth, Texas, Riggs graduated magna cum laude from Harvard University in 1978 with a B.A. in history. He earned his M.A. in journalism from the University of California, Berkeley, in 1981, and returned there to teach documentary film in 1987. He was the recipient of numerous awards, including **Emmy Awards** in 1987 and 1991, a Peabody Award in 1989, and an Erik Barnouw

Award in 1992. His writings have appeared in scholarly and literary journals, and his video productions brought him both praise and controversy. His video works on the ethnic **stereotyping** of African Americans in the media and various other forms of popular culture, *Ethnic Notions*, 1987, and *Color Adjustment*, 1989, were well received when they aired on public television stations across the country. However, his 55-minute poetic essay on black gay males, *Tongues Untied*, 1988, was considered obscene by some, and caused a rage of controversy over government funding and censorship. The project received numerous awards, including Best Documentary of the Berlin International Film Festival, Best Independent Experimental Work by the Los Angeles Film Critics, and Best Video by the New York Documentary Film Festival. Riggs died of AIDS in April 1994.

Filmography: *Ethnic Notions*, 1986; *Tongues Untied*, 1988; *Color Adjustment*, 1989; *Non, Je Ne Regrette Rein (No Regret)*, 1992; *Black Is ... Black Ain't*, 1994.

RIVER NIGER, THE. 1976. (R) 105 min. Drama. This is a film adaptation of the Tony-award winning play about the often-hard life of inner-city living. A hard-working painter questions his faith when his wife falls ill. Their son returns home from the military, but is not in uniform. His parents are proud and happy to see him, but wonder why he is home. The street gang he was once a member of has turned militant, and they pressure him to come back to the fold. He refuses. When a planned heist goes bad because there is a traitor among them, they escape to his parents' home, where the truth is revealed, and bad things start to happen. Cast: **James Earl Jones, Cicely Tyson, Glynn Turman, Louis Gossett Jr., Roger E. Mosley**, Jonelle Allen. Director: Krishna Shah. Writer: Joseph A. Walker.

RIZE. 2005. (PG-13) 124 min. Dance/Music/Documentary. This film explores the dance phenomenon born in the mean streets of south central Los Angeles known as "krumping." The spastic movements often look like epileptic convulsions set to music. The young, mostly African American, dancers appear to lose total control of their bodies, but know exactly what they are doing. Not dancing "with" each other, they dance "at" each other, erupting in a duel of frenzied motion. Their dance is said to be a way to release their hostilities in a positive manner, rather than through the obvious gang warfare and crime on the streets. The film culminates in an exciting dance-off called Battle Zone V, held at a packed Los Angeles sports arena. Cast: Tommy the Clown, Dragon, Lil C, Ms.

Prissy, Tight Eyez, Larry, La Nina, Lil Tommy. Director: David LaChapelle.

ROBERT MOTT'S PEKING THEATER STOCK COMPANY. This distinctive Chicago-based acting troupe was active on the vaudeville stage circuit. Talent from this group was cast in a series of four short films produced by the **Foster Photoplay Company** between 1910-1913.

ROBERTSON, HUGH A. (1932-1988). Editor, director. He is the first African American to be nominated for a technical **Oscar** for his editing of the film *Midnight Cowboy*, 1969. He began his career as an assistant editor on *Something Wild*, 1961. Other editing credits include *Shaft*, 1971, and *Harvey Middleman, Fireman*, 1965. As a director, he helmed the feature films *Melinda*, 1972; *Obeah*, 1978; and, for **television**, the "Love and the Lady Prisoner" episode of *Love American Style*, 1969.

ROBESON, PAUL (1898-1976). Actor, singer, civil rights activist. Born in Princeton, New Jersey, Paul Robeson gained a worldwide reputation as an actor, singer, scholar, and activist. The son of a runaway slave, he educated himself at Lincoln University and won a scholarship to Rutgers University. A tremendous athlete, he earned 12 letters in football, baseball, track, and basketball. He was named as an All American in both 1917 and 1918, and was honored as a Phi Beta Kappa for his academics in his junior year. Robeson received his law degree from Columbia in 1923, and financed it while playing professional football. While performing in a play at Columbia, he was spotted by noted playwright Eugene O'Neill, and made his professional stage debut in *Taboo*. Robeson followed his stage success with O'Neill's *All God's Chillun Got Wings* and *The Emperor Jones*. Other important stage roles included *Othello*, *Porgy*, and *Showboat*. Robeson became a world traveler and spoke several languages, including Chinese, Russian, and Spanish. His first film role was in **Oscar Michueax's** *Body and Soul*, 1924. He was later brought to Hollywood from the European stage to play the title character in the film version of *The Emperor Jones*, 1933, a role that would bring him international stardom. Robeson's other films include *Sanders of the River*, 1935; *Showboat*, 1936; and *Tales of Manhattan*, 1942. Well known for his powerful singing voice, Robeson also recorded over 300 records in his multi-faceted career. His political views and affiliations often surrounded him in controversy. He protested against lynching, picketed the White House, and refused to perform before segregated audiences. In 1951, during the McCarthy era, his passport was denied when he was called to testify and refused to deny that he was a member of the Communist Party. With limited work and career opportunities, Robeson's annual income plummeted from $104,000.00 to $2,000. The decision was overturned eight years later by the Supreme Court and his passport was returned, but his career never recovered.

Filmography: *Body and Soul*, 1924; *Emperor Jones*, 1933; *Sanders of the River*, 1935; *Song of Freedom*, 1936; *Show Boat*, 1936; *King Solomon's Mines*, 1937; *Big Fella*, 1937; *Jericho*, 1938; *Tales of Manhattan*, 1942.

ROBINSON, BILL "BOJANGLES" (1878-1949). Dancer, actor. He was seemingly born to dance in Richmond, Virginia. After the death of his parents while he was still a baby, his grandmother raised Robinson, and she was not pleased when he began dancing on street corners to make money. Regardless, he became a "hoofer" or song-and-dance man by age six, and worked the local beer taverns. By age eight, he was performing with Mayme Remington's vaudeville troupe based in Washington, D. C., and by the time he was 12, Robinson was performing with a traveling company in *The South, Before the War*. He later formed a vaudeville team with George Cooper, and his early career was exclusively playing the black theater circuit. Robinson did not dance for white audiences until he was 50. When Chicago agent Marty Forkins became his lifelong manager in 1908, Robinson began to nurture his solo act, and became one of the toasts of Broadway. As the vaudeville era waned, white impresario Lew Leslie produced his highly successful *Blackbirds of 1928*, a black, musical review specifically for white audiences that featured Robinson and other black stars. Robinson soon became very popular and received the nickname "Bojangles." He was in a total of 17 motion pictures, including *Hello, Bill*, 1929; *Dixiana*, 1930; and *King for a Day*, 1934. After the financial failure of **Harlem is Heaven**, 1932, Robinson shied away from all-black independent productions and hit mainstream success as the antebellum butler dancing with Shirley Temple in such films as *The Littlest Colonel*, 1935; *The Littlest Rebel*, 1935; and *Rebecca of Sunnybrook Farm*, 1937. He returned to all-black cast films with **One Mile from Heaven**, 1937, and **Stormy Weather**, 1943, both opposite the lovely **Lena Horne**. He was married twice. The first just after World War I to Fannie S. Clay in Chicago, ended in divorce, in 1943. He married Elaine Plaines in Columbus, Ohio, in 1944. He was well-known in gambling circles and, other than giving freely to charity, he spent little time managing his estimated

$3,500 per week earnings. **Bojangles**, 2001, a film depicting Robinson's life and times was made with master tap dancer **Gregory Hines** in the title role.

Filmography: *Hello, Bill*, 1929; *Dixiana*, 1930; *Harlem Is Heaven*, 1932; *King for a Day*, 1934; *The Littlest Rebel*, 1935; *The Little Colonel*, 1935; *One Mile from Heaven*, 1937; *Rebecca of Sunnybrook Farm*, 1938; *Just Around the Corner*, 1938; *Stormy Weather*, 1943.

ROCHON, LELA (1964-). Actress. Born and raised in Los Angeles, California, Rochon studied journalism and theater at Cal State University while modeling on the side. After being in music videos for Luther Vandross and Lionel Ritchie, as well as starring in 28 Spuds Bud Light beer commercials, Rochon was ready for the bright lights of Hollywood. Her big break came from small parts in *Harlem Nights*, 1989, as a memorable character named Sunshine. Larger roles eventually followed in *Waiting to Exhale*, 1995, and *Why Do Fools Fall in Love*, 1998. Rochon has made guest appearances on **television** shows, such as *Amen*, *The Cosby Show*, *Roc*, and *Hangin' with Mr. Cooper*, and she was a regular on *The Wayans Brothers*, and *The Division*. She is married to film director **Antoine Fuqua**.

Filmography: *Breakin'*, 1984; *Foxtrap*, 1986; *The Wild Pair*, 1987; *Stewardess School*, 1987; *Harlem Nights*, 1989; *Boomerang*, 1992; *The Meteor Man*, 1993; *Waiting to Exhale*, 1995; *The Chamber*, 1996; *Gang Related*, 1997; *Legal Deceit*, 1997; *Ruby Bridges*, 1998; *The Big Hit*, 1998; *Knock Off*, 1998; *Why Do Fools Fall in Love*, 1998; *Any Given Sunday*, 1999; *Labor Pains*, 2000; *First Daughter*, 2004.

ROCK, CHRIS (1966-). Comedian, actor, producer. Born in South Carolina and raised in Brooklyn, New York, Rock was a stand-up comic who distinguished himself on NBC's *Saturday Night Live*, 1990-93. After headlining two HBO specials, he got his own talk show on HBO, *The Chris Rock Show*, 1997. He has also guest starred on TV series, such as *The Fresh Prince of Bel-Air*, *Martin*, and *Homicide: Life on the Street*. While building his film career, Rock started out in bit parts in films like *Beverly Hills Cop II*, 1987, and *I'm Gonna Git You Sucka*, 1988. His roles increased in films like *New Jack City*, 1991, and *Boomerang*, 1992. He then co-wrote, produced, and starred in *CB4*, 1993. A variety of roles followed, including providing the voice for the guinea pig in the remake of *Dr. Dolittle*, 1998, and the voice of the title character in the animated feature film *Osmosis Jones*, 2001. His costarring roles include *Beverly Hills Ninja*, 1997, and **Down to Earth**, 2000.

Filmography: *Beverly Hills Cop II*, 1987; *I'm Gonna Git You Sucka*, 1988; *New Jack City*, 1991; *Boomerang*, 1992; *Coneheads*, 1993; *CB4: The Movie*, 1993; *Beverly Hills Ninja*, 1996; *Lethal Weapon 4*, 1998; *Dogma*, 1999; *Nurse Betty*, 2000; **Pootie Tang**, 2001; *Jay and Silent Bob Strike Back*, 2001; *Down to Earth*, 2001; *Bad Company*, 2002; **Head of State**, 2003.

ROCK, THE (1972-). Professional wrestler, actor. He was born Dwayne Douglas Johnson in Hayward, California. He attended the University of Miami on a full football scholarship, but a back injury kept him from playing in the NFL. He played football with the Canadian league for one year and then left to pursue his wrestling career. He made his wrestling debut in the United States Wrestling Association (USWA) under the name Flex Kavanah, and joined the World Wrestling Entertainment Group (WWE) as Rocky Maivia, eventually taking the persona of The Rock. He made his film debut as The Scorpion King in *The Mummy Returns*, 2001, and returned to the big screen in the title role for the prequel, *The Scorpion King*, 2002.

Filmography: *The Mummy Returns*, 2001; *The Scorpion King*, 2002; *The Rundown*, 2003; *Walking Tall*, 2004; *Be Cool*, 2005; *Doom*, 2005; *Instant Karma*, 2005; *Spy Hunter*, 2005; *Johnny Bravo*, 2005; *Gridiron Gang*, 2006.

ROLL BOUNCE. 2005. (PG-13) Comedy/Romance. This film is like *Saturday Night Fever* on roller skates. A group of five teenage friends rule their local roller rink with their fancy moves and synchronized skating routines. When their home base closes down, they are forced to go across town to skate, only to find stiffer competition for the girls and for their suddenly lackluster routines. They go home and practice even harder in hopes of coming back to win an upcoming performance skate competition. Cast: **Bow Wow**, **Chi McBride**, Westley Jonathan, **Meagan Good**, **Mike Epps**, Charles Q. Murphy, **Nick Cannon**, J. D. Ballew, Tai'isha Davis, Diane Frances Fisher, Rick Gonzalez, Busisiwe Irvin, Brandon T. Jackson, Tim Kazurrinsky, Bob Kolbey, Bryan Lukasik, Justin Menntell, Amy Moore, Marcus T. Paulk, Antonio Polk, Steve Rollins Jr., Michael Rollins, Sean Skowronski, **Jurnee Smollett.** Director: **Malcolm D. Lee**. Writer: Norman Vance Jr.

ROLLE, ESTHER (1920-1998). Actress. This native of Pompano Beach, Florida, became an accomplished actress in **television** and film, best known as Florida Evans, the outspoken maid from the sitcom *Maude*, and the spin-off series *Good Times*. Before accepting the part, Rolle insisted that *Good Times* should have a strong father figure and be based around her home and family life, not on her work as a maid. She often clashed with the producers, fighting against racial **stereotypes** and insisting on more role models and a positive direction for the show. She began acting in stage productions with the Negro Ensemble Company in their productions of *The Blacks, The Amen Corner*, and *A Raisin in the Sun*.

Filmography: *The Summer of My German Soldier*, 1978; *I Know Why the Caged Bird Sings*, 1979; *P. K. and the Kid*, 1985; *A Raisin in the Sun*, 1989; *The Mighty Quinn*, 1989; *Driving Miss Daisy*, 1989; *Age Old Friends*, 1989; *The Kid Who Loved Christmas*, 1990; *House of Cards*, 1992; *To Dance with the White Dog*, 1993; *Scarlet*, 1994; *How to Make an American Quilt*, 1995; *Rosewood*, 1996; *My Fellow Americans*, 1996; *Down in the Delta*, 1998.

ROLLINS, HOWARD E., JR. (1950-1996). Actor. Rollins began his film career as famed musician Coalhouse Walker Jr. in *Ragtime*, 1981. After performing the role of a military lawyer investigating the murder of a black GI on stage, Rollins joined the rest of his onstage cast in the film version of *A Soldier's Story*, 1984. Moving to **television**, he portrayed a wide range of character roles, including Andrew Young in the miniseries *King*, 1978, and George Haley in the miniseries *Roots: The Next Generation*. He is perhaps best remembered as detective Virgil Tibbs in the hit TV series *In the Heat of the Night*.

Filmography: *King*, 1978; *Ragtime*, 1981; *The Member of the Wedding*, 1983; *A Soldier's Story*, 1984; *The Children of Times Square*, 1986; *Johnny Gibson F. B. I.*, 1987; *For Us, the Living*, 1988; *Drunks*, 1996.

ROLL OF THUNDER, HEAR MY CRY. 1978. (TV) 110 min. Drama. In this **television** film based on the novels of Mildred Taylor, an African American family tries to live and survive in Mississippi during the Depression. Cast: **Claudia McNeil, Janet MacLachlan, Morgan Freeman**. Director: Jack Smight.

ROOTS. 1977. (TV) 573 min. Drama. An eight-part **television** miniseries based on **Alex Haley**'s best-selling book that recounts his family history all the way back to Africa. The series aired for eight consecutive nights on ABC-TV and broke viewing records around the world. The story begins with Kunta Kinte, a young boy in a

Gambian village in West Africa, who is completing his manhood trials. He is captured by slave traders and taken to America, where he is sold into slavery. From his story, to his daughter's, to the stories of his grandchildren, the cruelty and brutality of slavery is unmasked, and the strength and fortitude of a resilient African people is revealed. The sequel *Roots: The Next Generation* aired on ABC in 1979. Cast: **John Amos, Maya Angelou**, Ed Asner, Lloyd Bridges, **LeVar Burton**, Chuck Conners, **Cicely Tyson, Ben Vereen**, Sandy Duncan, Tanya Boyd, Lynda Day George, Lorne Greene, Burl Ives, **O. J. Simpson**, Todd Bridges, **Georg Stanford Brown**, MacDonald Carey, Olivia Cole, Leslie Uggams, **Ossie Davis**. Directors: David Greene, Marvin J. Chomsky, John Erman, Gilbert Moses. Writers: William Blinn, Ernest Kinoy, M. Charles Cohen, James Lee. Cinematographers: **Joseph M. Wilcots**, Stevan Lamer. Music: Quincy Jones, Gerald Fried.

ROOTS: THE GIFT. 1988. (TV) 94 min. Drama. This is a story based on characters from the **television** miniseries *Roots*, 1977. Kunta Kinte and Fiddler escape their bondage with the help of the Underground Railroad. Along the way, they show several more of their enslaved comrades the way, thus giving them the gift of freedom. Cast: **Louis Gossett Jr.**, **LeVar Burton**, Michael Learned, **Averi Brooks**, Kate Mulgrew, Shaun Cassidy, John McMartin. Director: **Kevin Hooks**. Cinematographer: John A. Alonzo.

ROOTS: THE NEXT GENERATION. 1979. (TV) 685 min. Drama. The television miniseries sequel to **Alex Haley's** epic saga *Roots*, 1977. The story picks up in the 1880s during the Reconstruction era and moves forward to the volatile 1960s. The film ends full circle back in Gambia, where Haley first discovered the story of his historical ancestor Kunta Kinte. Cast: **Georg Stanford Brown, Lynne Moody**, Henry Fonda, Richard Thomas, Marc Singer, Olivia de Havilland, Paul Koslo, **Beah Richards, Stan Shaw**, Harry Morgan, **Irene Cara, Dorian Harewood, Ruby Dee, Paul Winfield, James Earl Jones, Debbie Allen**. Cameos: **Al Freeman Jr.**, Marlon Brando.

ROSA PARKS STORY, THE. 2002. (PG) 96 min. Biopic. Made-for-TV movie based on the civil rights heroine who refused to obey racial bus segregation laws in 1955 and helped to start the civil rights movement. The story follows Parks from a little girl first arriving in Montgomery, Alabama, to her involvement with the National Association for the Advancement of Colored People, through her arrest for not giving up her seat on the bus to a white passenger, and the resulting Montgomery bus boycott. The aftermath would change the course of American history. Cast: **Angela Bassett**, Peter Francis James, Tonea Stewart, **Cicely Tyson**, Sonny Shroyer. Director: **Julie Dash**. Writer: Paris Qualles.

ROSEWOOD. 1996. (R) 142 min. Historical Drama. A film based on a true story about the destruction of an affluent African American community by a white mob in Rosewood, Florida, back in 1923. When a white woman falsely claims she was beaten and raped by a black man, the simmering racial tensions explode into an orgy of death and violence, with the town's black population mainly on the receiving end. Cast: **Ving Rhames**, Jon Voight, **Don Cheadle**, Michael Rooker, Bruce McGill, Loren Dean, **Esther Rolle**, **Elise Neal**, Catherine Kellner, **Akosua Busia**, Paul Benjamin, Mark Boone Jr., Muse Watson, Badja Djola, Kathryn Meisle, Jaimz Woolvett. Director: **John Singleton**. Writer: Gregory Poirier. Cinematographer. Johnny E. Jensen. Music: John Williams.

ROSS, DIANA (1944-). Singer, actress. Diana Ross began her career as the lead singer of the Supremes, one of the most successful singing groups in musical history. She was born in Detroit and raised in a housing project. After losing a role in a school musical, she teamed with friends Mary Wilson and Florence Ballard to form their own group. In 1960, while high school seniors, the trio was hired by **Motown** Records to sing background for Marvin Gaye and Mary Wells. After graduation, they were named the Supremes and toured with the Motor Town Revue. Their first number one hit was "Where Did Our Love Go?" Over the next 10 years, they charted 15 back-to-back hit singles with five number one hits in a row. Ross went solo in 1969. Along with recording albums, she scheduled a nightclub tour and starred on her own self-named television show. She portrayed legendary singer Billy Holiday in the Motown-produced film *Lady Sings the Blues*, 1972, and received an **Academy Award** nomination. She would also star as Dorothy in the film version of the highly successful stage play *The Wiz*, inspired by the popular Hollywood film *The Wizard of Oz*.

   Filmography: *Lady Sings the Blues*, 1972; *Mahogany*, 1975; *The Wiz*, 1978; *Double Platinum*, 1999.

ROSS, TRACEE ELLIS (1972-). Actress, model, writer, producer. She was born in Los Angeles, California, and is a graduate of Brown University and the William Asper Acting Studio. She has worked in the fashion industry as a model and began acting in small independent film productions like *Far Harbor*, 1996. She hosted the Lifetime TV magazine show *The Dish*, appeared on the MTV series *The Lyricist Lounge Show*, and stars in the UPN series *Girlfriends*. She is the daughter of singer/actress **Diana Ross**. Filmography: *Far Harbor*, 1996; *Sue*, 1997; *Race Against Fear*, 1998; *A Fare to Remember*, 1998; *Hanging Up*, 2000.

'ROUND MIDNIGHT. 1986. (R) 132 min. Music/Drama. This jazz film is about an alcoholic American sax player who goes to Paris in the 1950s to start a new life. He meets a young fan and admirer who eventually inspires him to once again pick up his saxophone and play. Cast: Dexter Gordon, **Lonette McKee**, Francois Cluzet, Martin Scorsese, **Herbie Hancock**, Sandra Reaves-Phillips. Director: Bertrand Tavernier. Writers: Bertrand Tavernier, David Rayfiel. Cinematographer: Bruno de Keyzer. Awards: Oscars 1986: Best Original Score.

ROUNDTREE, RICHARD (1942-). Actor. Born in New Rochelle, New York, Roundtree graduated from New Rochelle High School and attended college on a football scholarship to Southern Illinois University. He enjoyed a short career as a model before joining the Negro Ensemble Company and taking to the stage. The big-screen opportunity that catapulted him to stardom was his role as black private eye John Shaft in *Shaft*, 1971, and the two sequels, *Shaft's Big Score*, 1972, and *Shaft in Africa*, 1973. Roundtree became a pop icon and continued to work in film and **television** throughout the 1970s, 1980s, and 1990s. Television appearances include *Cop Files, Rescue 77,* and the TV miniseries *Roots.* Years later, he would again play John Shaft, but as the uncle of that film's main character, played by **Samuel L. Jackson** in *Shaft 2000.*

Filmography: *Shaft*, 1971; *Shaft's Big Score*, 1972; *Firehouse*, 1972; *Embassy*, 1972; *Shaft in Africa*, 1973; *Earthquake*, 1974; *Man Friday*, 1975; *Portrait of a Hitman*, 1977; *Day of the Assassin*, 1981; *One Down, Two to Go*, 1982; *Big Score*, 1983; *Killpoint*, 1984; *City Heat*, 1984; *The Last Contract*, 1986; *Opposing Force*, 1987; *Jocks*, 1987; *Party Line*, 1988; *Manic Cop*, 1988; *Angel 3: The Final Chapter*, 1988; *Miami Cops*, 1989; *Crack House*, 1989; *Bad Jim*, 1989; *A Time to Die*, 1991; *Getting Even*, 1992; *Deadly Rivals*, 1992; *Bloodfist 3: Forced to Fight*, 1992; *Body of Influence*, 1993; *Amityville: A New Generation*, 1993; *Ballistic*, 1994; *Theodore Rex*, 1995; *Seven*, 1995; *Once Upon a Time When We Were Colored*, 1995; *Original Gangstas*, 1996; *George of the Jungle*, 1997; *Having Our Say: The Delany Sisters' First 100 Years*, 1999; *Shaft 2000*, 2000; *Antitrust*, 2000; *Corky Romano*, 2001; *Joe and Max*, 2002; *Boat Trip*, 2003.

ROYAL GARDENS FILM COMPANY. This early race movie production company produced the silent film *In the Depths of Our Hearts*, 1920.

RUBY BRIDGES. 1998. (TV) 90 min. Biopic. This is a biopic based on the first black student to integrate the public school system in New Orleans, Louisiana, on 14 November 1960. Escorted by four federal marshals, she was met with hostile crowds and death threats but maintained her pride and her dignity to help bring about equality in education. Cast: **Michael Beach**, Penelope Ann Miller, **Lela Rochon**, Chaz Monet, Kevin Pollak, Diana Scarwid. Director: **Euzhan Palcy**. Writer: Toni Ann Johnson.

RUDE. 1996. (R) 90 min. Urban Drama. This is a trilogy of urban-based stories told by a Jamaican–Canadian pirate-radio deejay. A woman deals with having an abortion after her boyfriend abandons her. A gay man struggles to live with himself after participating in a gay-bashing incident with a couple of his straight friends. And, a former drug dealer returns to his family after spending time in jail, and struggles to stay on the up-and-up. Cast: Sharon M. Lewis, Richard Chevilleau, Rachael Crawford, Maurice Dean Wint, Stephen Ellen, Clark Johnson, Melanie Nicholls-King, Stephen Shellen. Writer/Director: Clement Virgo. Cinematographer: Barry Stone. Music: Aaron David.

RUN FOR THE DREAM: THE GAIL DEVERS STORY. 1996. (PG-13) 99 min. Drama. This was a cable television biopicture about U.S. track star Gail Devers, who overcame a debilitating thyroid condition to win a gold medal in the 100-meter dash in the 1992 Olympics. Cast: **Alfre Woodard, Louis Gossett Jr., Robert Guillaume**.

RUSSELL, ALICE B. (1892-1984). Actress. She was born Alice Burton Russell in Maxton, North Carolina. She not only starred in many of pioneer filmmaker **Oscar Micheaux**'s movies, including *Wages of Sin*, 1929; *Murder in Harlem*, 1935; and *God's Step Children*, 1938, but she also married him. She was known for her many emotionally charged, sympathetic mother roles.

Filmography: *The Broken Violin*, 1927; *Wages of Sin*, 1929; *Easy Street*, 1930; *Murder in Harlem*, 1935; *God's Step Children*, 1938; *The Betrayal*, 1948.

RUSSELL, NIPSEY (1925-2005). Actor, singer. He was born in Atlanta, Georgia, and began his career in the 1950s performing in music reviews. He began acting on **television** in 1961 when he landed a role on *Car 54, Where Are You?* He appeared on many television variety shows, such as *Laugh In, The Dean Martin Show*, and *The Jackie Gleason Show*. He became known as television's Poet Laureate, and appeared on *The Tonight Show*, and several game shows of the day, including *To Tell the Truth, Match Game PM*, and he hosted *Juvenile Jury*. Russell portrayed the Tin Man in the movie musical *The Wiz*, 1978, and has performed for many years on the Broadway stage.

Filmography: *The Wiz*, 1978; *Nemo*, 1984; *Wildcats*, 1986; *Posse*, 1993; *Car 54, Where Are You?* 1994.

S

ST. JACQUES, RAYMOND (1930-1990). Actor, director. He was born in Hartford, Connecticut, and made his film debut in *Black Like Me*, 1964. Many more roles followed in films like *The Pawnbroker*, 1964; *The Comedians*, 1967; and *The Green Berets*, 1968. He portrayed detective Coffin Head Johnson in the comedy *Cotton Comes to Harlem*, 1970, and the sequel, *Come Back, Charleston Blue*, 1972. He produced, directed, and starred in *Book of Numbers*, 1973.

Filmography: *Black Like Me*, 1964; *The Pawnbroker*, 1964; *The Comedians*, 1967; *The Green Berets*, 1968; *Dead Right*, 1968; *Cotton Comes to Harlem*, 1970; *Come Back, Charleston Blue*, 1972; *Final Comedown*, 1972; *Book of Numbers*, 1973; *Search for the Gods*, 1975; *The Private Files of J. Edgar Hoover*, 1977; *Mercenaries*, 1980; *Kill Castro*, 1980; *Sophisticated Gents*, 1981; *The Evil that Men Do*, 1984; *The Wild Pair*, 1987; *They Live*, 1988; *Voodoo Dawn*, 1989; *Glory*, 1989; *Time Bomb*, 1991.

ST. LOUIS BLUES. 1958. 93 min. Music/Drama. This is a film based on the life and the music of composer W. C. Handy, who became known as the father of jazz music. The film begins with a young Handy, playing organ for his father's church. His strict and traditionalist father harshly reprimands him for buying a cornet from a pawnshop. He grows into a reserved, college-educated piano teacher who suppresses the true sounds he hears and feels inside. Handy eventually meets a nightclub singer who encourages and records his music, which becomes a national phenomenon and eventually recognized as an original musical art form. Cast: **Nat King**

Cole, **Eartha Kitt, Pearl Bailey, Cab Calloway**, Ella Fitzgerald, Mahalia Jackson, **Ruby Dee, Juano Hernandez**, Billy Preston.

SACK AMUSEMENT COMPANY. White businessman Richard C. Khan based his production and distribution company in Dallas, Texas. After distributing the successful all-black-cast Western *Harlem on the Prairie*, 1938, Khan formed a partnership with the film's star, **Herb Jeffries**, to make three additional films that would continue the story of the black cowboy. These films are *Two-Gun Man from Harlem*, 1939; *Harlem Rides the Range*, 1939; and *The Bronze Buckeroo*, 1939. The company's other African American films include the thriller *Professor Creeps*, 1941, and nine films written and produced by **Spencer Williams Jr.**

SADAT. 1983. (PG) 195 min. Biopic. This was a powerful made-for-TV biopic about the life and efforts of former Egyptian president and Nobel Peace Prizewinner Anwar Sadat, to bring peace to the Middle East, until his assassination in 1981. Cast: **Louis Gossett Jr.**, John Rhys-Davies, Jeremy Kemp, Nehemiah Persoff, Madolyn Smith, Anne Haywood, Jeffrey Tambor, Barry Morse. Director: Richard Michaels. Music: Charles Bernstein.

SALLY HEMINGS: AN AMERICAN SCANDAL. 2000. (TV) 173 min. Biopic. A film based on the 38-year romance between the third U.S. president, Thomas Jefferson, and Sally Hemings, one of his enslaved housekeepers. Cast: Carmen Ejogo, Sam Neil, **Diahann Carroll**, Mare Winningham, Rene Auberjonois, **Mario Van Peebles**. Director: Charles Haid. Writer: Tina Andrews. Cinematographer: Donald M. Morgan. Music: Joel McNeely.

SANDERS OF THE RIVER. 1935. 116 min. Drama. When a rebellion erupts in colonial Africa, a British office is dispatched to see the local chief and bring the situation under control. Cast: **Paul Robeson**, Leslie Banks, **Nina Mae McKinney**, Robert Cochran. Director: Zoltan Korda. Cinematographer: Georges Perinal.

SANFORD, ISABEL (1917-2004). Actress. This New York City-born actress spent 30 years on Broadway and the stage before moving to Hollywood. She made numerous guest appearances on *The Carol Burnett Show*, and became well known as Louise "Weezy" Jefferson on the hit sitcom *The Jeffersons*. Years later, she made a series of Old Navy store commercials with *Jefferson's* co-star Sherman Hemsley. She made her film debut as Tillie the maid in *Guess Who's Coming to Dinner*, 1967. Other notable film roles include

Lady Sings the Blues, 1972; *Desperate Moves*, 1981; **Original Gangstas**, 1996; and ***Sprung***, 1997.

Filmography: *Guess Who's Coming to Dinner*, 1967; *The Young Runaways*, 1968; *Pendulum*, 1969; *The Red, White, and Black*, 1970; *The New Centurions*, 1972; *Hickey & Boggs*, 1972; *Lady Sings the Blues*, 1972; *Up the Sandbox*, 1972; *The Photographer*, 1975; *Love at First Bite*, 1979; *Desperate Moves*, 1981; *South Beach*, 1992; *Original Gangstas*, 1996; *Sprung*, 1997; *Click Three Times*, 1999.

SANDS, DIANA (1934-1973). Actress. This New York City-born actress graduated from Manhattan High School for the Performing Arts and made her stage debut in George Bernard Shaw's *Major Barbara*. She continued to work on stage in productions like *Land Beyond the River*, *A Raisin in the Sun*, *Blues for Mr. Charlie*, and *Tiger, Tiger Burning Bright*. She was cast opposite Alan Alda in *The Owl and the Pussycat*, the first Broadway production with an interracial romance with no mention of color. She won an Obie Award for her role in *Living Premise*, the Outer Circle Critics Award for her role as Beneatha Younger in *A Raisin in the Sun*, and a Tony Award nomination for *Blues for Mr. Charlie*. Her **television** guest appearances include *East Side/West Side*, *The Outer Limits*, *I Spy*, and *Medical Center*. Sands reprised her stage role in the film version of *A Raisin in the Sun*, 1961. She also starred in *The Landlord*, 1970, and *Willie Dynamite*, 1974.

Filmography: *Caribbean*, 1952; *Four Boys and a Gun*, 1957; *A Raisin in the Sun*, 1961; *An Affair of the Skin*, 1963; *Ensign Pulver*, 1964; *The Landlord*, 1970; *Doctors' Wives*, 1971; *Georgia, Georgia*, 1972; *Willie Dynamite*, 1974; *Honeybaby, Honeybaby*, 1974.

SANKOFA. 1993. (NR) 125 min. Drama. Mona is a narcissistic black model on a fashion photo shoot on the sacred grounds of an African slave castle in Ghana. When she disrespects the location and the memory of its tragic history, she is spititually transported back in time and forced to experience the cruelty of life as an enslaved African. After no distributor would release the film its director adapted the **Oscar Micheaux** method of **four-walling** his unique movie from city to city and grossed a respectable three million dollars. Cast: Oyafunmike Ogunlano, Kofi Ghanaba, Alexandra Duah, Nick Medley, Mutabaruka, Afemo Omilami, Reggie Carter, Mzuri, Jimmy Lee Savage, Hasinatu Camara, Jim Faircloth, Stanley Michelson, John A. Mason, Louise Reid, Roger Doctor.

Writer/Director: **Haile Gerima**. Cinematographer: Augustin Cubano. Music: David J. White.

SARAFINA! 1992. (PG-13) 98 min. Musical Drama. This film was adapted from Mbongeni Ngema's musical stage play about a young girl's political awakening in the midst of the Soweto riots in South Africa during the 1970s. Emotional, musical, and powerful, she is motivated by an outspoken teacher to be defiant and take a stand against the cruelties of the apartheid system. Cast: Leleti Khumalo, **Whoopi Goldberg**, Miriam Makeba, John Kani, Mbongeni Ngema. Director: Darrell Roodt. Writers: Mbongeni Ngema, William Nicholson. Music: Stanley Myers.

SAVAGE! 1973. (R) 103 min. Drama. Also known as *Black Valor*, a foreign agent uses a baseball bat and a bevy of lethal beauties to stop a diabolical plot. Cast: James Inglehart, Lada Edmund, **Carol Speed**, Rosanna Ortiz, Sally Jordan, Aura Aurea, Vic Diaz. Director: Cirio H. Santiago.

SAY AMEN, SOMEBODY. 1982. (NR) 100 min. Documentary. This is a film that explores the richness and depth of gospel music through interviews and performances by the some of the pioneers of modern gospel music and a few of its rising stars. It is a spirit-filled film, expressing the power and the history of gospel music, told with a great and mighty joy by people who sing it, share it, and live with the bliss of gospel music every day. Cast: Thomas A. Dorsey, DeLois Barrett Cambell, Billie Barrett Greenbey, Sallie Martin, Edward O'Neal, Rhodessa Barrett Porter, Zella Jackson Price, Bertha Smith, Michael Keith Smith, Willie May Ford Smith. Director: George T. Nierenberg. Cinematographer: Edward Lachman.

SAYEED, MALIK HASSAN. Cinematographer. Sayeed is a graduate of Howard University's School of Communications and began his cinematic career as best boy on director **Spike Lee's** *Crooklyn*, 1994. He later lensed three films for Lee, *Clockers*, 1995; *Girl 6*, 1996; and *He Got Game*, 1998.

　　　Filmography: *Clockers*, 1995; *Girl 6*, 1996; *Cold Around the Heart*, 1997; *The Players Club*, 1998; *He Got Game*, 1998; *Belly*, 1998; *The Original Kings of Comedy*, 2000; *Life and Debt*, 2001.

SCAR OF SHAME. 1927. 90 min. Drama. The color caste system in America is tested when a prosperous concert pianist marries a lower-class neighbor woman and saves her from her abusive, drunken father. He is unable to take her home to meet his parents for fear of the problems it would cause, and their ill-fated union seems doomed amidst the racial strife and perceived class-divisions of the black community. The film was produced by the **Colored Players of Philadelphia**. Cast: Harry Henderson, Lucia Lynn Moses, Ann Kennedy, Norman Johnstone. Director: Frank Peregini.

SCARY MOVIE. 2000. (R) 85 min. Comedy/Horror. This film is a parody of the successful Wes Craven horror trilogy *Scream 1*, *2*, and *3*, 1996, 1997, and 2000. It includes a genre spoof with plenty of satirical jokes, sight gags, and profanity, mostly patterned from other horror films only with a twist. The film was hugely successful with a big box office take. It became the highest-grossing film directed by an African American. Cast: **Keenen Ivory Wayans**, **Marlon Wayans**, **Shawn Wayans**, Carmen Electra, Jon Abrahams, Shannon Elizabeth, **Regina Hall**, Kurt Fuller, David Lander, Dave Sheridan, Dan Joffre. Director: Keenen Ivory Wayans. Writers: Marlon Wayans, Shawn Wayans. Cinematographer: Francis Kenny. Music: David Kitay.

SCARY MOVIE 2. 2001. (R) 82 min. Comedy/Horror. Under the guise of conducting an insomnia study, an eerie scientist persuades most of the original *Scary Movie* cast to spend the night in a haunted house. There are lots of parodies on other movies with plenty of sex jokes and body fluids. Cast: Anna Faris, Time Curry, **Shawn Wayans**, **Marlon Wayans**, Chris Elliott, Torri Spelling, Christopher K. Masterson, Kathleen Robertson, **Regina Hall**, James Woods, David Cross, Andy Richter, Natasha Lyonne, Veronica Cartwright, Richard Moll. Director: **Keenen Ivory Wayans**. Writers: Shawn Wayans, Marlon Wayans, Alyson Fouse, Greg Grabianski, Dave Polsky, Michael Anthony Snowden, Craig Wayans. Cinematographer: Steven Bernstein.

SCHOOL DAZE. 1988. (R) 114 min. Drama. This film was hyped as a serious look at the light-skinned vs. dark-skinned conflict simmering beneath the surface of the African American community. A Southern black college is the backdrop as fraternities and sororities clash, sing about, and debate about class, skin-color, and culture during the festivities of homecoming weekend. It was **Spike Lee**'s second film. Cast: Spike Lee, **Laurence Fishburne**, **Giancarlo Esposito**, **Tisha Campbell**, **Ossie Davis**, **Joe Seneca**, **Art Evans**, Ellen Holly, Branford Marsalis, **Bill Nunn**, **Kadeem Hardison**, Darryl M. Bell, Joie Lee, **Tyra Ferrell**, **Jasmine Guy**, Greg Burge, **Kasi Lemmons**, **Samuel L. Jackson**, Phyllis Hyman,

James Bond III. Writer/Director: Spike Lee. Cinematography: **Ernest Dickerson**. Music: Bill Lee.

SCHULTZ, MICHAEL (1938-). Director. He was born in Milwaukee, Wisconsin, and attended the University of Wisconsin, Marquette University, and Princeton University, where he directed his first stage play in 1966. He joined the Negro Ensemble Company in 1968 and directed *To Be Young, Gifted and Black* for **television** in 1971. His early film projects include *Honeybaby, Honeybaby*, 1974, and *Cooley High*, 1975. He worked with comedian **Richard Pryor** in films like *Car Wash*, 1976, and *Which Way Is Up*, 1977, and later helmed the early rap music movies *Krush Groove*, 1985 and *Disorderlies*, 1987. He has kept busy in television directing made-for-TV movies and series, such as *Young Indiana Jones, City of Angels, Boston Public,* and *Everwood.*

Filmography: *Honeybaby, Honeybaby*, 1974; *Cooley High*, 1975; *Car Wash*, 1976; *Which Way Is Up?* 1977; *Greased Lighting*, 1977; *Sgt. Pepper's Lonely Hearts Club Band*, 1978; *Scavenger Hunt*, 1979; *Carbon Copy*, 1981; *Three Days in Beirut*, 1983; *The Last Dragon*, 1985; *Krush Groove*, 1985; *Timestalkers*, 1987; *Disorderlies*, 1987; *For Us, The Living*, 1988; *Livin' Large*, 1981; *The Great American Sex Scandal*, 1994; *Woman Thou Art Loosed*, 2004.

SCOTT, EMMITT J. He was a personal secretary to Booker T. Washington and spearheaded the production of the early **race movie** *Lincoln's Dream*, which was eventually released as *Birth of a Race*, 1918.

SCOTT, LARRY B. (1961-). Actor. This New York City-born actor began his career as a teenager in *A Hero Ain't Nothin' But a Sandwich*, 1978. He is perhaps best remembered as Tri-Lam Lamar Latrell in the *Revenge of the Nerds I-IV*, series of films. Other notable appearances include *Roll of Thunder, Hear My Cry*, 1978; *One in a Million: The Ron LeFlore Story*, 1978; and *Fear of a Black Hat*, 1994.

Filmography: *A Hero Ain't Nothin' But a Sandwich*, 1978; *Roll of Thunder, Hear My Cry*, 1978; *The Ron LeFlore Story*, 1978; *The Karate Kid*, 1984; *Revenge of the Nerds*, 1984; *That Was Then...This is Now*, 1985; *My Man Adam*, 1985; *Iron Eagle*, 1986; *Space Camp*, 1986; *Extreme Prejudice*, 1987; *Revenge of the Nerds II: Nerds in Paradise*, 1987; *Instant Karma*, 1990; *Snake Eater II: The Drug Buster*, 1991; *Revenge of the Nerds III: The Next Generation*, 1992; *Another Stake Out*, 1993; *Revenge of the*

Nerds IV: Nerds in Love, 1994; *Fear of a Black Hat*, 1994; *The Bad Pack*, 1998; *Champions*, 1998; *Butter*, 1998; *The Breaks*, 1999; *The Cheapest Movie Ever Made*, 2000; *Judge Koan*, 2003; *Getting Played*, 2005.

SCREAM BLACKULA SCREAM. 1973. (R) 96 min. Horror. This is the sequel to *Blackula*, 1972. Mamuwalde, accursed African prince and creature of the night, again returns from the dead. This time, a voodoo priestess is out to stop him. Cast: **William Marshall, Pam Grier,** Michael Conrad, Don Mitchell, **Richard Lawson, Lynne Moody,** Janee Michelle, Barbara Rhoades, **Bernie Hamilton.** Director: Bob Kelljan.

SECRET AGENT 00 SOUL. 1989. (TV) 71 min. Drama. A former international spy returns home and opens a detective agency in his old neighborhood. Cast: **Billy Dee Williams,** Amanda Le Flore, Marjean Holden, Tommy (Tiny) Lister. Director: Julius Le Flore.

SELMA, LORD, SELMA. 1999. (TV) 88 min. Drama. This is a made-for-TV movie based on the book by Webb-Christburg, Nelson and Frank Sikora. Inspired by Dr. Martin Luther King Jr., a young girl becomes involved in the civil rights movement. The year is 1965, and on 7 March, she is one of the youngest Selma to Montgomery protest marchers to be attacked by state troopers at the Edmund Pettus Bridge in Selma, Alabama. Cast: Jurnee Smollett, Stephanie Zandra Peyton, Clifton Powell, Yolanda King. Director: Charles Burnett. Writer: Cynthia Whitcomb.

SENECA, JOE (1919-1996). Actor. He was born in Cleveland, Ohio, and started his entertainment career as a singer and songwriter, working the New York City supper clubs with the vocal group The Three Riffs. His notable film roles include *The Fish That Saved Pittsburgh*, 1979; *Crossroads*, 1986; and *A Time to Kill*, 1996. He appeared in the telefilms *Wilma*, 1977; *Solomon Northup's Odyssey*, 1984; and *A Gathering of Old Men*, 1987. He made **television** guest appearances on the series *Spencer for Hire, The Golden Girls, 227, A Man Called Hawk, Matlock, Law & Order, Sea Quest DSV,* and *In the Heat of the Night.*

Filmography: *The Taking of Pelham One Two Three*, 1974; *Wilma*, 1977; *Solomon Northup's Odyssey*, 1984; *A Gathering of Old Men*, 1987; *The Fish That Saved Pittsburgh*, 1979; *Kramer vs. Kramer*, 1979; *The Verdict*, 1982; *The Evil That Men Do*, 1984; *Silverado*, 1985; *Crossroads*, 1986; *Big Shots*, 1987; *School Daze,* 1988; *The Blob*, 1988; *Mo' Better Blues*, 1990; *Mississippi Ma-*

sala, 1991; ***Malcolm X***, 1992; *Saint of Fort Washington*, 1993; *A Time to Kill*, 1996.

SERGEANT RUTLEDGE. 1960. 112 min. Western. This film is based on the novel *Captain Buffalo*, by James Warner Bellah, a proud Buffalo Soldier goes AWOL to keep from being falsely accused of rape and murder. His commanding officer tracks him down and they fight their own distrust and hostile Indians on their trek back to the fort. Told mostly in flashback during the trial, it shows various views of the events that led up to his reason for running away until the truth is revealed. Cast: **Woody Strode**, Jeffrey Hunter, Constance Towers, Billie Burke, **Juano Hernandez**, Carleton Young, Charles Steel, Jan Styne, Mae Marsh. Director: John Ford. Writers: Willis Goldbeck, James Warner Bellah. Music: Howard Jackson.

SET IT OFF. 1996. (R) 121 min. Urban Drama. Four over-worked and over-stressed female co-workers employed by a sleazy janitorial firm decide to rob banks to help make ends meet. Friends since childhood, their sisterly bonds are torn and tested as greed, guilt, and grief lead to a downward spiral of pursuit, death, and retribution. Cast: **Jada Pinkett Smith, Queen Latifah, Vivica A. Fox, Kimberly Elise, Blair Underwood**, John C. McGinley, **Anna Marie Horsford**, Ella Joyce, Charles Robinson, Chaz Lamas Shepard, Vincent Baum, Van Baum, Tom Byrd, Samantha MacLachlan. Director: **F. Gary Gray**. Writers: Kate Lanier, Takashi Bufford. Cinematographer: Marc Reshovsky. Music: Christopher Young.

SHAFT. 1971. (R) 98 min. Drama. Based on the novel by Ernest Tidyman, a hip, black private eye is hired to find the kidnapped daughter of a Harlem gangster. A gang war is brewing, and Shaft must navigate on both sides of the law. He teams up with a local militant group to stage the girl's dramatic rescue and saves the day. Musician **Isaac Hayes** won an **Academy Award** for his theme song. This film was highly successful and helped to solidify what became known as the **blaxploitation** era of filmmaking during the early 1970s. It spawned the sequels ***Shaft's Big Score***, ***Shaft in Africa***, and the much later, short-lived TV series with a different leading actor. Cast: **Richard Roundtree, Moses Gunn**, Charles Cioffi. Director: **Gordon Parks**. Writer: John D. F. Black. Awards: Academy Awards 1971: Best Song, "Theme From Shaft." Golden Globe Awards 1972: Best Score.

SHAFT. 2000. (R) 98 min. Drama. Also known as *Shaft Returns*, this version actually follows the original character's nephew, a disgruntled cop who throws away his badge to pursue a wealthy killer. Out to silence the only witness to his crime, the killer uses his money and contacts to hire a ruthless Latino drug lord to find and kill not only the beautiful witness, but Shaft as well. The original Shaft, **Richard Roundtree**, makes a cameo appearance. Cast: **Samuel L. Jackson**, Christian Bale, **Vanessa L. Williams**, **Jeffrey Wright**, Philip Bosco, Toni Collette, Angela Pietropinto, Dan Hedaya, Josef Sommer, Richard Roundtree, Ruben Santiago-Hudson, **Lynn Thigpen**, Pat Hingle, Busta Rhymes, **Mekhi Phifer**, Zach Grenier, Catherine Kellner, **Isaac Hayes**, Lee Tergesen, Gloria Reuben, Gordon Parks, Daniel von Bargen. Director: **John Singleton**. Writer: Richard Price. Cinematographer: Stuart Dryburgh. Music: Isaac Hayes, David Arnold.

SHAFT IN AFRICA. 1973. (R) 112 min. Drama. This is the second sequel to *Shaft*, 1971. The Harlem private eye leaves the United States and helps an African country stop a ring of present-day slave traders. Cast: **Richard Roundtree**, Frank Fuinlay, **Vonetta McGee**, Neda Arneric, Jacques Marin. Director: John Guillermin. Writer: Stirling Silliphant.

SHAFT'S BIG SCORE. 1972. (R) 105 min. Drama. This is the first sequel to *Shaft*, 1971. In this one, the Harlem private detective must investigate a friend's murder while trying to keep the peace between feuding mobsters. There is lots of action and a big chase scene. It was followed by *Shaft in Africa*, 1973. Cast: **Richard Roundtree**, **Moses Gunn**, Joseph Macolo, Drew Bundi Brown, Wally Taylor, Kathy Imrie, **Julius W. Harris**, Rosalind Miles, Joe Santos. Director: **Gordon Parks**. Writer: Ernest Tidyman. Music: Gordon Parks.

SHAKA ZULU. 1987. (PG) 300 min. Drama. A miniseries based on Joshua Sinclair's novel, this is hailed as the true story of the life of the greatest leader in Zulu history, Shaka, from his birth to his rise to power. The story itself is based on the oral tradition of the Zulu people. Cast: Henry Cele, Vuyisile Bojana, Graham Armitage, Bingo Bentley, John Carson, Roy Dotrice, Edward Fox, Fiona Fullerton, Kenneth Griffith, Alex Heyns, Trevor Howard, Gordon Jackson, Christopher Lee, Conrad Magwaza, Dudu Mkhize, Roland Mqwebu, Patrick Ndlovu, Tu Nokwe, Gugu Nxumalo, Robert Powell, Simon Sabela, Sam Williams, Nomsa Xaba. Directors: William C. Faure, Joshua Sinclair. Writer: Joshua Sinclair.

SHAKUR, TUPAC (1971-1996). Rapper, actor. He was born Tupac Amaru Shakur in New York City and moved with his family to Baltimore, Maryland, at age 15, where he wrote his first rap. He enrolled in a school of the arts to study ballet and acting until the family relocated to Marine City, California. He joined the rap group Digital Underground in 1990 as a roadie, dancer, and rapper, and released his first controversial album, *2pacalypse Now*, a year later. He began a long-running feud with the police involving lawsuits, drugs, guns, and alleged brutality, and his life would be constantly involved in controversy and tragedy. Shakur made his film debut in *Juice*, 1992, and followed with a costarring role in *Poetic Justice*, 1993. He was dropped from the cast *of Higher Learning* and *Menace II Society* due to bad publicity in his personal life and a case of on-the-set violence. He was then cast in the street basketball-driven film *Above the Rim*, 1994, and his music was prominently featured in the movie soundtrack. A major rift erupted between the East Coast and West Coast rappers and Tupac was right at the center of this major dispute, much of his music and lyrics only fueled the flames. More legal turmoil followed and he was shot and robbed while entering a New York recording studio. Tupac survived this attack, but was sentenced to four years and six months in jail on sexual abuse and weapons charges. Upon his early release, he returned to Los Angeles and began work on his album *All Eyes on Me*, and *2 of Americaz Most Wanted* with rapper **Snoop Dog**, which continued to exploit the ongoing East Coast–West Coast rivalry. On 7 September 1996, while leaving a Mike Tyson fight in Las Vegas, Nevada, Tupac Shakur was shot four times while sitting in a car at a traffic light. He died four days later. His posthumously released album *Makaveli* was a big hit. The documentary *Tupac: Resurrection*, 2003, explores his life and music. It received an **Academy Award** nomination for Best Documentary in 2005.

Filmography: *Juice*, 1992; *Poetic Justice*, 1993; *Bullet*, 1994; *Above the Rim*, 1994; *Gridlock'd*, 1996; *Gang Related*, 1996.

SHARP, SAUNDRA PEARL (1942-). Actress, director. She was born in Cleveland, Ohio, and landed her first film role as Prissy, in the autobiographical **Gordon Parks** film *The Learning Tree*. She continued to work in a string of made-for-TV movies and popular sitcoms, such as *The Jeffersons, Good Times, Different Strokes*, and *Benson*. In the 1980s, she was cast in the supporting roles of Nurse Carolee Wilson in the series *Knot's Landing*, and as Nurse Peggy Shotwell on the medical drama series *St. Elsewhere*. Sharp is an independent filmmaker and director of the award-winning films *Back Inside Herself*, 1984; *Picking Tribes*, 1989; and *The Healing Passage: Voices from the Water*, 2005. Filmography: *The Learning Tree*, 1969; *Minstrel Man*, 1977; *The Greatest Thing That Almost Happened*, 1977; *Night Cries*, 1978; *Hollow Image*, 1979.

SHAW, STAN (1952-). Actor. He was born in Chicago, Illinois, and was a karate and ju jitsu instructor before becoming an actor. With his fighting skills, he has played a professional fighter in many films, including *Snake Eyes*, 1998; *Tough Enough*, 1983; and *Harlem Nights*, 1989. He also portrayed boxing champion Joe Lewis in the telemovie *The Court-Martial of Jackie Robinson*, 1990. He began his acting career in the Chicago productions of the Broadway musicals *Hair* and *The Me Nobody Knows*. His **television** guest appearances include the series *Starsky and Hutch*, *Matt Houston*, *Murder She Wrote*, *Hill Street Blues*, *Fame*, *Wise Guy*, *L. A. Law*, *Matlock*, *Early Edition*, and *The X Files*. Filmography: ***Truck Turner***, 1974; ***T. N. T. Jackson***, 1975; ***Darktown Strutters***, 1975; ***The Bingo Long Traveling All-Stars and Motor Kings***, 1976; *Rocky*, 1976; ***Roots: The Next Generation***, 1979; ***Buffalo Soldiers***, 1979; *The Great Santini*, 1979; *Tough Enough*, 1983; *Runaway*, 1984; *Busted Up*, 1986; *The Monster Squad*, 1987; *Harlem Nights*, 1989; *Fried Green Tomatoes*, 1991; *Body of Evidence*, 1993; *Rising Sun*, 1993; *Houseguest*, 1995; *Cutthroat Island*, 1995; *Daylight*, 1996; *Snake Eyes*, 1998; *Detonator*, 2003.

SHEBA, BABY. 1975. (PG) 90 min. **Blaxploitation**. A female private eye returns to Louisville, Kentucky, to help take down some local hoods out to steal her father's loan company. Cast: **Pam Grier**, Rudy Challenger, Austin Stocker, **D'Urville Martin**, Charles Kissinger. Director: William Girdler.

SHE HATE ME. 2004. (R) 138 min. Comedy/Drama. In this multi-topic message film, a young vice president at a biotech firm is fired for blowing the whistle on his company's corrupt business practices. After losing access to his financial accounts, he accepts an offer from a former girlfriend, who is now a lesbian, to be a surrogate father for her and her female lover. He earns $10,000 for his efforts and from this first lucrative encounter, he goes into business for himself, impregnating wealthy lesbians for profit. Cast: Andrew Mackie, **Kerry Washington**, Ellen Barkin, Monica Bellucci, **Jim Brown**, **Ossie Davis**, Jamel Debbouze, Brian Dennehy, Woody

Harrelson, Ling Bai, **Lonette McKee**, Paula Jai Parker, Q-Tip, Dania Ramirez, John Turturro. Director: **Spike Lee**. Writer: Michael Genet.

SHELBY, LARITA. Actress. She was born in Memphis, Tennessee, and moved to Los Angeles to pursue an acting career. She made her film debut in *South Central*, 1992, and starred in the independent film on AIDS, *Silent Bomb*, 1994, directed by actress Kim Fields. Her **television** guest-starring roles include the series *Martin*, *A Different World*, *Hunter*, *Dr. Quinn, Medicine Woman*, *Babylon 5*, *Jag*, *City of Angels*, and *ER*.

Filmography: *South Central*, 1992; *Silent Bomb*, 1994; *No Way Back*, 1995; *Black Sheep*, 1996; **Woman Thou Art Loosed**, 2004.

SHE'S GOTTA HAVE IT. 1986. (R) 84 min. Comedy. A rough-edged romantic comedy about a strong and independent woman living in Brooklyn, New York, with three men and a woman aggressively competing for her attention. The film was shot in black and white but for one dreamlike dance scene. It was director **Spike Lee**'s first feature-length film and ushered in a new crop of black films and young African American directors. Cast: Tracy Camila Johns, Tommy Redmond Hicks, John Canada Terrell, Spike Lee, Raye Dowell, Joie Lee, S. Epatha Merkinson, Bill Lee. Writer/Director: Spike Lee. Cinematographer: **Ernest Dickerson**. Music: Bill Lee.

SHROPSHIRE, TERILYN. Editor. She began her career as an assistant editor on the films *Glengary Glen Ross*, 1992, and *The Saints of Fort Washington*, 1993. She moved up to editor on the independent films *Embrace of the Vampire*, 1994, and *The Beast*, 1995. Shropshire has cut two films for director **Kasi Lemmons**: *Eve's Bayou*, 1997, and *The Caveman's Valentine*, 2001. She was also chosen to cut director **Gina Prince-Bythewood**'s *Love & Basketball*, 2000, and **Reggie "Rock" Bythewood**'s *Biker Boyz*, 2003. She has recently worked with actor/playwright Tyler Perry on his first film venture, *Diary of a Mad Black Woman*, 2005.

Filmography: *Embrace the Vampire*, 1994; *The Beast*, 1995; *Poison Ivy II*, 1996; *Love in Paris*, 1997; *Eve's Bayou*, 1997; *The Joyriders*, 1999; *Love & Basketball*, 2000; *Luminarias*, 2000; *The Caveman's Valentine*, 2001; *Never Get Outta the Boat*, 2002; *Biker Boyz*, 2003; **Redemption: The Tookie Williams Story**, 2004; *Diary of a Mad Black Woman*, 2005.

SILENT FILMS. At the birth of motion pictures in the late 1890s, this exciting new technology was relegated to a pure visual experience. Later, title cards with the actor's lines and pertinent story information were spliced in between the images to move the plot forward while live piano or organ music accompanied this neoteric form of entertainment. The first filmed images of African Americans were nothing more than degrading coon shows, often with white actors performing comic dance routines in **blackface**. In Chicago, vaudeville booking agent **William Foster** was the first African American to take his filmed image into his own hands when he produced *The Railroad Porter*, 1912. After the deplorable depiction of blacks in *Birth of a Nation*, 1915, several other African American producers mobilized to counteract the negativity of the portrayals. These included **Noble Johnson**'s *Realization of a Negroes Ambition*, 1916, **Emmitt Scott**'s, *The Birth of a Race*, 1918, and **Oscar Micheaux**'s *The Homesteader*, 1918. Although the company was white owned, the **Norman Film Manufacturing Company** contributed several silent films, including *The Crimson Skull*, 1921, and *The Flying Ace*, 1926. Toward the end of the silent era, husband and wife evangelists **James and Eloyce Gist** released their faith-based *Hellbound Train*, 1929. The high cost of sound picture technology forced most early silent film production companies to close down.

SILVERA, FRANK (1914-1970). Actor. He was born in Kingston, Jamaica, but raised in Boston, Massachusetts, and became an actor and stage director during the Harlem Renaissance. He began his stage career with the American Negro Theater in Harlem, and was also involved with the famed Actor's Studio. His light complexion allowed him to play non-ethnic roles. His television guest appearances include *Bonanza*, *The Twilight Zone*, *Rawhide*, *Gunsmoke*, *I Spy*, *The Wild Wild West*, and *Hawaii Five-O*. He was very active and vocal during the civil rights movement and encouraged his industry associates to support the cause of African Americans as well. The Frank Silvera Writers' Workshop Foundation, Inc. was founded in his honor to sponsor up-and-coming playwrights.

Filmography: *The Fighter*, 1952; *The Cimarron Kid*, 1952; *Viva Zapata!* 1952; *The Miracle of Our Lady of Fatima*, 1952; *Crin-Blanc*, 1952; *Fear and Desire*, 1953; *Killer's Kiss*, 1955; *Crowded Paradise*, 1956; *Death Tide*, 1958; *Crime & Punishment, USA*, 1959; *Heller in Pink Tights*, 1960; *The Mountain Road*, 1960; *Key Witness*, 1960; *Mutiny on the Bounty*, 1963; *Toys in the Attic*, 1963; *Lonnie*, 1963; *The Greatest Story Ever Told*, 1965; *The Appaloosa*, 1966; *Hombre*, 1967; *The St. Valentines Day Mas-*

sacre, 1967; **Up Tight!**, 1968; *The Stalking Moon*, 1969; *Che!* 1969; *Guns of the Magnificent Seven*, 1969; *Valdez is Coming*, 1971.

SIMMONS, JOHNNY. Cinematographer. Simmons began his cinematic career as an assistant camera and camera operator. He has since become a sought-after director of photography with feature film credits that include *Once Upon a Time When We Were Colored*, 1995, and *Asunder*, 1998 for director **Tim Reid**. His **television** work includes *Mo' Funny: Black Comedy in America*, 1993; *Motown 40: The Music is Forever*, 1998; *All of Us*, 2003; and *The Tracy Morgan Show*, 2003. Simmons has also conducted lighting workshops for students at the Howard University Department of Radio, Television, and Film.

Filmography: *Once Upon a Time When We Were Colored*, 1995; *The Show*, 1995; *The Dinner*, 1997; *The Race to Save 100 Years*, 1997; *Sistuhs*, 1998; *Asunder*, 1998; **Ruby Bridges**, 1998; **Selma, Lord, Selma**, 1999; **3 Strikes**, 2000; **The Old Settler**, 2001; *The Gin Game*, 2003; *Dirty and Dirtier*, 2004.

SIMPSON, O. J. (1949-). Football player, athlete, actor. He was born as Orenthal James Simpson in San Francisco, California. Simpson became a football star at the University of Southern California and was awarded the prestigious Heisman Trophy in 1968. He gained a record-setting 2,000 yards rushing during the 1973 season with the Buffalo Bills, and was inducted into the Pro Football Hall of Fame in 1985. He began acting in such films as *The Towering Inferno*, 1974, and the *Naked Gun* trilogy. As the spokesman for Hertz Rent-a-Car, he sprinted through airports, and often announced on ABC's Monday Night Football. Simpson starred in a few failed TV pilots, such as *Cocaine and Blue Eyes*, and was cast on the syndicated series *Frogmen*. His career came to a halt when he was accused of murdering his ex-wife Nicole Simpson and her friend Ronald Goldman. In October of 1995, he was found not guilty after a highly publicized criminal trial, yet he was found liable for their deaths in civil court.

Filmography: *The Towering Inferno*, 1974; *The Klansman*, 1974; *The Cassandra Crossing*, 1976; **Roots**, 1977; *Capricorn One*, 1978; *Firepower*, 1979; *Hambone & Hillie*, 1984; *The Naked Gun: From the Files of Police Squad*, 1988; *Naked Gun 2 1/2: The Smell of Fear*, 1991; *C. I. A.: Code Name Alexa*, 1992; *No Place to Hide*, 1993; *Naked Gun 33 1/3: The Final Insult*, 1994.

SINBAD (1956-). Comedian, actor. He was born in Benton Harbor, Michigan, and began doing stand-up comedy while serving in the military. He made his **television** debut on *The Redd Foxx Show* in 1986, and starred as Coach Walter Oakes on the TV sitcom *A Different World*. He starred in his own comedy special *Sinbad: Brain Damaged*, 1990, and appeared in his own TV series *The Sinbad Show*. His film roles include *Coneheads*, 1993; *The Meteor Man*, 1993; and *Jingle All the Way*, 1996.

Filmography: *That's Adequate*, 1989; *Necessary Roughness*, 1991; *Coneheads*, 1993; *The Meteor Man*, 1993; *Houseguest*, 1995; *First Kid*, 1996; *Jingle All the Way*, 1996; *Good Burger*, 1997; *Crazy as Hell*, 2002; *Treading Water*, 2002.

SINCLAIR, MADGE (1938-1995). Actress. This island girl from Kingston, Jamaica, married young, raised her family, and taught school until she was 30. She moved to New York City and did some modeling while she pursued an acting career. Sinclair acted with the New York Shakespearean Festival and at Joseph Papp's Public Theater before making her **television** debut in *The Witches of Salem: The Horror and the Hope*, 1972, and her film debut in *Conrack*, 1974. She was nominated for an **Emmy Award** for her portrayal of Belle in the mini series *Roots*, 1977, and later joined the cast of the TV series *Trapper John, M. D.*

Filmography: *The Witches of Salem: The Horror and the Hope*, 1972; *Conrack*, 1974; *Cornbread, Earl & Me*, 1975; *Leadbelly*, 1976; *I Will, I Will...for Now*, 1976; *Roots*, 1977; *Uncle Joe Shannon*, 1978; *Convoy*, 1978; *One in a Million: The Ron LeFlore Story*, 1978; *I Know Why the Caged Bird Sings*, 1979; *Star Trek IV: The Voyage Home*, 1986; *Coming to America*, 1988; *The End of Innocence*, 1990; *Queen*, 1993; *The Lion King*, 1994.

SINGLETON, JOHN (1968-). Filmmaker, screenwriter. A native of Los Angeles, Singleton graduated from the University of California's Film Writing program and rose to prominence after writing and directing a film version of his growing up in South Central Los Angeles. His film *Boyz N the Hood*, 1991, was made from his thesis screenplay and produced by Columbia Pictures. His hardcore urban-drama was a realistic portrayal of the violence and hardships of growing up black in the inner cities, and gang violence sometimes erupted in the theater. As a first-time director, he became the first African American and the youngest person ever nominated for a Best Director **Academy Award**. Singleton was tapped by **Michael Jackson** to direct his *Remember the Time* music video, and has continued to make films, including *Poetic Justice*, 1993;

Higher Learning, 1995; and *Rosewood*, 1996. He directed a loosely based remake of the 1970s black detective film *Shaft 2000*, and became the highest-grossing African American director of all time with the film sequel *2 Fast, 2 Furious*, 2003.

Filmography: *Boyz N The Hood*, 1991; *Poetic Justice*, 1993; *Higher Learning*, 1994; *Rosewood*, 1996; *Shaft 2000*, 2000; *Baby Boy*, 2001; *2 Fast 2 Furious*, 2003.

SISTER, SISTER. 1982. (TV) 98 min. Drama. Three siblings struggle to maintain peace, love, and morality in their family home. The oldest condemns her baby sister's coming-of-age desires to date and live a full life while maintaining an immoral relationship of her own. Meanwhile, the prodigal middle daughter returns and reveals family secrets better left forgotten. Cast: **Diahann Carroll, Rosalind Cash, Irene Cara, Paul Winfield, Dick Anthony Williams, Robert Hooks**, Diana Douglas, Lamont Johnson, Kristoff St. John, Albert Popwell, **Frances E. Williams**, Alvin Childress, Gloria Edwards. Director: John Berry. Writer: **Maya Angelou.**

SLAUGHTER. 1972. (R) 92 min. Blaxploitation. A former Green Beret returns home to seek his revenge on the men who murdered his parents. It spawned the sequel *Slaughter's Big Rip-Off*. Cast: **Jim Brown**, Stella Stevens, Rip Torn, Cameron Mitchell, Don Gordon, Marlene Clark. Director: Jack Starrett.

SLAUGHTER'S BIG RIP-OFF. 1973. (R) 92 min. Blaxploitation. The former Green Beret is back to fight the mob this time. Cast: **Jim Brown, Brock Peters**, Don Stroud, Ed McMahon, Art Metrano, **Gloria Hendry**. Director: Gordon Douglas.

SMALL TIME. 1991. (NR) 88 min. Urban Drama. A small-time Harlem thief struggles to survive the streets and resist peer pressure until an abusive encounter with the police leads him to commit a fatal crime. Cast: Richard Barboza, Carolyn Hinebrew, Keith Allen, Scott Ferguson, Jane Williams. Writer/Director: Norman Loftis. Music: Arnold Bieber.

SMITH, KELLITA (1969-). Actress. She was born in Chicago, Illinois, raised in Oakland, California, and earned her Associate's Degree in Political Science from Santa Rosa Junior College. She joined an acting workshop and toured in the play *Tell It Like It Tiz*. She also appeared on stage in *The Thirteenth Thorn*, *No Place to Be Somebody*, and won an NAACP **Image Award** for Best Supporting Actress for her work in *Feelings*. She has guest starred in the **television** series *Living Single, Martin, The Steve Harvey Show*, and *The Parent Hood*. She landed recurring roles in *Sister, Sister, Malcolm & Eddie*, and *The Jamie Foxx Show*. She stars in the Fox TV series *The Bernie Mac Show*.

Filmography: *The Crossing Guard*, 1995; *Retiring Tatiana*, 2000; *Masquerade*, 2000; **Kingdom Come**, 2001; *Hair Show*, 2004; *King's Ransom*, 2005; *Roll Bounce*, 2005.

SMITH, ROGER GUENVEUR (1959-). Actor, writer. This Berkeley, California-born actor grew up in Los Angeles and made his film debut in director **Spike Lee**'s *School Daze*, 1988. He has appeared in nearly all of Lee's movies since. Smith wrote and performed the one-man stage play *A Huey P. Newton Story*, and he was a reader on the performance **documentary** *Unchained Memories: Readings from the Slave Narratives*, 2003. His **television** work includes roles in *A Different World, New York Undercover, Oz, City of Angels*, and *Third Watch*.

Filmography: *School Daze*, 1988; **Do the Right Thing**, 1989; **King of New York**, 1990; **Deep Cover**, 1992; **Malcolm X**, 1992; **Poetic Justice**, 1993; *The O. J. Simpson Story*, 1995; **Panther**, 1995; **Tales From the Hood**, 1995; **Get on the Bus**, 1996; **Eve's Bayou**, 1997; **He Got Game**, 1998; **The Color of Courage**, 1999; *Summer of Sam*, 1999; *Incognito*, 1999; *Final Destination*, 2000; *Façade*, 2000; **All about the Benjamins**, 2002; *MVP*, 2003; *Shade*, 2003; *Justice*, 2004; *Lesser of Three Evils*, 2005; *God's Waiting List*, 2005; *Fatwa*, 2005.

SMITH, WILL (1968-). Rapper, actor, producer. Smith was born and raised in Philadelphia, Pennsylvania, and pursued music at an early age. Calling himself The Fresh Prince, he began performing with his friend Jeff Townes, known as DJ Jazzy Jeff. The rap duo's careers flourished with their fresh, up-beat, positive sound, and it was not long before Hollywood came knocking. He starred in the NBC sitcom *The Fresh Prince of Bel-Air* for six seasons, basically playing himself as a street-smart kid from Philadelphia who comes to live with rich relatives in Beverly Hills. His first film role was in *Six Degrees of Separation*, 1993, in which he earned critical acclaim. His first starring role was in the action hit **Bad Boys**, 1995, and the disaster thriller *Independence Day*, 1996, made him a star. Smith joined the $20 million dollar club for his portrayal of boxing champion Muhammad Ali in the biopic *Ali*, 2001. His first solo-starring role was in the high-tech, sci-fi thriller *I-Robot*, 2004. He is married to actress **Jada Pinkett Smith**, and they produce the TV sitcom *All of Us,* based on their early relationship dealing with his ex-wife and baby's mama.

Filmography: *Made in America,* 1993; *Six Degrees of Separation,* 1993; *Bad Boys,* 1995; *Independence Day,* 1996; *Men in Black,* 1997; *Enemy of the State,* 1998; *Wild Wild West,* 1999; *Legend of Bagger Vance,* 2000; *Ali,* 2001; *Men in Black II,* 2002; *I-Robot,* 2004.

SMOLLETT, JURNEE (1986-). Actress. She was born in New York City and began acting at an early age. She came to prominence when she landed the lead role in writer/director **Kasi Lemmon**'s *Eve's Bayou,* 1997. She received rave reviews for her performance and moved on to do recurring roles in such **television** series as *Full House, Hangin' with Mr. Cooper,* and *Cosby.* Her other film work includes roles in *Selma, Lord, Selma,* 1999, and *Roll Bounce,* 2005.

Filmography: *On Our Own,* 1994; *Jack,* 1996; *Eve's Bayou,* 1997; *Selma, Lord, Selma,* 1999; *Beautiful Joe,* 2000; *Roll Bounce,* 2005; *Gridiron Gang,* 2006.

SNIPES, WESLEY (1962-). Actor. Born in Orlando, Florida, and raised in the Bronx, New York, he appeared in the off-Broadway production of *The Me Nobody Knows* at age 12. He was also interested in dance and attended New York's High School for the Performing Arts for a while, but completed his education back in Orlando. Snipes enrolled at the State University of New York at Purchase on a theater scholarship and continued to perform in off-Broadway productions, such as *Death and the King's Horsemen, Execution of Justice,* and *The Boys of Winter.* He landed several minor roles in films, including *Wildcats,* 1986; *Major League,* 1989; and *King of New York,* 1990, but it was his role as a rival musician and band leader in *Mo' Better Blues,* 1990, that led to his leading-man status. Lead roles in *New Jack City,* 1991, and *Jungle Fever,* 1991, soon followed, and he continued on in films like *White Men Can't Jump,* 1992; *Passenger 57,* 1992; and *Sugar Hill,* 1994. Snipes ventured deep into horror as a half-human, half-vampire in the highly successful films *Blade* and *Blade 2.*

Filmography: *Wildcats,* 1986; *Streets of Gold,* 1986; *Major League,* 1989; *Mo' Better Blues,* 1990; *King of New York,* 1990; *The Waterdance,* 1991; *Jungle Fever,* 1991; *White Men Can't Jump,* 1992; *Passenger 57,* 1992; *Rising Sun,* 1993; *Demolition Man,* 1993; *Boiling Point,* 1993; *Sugar Hill,* 1994; *Drop Zone,* 1994; *Waiting to Exhale,* 1995; *To Wong Foo, Thanks for Everything, Julie Newmar,* 1995; *Money Train,* 1995; *America's Dream,*

1995; *The Fan*, 1996; *One Night Stand*, 1997; *Murder at 1600*, 1997; *U.S. Marshals*, 1998; **Down in the Delta**, 1998; *Blade*, 1998; **Disappearing Acts**, 2000; *The Art of War*, 2000; *ZigZag*, 2002; *Undisputed*, 2002; *Liberty Stands Still*, 2002; *Blade 2*, 2002; *Blade: Trinity*, 2004.

SNOOP DOGG (1971-). Rapper, composer, actor, producer. He was born in Long Beach, California, as Calvin Cordozar Broadus, and he is one of the most popular and successful gangsta emcees on the West Coast. His star persona led to film appearance in primarily urban-based comedies and dramas, and his **television** appearances include countless music videos, comedy specials, and music award shows, and the short-lived series *Doggy Fizzle Televizzle*, 2002, which he also executive produced.

Filmography: *Half Baked*, 1998; **Caught Up**, 1998; **Ride**, 1998; **I Got the Hook-Up**, 1998; *The Wrecking Crew*, 1999; *Hot Boyz*, 1999; *Urban Menace*, 1999; *Tha Eastsidaz*, 2000; **Baby Boy**, 2001; **Training Day**, 2001; **Bones**, 2001; **The Wash**, 2001; *Starsky and Hutch*, 2004; **Soul Plane**, 2004; *The Tenants*, 2005; *Boss'n Up*, 2005; *Coach Snoop*, 2006.

SOLDIER STORY, A. 1984. (PG) 101 min. Drama. This is a film based on the stage play by Charles Fuller. An Army attorney is sent to a military base in the South during World War II to investigate the suspicious murder of a black drill sergeant. White racism and the Ku Klux Klan are the initial suspects until the inquest reveals a much deeper possibility that lies closer to home. It was produced with most of the Broadway cast. Cast: **Howard E. Rollins Jr.**, Adolph Caesar, **Denzel Washington**, Patti LaBelle, **Robert Townsend**, Scott Paulin, Wings Hauser, **Art Evans**, Larry Riley, **David Alan Grier**. Director: Norman Jewison. Music: **Herbie Hancock**. Awards: Edgar Allan Poe Awards 1984: Best Screenplay; Los Angeles Film Critics Association Awards 1984; Best Supporting Actor (Caesar). Nominations: Academy Awards 1984: Best Adapted Screenplay, Best Picture, Best Supporting Actor (Caesar).

SOLOMON NORTHUP'S ODYESSEY (a.k.a. *Half Man Half Slave*). 1985. (TV) 113 min. Drama. A freedman is kidnapped by paddy rollers and forced into slavery back in the 1840s. Cast: **Avery Brooks**, Mason Adams, Petronia Paley, John Saxon, **Joe Seneca**, Michael Tolan, Lee Bryant, Rhetta Greene, Janet League. Director: **Gordon Parks**.

SOME KIND OF HERO. 1982. (R) 97 min. Comedy/Drama. A Vietnam veteran returns home after spending several years as a prisoner of war. Things have changed on the home front and he must reinvent himself to survive and fit into the world around him. Cast: **Richard Pryor**, Margot Kidder, Ray Sharkey, Ronny Cox, **Lynne Moody**, Olivia Cole. Director: Michael Pressman. Writer: Robert Boris.

SOMETHING OF VALUE. 1957. 113 min. Drama. This film is based on the book by Robert Ruark. Two men must choose between their long-standing friendship and their personal loyalties during the Mau Mau rebellion in Kenya to overthrow the colonial occupation. Cast: **Sidney Poitier**, Rock Hudson, Wendy Hiller, Dana Wynter, **Juano Hernandez**. Writer/Director: Richard Brooks. Music: Miklos Rozsa.

SON OF INGAGI. 1940. 70 min. Horror. A female scientist befriends a newlywed couple. She has some connection to the bride's father through an African adventure year earlier. The scientist secretly keeps an ape-like creature in her basement as a servant, until it rises up and turns against her. The creature then kidnaps the bride, who has to be rescued by her husband, and a bumbling policeman. Cast: Zack Williams, Laura Bowman, Alfred Grant, Daisy Bufford, Arthur Ray, **Spencer Williams Jr.**, Jesse Graves, Earle Morris, The Four Toppers. Director: Richard C. Kahn. Writer: Spencer Williams Jr.

SONG OF FREEDOM. 1936. 80 min. Drama. A black dockworker with a powerful singing voice is recruited to sing opera. After a successful concert career, he goes to Africa in search of his roots, and discovers he is of royal blood. Cast: **Paul Robeson**, Elizabeth Welch, George Mozart. Director: J. Elder Willis.

SOPHISTICATED GENTS. 1981. (TV) 200 min. Drama. This is a made-for-television movie based on the novel *The Junior Bachelor Society* by John A. Williams. Nine childhood friends are reunited after 25 years to honor their old coach. Their lives and relationships have been changed and strained over their many years of being black in America, and some have secrets they have not told. Cast: **Paul Winfield, Roosevelt Grier, Bernie Casey, Raymond St. Jacques, Thalmus Rasulala, Dick Anthony Williams, Ron O'Neil, Rosalind Cash, Denise Nicholas, Alfre Woodard, Melvin Van Peebles**. Director: Henry Falk. Writer: Melvin Van Peebles.

SOUL FOOD. 1997. (R) 114 min. Drama. The close and loving relationships of three sisters is tested and torn when the family matriarch falls ill. A corporate attorney, a hardworking housewife, and a
newlywed whose husband is fresh out of jail must let go of the family anchor and learn to rely on themselves and each other. The film
is narrated by a son/nephew who sees the opportunity to save their
family ties by continuing the tradition of the family Sunday meal.
Music producer **Kenneth "Babyface" Edmonds** and his wife
Tracey Edmonds produced the film. Cast: **Vanessa L. Williams,
Vivica A. Fox, Nia Long, Michael Beach, Mekhi Phifer, Irma
P. Hall,** Jeffrey D. Sams, Gina Ravera, Brandon Hammond, Carl
Wright, **Mel Jackson,** Morgan Michelle Smith, John M. Watson
Sr. Writer/Director: George Tillman Jr. Cinematographer: Paul
Elliott. Music: Wendy Melvion, Lisa Coleman.

SOUL OF NIGGER CHARLIE, THE. 1973. (R) 109 min. Western/
Blaxploitation. In the middle of the Civil War, escaped slaves
Charlie and Toby free other renegade black slaves that have been
captured by a Southern colonel determined to deliver them to a
group of aristocrats living in Mexico. The movie is a sequel to *The
Legend of Nigger Charlie*, 1972. Cast: **Fred Williamson,
D'Urville Martin, Denise Nicholas,** Pedro Armendariz Jr., Kirk
Calloway, George Allen, Kevin Hagen, Nai Bonet, Robert Miner,
Johnny Greenwood, James Garbo, Michael Cameron, Fred Lerner,
Joe Henderson. Director: Larry G. Spangler. Writers: Larry G.
Spangler, Harold Stone.

SOUL OF THE GAME. 1996. (PG-13) 105 min. Biopic. Made-for-
cable. In 1945, at the dawn of the integration of baseball, Negro
league greats Satchel Paige, Josh Gibson, and Jackie Robinson are
heavily scouted by the pros. The film explores their thoughts, their
talents, and their different lives during this transitional time frame.
Cast: **Delroy Lindo, Mykelti Williamson, Blair Underwood,**
Edward Herrmann, R. Lee Ermey, Gina Ravera, **Salli Richardson,
Obba Babatunde,** Brent Jennings, Edwin Morrow, Richard
Riehle. Director: **Kevin Rodney Sullivan.** Writer: David Himmel-
stein. Cinematographer: Sandi Sissel. Music: Lee Holdridge.

SOUL PATROL. 1980. (R) 90 min. Comedy. The all-white police department in a racist town gives a black local newspaper reporter the
blues. Cast: Nigel Davenport, Ken Grampus, Peter Dyneley. Director: Christopher Rowley.

SOUL PLANE. 2004. (R) 92 min. Urban Comedy. A man sues an airline after a humiliating experience and uses the huge settlement money to start his own airline. It is a full service airline with sexy flight attendants, a bathroom attendant, an on-board nightclub/disco with lots of funky music, and a pot-smoking pilot. This is their maiden flight and it will be like no other. Cast: Kevin Hart, Method Man, **Snoop Dogg**, Tom Arnold, K. D. Aubert, Godfrey, Brian Hooks, **D. L. Hughley**, Arielle Kebbel, Loni Love, Mo'Nique Imes-Jackson, Ryan Pinkston, Missi Pyle, Sommore, Sofia Vergara. Director: Jessy Terrero. Writers: Bo Zenga, Chuck Wilson.

SOUL VENGENCE (a.k.a. *Welcome Home Brother Charles*). 1975. (R) 91 min. Drama. A falsely accused black man is beaten and castrated by racist white cops who trump up their case to have him locked away. While in prison, he somehow receives special powers that allow him to extend, control, and manipulate his male organ to kill. Upon his release from prison, he sets about seeking his deadly revenge on those who have wronged him. Cast: Marlo Monte, Reatha Grey, Stan Kamber, Tiffany Peters, Ven Bigelow, Jake Carter. Writer/Director: **Jamaa Fanaka**.

SOUNDER. 1972. (G) 105 min. Drama. In this film based on the novel by William Armstrong, a Louisiana sharecropper and his family must struggle to survive after he is jailed for stealing food during the hard times of the Depression. While the wife works hard to hold down the farm, the son receives an opportunity to go to school and get an education, possibly his family's only way out of poverty. Cast: **Paul Winfield, Cicely Tyson, Kevin Hooks**, Taj Mahal, Carmen Mathews, James Best, **Janet MacLachlan**. Director: Martin Ritt. Writer: **Lonne Elder III**. Cinematographer: John A. Alonzo. Music: Taj Mahal. Awards: National Board of Review Awards 1972; 10 Best Films of the Year, Best Actress (Tyson). Nominations: Academy Awards 1972; Best Actor (Winfield), Best Actress (Tyson), Best Adapted Screenplay, Best Picture.

SOUND FILMS (Talkies). With the advent of sound picture technology in 1923, moving pictures eventually found a voice and visual story telling took on another dimension. Shortly after *The Jazz Singer*, 1927, became the first theatrically released talking film, and more theaters were wired for sound, the race for the first all-black talking film began. Acknowledging the vast talents of black performers when it came to song and dance, Fox released *Hearts in Dixie*, 1929, while MGM followed with *Hallelujah*, 1929, released in both a silent and a sound version. Despite this modern, state-of-the-art technology, many of the early talkies maintained derogatory stereotypes, such as **blackface**, when it came to depicting black characters. A suitable black dialect was also introduced. The Maverick filmmaker **Oscar Micheaux** partnered with two white Harlem theater owners to continue making films into the sound era. His first talkie was *A Daughter of the Congo*, 1930. Several popular actors of the silent screen were forced to retire because the sound of their voice did not match their strong, visual, on-screen presence.

SOUTH CENTRAL. 1992. (R) 99 min. Urban Drama. A former gang-banger returns home after spending 10 years in prison for murder. His drug-addicted wife has done little to keep their son from running with his old gang and heading down the same dead-end path. Life becomes a constant struggle to stay clean, do what is right, and give his son the guidance and nurturing that he never received. Cast: **Glenn Plummer, Carl Lumbly**, Christian Coleman, **LaRita Shelby**, Byron Keith Minns. Writer/Director: Steve Anderson.

SPARKLE. 1976. (PG) 98 min. Music/Drama. A trio of singing sisters must balance their home life, love life, and inter-personal relationships while trying to move their music up the charts to achieve stardom. All the old haunts of drugs, jealousy, and mob manipulation endanger their efforts. Cast: **Irene Cara, Lonette McKee**, Dwan Smith, **Philip Michael Thomas, Mary Alice, Dorian Harewood**, Tony King. Director: Sam O'Steen. Writer: Joel Schumacher. Music: **Curtis Mayfield**.

SPAWN. 1997. (PG-13) 97 min. Sci-Fi. In a tale based on the comic book, a murdered CIA assassin returns to life after six years to seek his revenge and protect his family. He reappears with a burned and disgusting face, and supernatural powers provided by Satan, to whom he sold his soul to see his wife again. It is a dark, twisted attempt at exploring the superhero genre. Cast: **Michael Jai White**, Michael Papajohn, John Leguizamo, Martin Sheen, **Theresa Ranle**, D. B. Sweeney, Nicol Williamson, Melinda Clarke, Miko Hughes. Director: Mark Dippe. Writer: Alan B. McElroy. Cinematographer: Guillermo Navarro. Music: Graeme Revell.

SPEED, CAROL (1945-). Actress. She was born in Bakersfield, California, and began her film career in *The Big Bird Cage*, 1972; Her **television** appearances include *Getting Away from It All*, 1972; *The New Centurions*, 1972; and *The Girls of Huntington House*, 1973.

She also played in several **blaxploitation** films, including *Black Sampson*, 1974; *The Mack*, 1973; and *The Avenging Disco Godfather*, 1976.

Filmography: *The Big Bird Cage*, 1972; *Savage!* 1973; *The Mack*, 1973; *Bummer*, 1973; *Abby*, 1974; *Dynamite Brothers*, 1974; *Black Sampson*, 1974; *The Avenging Disco Godfather*, 1976.

SPRUNG. 1997. (R) 105 min. Romantic Comedy. This is a story about friendship and sex. Two male friends meet two female friends at a party one night. One couple cannot stand each other while the other two fall in love. When wedding plans are announced, the feuding couple calls a truce and combines forces to try to stop them. Cast: **Tisha Campbell**, **Rusty Cundieff**, Paula Jai Parker, **Joe Torry**, Moon Jones, Bobby Mardis, **John Witherspoon**, Jennifer Lee, **Clarence Williams III**, Loretta Jean, Ronnie Willis, John Ganun, David McKnight, Ron Brooks. Director: Rusty Cundieff. Writers: Rusty Cundieff, Darin Scott.

SPENCER, KENNETH (1913-1964). Actor, singer. He was born in Los Angeles, California, and matured into a talented actor with a rich, bass baritone voice. He appeared as Joe in the 1946 Broadway production of *Show Boat*, and sang "Ol' Man River." He made two films at MGM: *Cabin in the Sky*, 1943, and *Bataan*, 1943. He moved to Germany in 1951 and continued to act in local films.

Filmography: *Cabin in the Sky*, 1943; *Bataan*, 1943; *Joyeux pelerins, Les*, 1951; *Tanzende Sterne*, 1952; *An jedem Finger zehn*, 1954; *Mein Bruder Josua*, 1956; *Grub und Kub vom Tegernsee*, 1957; *Tausend Sterne leuchten*, 1959; *Unser Haus in Kamerun*, 1961.

SPIRIT OF YOUTH. 1938. 70 min. Drama. In this film, a hardworking young man struggles to support his family until he discovers his boxing ability and eventually does well. Cast: Joe Lewis, **Clarence Muse**, **Mantan Moreland**, Edna Mae Harris, Cleo Desmond, **Clarence Brooks**. Director: Harry L. Fraser. Writer: Arthur Hoerl. Cinematographer: Robert E. Cline. Music: Elliot Carpenter, Clarence Muse.

SPOOK WHO SAT BY THE DOOR, THE. 1973. (PG) 95 min. Drama. Based on the novel by Sam Greenlee, the film is about the U.S. government's search for the first ever-black CIA agent back in the 1970s. Upon completing his training, the selected candidate is used as a token to give diplomats tours when he is not at his post as a copy machine specialist. When he leaves the agency for a social worker job in Chicago, he organizes the youth in his old street gang, The Cobras, and uses his acquired covert skills and training to start a revolution. Cast: Lawrence Cook, **Paula Kelly, J. A. Preston**, Jack Aaron, Elaine Aiken, Kathy Berk, Don Blakely, Paul Butler, John Charles, Beverly Gill, Anthony Ray, Stephen Ferry II. Director: **Ivan Dixon**. Writers: Melvin Clay, Sam Greenlee. Cinematography: Michel Hugo. Music: **Herbie Hancock**.

STEREOTYPE. Many African American images in film are considered to be stereotypes that represent preset patterns of speech, actions, or personalities that degrade or reflect upon the subject in a negative way. Many of these depictions were merely throwbacks from the characters and comedy routines from the vaudeville stage. In the early days when there was a limited black presence on the screen, many of these stereotypical depictions were thought to represent the entire race, and often, for the sake of comedy, were purposely meant to undermine and belittle them. The National Association for the Advancement of Colored People (NAACP) and other civil rights organizations have constantly fought for the elimination of such negative portrayals on the screen. There has been much progress, but the practice has not been totally eliminated, and many modern versions of these old and disgraceful characters can still be seen on the screen today. The most criticized examples of black stereotypes are:

The Sambo is a black man with child-like ways. He is usually docile and happy with a wide grin. Helen Bannerman first established this character in the popular children's book *The Little Black Sambo*. This stereotype has been used in many of the *Tarzan* and African jungle-based films, and has morphed into other modern-day on-screen interpretations.

The Uncle Tom is a faithful, older, black male servant. He is well behaved and respectful of the master despite being mistreated and disrespected. The most well-known Uncle Tom appeared in **Uncle Tom's Cabin**, 1914, the film that gave birth to the name, based on the book by Harriet Beecher Stowe.

The Coon is a lazy, worthless black man. He talks slowly in an ethnic dialect and walks slowly sometimes slumped over. He is considered stupid and illiterate. **Stepin Fetchit** was both criticized and acclaimed for opening doors in Hollywood with his portrayal of the typical coon character in films like *Judge Priest*, 1934, and its remake *The Sun Shines Bright*, 1953.

The Zip Coon is a crude, stupid, and trifling buffoon who often makes a fool of himself. An obnoxious personality, ill-fitting and loud clothes are typical traits. He also has difficulty understanding and pronouncing big words. Willie Best in *Ghost Breakers*, 1940, is one of the best-known zip coon caricatures.

The Mammy is a loyal servant and nurturing mother figure. She is usually heavy-set, and considered asexual as a woman. She is depicted with a strong and controlling personality, **Hattie McDaniel** won an **Oscar** for her role as Mammy in *Gone with the Wind*, 1939.

The Black Buck or Savage Brute is a violent, angry black male. He tends to have a violent nature and an uncontrollable sexual appetite, often for white women. The quintessential example is perhaps Gus or Silas Lynch from the film *Birth of a Nation*, 1915.

The Pickanny is a black child with his or her hair uncombed, nappy, and often shooting straight up on the head. With clothes that are sometimes dirty and raggedy, they are usually depicted as dim-witted. Stymie and Buckwheat, two of the Little Rascals in *The Our Gang* series, are early examples.

The Tragic Mulatto stereotype reflects a mixed-race child, the product of a black/white relationship. They are usually light-skinned and attempt to pass for white in a society that considers black a bad thing. Being chronically unhappy and confused are standard traits. The Peola role in both the 1934 and 1959 versions of *Imitation of Life* was a tormented mulatto stereotype.

The Jezebel stereotype involves a sexually loose, hot, erotic black woman. It evolved during slavery to justify the rape and other sexual violence that occurred between white men and slave women. One of the most prominent historical examples is **Nina Mae McKinney** in *Hallelujah!* 1929.

STEWART, NICK (1910-2000). Actor. Also known as Nicodemus, Stewart was born in New York City, and had a long career in entertainment. He is perhaps best remembered for his role as Lightnin' in the *Amos 'n' Andy* TV series. Other TV roles included *Ramar of the Jungle*, and he was the host of the 1950s series *Ebony Showcase Presents*. For years, he ran the Ebony Showcase Theater in Los Angeles. His film roles include parts in *Go West Young Man*, 1936; *Cabin in the Sky*, 1943; and *Carmen Jones*, 1954.

Filmography: *Go West Young Man*, 1936; *Mind Your Own Business*, 1936; *Dark Manhattan*, 1937; *Wall Street Cowboy*, 1939; *My Son the Hero*, 1943; *Cabin in the Sky*, 1943; *False Faces*, 1943; *Hoosier Holiday*, 1943; *Follow the Boys*, 1944; *And Hardy's Blonde Trouble*, 1944; *Gildersleeve's Ghost*, 1944; *I Love A Bandleader*, 1945; *Dakota*, 1945; *Night Train to Memphis*, 1946; *No Holds Barred*, 1952; *Carmen Jones*, 1954; *Thunder Over*

Sangoland, 1955; *Phantom of the Jungle*, 1955; *Flame of the Islands*, 1956; *Tarzan's Fight for Life*, 1958; *It's a Mad Mad Mad Mad World*, 1963; *Silver Streak*, 1976; **Hollywood Shuffle**, 1987.

STICKNEY, PHYLLIS YVONNE. Actress. This native of Little Rock, Arkansas, started her entertainment career performing stand-up comedy and was one of the first comediennes of color to perform at the Juste Pour Rire Comedy Festival in Montreal, Canada. Her comedy routine was on the pilot episode of the TV series *Showtime at the Apollo*, and she was initially considered as a possible host. Stickney's first acting role came in the telepic **The Women of Brewster Place**, and she followed with a role as a stand-up comic in writer/director **Topper Carew**'s *Talkin' Dirty after Dark*. She was named as one of the 200 African American women who changed the world in the 25th anniversary issue of *Essence* magazine.

Filmography: *The Women of Brewster Place*, 1989; *Talkin' Dirty After Dark*, 1991; **New Jack City**, 1991; **Jungle Fever**, 1991; **Malcolm X**, 1992; **What's Love Got to Do with It?** 1993; **The Inkwell**, 1994; *My Teacher's Wife*, 1995; *Die-Hard: With a Vengeance*, 1995; *Tendrils*, 1996; **How Stella Got Her Groove Back**, 1998; *Big Ain't Bad*, 2002.

STORMY WEATHER. 1943. 77 min. Musical. This is considered one of the most important black musical films of all times. A retired hoofer recounts his days of dancing on the stage to a group of neighborhood children and tells them of the woman he loved, but lost to show business. Later, his old showbiz friends return to perform in a tribute show for the troops who are headed off to fight in World War II. They all return, including his lost love, and they put on a show that is unforgettable. Cast: **Lena Horne, Bill Robinson**, Fats Waller, **Dooley Wilson, Cab Calloway, The Nicholas Brothers**. Director: Andrew L. Stone. Cinematographer: Leon Shamroy.

STORY OF A THREE DAY PASS, THE. 1968. 87 min. Drama. Also known as *La Permission.* This is a love story between a black American soldier in Paris who falls for a French girl. Cast: Harry Baird, Nicole Berger, Pierre Doris. Writer/Director: **Melvin Van Peebles**.

STRAIGHT OUT OF BROOKLYN. 1991. (R) 91 min. Urban Drama. This film takes a look at the often rough and unseemly life in a Brooklyn housing complex and the inhabitants' desires to break free. One escapes into the bottle while his son moves toward a life of crime. Cast: George T. Odis, Ann D. Sanders, Lawrence Gillard, Mark Malone Jr., Reana E. Drummond, Barbara Sanon. Writer/Director: **Matty Rich**. Awards: Independent Spirit Awards 1992: Best First Feature. Sundance Film Festival 1991: Special Jury Prize.

STRANGE JUSTICE: THE CLARENCE THOMAS AND ANITA HILL STORY. 1999. (R) 111 min. Drama. This cable-drama based on a true story about the hardball politics surrounding the 1991 confirmation hearings for Supreme Court Justice Clarence Thomas and the claims of sexual harassment by former employee Anita Hill. Cast: **Delroy Lindo, Regina Taylor**, Mandy Patinkin, **Paul Winfield, Louis Gossett Jr.** Director: **Ernest R. Dickerson**. Writer: Jacob Epstein.

STRAPPED. 1993. (TV) 102 min. Urban Drama. An inner-city youth tries to sell guns to raise bail money for his pregnant, crack-selling girlfriend. Pressured by the cops and by his partner in crime, dangerous secrets are revealed. Cast: **Bokeem Woodbine**, Kia Joy Goodwin, Fred Scruggs, Michael Biehn, Craig Wasson. Director: **Forest Whitaker**. Writer: Dena Kleiman.

STREET WARS. 1992. (R) 90 min. Urban Drama. A 17-year-old military school graduate takes over his murdered older brother's Los Angeles drug operation. When a rival gang tries to move in, they use machine-gun strapped, ultra-light airplanes to stage battles high over the city. Cast: Alan Joseph, Bryan O'Dell, Clifford Shegog, Jean Pace, Vaughn Cromwell, Cardella Demilo. Writer/Director: **Jamaa Fanaka**. Music: Michael Dunlap, Yves Chicha.

STRICTLY BUSINESS. 1991. (PG-13) 83 min. Comedy/Romance. A bland and boring stockbroker seeks the advice of a hip mailroom worker to change his image and help him woo a sexy club promoter. Cast: **Halle Berry, Tommy Davidson**, Joseph C. Phillips. Director: **Kevin Hooks**. Music: Michel Colombier.

STRODE, WOODY (1914-1994). Actor, athlete. He was born Woodrow Wilson Woolwine Strode in Los Angeles, California. He became a top-notch decathlete and was a star football player at the University of California, Los Angeles. Strode got into acting after meeting famed director John Ford, who cast him in nearly a dozen of his Westerns, including the title role in *Sergeant Rutledge*, 1961. His television appearances include *Ramar of the Jungle*,

1952; *How the West Was Won*, 1977; and *A Gathering of Old Men*, 1987. Strode played many powerful black male roles throughout the 1960s, including a hard-working ranch hand in *The Man Who Shot Liberty Valance*, 1962, and a gunfighter in *Once Upon a Time in the West*, 1968. He is well remembered for his gladiator fight scene against Kirk Douglas in *Spartacus*, 1960.

Filmography: *Pork Chop Hill*, 1949; *Spartacus*, 1960; *Sergeant Rutledge*, 1960; *The Last Voyage*, 1960; *The Man Who Shot Liberty Valance*, 1962; *The Professionals*, 1966; *Shalako*, 1968; *Once Upon a Time in the West*, 1968; *Black Jesus*, 1968; *Boot Hill*, 1969; *Ride to Glory*, 1971; *The Gatling Gun*, 1972; *Manhunt*, 1973; *Hit Men*, 1973; *Hired to Kill*, 1973; *Loaded Guns*, 1975; *Winterhawk*, 1976; *Kingdom of the Spiders*, 1977; *Oil*, 1978; *The Mercenaries*, 1980; *Kill Castro*, 1980; *Violent Breed*, 1983; *Vigilante*, 1983; *Scream*, 1983; *Jungle Warriors*, 1984; *Lust in the Dust*, 1985; *Super Brother*, 1990; *Murder on the Bayou*, 1991; *Storyville*, 1992; *Posse*, 1993.

SUBLETT, JOHN "BUBBLES" (1902-1986). Dancer, singer, actor. This native of Louisville, Kentucky, began his entertainment career on the vaudeville stage as one part of the dance duo Buck & Bubbles. He often sang and danced in the films he performed in, including *On with the Show*, 1929; *Dark Town Follies*, 1929; *Variety Show*, 1937; and *Calling All Stars*, 1937. He is perhaps best remembered as the high-rolling gambler Domino Johnson in the musical *Cabin in the Sky*, 1943.

Filmography: *Speed Boys*, 1924; *Don't Fall*, 1924; *On With the Show*, 1929; *High Toned*, 1929; *Dark Town Follies*, 1929; *In and Out*, 1930; *Honest Crooks*, 1930; *Foul Play*, 1930; *Varsity Show*, 1937; *Calling All Stars*, 1937; *Cabin in the Sky*, 1943; *I Dood It*, 1943; *Atlantic City*, 1944; *Laff Jamboree*, 1945; *Mantan Messes Up*, 1946; *A Song Is Born*, 1948.

SUGAR HILL. 1994. (R) 123 min. Urban Drama. Two-drug dealing brothers go head to head when one falls in love with an aspiring actress and decides to get out of the business. Flashbacks reveal their relationship and career path while growing up with a drug addict for a father. Cast: **Wesley Snipes, Michael Wright, Theresa Randle, Clarence Williams III**, Abe Vigoda, **Ernie Hudson**, Larry Joshua, Leslie Uggams, **Khandi Alexander**, Raymond Serra, Joe Dallesandro, **Vondie Curtis-Hall**. Director: Leon Ichaso. Writer: Barry Michael Cooper. Cinematographer: Bojan Bazelli. Music: **Terence Blanchard**.

SULLIVAN, KEVIN RODNEY (1958-). Director, producer, actor. He began his career as an actor in the recurring role of Tommy in the hit comedy series *Happy Days*. He began directing **television** with the series *Frank's Place*, and he helmed the feature films *Soul of the Game*, 1996; *How Stella Got Her Groove Back*, 1998; and *Barbershop 2: Back in Business*, 2004. Sullivan is one of the first African American executive producers of a network television series for *Knightwatch*, 1988.

Filmography: *Moe's World*, 1990; *Boy Meets Girl*, 1993; *Cosmic Slop*, 1994; *America's Dream*, 1996; *Soul of the Game*, 1996; *How Stella Got Her Groove Back*, 1998; *Barbershop 2: Back in Business*, 2004; *Guess Who*, 2005.

SUPERFLY. 1972. (R) 98 min. **Blaxploitation**. A Harlem drug dealer, Youngblood Priest, decides to get out of the game, but finds that his partner, the big-time suppliers, and some crooked cops block his efforts. When his life is threatened, he devises a masterful plan to get away safely with his life, his money, and the woman he loves. It spawned the sequel *Superfly T. N. T.* This film includes an excellent soundtrack and score by **Curtis Mayfield**. Cast: **Ron O'Neil, Carl Lee, Sheila Frazier, Julius W. Harris**, Charles McGregor, Nate Adams, Polly Niles, Yvonne Delaine, Henry Shapiro, Jim Richardson. Director: **Gordon Parks Jr.** Writer: Philip Fenty. Cinematographer: James Signorelli. Music: Curtis Mayfield.

SUPERFLY T. N. T. 1973 (R) 87 min. **Blaxploitation**. Now retired from the drug trade and living with his girlfriend in Rome, Priest becomes involved in a revolution with an African weapons dealer to help overthrow an oppressive regime. Cast: **Ron O'Neil, Roscoe Lee Brown, Sheila Frazier, Robert Guillaume**, Jacques Semas, William Berger. Director: Ron O'Neil. Writer: **Alex Haley**.

SURVIVING THE GAME. 1994. (R) 94 min. Drama. A down-and-out homeless man is recruited for a job as a wilderness hunting guide assistant only to find that he is fair game. He uses his street smarts and raw survival instincts to turn the tables on his would-be killers and escape with his life as a new man. Cast: **Ice T**, Rutger Hauer, F. Murray Abraham, Gary Busey, **Charles S. Dutton**, John C. McGinley, William McNamara, Jeff Corey. Director: **Ernest Dickerson**. Writer: Eric Bernt. Cinematographer: Bojan Bazelli. Music: Stewart Copeland.

SWEET JESUS PREACHER MAN. 1973. (R) 99 min. Urban Drama. A hit man is double-crossed by his boss, so he poses as a Baptist preacher at an inner-city church while he makes plans to get his revenge and take over the local rackets. Cast: **Roger E. Mosley**, William Smith, Chuck Wells, **Marla Gibbs**, Bobby Angelle, Diego Barquinero, Daniel Black, Joanne Bruno, Betty Coleman, Nick Dimitri, Chuck Douglas Jr., Patricia Edwards, T. C. Ellis. Director: Henning Schellerup. Writer: John Cerullo, Abbey Leitch.

SWEET SWEETBACK'S BAADASSSSS SONG. 1971. (R) 97 min. **Blaxploitation.** A homeless boy is taken in by the women of a bordello and grows up to become Sweet Sweetback, a live sex-show performer. Arrested one night by a couple of crooked cops on the take, he is driven to a distant location and forced to watch as they beat a black militant nearly to death. Using his handcuffs as weapons, Sweetback kills the crooked cops, saves the militant's life, and makes a run for Mexico, stopping only for sex and assistance along the way from a variety of strangers and acquaintances. This film is credited with kicking the 1970s blaxploitation era of filmmaking into full gear. Cast: **Melvin Van Peebles**, Simon Chuckster, Hubert Scales, John Dullaghan, Rhetta Hughes, **John Amos**, West Gale, Niva Rochelle, Nick Ferrari, **Mario Van Peebles**, Megan Van Peebles. Writer/Director: Melvin Van Peebles. Cinematographer: Robert Maxwell. Music: Earth Wind and Fire, Melvin Van Peebles.

SYKES, BRENDA (1949-). Actress. She was born in Shreveport, Louisiana, and moved to Baldwin Hills, California, where she became a 19-year-old teaching assistant in black history through the UCLA High Potential Program. An appearance on the TV show *The Dating Game* got her noticed by director William Wyler, who cast her in his film *The Liberation of L. B. Jones,* 1970. She worked throughout the 1970s in films like *Cleopatra Jones,* 1973; *Mandingo,* 1975; and *Drum,* 1976. Her **television** roles included work in *The Streets of San Francisco, The Love Boat, Ozzie's Girls,* and *Executive Suite.*

Filmography: *The Liberation of L. B. Jones,* 1970; *The Baby Maker,* 1970; *Getting Straight,* 1970; *The Skin Games,* 1971; *Pretty Maids All in a Row,* 1971; *Honky,* 1971; *Black Gunn,* 1972; *Cleopatra Jones,* 1972; *Mandingo,* 1975; *Drum,* 1976.

T

TAKE A HARD RIDE. 1975. (R) 103 min. Drama. This is an action-packed take-off of a spaghetti Western with a much darker sauce. A group of black cowboys dodge bounty hunters and bandits while hauling a load of cash to Mexico. Cast: **Jim Brown, Fred Williamson**, Lee Van Cleef, **Jim Kelly**, Barry Sullivan. Director: Anthony M. Dawson. Music: Jerry Goldsmith.

TALES FROM THE HOOD. 1995. (R) 97 min. Comedy/Horror. This is an anthology film and trilogy of horror. Three young gang members go to a funeral parlor in search of a stash of hidden drugs. The creepy funeral director begins to tell them tales. He gives the back story on each dead body that lies in state at his establishment and how they each ended up that way. Scary, but often-comical reasons are given for these untimely deaths. From drugs, to white racism, to black-on-black crime, these causes of death turn out to be linked to their own demises. Cast: Lamont Bentley, **De'Aundre Bonds**, Tom Wright, Michael Massee, Duane Whitaker, Brandon Hammond, Paula Jai Parker, **Roger Guenveur Smith**, **Art Evans**, **Clarence Williams III**, Corbin Bernsen, **David Allen Grier**, Wings Hauser, **Rosalind Cash**, **Rusty Cundieff**, **Joe Torry**, Anthony Griffith, Darin Scott. Director: Rusty Cundieff. Writers: Rusty Cundieff, Darin Scott. Cinematographer: Anthony B. Richmond. Music: Christopher Young.

TALL, TAN AND TERRIFIC. 1946. 40 min. Music/Drama. Things get out of hand after the proprietor of a Harlem nightclub is accused of murder. Cast: **Mantan Moreland, Monte Hawley**, Francine Everett, Dots Johnson. Director: Bud Pollard.

TAMANGO. 1959. 98 min. Drama. Tamango is the leader of a revolt on a slave ship making its way from Africa to Cuba in 1830. The captain takes on a beautiful black mistress, but their relationship is doomed when she becomes a conspirator with the African captives. Cast: **Dorothy Dandridge**, Curt Jurgens, Jean Servais, Alex Cressan. Director: John Berry.

TAP. 1989. (PG-13) 106 min. Drama. A reformed criminal helps an aging hoofer open a dance studio to bolster the dying art of tap dancing. It is renowned for its challenge dance scenes when a group of vintage old hoofers try to outdo each other on the dance floor, and prove that they still have what it takes. This was Sammy Davis Jr.'s last film role. Cast: **Gregory Hines, Sammy Davis Jr.**,

Suzzanne Douglass, **Joe Morton**, Terrence McNally, Steve Condos, Jimmy Slyde, **Harold Nicholas**, Etta James, **Savion Glover**, **Dick Anthony Williams**, Howard "Sandman" Sims, Bunny Briggs, Pat Rico, Arthur Duncan. Writer/Director: Nick Castle. Music: James Newton Howard.

TATE, LARENZ (1975-). Actor. This Chicago-born actor began his theatrical training at the Inner City Cultural Center in Los Angeles, California. He began to land **television** roles on series, such as *The Twilight Zone*, *Hunter*, *Amen*, *21 Jump Street*, and *The Wonder Years*. His breakout film role was as the out-of-control ghetto thug "O-Dog," in the **Hughes Brothers'** hard-hitting, *Menace II Society*, 1993. Leading roles quickly followed in films like *The Inkwell*, 1994, *Love Jones*, 1997, and *Why Do Fools Fall in Love?*, 1998, where he portrayed teen singing idol Frankie Lymon.

Filmography: *The Women of Brewster Place*, 1989; *Clippers*, 1991; *Seeds of Tragedy*, 1991; *Menace II Society*, 1993; *The Inkwell*, 1994; *Dead Presidents*, 1995; *Love Jones*, 1997; *The Postman*, 1997; *Why Do Fools Fall in Love?* 1998; *Love Come Down*, 2000; *Biker Boyz*, 2003; *A Man Apart*, 2003; *Crash*, 2004; *Ray*, 2004; *Waist Deep*, 2006.

TAYLOR, MESHACH (1947-). Actor. He was born in Boston, Massachusetts, and earned his bachelor's degree from Florida A&M University in Tallahassee. He is perhaps best known for his portrayal of Anthony Bouvier on the TV series *Designing Women*.

Filmography: *Damien: Omen II*, 1978; *The Howling*, 1981; *The Beast Within*, 1982; *The Haircut*, 1982; *Explorers*, 1985; *Warning Signs*, 1985; *One More Saturday Night*, 1986; *Mannequin*, 1987; *Inside Out*, 1987; *House of Games*, 1987; *Ultra Warrior*, 1990; *Mannequin: On the Move*, 1991; *Class Act*, 1992; *Jacks or Better*, 2000; *Friends and Family*, 2001.

TAYLOR, REGINA (1960-). Actress, playwright, director. Born in Dallas, Texas, she attended Southern Methodist University and appeared in the telefilm *Crisis at Central High*, 1981, while she was still a student. She has appeared on and off Broadway and was the first African American actress to portray Juliet in *Romeo and Juliet* on Broadway. She became well-known on **television** in the series I'll Fly Away, for which she earned numerous awards, including a **Golden Globe Award** and an NAACP **Image Award**. She also starred in the television series *The Education of Max Bickford*, and portrayed Anita Hill in the made-for-TV film *Strange Justice: The Clarence Thomas Story*. She made her film debut in *Lean on Me*,

1989. Taylor is a Distinguished Artistic Associate at Chicago's Goodman Theater.

Filmography: *Lean on Me*, 1989; *A Good Day to Die*, 1995; ***Losing Isaiah***, 1995; ***Clockers***, 1995; *Spirit Lost*, 1996; ***The Keeper***, 1996; *A Family Thing*, 1996; *Courage Under Fire*, 1996; *Hostile Waters*, 1997; *The Negotiator*, 1998; ***Strange Justice: The Clarence Thomas and Anita Hill Story***, 1999; *Cora Unashamed*, 2000.

TELEVISION. This visual form of in-home entertainment was at one time the subject of science fiction novels and fantasy cartoons, but by the 1950s, just like with radio decades before, the technology had been developed to bring both sound and pictures into living rooms across America and throughout the world. Research had begun some 30 years earlier in both a mechanical and an electronic system for producing and transmitting visual images. By the mid-1930s, there were limited test broadcasts to a controlled number of receivers using the electronic system. The National Broadcasting Company (NBC) began a regular program service to about a thousand receiver sets with a network telecast of President Franklin D. Roosevelt at the opening ceremonies of the 1939 New York World's Fair. As interest in television dramatically increased after World War II, networks relied heavily on established radio stars for their broadcast programs, but the huge amounts of lighting required to produce an image, along with the poor quality of the transmitted signal, did not lend itself to dramatic applications. After vast improvements in broadcast technology, commercial television began in 1948 with four television networks on the air: NBC, Colombia Broadcasting System (CBS), American Broadcasting Company (ABC), and the DuMont Television Network. The first African American entertainer to host a television program was Bob Howard, with his 15-minute program on CBS, *The Bob Howard Show*, 1948-1950. The DuMont Network signed singer Hazel Scott to host the 15-minute, three-nights-a-week, *The Hazel Scott Show*, 1950. These were both musical performance programs. Popular Hollywood actress **Ethel Waters** became the first African American to star in a series when she was cast in the title role of *Beulah*, 1950-1953. In this weekly sitcom, Waters portrayed a black maid working for a white family who operates in both worlds, maintaining the status quo in an ideal setting of wistful camaraderie with no indication of the cultural or racial dissentions that existed in the real world. Waters left the series after only one season and Louise Beavers replaced her. Many established film actors found work on the small screen, including **Spencer Williams Jr.**, who portrayed the title role of Andy Brown in the controversial TV series *Amos 'n' Andy*, 1951-1953. **Eddie Anderson** became better known as Rochester on *The Jack Benny Show*, 1950-1965, and **Willie Best** appeared as Willie the Handyman on *The Stu Erwin Show*, 1950-1955. Ruby Dandridge, mother of famed film star **Dorothy Dandridge**, was cast as Delilah, a housekeeper on *Father of the Bride*, 1961-1962. As the popularity of television increased, opportunities for African Americans on the tube failed to keep up and the black images that did appear were often cast, created, and manipulated by white hands. Just like with Hollywood films decades before, the portrayal of black characters was often called into question and criticized for being demeaning and stereotypical.

Regardless of this, many African American actors got their start on television before transitioning into film roles. Comedian **Bill Cosby** was cast as a co-star in *I Spy*, 1965, before making films and remains active in both mediums. In fact, when his hugely successful 1980s family-oriented sitcom *The Cosby Show*, took the network to #1, the NBC acronym jokingly became known as "N-othing B-efore C-osby." **Sidney Poitier**'s early career included appearances in *Pond's Theater* and *The Philco Playhouse* productions, but he has not returned to work on the small screen since his acting career soared. Neither has **Denzel Washington**, who was once a regular in the medical series *St. Elsewhere*. Many actors started on television and mostly remained there, including Don Mitchell, *Ironside*; Don Marshall, *Land of the Giants*; Gail Fisher, *Mannix*; Lloyd Haynes, *Room 222*; Sherman Hemsley, *The Jeffersons*. Others, such as **Vivica A. Fox**, **Blair Underwood**, **Hill Harper**, and many others, work freely between the two mediums.

TEMPTATIONS, THE. 1998. (TV) 150 min. Music/Drama. This made-for-cable biopic miniseries features the famous **Motown** recording group. The story starts in 1958 with their high school, doo-wop beginnings, and follows the group through the highs and lows of their careers. From meeting Motown founder **Berry Gordy** and signing with his label, through the tours, the records, and the successes, to the lead singer going solo and the spiraling downfall of one of the group's original members. Based on the book by original member Otis Williams. Cast: Charles Malik Whitfield, D. B. Woodside, Terron Brooks, Christian Payton, **Leon**, Alan Rosenberg, **Obba Babatunde**, Charles Ley, Tina Lifford, Gina Ravera, **Vanessa Bell Calloway**, Chaz Lamar Shepherd, **Mel Jackson**. Director: Alan Arkush. Writers: Kevin Arkadie, Robert P. Johnson. Cinematographer: Jamie Anderson.

TERRELL, JOHN CANADA. Actor. He began his career as a model and came to prominence as Greer Childs in *She's Gotta Have It*, 1986. His other film work includes roles in *Def by Temptation*, 1990; *The Five Heartbeats*, 1991; and *White Men Can't Rap*, 2005. Filmography: *The Brother from Another Planet*, 1984; *Recruits*, 1986; *She's Gotta Have It*, 1986; *Magic Sticks*, 1987; *Rooftops*, 1989; *Elliot Fauman, Ph.D.*, 1990; *Def by Temptation*, 1990; *Mo' Better Blues*, 1990; *The Return of Superfly*, 1990; *The Five Heartbeats*, 1991; *Boomerang*, 1992; *Crooked Lines*, 2003; *The Story of Breakout*, 2004; *White Men Can't Rap*, 2005.

THAT MAN BOLT. 1973. (R) 102 min. Drama. Karate expert Jefferson Bolt is hired to deliver $1 million dollars in cash from Hong Kong to clients waiting in Mexico City with a government agent on his trail. Cast: **Fred Williamson**, Tereasa Graves, Byron Webster, Miko Mayama, Satoshi Nakamura, Jack Ging, Vassili Lambrinos, John Orchard. Director: Henry Levin, David Lowell Rich. Writer: Quentin Werty. Cinematographer: Gerald Perry Finnerman. Music: Charles Bernstein.

THEIR EYES WERE WATCHING GOD. 2005. (TV-14) Drama. A film based on the novel by Zora Neal Hurston. Janie Crawford is a free-spirited woman in the 1920s who seeks happiness and fulfillment through a series of marriages. Betrothed at an early age to a much older farmer, she runs off with a sweet-talking politician, and later falls for a much younger man. Her behavior challenges the strict, conservative mores of her small Southern town. Cast: **Halle Berry**, Ruben Santiago-Hudson, **Michael Ealy**, Nicki Micheaux, Lorraine Toussaint, **Ruby Dee**, **Terrence Dashon Howard**, Gabriel Casseus, Artel Kayaru, Kevin Daniels, Henry Brown, Taji Coleman, Wayne Duvall, Lisa Lovelace, Rhonda Stubbins White, Mark Anthony Williams, Raymond T. Williams. Director: **Darnell Martin**. Writer: Suzan-Lori Parks. Cinematographer: Checco Varese. Music: **Terence Blanchard**.

THERE ARE NO CHILDREN HERE. 1993. (TV) 120 min. Drama. This is a film based on the book by Alex Kotlowitz. An inner-city family must cope with the legacy of poverty and violence that surrounds them every day. A mother lives in a housing project on Chicago's West Side with her two sons with little support from their father. When the oldest son joins a gang, the family bonds become tested and strained. Cast: **Oprah Winfrey**, **Keith David**, Mark Lane, Norman D. Golden II, **Maya Angelou**, Vonte Sweet, Crystal

Laws Green, Ellis Peal, Eric McNeal, Ashley Magby, Tiffany Magby, Phillip Edward Van Lear, Earl Johnson, Cheryl Lynn Bruce, Nancy Sheeber. Director: Anita W. Addison. Writer: Bobby Smith Jr.

THEY CALL ME MR. TIBBS. 1970. (R) 108 min. Drama. In this sequel to ***In the Heat of the Night***, detective Virgil Tibbs investigates a prostitute's murder. His good friend, who is a reverend, soon becomes the main suspect. Cast: **Sidney Poitier**, Barbera McNair, Martin Landau, **Juano Hernandez**, Anthony Zerbe, Ed Asner, Norma Crane, Jeff Corey. Director: Gordon Douglas. Writer: Alan R. Trustman. Cinematographer: Gerald Perry Finnerman. Music: Quincy Jones.

THIGPEN, LYNNE (1948-2003). Actress. She was born Cherlynne Thigpen in Joiliet, Illinois. She taught high school English before pursuing an acting career. In 1971, she was part of an ensemble in the musical *Godspell* and was part of the original stage cast that took the play to film in 1973. She continued in stage musicals and received a Tony nomination for her role in *Tintypes*, and she won the 1997 Tony award for Best Actress in a featured role for her performance in *An American Daughter*. On **television**, she appeared in *L.A. Law*, the daytime soap *All My Children*, and the kiddie show *Where in the World is Carmen Sandiego?* She also portrayed Ellen Farmer in the dramatic series *The District*. Her many notable film appearances include **Lean on Me**, 1989; *Tootsie*, 1982; *Running on Empty*, 1988; and *Random Hearts*, 1999.

Filmography: *Godspell*, 1973; *Streets of Fire*, 1984; *Rockabye*, 1986; **Lean on Me**, 1989; *Impulse*, 1990; **Separate but Equal**, 1991; *Bob Roberts*, 1992; *Article 99*, 1992; *Naked in New York*, 1993; *The Paper*, 1994; *Just Cause*, 1994; *The Boys Next Door*, 1996; *Random Hearts*, 1999; *The Insider*, 1999; *Bicentennial Man*, 1999; *Trial by Media*, 2000; **Shaft**, 2000; *Novacaine*, 2001; *Anger Management*, 2003.

THIN LINE BETWEEN LOVE AND HATE, A. 1996. (R) 106 min. Comedy/Romance. A smooth-talking womanizer pursues a beautiful and successful businesswoman who is out of his league, and ruins her life. Known for using and then discarding his conquests, he does the same to her, but this femme fatale harbors baggage from a former abusive relationship and makes him pay for his heartless transgressions. He lands in the hospital while she lands in jail. Cast: **Martin Lawrence, Lynn Whitfield**, Tracy Morgan, **Regina King, Bobby Brown, Della Reese, Roger E. Mosley**, Malinda Williams,

Daryl Mitchell, Simbi Khali. Director: Martin Lawrence. Writers: Martin Lawrence, Bentley Kyle Evans, Kenny Buford, Kim Bass. Cinematographer: Francis Kenny. Music: Roger Troutman.

THING WITH TWO HEADS, THE. 1972. (PG) 93 min. Horror. In an attempt to prolong his life, a racist white surgeon has his head surgically attached to a younger, healthier body. His new body happens to belong to a black man, with the original head still attached. Cast: **Rosey Grier**, Ray Milland, Don Marshall, Roger Perry, Katherine Baumann, Lee Frost, Wes Bishop, Rick Baker. Director: Lee Frost. Writer: James Gordon White. Cinematographer: Jack Steely. Music: Robert O. Ragland.

30 YEARS TO LIFE. 2001. (R) 110 min. Comedy/Romance. A group of six buppie friends in New York City begin to evaluate their lives, loves, careers, and friendships with each other as they each approach their 30th birthdays. Cast: **Erika Alexander**, **Melissa De Sousa**, Tracy Morgan, Paula Jai Parker, **Allen Payne**, T. E. Russell, **Kadeem Hardison**, Eddie Brill, Janet Hubert-Whitten, Laz Alonzo, Dominique, Wil Slyvince, Godfrey. Writer/Director: Vanessa Middleton.

THOMAS, SEAN PATRICK (1970-). Actor. He was born in Wilmington, Delaware, and studied law at the University of Virginia before deciding to become an actor. He eventually earned his master's degree in drama from New York University in 1996. Guest-starring roles soon followed in television series, such as *New York Undercover*, *The Agency*, *Static Shock*, and a costarring role as Detective Temple Page in *The District*. His film work includes roles in *Courage Under Fire*, 1996; *Save the Last Dance*, 2001; and ***Barbershop***, 2002.

Filmography: *Courage Under Fire*, 1996; *Picture Perfect*, 1997; *Conspiracy Theory*, 1997; *Can't Hardly Wait*, 1998; *Graham's Dinner*, 1999; *Cruel Intentions*, 1999; *The Sterling Chase*, 1999; *Dracula 2000*, 2000; *Save the Last Dance*, 2001; *Halloween Resurrection*, 2002; *Barbershop*, 2002; ***Barbershop 2***, 2004; *The Fountain*, 2005; *Saint Louis Blues*, 2005.

THOMASINE & BUSHROD. 1974. (PG) 95 min. Western. Robin Hood meets Bonnie and Clyde. A pair of goodhearted thieves roams the American South between 1911-1915, robbing from the rich and giving to the poor. Cast: **Max Julien**, **Vonetta McGee**, George Murdock, **Glynn Turman**, **Juanita Moore**, **Joel Fluellen**, Jackson D. Kane, Bud Conlan, Kip Allen, Ben Zeller, Herb Robins, Harry Luck, Jason Bernard, Paul Barby, Scott Britt. Director: **Gordon Parks Jr.** Writer: Max Julien.

THOMPSON, KENAN (1978-). Actor. He was born in Atlanta, Georgia, and began his career as a child actor with roles in *The Mighty Duck* series of films. After costarring in the series *Kenan & Kel*, 1996, the TV duo starred in the comedy film *Good Burger*, 1997. The first impression the youngster performed on *Saturday Night Live* was of actor/comedian **Bill Cosby**, and he would later portray the title role in *Fat Albert*, 2004.

Filmography: *D2: The Mighty Ducks*, 1994; *Heavy Weights*, 1995; *D3: The Mighty Ducks*, 1996; *Good Burger*, 1997; *The Adventures of Rocky and Bullwinkle*, 2000; *Big Fat Liar*, 2002; *The Master of Disguise*, 2002; *My Boss's Daughter*, 2003; *Love Don't Cost a Thing*, 2003; *Barbershop 2: Back in Business*, 2004; *Fat Albert*, 2004; *Candy Paint*, 2005; *Peter Cottontail: The Movie*, 2005.

THREE STRIKES. 2000. (R) 83 min. Urban Comedy. Determined not to get caught up in California's "Three Strikes" law, and get put away for life, a two-time felon is released from prison with plans to stay on the right path. Things go wrong when his homeboy picks him up from jail in a stolen car, they have a shoot-out with the police, and later, have to run from rival gang members. All he wants to do is stay out of trouble and get home. Cast: Brian Hooks, **N'Bushe Wright, Faizon Love, Starletta DuPois, David Allen Grier**, Dean Norris, **Meagan Good, De'Aundre Bonds, Antonio Fargas**, Vincent Schiavelli, David Leisure, Gerald S. O'Loughlin, George Wallace. Writer/Director: DJ Pooh. Cinematographer: Johnny Simmons. Music: Aaron Anderson, Andrew Slack.

THREE THE HARD WAY. 1974. (R) 93 min. Drama. A trio of hard-hitting brothers must stop a racist white supremist from annihilating the black race. Three vials of a virus designed to only affect blacks are to be released in the water supply of three major cities, and tens of thousands will die, unless the three heroes get there first. Cast: **Jim Brown, Fred Williamson, Jim Kelly, Sheila Frazier**, Jay Robinson, Alex Rocco. Director: **Gordon Parks**.

THOMAS, PHILIP MICHAEL (1949-). Actor. This native of Columbus, Ohio, is perhaps most remembered as Detective Ricardo Tubbs from the flashy, 1980s TV cop series *Miami Vice*. He got his start in 1970s **blaxploitation** films, such as *Come Back, Charleston Blue*, 1972; *Book of Numbers*, 1973; and *Black Fist*, 1975.

His big film break came when he was cast as the lead in *Sparkle*, 1976. Filmography: *Come Back, Charleston Blue*, 1972; *Stigma*, 1972; *Toma*, 1973; *Book of Numbers*, 1973; *Mr. Ricco*, 1975; *Black Fist*, 1975; *Coonskin*, 1975; *Sparkle*, 1976; *Death Drug*, 1978; *The Dark*, 1979; *The Wizard of Speed and Time*, 1989; *Miami Shakedown*, 1993; *River of Stone*, 1994; *Fate*, 2003.

...tick...tick...tick... 1970. (G) 100 min. Drama. It is the 1950s in the deep South. A black man, Jimmy Price, is elected as sheriff of a racially divided county and tensions are high. When a child is killed in a hit-and-run, a white man from a neighboring county is arrested for the crime. The town becomes a ticking time bomb about to explode as the jailed boy's father forms a white mob to bust his son out. Cast: **Jim Brown**, George Kennedy, Fredric March, Lynn Carlin, Don Stroud, **Janet MacLachlan**, Richard Elkins, Clifton James, Robert Random, Mills Watson, **Bernie Casey**, Anthony James, Dub Taylor, Ernest Anderson, Karl Swenson. Director: Ralph Nelson. Writer: James Lee Barrett.

TIGER WOODS STORY, THE. 1998. (PG-13) 103 min. Biopic. Based on the book *Tiger* by John Strege. This is a TV movie about golf phenomenon Tiger Woods, the youngest player to ever win a Masters Golf Tournament. Cast: Khalil Kain, Keith David, Freda Foh Shen. Director: **LeVar Burton**. Writer: Takashi Bufford.

TIME TO KILL, A. 1996. (R) 150 min. Drama. A black father goes vigilante and kills the two Southern rednecks that beat and raped his young daughter before leaving her for dead. The small-town lawyer assigned to represent him fights the good fight with the help of a former mentor and an ambitious law student. Cast: **Samuel L. Jackson**, Matthew McConaughey, Sandra Bullock, Kevin Spacey, Donald Sutherland, Brenda Fricker, Oliver Pratt, **Charles S. Dutton**, Kiefer Sutherland, Chris Cooper, Ashley Judd, Patrick McGoohan, Rae'ven Kelly, John Diehl, Tonea Stewart, M. Emmet Walsh, Anthony Heald, Kurtwood Smith. Director: Joel Schumacher. Writer: Akiva Goldsman. Cinematographer: Peter Menzies Jr. Music: Elliot Goldenthal. Awards: MTV Movie Awards 1997: Breakthrough Performance (McConaughey).

TNT JACKSON. 1975. (R) 73 min. **Blaxploitation**. A karate-kicking sister goes to Hong Kong in search of her brother, but no one seems to want her there, and she has to fight to find him. Cast: Jeanie Bell. Director: Cirio H. Santiago.

TODD, BEVERLY (1946-). Actress. This native of Chicago, Illinois, made her screen debut on the 1968 season of the **television** soap opera *Love of Life*. Other TV guest appearances include *The Wild Wild West, Barnaby Jones, Lou Grant, Benson, St. Elsewhere, Magnum P. I., Hill Street Blues, Sparks,* and *Six Feet Under.* Her notable film roles include ***Brother John***, 1971; ***Moving***, 1988; and ***Lean on Me***, 1989.

Filmography: *The Lost Man*, 1969; *Deadlock*, 1969; *They Call Me Mister Tibbs!* 1970; *Brother John*, 1970; *Six Characters in Search of an Author*, 1976; *The Ghost of Flight 401*, 1978; *Having Babies*, 1978; *The Jericho Mile*, 1979; *Don't Look Back: The Story of Leroy "Satchel" Paige*, 1981; *Vice Squad*, 1982; *Homework*, 1982; *A Touch of Scandal*, 1984; *The Ladies Club*, 1986; *Happy Hour*, 1987; *Different Affair*, 1987; *Baby Boom*, 1987; *Moving*, 1988; *Clara's Heart*, 1988; *Lean on Me*, 1989; *The Surgeon*, 1995; *Ali: An American Hero*, 2000; *Crash*, 2004; *Animal*, 2005.

TODDY, TED (1900-1983). Producer. He was a top independent film producer in the 1940s. Toddy Pictures comedy films employed former vaudeville performers such as **Pigmeat Markham, Eddie Green,** and **Mantan Moreland**. His light musical adventures featured famed singer **Louis Jordan**.

Filmography: *Polygamy*, 1939; *Take My Life*, 1942; *Professor Creeps*, 1942; *Fighting Americans*, 1944; *Mantan Runs for Mayor*, 1946; *Mantan Messes Up*, 1946; *House-Rent Party*, 1946; *Fight that Ghost*, 1946; *She's Too Mean for Me*, 1948; *The Return of Mandy's Husband*, 1948; *Come On, Cowboy*, 1948.

TOGETHER BROTHERS. 1974. (PG) 94 min. Drama. When a uniformed police officer and community youth mentor is brutally murdered, the young men under his tutelage decide to band together and find the killer. One kid who witnessed the murder is traumatized by the event and unable to speak as the killer closes in to shut him up permanently. Barry White composed the musical score. Cast: Ahmad Nurradin. Anthony Wilson, Nelson Sims, Kenneth Bell, Owen Pace, Kim Dorsey, Ed Bernard, Lincoln Kilpatrick, **Glynn Turman**, Richard Yniquez, Mwako Cumbuka, **Frances E. Williams**, Craig Campfield, Bessie Griffin, Lynne Holmes. Director: William A. Graham. Writers: Jack DeWitt, Joe Green.

TOP OF THE HEAP. 1972. (R) 91 min. Drama. When an overly dedicated officer of the peace is passed over for promotion, he takes the law into his own hands, goes on a killing spree, and rids the streets of as many criminals as he can. Cast: Christopher St. John, **Paula Kelly**, Patrick McVey. Director: Christopher St. John.

TORRY, JOE (1965-). Comedian, actor. Torry honed his stand-up comic skills at clubs and on comedy TV specials, such as *Uptown Comedy Club*, *BET Comedy Awards*, and *Def Comedy Jam*. He was the host of the series *On the Beat*. His big film break came in *Poetic Justice*, 1993, and he landed costarring roles in *Tales from the Hood*, 1995, and *Sprung*, 1997. On **television**, he guest starred on *Amen*, *Roc*, *ER*, *NYPD Blue*, and *Girlfriends*.

Filmography: *The Three Muscatels*, 1991; *Poetic Justice*, 1993; *House Party 3*, 1994; *Exit to Eden*, 1994; *Tales From the Hood*, 1995; *Fled*, 1996; *Sprung*, 1997; *Back in Business*, 1997; *Lockdown*, 2000; *The Great Commission*, 2003; *Motives*, 2004; *Hair Show*, 2004; *Getting Played*, 2005; *Halloween House Party*, 2005.

TO SIR, WITH LOVE. 1967. (NR) 105 min. Drama. A film based on the E. R. Braithwaite novel about a lone black high school teacher who breaks all the rules to connect with, bond with, and teach his class of rowdy and sometimes racist students in London's tough East End. Cast: **Sidney Poitier**, Lulu, Judy Geeson, Christian Roberts, Suzy Kendall, Faith Brook. Writer/Director: James Clavell. Cinematographer: Paul Beeson. Music: Ron Granier.

TO SLEEP WITH ANGER. 1990. (PG) 105 min. Drama. An older Southern couple living in Los Angeles for 30 years have not forgotten, nor given up all of their deep-South cultural ways. Tradition and superstition still play a part in their everyday lives, and they have tried to pass these traditions down to their two sons who now have families of their own. All is going relatively well until an old friend visiting from the South knocks on their door, and their lives are inextricably changed. Cast: **Danny Glover, Mary Alice**, Paul Butler, **Richard Brooks, Carl Lumbly, Vonetta McGee, Sheryl Lee Ralph**. Writer/Director: **Charles Burnett**. Cinematographer: Walt Lloyd. Awards: Independent Spirit Awards 1991: Best Actor-Glover, Director and Screenplay-Burnett, Supporting Actress-Ralph. National Society of Film Critics Award 1990: Best Screenplay. Sundance 1990: Special Jury Prize.

TOUGHER THAN LEATHER. 1988. (R) 92 min. Music/Drama. A rap group turns vigilante to fight criminals and clean up their neighborhood. Cast: Run-DMC, The Beastie Boys, Slick Rick, Richard Edson, Jenny Lumet. Director: Rick Rubin.

TOWNSEND, ROBERT (1957-). Comedian, actor, director. Born in Detroit, Michigan, Townsend began as a stand-up comedian before he turned to acting. He had bit parts in *Cooley High* and *A Soldier's Story*, before co-writing, co-producing, and directing *Hollywood Shuffle*, 1987. As a director, he has helmed the Eddie Murphy concert film *Raw*, 1987; *The Five Heartbeats*, 1991; *The Meteor Man*, 1993; and *B*A*P*S*, 1997. On **television**, he hosted a series of comedy specials, *Robert Townsend and His Partners in Crime*, and was star of the long-running sitcom, *The Parent Hood*.

Filmography: *Streets of Fire*, 1984; *A Soldier's Story*, 1984; *Odd Jobs*, 1985; *American Flyers*, 1985; *Ratboy*, 1986; *Hollywood Shuffle*, 1987; *I'm Gonna Git You Sucka*, 1988; *The Mighty Quinn*, 1989; *That's Adequate*, 1990; *The Five Heartbeats*, 1991; *The Meteor Man*, 1993; *Mercenary 2: Thick and Thin*, 1997; *The Taxman*, 1998; *Love Songs*, 1999.

TRAINING DAY. 2001. (R) 120 min. Drama. An undercover narc gets above the law until he is brought back down for an enraged murder for which he must pay...or die. He goes even further out of bounds to try to raise the cash, setting up his neophyte partner, and going against a friend. His maverick bravado turns against him in the end, and the many bridges he has burned leave him no way to get back. **Denzel Washington** won his second **Oscar** for his portrayal of the rogue cop. Cast: Denzel Washington, Ethan Hawke, Scott Glenn, Clifford Curtis, Dr. Dre, **Snoop Dogg**, Tom Berenger, Harris Yulin, Raymond J. Barry, Charlotte Ayanna, Macy Gray, Eva Mendes, Nicholas Chinlund, Jaime Gomez, Raymond Cruz. Director: **Antoine Fuqua**. Writer: David Ayer. Cinematographer: Mauro Fiore. Music: Mark Mancina. Awards: Oscars 2001: Best Actor-Washington. L.A. Film Critics Award 2001: Best Actor-Washington.

TREACH (1970-). Actor, rapper. He was born Anthony Criss in East Orange, New Jersey, and is a member of the popular rap group Naughty by Nature. He began his acting career in *Juice*, 1992 and went onto star in other popular films like *Jason's Lyric*, 1994; *Playas Ball*, 2003; *Love and a Bullet*, 2002; and *Today You Die*, 2005. His television credits include such programs as *Law and Order*, *Soul Food*, *Third Watch*, *Oz,* and *New York Undercover*.

Filmography: *Juice*, 1992; **The Meteor Man**, 1993; *Jason's Lyric*, 1994; *The Contract*, 2000; *Love and a Bullet*, 2002; *Empire*, 2002; *Book of Love*, 2002; *Playas Ball*, 2003; *The Orphan King*, 2005; *Today You Die*, 2005; *Park*, 2006; *Conner's War*, 2006.

TRIPPIN' 1999. (R) 92 min. Comedy. A below-average student with a pension for daydreaming decides to raise his grades in hopes of attracting his dream prom date, who only goes out with the studious type. Cast: Deon Richmond, Maia Campbell, Donald Faison, Guy Torry, Harold Sylvester, **Stoney Jackson**, **Michael Warren**, Aloma Wright, Bill Henderson. Director: David Raynr. Writer: Gary Hardwick. Cinematographer: John Aronson.

TROIS. 2000. (R) 93 min. Drama. A young professional man has married a woman who is still mentally recovering from a previous abusive relationship. He loves his wife, but yearns for the experience of ménage-a-trios, and convinces his reluctant wife to go along with his plan. On the recommendation of a friend, he hires a troubled, bisexual stripper to share in their night of passion, but the aftermath goes wrong. Cast: Gary Dourdan, Gretchen Palmer, Kenya Moore, Soloman K. Smith, Thomas Jefferson Byrd, Chrystale Wilson, Bryce Wilson, Jay Jones, Tariq Holloway, Donna Briscoe, George Williams, Ron N. Binder, Gregory W. Anderson, Tom Rowley, Chato Waters. Director: **Rob Hardy**. Writers: Rob Hardy, William Packer.

TROOPER OF COMPANY K, A. 1918. Drama. A good-for-nothing man joins the U.S. Army. As a member of the historic all-black 10th Calvary, he is dispatched to Mexico and fights bravely against the Carranzista soldiers at Carrizal. He proves himself a man in battle and returns home a hero. This was the second film produced by **George** and **Noble Johnson**'s **Lincoln Motion Picture Company**. Cast: Noble Johnson, Beulah Hall, James Smith. Director: Harry A. Gant.

TROUBLE MAN. 1972. (R) 99 min. **Blaxploitation**. A hard-core brother takes his troubles out on the mob to the sounds of a Marvin Gaye soundtrack. Cast: **Robert Hooks**, **Paul Winfield**, Ralph Waite, William Smothers, **Paula Kelly**, **Julius Harris**, Bill Henderson, Wayne Storm, Alkali Jones, Vince Howard, Stack Pierce, Lawrence Cook, Virginia Capers, Rick Ferrell. Director: **Ivan Dixon**. Writer: John D. F. Black.

TRUCK TURNER. 1974. (R) 91 min. **Blaxploitation.** A bounty hunter seeks his revenge on those responsible for his partner's death. Cast: **Isaac Hayes, Yaphet Koto,** Annazette Chase, Nichelle Nichols, **Scatman Crothers,** Dick Miller. Director: Jonathan Kaplan. Writer: Leigh Chapman. Cinematographer: Charles F. Wheeler. Music: Isaac Hayes.

TRUE IDENTITY. 1991. (R) 94 min. Comedy. Afraid for his life, an innocent black man uses make-up and disguises to pass for white and hide from the mob that is after him. It was inspired by a *Saturday Night Live* television show skit by **Eddie Murphy.** Cast: Lenny Henry, Frank Langelia, **Anne-Marie Johnson,** Charles Lane. Director: Charles Lane. Writer: Andy Breckman.

TUCKER, CHRIS (1972-). This Atlanta, Georgia-born comic has become one of the highest-paid actors in Hollywood. His breakout role was as Smokey in the film *Friday,* 1995, and he has steadily moved up the film ladder with roles in *Dead Presidents,* 1995; **Money Talks,** 1997, which he also executive produced; and the highly successful *Rush Hour* trilogy of films with karate expert Jackie Chan. On **television,** Tucker has appeared on *Def Comedy Jam.*

Filmography; *House Party 3,* 1994; *Friday,* 1995; *Panther,* 1995, *Dead Presidents,* 1995; *The Fifth Element,* 1997; *Money Talks,* 1997; *Jackie Brown,* 1997; *Rush Hour,* 1998; *Rush Hour 2,* 2001; *Rush Hour 3,* 2006.

TUCKER, LORENZO (1907-1986). Actor. This native of Philadelphia, Pennsylvania, began his acting career after **Oscar Micheaux** spotted him in a theater audience and asked him to appear in one of his films. Thus began a long working relationship with the famed director, and Tucker became known as "The Black Valentino." He acted in many of Micheaux's pictures, including *Veiled Aristocrats,* 1932; *Ten Minutes to Live,* 1932; and *Temptation,* 1935.

Filmography: *When Men Betray,* 1928; *Wages of Sin,* 1929; *Easy Street,* 1930; *Veiled Aristocrats,* 1932; *The Black King,* 1932; *Ten Minutes to Live,* 1932; *Harlem after Midnight,* 1934; *Temptation,* 1935; *Underworld,* 1937; *Straight to Heaven,* 1939; *Reet, Petite, and Gone,* 1947.

TURMAN, GLENN (1946-). Actor. A stage-trained actor, Turman burst onto the big screen in *Cooley High,* 1975. A string of roles followed, including *The River Niger,* 1976, and *J. D.'s Revenge,* 1976. His multiple theater credits include *The Wine Sellers,* for which he won a Los Angeles Critics Award and a Dramalogue Award. On **television**, he has been seen in the hit series *A Different World* and Showtime's *The Wire.* Filmography: *Cooley High*, 1975; *The Blue Knight*, 1975; *The River Niger*, 1976; *J. D.'s Revenge*, 1976; *A Hero Ain't Nothin' but a Sandwich*, 1978; *Penitentiary 2*, 1982; *Secrets of a Married Man*, 1984; *Gremlins*, 1984; *Deep Cover*, 1992; *Race to Freedom: The Story of the Underground Railroad*, 1994; *Buffalo Soldiers*, 1997; *Light It Up!* 1999; *How Stella Got Her Groove Back*, 1999; *The Visit*, 2000; *Men of Honor*, 2000; *Freedom Song*, 2000.

TURN IT UP. 2000. (R) 87 min. Music/Drama. A drug dealer wants to go straight and concentrate on his music but his partner in crime takes him down a dark and troubled path. Things get worse when his mom dies, his girlfriend becomes pregnant, and his dead-beat dad shows up. How will he ever be able to pursue his musical talents and fulfill his dreams? Cast: Pras, **Vonde Curtis-Hall**, Ja Rule, **Tamala Jones**, Jason Statham, Eugene C. Clark. Writer/Director: Robert Adetuyi. Cinematographer: Hubert Taczanowski. Music: Gar Jones, Happy Walter.

TUSKEGEE AIRMEN, THE. 1995. (PG-13) 107 min. Biopic. Cable drama based on a book by former Tuskegee airman Robert W. Williams about the formation and service accomplishments of the first black fighter squadron during World War II, who faced scorn, doubt, and racism at every turn. The story begins with their induction and training at a segregated airbase in Tuskegee, Alabama. After proving they were intelligent enough to even fly a plane, the "Fighting 99th" of the 332nd fighter group were stationed in Europe, where they never lost an escorted B-52 bomber to an enemy fighter. Several of the fighters' lives are highlighted, including Captain Benjamin O. Davis, who would become the first black general in the U.S. Air Force. Cast: **Laurence Fishburne**, **Cuba Gooding Jr.**, **Allen Payne**, Malcolm Jamal Warner, **Courtney B. Vance**, **Andre Braugher**, John Lithgow, Rosemary Murphy, Christopher McDonald, **Vivica A. Fox**, Daniel Hugh-Kelly, David Harrod, Eddie Braun, Bennet Guillory. Director: Robert Markowitz. Writers: Paris Qualles, Ron Hutchinson, Trey Ellis. Music: Lee Holdridge.

TWO CAN PLAY THAT GAME. 2001. (R) 90 min. Comedy/Romance. A romantically dumped young woman goes on a 10-day plan to get her man back. She works her game well, but her man's best friend is well versed in the rules of the game and advises him on how to thwart her well-planned moves. It becomes a cat-and-mouse game of one-upsmanship before they realize that true love and understanding will conquer all. Cast: **Vivica A. Fox, Morris Chestnut, Anthony Anderson, Gabrielle Union**, Wendy Raquel Robinson, **Tamala Jones**, Mo'Nique, Ray Wise, **Bobby Brown**, Dondre T. Whitfield. Writer/Director: Mark Brown. Cinematographer: Alexander Grusynski. Music: Marcus Miller.

TWO-GUN MAN FROM HARLEM. 1938. 60 min. Western. This was a sequel to ***Harlem on the Prairie*** but produced under a new partnership with a new lead character. A ranch hand is falsely accused of killing his boss and escapes to Harlem, where he runs into a hot-tempered gangster who could be his own twin brother. He takes on the identity and reputation of this feared city slicker, including manner of dress, dialect, and a pair of glasses as a disguise, and returns to the Wild West to clear his good name. Two more films followed: ***Harlem Rides the Range*** and ***The Bronze Buckaroo***.

TYRESE (1978-). Actor, singer. Tyrese Darnell Gibson was born in the Watts area of Los Angeles, California. He won his first talent show when he was 14 years old, and began a modeling career when he was 17. His debut, self-titled album, *Tyrese* went platinum and he became the host for Music Television's (MTV) *Jams Countdown*. He moved into acting with guest appearances in sitcoms, such as *Hangin' with Mr. Cooper, Martin, The Parenthood*, and *Moesha*. His acting career gained prominence when he was cast in the title role of director **John Singleton**'s ***Baby Boy***, 2001.

Filmography: *Baby Boy*, 2001; *2 Fast 2 Furious*, 2003; *Flight of the Phoenix*, 2004; *Four Brothers*, 2005; *Annapolis*, 2006; *Waist Deep*, 2006.

TYSON. 1995. (TV) 90 min. Biopic. This film was based on the book *Fire and Fear: The Inside Story of Mike Tyson* by Jose Torres, about the life and times of former world heavyweight boxing champion "Iron" Mike Tyson. Cast: **Michael Jai White, Paul Winfield**, George C. Scott, Malcolm Jamal Warner, Tony LoBianco, James B. Sikking, Clark Gregg, Kristen Wilson, Sheila Wills, Holt McCallany, Lilyan Chauvin, **Georg Stanford Brown**, Joe Santos, Charles Napier. Director: Uli Edel. Writer: Robert P. Johnson. Music: Stewart Copeland.

TYSON, CICELY (1939-). Actress. Born in New York City, Cicely Tyson went from being a secretary to a magazine fashion model before becoming an actress. She is probably best known for portraying two strong-willed Southern women. She portrayed Rebecca in the film *Sounder*, 1972, for which she received an **Academy Award** nomination, and Jane Pittman, in the television movie *The Autobiography of Miss Jane Pittman*, 1974, for which she won an **Emmy Award**. In 1959, Tyson was the first woman to wear a "natural" hairstyle on television, when she appeared on the CBS culture series *Camera Three*. On stage, she was cast in Jean Genet's off-Broadway play *The Blacks*, and later landed a leading role in the CBS TV Series *East Side, West Side*. She moved on to motion pictures with *The Comedians*, 1967; *The Heart Is A Lonely Hunter*, 1968; and *The River Niger*, 1976. Her television record includes *Roots*, 1977; *King*, 1978; and *Wilma*, 1977, based on the life of tennis star Wilma Rudolph. Tyson also portrayed Harriet Tubman in *A Woman Called Moses*, 1978, and a schoolteacher in the made-for-TV movie, *The Marva Collins Story*. She was at one time married to world-renowned jazz trumpeter Miles Davis.

Filmography: *A Man Called Adam*, 1966; *The Heart is a Lonely Hunter*, 1968; *Sounder*, 1972; *The Autobiography of Miss Jane Pittman*, 1974; *The River Niger*, 1976; *Wilma*, 1977; *Roots*, 1977; *A Woman Called Moses*, 1978; *King*, 1978; *A Hero Ain't Nothin' But a Sandwich*, 1978; *The Concorde: Airport '79*, 1979; *Bustin' Loose*, 1981; *Acceptable Risks*, 1986; *The Women of Brewster Place*, 1989; *Heat Wave*, 1990; *Fried Green Tomatoes*, 1991; *The Road to Galveston*, 1996; *Riot in the Streets*, 1996; *Hoodlum*, 1996; *Ms. Scrooge*, 1997; *Mama Flora's Family*, 1998; *Always Outnumbered, Always Outgunned*, 1998; *Life*, 1999; *A Lesson Before Dying*, 1999; *Aftershock Earthquake in New York*, 1999; *The Rosa Parks Story*, 2003.

U

UCLA REBELLION, THE. This is a term coined by film scholar Clyde Taylor when referring to a group of African American and other minority students who attended film school at the the University of California, Los Angeles during the 1970s and initiated a black independent filmmaking movement. Galvanized by the political and cultural awareness of the civil rights movement, they were inspired by the revolutionary ideologies of Marxism, Maoism and Guevarism, and their films often stressed Black Nationalism and addressed the class warfare being waged against the black family. These students often had to resort to guerilla-style tactics to obtain production equipment and post-production facilities to make their films and developed a proclivity to rebel against the Hollywood system and remain independent. These filmmakers included

Abdosh Abdulhafiz, Carol Blue, **Charles Burnett**, Ben Caldwell, Larry Clark, **Julie Dash**, **Jamaa Fanaka**, Teshome Gabriel, David Garcia, **Haile Gerima**, Pamela Jones, Alile Sharon Larkin, Francis Martinez, John Reir, Billy Woodberry, and Tommy Wright. A larger, but perhaps less rebellious wave transitioned through the UCLA film program in the early 1980s, including Gay Abel-Bey, Melvonna Ballenger, S. Torriano Berry, Dalili Davis, Zeinabu irene Davis, Willy Dawkins, Derek Deterville, Nancy Jones, Marie Kellier, Bernard Nicholas, Rico Richardson, Valencia Sinclair, Valorie Thomas, Robert Wheaton, and Iverson White.

UNCLE TOM'S CABIN. 1903, 1914, 1927, 1969, 1987. Drama. This multi-remade tale of slavery and the old South is based on the Harriet Beecher Stowe novel. The 1914 first silent version is credited with being the first major motion picture to cast a black man, Sam Lucas, in a lead role. The 1903 production utilized white actors in blackface. In 1927, Universal Studios put a record $2 million into the second silent production of the abolitionist novel with a huge cast and long shooting schedule to match the big budget. The first sound version was made in 1969. Although the story is about a Kentucky family suffering through the oppression of slavery the production was filmed in Yugoslavia and had an international cast. The next U. S. version was a TV movie made in 1987 and was the first to hire an African American director. Cast: *1914 version (54 min.):* Mary Eline, Irving Cummings, Sam Lucas. Director: William Robert Daly. *1927 version (112 min.):* James B. Lowe, Margarita Fischer, George Siegmann, Virginia Grey. Director: Harry A. Pollard. Writers: Harry A. Pollard, Harvey Thew. Cinematographers: Charles Stumar, Jacob Kull. Music: Emo Rapee. *1969 version (120 min):* Herbert Lom, John Kitzmiller, O.W. Fischer, Eleanora Rossi-Drago, Mylene Demongeot, Juliette Greco. Director: Geza von Radvanyi. Voiceover: Ella Fitzgerald. *1987 version (110 min.):* **Averi Brooks**, Kate Burton, Bruce Dern, **Paula Kelly**, **Phylicia Rashad**, Kathryn Walker, Edward Woodward, Frank Converse, George Coe, **Albert Hall**. Director: **Stan Lathan**.

UNDERCOVER BROTHER. 2002. (PG-13) 85 min. Comedy. This is a satire on the 1970s **blaxploitation** films. A hip-funky secret agent is assigned to stop a brainwashed black war hero being controlled by The Man. As a presidential candidate, the plan is to pass legislation that would destroy black culture by flooding African American communities with unhealthy products. Cast: **Eddie Griffin**, Chris Kattan, Denise Richards, **Dave Chappelle**, **Chi McBride**, Aunjannue Ellis, Neil Patrick Harris, **Billy Dee Williams**, Jack Noseworthy, Gary Anthony Williams, **James Brown**, Robert Trumbull. Director: **Malcolm Lee**. Writers: John Ridley, Michael McCullers. Cinematography: Tom Priestley. Music: **Stanley Clarke**. Narration: J. D. Hall.

UNDER THE CHERRY MOON. 1986. (PG-13) 98 min. Musical/Drama. Two jive-talking gigolos move from Miami to the Mediterranean to live the good life while scamming rich women out of their money. One of them falls for a mark that is about to inherit $50 million, which creates friction between the scamming partners, and their plan falls apart. Cast: **Prince**, Jerome Benton, Kristin Scott Thomas, Steven Berkoff, Emmanuelle Sallet, Alexandra Stewart, Francesca Annis, Pamela Ludwig, Barbera Stall, Karen Geerlings, Victor Spinetti, Myriam Tadesse, Moune De Vivier, Amoury Desjardins, Garance Tesello. Director: Prince. Writer: Becky Johnson.

UNDERWOOD, BLAIR (1964-). Actor. A native of Tacoma, Washington, Underwood is a graduate of Carnegie Mellon University who began his acting career on *The Cosby Show* in 1985. He was then cast in the court drama *L. A. Law*, and appeared on the daytime drama *One Life to Live*. He also starred in the TV series *City of Angels* and *L.A.X.* He made his film debut in the rap movie *Krush Groove*, 1985.

Filmography: *Krush Groove*, 1985; *The Second Coming*, 1992; *Posse*, 1993; *Just Cause*, 1995; *Set It Off*, 1996; *Gattaca*, 1997; *Deep Impact*, 1998; *Asunder*, 1998; *The Wishing Tree*, 1999; *Rules of Engagement*, 2000; *Final Breakdown*, 2002; *G*, 2002; *Full Frontal*, 2002; *Malibu's Most Wanted*, 2003; *How Did It Feel?* 2003.

UNDISPUTED. 2002. (R) 96 min. Drama. A champion boxer is convicted of a rape he did not commit. Sent to prison, he becomes involved in a series of boxing matches that allows him to regain a bit of his pride and dignity. He sets his sights on the prison's undisputed and undefeated champion who has reasons to elude such a match. Cast: **Wesley Snipes**, **Ving Rhames**, Peter Falk, Michael Rooker, Jon Seda, Wes Studi, Fisher Stevens, Dayton Callie, Amy Aquino, Nils Allen Stewart, Denis Arndt, Rose Collins. Director: Walter Hill, David Giler. Cinematographer: Lloyd Ahern II. Music: **Stanley Clarke**.

UNION, GABRIELLE (1973-). Actress. Born in Omaha, Nebraska, Union moved with her family to Pleasanton, California, when she was eight years old. An athlete, she participated in soccer, basketball, and track in high school. Upon graduation, she attended the University of Southern California, Los Angeles to study law. While an intern at a modeling agency, she gained much attention, and signed on as a model herself. After shooting a spread for *Teen Magazine*, she began to audition for **television** appearances and landed a spot on *Saved by the Bell: The New Class*. Union began to gain recognition with guest roles on TV's *Moesha*, *7th Heaven*, and *Clueless*. She broke new ground on the 2001 season of *Friends* as the first African American love interest of one of the characters. Early big-screen roles included *She's All That*, 1999, and *Bring It On*, 2000. Her more popular roles have been in *Two Can Play That Game*, 2001, and *Bad Boys II*, 2003.

Filmography: *Ten Things I Hate About You*, 1999; *She's All That*, 1999; *Bring It On*, 2000; *Two Can Play That Game*, 2001; *The Brothers*, 2001; *Welcome to Collinwood*, 2002; *Abandon*, 2002; *Deliver Us from Eva*, 2003; *Cradle 2 the Grave*, 2003; *Bad Boys II*, 2003. *Breakin' All the Rules*, 2003. *Something the Lord Made*, 2004.

UP TIGHT! 1968. (R) 104 min. Drama. This is a remake of John Ford's political drama *The Informer*, 1935, depicting the thoughts and actions of a band of Irish rebels in pursuit of their revolutionary goals. In this version, Martin Luther King Jr. has just been assassinated. A band of black revolutionaries in Cleveland, Ohio, take up arms and prepare to fight, proclaiming that nonviolence died in Memphis along with King. When another militant rats out the group leader to the police, he is tracked down and dealt with accordingly. Cast: **Raymond St. Jacques**, **Ruby Dee**, Frank Silvera, **Roscoe Lee Brown**, Julian Mayfield, **Janet MacLachlan**, **Max Julien**, **Juanita Moore**, **Dick Anthony Williams**, Michael Baseleon, Ji-Tu Cumbuka, John Wesley, Ketty Lester, **Robert DoQui**, Leon Bibb. Director: Jules Dassin. Writers: Jules Dassin, Ruby Dee.

UPTOWN ANGEL. 1990. (R) 90 min. Drama. A young woman is determined to get out of the ghetto, improve her life, and become a star of the theatrical stage. She quickly learns that it will come at a price. Cast: Caron Tate, Cliff McMullen, Gloria Davis Hill, Tracy Halima Williams. Writer/Director: Joy Shannon. Cinematographer: **Charles Burnett**.

UPTOWN SATURDAY NIGHT. 1974. (PG) 104 min. Comedy. A couple of ordinary working stiffs devise a plan to retrieve a winning lottery ticket from gangsters who stole it during a robbery while they were at an illegal gambling joint. It spawned the sequel *Let's Do It Again*. Cast: **Sidney Poitier, Bill Cosby, Harry Belafonte,** Flip Wilson, **Richard Pryor,** Calvin Lockhart. Director: Sidney Poitier. Writer: **Richard Wesley.** Cinematographer: Fred W. Koenekamp.

URBAN ENTERTAINMENT. This African American-owned film distribution company was founded in January 2000 by former Fox Films vice president of feature film production Michael Jenkinson. It is based in Los Angeles, California. Urban Entertainment was the first company to sell a web-based property to a major studio and relies heavily on Macromedia Flash animation as a distribution and audience building vehicle. Universal Studios and Imagine Entertainment purchased the popular animated web series, *Undercover Brother*, for $3 million and produced a live action version starring comedian-actor **Eddie Griffin.** The company has "first look" deals with New Line Cinema and Warner Brothers Online, and represents many independent films. It will soon release the animated feature *The Golden Blaze*, 2005, a G-rated animated feature film for the whole family with an exciting new African American superhero.

URBANWORLD. The Urbanworld Film Festival was launched in August 1997 by founder Stacy Spikes, a former executive at Miramax and October Films. Urbanworld has presented over 400 features, shorts, and documentaries and has become one of the largest internationally competitive festivals of its kind. The five-day festival also includes panel discussions, live staged screenplay readings, and the celebrated Actor's Spotlight. The Urbanworld Film Festival is an initiative delivered by the Urbanworld Foundation, a nonprofit organization dedicated to redefining the role of minorities in contemporary cinema by implementing programs and events that support the development and success of the urban filmmaking community. The distribution arm, Urbanworld Films, received a $15 million investment from the Sony Corporation and the Black Enterprise/Greenwich Street Fund, to acquire independent, commercially viable black and Latin films to distribute in limited release.

V

VAMPIRE IN BROOKLYN, A. 1995. (R) 100 min. Comedy/Horror. The last survivor of a race of Caribbean vampires comes to New York to find his predestined mate, who is unknowingly part vampire herself. Desperate to keep his bloodline from ending, he finds her and tries to bring her into his imprisoning fold of the living dead, while her male partner fights to keep her alive and free. Cast: **Eddie Murphy, Angela Bassett, Allen Payne, Kadeem Hardison, John Witherspoon, Zakes Mokae,** Joanna Cassidy, Simbi Khali, Messiri Freeman, Kelly Cinnante, Jsu Garcia, W. Earl Brown, Ayo Adeyemi, Troy Curvey Jr., Vickilyn Reynolds. Director: Wes Craven. Writers: Eddie Murphy, Vernon Lynch.

VAN PEEBLES, MARIO (1957-). Actor, director, producer. Born in Mexico City, Mexico, to filmmaker father, **Melvin Van Peebles,** Mario seemed destined to follow in his father's cinematic footsteps. He began his career acting in his father's controversial blockbuster hit *Sweet Sweetback's Baadasssss Song,* 1971, and has since carved out an impressive film career of his own. His feature directing debut was *New Jack City,* 1991. His latest directing project is *Baadasssss!,* 2004, based on his father's struggling efforts to produce his Sweetback project in the 1970s.

Filmography: *Sweet Sweetback's Baadasssss Song,* 1971; *Exterminator 2,* 1984; *The Cotton Club,* 1984; *Rappin',* 1985; *3:15,* 1986; *Heartbreak Ridge,* 1986; *Jaws: The Revenge,* 1987; *The White Girl,* 1990; *Identity Crisis,* 1990; *New Jack City,* 1991; *Posse,* 1993; *Gunmen,* 1994; *Highlander,* 1995; *Solo,* 1996; *Ali,* 2001; *The Hebrew Hammer,* 2003; *Baadasssss!* 2004.

VAN PEEBLES, MELVIN (1932-). Filmmaker, actor, writer. Born in Chicago, Illinois, and raised in Phoenix, Illinois, Van Peebles attended Wesleyan University, graduating with a BA degree in English literature in 1953. He spent several years in the U. S. Air Force as a flight navigator before relocating to San Francisco, where he began to make films. With several films in the can, including *Three Pickup Men for Herrick,* 1958, Van Peebles headed for Hollywood. After a series of rejections, he moved to Holland and became involved with the Dutch National Theater. He later relocated to Paris and wrote several novels while transitioning back into filmmaking. His film *Story of a Three-Day Pass* garnered critical success when it premiered at the San Francisco International Film Festival. Now that he had Hollywood's attention, he was hired to direct *Watermelon Man,* and later wrote, produced, and directed the highly successful *Sweet Sweetback's Baadasssss Song*, the film credited with giving birth to the so-called **blaxploitation** era of filmmaking during the early 1970s. His stage plays *Ain't Supposed to Die a Natural Death* and *Don't Play Us Cheap*, had long runs on Broadway but received mixed reviews from the critics. The latter won first prize at a Belgian Theater festival, and his teleplay *The Day They Came to Arrest the Book* won him an **Emmy Award**. Working with his son **Mario Van Peebles**, he directed *Identity Crisis*, 1990, a film written by and starring Mario. They again teamed up to produce *Panther*, 1995, based on the rise and fall of the Black Panther Party.

Filmography: *Sweet Sweetback's Baadasssss Song*, 1971; *Sophisticated Gents*, 1981; *O. C. and Stiggs*, 1987; *Boomerang*, 1992; *Posse*, 1993; *Terminal Velocity*, 1994; *Fist of the North Star*, 1995; *Riot in the Streets*, 1996; *Gang in Blue*, 1996; *Calm at Sunset*, 1996; *Love Kills*, 1998.

VEREEN, BEN (1946-). Actor, singer, dancer. This all-around entertainer was born in Miami, Florida, and made his film debut as a Frug dancer in *Sweet Charity*, 1969. He gained prominence for his portrayal of Chicken George in the miniseries *Roots*, 1977, and received acclaim for his performance as O'Connor Flood in *All That Jazz*, 1979. On **television**, he acted in the telepics *Louis Armstrong, Chicago Style*, 1976; *Tenspeed and Brown Shoe*, 1980; *Pippin: His Life and Times*, 1981; and *The Kid Who Loved Christmas*, 1990. He guest starred on such series as *J. J. Starbuck, Silk Stalkings*, and *Oz*. In 1985, he hosted his own show: *Ben Vereen...Comin' at Ya.*

Filmography: *Sweet Charity*, 1969; *Funny Lady*, 1975; *Roots*, 1977; *All That Jazz*, 1979; *Sabine*, 1982; *The Jesse Owens Story*, 1984; *The Zoo Gang*, 1985; *Buy & Cell*, 1989; *Once Upon a Forest*, 1993; *Why Do Fools Fall in Love?*, 1998; *I'll Take You There*, 1999; *Fosse*, 2001; *Feast of All Saints*, 2001.

W

WAITING TO EXHALE. 1995. (R) 120 min. Drama. This film is based on Terry McMillan's best-selling novel about four female friends all trying to find a good man, or get rid of the bad ones they already have. Cast: **Whitney Houston, Angela Bassett, Loretta Devine, Lela Rochon, Gregory Hines, Dennis Haysbert, Mykelti Williamson, Michael Beach, Leon, Wendell Pierce, Wesley Snipes**, Donald Adeosun Faison, Jeffrey D. Sams, Toyomichi Kurita. Director: **Forest Whitaker**. Writer: Ronald Bass. Music: **Kenneth "Babyface" Edmonds**.

WALKER, BILL (1896-1992). Actor. Walker first appeared on screen in *The Killers*, 1946, and was later cast as the male lead in the musical *No Time for Romance*, 1948, the first all-black cast movie filmed in color. His other notable film appearances include *A Kiss Before Dying*, 1956; *Ride a Crooked Mile*, 1958; and *To Kill a Mocking Bird*, 1962. Walker has appeared in **television** series, such as *Perry Mason*, 1972; *McCloud*, 1973; *The Rockford Files*, 1976; and *What's Happening*, 1978.

Filmography: *The Killers*, 1946; *No Time for Romance*, 1948; *Bad Boy*, 1949; *The Harlem Globetrotters*, 1951; *The Family Secret*, 1951; *Lydia Bailey*, 1952; *A Man Called Peter*, 1955; *A Kiss Before Dying*, 1956; *Ride a Crooked Mile*, 1958; **Porgy and Bess**, 1959; *To Kill a Mockingbird*, 1962; *Kisses for My President*, 1954; *The Third Day*, 1965; *Riot*, 1969; **The Great White Hope**, 1970; *...tick...tick...tick*, 1970; *Maurie*, 1973; *The Choirboys*, 1977; *A Piece of the Action*, 1977.

WALKER, JIMMIE (1947-). Comedian, actor. He was born in the Bronx, New York, and is perhaps best known as J. J. from the hit TV sitcom *Good Times*. His film roles include **Let's Do It Again**, 1975; *Rabbit Test*, 1978; and *Doin' Time*, 1985.

Filmography: *Let's Do It Again*, 1975; *Rabbit Test*, 1978; *Airport '79*, 1979; *B. A. D. Cats*, 1980; *Airplane!* 1980; *Doin' Time*, 1985; *Water*, 1985; *Stiffs*, 1985; *Kidnapped*, 1986; *Going Bananas*, 1988; *The Guyver*, 1991; *Home Alone 2: Lost in New York*, 1992; *Monster Mash: The Movie*, 1995; *Open Season*, 1996; *Plump Fiction*, 1997; *Shriek If You Know What I Did Last Friday the Thirteenth*, 2000.

WARD, RICHARD (1915-1979). Actor, writer, director. He was born in Glenside, Pennsylvania, and educated at Tuskegee Institute. After performing on the vaudeville stage with Florida Blossoms as part of the comedy team of Dot, Flo, and Dick, Ward joined the American Negro theater and toured the United States and Canada as the troop emcee. His first film work came in a series of *Tarzan* movies from 1937-1939, and he appeared on the theatrical stage in countless productions, including *St. Louis Woman*, 1946; *Shuffle Along*, 1952; and the European tour of *Anna Lucasta*, 1954. He returned to the big screen in the 1960s in a string of important bit parts in films, such as **Black Like Me**, 1964; **Nothing But a Man**, 1964; and **The Learning Tree**, 1969. In 1947, Ward won a best short story award from the *Saturday Evening Post*. He was founder and director of the drama department at the International School of Performing Arts, 1960, and he directed at the Hartford Stage Co. of Hartford, Connecticut, and Center Stage in Baltimore, Maryland.

Filmography: *Tarzan Series*, 1937-1939; *Public Enemy #1*, 1962; *Black Like Me*, 1964; *The Cool World*, 1964; *Nothing But a Man*, 1964; *The Learning Tree*, 1969; *Brother John*, 1971; *Across 110th Street*, 1972; *Cops and Robbers*, 1973; *Mandingo*, 1975; *The Jerk*, 1979; *Brubaker*, 1980.

WARREN, MICHAEL (1946-). Actor. He was born in South Bend, Indiana, and played basketball at the University of California, Los Angeles. He began his acting career as a referee in *Halls of Anger*, 1970, and his big film break came when he was cast in the title role of *Norman...Is That You?* 1976. On television, he portrayed Officer Bobby Hill in the long-running series *Hill Street Blues*, Ron Harris in *City of Angels*, and Baron Marks in *Soul Food*.

Filmography: *Halls of Anger*, 1970; *Drive, He Said*, 1971; *Butterflies Are Free*, 1973; *Cleopatra Jones*, 1973; *Norman...Is That You?* 1976; *Fast Break*, 1979; *Dreamaniac*, 1986; *Cold Steel*, 1987; *Heaven is a Playground*, 1991; *Stompin' at the Savoy*, 1992; *Storyville*, 1992; *A Passion to Kill*, 1994; *The Hunted*, 1995; *Buffalo Soldiers*, 1997; *Species III*, 2004; *Anderson's Cross*, 2004.

WARREN, SHARON. Actress. Born in Opelika, Alabama, she made her film debut as Aretha Robinson, the mother of Ray Charles, in the biopic *Ray*, 2004. She attended Stillman College in Tuscaloosa, Alabama, and got the opportunity to attend a casting call for Ray while performing at the Alliance Theater in Atlanta in a local stage production called *Music by Tamie Ryan*.

Filmography: *Ray*, 2004; *Glory Road*, 2006.

WASH, THE. 2001. (R) 96 min. Comedy. A down-and-out man takes a job at a carwash and soon becomes an assistant manager. Now resented by his good friend, who helped to get him the job, he must cope with a variety of odd characters and plot twists that include his boss's kidnapping. It was meant to be a tribute to the comedy hit *Car Wash*, 1976. Cast: Dr. Dre, **Snoop Dogg**, DJ Pooh, George Wallace, Tommy "Tiny" Lister, Alex Thomas, Arif S. Kinchen, Demetrius Navarro, Tommy Chong, Pauly Shore, Lamont Bentley, Bruce Bruce, Shari Watson, Shawn Fonteno, Angell Conwell. Writer/Director: DJ Pooh. Cinematographer: Keith L. Smith.

WASHINGTON, DENZEL (1954-). Actor, director. The Mt. Vernon, New York, native graduated from Oakland Academy, a private high school, before going to Fordham University to study medicine. After being cast in a student production of *Othello*, he decided to pursue acting. After costarring in the film *Carbon Copy*, 1981, his stage role in the off-Broadway production of *A Soldier's Story* led to an important film opportunity when the play was adapted to the big screen. He played a doctor for several seasons on the 1980s **television** series *St. Elsewhere*, before moving on to other notable film roles, including *Cry Freedom*, 1987; *The Mighty Quinn*, 1989; and *Glory*, 1989, for which he received an **Academy Award** for best supporting actor. The 1990s brought about a series of collaborations with director **Spike Lee** in such films as *Mo' Better Blues*, 1990; *Malcolm X*, 1992; and *He Got Game*, 1998. As an established leading man, Washington starred in many more films throughout his career and received his second Academy Award for his controversial role as a rogue cop in *Training Day*, in 2001. He made his directorial debut with *Antwone Fisher*, 2002.

Filmography: *Carbon Copy*, 1981; *A Soldier's Story*, 1984; *License to Kill*, 1984; *Power*, 1986; *Hard Lessons*, 1986; *Cry Freedom*, 1987; *The Mighty Quinn*, 1989; *Glory*, 1989; *Mo' Better Blues*, 1990; *Heart Condition*, 1990; *Ricochet* 1991; *Mississippi Masala*, 1992; *Malcolm X*, 1992; *Philadelphia*, 1993; *The Pelican Brief*, 1993; *Much Ado about Nothing*, 1993; *Virtuosity*, 1995; *Devil in a Blue Dress*, 1995; *Crimson Tide*, 1995; *The Preacher's Wife*, 1996; *Courage Under Fire*, 1996; *Fallen*, 1997; *The Siege*, 1998; *He Got Game*, 1998; *The Hurricane*, 1999; *The Bone Collector*, 1999; *Remember the Titans*, 2000; *Training Day*, 2001; *John Q*, 2002; *Antwone Fisher*, 2002; *The Manchurian Candidate*, 2004.

WASHINGTON, FREDDIE (1903-1994). Actress. She was born Fredericka Carolyn Washington in Savannah, Georgia, and spent time at a convent in Pennsylvania after her mother died. She was eventually raised by her grandmother in New York City and began taking acting and dancing lessons. She appeared in the stage productions of *Shuffle Along*, *Black Boy*, and *Hot Chocolates*, before making her film debut in *Black and Tan*, 1929. She gained national attention for her portrayal of Peola, a light-skinned woman who tries to pass for white in *Imitation of Life*, 1934. She was disappointed by the lack of non-**stereotypical** roles she was being offered in Hollywood and returned to the stage in *Mamba's Daughter* and *Lysistrata*. She also became involved in more political activities and was a founding member of the Negro Actors Guild in 1937. She wrote a regular feature for *The People's Voice* newspaper under the banners "Headlines and Footlights" and "Freddie Speaks." She continued her activism throughout the 1940s and 1950s through her involvement in the Cultural Division of the National Negro Congress and the Committee for the Negro in the Arts. She was once married to Lawrence Brown, a trombonist with Duke Ellington's orchestra, from 1933 to 1948. In 1952, she married dentist Anthony Bell.

Filmography: *Black & Tan*, 1929; ***The Emperor Jones***, 1933; *Imitation of Life*, 1934; *Mills Blue Rhythm Band*, 1934; *Ouanga*, 1936; *One Mile From Heaven*, 1937.

WASHINGTON, ISAIAH (1963-). Actor. He was born in Houston, Texas, and graduated from Willowridge High School class of 1981. He plays prominent heart surgeon Preston Burke in the ensemble cast of the **television** drama *Grey's Anatomy* on ABC. He joined the U. S. Air Force before attending Howard University then moved to New York to build his stage career in well-known productions like *Fences* and *Skin of Our Teeth*. He has since become an accomplished actor with notable roles in ***Get on the Bus***, 1996; ***Love Jones***, 1997; ***Dancing in September***, 2000; and *Romeo Must Die*, 2000.

Filmography: ***Crooklyn***, 1994; ***Clockers***, 1995; *Mr. & Mrs. Loving*, 1996; ***Girl 6***, 1996; *Get on the Bus*, 1996; *Love Jones*, 1997; *Out of Sight*, 1998; *Mixing Nia*, 1998; *Bulworth*, 1998; ***Always Outnumbered, Always Outgunned***, 1998; *True Crime*, 1999; *A Texas Funeral*, 1999; *Romeo Must Die*, 2000; *Dancing in September*, 2000; *Exit Wounds*, 2001; *Welcome to Collinwood*, 2002; *Ghost Ship*, 2002; *Hollywood Homicide*, 2003; *Dead Birds*, 2004; *The Escort*, 2004; *The Moguls*, 2005.

WASHINGTON, KERRY (1977-). Actress. She was raised in the Bronx, New York, and attended the Spence School in Manhattan. She is also a graduate of George Washington University. She has guest starred in **television** shows, such as *NYPD Blue*, *The Guardian*, and *Law & Order*. She had a recurring role in *100 Centre Street*. On film, she portrayed the wife of Ray Charles in the biopic ***Ray***, 2004. She won a Teen Choice Award for Best Breakout Performance for her role in *Save the Last Dance*, 2001, and an Independent Spirit Award nomination for Best Actress for her work in the Showtime cable movie *Lift*, 2002.

Filmography: *Our Song*, 2000; *3D*, 2000; *Save the Last Dance*, 2001; *Bad Company*, 2002; *Take the A Train*, 2002; *Sin,*

2003; *The Human Stain*, 2003; *The United States of Leland*, 2003; *Against the Ropes*, 2004; *She Hate Me*, 2004; *Sexual Life*, 2004; *Ray*, 2004; *Mr. and Mrs. Smith*, 2005; *Fantastic Four*, 2005.

WATERMELON MAN. 1970. (R) 97 min. Comedy/Drama. A white bigot wakes up one morning to find that he has turned black, and must now live his life learning to understand something he hates. Cast: **Godfrey Cambridge**, Erin Moran, Estelle Parsons, Howard Caine, **D'Urville Martin**, Kay Kimberly, Paul Williams. Director/Music: **Melvin Van Peebles**. Writer/Cinematographer: Herman Raucher.

WATERMELON WOMAN, THE. 1997. (NR) 85 min. Drama. A lesbian clerk at a video store does research to find the identity of a 1930s movie actress credited only as the "Watermelon Woman." She discovers that their personal lives have many parallels. Cast: Cheryl Dunye, Valerie Walker, Guinevere Turner, Lisa Marie Bronson. Writer/Director: Cheryl Dunye. Cinematographer: Michelle Crenshaw. Music: Bill Coleman.

WATERS, ETHEL (1900-1977). Actress, singer. After spending her childhood in Chester, Pennsylvania, Ethel Waters became a distinguished entertainer of stage and screen. She began singing professionally at the Lincoln Theater in Baltimore, Maryland, at age 17, and was the first woman to perform in W. C. Handy's stage play *St. Louis Blues*. After performing in vaudeville and nightclubs, she made her Broadway debut in the 1927 review *Africana*. Waters later appeared on stage in *Blackbirds*, 1930, and starred in *Rhapsody in Black*, in the 1931 and 1932 seasons. She was featured in Irving Berlin's *As Thousands Cheer*, and later played the lead role in *Mamba's Daughters*. Her greatest stage role came in 1940 when she portrayed the character of Petunia in *Cabin in the Sky*, and she took that role to the big screen in the 1943 movie version. Other film roles include *Rufus Jones for President*, 1933; *Tales of Manhattan*, 1942; *Cairo*, 1942; and *Pinky*, 1949. Another major stage role came in 1950 in *Member of the Wedding*. Her autobiography, *His Eye Is on the Sparrow*, was published in 1951.

Filmography: *Tales of Manhattan*, 1942; *Cairo*, 1942; *Stage Door Canteen*, 1943; *Cabin in the Sky*, 1943; *Pinky*, 1949; *The Member of the Wedding*, 1952.

WAYANS, DAMON (1960-). Comedian, actor, writer, producer. Born in New York City, he is part of a talented and very funny family of entertainers. Damon established his comedy and acting career on NBC's popular comedy skit show *Saturday Night Live*. Film roles quickly followed with parts in **Hollywood Shuffle**, 1987; **I'm Gonna Git You Sucka**, 1988; and *Earth Girls Are Easy*, 1989. He returned to **television** in his brother **Keenen Wayans**'s comedy series *In Living Color*, 1990-92, wrote and produced his own series *Damon*, and starred in the ABC sitcom *My Wife and Kids*. On the big screen, Damon wrote and starred in the comedy romance **Mo' Money**, 1992, the superhero spoof **Blankman**, 1994, and the military comedy *Major Payne*, 1995.

Filmography: *Beverly Hills Cop*, 1984; *Hollywood Shuffle*, 1987; *Roxanne*, 1987; *Colors*, 1988; *Punchline*, 1988; *I'm Gonna Git You Sucka*, 1988; *Earth Girls Are Easy*, 1989; *The Last Boy Scout*, 1991; *Mo' Money*, 1992; *Last Action Hero*, 1993; *Blankman*, 1994; *Major Payne*, 1995; *Celtic Pride*, 1996; **The Great White Hype**, 1996; *Bulletproof*, 1996; *Harlem Aria*, 1999; *Goosed*, 1999; **Bamboozled**, 2000; *Marci X*, 2003.

WAYANS, KEENEN IVORY (1958-). Comedian, actor, writer, producer, director. The New York City-born filmmaker began doing stand-up comedy, and worked with fellow comedian **Robert Townsend** on his independent spoof on the motion picture industry **Hollywood Shuffle**, 1987. A quadruple threat when it comes to making films, he went on to write, produce, direct, and star in the comedic take-off on the action-packed **blaxploitation** films of the 1970s, **I'm Gonna Git You Sucka**, 1988. Many more film roles followed and he also took to **television** with his very own comedy skit series, *In Living Color*, 1990-92, which helped to launch the careers of his brother, **Damon Wayans**, and mega-film-star Jim Carrey. Realizing the limited box office returns the industry afforded to all-black cast films, Wayans set out to create an all-encompassing mainstream concept that would have a broad box office appeal. His **Scary Movie**, 2000, which made fun of the horror genre of filmmaking, became the highest-grossing motion picture directed by an African American. His **Scary Movie 2**, 2001, was another big hit, and helped to make stars out of **Marlon** and **Shawn Wayans**, two of his other brothers.

Filmography: *Hollywood Shuffle*, 1987; *I'm Gonna Git You Sucka*, 1988; **A Low Down Dirty Shame**, 1994; **Don't Be a Menace to South Central While Drinking Your Juice in the Hood**, 1995; *The Glimmer Man*, 1996; *Most Wanted*, 1997; *Scary Movie*, 2000, *Scary Movie 2*, 2001.

WAYANS, KIM (1961-). Actress. She is a member of the talented Wayans family of actors, filmmakers, and comedians. She attended

Wesleyan University and first appeared in a cameo role in *I'm Gonna Git You Sucka*, 1988. On **television**, she appeared on her brother **Keenen Wayans'** comedy series *In Living Color*, and had a regular role in the television sitcom *In the House*.

Filmography: *I'm Gonna Git You Sucka*, 1988; *Floundering*, 1994; *Talking about Sex*, 1996; ***Don't Be a Menace to South Central While Drinking Your Juice in the Hood***, 1995; ***Juwanna Mann***, 2002.

WAYANS, MARLON (1972-). Actor. Before making it big in Hollywood, he graduated from the School of Performing Arts in New York, and studied filmmaking at Howard University in Washington, D. C. With his brother **Shawn Wayans**, he costarred, wrote, and produced the TV sitcom *The Wayans Bros.* The two were also a team in the comedy flicks ***Don't Be a Menace to South Central While Drinking Your Juice in the Hood***, 1996, and ***White Chicks***, 2004.

Filmography: ***Mo' Money***, 1992; ***Above the Rim***, 1994; *Don't Be a Menace to South Central While Drinking Your Juice in the Hood*, 1995; *The Sixth Man*, 1997; *Senseless*, 1998; ***Scary Movie***, 2000; *Requiem for a Dream*, 2000; *Dungeons and Dragons*, 2000; *Scary Movie 2*, 2001; *White Chicks*, 2004; *Behind the Smile*, 2004; *Little Man*, 2006.

WAYANS, SHAWN (1971-). Actor. He graduated from Bayard Rustin High School for the Humanities class of 1989. He began his entertainment career as deejay Sw.1 for brother **Keenen Wayans's** comedy series *In Living Color*. He costarred, wrote, and produced the TV sitcom *The Wayans Bros.*, with his brother **Marlon Wayans**, and they also collaborated on the comedy films ***Don't Be a Menace to South Central While Drinking Your Juice in the Hood***, 1996, and ***White Chicks***, 2004, directed by brother Keenen.

Filmography: *Don't Be a Menace to South Central While Drinking Your Juice in the Hood*, 1995; *New Blood*, 1999; ***Scary Movie***, 2000; *Scary Movie 2*, 2001; *White Chicks*, 2004; *Little Man*, 2006.

WEATHERS, CARL (1948-). Actor, football player, athlete. He is perhaps best known as the husky, sharp-witted boxer in the first four *Rocky* films. He began acting in 1975 after a successful career on the gridiron and gravitated toward action-packed film projects. He appeared in *Predator*, 1987, and landed the title role in ***Action Jackson***, 1988. On the small screen, he could be seen in a recurring role in the TV series *In the Heat of the Night*, 1993-94.

Filmography: *Friday Foster*, 1975; *Rocky*, 1976; *Semi-Tough*, 1977; *Force 10 from Naverone*, 1978; *Rocky 2*, 1979; *Death Hunt*, 1981; *Rocky 3*, 1982; *Rocky 4*, 1985; *Fortune Dane*, 1986; *Predator*, 1987; *Action Jackson*, 1988; *Hurricane Smith*, 1992; *Dangerous Passion*, 1995; *Happy Gilmore*, 1996; *Shadow Warriors*, 1992; *Shadow Warriors II: Hunt for the Death Merchant*, 1997; *Little Nicky*, 2000.

WEDDING, THE. (1998). (PG) 180 min. Drama. This is a film based on the novel by Dorothy West. In this story of class and caste, a young mulatto woman who is half-black must choose between marrying a successful white jazz musician, or an honest, working-class black man. Cast: **Halle Berry**, Eric Thal, **Lynn Whitfield**, **Carl Lumbly**, **Michael Warren**, **Marianne Jean-Baptiste**, Shirley Knight, **Cynda Williams**, Charlayne Woodard, **Richard Brooks**, Gabriel Casseus, Ethel Ayler, Kelsey Walker, Peter Francis James, Carl Gordon. Director: **Charles Burnett**. Writer: Lisa Jones.

WESLEY, RICHARD (1945-). Writer. This Newark, New Jersey-born screenwriter first came to prominence when he penned the hit films *Uptown Saturday Night*, 1974, and the sequel *Let's Do It Again*, 1975. He studied playwriting and dramatic literature at Howard University and won an Honorable Mention in the Samuel French National Collegiate Playwriting Competition. After graduation, Wesley joined the writer's workshop at the New Lafayette Theater in Harlem. His first produced play was the political drama *The Black Terror*.

Filmography: *Uptown Saturday Night*, 1974; *Let's Do It Again*, 1975; *Fast Forward*, 1985; *Native Son*, 1986; *Murder without Motive: The Edmund Perry Story*, 1992; *Mandela and De Klerk*, 1997; *Bojangles*, 2001; *Deacons for Defense*, 2003.

WHAT'S LOVE GOT TO DO WITH IT? 1993. (R) 118 min. Music/Drama. Based on the book *I Tina* by Tina Turner and Kurt Loder. A biopic of the life and times of singer and pop diva Tina Turner, from her humble beginnings to her rise to success beside Ike Turner, her musical director and often-abusive husband, to their subsequent separation and her successful, self-orchestrated comeback in the rock arena. Cast: **Angela Bassett, Laurence Fishburne, Vanessa Bell Calloway, Jenifer Lewis, Phyllis Yvonne Stickney, Khandi Alexander**, Pamela Tyson, Penny Johnson, Rae'ven Kelly, Robert Miranda, **Chi McBride**. Director: Brian Gibson. Writer: Kate Lanier. Cinematographer: Jamie Anderson. Music: **Stanley Clarke**. Awards: Golden Globes 1994:

Best Actress in a Musical/Comedy (Bassett). Blockbuster Awards 1995: Best Female Newcomer (Bassett).

WHEN WE WERE KINGS. 1996. (PG) 94 min. Documentary. A film that chronicles the historic heavyweight championship fight between Muhammad Ali and George Forman held in Zaire. It contains original footage mixed with contemporary interviews. Director: Leon Gast. Awards: Oscars 1996: Best Feature Documentary. Broadcast Film Critics 1996: Best Feature Documentary.

WHIPPER, LEIGH (1877-1975). Actor. He was born in Charleston, South Carolina, and earned his LLB degree in 1895 from the Howard University Law School. He began his theatrical career in 1899 with the Philadelphia Standard Theater stock company and became the first African American member of Actors Equity Association in 1920. He formed Renaissance Company in 1922 to produce all-black newsreels. Whipper appeared on the Broadway stage in *Talk of the Town*, *The Squaw Man*, and *Porgy*. He also wrote many plays, including "De Board Meeting" and *Runnin' de Town*. His early films include *Of Mice and Men*, 1939, with Lon Chaney, and *The Ox-Bow Incident*, 1943, with Henry Fonda, in which he plays a Negro preacher who pleads with a lynch mob about to hang three men for murder despite their innocence. Whipper brought compassion and intelligence to the roles he played and refused to accept roles that he felt were racist or insulting to black people, which eventually resulted in professional suicide.

Filmography: *Of Mice and Men*, 1939; *Virginia*, 1941; *King of the Zombies*, 1941; *White Cargo*, 1942; *Bahama Passage*, 1942; *The Ox-Bow Incident*, 1943; *The Negro Sailor*, 1943; *Untamed Fury*, 1947; ***Lost Boundaries***, 1949; *The Harder They Fall*, 1956; *The Young Don't Cry*, 1957; *Marjorie Morningstar*, 1958.

WHITAKER, FOREST (1961-). Actor, director. He was born in Longview, Texas, and attended college on a football scholarship but switched to studying music when he transferred to the University of Southern California. He later entered the drama program at the University of California, Berkeley, and appeared in his first film, as a high school football player in *Fast Times at Ridgemont High*, 1982. He gained credibility as a young pool shark in *The Color of Money*, 1986; as jazz great Charlie "Bird" Parker in ***Bird***, 1988; as a captured British soldier in *The Crying Game*, 1992; and has continued working ever since. After directing stage plays and music videos, Whitaker made his feature directorial debut with the film version of Terry McMillan's best-selling novel ***Waiting to***

Exhale, 1995. He also directed *Hope Floats*, 1998. On **television**, he hosted the contemporary version of the famed sci-fi series *The Twilight Zone.*

Filmography: *Fast Times at Ridgemont High*, 1982; *Tag: The Assassination Game*, 1982; *Vision Quest*, 1985; *Platoon*, 1986; *The Color of Money*, 1986; *Bloodsport*, 1986; *Good Morning, Vietnam*, 1987; *Stakeout*, 1987; *Hands of a Stranger*, 1987; *Bird*, 1988; *Johnny Handsone*, 1989; *Downtown*, 1989; *Criminal Justice*, 1990; ***A Rage in Harlem***, 1991; *Diary of a Hitman*, 1991; *The Crying Game*, 1992; *Article 99*, 1992; *Consenting Adults*, 1992; ***Strapped***, 1993; *Last Light*, 1993; *Body Snatchers*, 1993; *Bank Robber*, 1993; *The Enemy Within*, 1994; ***Jason's Lyric***, 1994; *Blown Away*, 1994; *Lush Life*, 1994; *Waiting to Exhale*, 1995; *Smoke*, 1995; *Species*, 1995; *Phenomenon*, 1996; *Hope Floats*, 1998; *Body Count*, 1998; *Ghost Dog: The Way of the Samurai*, 1999; ***Light It Up***, 1999; *Witness Protection*, 1999; *Four Dogs Playing Poker*, 1999; *Battlefield Earth*, 2000; *Green Dragon*, 2001; *The Follow*, 2001; *The Fourth Angel*, 2001; ***Feast of All Saints***, 2001; *The Panic Room*, 2002; *Phone Booth*, 2002; *The Last King of Scotland*, 1976.

WHITE CHICKS. 2004. (PG-13) 109 min. Comedy. This film is a comedy spoof about two bumbling FBI agents assigned to escort hotel heiresses the Wilson Sisters to the Hamptons for a highly anticipated annual fashion show, and protect them from a kidnapping plot. When the girls are accidentally injured and cannot make the trip, the black agents undergo high-tech makeovers to look like the white girls, and go undercover in an effort to foil the plot and save their jobs. Cast: **Shawn Wayans**, **Marlon Wayans**, Jaime King, Frankie Faison, Lochlyn Munro, John Heard, Busy Philipps, Terry Crews, Brittany Daniel, Eddie Velez, Jessica Cauffiel, Maitland Ward, Anne Dudek, Rochelle Aytes, Jennifer Carpenter. Writer/Director: **Keenen Ivory Wayans**.

WHITE GIRL, THE. 1988. (PG) 94 min. Drama. This film's title is taken from a slang term used for cocaine, and also represents the main character's desire to deny her culture and assimilate into white society. A young girl enters college with a colorblind mindset, but soon finds herself in a tug-of-war between a drug habit, her blackness, and manipulating forces beyond her control. The producer-director-TV journalist Tony Brown billed it as the first "Buy Freedom" motion picture. Profits from this film were to be used to help build an independent, self-sustaining, black-owned-and-controlled film community. This was a noble concept that has yet to be revisited. Cast: **Troy Beyer**, Taimak, Teresa Yvon Farley, Diane B. Shaw, O. L. Duke, Petronia Paley, Donald Craig, Don Hannah, Michael Duerloo, Sherry Williams, Twila Wolfe, Kevin Campbell. Writer/director: Tony Brown. Cinematographers: **Joseph M. Wilcots**, Tony Vigna. Music: George Porter Martin, Jimmy Lee Brown.

WHITE MAN'S BURDEN. 1995. (R) 89 min. Drama. In a world where African Americans control the wealth and power, and Caucasians are relegated to the poverty-stricken underclass, a bigoted black manager fires a white factory worker. In an act of social rebellion, the worker kidnaps his former boss to show him life on the other side of the color line. Many reversed **stereotypes** are presented in this attempt to make a serious social statement on the wrongs of racism. Cast: John Travolta, **Harry Belafonte**, Kelly Lynch, **Magaret Avery**, Tom Bower, Carrie Snodgrass, **Sheryle Lee Ralph**. Writer/Director: Desmond Nakano. Cinematographer: Willy Kurant. Music: Howard Shore.

WHITE MEN CAN'T JUMP. 1992. (R) 115 min. Comedy/Drama. Originally titled "White Boys Can't Jump," a white hoop hustler joins forces with a black ball player to run a game on the basketball courts of Los Angeles. The salt-and-pepper team devises a scam based on the stereotype that white boys can't really play basketball, let alone jump high enough to slam dunk the ball. They make lots of money and their friendship grows until unfortunate circumstances and financial pressure force one to scam the other. Cast: **Wesley Snipes**, Woody Harrelson, **Rosie Perez**, **Tyra Ferrell**, Cylk Cozart, **Kadeem Hardison**, Ernest Harden, John Jones. Writer/Director: Ron Shelton. Cinematographer: Russell Boyd. Music: Bennie Wallace.

WHITEWASH: THE CLARENCE BRANDLEY STORY. 2002. (R) 108 min. Drama. Racism in the judicial system is alive and well in Conroe, Texas. In this made-for-cable movie, a young black kid finds the body of a white girl and is convicted of her murder. Ironically, 40 years before, a white man shot his grandfather to death and no one was even brought to trial. An attorney must fight to sort it all out. Cast: **Courtney B. Vance**, Gil Bellows, Eamonn Walker, Chuck Shamata, Richard Eden, Joseph Ziegler. Director: Tony Bill. Writer: Abby Mann. Cinematographer: Jean Lepine.

WHITFIELD, LYNN (1953-). She was born in Baton Rouge, Louisiana, and first appeared on TV in *For Colored Girls Who Have*

Considered Suicide When the Rainbow Is Enuf, 1982. She has since portrayed the title roles in the telepictures *Johnnie Mae Gibson: FBI*, 1986; *The Josephine Baker Story*, 1991; *Sophie & The Moonhanger*, 1996; and *Dangerous Evidence: The Lori Jackson Story*, 1999. Her film roles include *Silverado*, 1985; *A Thin Line Between Love and Hate*, 1996; *Eve's Bayou*, 1987; and *Redemption: The Stan Tookie Williams Story*, 2004.

Filmography: *Doctor Detroit*, 1983; *The Slugger's Wife*, 1985; *Hard Lessons*, 1986; *Johnnie Mae Gibson: FBI*, 1987; *Jaws: The Revenge*, 1987; *The Josephine Baker Story*, 1991; *A Thin Line Between Love and Hate*, 1996; *Sophie & The Moonhanger*, 1996; *Gone Fishin'*, 1997; *Eve's Bayou*, 1997; *Stepmom*, 1998; *The Color of Courage*, 1998; *Love Songs*, 1999; *Dangerous Evidence: The Lori Jackson Story*, 1999; *A Girl Thing*, 2001; *Head of State*, 2003; *Redemption*, 2004; *Redemption: The Stan Tookie Williams Story*, 2004.

WHY DO FOOLS FALL IN LOVE? 1998. (R) 115 min. Music/ Drama. This is a biopic on the life and times, and the multiple marriages, of 1950s' doo-wop singing sensation Frankie Lymon. It follows his rise and fall due to drugs and his immature actions. After his untimely death at age 25, his three widows must come together to do battle over his estate. Cast: **Larenze Tate**, **Halle Berry**, **Lela Rochon**, **Vivica A. Fox**, Paul Mazursky, Pamela Reed, Little Richard, **Ben Vereen**, Lane Smith, Alexis Cruz. Director: Gregory Nava. Writer: Tina Andrews. Cinematographer: Edward Lachman. Music: Stephen James Taylor.

WILCOTS, JOSEPH M. (1939-). Cinematographer, producer, director. He was born in Des Moines, Iowa, and became a freelance still photographer at an early age. After shooting many films on his 8mm movie camera, he trained as a motion-picture newsman at WHO-TV and worked as a cameraman for the Iowa State Department of Health. In 1959, he moved to Hollywood to pursue a career in motion pictures, only to meet with considerable resistance due to racism in the industry. Wilcots joined the U.S. Navy and was sent to the Naval School of Photography in Pensacola, Florida, where he was trained as a photonavigator. He left the Navy in 1963 and returned to Hollywood. This time, he weathered the resistance and became the first African American to join Hollywood's camera operators' union in 1966. Wilcots worked as a camera operator on films like *The Long Goodbye*, 1973; *Thomasine & Bushrod*, 1974; and *Cornbread, Earl & Me*, 1975. He was later hired as director of photography on the **television** miniseries *Roots*, 1977, and *Roots:*

The Next Generation, 1979. He was associate producer on the live comedy-performance film *Bill Cosby: Himself*, 1983; he produced **Michael Jackson**'s "Dangerous Tour;" and directed the TV movie *Trials of Life*, 1997.

Filmography: *Roots*, 1977; *Roots: The Next Generation*, 1979; *Palmerstown, U. S. A.*, 1980; *Grambling's White Tiger*, 1981; *Bill Cosby: Himself*, 1983; *Mountaintop Motel Massacre*, 1986; *The Aurora Encounter*, 1986; *Where the Red Fern Grows: Part 2*, 1992; *Simple Justice*, 1993.

WILLIAMS, BERT (1874-1922). Singer, actor, vaudeville performer. He was born Egbert Austin Williams and became a popular singer and performer on the vaudeville stage. He often performed in **blackface** as part of the comedy team Walker and Williams, and he was the first African American to be featured as a star in a motion picture, *Darktown Jubilee*, 1914.

Filmography: *Darktown Jubilee*, 1914; *A Natural Born Gambler*, 1916; *Fish*, 1916.

WILLIAMS, BILLY DEE (1937-). Actor, artist. William December Williams was born in Harlem, New York. Interested in art, he won a scholarship to the School of Fine Arts in the National Academy of Design. A casting director at CBS cast him as a bit-actor in **television** shows, including *Look Up and Live* and *Lamp Unto My Feet*. He studied acting at the Actors Workshop in Harlem under Paul Mann and **Sidney Poitier**. His first film was *The Last Angry Man*, 1959, and he was also cast in the stage productions of **The Cool World**, **A Taste of Honey**, 1960; and *The Blacks*, 1962. He appeared on Broadway in **Hallelujah Baby**, 1967, and off-Broadway in **Ceremony in Dark Old Men**. Williams' first major television role was as football player Gale Sayers in *Brian's Song*, 1970. His appearance in **Motown**'s film production of *Lady Sings the Blues*, 1972, made him a matinee screen idol, and he was again teamed with **Diana Ross** in *Mahogany*, 1976. During the 1980s, Williams was cast as Lando Calrizion in the popular and highly successful *Star Wars* sequels *The Empire Strikes Back* and *Return of the Jedi*. On television, he was cast in the TV series *Dynasty*. Williams is also an acclaimed painter and visual artist.

Filmography: *Black Brigade*, 1969; *The Out-of-Towners*, 1970; *Brian's Song*, 1971; *Lady Sings the Blues*, 1972; *The Glass House*, 1972; *The Final Comedown*, 1972; *Hit*, 1973; *Mahogany*, 1975; *Bingo Long Traveling All-Stars and Motor Kings*, 1976; *The Empire Strikes Back*, 1980; *Nighthawks*, 1981; *Return of the Jedi*, 1983; *Chiefs*, 1983; *Marvin and Tige*, 1984; *Shooting Stars*,

1995; *Fear City*, 1985; *Oceans of Fire*, 1986; *Courage*, 1986; *Number One with a Bullet*, 1987; **Secret Agent 00 Soul**, 1989; *Batman*, 1989; *Driving Me Crazy*, 1991; **The Jacksons: An American Dream**, 1992; **Percy & Thunder**, 1993; *Alien Intruder*, 1993; *Dangerous Passion*, 1995; *Moving Target*, 1996; *Mask of Death*, 1997; *The Contract*, 1998; *Fear Runs Silent*, 1999; **The Visit**, 2000; **The Ladies Man**, 2000; **Undercover Brother**, 2002.

WILLIAMS, CLARENCE, III (1939-). Actor. Williams became interested in acting as a teenager while attending a local branch of the Young Men's Christian Association (YMCA). After spending two years in the U.S. Air Force, he began his acting career in *The Long Dream* and worked often on the Broadway stage during the 1960s. His first film role was in director Shirley Clarke's independent film **The Cool World**, 1963, and he received national prominence as Link Hayes, a hip undercover cop in the hit TV series *The Mod Squad*. Later film roles include **Purple Rain**, 1984; **Tales from the Hood**, 1995; **Hoodlum**, 1997; and **Life**, 1999. He married actress **Gloria Foster**.

Filmography: *The Cool World*, 1963; *Purple Rain*, 1984; *52 Pick-Up*, 1986; *Tough Guys Don't Dance*, 1987; *The Last Innocent Man*, 1987; **I'm Gonna Git You Sucka**, 1988; *Manic Cop 2*, 1990; **Deep Cover**, 1992; *Dangerous Relations*, 1993; **Sugar Hill**, 1994; *Tales from the Hood*, 1995; *The Silencers*, 1995; *The Immortals*, 1995; **Sprung**, 1996; *The Road to Galveston*, 1996; *Hoodlum*, 1996; *The Love Bug*, 1997; *George Wallace*, 1997; *Malicious Intent*, 1999; *Life*, 1999; *The General's Daughter*, 1999; *Reindeer Games*, 2000; *Mindstorm*, 2001.

WILLIAMS, CYNDA (1966-). Actress. This native of Chicago, Illinois, is a graduate of Ball State University in Indiana. She made her film debut in **Spike Lee**'s music-driven **Mo' Better Blues**, 1990, and followed with a starring role in Carl Franklin's gritty **One False Move**, 1992. She appeared in the TV movies **The Wedding**, 1998; **Introducing Dorothy Dandridge**, 1999; and *Hidden Blessings*, 2000.

Filmography: *Mo' Better Blues*, 1990; *One False Move*, 1992; *Tales of Erotica*, 1993; *The Ghost Brigade*, 1993; *The Tie That Binds*, 1995; *The Sweeper*, 1995; *Machine Gun Blues*, 1995; *Condition Red*, 1995; *Spirit Lost*, 1996; *Gang in Blue*, 1996; *Caught Up*, 1998; *The Wedding*, 1998; *Introducing Dorothy Dandridge*, 1999; *Hidden Blessings*, 2000.

WILLIAMS, DICK ANTHONY (1938-). Actor. This Chicago, Illinois-born actor has spent the most of his life on both the big and the small screen. He made his film debut in *Uptight*, 1968, and worked consistently throughout the 1970s. Other film roles include *The Mack*, 1973; *Five on the Black Hand Side*, 1973; and *Omen III: The Final Conflict*, 1981. His made-for-TV movies include *A Woman Called Moses*, 1978; *The Sophisticated Gents*, 1981; *Sister, Sister*, 1982; and *For Us the Living: The Medgar Evers Story*, 1983. He has also guest starred on the **television** series *L. A. Law*, *Roc*, *JAG*, *NYPD Blue*, *That's Life*, and *The Shield*.

Filmography: *Uptight*, 1968; *The Mack*, 1973; *Five on the Black Hand Side*, 1973; *The Deep*, 1977; *A Woman Called Moses*, 1978; *An Almost Perfect Affair*, 1979; *The Night the City Screamed*, 1980; *Sophisticated Gents*, 1981; *Keeping On*, 1981; *Sister, Sister*, 1982; *For Us the Living: The Medgar Evers Story*, 1983; *Gardens of Stone*, 1987; *For Us, the Living*, 1988; *Tap*, 1989; *Mo' Better Blues*, 1990; *Edward Scissorhands*, 1990; *The Player's Club*, 1998; *Blacklisted*, 2003.

WILLIAMS, FRANCES E. (1905-1995). Actress. This native of Ohio made her film debut in **Oscar Micheaux**'s *Lying Lips*, 1939, and continued a long career on both the big and small screen. Her notable guest appearances include the **television** series *The Waltons*, *The White Shadow*, *Little House on the Prairie*, *Hill Street Blues*, *Amen*, *Frank's Place*, and *Designing Women*. She appeared in the telefilms *A Woman Called Moses*, 1978, and *Sister, Sister*, 1982.

Filmography: *Lying Lips*, 1939; *Her Sister's Secret*, 1946; *Magnificent Doll*, 1946; *The Reckless Moment*, 1946; *Three Secrets*, 1950; *Queen for a Day*, 1951; *Show Boat*, 1951; *The Family Secret*, 1951; *Week-End with Father*, 1951; *Lydia Bailey*, 1952; *The Black Klansman*, 1966; *Baby Needs a New Pair of Shoes*, 1974; *Together Brothers*, 1974; *Switchblade Sisters*, 1975; *A Piece of the Action*, 1977; *A Woman Called Moses*, 1978; *The Jerk*, 1979; *Sister, Sister*, 1982; *There Goes My Baby*, 1994.

WILLIAMS, GREGALAN. Actor, writer. Williams is an **Emmy Award**-winning actor from Des Moines, Iowa, with a long list of credits in **television** and film. For seven seasons, he played Officer Garner Ellerbee, a beach cop on the television series *Baywatch*. He has guest starred on *The Sopranos*, *The West Wing*, and *Boston Public*. He was a regular as Dr. Nathan Ambrose on *City of Angels*, the first black medical drama in primetime. His **Emmy Award**-nominated PBS special *1534 Cleveland*, won second place in the Black Filmmakers Hall of Fame Competition. He has written one nonfiction book *A Gathering of Heroes, Boys to Men: Maps for the Journey*, and is finishing a second *Courage to Love: Loving and Celebrating the Plus Size Woman*. He is co-founder of The Journey Foundation, a nonprofit curriculum development teaching organization in Georgia.

Filmography: *Above the Law*, 1988; *Major League*, 1989; *The Package*, 1989; *In the Line of Fire*, 1993; *Stag*, 1997; *Acts of Betrayal*, 1997; *Remember the Titans*, 2000; *The Beat*, 2003; *Old School*, 2003.

WILLIAMS, SPENCER, JR. (1893-1969). Actor, writer, producer, director. He was born in Vidalia, Louisiana, and moved to New York City at the age of 23, where he studied acting and comedy with vaudeville star Bert Williams. He served in the U.S. Army during World War II but returned to show business and worked behind the scenes after the war. He assisted in the installation of sound systems for making sound movies and later co-wrote several black-cast comedy films with Octavus Cohen while working for producer Christie Williams. He began acting and writing his own scripts and landed his first film role in *Tenderfeet*, 1928. He was a natural on the screen and many more roles followed, including the black Westerns ***Harlem Rides the Range*** and ***The Bronze Buckaroo***. During the 1940s, Williams developed an association with Sack Amusement Company of Dallas, Texas, to write and direct his own screenplays. He made nine films in seven years, including ***The Blood of Jesus***, 1941; ***Go Down Death***, 1944; ***Beale Street Mama***, 1946; and ***Juke Joint***, 1947. When CBS visualized bringing the popular radio series ***Amos 'n' Andy*** to television in the 1950s, they cast Williams in the title role of Andy Brown.

Filmography: *Harlem Rides the Range*, 1939; *Bronze Buckaroo*, 1939; ***Son of Ingagi***, 1940; *Go Down Death*, 1941; *Blood of Jesus*, 1941; *Beale Street Mama*, 1946; *Dirty Gertie from Harlem U.S.A.*, 1946; *Juke Joint*, 1947.

WILLIAMS, STEVEN (1949-). Actor. This Memphis, Tennessee-born actor has amassed a massive list of credits on both the big and the small screen. He made his film debut as Jimmy Lee in *Cooley High*, 1975. His major film roles include Captain Adam Fuller in *21 Jump Street* and the mysterious Mr. X in *The X Files*.

Filmography: *Cooley High*, 1975; ***The Monkey Hustle***, 1976; *Big Apple Birthday*, 1978; *The Blues Brothers*, 1980; *Doctor Detroit*, 1983; *Twilight Zone: The Movie*, 1983; *Missing in Action 2: The Beginning*, 1985; *Rambo: First Blood Part II*, 1985; *Better Off Dead*, 1985; *House*, 1986; *Under the Gun*, 1988; ***The Court-***

Martial of Jackie Robinson, 1990; *Dance with Death*, 1991; *Jason Goes to Hell: The Final Friday*, 1993; *Deep Red*, 1994; *Corina, Corina*, 1994; *Bloodfist VII: Manhunt*, 1995; *The Sender*, 1998; *Elite*, 2000; *Van Hook*, 2001; *The Assistant*, 2001; *Firetrap*, 2001; *Route 666*, 2001; *Halfway Decent*, 2003; *Dark Wolf*, 2003; *Guarding Eddy*, 2004.

WILLIAMS, VANESSA (1963-). Actress. She was born and raised in Brooklyn, New York. She began her theatrical training at age 11 with the Children's Chorus of the New York City Opera, and attended the High School for the Performing Arts in New York City. Her professional acting debut came with an appearance on the **television** series *A Different World*, and she made guest appearances on *The Cosby Show*, *NYPD Blue*, and *Malcolm and Eddie*. She also starred in the first season of *Melrose Place*, and costars in the Showtime cable series *Soul Food*. She has appeared on stage in *Sarafina* and *Mule Bone*. Her feature film debut came in *New Jack City*, 1991.

Filmography: *New Jack City*, 1991; *Candyman*, 1992; *Fatal Bond*, 1992; *Drop Squad*, 1994; *Mother*, 1996; *Breakdown*, 1997; *Incognito*, 1999; *Punks*, 2000; *Like Mike*, 2002; *Baby of the Family*, 2002; *Black Listed*, 2003; *Allergic to Nuts*, 2003.

WILLIAMS, VANESSA L. (1963-). Actress, singer. Originally from New York City, Vanessa Lynne Williams became the first black Miss America in 1983. She was forced to give up her title for having posed nude in a series of photos that appeared in *Penthouse* magazine. She weathered the scorn and criticism, moving forward with a very successful career in music and film. Her debut album, *The Right Stuff*, went gold and included the hit single "Dreamin'." Future hits included "Save the Best for Last," and the theme song for the Disney animated film *Pocahontas*. That song, "Colors of the Wind," won an **Academy Award**, a **Golden Globe Award**, and a Grammy Award. Her first film, *Under the Gun*, 1988, led to much larger roles in *Eraser*, 1996; *Hoodlum*, 1997; *Soul Food*, 1997; and *Dance with Me*, 1998. Her made-for-television movies include *Stompin' at the Savoy*, 1992; *The Jacksons: An American Dream*, 1992; and *The Odyssey*, 1997. Williams made her Broadway debut in 1994 in the hit musical *Kiss of the Spider Woman*.

Filmography: *The Pick-Up Artist*, 1987; *Under the Gun*, 1988; *Full Exposure: The Sex Tape Scandals*, 1989; *The Kid Who Loved Christmas*, 1990; *Harley Davidson and the Marlboro Man*, 1991; *The Jacksons: An American Dream*, 1992; *Bye Bye Birdie*, 1995;

Hoodlum, 1996; *Eraser*, 1996; *Soul Food*, 1997; *The Odyssey*, 1997; *Futuresport*, 1998; *Dance with Me*, 1998; **Light It Up**, 1999; **Shaft 2000**, 2000; *Don Quixote*, 2000; *Winds of Terror*, 2001.

WILLIAMSON, FRED (1938-). Football player, actor, producer. Born in Gary, Indiana, Williamson studied architecture and played college ball at Northwestern University in Evanston, Illinois. An all-pro defensive cornerback, he was nicknamed "The Hammer" for his hard-hitting style of play and took to the field for the Kansas City Chiefs and for the Oakland Raiders during the 1960s. By 1972, he was in Hollywood starring opposite Diahann Carrol on her TV series *Julia*. On film, he was cast as *Spearchucker Jones* in director Robert Altman's film *M*A*S*H*, and in Otto Preminger's *Tell Me You Love Me, Junie Moon*. He became interested in producing and directing and set up his own production company, Po' Boy Productions, in 1974. Williamson hit hard during the 1970s **blaxploitation**-era films by starring as **That Man Bolt**, 1973; **Black Caesar**, 1973; and in the **Legend of Nigger Charley**. His other action-packed films included **Three the Hard Way**, 1974, and **One Down, Two to Go**, 1972. His company produced the action-packed retro film **Original Gangstas**, 1996. On **television**, he has worked in *Police Story*, *The Equalizer*, and in the sitcoms *Amen* and *The Jaimie Foxx Show*. He has continued to act and produce films in the United States and internationally.

Filmography: *M*A*S*H*, 1970; *That Man Bolt*, 1973; **Hell Up in Harlem**, 1973; *Black Caesar*, 1973; *Three the Hard Way*, 1974; **No Way Back**, 1974; *Boss*, 1974; **Take a Hard Ride**, 1975; **Bucktown**, 1975; *Adios Amigo*, 1975; *Mister Mean*, 1977; *Blind Rage*, 1978; *Fist of Fear, Touch of Death*, 1980; *Fear in the City*, 1981; *One Down, Two to Go*, 1982; *The Last Fight*, 1982; *White Fire*, 1983; *Warriors of the Wasteland*, 1983; *Vigilante*, 1983; *The New Gladiators*, 1983; *Big Score*, 1983; *Deadly Impact*, 1984; *Foxtrap*, 1985; *Delta Force Commando*, 1987; *The Black Cobra*, 1989; *Three Days to a Kill*, 1991; *Steele's Law*, 1991; *South Beach*, 1992; *Silent Hunter*, 1994; *From Dusk till Dawn*, 1995; *Original Gangstas*, 1996; *Night Vision*, 1997; *Blackjack*, 1997; *Children of the Corn 5: Fields of Terror*, 1998; *Active Stealth*, 1999; *Submerged*, 2000; *Rhapsody*, 2001.

WILLIAMSON, MYKELTI (1960-). Actor. This native of St. Louis, Missouri, began acting in plays at age nine, and moved with his family to Los Angeles when he was 15. He became an athlete playing football and basketball, until he quit to perform with the cheerleading squad. He began acting professionally at age 18 after graduation, landing parts in **television** series, such as *Starsky and Hutch, Hill Street Blues,* and *China Beach.* He made his film debut in *Streets of Fire,* 1984, but it was his performance as Bubba in *Forrest Gump,* 1994, that gave him his big break. On television, he portrayed baseball great Josh Gibson in the HBO telefilm *Soul of the Game,* 1996. His other film roles include *Waiting to Exhale,* 1995; *Heat,* 1995; and *Con Air,* 1997. Getting back to the stage, he performed in *What Lies Beneath* and the L. A. Theater Award-winning ensemble drama *Distant Fires.*

Filmography: *Streets of Fire,* 1984; *Number One with a Bullet,* 1987; *Miracle Mile,* 1989; *The First Power,* 1989; *Forrest Gump,* 1994; *Waiting to Exhale,* 1995; *How to Make an American Quilt,* 1995; *Heat,* 1995; *Soul of the Game,* 1996; *Twelve Angry Men,* 1997; *Con Air,* 1997; *Buffalo Soldiers,* 1997; *Species 2,* 1998; *Primary Colors,* 1998; *Double Tap,* 1998; *Three Kings,* 1999; *Having Our Say: The Delaney Sisters' First 100 Years,* 1999; *Holiday Heart,* 2000; *Ali,* 2001; *The Assassination of Richard Nixon,* 2004; *After the Sunset,* 2004; *Fatwa,* 2005.

WILLIE DYNAMITE. 1974. (R) 102 min. Blaxploitation. A concerned social worker tries to get a flamboyant pimp to give up his scantily clad stable of women and change his pimping ways. Cast: Roscoe Orman, **Diana Sands, Thalmus Rasulala,** Joyce Walker, Roger Robinson, George Murdock, **Albert Hall,** Norma Donaldson, Juanita Brown, Royce Wallace, Judith M. Brown, Marilyn Coleman, Mary Charlotte Wilcox, Marcia McBroom, Jack Bernardi.

WILSON, DOOLEY (1886-1953). He was born in Tyler, Texas, and became a fine actor on stage and screen. He was perhaps best known as the piano player performing at Rick's bar in the film *Casablanca,* 1942, and was the recipient of that famous Humphrey Bogart line that never was..."Play it again, Sam." Other film performances include *Keep Punching,* 1939; *Cairo,* 1942; *Stormy Weather,* 1943; and *Passage West,* 1951. On **television,** he could be seen in the series *The Beulah Show,* 1952-1953.

Filmography: *Racing Luck,* 1935; *Keep Punching,* 1939; *Night in New Orleans,* 1942; *Take a Letter Darling,* 1942; *My Favorite Blonde,* 1942; *Cairo,* 1942; *Casablanca,* 1942; *Stormy Weather,* 1943; *Higher and Higher,* 1943; *Two Tickets to London,* 1943; *Seven Days Ashore,* 1944; *Racing Luck,* 1948; *Triple Threat,* 1948; *Free for All,* 1949; *Tell It to the Judge,* 1949; *Knock on Any Door,* 1949; *Father is a Bachelor,* 1950; *No Man of Her Own,* 1950; *Passage West,* 1951.

WINFIELD, PAUL (1941-2004). Actor. The Los Angeles-born actor pursued an early education at several colleges and universities before leaving UCLA for an acting career. He was in various **television** series, including a stint on *Julia.* He received an **Academy Award** nomination for his role in *Sounder,* 1972, and went on to appear in the films *Gordon's War,* 1973; *Conrack,* 1974; and *A Hero Ain't Nothing But a Sandwich,* 1978. Going back to television, he received an **Emmy** nomination for his portrayal of civil rights leader Martin Luther King Jr., in NBC's *King,* 1978, and a second nomination for the miniseries *Roots: The Next Generation.* He continued to work extensively in television and film throughout the 1980s. In 1995, he received an Emmy Award for best guest actor on a drama series for his appearance in the *Picket Fences* episode "Enemy Lines." His stage work includes *A Midsummer Night's Dream, Othello, The Seagull,* and he appeared on Broadway in *A Few Good Men.*

Filmography: *The Lost Man,* 1969; *Brother John,* 1970; *Sounder,* 1972; *Gordon's War,* 1973; *It's Good to be Alive,* 1974; *Huckleberry Finn,* 1974; *Conrack,* 1974; *High Velocity,* 1976; *Green Eyes,* 1976; *The Greatest,* 1977; *Damnation Alley,* 1977; *King,* 1978; *A Hero Ain't Nothin' But a Sandwich,* 1978; *Roots: The Next Generation,* 1979; *Sophisticated Gents,* 1981; *Carbon Copy,* 1981; *Star Trek 2: The Wrath of Khan,* 1982; *The Terminator,* 1984; *Go Tell It on the Mountain,* 1984; *The Serpent and the Rainbow,* 1987; *For Us the Living,* 1988; *The Women of Brewster Place,* 1989; *Presumed Innocent,* 1990; *Queen,* 1993; *Dennis the Menace,* 2003; *Cliffhanger,* 1993; *White Dwarf,* 1995; *Tyson,* 1995; *Original Gangsters,* 1996; *Mars Attacks!* 1996; *Strange Justice: The Clarence Thomas and Anita Hill Story,* 1999; *Catfish in Black Bean Sauce,* 2000.

WINFREY, OPRAH (1954-). Businesswoman, talk show host, actress. Winfrey graduated from Tennessee State University in 1976 and began her career as a reporter for a local radio station in Nashville, Tennessee. She worked for Nashville's CBS affiliate while in college and became the city's first African American TV anchorwoman in 1971. Winfrey took a position at WJZ-TV in Baltimore, Maryland, and became co-host of *Baltimore Is Talking,* its popular morning show. *A.M. Chicago* lured her away in 1984, and it quickly surpassed *The Phil Donahue Show* in ratings. Her show became so popular it was renamed *The Oprah Winfrey Show.* Her multi-**Emmy Award** winning show is now widely syndicated. It has become one of the most successful and popular shows in television history. Her Oprah's Book Club segment has made millionaires out of most of the authors on her list. And her production company, Harpo Productions, produces films and TV miniseries based on books, including Gloria Naylor's *The Women of Brewster's Place*, 1989; Toni Morrison's *Beloved*, 1998; and Dorothy West's *The Wedding*, 2000. She has her own magazine called *O*. Winfrey earned an **Academy Award** nomination for her very first role in the film *The Color Purple*, 1985. Due to her success and her business savvy, she has become a media powerhouse and the first African American female billionaire.

Filmography: *The Color Purple*, 1985; *Native Son*, 1986; *The Women of Brewster Place*, 1989; *There Are No Children Here*, 1992; *Beloved*, 1998.

WITHERSPOON, JOHN (1942-). Comedian, actor. He was born in Detroit, Michigan, and made his film debut as an emcee in *The Jazz Singer*, 1980. Other notable film roles include *Hollywood Shuffle*, 1987; *I'm Gonna Git You Sucka*, 1988; *The Meteor Man*, 1993; and *Friday*, 1995. His TV guest appearances include: *The Incredible Hulk, Good Times, Hill Street Blues, Amen, L. A. Law, The Fresh Prince of Bel Air, Living Single*.

Filmography: *The Jazz Singer*, 1980; *Ratboy*, 1986; *Kidnapped*, 1986; *Hollywood Shuffle*, 1986; *Bird*, 1988; *I'm Gonna Git You Sucka*, 1988; *House Party*, 1990; *Killer Tomatoes Strike Back*, 1990; *The Five Heartbeats*, 1991; *Talkin' Dirty After Dark*, 1991; *Boomerang*, 1992; *The Meteor Man*, 1993; *Fatal Instinct*, 1993; *Cosmic Slop*, 1994; *Vampire in Brooklyn*, 1995; *Friday*, 1995; *Sprung*, 1997; *Fakin' Da Funk*, 1997; *Ride*, 1998; *Bulworth*, 1998; *I Got the Hook Up*, 1998; *High Frequency*, 1998; *Next Friday*, 2000; *The Ladies Man*, 2000; *Little Nicky*, 2000; *Friday after Next*, 2002; *Soul Plane*, 2004.

WITHIN OUR GATES. 1920. 79 min. Drama. **Oscar Micheaux**'s second film, it was produced with a budget of $15,000. It is a silent film about a woman who goes North to help a Southern minister raise money to keep his school for poor black children open. The story is filled with a convoluted mix of love, lies, death, and deceit. Controversial for its time, it was banned in Chicago for fear that a vivid lynching scene and an attempted rape scene might spark a riot. Lost for 75 years, a print of the film, entitled *La Negra*, was rediscovered in Spain. In 1993, the Library of Congress Motion Picture Conservation Center restored the print as close to the original as possible and it is available for public viewing. *Within Our Gates* is the oldest-known surviving film made by an African American director. Cast: **Evelyn Preer**, Flo Clements, James D.

Ruffin, Jack Chenault, William Smith, Charles D. Lucas. Writer/director: Oscar Micheaux.

WIZ, THE. 1978. (G) 133 min. Musical. This is a film based on the Broadway musical that was inspired by *The Wizard of Oz* with an inner-city twist. Far away from the innocence of youth, and from the plains of Kansas, a frigid schoolteacher in Harlem embarks on a magical journey through a fantasy version of the "Big Apple" (New York City) in search of herself. In the process, she meets the usual characters—The Tin Man, the Scarecrow, and the Cowardly Lion—and figures out just what each needs when the false and incompetent black wizard cannot. It is full of powerful musical numbers, lavish costumes and sets, and was one of the highest-budget black films ever made. Cast: **Diana Ross, Michael Jackson, Nipsey Russell**, Ted Ross, Mabel King, Thelma Carpenter, **Richard Pryor, Lena Horne**. Director: Sidney Lumet. Writer: Joel Schumacher. Cinematographer: Oswald Morris. Music: **Quincy Jones**.

WOMAN CALLED MOSES, A. 1978. (TV) 200 min. Drama. This made-for-TV movie is based on the novel by Marcy Heldish about the life of underground railroad founder Harriet Ross Tubman, who bought her freedom from slavery and spent the rest of her life leading others to freedom as well. Cast: **Cicely Tyson, Dick Anthony Williams**, Will Geer, **Robert Hooks**, Hari Rhodes, James Wainwright. Director: Paul Wendkos. Writer: **Lonnie Elder III**. Music: Coleridge-Taylor Perkinson.

WOMAN THOU ART LOOSED. 2002. (R) 94 min. Drama. This film adaptation of the self-help book by Bishop **T. D. Jakes** chronicles the life of a woman on death row who fights to overcome a legacy of abuse, poverty, and addiction. Cast: **Kimberly Elise, Loretta Devine, Debbi Morgan, Michael Boatman, Clifton Powell**, Idalis DeLeon, T. D. Jakes, Sean Blakemore, Jordan Moseley, Philip Bolden, Destiny Edmond, J. Karen Thomas, Louisa Abernathy, Amy Aquino, Malik Barnhardt. Director: **Michael Schultz**. Writers: T. D. Jakes, Stan Foster. Cinematographer: Reinhart "Rayteam" Peschke. Music: Todd Cochran.

WOMEN OF BREWSTER PLACE, THE. 1989. (TV) 180 min. Drama. This made-for-TV series pilot is based on the novel by Gloria Naylor. Seven women living in a tenement apartment building together face life and the daily struggle to survive. Cast: **Oprah Winfrey, Mary Alice**, Olivia Cole, **Robin Givens, Moses Gunn**,

Jackee, **Paula Kelly, Lonette McKee, Paul Winfield, Cicely Tyson**. Director: Donna Deitch. Writer: Karen Hall. Cinematographer: Alexander Grusynski. Music: David Shire.

WOO. 1998. (R) 84 min. Romantic Comedy. A beautiful, extroverted woman with a sad history of not being able to hold on to a man goes on a blind date with a straight-laced, insecure law clerk, who is so much her opposite. They make a strange couple and clash throughout much of their date, but after this night in Manhattan, both they and the city will never be the same. Cast: **Jada Pinkett Smith, Tommy Davidson, Duane Martin**, Michael Ralph, Darrel Heath, **David Chappelle**, Paula Jai Parker, **L. L. Cool J**, Aida Turturro, Lance Slaughter, Dartanyan Edmonds, Foxy Brown, Sam Moses, Tiffany Hall, Girlina. Director: Daisy von Scherler Mayer. Writer: David C. Johnson.

WOOD, THE. 1999. (R) 107 min. Romantic Comedy. A wedding brings three childhood friends together to strengthen their fraternal bonds, and to make sure the vacillating groom makes it to the church on time. Much of the film is told in flashback to reveal how the trio met, learned to rap to women, and managed to remain friends throughout the years. Cast: **Omar Epps, Sean Nelson**, Richard T. Jones, **Taye Diggs**, Trent Cameron, Malinda Williams, Duane Finley, **Sanaa Lathan, De'Aundre Bonds, LisaRaye**, Cynthis Martells, **Tamala Jones**, Elayne J. Taylor. Writer/Director: Rick Famuyiwa. Cinematographer: Steven Bernstein. Music: Robert Hurst.

WOODARD, ALFRE (1953-). Actress. A native of Oklahoma, she was a track star and cheerleader in high school, until she auditioned for schools play. She studied acting at Boston University and spent some time on Broadway before relocating to Los Angeles. Her film break came with a role in *Remember My Name*, 1978. She has won **Emmy Awards** for her appearances in the TV series *Hill Street Blues, L.A. Law,* and *The Practice.* Her wide emotional range landed her in roles in ***Go Tell It on the Mountain***, 1984; **Spike Lee's *Crooklyn***, 1994; and as Winnie Mandela in the cable TV movie ***Mandela***, 1987. Woodard became the most honored African American actress in primetime Emmy history with her forth award for ***Miss Evers' Boys***, 1997.

Filmography: *Remember My Name*, 1978; ***Freedom Road***, 1979; ***Sophisticated Gents***, 1981; *The Ambush Murders*, 1982; *Cross Creek*, 1983; *Words by Heart*, 1984; *Go Tell It on the Mountain*, 1984; ***Killing Floor***, 1985; *Unnatural Causes*, 1986; *Man-*

dela, 1987; *Scrooged*, 1988; *Grand Canyon*, 1991; *Passion Fish*, 1992; *Heart and Souls*, 1993; ***Bopha!*** 1993; ***Race to Freedom: The Story of the Underground Railroad***, 1994; ***The Piano Lesson***, 1994; *Crooklyn*, 1994; *Blue Chips*, 1994; *How to Make an American Quilt*, 1995; *Star Trek: First Contact*, 1996; ***Run for the Dream: The Gail Devers Story***, 1996; *Primal Fear*, 1996; *Miss Evers' Boys*, 1997; *The Member of the Wedding*, 1997; ***Down in the Delta***, 1998; ***Love and Basketball***, 2000; *Holiday Heart*, 2000; *K-PAX*, 2001; *The Core*, 2003.

WOODBINE, BOKEEM (1973-). Actor. He was born in Harlem, New York, and attended LaGuardia High School of Music and Art in New York City. He made his **television** acting debut in the telepic ***Strapped***, 1993, and his feature film debut in ***Crooklyn***, 1994. His TV guest appearances include *The X Files*, *New York Undercover*, *The Sopranos*, *Soul Food*, *City of Angels*, and *CSI: Miami*.

    Filmography: *Crooklyn*, 1994; ***Jason's Lyric***, 1994; ***Panther***, 1995; ***Dead Presidents***, 1995; *The Rock*, 1996; ***Gridlock'd***, 1997; ***Caught Up***, 1998; *The Big Hit*, 1998; *Almost Heroes*, 1998; ***Life***, 1999; *The Runner*, 1999; *BlackMale*, 2000; *3000 Miles to Graceland*, 2001; *The Breed*, 2001; *Run for the Money*, 2002; *Detonator*, 2003; ***Ray***, 2004; *The Circle*, 2004; *Blood of a Champion*, 2004; *18 Fingers of Death*, 2004.

WOODS, REN. (1958-). Actress. She was born in Portland, Oregon, and began acting after high school in an uncredited role as a singer in ***Sparkle***, 1976. Small roles in ***Car Wash***, 1976, and the TV miniseries ***Roots***, 1977, followed. Her **television** appearances include guest roles on such TV series as *What's Happening*, *The White Shadow*, *The Jeffersons*, and *Hill Street Blues*. In 1982, the **Black Filmmakers Hall of Fame** honored her with the Clarence Muse Youth Award.

    Filmography: *Sparkle*, 1976; *Car Wash*, 1976; *Roots*, 1977; *Youngblood*, 1978; *The Jerk*, 1979; *Xanadu*, 1980; *Nine to Five*, 1980; ***Penitentiary II***, 1982; ***Brother from Another Planet***, 1984; *Beer*, 1985; *Jumpin' Jack Flash*, 1986; *Judgement*, 1989; *From Hollywood to Deadwood*, 1989; *Crazy World*, 1996.

WORDS BY HEART. 1984. (TV) 116 min. Drama. This is a made-for-**television** movie based on the book by Ouida Sebestyen. A 12-year-old girl in turn-of-the-century Missouri wins a speech contest, only to be stifled in her success by race prejudice and discrimination. Cast: Charlotte Rae, **Robert Hooks**, **Alfre Woodard**. Director: Robert Thompson.

WRIGHT, MICHAEL (1961-). Actor. Wright made his film debut in *The Wanderers*, 1979, and worked in a series of made-for-television movies before landing costarring roles in *Streamers*, 1983; *The Five Heartbeats*, 1991; and *Sugar Hill*, 1994. He also appeared in the science fiction miniseries *V*, 1984.

Filmography: *The Wanderers*, 1979; *Streamers*, 1983; *Bedtime Eyes*, 1987; *The Principal*, 1987; *The Five Heartbeats*, 1991; *Confessions of a Hitman*, 1994; *Sugar Hill*, 1994; *The Cottonwood*, 1996; *Point Blank*, 1997; *Money Talks*, 1997; *Rage*, 1999; *Light and the Sufferer*, 2004; *Coalition*, 2004; *Downtown: A Street Tale*, 2004; *The Interpreter*, 2005.

WRIGHT, N'BUSHE (1970-). Actress. She was born and raised in Brooklyn, New York, where she attended the High School for the Performing Arts in Manhattan. She began her career as a dancer with Alvin Ailey and Martha Graham. She studied acting at Stella Adler's New York studio, which helped prepare her for the lead role in *Zebrahead*, 1992. On television, she has guest starred on *Homicide: Life on the Street*, *Third Watch*, and *Law & Order*. Her recurring TV roles include *I'll Fly Away*, *New York Undercover*, and *U. C. Undercover*. She starred in the miniseries *Widows* and the short-lived entertainment industry-based series *Platinum*.

Filmography: *Zebrahead*, 1992; *Fresh*, 1994; *Dead Presidents*, 1995; *Johns*, 1996; *A Woman Like That*, 1997; *His & Hers*, 1997; *Blade*, 1998; *3 Strikes*, 2000; *Civil Brand*, 2003; *MVP*, 2003; *God's Forgotten House*, 2005.

WRIGHT, RICHARD (1908-1960). Author, actor. After leaving home at age 17, Wright worked at menial jobs in Memphis and Chicago. Becoming a writer, he published his book *Uncle Tom's Children* in 1938, a collection of short stories reflecting racism and discrimination in the South. His most famous book, *Native Son*, sold over 200,000 copies in the first month of its publication. A film version of *Native Son* was released in 1951 with Wright himself in the lead role of Bigger Thomas.

Filmography: *Native Son*, 1951.

Y

YOU GOT SERVED. 2003. (PG-13). 95 min. Music/Drama. Two friends enter a dance contest in hopes of using the prize money to open a recording studio. Now thrust into the competitive world of street dancing, they are challenged to do battle with another top dance crew, and learn that earning respect from the street and each other will be just as hard as winning the prize money. Cast: Omarion Grandberry, Marques Houston, Jennifer Freeman, J-Boog, Lil' Fizz, Raz B, Marty Dew, Jerome Jones, Tanee McCall, Amanda Rodriguez, Malcolm David Kelley, **Meagan Good**, **Steve Harvey**, Christopher Jones, Robert Hoffman. Writer/Director: Chris Stokes.

YOU MUST REMEMBER THIS. 1992. (TV) 110 min. Drama. Made-for-TV movie about a woman who discovers a stash of old movies in a storage trunk and learns that her uncle was an early black film pioneer who is now embarrassed about the images he once portrayed. After further research on early black movies, she eventually makes him proud of his maverick role in cinematic history. Cast: **Robert Guillaume**, **Tim Reid**, **Daphne Maxwell Reid**, **Vonetta McGee**. Director: Helaine Head. Writer: Daryl G. Nickens.

YOU SO CRAZY. 1994. (R) 85 min. Comedy. This is an uncut, unrated stand-up comedy act by comedian **Martin Lawrence**. Filmed live at the Brooklyn Academy of Music, the original distributor backed out when the film received an NC-17 rating. Lawrence is in the intensely profane and vulgar form that he has since become known for. Cast: Martin Lawrence. Director: Thomas Schlamme. Writer: Martin Lawrence. Cinematographer: Arthur Albert.

Z

ZEBRAHEAD. 1992. (R) 102 min. Drama. An interracial love story about two Detroit high school students who must maintain their loving relationship despite their respective skin color and the societal backlash it causes. It was produced and developed through the Sundance Institute. Cast: **N'Bushe Wright**, Michael Rapaport, Ray Sharkey, DeShonn Castle, Ron Johnson, Marsha Florence, Paul Butler, Abdul Hassan Sharif, Dan Ziskie, Candy Ann Brown, Helen Shaver, Luke Reilly, Martin Priest, Kevin Corrigan. Writer/Director: Tony Drazan. Cinematographer: Maryse Alberti. Music: Taj Mahal. Awards: Sundance 1992: Filmmaker's Trophy.

ZOOMAN. 1995. (R) 95 min. Drama. A cable movie based on the Charles Fuller 1978 stage play *Zooman and the Sign.* A Brooklyn gang banger accidentally kills a little girl sitting on her stoop while shooting at a rival gang member. Witnesses will not talk for fear of their own safety, so the police investigation becomes stalled until a preacher hangs a sign to protest their plight, which attracts media attention. Cast: **Louis Gossett Jr.**, **Charles S. Dutton**, Khalil Kain, Cynthia Martells, **CCH Pounder**, **Vondie Curtis-Hall**, **Hill Harper**. Director: Leon Ichaso. Writer: Charles Fuller.

ZORA IS MY NAME. 1990. (TV) 90 min. Biopic. This PBS American Playhouse production is based on the life and works of Harlem Renaissance writer Zora Neal Hurston. Cast: **Ruby Dee, Louis Gossett Jr.** Director: Neema Barnette.

Appendix A
NAACP Image Award Winners

1988 Outstanding motion picture: *The Color Purple*; Outstanding actor in a motion picture: Gregory Hines, *Running Scared*; Outstanding actress in a motion picture: Whoopi Goldberg, *The Color Purple*; Outstanding supporting actor in a motion picture: Denzel Washington, *Power*.

1989 Outstanding motion picture: *Lethal Weapon*; Outstanding actor in a motion picture: Danny Glover, *Lethal Weapon*; Outstanding supporting actor in a motion picture: Mario Van Peebles, *Heartbreak Ridge*; Outstanding supporting actress in a motion picture: Traci Wolfe, *Lethal Weapon*.

1990 Outstanding motion picture: *Coming to America*; Outstanding actress in a motion picture: Whoopi Goldberg, *Fatal Beauty*; Outstanding supporting actor in a motion picture: Arsenio Hall, *Coming to America*; Outstanding supporting actress in a motion picture: Juanita Waterman, *Cry Freedom*.

1991 Outstanding motion picture: *Lean on Me*; Outstanding actor in a motion picture: Morgan Freeman, *Lean on Me*; Outstanding actress in a motion picture: Ruby Dee, *Do the Right Thing*; Outstanding supporting actor in a motion picture: Ossie Davis, *Do the Right Thing*.

1992 Outstanding motion picture: *Glory*; Outstanding actor in a motion picture: Morgan Freeman, *Driving Miss Daisy*: Outstanding actress in a motion picture: Whoopi Goldberg, *Ghost*: Outstanding supporting actor in a motion picture: Denzel Washington, *Glory*.

1993   Outstanding motion picture: *Boyz N the Hood*; Outstanding actor in a motion picture: Wesley Snipes, *New Jack City*; Outstanding actress in a motion picture: Whoopi Goldberg, *The Long Walk Home*.

1994   Outstanding motion picture: *Sister Act*; Outstanding actor in a motion picture: Denzel Washington, *Mississippi Masala*; Outstanding actress in a motion picture: Whoopi Goldberg, *Sister Act*.

1995   Outstanding motion picture: *Malcolm X*; Outstanding actor in a motion picture: Denzel Washington, *Malcolm X*; Outstanding actress in a motion picture: Angela Bassett, *What's Love Got to Do with It*; Outstanding supporting actor in a motion picture: Al Freeman Jr., *Malcolm X*; Outstanding supporting actress in a motion picture: Angela Bassett, *Malcolm X*.

1996   Outstanding motion picture: *Waiting to Exhale*; Outstanding actor in a motion picture: Denzel Washington, *Crimson Tide*; Outstanding actress in a motion picture: Angela, Bassett, *Waiting to Exhale*; Outstanding supporting actor in a motion picture: Laurence Fishburne, *Higher Learning*; Outstanding supporting actress in a motion picture: Loretta Devine, *Waiting to Exhale*.

1997   Outstanding motion picture: *A Time to Kill*; Outstanding actor in a motion picture: Denzel Washington, *Courage Under Fire*; Outstanding actress in a motion picture: Whitney Houston, *The Preacher's Wife*; Outstanding supporting actor in a motion picture: Samuel L. Jackson, *A Time to Kill*; Outstanding supporting actress in a motion picture: Loretta Devine, *The Preacher's Wife*.

1998   Outstanding motion picture: *Soul Food*; Outstanding actor in a motion picture: Djimon Hounsou, *Amistad*; Outstanding actress in a motion picture: Vanessa L. Williams, *Soul Food*; Outstanding supporting actor in a motion picture: Morgan Freeman, *Amistad*; Outstanding supporting actress in a motion picture: Irma P. Hall, *Soul Food*; Outstanding youth actor/actress: Brandon Hammond, *Soul Food*.

1999   Outstanding motion picture: *How Stella Got Her Groove Back*; Outstanding actor in a motion picture: Danny Glover, *Beloved*; Outstanding actress in a motion picture: Angela Bassett, *How Stella Got Her Groove Back*; Outstanding supporting actress in a motion picture: Whoopi Goldberg, *How Stella Got Her Groove Back*.

2000 Outstanding motion picture: *The Best Man*; Outstanding actor in a motion picture: Denzel Washington, *The Hurricane*; Outstanding actress in a motion picture: Nia Long, *The Best Man*; Outstanding supporting actor in a motion picture: Terrence Howard, *The Best Man*; Outstanding supporting actress in a motion picture: Angela Bassett, *Music of the Heart*.

2001 Outstanding motion picture: *Remember the Titans*; Outstanding actor in a motion picture: Denzel Washington, *Remember the Titans*; Outstanding actress in a motion picture: Sanaa Lathan, *Love and Basketball*; Outstanding supporting actor in a motion picture: Blair Underwood, *Rules of Engagement*; Outstanding supporting actress in a motion picture: Alfre Woodard, *Love and Basketball*.

2002 Outstanding motion picture: *Ali*; Outstanding actor in a motion picture: Denzel Washington, *Training Day*; Outstanding actress in a motion picture: Halle Berry, *Swordfish*; Outstanding supporting actor in a motion picture: Jamie Foxx, *Ali*; Outstanding supporting actress in a motion picture: Angela Bassett, *The Score*.

2003 Outstanding motion picture: *Antwone Fisher*; Outstanding actor in a motion picture: Denzel Washington, *John Q*; Outstanding actress in a motion picture: Angela Bassett, *Sunshine State*; Outstanding supporting actor in a motion picture: Denzel Washington, *Antwone Fisher*; Outstanding supporting actress in a motion picture: Halle Berry, *Die Another Day*.

2004 Outstanding motion picture: *The Fighting Temptations*; Outstanding actor in a motion picture: Cuba Gooding Jr., *Radio*; Outstanding actress in a motion picture: Queen Latifah, *Bringing Down the House*; Outstanding supporting actor in a motion picture: Morgan Freeman, *Bruce Almighty*; Outstanding supporting actress in a motion picture: Alfre Woodard, *Radio*.

2005 Outstanding motion picture: *Ray*; Outstanding actor in a motion picture: Jamie Foxx, *Ray*; Outstanding actress in a motion picture: Kerry Washington, *Ray*; Outstanding supporting actor in a motion picture: Morgan Freeman, *Million Dollar Baby*; Outstanding supporting actress in a motion picture: Regina King, *Ray*; Outstanding independent or foreign film: *Woman Thou Art Loosed*.

Appendix B
African American Academy Award Winners

1939	Hattie McDaniel, best supporting actress, *Gone With the Wind*
1948	James Baskeet, honorary award
1963	Sidney Poitier, best actor, *Lilies of the Field*
1971	Isaac Hayes, best original song, *Shaft*
1982	Louis Gossett Jr., best supporting actor, *An Officer and a Gentleman*
1983	Irene Cara, best original song, *Flashdance*
1984	Stevie Wonder, best original song, *The Woman in Red*
1985	Lionel Richie, best original song, *White Nights*
1989	Russell Williams II, best sound, *Glory*
1989	Denzel Washington, best supporting actor, *Glory*
1990	Russell Williams II, best sound, *Dances with Wolves*
1990	Whoopi Goldberg, best supporting actress, *Ghost*
1995	Quincy Jones, honorary award
1996	Cuba Gooding Jr., best supporting actor, *Jerry Maguire*
2001	Denzel Washington, best actor, *Training Day*
2001	Halle Berry, best actress, *Monster's Ball*
2001	Sidney Poitier, honorary award
2004	Jamie Foxx, best actor, *Ray*
2004	Morgan Freeman, best supporting actor, *Million Dollar Baby*
2005	Three 6 Mafia, best original song, *It's Hard Out Here for a Pimp*

Appendix C
African American Golden Globe Award Winners

1954 *Carmen Jones*, best picture, musical/comedy
1958 *The Defiant Ones*, best picture, drama
1959 *Porgy and Bess*, best picture, musical
1962 Nat King Cole, special achievement award
1963 Sidney Poitier, actor in leading role, drama, *Lilies of the Field*
1968 Sidney Poitier, Henrietta Award, world film favorites
1970 James Earl Jones, new male star, *The Great White Hope*
1971 Issac Hayes, original score, *Shaft*
1972 Diana Ross, new female star, *Lady Sings the Blues*
1981 Sidney Poitier, Cecil B. Demille Award
1982 Louis Gossett Jr., actor in supporting role, *An Officer and a Gentleman*
1984 Stevie Wonder, best original song, "I Just Called to Say I Love You," *Woman in Red*
1984 Prince, best music score, *Purple Rain*
1985 Lionel Richie, best original song, "Say You, Say Me," *White Nights*
1985 Whoopi Goldberg, actress in leading role, drama, *The Color Purple*
1986 Herbie Hancock, best music score, *'Round Midnight*
1989 Suzanne DePasse, best miniseries/TV movie, *Lonesome Dove*
1989 Denzel Washington, actor in supporting role, *Glory*
1989 Morgan Freeman, actor in leading role, *Driving Miss Daisy*
1990 Whoopi Goldberg, actress in supporting role, *Ghost*
1993 Angela Bassett, actress in leading role, *What's Love Got to Do With It?*
1999 Denzel Washington, actor leading role, drama, *The Hurricane*
2005 Jamie Foxx, actor in leading role in musical/comedy, *Ray*

Appendix D
Black Filmmakers Hall of Fame Inductees

1974   Alvin Childress, Lillian Cumber, Ossie Davis, Sammy Davis Jr., Katherine Dunham, Teresa Harris, Eugene Jackson, Juanita Moore, Clarence Muse, Gordon Parks Sr., Lincoln Theodore Perry (Stepin Fetchit), Beah Richards, Paul Robeson, Vincent Tubbs, Lorenzo Tucker, Leigh Whipper

1975   William Alexander, Eddie "Rochester" Anderson, Ruby Dee, Edward Kennedy "Duke" Ellington, Joel Fluellen, Lorraine Hansberry, Lena Horne, Allen Clayton Hoskins, Rex Ingram, Hall Johnson, Quincy Jones, Robert Earl Jones, Eartha Kitt, Abbey Lincoln, Hattie McDaniel, Butterfly McQueen, Frederick O'Neal, Louis Peterson, Sidney Poitier, Fredi Washington, Joseph M. Wilcots

1976   Josephine Baker, Louise Beavers, Harry Belafonte, Eubie Blake, Diahann Carroll, Alfred "Slick" Chester, Bernie Hamilton, John Oliver Killens, Canada Lee, Lucia Lynn Moses, The Nicholas Brothers (Harold and Fayard), Brock Peters, Melvin Van Peebles, Ethel Waters

1977   Roscoe Lee Brown, Dorothy Dandridge, Bee Freeman, Bernard Johnson, James Earl Jones, Maidie Norman, Cicely Tyson

1978   William "Count" Basie, Bennett L. Carter, Nat "King" Cole, Ella Fitzgerald, Nina Mae McKinney, Bill "Bojangles" Robinson, Hazel Scott

1979   Lonne Elder III, Earl "Fatha" Hines, Herb Jeffries, Etta Moten, Floyd Norman, Diana Sands, Leo D. Sullivan, Paul Winfield

1980   Vinnette Carroll, Ivan Dixon, James Edwards, William Greaves, Lilian Randolph, Frank Silvera, Woody Strode

1981   Maya Angelou, Louis Gossett Jr., Geoffrey Holder, Phil Moore, Raymond St. Jacques

1982   Cab Calloway, Jester Hairston, Yaphet Kotto, Hugh Robertson

1983   Special Retrospective for the 10th Anniversary of BFHFI

1984   Carmen de Lavallade, Mantan Moreland, Richard Pryor, Billy Dee Williams

1985   Jim Brown, Gloria Foster, Robert Hooks

1986   Moses Gunn, Madame Sul-te-Wan

1987   Jeni LeGon, Ernest "Sunshine Sammy" Morrison, Benjamin "Scatman" Crothers

1988   Louis "Satchmo" Armstrong, John Birks "Dizzy" Gillespie

1989   Lola Falana, Elisabeth Welch

1990   Danny Glover, Suzanne de Passe

1991   Esther Rolle, Michael Schultz

1992   Madeline Anderson, Rosalind Cash, Helen Martin, Denise Nicholas, Madge Sinclair

Appendix E
Top-Grossing African American Films

1998	*Doctor Dolittle*	Fox	$144,156,605
2003	*Bad Boys II*	Sony	$138,608,444
2003	*Bringing Down the House*	Buena Vista	$132,716,677
1996	*Nutty Professor*	Universal	$128,814,019
1988	*Coming to America*	Paramount	$128,152,301
2000	*The Nutty Professor II*	Universal	$123,309,890
2000	*Big Momma's House*	Fox	$117,559,438
2000	*Remember the Titans*	Buena Vista	$115,654,751
2001	*Dr. Dolittle 2*	Fox	$112,952,899
2003	*Daddy Day Care*	Sony	$104,297,061
1985	*The Color Purple*	Warner Bros.	$ 94,175,854
2005	*Are We There Yet?*	Sony/Col.	$ 82,674,398
2001	*Training Day*	Warner Bros.	$ 76,631,907
1992	*White Men Can't Jump*	Fox	$ 76,253,806
2003	*The Haunted Mansion*	Buena Vista	$ 75,847,266
2002	*Barbershop*	MGM	$ 75,782,105
2004	*Ray*	Universal	$ 73,331,600
2002	*John Q*	New Line	$ 71,756,802
2004	*White Chicks*	Sony	$ 70,831,760
2000	*Shaft*	Paramount	$ 70,334,258
1992	*Boomerang*	Paramount	$ 70,052,444
2005	*Guess Who*	Sony	$ 68,915,888
1993	*Cool Runnings*	Buena Vista	$ 68,856,263
1999	*Blue Streak*	Sony	$ 68,518,533
1984	*Purple Rain*	Warner Bros.	$ 68,392,977
2005	*Coach Carter*	Paramount	$ 67,264,877
1995	*Waiting to Exhale*	Fox	$ 67,052,156
1995	*Bad Boys*	Sony	$ 65,807,024

2004	*Barbershop 2*	MGM	$ 65,111,277
2001	*Down to Earth*	Paramount	$ 64,186,502
1999	*Life*	Universal	$ 63,886,029
1989	*Harlem Knights*	Paramount	$ 60,864,870
2001	*Ali*	Sony	$ 58,203,105
1991	*Boyz N the Hood*	Columbia	$ 57,504,069
2000	*Next Friday*	New Line	$ 57,328,603
2002	*Drumline*	Fox	$ 56,399,184
2005	*Crash*	Lionsgate	$ 54,580,300
2001	*Exit Wounds*	Warner Bros.	$ 51,758,599
2002	*Like Mike*	Fox	$ 51,432,760
1999	*The Hurricane*	Universal	$ 50,699,241
2005	*Diary of a Mad Black Woman*	Lionsgate	$ 50,633,099
1987	*Eddie Murphy Raw*	Paramount	$ 50,504,655
1992	*Malcolm X*	Warner Bros.	$ 48,169,910
2004	*Fat Albert*	Fox	$ 48,116,322
1996	*The Preacher's Wife*	Buena Vista	$ 48,102,795
1991	*New Jack City*	Warner Bros.	$ 47,624,353
1988	*Colors*	Orion	$ 46,616,067
1997	*Amistad*	Dreamworks	$ 44,229.441
2004	*You Got Served*	Sony/SGem	$ 40,363,810
1992	*Mo' Money*	Columbia	$ 40,227,006

(Totals from Box Office Mojo as of September 23, 2006)

Appendix F
Top-Grossing Films Directed by African American Women

2005	*Herbie: Fully Loaded* Angela Robinson	Buena Vista	$66,023,816
2000	*Love & Basketball* Gina Prince-Bythwood	New Line	$27,459,615
2003	*Love Don't Cost a Thing* Troy Beyer	Warner Bros.	$21,924,226
2004	*My Baby's Daddy* Cheryl Dunye	Miramax	$17,669,317
1997	*Eve's Bayou* Kasi Lemmons	Trimark	$14,842,388
1998	*Down in the Delta* Maya Angelou	Miramax	$ 5,672,903
1998	*Ride* Millicent Shelton	Miramax	$ 5,485,295
1989	*A Dry White Season* Euzhan Palcy	MGM	$ 3,766.879
1994	*I Like It Like That* Darnell Martin	Sony	$ 1,760,527
1992	*Daughters of the Dust* Julie Dash	Kino Intl.	$ 1,642,436
2001	*Caveman's Valentine* Kasi Lemmons	Universal	$ 687,194
1993	*Just Another Girl on the IRT* Leslie Harris	Miramax	$ 479,169

(Totals from Box Office Mojo as of September 23, 2006)

Appendix G
Top-Grossing Films Directed by African American Men

Year	Film / Director	Studio	Gross
2000	*Scary Movie* Keenen Ivory Wayans	Miramax	$157,019,771
2003	*2 Fast 2 Furious* John Singleton	Universal	$127,154,901
2003	*S.W.A.T.* Clarke Johnson	Sony	$116,934,650
2003	*The Italian Job* F. Gary Gray	Paramount	$106,128,601
2001	*Training Day* Antoine Fuqua	Warner Bros.	$ 76,631,907
2002	*Barbershop* Tim Story	MGM	$ 75,782,105
2001	*Scary Movie 2* Keenen Ivory Wayans	Miramax	$ 71,308,997
2004	*White Chicks* Keenen Ivory Wayans	Sony	$ 70,831,760
2000	*Shaft 2000* John Singleton	Paramount	$ 70,334,258
1992	*Boomerang* Reginald Hudlin	Paramount	$ 70,052,444
2005	*Coach Carter* Thomas Carter	Paramount	$ 67,264,877
1995	*Waiting to Exhale* Forest Whitaker	Fox	$ 67,052,156
2004	*Barbershop 2* Kevin Rodney Sullivan	MGM	$ 65,111,277
1989	*Harlem Knights* Eddie Murphy	Paramount	$ 60,864,870

1991	*Boyz N the Hood*	Columbia	$ 57,504,069
	John Singleton		
2000	*Next Friday*	New Line	$ 57,328,603
	Steve Carr		
2002	*Drumline*	Fox	$ 56,399,184
	Charles Stone III		
2005	*Diary of a Mad Black Woman*	Lionsgate	$ 50,633,099
	Tyler Perry		
1987	*Eddie Murphy Raw*	Paramount	$ 50,504,655
	Robert Townsend		
1992	*Malcolm X*	Warner Bros.	$ 48,169,910
	Spike Lee		
1991	*New Jack City*	Warner Bros.	$ 47,624,353
	Mario Van Peebles		
1998	*The Negotiator*	Warner Bros.	$ 44,547,681
	F. Gary Gray		
2004	*You Got Served*	Sony SGems	$ 40,363,810
	Chris Stokes		

(Totals from Box Office Mojo as of September 23, 2006)

Bibliography

Altman, Susan. *The Encyclopedia of African American Heritage.* New York: Facts on File, 2000.

Antonio, Sheril D. *Contemporary African American Cinema.* New York: Peter Lang Publishers, 2002.

Berry, S. Torriano, and Venise T. Berry. *The 50 Most Influential Black Films.* New York: Citadel Press, 2001.

Bogle, Donald. *Blacks in American Films and Television.* New York: Garland Publishing, 1988.

———. *Brown Sugar: Eighty Years of America's Black Female Superstars.* New York: Da Capo Press, 1980.

———. *Toms, Coons, Mulattoes, Mammies, and Bucks: An Interpretive History of Blacks in American Films.* New York: Continuum, 2001.

Bowser, Pearl, and Louise Spence. *Writing Himself into History: Oscar Micheaux, His Silent Films and His Audiences.* New Brunswick, N. J.: Rutgers University Press, 2000.

Bowser, Pearl, Jane Gaines, and Charles Musser. *African-American Filmmaking and Race Cinema of the Silent Era: Oscar Micheaux & His Circle.* Bloomington: Indiana University Press, 2001.

Buhle, Paul, and Dave Wagner. *Blacklisted: the Film Lover's Guide to Hollywood.* New York: Palgrave Macmillan, 2003.

Cripps, Thomas. *Slow Fade to Black: The Negro in American Film, 1900-1942.* New York: Oxford University Press, 1977.

———. *Black Film as Genre.* Indiana University Press, 1978.

———. *Making Movies Black: The Hollywood Message Movie WWII to the Civil Rights Era.* Oxford: Oxford University Press, 1993.

Dates, Jannette L., and William Barlow, eds. *Split Image: African Americans in Mass Media*. Washington, D. C.: Howard University, 1993.

Diawara, Manthia. *Black American Cinema*. New York: Routledge, 1993.

Fern-Banks, Kathleen. *Historical Dictionary of African American Television*. Lanham, Md.: Scarecrow Press, 2006.

Guerrero, Ed. *Framing Blackness: The African American Image in Film*. Philadelphia, Pa.: Temple, 1993.

Hooks, Bell. *Reel to Real: Race, Sex and Class at the Movies*. New York: Routledge, 1996.

Katz, Ephraim. *The Film Encyclopedia*. New York: Harper Perennial, 1994.

Kendall, Steven. *New Jack Cinema: Hollywood's African American Filmmakers*. New York: J. L. Denser, 1994.

Leab, Daniel. *From Sambo to Super Spade: The Black Experience in Motion Pictures*. Boston: Houghton Mifflin, 1976.

Leish, Kenneth W. *Cinema*. New York: Newsweek Books, 1974.

Manchel, Frank. *Film Study: An Analytical Bibliography, Volume I*. Milltown, N.J.: Fairleigh Dickinson University Press, 1995.

Murray, James. *To Find an Image: Black Films from Uncle Tom to Super Fly*. Indianapolis: Bobbs-Merrill, 1973.

Null, Gary. *Black Hollywood: The Negro in Motion Pictures*. Secaucus, N. J.: The Citadel Press, 1975.

———. *Black Hollywood: From 1970 to Today*. Secaucus, N. J.: The Citadel Press, 1993.

Parish, James Robert, and George H. Hill. *Black Action Films: Plots, Critiques, Casts and Credits for 235 Theatrical and Made-for-TV Releases*. Jefferson, N. C.: McFarland, 1989.

Reid, Mark A. *Redefining Black Film*. Berkeley: University of California Press, 1993.

Rocchio, Vincent. *Reel Racism: Confronting Hollywood's Construction of Afro-American Culture*. Boulder, Colo.: Westview, 2001.

Ross, Karen. *Black and White Media: Black Images in Popular Film and Television*. New York: Polity Press, 1996.

Sampson, Henry T., and Saundra Sharp. *History of Blacks in Film: A catalogue of an exhibition of posters, photographs and memorabilia of Black stars and pioneers in film*. Los Angeles: William Grant Still Community Arts Center, 1983.

Snead, James. *White Screens Black Images: Hollywood from the Dark Side*. New York: Routledge, 1994.

VideoHound's Golden Movie Retriever 2004. Farmington Hills, Mich.: Thompson Gale, 2003.

VideoHound's Golden Movie Retriever 1997. Detroit, Mich.: Visible Ink Press, 1996.

Yearwood, Gladstone. ed. *Black Cinema Aesthetics: Issues in Independent Black Filmmaking.* Athens, Ohio: Ohio University Center for Afro-American Studies, 1982.

———. *Black Film as a Signifying Practice.* New York: Africa World Press, 2000.

Internet Sources

www.imdb.com
www.eonline.com
www.hollywood.com
www.mahoganycafe.com
www.movies.com
www.moviemojo.com
www.thehistorymakers.com
www.wmm.com

About the Authors

S. Torriano Berry is an award-winning independent filmmaker who has created and executive produced the anthology series *Black Independent Showcase* and *Black Visions/Silver Screen: Howard University Student Film Showcase* for WHUT-TV 32, in Washington, D.C. His two half-hour, made-for-television movies *The Light* and *When It's Your Turn* were produced through the Minority Advisory Board of WPVI-TV 6, in Philadelphia, Pennsylvania. Berry is creator of the science-fiction anthology series *The Black Beyond*, and his feature-length horror film *EMBALMER* is available on home video. A 30-minute version of *EMBALMER* was a 1998 finalist in Showtime Network Inc.'s Black Filmmaker's Short Film Showcase. In 2005, he spent a year in Belize, Central America, directing and editing *Noh Matta Wat*, that country's first dramatic television series.

As a writer, Berry co-authored the film resource book *The 50 Most Influential Black Films*, published by Citadel Press in 2001. He has also written two fiction novels: *Tears*, based on his feature-length screenplay addressing the roots of racism in America, and *The Honeyman's Son*, a coming-of-age adventure set in the early 1940s.

Berry is an associate professor at Howard University's Department of Radio, Television, and Film. He received his BA in Art/Photography from Arizona State University, and earned his MFA in Motion Picture Production from the University of California, Los Angeles. He lives in Washington, D.C.

Venise T. Berry is the author of three best-selling novels: *Colored Sugar Water* (Dutton, 2002); *All of Me, A Voluptuous Tale* (Dutton 2000); and *So Good, An African American Love Story* (Dutton 1996). She is co-author of *The 50 Most Influential Black Films*, published in 2001 by Citadel Press, and co-editor of *Mediated Messages and African-American Culture: Contemporary Issues*, which won the Meyers Center Award for the Study of Human Rights in North America in 1997. She is currently completing a nonfiction book titled *I Used to Be a Rap Music Fan: Racialism and the Media*, and is working on her fourth novel, *Pockets of Sanity.*

In 2003, the Zora Neale Hurston Society honored Berry for her Creative Contribution to Literature. Her novel *All of Me* received an Honor Book Award from the Black Caucus of the American Library Association in 2001, and she received an Iowa Author Award from the Public Library Foundation of Des Moines that same year. Berry teaches a one-week workshop called "Powerful Plots: A Blueprint for Popular Novel Writing" at the University of Iowa's Annual Summer Writers' Festival, and conducts a series of seminars, including "Women, Weight and Wellness: Challenging the Myths," "Racialism and the Media," "Words That Set Us Free," and "Success in the 21st Century."

Berry is currently an associate professor of journalism and mass communication at the University of Iowa in Iowa City, Iowa. She received a BA in Journalism, 1977, and an MA in Communication Studies, 1979, from the University of Iowa. Her PhD was awarded in 1989 in Radio, Television, and Film, with a minor in Ethnomusicology, at the University of Texas in Austin. She lives in Coralville, Iowa.

Cover Photo Credits

top left   Black Filmmaker Hall of Fame. Patti LaBelle honors 1974 Hall of Fame inductee Lincoln Perry (Stepin Fetchit). Photo by Jim Dennis, courtesy Black Filmmaker Hall of Fame, Inc.

top center   Halle Berry and Denzel Washington with Oscars at 2002 Academy Awards Ceremony, courtesy of Photofest.

top right   Jack Johnson and Jim Jeffries 1910 fight film.

right center   *Harlem on the Prairie*, starring Herbert Jeffrey, 1938.

bottom right   Euzhan Palcy, first black woman to direct a feature-length Hollywood film (*Dry White Season*).

bottom center   Suzanne de Passe, de Passe Entertainment.

bottom left   *Daughters of the Dust* poster, 1991. Courtesy of Kino International, courtesy of the Black Film Center/Archive, Department of African American and African Diaspora Studies, Indiana University.

left center   Haile Gerima, Sankofa, Mypheduh Films.

center   Will Smith in *Ali*, 2001, Columbia Pictures Industries, Inc. All rights reserved. Courtesy of Columbia Pictures, courtesy of Initial Entertainment Group.